MW01076631

SUPERNATURAL
AS NATURAL

SUPERNATURAL AS NATURAL

A Biocultural Approach to Religion

Michael Winkelman

Arizona State University

John R. Baker

Moorpark College

Routledge
Taylor & Francis Group

LONDON AND NEW YORK

First published 2010 by Pearson Education, Inc.

Published 2016 by Routledge
2 Park Square, Milton Park, Abingdon, Oxon OX14 4RN
711 Third Avenue, New York, NY 10017, USA

Routledge is an imprint of the Taylor & Francis Group, an informa business

Copyright © 2010 Taylor & Francis. All rights reserved.

All rights reserved. No part of this book may be reprinted or reproduced or utilised in
any form or by any electronic, mechanical, or other means, now known or hereafter
invented, including photocopying and recording, or in any information storage or
retri eval system, without permission in writing from the publishers.

Notice:
Product or corporate names may be trademarks or registered trademarks, and are
used only for identification and explanation without intent to infringe.

Credits and acknowledgments borrowed from other sources and reproduced,
with permission, in this textbook appear on the appropriate page within text.

ISBN: 9780131893030 (pbk)

Cover Designer: Bruce Kenselaar

Library of Congress Cataloging-in-Publication Data

Winkelman, Michael.
  Supernatural as natural : a biocultural approach to religion / Michael
Winkelman, John R. Baker.
    p. cm.
 ISBN-13: 978-0-13-189303-0
 ISBN-10: 0-13-189303-3
 1. Supernatural. I. Baker, John R, 1953—II. Title.
 BL100.W56 2010
 200—dc22
                              2008039383

To all of our past, present, and future students

and

*to our ancestors, who had the wisdom, curiosity, and courage
to ponder their origins and contemplate the meaning of it all.*

Brief Contents

Contents

7 RELIGION AND COGNITION: HOW RELIGION SHAPES THE WAY WE THINK   178

Special Features

Special Features

Preface

For more than a century, leading scientists and scholars have declared that religions were on their way to extinction and that the rational ideas discovered by science would replace the irrational beliefs and superstitions that have been passed down by religion. It was said that this change would usher in a new era of maturity in our species and would represent a significant advance in our knowledge of the Universe, as science provided explanations of a reality vastly larger and perhaps even more strange and mysterious than anything conceived of by any religion.

This shift to secularism and the abandonment of religion has not occurred. Across the globe, religions continue to shape our lives, influence our political decisions, help us recover from illness, define our limits of acceptable behavior, and provide a way for us to distinguish our own group from others. Moreover, the persistence and even reinvention of religion among the peoples of advanced industrial societies suggest that religious beliefs and scientific insights are not incompatible.

Those who predicted the demise of religion may have difficulty understanding why religious beliefs and practices continue to exert such important influences in our world today. In our opinion, the continuing presence and apparently irresistible appeal of religious beliefs and behaviors in cultures across the globe are consequences of some of the most deep-seated aspects of what makes us uniquely human. Religiosity is a product not merely of our cultural traditions, but also of our biological evolution.

For some, looking at religiosity as a product of our biology might seem like mixing oil and water. But humans are biological organisms, and everything we do—whether it concerns the way we move or the things that move us—is a product of our evolution. It is not always easy to understand the role that evolution has played in the development of a particular trait or behavior. This is because any characteristic that contributes to the survival and reproductive success of an individual—whether it has to do with religion or with something else—may be a direct product of natural selection or a by-product that originally served one function but was later used to fulfill another. We can understand how this might occur by considering another virtual universal of human cultures: playing soccer.

Few people would argue that we evolved to play soccer. Our abilities to play soccer are based on many other skills—such as our ability to walk on two legs, to judge distance, and to kick—that were themselves selected for in the course of human evolution because they helped our ancestors survive and reproduce. Once these abilities became established in the human species, however, they could then be used for other purposes, including soccer, dancing, and a whole host of other activities. Might a similar set of independent abilities account for religion?

Without question, religions make use of many human traits—such as our ability to relate to and emotionally bond with others, to infer what other people are thinking, to submit to authority, to offer one thing in exchange for something else, and more. All of these complex abilities are the products of millions of years of evolution. But are they enough to explain religion? In other words, is religion nothing more that a by-product of evolution? Or are there at least some aspects of religion that are the direct products of evolution?

The dominant voices in biology and anthropology have long answered this last question with a resounding "No!" Religions have been described as quaint cultural traditions, misguided attempts to explain the world, and even "parasites" that exploit human nature. We do not think that this view is correct, and that is why we have written this book. In it, we will draw together many threads of evidence as we consider why our ancestors came to adopt certain religious beliefs and behaviors. We will consider the evolutionary origins of those traits and assess how these religious features may have helped our ancestors to adapt to the world in which they lived. We will also address whether what may have been *adaptive* in the past (e.g., as a means of integrating a group and distinguishing it from others) has social effects that have become *maladaptive* in our modern world. Yet even if some aspects of religiosity are now indeed maladaptive, we cannot easily abandon them. Religions will continue to be a potent force in human life; of that we may be certain. For many reasons, humans are "wired" for religion.

About this Book: The Biocultural Perspective

The title of this book, *Supernatural as Natural*, states one of our main theses: Thinking about, and even having an experience of the "supernatural" is a completely natural thing to do. For many people, the supernatural focus of religion concerns itself with a domain that is somehow "above" or "beyond" the natural forces of the Universe. This widespread notion of the "otherworldly" focus of religious belief systems makes religion seem very different from other, more down-to-earth, aspects of culture, such as economics, family, or politics. But these practical aspects of culture are often shaped by religious beliefs, and they shape religion in return. For example, a religion may instruct its followers to contribute money, goods, and time to a church. Religious myths about the Gods and their families provide role models for how human families should (and should not) behave. And while religion and politics do indeed make strange bedfellows, the two are intimately entwined in most societies of the world—including our own.

To many Westerners, the "natural" is regarded as the domain of science, while the "supernatural" is the domain of religion. Consequently, many people think that these two domains are mutually exclusive and perhaps even contradictory. But in many other societies, the most important supernatural forces are natural, and the wind, the rain, different species of plants and animals, and even features of the landscape are conceptualized in religious terms and addressed through rituals.

The perspective we will be using in this text is different from each of these views, and we believe that it can encompass the perspectives of both science and religion and help us to understand why people hold each. Our core idea is simple: *It is natural to think about the supernatural.* This does not mean that all of the "otherworldly" things that religions talk about actually exist. Rather, we believe that it is a natural condition of human beings to have religions, which we *talk* about as beliefs and we *do* as rituals.

The presence of religious beliefs and rituals in every society suggests that we are religious by nature, that we could with justification call ourselves *Homo*

religioso. But why? What happened to our ancestors that caused them to develop this capacity for religion? To answer this question, we need to examine what it means to be human from both the biological and the cultural perspective. The subtitle of this book, *A Biocultural Approach to Religion*, reflects that view.

Many fields of knowledge, including biology, animal behavior, psychology, sociology, art, economics, politics, and even medicine, can help us understand the nature of religion. Anthropology's interdisciplinary perspective integrates these many fields of knowledge to enhance our understanding of the reasons that humans are religious and the impacts that religion can have on human life. Anthropology offers a perspective for understanding the importance of religious beliefs and practices by comparing and contrasting them in different cultures so that we may identify what is common to all. By examining the ways in which human biology and human cultures interact, anthropology can help us understand why religion has been so adaptive—and maladaptive—and why religious differences remain so important today.

Discussions of religion can easily provoke strong opinions and emotions, whether they occur among believers, atheists, or agnostics. It is important to note that, when studying religions, anthropologists attempt to avoid making judgments about them. Accordingly, we will not be advocating for or against any particular religious system. Some people, of course, believe that their own religion is the only one worth considering. In their eyes, the very idea of looking objectively at all religions is a type of advocacy. We see it as a scientific attitude directed toward helping you, our readers, gain a better understanding of all religions, regardless of whatever faith you may hold and whether you are religious or not.

Regardless of your beliefs, this book will likely provoke you. Learning about the unfamiliar can have that effect. That would be true even if our subject were politics or gender roles, but it is much more likely with religion, the source of many of our most important values. Furthermore, we bring a relatively new paradigm to understanding religion, one that regards it as a product of our evolved capacities as humans. This approach leads us to look for the roots of religion in the adaptive behaviors of other animal species.

You may find these and other ideas irreligious. The scientific approach often forces us to confront the limitations of our own personal and cultural thinking and to develop much more expansive and complete ways of looking at the Universe. You will likely find some of the religious practices we will examine strange or even offensive. This is one of the risks—and a great deal of the value—of the anthropological approach, which confronts us with beliefs quite unlike our own. The cross-cultural and biocultural perspectives of anthropology can help us understand the importance of other people's beliefs and why religious impulses are so important the world over. At the same time, anthropology's humanistic perspective reminds us that these beliefs and impulses are held by people who live and die, and laugh and cry, in essentially the same way as we do.

Religion, like anything else, can be viewed and interpreted only through some type of conceptual framework. We feel that the biocultural approach is the most appropriate, for it enables us to use scientific methods in our inquiry. By incorporating insights from biology, we can reframe questions about the origins and functions of religion in a way that views humans as sharing many features in common with other animals. This can help us understand how and why certain behaviors can aid humans and other animals in adapting to their environments by coordinating their societies. By considering the range of religious beliefs and behaviors around the world, we can ascertain which features are common to all societies and which are found in only a few. This can help us distinguish those aspects of religiosity which are the direct products of our biology from those which are the products of specific kinds of cultures.

The biocultural examination of religion can also help us overcome our personal biases and view religion from the perspective of religious traditions other than our own. This integrative approach provides us with both a deeper understanding of the role of religion in shaping what it means to be human and a greater awareness of the different ways that religion affects people's relationships with the Universe.

Purpose of this Book

Our purpose is to explore the nature of religion, to appreciate the diversity of ways in which it is manifested, and to understand the different roles that religious beliefs and behaviors play in human life. The biocultural approach looks at how religions help humans adapt, and examines whether or not the process of natural selection selected for our religious capacities and features during our biological and cultural evolution. It also considers how our religious beliefs and behaviors, our individual spiritual experiences, and our collective religious rituals are rooted in aspects of our

nature that are as fundamental to being human as our need to live in families and our innate capacities as children to learn a language and acquire a culture without conscious effort.

Today, our biologically based tendencies toward spirituality and religion are interpreted through the cultural and religious filters we have acquired from the other members of our society. It is from others that we learn what spirits are, how to interact with them, and what our experiences with them mean. Our cultures even tell us how to induce spirits to appear and how to value the spiritual aspects of life. Our biological propensities for religion—whatever they might be—are profoundly shaped by socialization, which, in turn, is often controlled by religious processes. What affects how humans today make use of the religious traits that our ancestors acquired as they evolved, and how might these traits and the potentials they provide affect our further evolution?

We have written this book to help answer these questions. By applying a biocultural approach to the study of religion, we can consider what religion is, why it exists, and why it is important to humans in cultures around the world. We hope that, as a consequence, your own understanding of religion—and your appreciation and tolerance of religious differences—will be advanced. If, by the time you have finished this book, you have gained a better understanding of why religion is so central to human nature and culture and why it is still important today, the book will have fulfilled its purpose.

ACKNOWLEDGMENTS

Both of us would like to acknowledge the many researchers who have bravely countered the scientific ethos by asking questions about what is adaptive about religion and spirituality.

We would also like to express our gratitude to the following individuals who reviewed parts or all of this text:

Brian Hayden, *Simon Fraser University*
Rebecca M. Keith, *Ball State University*
Frank J. Korom, *Boston University*
William M. Leons, *University of Toledo*
Scott Lukas, *Lake Tahoe Community College*
Ronald Lukens-Bull, *University of North Florida*
James McClenon, *Elizabeth City State University*
Patrick McNamara, *Boston University*

Liam D. Murphy, *California State University-Sacramento*
Lin Poyer, *University of Wyoming*
Frank Salomon, *University of Wisconsin-Madison*
Leslie E. Sponsel, *University of Hawaii-Honolulu*

and several anonymous reviewers.

We are grateful to the many amazing people at Prentice Hall who provided us with support and encouragement while we were preparing the manuscript and during the subsequent process of turning it into a book and helping it reach its audience. Our heartfelt thanks go to Nancy Roberts, publisher extraordinaire. We also thank Vanessa Gennarelli, project manager; Cheryl Keenan, production liaison; Lindsey Prudhomme, marketing manager; and their teams.

We are deeply appreciative of the hard work and effort that Heather Sisan and Brian Baker of Write With Inc. and Peggy Kellar of Aptara put into turning our manuscript into a book.

We are also grateful to Sue Winkelman for her assistance during the final editing process and to Cindy Winkelman for preparing the list of references.

MW would like to thank JB for the invitation to engage in this project.

JB would like to thank MW for helping to bring a long-held dream to fruition. I would also like to acknowledge the support provided by Moorpark College and the Ventura County Community College District in the form of a sabbatical leave during the early phase of this work. Thanks, too, go to Janice Daurio and Nenagh Brown, two of my wonderful colleagues at Moorpark College, who graciously provided feedback on some of the ideas discussed in these pages. Erik Clark set me straight on some aspects of Germanic mythology. A. Muhammad Mà'ruf reminded me of the parable of the elephant. Finally, I wish to express my deep love and gratitude to Min for her patience and understanding during the many hours I was "in here," "out there," and "nowhere."

Biocultural Frameworks for the Study of Religiosity

HORATIO
O day and night, but this is wondrous strange!

HAMLET
And therefore as a stranger give it welcome.
There are more things in heaven and earth, Horatio,
Than are dreamt of in your philosophy.

—Hamlet Act I, Scene 5

In Shakespeare's England, ghosts were common, witches caused misfortune, and comets were portents of impending doom. Today, such beliefs might seem quaint and unsophisticated, but they continue to exert an influence on people throughout the world. A 2005 Harris Poll of 889 U.S. adults found that 40% believed in ghosts, 28% believed in witches, and 34% believed in UFOs (Harris 2005). Some people take these beliefs further than others. On March 26, 1997, 39 members of the Heaven's Gate cult living in a San Diego suburb used a mixture of barbituates and vodka to liberate themselves from the "vehicles" of their bodies and join up with an alien spaceship they believed to be traveling behind a comet that was visible in the night sky.

Shakespeare's continued relevance today is due in no small part to the brilliance of his perceptions into human nature. In the passage above, Hamlet is responding to his friend Horatio's report that he has just encountered the ghost of Hamlet's father. His few words convey a deep insight: How we experience the Universe is affected by what we think we know. In anthropological terms, culture filters and shapes our perceptions of the Universe.

For many people, the most important cultural filter of all is their religion. People's religions tell them how to carry out their everyday activities and provide them with many of the meanings, concepts, and values they use to understand the Universe. But while all cultures have religions, the differences between them can be so profound that one culture's God may literally be another culture's devil. The expressions of religion are so diverse that virtually anything—a mountain, a stream, an animal, a rock, a cloud, a star in the sky, a feather, or an intangible concept not expressible in words—can have religious significance and even be a God.

It is not easy to define religion. What features make something religious? Is religion different from magic, superstition, and witchcraft? Or are all of these manifestations of religion? How do we even decide if something is a religion? Is Satanism a religion? What about Scientology? Communism? Capitalism? All of these have been called religions, but not everyone would agree that they are.

What criteria should be used to define religion? Should they be based on a kind of experience, such as the emotional feelings of awe and visions often reported by persons who say they have been touched by the divine? Must religion involve a particular behavior, such as visiting a temple or saying a prayer? Or is religion defined by belief in a world of supernatural beings? Is the core concern of religion the "supernatural," something that is "beyond" nature? Or is a feeling that there are spirits in nature itself, including plants, animals, and rocks, also religious? Is a deep sense of connection with nature, the planet, and the entire Universe a religious experience—even when a person doesn't believe in a God?

Religion's Family Resemblances

The study of comparative religion generally suggests that we understand religion not as a single thing, but as a range of activities and beliefs that are typically found in what we call religions. By looking at religion in this way, we can identify the shared "family resemblances" across different religious traditions. Thus, while all religions are not identical, they do tend to share many core features. For example, divination or prophecy—the act of obtaining information from the spirit world—is a universal feature of religion. But the spirits people attempt to contact may be quite different, even in otherwise similar religions. Christians emphasize the central role of Jesus, while Muslims focus on Allah. Within the Christian religion, various sects differ over the roles of other supernatural beings, such as the Virgin Mary, and disagree about which texts are most sacred. The Roman Catholic Church has a very different leadership structure than the Southern Baptist Church or the Church of the Latter Day Saints. Like the members of any family, religions share features that are related but different.

While their specific features will vary, all religions provide their followers with a basic understanding about the nature of reality and the purposes of their lives, providing justifications for various activities and beliefs that often dominate social life. Other common features of the "family resemblances" shared across different religions are:

- ritual activities, which organize people into socially defined communities;
- beliefs in supernatural beings, their spirits, Gods, and demons, who typically come from a dimension distinct from the ordinary physical world and who can affect both nature and humans;
- socialization processes, which instill attitudes and evoke powerful personal experiences and emotions;
- public ceremonies, during which social leaders may communicate with, and attempt to influence, supernatural beings;
- worldview, which is embodied in a cosmological system that explains the nature and origins of the Universe, of humans, and of the activities of supernatural and natural beings; and

- a sacred domain, which is distinct from the ordinary profane social world and which organizes social life through a moral system established by supernatural beings to govern human behavior.

Religion, Spirituality, and Religiosity

Many of the most important family resemblances among religions reflect the social side of religion. Accordingly, in this book we will be using the term **religion** to refer to institutionalized social and cultural beliefs and practices about spirits and the supernatural. That is, *religion is a group phenomenon* manifested in material forms and organized social practices. Religion involves groups of people who visit special locations, such as churches or shrines and who engage in specific ritually standardized activities, such as using special garments and objects or reciting sacred texts. Religion involves collective social rituals that focus on ceremonial interaction with the supernatural through many activities, such as praying, feasting, and fasting.

It is important that we distinguish these group activities from the very personal experiences they may invoke. To do this, we will be using the term **spirituality** to refer to an individual's experiences, particularly of spirit entities, supernatural realities, and one's own soul and other personal spiritual aspects. In this view, *spirituality is an individual phenomenon*, an experience, which while personal and subjective, is also shaped by culture.

Although spiritual experiences are generally very individual, internal, and personal, they also exhibit remarkably similar patterns in cultures around the world. This indicates that some aspects of spirituality have a biological basis manifested in the many universals and cross-culturally recurrent patterns of religiosity. By studying these universals, we can uncover the biological principles—the basic functions and processes of the brain and consciousness—that are involved in these experiences.

But while the universalities of spiritual experiences reflect a biological basis, these experiences are shaped by culture. How a culture prepares people for these experiences can determine whether those people feel great confusion and distress when they occur or whether they integrate their experiences into their personal development. When cultures train people to seek such experiences, the episodes often culminate in a life-shaping event. In cultures without guidance in these matters, spiritual experiences may appear as "spiritual emergencies" that cause the people to seek psychiatric care. The cultural resources a person brings to a spiritual experience, including the language he or she uses to describe the experience, reflect the categories, assumptions, and concepts of that person's culture. The shaping of spiritual experiences by a particular culture, as well as their expression through the concepts of that culture, effectively "standardize" those personal experiences.

In many ways, religion and spirituality are the two sides of one coin. Spiritual experiences can lead to new religions, and religions can create the conditions necessary for a spiritual experience. We will use **religiosity** as an inclusive term that encompasses all forms of "spirituality" and "religion," and also the phenomena referred to by such terms as "magic," "witchcraft," "sorcery," and "possession." Religiosity is a basic human capacity that is manifested differently in each society and every individual.

Overview of this Book

In Chapter 1, we provide a general introduction to how religion has been understood in Western history, and we illustrate how anthropology can give us a more comprehensive view of religiosity. We introduce the four subfields of anthropology—cultural, archaeological, linguistic, and biological anthropologies—and discuss how the interdisciplinary and cross-cultural approaches of anthropology can help us to understand religiosity.

Chapter 2 examines how biological and cultural factors interact to produce our experience and understanding of reality, and considers how these capacities relate to religious and scientific ways of knowing the Universe. By understanding the brain processes associated with different kinds of experiences, we can understand the biological bases associated with scientific and religious thinking and experiences.

In Chapter 3, we examine the states of consciousness involved in religious experiences. Cross-cultural studies establish that there are identifiable universal patterns in the ways that these experiences provoke individuals to act and experience reality. Mystical experiences can be investigated in terms of the patterns of brain activity that appear when they are occurring, and by examining the effects of social behaviors on the development of consciousness. These perspectives allow for an understanding of the bases of universal spiritual experiences and their role in human adaptation.

Chapter 4 examines the origins of religiosity in ritualized animal behaviors. This enables us to consider the adaptive functions of these behaviors and to consider how they provided the antecedents to human religiosity. The evolutionary perspective allows us to see how our commonalities with other animals' behaviors reveal preadaptations for religiosity that illustrate the biological roots of religion. By examining these complex behavioral routines in our closest animal "cousins," the chimpanzees, we can also determine what is unique about human religiosity.

Chapter 5 introduces prehistorical and cross-cultural evidence that suggests when and how different features of religiosity first emerged and what our first religious practices were probably like. The shamanic paradigm—developed from cross-cultural and neurological data—provides a biocultural framework that illustrates the origins of human religiosity in the integration of cognitive capacities that gave rise to symbolism and culture.

Chapter 6 addresses healing as one of the key adaptive aspects of religion and a human universal; all cultures have religious healing practices and view health in spiritual terms. The animistic theories of illness, in which we view our well-being and distress in relation to the spirit world and moral systems, are human universals. Humans' ritual healing systems are distinct from ritualized animal behaviors and involve many universal features that have biological effects and provide functional adaptations.

In Chapters 7–9, we examine the historical development of the major paradigms of the anthropology of religion: the intellectualist (cognitive), psychological (emotional), and social (political) traditions. These traditional approaches are then reexamined through the lens of the biocultural paradigm, revealing new reasons to consider religion as being based in a variety of human adaptations. Many aspects of these traditional theories of religion attain a new vitality when reinterpreted from the biocultural, evolutionary, and adaptationist perspectives. These chapters collectively speak to the adaptive nature of religion in cognitive processing, emotional socialization, self-representation and social identity transformation, and social organization and integration.

Chapter 10 looks at the evil side of religion. We examine various forms of destructive religious behavior and ask what might be adaptive about these behaviors. Do such negative activities reflect the ends of the adaptationist paradigm of religion? It seems clear that religion can be maladaptive for the human species as a whole, as it pits group against group and threatens humanity with extinction.

Chapter 11 provides a short overview that summarizes the diverse lines of evidence concerning the bases and functions of religiosity that we have sketched out throughout the text. Using the evidence available, we examine some of the primary ways in which religious beliefs and behaviors can be seen as adaptive for humans. Although this evidence does not enable us to determine conclusively whether religion is an evolutionary adaption or a functionless by-product of other evolutionary events, it does allow us to draw preliminary conclusions about the relationship of religiosity to human nature. Our conclusions focus on the implications of these understandings about religion for humanity today and in the future.

Although religiosity is a universal feature of human life, religious impulses, experiences, and behaviors are not equally manifested in every one of us. The biocultural perspective tells us to expect that some people will be extremely prone to what they will construe as an encounter with a spirit while others may not have a religious "bone" in their bodies. Just as humans differ in terms of size, strength, and intelligence, we also vary in the extent of our various capacities for religiosity. In addition, the degree to which our religious inclinations are expressed will be affected by the things we learn as we grow up in our society. The religions of some societies encourage spiritual experiences, while others literally demonize them. Together, biology and culture help us understand our similarities and diversity in these complex behaviors we call religion.

Glossary

religion a group phenomenon involving cultural beliefs and practices related to spirits and the supernatural

religiosity an inclusive term that encompasses spirituality, religion, and all other concepts and behaviors related to spirits and the supernatural

spirituality a personal phenomenon that concerns an individual's experiences of spirit entities, and supernatural realities, and one's own soul and other spiritual aspects

Anthropology and the Study of Religion

CHAPTER OUTLINE

Introduction: The Anthropological Study of Religion
Western Perspectives on Religion
The Development of Anthropological Approaches to Religion
The Four-Field Approach of Anthropology
Conclusions: The Biocultural Approach to the Study of Religion

CHAPTER OBJECTIVES

- Describe the development of several Western approaches to studying religion, and show how these ultimately led to the anthropological perspective.
- Introduce the four-field approach of contemporary American anthropology, and demonstrate how each of these fields can contribute to an understanding of religiosity.
- Introduce several core evolutionary principles, and consider how these can help us to comprehend the emergence of religiosity.
- Describe the biocultural approach to the study of religiosity, and demonstrate how using both humanistic and scientific approaches can enable us to more accurately assess the manifestations of religiosity and the role these manifestations play in human life.

A YOUNG MAN TROUBLED BY DISTURBING DREAMS is led out of the village by an old man, who carries a rattle, a drum, and a blanket. They walk for two days and climb to the top of the "spirit" mountain. After spending a night drumming and chanting over the youth, the old man prepares to leave, taking with him all food and water. As he departs, he tells the youth, "When the spirits come for you, you will die. When you come back to life, then you may come back and live with us again."

* * *

A monk sits calmly in the street amid the crowds of people and slowly pours a can of gasoline over his head, chanting in a low voice. The crowd parts, leaving

a large circle of empty space around him. The monk then takes a box of matches and lights one as he continues his chanting. As the horrified onlookers watch, he bursts into flames.

* * *

The small room is filled with worshippers moving to the music played by the band in the front. Suddenly, a man lifts the lid off a box that has been sitting on the floor and removes a rattlesnake from within. Others come over and take snakes from the box as well. Some drink strychnine. Confident that the Holy Ghost will keep them safe, the worshippers hold the snakes in the air and shout "Hallelujah!"

Introduction: The Anthropological Study of Religion

Although we may have difficulty understanding the behaviors just described, it is not difficult to see them as expressions of religion. While all cultures have religion, the behaviors these religions justify are astonishingly diverse and seem to challenge the notion that there could be any elements common to every religion. Religion has effects on many aspects of our lives, including the personal, the social, the political, the economic, and even the artistic and the culinary. Religions can motivate people to undertake long fasts and to hold feasts, to engage in orgies, and to abstain from ever having sex. Some religions encourage their believers to risk their lives traveling to other countries to preach their religion to nonbelievers. Religions can induce people to lead better lives, and they can also inspire their followers to disobey laws, deny medical care to their own children, and even commit suicide and murder. Religions influence healing practices, define families, and shape political policies. They have provided the rationales for war and have given birth to international peace movements. Some of the greatest art and literature in history have been motivated by religion, and some of the most terrible deeds that humans have ever done have been justified by religion. The effects of religion are so extensive that some scholars regard religion as the very foundation of culture.

How is religion able to exert such a wide range of influences on peoples and cultures? Perhaps the easiest and most obvious answer is that religion deals with essential issues such as right and wrong, life and death. But right and wrong mean different things in different places, and although we all must die, not all religions teach their followers to fear or fret about this fact.

We will never understand religion if we regard it as simply a belief system about spirits or issues of ultimate meaning, as just a mechanism of social control, or as a means to allay fear. Religions do indeed serve these purposes, but they also do much more. Religions structure our perceptions of the Universe, linking the present to both the past and the future. Religions inform us about unseen beings and powers that are responsible for the phenomena we perceive in the everyday world, and postulate unseen aspects of our own nature that motivate our behaviors. To even begin to understand these complex aspects of religion, we need a comprehensive framework that views all manifestations of religion as expressions of deeper, more fundamental characteristics of the species we call *Homo sapiens*. Such a framework should provide a broad and integrative context that accounts for all types of religious beliefs and behaviors and provides

a suitable approach for understanding them with the rigor and the objective attitudes of science. But it should also consider the perspectives and experiences of the insider—the believer—and it should do so with respect.

The one field that offers this comprehensive and yet respectful approach to religion is anthropology. Anthropology uses the ideas and methods of the life sciences, behavioral sciences, and social sciences, thereby combining the scientific with the humanistic perspectives. Anthropology is scientific because it focuses on the recording and analysis of observable phenomena and the development of theories to explain these phenomena. It is humanistic because it takes seriously the importance of the things that people experience and report, and attempts to understand their cultures through the information they provide about their beliefs and experiences. This broad approach has enabled anthropology to enhance our awareness of the diversity of cultures and to see more clearly the nature of the features that all humans share, including religion.

Anthropology and the Biocultural Approach

The word "anthropology" is derived from two roots: *ánthrōpos* (the Greek term for "human") and *logos* (the Greek term for "word," now used to refer to a field of study). As its very name indicates, **anthropology** is the scholarly discipline that studies humans. In a very real sense, *anything* about humans can be studied from an anthropological perspective. Many anthropologists travel to other countries to learn about such aspects of cultural life as family structures, political organizations, economic systems, the settling of disputes, and—not surprisingly—religions. Others carry out excavations to uncover information about ancient societies. Some study languages to understand how this important human capacity shapes the way we perceive the world. And some even observe other animals to determine which features we share with these animals and which are found only in our species. Of course, each of these topics may also be studied by researchers from other disciplines. What sets anthropology apart is that it brings together all of these different lines of evidence to provide an all-encompassing perspective for understanding the human condition.

In practice, most anthropologists focus on just one or a few aspects of what it means to be human. But they also integrate other perspectives into their work. They may make use of cultural, archaeological, linguistic, or biological data, and they also draw upon insights from other disciplines. Because they strive to take all relevant data into consideration, anthropologists tend to work from an interdisciplinary, **holistic,** and integrative perspective. As we shall see, this broad approach is very useful for considering one of humankind's most unique traits: religiosity, our capacity for religious thought and spiritual experience.

This religious capacity is central to what it means to be human. Religion represents one of the central divides between *Homo sapiens* and every other species of animal alive today. The universality of religious *beliefs* in our species—but not in others—indicates that they arose after our ancestors had already taken their first steps down that unique path that has taken us ever further from the paths taken by other animals. Our beliefs, in other words, are products of something unique about human biology: our ability to develop culture. But if we trace our path back far enough, we can see that at least some of the *behaviors* associated with religion are present in other species, indicating that those behaviors arose before our ancestors parted ways with their ancestors. Such behaviors are products of our shared biology.

The **biocultural approach** to explaining religiosity that is the premise of this book is based on the insight that religiosity is a product of both our biological makeup and our socialization into a particular culture. This view is derived from a more far-reaching insight: the idea that *humans are biological organisms whose most important means of adapting to the world is culture*. The biocultural perspective attempts to explain both why humans have a natural, biologically based propensity for religiosity and how this propensity finds expression in different places and times.

The insight that religiosity is rooted in our biology does not mean that every one of us shares the same interest in religion or tendency to have spiritual experiences. All biological organisms differ from one another, so we can expect that religiosity, too, will be expressed differently from one individual and culture to the next. For example, some people are very susceptible to spontaneous extraordinary experiences that they may interpret as being religious in nature, while others spend their entire lives with their "feet on the ground." Some people have a tendency to believe whatever it is that the people around them believe, while others are more likely to be skeptical about everything, no matter what anyone else may tell them. In short, the biological perspective of the biocultural approach views religiosity as the product of certain innate characteristics of our species that—like any other biological traits—are manifested in different ways in different people and in different situations.

The cultural perspective of the biocultural approach recognizes that the values, beliefs, and language of each society shape the way that religiosity will be experienced, practiced, and expressed by the members of that society. Culture provides the explanations that people who have extraordinary experiences use to understand their experiences and also tells its members why only some of them have such experiences. Because culture teaches us what to "naturally" believe in, our capacity for religiosity is molded by the same forces that shape the many other aspects of our thoughts and behaviors.

The integrative and holistic perspective provided by the biocultural approach also directs us to consider how biology and culture interact with and influence one another. As a consequence, the biocultural approach provides us with a framework that enables us to consider such questions as why only some people have certain religious experiences, which people are more prone to having such experiences, what functions religion plays in human life, how religions change, and when and why new religions emerge. The biocultural approach moves religiosity from an often marginal position—in which religion is seen as opposing science and is frequently viewed with skepticism—and instead places it at the very foundations of the evolution of human thought and culture.

Anthropological Approaches and Perspectives: Becoming Aware of Our Biases

Like anything else, religion can be viewed and interpreted only through some type of conceptual framework. Anthropology is unique because it looks at religion from both the outside and the inside, making it easier to understand the biases introduced by our own framework. Because it examines many different societies, anthropology also affords a **cross-cultural** perspective that makes it possible to understand the universal features of all humans as well as the ways these are expressed in each individual and in every culture. And finally, because it combines scientific, humanistic, and cross-cultural perspectives, anthropology offers a way past the cultural blinders that has affected many other attempts to understand religion.

Most people regard their own ways of doing things as "better" and "more natural" than the ways that people in other cultures do things. It is easy to understand why. Because the people around us typically tend to think and act much as we do, our interactions with them tend to reinforce our cultural worldview as being the best. Moreover, the things that we already know enable us to expect what will happen next and thus provide us with reassurance in an otherwise uncertain world. Consequently, it is entirely normal for us to interpret things from the perspectives of our own cultural knowledge and personal experiences. Indeed, what else could we do?

This tendency to view the world through the framework of our own culture is called **ethnocentrism**. Ethnocentrism, which is normal for individuals and for cultures, causes us to prefer our own culture over another. Consequently, ethnocentrism is an important force that promotes group cohesion. But it can also cause us to misinterpret what other people think and do. Because religions express many of a society's core values, the ways in which people look at other religions are particularly susceptible to ethnocentrism. Over the course of Western history, feelings of cultural superiority have frequently colored the ways in which people have looked at and evaluated other societies and their religions. This effect has prevented us from achieving a fuller understanding of why people believe and behave the way that they do.

Western Perspectives on Religion

During the last 1600 or so years of European history, outside religions have provoked curiosity, disbelief, apprehension, scorn, and even hatred, but only rarely appreciation. An awareness of other religious systems can inspire us to compare these systems with our own and to consider their differences. But not all comparisons have the same purpose. Some people make comparisons in order to demonstrate that one particular religion is superior to all others. Others compare religions to identify their universal features. And others look at different religions to gain a greater comprehension of the diversity of ways that humans live and to uncover the reasons for this diversity. So that we may more clearly recognize the biases that are often brought into any comparison of religious phenomena, we will now briefly consider three perspectives that have played a prominent role in the ways that Westerners have thought about religion. This discussion will also enable us to better understand the emergence of the modern anthropological perspective on religions.

Early Christian Thinking: "There Is But One Path to God"

For most of the last 1600 years, Western thinking about religion has been largely shaped by Christianity. Because it regards itself as the fulfillment of a promise that its God made to the Jewish people, Christianity has traditionally considered itself to be the only "true" religion and has often looked down on other beliefs. As a consequence of this **exclusivism**, Christianity has long regarded Judaism, Islam, Buddhism, and Hinduism as erroneous religions. And it has tended to lump all the other religious systems in the world, including the Gods of the ancient Europeans and of the people encountered in the New World, into the category of "paganism." This ethnocentric attitude has led to a great deal of violence and has long impeded Westerners' understanding of other peoples and their religions.

The standard used to evaluate other religions was Christianity itself. Seen from the Christian perspective, Judaism is the religion of a small group of people chosen by God, and Christianity is the realization of the promise of that religion. Islam is a heretical upstart that emerged in an alien land, the product of a "false prophet" known as Muhammad. The "pagans" of the Old and New Worlds were living in "darkness" and needed to be "shown the light." To be redeemed, the adherents of all of these other religious traditions needed to learn about and adopt Christianity, the one "true" religion that had developed in the West. Similar thinking demanded that other societies also adopt Western systems of politics and economics, and even dress.

It was not always like this. During the Roman Republic and in the early Empire, the Roman government permitted the peoples it conquered to retain most of their customs, including their religions. As the Empire expanded, new temples to "foreign" deities were built alongside established temples, often in the capital itself. As a result, Rome was long a center of religious pluralism and tolerance.

All this changed when the Emperor Theodosius recognized Christianity as the state religion of Rome in 380 C.E. ("Current Era"). With that the Christian claim to a superior and exclusive truth could be enforced by the power of the state, and it was. By 435, all non-Christian shrines and temples in the Empire had been shuttered and all non-Christian rituals and beliefs had been declared illegal under penalty of death. All citizens of the Empire were required to be Roman Catholic (from the Greek word *katholikos*, meaning "universal"), with the exception of Jews. Judaism remained legal, but its followers were typically kept apart from Christians. (The European "two-class" system of Christians and Jews has its roots in this time.)

These new imperial policies primarily affected the people of the cities. For several more centuries, the people who lived in the towns and villages and in the countryside continued their ancient practices. During those centuries, the Roman Catholic Church exerted a great deal of effort to expand its sphere of influence outside the cities and ensure that only those doctrines which it approved were promulgated. Aided by the very nobility whose rule it legitimized, the Church acted—often with great force—to eradicate alternative beliefs. The

In 380 C.E., the Roman Emperor Theodosius I issued a decree that declared all citizens of the empire "Catholic Christians" and banned the practice of all other religions.

> It is Our will that all the peoples who are ruled by the administration of Our Clemency shall practice that religion which the divine Peter the Apostle transmitted to the Romans, as the religion which he introduced makes clear even unto this day. It is evident that this is the religion that is followed by the Pontiff Damasus and by Peter, Bishop of Alexandria, a man of apostolic sanctity; that is, according to the apostolic discipline and the evangelic doctrine, we shall believe in the single Deity of the Father, the Son, and the Holy Spirit, under the concept of equal majesty and of the Holy Trinity.
>
> 1. We command that those persons who follow this rule shall embrace the name of Catholic Christians. The rest, however, whom We adjudge demented and insane, shall sustain the infamy of heretical dogmas, their meeting places shall not receive the name of churches, and they shall be smitten first by divine vengeance and secondly by the retribution of Our own initiative, which We shall assume in accordance with the divine judgment.

Theodosian Code, XVI, 1, 2

(cited in Hillgarth 1969; original translation by Clyde Pharr, Theodosian Code, Princeton, 1952)

Inquisition was established to root out heresy at home, and the Crusades took the battle abroad.

The Church's desire to maintain its monopoly on thought even embroiled it in matters usually regarded as belonging to the purview of science, such as the controversy between the geocentric ("earth-centered") and the heliocentric ("sun-centered") models of the solar system. By the sixteenth century, however, the Catholic Church's internal problems and the excesses brought about by centuries of wielding power led reformers like Martin Luther, John Calvin, and John Wycliffe to offer correctives to a faith that they believed had strayed far from the truth. Their messages attracted followers for both religious and political reasons, and brought new churches into being that soon became powerful enough to openly oppose the Catholic Church. Most of these, moreover, now asserted their own exclusivist claims to the truth, resulting in the clashes known as the Thirty Years' War (1618–1648). The conflicting forces of religion and politics produced some strange bedfellows. Catholic Spain and Austria joined forces against Denmark, the Netherlands, Sweden, and parts of Germany, all of which had adopted Protestant ideas. To thwart the ambitions of the Spanish and Austrians, Catholic France allied itself with the Protestant countries. Finally, after an entire generation of warfare, the combatants agreed to the Peace of Westphalia, which ended the conflict and left a patchwork of competing interpretations of Christianity across the European continent. Weary of religious tensions and excited by the prospect of a new political landscape in which religions could peacefully coexist, many people became open to different ways of looking at religion.

Rationalist Thinking: "There Are Many Paths to God"

As the struggles between the various sects of Christianity destroyed both lives and property, new ways of regarding religion began to emerge. These perspectives did not negate religion, but viewed different religions as specific expressions of a single deeper underlying truth. These **rationalist** movements emphasized reason over revelation and argued for a more universal understanding of religion by emphasizing the similarities between religions rather than their differences. One variety of this thinking was known as **deism**. The word was first used in the seventeenth century to refer to a belief in God but lack of adherence to any specific dogma. Deists rejected the idea that religious truths had been "revealed" by God and argued instead that *all* religious ideas should be exposed to critical and even skeptical scrutiny. They were incensed by the power of the churches to enforce adherence to dogmatic notions that had to be accepted solely on the basis of faith. In their eyes, it was these demands of unquestioning obedience that had led to many of the excesses that had occurred in the name of God. The deists believed that religion's true purpose was to promote morality and that, apart from moral teachings, no other doctrines were needed. The deists believed in a God, who was conceived of as the "First Cause" of the Universe, which had established the laws of nature that were then being discovered by scientists such as Nicolaus Copernicus, Isaac Newton, and others. But the deists thought that once God had created the Universe, he no longer intervened in its workings, but rather allowed the Universe to run itself according to the principles he had established.

Deism was a popular belief among many of the early patriots and founders of the United States, including Thomas Jefferson, Benjamin Franklin, and George Washington. Because of his convictions and his awareness of the destructive potential of religious conflict, Washington went to great lengths to ensure that the U.S. Constitution did not contain a single reference to Christianity or even to God. Perhaps the clearest expression of the Founding Fathers' wariness of religious dogmatism and intolerance is found in Article VI, which states that "no religious Test shall ever be required as a Qualification to any office or public Trust under the United States." But deism was a product of rationalist thinking, and the wave of anti-intellectual evangelism that took place in the early 1800s (especially in the frontier regions) essentially ended the deist movement. Nonetheless, many of deism's core ideas—such as freedom of religion—remain with us today.

Deism influenced the development of **universalism,** the view that the common themes in different religions reflected different paths to the same end. In the United States, the universalist movement taught that God would never restrict his grace solely to people who adhered to a particular dogma, but would grant salvation to all. Although this was a relatively novel idea in the West, many Asian religions (especially Hinduism) have long held similar views. Indeed, some contemporary Hindus regard Jesus as a recent incarnation of the God Vishnu, and several modern Hindu temples have statues of Jesus alongside their many other deities.

Deist and universalist ideas were propounded in one form or another during the early Christian era. But the Church branded these ideas as heresies and persecuted those who espoused them. The ideas emerged once more in the atmosphere of religious tolerance that developed in Europe in reaction to the centuries of religious wars and persecution. These movements represent attempts to preserve and distill the common elements of different religious traditions and instill a profound appreciation of the role that religion plays in human life. Such rationalist perspectives, and the tolerance for diversity that they called for, provided the basis for a more objective approach to the study of religion.

Comparative Thinking: "Religions Are Objects for Study"

The nineteenth century witnessed an explosion in the European awareness of non-Western religions. Both sacred and mundane texts of other cultures were translated into European languages for the first time. Texts from India attracted considerable attention, for they demonstrated that sophisticated beliefs and elaborate rituals, as well as a complex priesthood, had been present in South Asia long before the rise of Christianity. Confucian and Buddhist texts also became available, providing additional evidence of the complexity of Asian religious thought.

In 1872, a curator at the British Museum in London named George Smith stunned the world when he announced that he had discovered an ancient cuneiform account of a flood that had numerous parallels to the version contained in Genesis. This *Epic of Gilgamesh* provoked many questions about the origins of the stories in the Old Testament, as did ancient Zoroastrian texts from Persia that contained some of the earliest evidence of monotheistic ideas. These discoveries not only suggested that the stories contained in the Old Testament might have been derived from earlier sources, but also implied that at least some aspects of religion are products of historical events.

This cuneiform text, which dates to the seventh century B.C.E. ("Before the Current Era"), was found at Nineveh (in modern Iraq). It contains a portion of the Gilgamesh epic that describes a great flood that destroyed most of humankind. (© Copyright The British Museum.)

These findings suggested that by comparing sacred texts and other evidence, one could discern universal aspects of religions and cast light on the functions of religion.

One of the first persons to put these ideas into practice in an academic context was F. Max Müller (1823–1900), a German scholar of languages who supervised the translation of numerous texts as part of a series entitled *Sacred Books of the East*. Müller became convinced that all religions contained some truths, but that these had often been obscured by the historical and cultural events that had shaped each religion. In 1868, he became the first Professor of Comparative Theology at Oxford University. Because he treated all religions as essentially equal, Müller was accused of undermining morality and the Christian faith. But Müller's attitude was a scientific one: In order to free the study of religion from bias, a researcher had to look at *all* religions with the same objectivity that he might bring to the study of rocks or clouds.

It was clear during Müller's time, and it is still clear today, that not everyone regards religious tolerance as a virtue. As we have seen, religious bias is nothing new. Today, some work in "comparative religion" is still carried out in support of a religious agenda that aims to bolster claims of superiority of one religion over another. Skeptical researchers who delight in pointing out the errors and flaws in all religions represent the other end of the spectrum. But the modern academic field of comparative religion attempts to avoid these extremes. It looks at historical trends, considers how religions have influenced one another, and attempts to determine the core features of religion and to identify the social factors that produce patterns in religious practices. Scholars in comparative religion are also working to develop new frameworks for the encounters between different religions, some of which we will examine in the last chapter of this book. This is an important effort for our time, for as the human population continues to grow, and as international trade, travel, and telecommunications whittle away at both geographic and cultural isolation, it is becoming increasingly clear that we humans need to develop new ways of "agreeing to disagree."

The Development of Anthropological Approaches to Religion

The comparative study of religion that began during the nineteenth century helped set the stage for the development of anthropology. As a product of Western thought, anthropology in its early history was shaped by many of the same trends in thinking that affected Western society at large, including the notion that Europeans had a superior culture and a more civilized way of life. It was only natural that the lenses through which outsiders were perceived and comprehended would be similar to those used to view other aspects of the world. Two of anthropology's major accomplishments have been to point out that these lenses do exist and to create ways to control them so that other cultures could be seen in their own light, in terms of their own cultural beliefs and meanings.

In some ways, anthropology originated in the notebooks and reports of the merchants, soldiers, colonial officials, missionaries, and others who wrote about their experiences with foreign peoples. In recording their encounters, these writers were exhibiting the same interest in the exotic as the ancient Greeks and other travelers in the ancient world did—and for many of the same reasons: the desire to trade, the urge for conquest, the need to administer colonies, and simple curiosity. But modern anthropology could emerge only when the human tendency to view others with an ethnocentric sense of superiority was overcome and the recording of anthropological data became more rigorous. How difficult this was can be seen by considering what is widely recognized as the first anthropological theory of religion.

The Englishman Edward Burnett Tylor (1832–1917) developed this first theory, which provided a framework both for comparing religions and for considering the manners in which religions developed. Tylor noted that all societies had a belief in spirits, and he attempted to explain this by asking which human experiences could be so profound and yet so common that they had led people everywhere to develop these religious concepts. His answers were the experiences of dreaming and death. Tylor argued that the universal human experience of dreaming—during which a nonphysical entity appears to leave the physical body—would inevitably lead people to make a distinction between a material body and a nonmaterial "soul." Death could then be explained as a permanent cutting of the ties between the two, while other religious phenomena (trance, possession, ghosts, etc.) could be construed as unusual relationships between them. Tylor used the term **anima** (from the Latin *anim*, meaning "air" or "breath") to refer to the nonmaterial aspect of our existence (e.g., spirits and souls) that resided within ordinary bodies and objects. Anima is the animating principle that is responsible for life and activity. Tylor proposed that the religious systems of every society had developed out of this recognition of the anima, making **animism** the original and universal basis of religion.

Tylor then applied one of the prevailing ideas of his time—the notion of progress—to religion. The idea of progress was based on the recognition that as time went by, both nature and societies produced increasingly complex forms, forms that were generally regarded as improvements. Tylor used his own religion (he was a Quaker), which teaches that there is just one deity, as the standard for his comparisons. He knew that the people of many past societies (such as the Egyptians, Greeks, and Romans) had believed in numerous deities, each of which was responsible for a particular facet of nature. Different Gods and Goddesses were responsible for the weather, plant growth, warfare, and love. Tylor suggested that the one God of Christianity had supplanted these many Gods when people came to realize that these were simply different aspects of the one. In Tylor's eyes, monotheism evolved out of polytheism.

Working in the opposite direction, Tylor then argued that the many Gods of polytheism developed out of earlier animistic beliefs that the world was populated by spirits. As more complex societies emerged and people became more sophisticated in their thinking, they realized that the many different groups of anima were controlled by a smaller number of more powerful anima (just as different groups of people are controlled by a smaller number of rulers). These "anima leaders" were the first deities. Eventually, these lesser deities came to be seen as nothing more than different aspects of one all-powerful deity.

This model of religious development—from animism to polytheism and ultimately monotheism—was central to Tylor's theory of **unilineal evolution**, his idea that all societies developed in essentially the same sequences, although at different rates and times. Because it provided a way to compare societies and determine where each stood on an evolutionary scale that stretched from "savagery" to "barbarism" and ultimately to "civilization," the unilineal evolutionary model is regarded as the first **comparative** theory of modern anthropology. Other scholars soon applied this theory to compare and classify societies on the basis of their technology, marriage and family forms, and political structures. But no matter which domain of human activity was being considered, one thing was constant. The "civilized," most highly evolved way of doing something was always the way that it was done in the scholar's own society; that is, in Europe or the United States. Consequently, not only monotheism, but also monogamy, writing, and nuclear families, came to be regarded as hallmarks of civilization.

Societies that lacked these traits were by definition something less than civilized.

As the unilineal evolutionary model was applied to an ever larger number of cultural traits, however, it became apparent that it was fundamentally flawed and that not all societies could be fitted into such a simple and rigid schema. The ancient Greeks were polytheistic, but practiced monogamy and had writing. The Moroccans of Tylor's time believed in one God and had writing, but many practiced polygamy. From the perspective of our time, it is clear that unilineal evolutionary thinking was simplistic, and the assertion that Western societies represented the pinnacle of social evolution was clearly self-serving and ethnocentric. Furthermore, the societies that Tylor and others used for their comparisons did not accurately reflect the diversity found in human societies, and much of the information about these societies was inaccurate. But in spite of these shortcomings, Tylor's unilineal evolutionary model deserves recognition as the first comparative theory of anthropology, and it spurred other anthropologists to think about the social determinants of different forms of religiosity.

Tylor's greatest legacy may be the fact that he introduced the word "culture" into the English language (although he used it as a synonym for "civilization"). Tylor viewed culture as something that a person or a society acquired *more* of while progressing along the path from savagery through barbarism to civilization. Like his theory, Tylor's definition has been replaced by a much more sophisticated understanding of culture that recognizes that all human groups possess a complex culture of their own.

Historical Particularism and Cultural Relativism: The Foundations of American Anthropology

The person most responsible for pointing out the inadequacies in the theory of unilineal evolution was Franz Boas (1858–1942), who is considered the "father" of American anthropology. Born and educated in Germany, Boas earned his doctorate in physics with a thesis titled "Contributions to the Understanding of the Color of Water" (1881). In 1883–1884, he lived in Baffinland (an island in eastern Canada) as part of a team conducting geographical research on the island. There, he encountered the Inuit ("Eskimo") people.

Boas was impressed by the sense of community he observed among the Inuit. When a hunter was successful, he shared his catch with the other members of his

Edward B. Tylor is credited with introducing the word "culture" into the English language. Because he equated culture with civilization, Tylor's definition implied that people in different societies have "more" or "less" culture. The anthropologists of today have a different view: Every society has its own unique culture, and each person learns his or her own unique version of their society's culture.

"Culture, or civilization, taken in its broad, ethnographic sense, is that complex whole which includes knowledge, belief, art, morals, law, custom, and any other capabilities and habits acquired by man as a member of society."

From Tylor, Edward. 1920 [1871]. *Primitive Culture*. New York: J.P. Putnam's Sons, p. 1.

the information that was used to support the unilineal evolutionary theory. His training in physics taught him that the development of theories requires accurate, replicable, and unbiased data. But many observations about other cultures—even those of experienced anthropologists—were unsystematic, superficial, and often tainted by the researchers' ethnocentric attitudes toward other peoples and customs. How, he wondered, could truly adequate theories about human society and behavior ever be produced from such poor data? Boas also recognized that the data which could be used to develop such theories were disappearing rapidly as native peoples around the world, especially in the Americas, were being changed and even destroyed before they had ever been studied.

These realizations led Boas to argue that the anthropologists of his time should focus on "salvage anthropology," collecting good field data while such data were still available and leaving the development of theories for a later time. He was a great advocate of **fieldwork**, a research method that involves living with the people being studied in order to understand their everyday lives and the ways in which they look at the world. To ensure the quality and the validity of the data, Boas argued that anthropologists needed to learn the language of the people they were studying and live among them for at least a year. This would give the fieldworkers an opportunity to observe the annual cycle of events and as many of the customs and practices as possible of the people they were studying. It also would allow the workers to actively participate in different aspects of those people's daily lives. This **participant-observation** would also enable the fieldworkers to understand the culture of the people they were studying from the perspective of those people, thereby helping the workers overcome their ethnocentrism.

While Boas recognized that fieldwork could demonstrate the ways in which societies differ from one another today, he also understood that historical and archaeological data would provide important information about how those societies had changed over time. Consequently, Boas argued that each culture was the product of a unique constellation of environmental and historical factors, and that each thus needed to be studied and understood on its own terms. This relativistic way of looking at societies—known as **historical particularism**—contrasted with the absolutist ideas of Tylor and other unilineal evolutionary thinkers, who argued that changes in human societies invariably follow the same sequence as they progress along the path to culture (= civilization).

group, and even with the visiting scientists. When there was no food, the community endured hunger together. This contrasted greatly with Boas' experiences in Germany, with its emphasis on private ownership and looking after oneself, as well as the treatment of the German Jews as second-class citizens. The Inuit, he found, did not make such distinctions.

These experiences led Boas to shift his focus from the study of the physical world to the study of humans. As he became familiar with the Inuit language and culture, Boas realized that their worldview was more abstract and sophisticated than previously thought. He began to question unilineal evolutionary thinking, which ranked the Inuit as "savages," far below the "civilized" peoples of Europe. His scientific sensibilities were also struck by the inadequacies of

Cultural Relativism

Boas did not make a distinction between "savage" or "civilized" societies, and he considered the ethnocentrism expressed in such rankings unscientific. (Would a scientist prejudge a planet or a chemical compound?) He revolutionized the study of humans by showing that each society has its own characteristic way of life and its own culture. Boas effectively pluralized the concept of culture that Tylor introduced into English. "Culture" became "cultures," and different cultures became equally relevant objects of study. This led to an insight that is one of anthropology's most important contributions to modern thought: **cultural relativism.** Cultural relativism is first and foremost a methodological strategy that reminds us that we should examine other cultures on their own terms rather than following the assumptions of our own culture. For example, if we want to understand why some people believe that handling venomous snakes is an appropriate expression of their religious faith, we need to take the reasons they give into consideration along with other information about the practice. Cultural relativism is also a humanistic position that reminds us to treat people and their beliefs with respect.

Cultural relativism is not, as some philosophers and critics have suggested, an ethical position that implies that "anything goes." Attempting to understand the worldview and motivation of other people does not mean that we should do nothing in the face of terrorism, genocide, religious persecution, or any other type of offensive or oppressive human behavior simply because it is practiced by the members of some culture. But it does mean that if we want to understand why people engage in such activities, we need to consider their own points of view, as well as the historical and social influences on their culture. Cultural relativism does not allow us to write off the members of a particular culture as "evil" simply because their beliefs and values are different from our own. Instead, it calls us to consider what people's beliefs and values mean to them. Cultural relativism is, in a sense, the anthropological version of the old maxim "Before you criticize someone, walk a mile in their shoes." Only then can we understand the people of a culture as they really are, within the system of meaning that is relevant to them. Cultural relativism moves us away from the notion that any one culture is inherently superior to another, and teaches us to regard each culture as a unique expression of the human propensity for culture.[1]

To avoid being judgmental when studying other cultures, anthropologists attempt to adapt and integrate themselves as fully as possible into the culture they are studying. They learn how to dress "appropriately" (that is, according to the standards of the society in which they are living), to use that society's language and conceptual system, and to participate in both the mundane and the significant events in the culture. Many anthropologists are adopted into the communities they study, thereby becoming recognized members in a system of kin relations. They may even participate in religious rituals.

[1]This is why we do not follow the common English practice of capitalizing the word "God" when referring to one particular deity while writing others in lowercase ("god," "goddesses"). We capitalize all occurrences as a way to emphasize the importance that these conceptions have for those who believe in them.

SOCIETY AND CULTURE

At this point, it is important to clarify two commonly used, but frequently misunderstood, terms. A human **society** is a group of people who are organized or structured in some way. The National Organization for Women, the U.S. Chamber of Commerce, and the National Council of Churches are all societies that were established to promote the shared interests of their members. Most of the time, however, the word refers to a nation or ethnic group. This is why we speak of American society, Jamaican society, or Cherokee society. But whether these groups formed voluntarily to pursue specific aims or whether their identity is the result of historical forces, the people in any society are linked together by shared ideas and values. They are linked, in fact, by a common culture.

Culture is something that all humans acquire by virtue of growing up in a society and learning society's ideas and values about such matters as the proper types of foods to eat, the causes of illness, and the types of behaviors that are considered appropriate in the presence of an elder. Although we are born into a society, we are not born with a culture. Culture is something we must learn. Humans have an innate propensity for learning culture by virtue of certain characteristics of our brains and bodies. If we think of our brains as our "mental hardware," then culture is the "social software" that stipulates how the hardware will be used.

Yet even anthropologists have limits on how far they are willing to step outside their own beliefs. Some are unwilling to abandon their own religious world-view; others have a skeptical attitude toward all religious thought. It is precisely with respect to the study of religion that cultural relativism is most difficult to achieve, for anthropologists and nonanthropologists alike. Could you accept a religion that viewed human sacrifice as a normal religious behavior, especially if it asked you to sacrifice your own child to that religion's God? Like most other people, anthropologists would be unwilling to participate in such behavior.

The Four-Field Approach of Anthropology

Franz Boas' emphasis on the collection of accurate and relevant data obtained by learning the local language and conducting long-term fieldwork laid the foundation for a scientific understanding of humans. His admonition to study each society and culture on its own terms also helped transform anthropology into a humanistic discipline. His focus on looking at humans from multiple points of view led to the development of a uniquely American anthropology based on the "four-field approach" provided by cultural anthropology, archaeology, linguistic anthropology, and biological anthropology. This four-field approach provides an integrative and interdisciplinary framework for investigating religiosity.

Cultural Anthropology

Cultural anthropology focuses on culture, those aspects of human life that we learn from members of our society and in turn pass on to others. While the focus of early fieldwork was on non-Western groups such as the Native Americans that were being devastated by Western expansion, many cultural anthropologists now work in modern societies. They may study faith healers or neopagans in the United States or conduct fieldwork to find out why so many people are now being drawn to "mega-churches" that meet in converted office buildings and sports arenas.

The Components of Culture. As humans, we have to learn a culture to survive. A person may be an American, a Kwakiutl, or a Samoan by birth. But the person does not automatically know all the things he or she needs to know to be an American, a Kwakiutl, or a Samoan. Each of us learns these things as we grow up among the people who, through their words and behavior, teach us their culture. This is why the things you learned about when you were a child probably seem so "natural" to you now.

Consider the things Americans eat and drink, and what the religion you were brought up in says about them. If you are a Christian or an atheist, it may seem perfectly normal and "natural" for you to have a hamburger and a milkshake when you go out. But if you are an Orthodox Jew, eating meat and dairy products at the same time is a violation of the dietary rules of *kahsrut* (kosher). You could have either the milkshake or the hamburger (provided that the latter was made of beef and *not* ham) and, after waiting for several hours, you could have the other. The foods would have to be prepared in separate dishes or at different times. If you are a Hindu, you would likely avoid hamburgers entirely because they are made from the flesh of cows, animals that are regarded as sacred. But you could have the milkshake. There are many reasons for religious dietary rules, which vary with the environment and the season and may have as much to do with affirming group identity as they do with the avoidance of parasites and diseases. Religious dietary rules, which are often based in beliefs and attitudes about what is "clean" and "unclean," also find their expression in objects and behaviors.

Thus, it is useful to think of culture as having three basic components: a material (or tangible) component; a behavioral (or action) component; and an ideational (or mental) component. The **material component** is quite literally the physical manifestation of culture and is typically the aspect that is most readily apparent to an outsider. Religious examples of the material component of culture include a Greek Orthodox church, a Hopi kachina doll, and a Jewish *talith* (prayer shawl).

The second component of culture is the **behavioral component**, which is culture in action. We easily notice behaviors that differ from what we know and expect, although we may not be able to precisely determine why a particular behavior strikes us as unusual. People talk differently, they walk differently, and they eat, drink, sleep, and greet one another differently in different societies. Religious examples of the behavioral component of culture include a Catholic going to confession, a Hindu placing flowers before an image of Krishna, and a Muslim slaughtering an animal according to the strict rules of *dhabh*.

The third component of culture is the **ideational component**. Although the term is related to the concept of "idea," it also refers to the emotional features of a culture. The ideational aspect is typically the most difficult to notice and to understand. It takes time to learn the concepts of a culture and the values associated with those concepts. You don't step off of an airplane and immediately see that firstborn sons have a responsibility to continue the family lineage or that elders have no fear of dying because they know they will be reborn. Since it is so abstract, the ideational component is the most complex aspect of culture to study. But it is also the most important, for it provides the rationale for both the behaviors of a person and the material objects he or she makes and uses. Religious examples of the ideational component of culture include the Buddhist emphasis on compassion, the Christian belief in heaven, and the Polynesian concept of *tabu*.

Although we distinguish these three components of culture, they are actually interwoven—intimately and necessarily interlinked. Our thoughts direct our behaviors and social relations, as well as our interactions with the material world. Think of one common article of Christian religious culture: a cross or crucifix. At the material level, we can easily discern its two perpendicular arms, one vertical and the other horizontal. But the behaviors that are associated with the crucifix might cause a person who is not a Christian to furrow his brow in bewilderment. Why do some people bow before it while others do not? Why do movies depict actors using crucifixes to ward off vampires, but not werewolves? And why, if crucifixes are such objects of veneration, do people use them for trivial purposes such as decorating their cars, making them into jewelry, and even putting them on their clothing? These behaviors, of course, are linked to ideas and emotions about the crucifix, which at the ideational level is a **symbol** for many things: the sacrifice of Jesus Christ, the membership in a community of believers, and, in a broader sense, the power of the Christian deity. Yet we must remember that the ideas and emotions are not present in the crucifix itself, but are projected onto it by the people who look at it. A Taoist, Jain, or Sikh will look at the same cross and see something very different from a Christian.

Methods of Cultural Anthropology: Ethnography and Ethnology.

One basic aim of anthropology is to understand how the people in one culture see the world and to translate this into terms that people from other cultures can understand. By learning the local language, conducting long-term fieldwork, and engaging in participant observation, anthropologists are able to develop a report or description of a society (or of some aspect thereof). Such a description is known as an **ethnography** (from the Greek *ethnos*, meaning "culture" or "people," and *graph(os)*, meaning "something drawn or written").

Ethnographies are the source of the data used in comparative or cross-cultural studies to develop more general theories of culture and models of culture change, a practice known as **ethnology**. Anthropologists use ethnological comparisons to discern the universal features of human societies (including features of religions) and identify the ecological, social, and other factors related to nonuniversal behaviors (e.g., spirit possession).

We can understand the value of cross-cultural comparisons by considering the practice of human sacrifice and ritual cannibalism among the ancient Aztecs who lived in the Valley of Mexico. During their rituals to honor and placate their Gods, the Aztecs sacrificed thousands of people over the course of a few days. The victims were often captured weeks or even months before their sacrifice, and Aztec beliefs dictated that the captives be well fed and looked after so that they would reflect well in the eyes of the Gods. The amount of resources (food, space, and labor) that this system required was enormous. Why did the Aztecs bother?

The Aztecs themselves believed that their Gods demanded these sacrifices. While this reason may have been all that an Aztec required, anthropologists consider other explanations as well. Why did the Aztecs conduct human sacrifice while many other groups did not? Did they need to eat human flesh because their normal diet was lacking in protein? Or was the practice a response to other ecological factors?

The Emic and Etic Distinction.

These different possible explanations for Aztec sacrifice demonstrate that there are two main perspectives for considering such practices. The first is the **emic**, or insider's, point of view—the explanations that the people themselves provide for their behaviors. The emic (Aztec) explanation for human sacrifice and ritual cannibalism was that their Gods demanded it. The second is the **etic**, or outsider's, point of view, which is derived from cross-cultural research. Here, scientific methods are used to investigate whether social, environmental, and other factors might have led to the practice of cannibalism in Aztec and other societies. (We will consider these factors in Chapter 10).

By comparing similar practices in different societies, we can discern the underlying causes of cultural phenomena and determine the dynamics and principles of culture that are valid in most—if not all—societies. By combining both the humanistic (emic) and scientific (etic) perspectives, anthropologists are able to develop a more comprehensive understanding of human behavior. In this book, we will use both of these approaches as we explore religiosity and attempt to understand the roles it likely played in the human past.

Universal Expressions of Religiosity. One method anthropologists use in their search for features common to all religions is to compare the variety of behaviors and beliefs found in the religious practices of a random sample of cultures. One cross-cultural comparison (Winkelman 1992) of a number of premodern societies and their religious beliefs has suggested that there are several types of universal expressions of religion. A feature that is a part of all aspects of anything religious can be considered as a **religious universal**. Given the diversity of religious activities, such universals are rare. One likely religious universal is the assumption of a spirit or supernatural domain.

Cultural universals of religion are features of religiosity found in all cultures, although not necessarily part of all of the rituals of any culture. For example, religious techniques for producing unusual experiences and states of consciousness are found in all cultures, but these cultures also have religious activities that do not involve such experiences. The following features are cultural universals of religion:

Spirit Power Beliefs. Humans hold a variety of beliefs about spirit entities (Gods, ghosts, etc.) and their abilities. These "supernatural" spirits are often said to have abilities that exceed or even defy the "natural" order. Yet in spite of these abilities, spirits are also said to possess many human features.

Magico-Religious Techniques. All societies have techniques for exerting an influence on the spirits they believe in. These techniques may involve language (spells, prayers) as well as material objects (amulets, symbols). The techniques may be directed toward affecting the spirits themselves or toward affecting or counteracting what they do, such as controlling the weather. Magic, in one form or another, is one of the most common of these culturally universal techniques.

Good and Malevolent Characteristics. The powers that humans attribute to spirits include powers to help and to harm, to reward and to punish. These beliefs find their expression in religious practices whose intention is to promote the beneficial effects of spirits and to ward off malevolent effects or protect people against them. Every society has practices that provide protection from the spirits and attempt to influence their actions; these actions may involve submission as well as dominance behaviors. All cultures have social rituals for acquiring power, protection, and information from spirits. Because spirits are understood to have both good and malevolent characteristics, they are

able to serve as "role models" that teach the members of a society about appropriate and inappropriate attitudes and behaviors.

Community Rituals. All societies have collective rituals for interacting with spirits. Some of these involve the entire community, while others focus on smaller groups, such as a clan or a family. In all societies, some leadership roles are associated with supernatural powers. Religious leaders are also social leaders and may rise to power because of their perceived connection with the spirit world, because of their heritage within a special clan, or because of power acquired through other spiritual interactions.

Altered States of Consciousness. All societies acknowledge and accept some types of special spiritual experiences distinct from ordinary experiences, and some people in every society will become religious specialists who enter into an altered state of consciousness for the purpose of contacting a spirit entity. While in this altered state, they are able to interact with the spirits and to invoke their powers and knowledge, especially for healing. All cultures teach at least some of their religious practitioners how to induce and utilize such states of consciousness.

Divination. All cultures have practices for acquiring information from the spirit world. A variety of procedures, including altered states of consciousness, are used to acquire information needed for subsistence, group movement, and protection. Divination is especially important in diagnosing and treating diseases.

Healing and Illness. Healing rituals are another cultural universal of religion. The belief that religion can play a role in health and healing is present in every culture. In most cultures, the central healing practices take place in a religious context, and there are always religious practitioners who have a responsibility for healing members of the group. One universal belief, manifested as the "spirit aggression" theory of illness, is that spirits can attack people and cause illness. There are also universal beliefs regarding the ability of humans to cause supernatural illness, manifested in sorcery and witchcraft beliefs and practices. Sorcery, a deliberately malevolent activity, is a cultural universal of religion. In contrast, witchcraft, which involves inadvertent or unconscious magical effects, is a social universal of religion (see next section). Although found in all cultures, these cultural universals of religion are expressed in distinct ways within each culture. Cultures differ with regard to the specific spirits in which they believe, the characteristics they attribute to these spirits, and the rituals and magical techniques they utilize to interact with the spirits.

Social universals of religion are found only in certain kinds of societies. Social universals of religion emerge under specific social circumstances and, consequently, differ from one society to the next. For example, priests are only found in politically integrated agricultural societies with a government hierarchy. The idea of spirit *possession*, the notion that a religious practitioner can be taken over and controlled by a spirit entity, appears to be a worldwide phenomenon, but it too is found only in societies with complex political hierarchies.

Hunter–gatherer societies are associated with different social universals of religion. It is in these societies that shamanism is found. In contrast, shamans are not found in the religious traditions of complex societies, where their functions have either disappeared or been taken over by more specialized religious practitioners, including witches, shamanic healers, sorcerers, and priests.

Archaeology

Archaeology is the field of anthropology that brings a **temporal** or "deep-time" perspective to anthropology. Archaeologists study ancient artifacts and other relevant materials (such as animal and plant remains) to reconstruct past societies and to understand the processes of social and culture change. Although the idea of searching for ancient artifacts may conjure up images of Indiana Jones or Lara Croft, the destructive activities of these fictional characters are very different from the work of real archaeologists, for whom unglamorous fragments of pottery or the outlines left behind by long-vanished structures may answer more questions than a crystal skull or golden statue. Archaeologists interpret artifacts using the insights and findings of the other fields of anthropology, as well as molecular biology, evolutionary psychology, geology, physics, botany, and zoology. By studying fossilized pollen and animal bones, for example, we can learn a great deal about the climate of a particular region in ancient times. By investigating the sediment layers found at a site, we can determine whether a society disappeared because of water shortages or as a result of a catastrophe, such as a volcanic eruption.

Because it takes the study of human culture into the past, archaeology provides us with one of our most important windows on early religiosity. Under the proper conditions, the material objects found at an archaeological site can provide important insights into the behavioral and ideational aspects of a culture. By analyzing the different features of artifacts (such as the materials from which they were made, the techniques used to make them, the locations where they were found, and the symbols they display), we can learn about the ways in which these objects were used and the beliefs and values of the people who made them. Differences in the spacing of bodies in a cemetery as well as the objects left with the bodies can provide insights into the presence of social hierarchies. The fact that the largest and most lasting structures that were built in the first cities were temples strongly supports the idea that religious belief systems and priestly leaders played important roles in the development of the first large-scale societies. Although we will never be able to completely reconstruct the past, archaeologists are able to provide important insights into how ancient humans lived and worshipped. One important technique is to compare archaeological artifacts from the past to analogous materials from present-day cultures.

Ethnographic and Ethnological Analogy. Archaeologists generally study the significance of artifacts by analogy, drawing upon information about historical and existing cultures to gain insights into the meaning of ancient objects and behaviors. Another method archaeologists use is **ethnographic analogy**, the practice of comparing the society they are excavating with ethnographic descriptions of recent or contemporary cultures that share similar features. Because cultures resemble one another in so many ways, archaeologists can reconstruct the broad outlines of long-dead cultures known only through their material remains (artifacts) by comparing these artifacts with objects from other cultures whose details are well known from anthropological fieldwork. This process of comparing archaeological and ethnographic data is one of the most important tools that archaeologists now use to describe past cultures and has provided us with important insights into many ancient cultures.

For example, evidence from Southwest Asia indicates that humans have been intentionally burying their dead for at least 100,000 years, sometimes with tools and other objects. But the material and behavioral evidence of these past cultural practices do not tell us much about the motivations of these long-dead people. What do these burials indicate? The method of ethnographic analogy can suggest an answer. In contemporary cultures around the world, burials are associated with beliefs in an afterlife. While we may never know the actual reasons why our ancestors began burying their dead, it is reasonable to assume that the people of those times had begun to think and feel in ways similar to modern humans and had a belief in an afterlife and souls.

The body of *il Giovane Principe* ("the little prince") was found at Arene Candide (Italy). The 20,000-year-old skeleton, which showed signs of disease, had been sprinkled with ochre and buried with a necklace made of mammoth ivory and a bracelet made of shells. The left hand held a flint blade.

Of course, such inferences can be wrong. A more reliable method of understanding the past by comparing it with the present can be achieved through **ethnological analogy**, which compares the patterns found in a sample of similar societies. The general insights about certain types of societies (such as hunter–gatherers or foragers) that have been derived through systematic cross-cultural research can reveal universal patterns of human social behavior and enable us to make much more secure inferences about the past. For instance, studies of recent and contemporary hunter–gatherer societies around the world allow us to safely infer that men have been the primary hunters in all hunter–gatherer societies that ever existed. These cross-cultural studies have provided important ethnological insights not only about people's subsistence method, lifestyle, and political organization, but also about their religious activities and beliefs (known as shamanism). This information

about the religious practices of known hunter–gatherer societies enables us to interpret and make inferences about the religious behaviors of hunter–gatherers in the past and even to reconstruct the origins of religiosity. By drawing upon models of human behavior derived from cross-cultural analysis, archaeology can help us to interpret the behaviors and beliefs of our ancestors and uncover the roots of religiosity.

Linguistic Anthropology

Linguistic anthropology—also known as anthropological linguistics—is the study of the role that language plays in human life. Language is the most important tool that humans use to express meaning and transmit cultural ideas, including ideas about religion. It is through language that we are able to communicate what we are thinking and feeling when we see an object like a crucifix, bow down before an image of God, or experience a sense of contact with a spirit. Language is so central to human life that many anthropologists and other scientists regard it as the single most important criterion for distinguishing humans from all other animals. Linguistic anthropologists record the languages of different societies and consider how these describe, shape, and even create different cultural worlds. They compare languages to investigate the extent to which language families and cultures have changed over time. They also investigate the reasons why humans have language and the role that languages play in shaping the natural and supernatural realities we experience. Of course, other animals also communicate. What makes human language different is the ways it enables us to communicate and the things we are able to communicate about. Much of what is conceptualized as religion would not be possible without the symbolic capacities that underlie language.

Unique Features of Human Language. Animals and even plants communicate in a variety of ways. Many forms of communication use chemicals. Animals mark their territories with urine and musk, and plants produce scents that attract insects and other animals in order to promote pollination and seed dispersal. A great deal of animal communication also occurs through ritualized behaviors, such as the courtship display of a male peacock when he fans open his tail feathers and the dance of a bee that tells the other members of a hive where and how far away a field of flowers is. Then there are the various grunts, howls, squeaks, and other sounds animals make to let others know about their position or the presence of predators. These communication systems used by nonhuman animals are **closed systems of language**. This means that the sounds a particular

Box 1.1 SYMBOLISM AND SPIRITUALITY

In his book *The Symbolic Species*, Terrence Deacon (1997) describes how the evolution of our symbolic capacity may have led our ancestors to develop an understanding of a spirit world. Social animals learn about the world around them in part because they are able to derive information from others. This enables them to develop a "theory of mind" that they can then use to understand the perceptions of others, thereby facilitating social communication and organization. This theory of mind involves interpreting the likely thoughts, feelings, and behaviors of other members of the group. Deacon argues that the development of symbols greatly expanded this ability to understand the minds and intentions of others and made it possible for our ancestors to develop ever more complex ideas about what was going on in the minds of others—including unseen others of the spirit world.

As our ancestors' symbolic abilities grew, they began to apply them to a wider range of perceptions. Now they not only attempted to understand the meanings and intentions that were being expressed in the behaviors of the other members of their species, but also began to do the same with the patterns and phenomena they perceived in the natural world. Eventually, their evolving predispositions to seek patterns and look for explanations led them to attribute meaning to the minds of unseen actors. The patterns of the natural world became cryptic messages, symbols communicated to us by imperceptible agents. According to Deacon, humans have an irrepressible need to assign meaning to the unseen agents that we experience as spirits.

Both the domain of spirits and the symbolic domain refer not to any physical reality, but to an imagined reality that is created through a network of associations shared by a cultural and linguistic community. Our experience of non-material, spiritual meaning is based in our experience of shared meaning in symbol systems expressed in the imagined minds of others. When we use these symbol systems, we mentally visualize disembodied abstractions, an exercise that prepares us to imagine a spirit world. Deacon suggests that even our sense that our self or mind exists independently of our body is a product of the symbols we use, for these have led us to assume that we possess a kind of "virtual" identity that is independent of our physical body.

The evolution of symbolic representations expanded our ancestors' abilities to use internalized abstract models to engage in the trial-and-error process of exploration of different possible circumstances. By providing them (and us) with a way of understanding the world that exceeded the "here and now" focus that has shaped so much of our evolution, symbols created a risk-free way to ponder alternate possibilities and realities without actually having to experience them. This option vastly extended our capacities for forethought and extended planning, and has made it possible for imagined goals and possible futures to take precedence over the immediate context in shaping our behavior.

species makes always mean essentially the same thing. In contrast, human languages are **open systems of language** in which a finite number of sounds can be combined into an infinite number of utterances, making it possible to create new words and communicate a virtually limitless range of ideas. This is the basis for our symbolic capacity, which allows us to associate meanings arbitrarily with behaviors or objects.

This symbolic capacity gives rise to another unique aspect of human language, **displacement**—the ability to speak of things that are not happening right now in our presence. Displacement enables humans to talk about things that happened in the past, speak of hopes or plans about the future, and even communicate about things that never happened at all. Displacement is key to many aspects of religiosity. It is what enables us to talk about our future rebirth or reward in heaven and exchange information about unseen forces and places that we will

never be able to directly perceive (see Box 1.1: Symbolism and Spirituality).

Language and Experience: The Sapir–Whorf Hypothesis. Our ability to use language to speak of things that are not occurring in the here and now brings up several important questions about the relationship between language and reality. To what extent does language mirror reality? Could certain things exist without language? Can language actually create reality? These questions were given expression by two American linguists, Edward Sapir (1884–1939) and Benjamin Whorf (1897–1934), in what has become known as the **Sapir–Whorf hypothesis**.

The hypothesis has two forms. The "weak" form, **linguistic relativism**, suggests that language *shapes* the way we think about reality. Because different languages structure the world in different ways, a speaker of one

Box 1.2 TRANSLATING THE IDEAS OF RELIGION

The Sapir–Whorf hypothesis raises important questions about translations of an original text or idea. Whether a translation can ever convey precisely the same sense in the target language as in the original is questionable. Translators must often choose among several more-or-less equivalent words, and the consequences of their choices can be significant. For example, in the Old Testament book of Isaiah (7:14), the Aramaic word *almah* is used to refer to the woman who would give birth to "Immanuel." *Almah* can be translated both as "maiden" (i.e., a young, unmarried woman) and "virgin," and the translator's choice of one term over another has had important implications for Christian (especially Roman Catholic) thought.

Islamic thinking explicitly recognizes that translation always involves interpretation. While the Qur'an has been translated into numerous languages, such translations are not regarded as authoritative. That is, the Islamic position on matters of faith cannot be determined by consulting translated versions of the Qur'an, but only by examining the original Arabic text. Muslims believe that the Qur'an was given to Muhammad by God in Arabic; as a result, most also believe that the Qur'an should be read in that language. Because of this belief, converts to Islam throughout the world exert themselves to learn Arabic. The fact that over one billion people strive to read their sacred scriptures in the same language has helped to create a linguistic and religious community that binds together people in countries with cultures as diverse as those of Indonesia, the Netherlands, Saudi Arabia, and the United States. Because the Qur'an also provides a durable example for the Arabic language, Arabic has changed less since the time of Muhammad (who died in 632 C.E.) than did English or any other language of Europe.

language will learn to perceive things differently than the speaker of another language. The "hard" form of the hypothesis, **linguistic determinism**, suggests that language actually *creates* the way we think about reality.

We find support for the idea of linguistic relativism in the distinctions provided by the vocabularies of different languages. For example, the ancient Greeks had three different words (*eros*, *philia*, and *agape*) to express the concept known to English speakers as "love," suggesting that they distinguished among three different emotions. The Hindu and Buddhist traditions have a large vocabulary of terms (e.g., *samadhi*, *zazen*) to describe their meditation experiences, indicating that they are able to discern—and thus experience—states of consciousness that were unknown in the West until Westerners learned about both the meditation practices and the experiences that they produce.

The idea of linguistic determinism suggests that such places as Hades, purgatory, or Valhalla may only exist because there are words for them. Since many of the concepts that religions talk about are not open to any type of objective evaluation, it is language that creates these realities. People's firm beliefs in heaven, hell, Gods, and other religious concepts illustrate the power of religion to create reality in people's minds and in their behaviors. Myths, the explanations of the world provided by religion, would be unthinkable without language. Language enables us to both develop and grasp such concepts as "redemption" and *nirvana*, it provides names for such unseen forces as "grace" and

mana, and it makes it possible for us to discuss the wrath of God and the powers of ancestors. Here again, we can see why it is so important for an anthropologist to learn the local language when conducting fieldwork. It is only when an anthropologist is able to speak of such concepts, forces, and beings in the same terms as the people she is studying that she can begin to understand the world in the same way as those people (see Box 1.2: Translating the Ideas of Religion).

Historical Linguistics. **Historical linguistics** is a subfield of anthropological linguistics that studies the origins of words and the ways in which languages change over time. It provides a tool for studying the concepts of religiosity in the past and examining changes in religious behaviors and beliefs over time. Historical linguists find the roots of ancient thought by comparing **cognates**, words that have similar sounds and meanings in different languages. By reconstructing the concepts present in common ancestral languages, the science of **etymology** (a subfield of historical linguistics that examines the derivations of words) can shed light on ancient religions in the origins of specific words. For example, the English word "religion" is derived from the Latin term *religiō*, which referred to a "bond between man and the gods" (AHD, p. 1099). The Latin *religiō* has its origins in words meaning "to bind" and is reflected in the Indo-European root *leig-* ("to bind"). Today, we still understand religion as something that binds people to a God or Gods and to one another. Many languages in the

Indo-European language family lack cognates for the word "religion." This indicates that the concept was not present in the original Indo-European languages and suggests that it was developed after these agricultural people had begun to spread across Europe.

The common roots of a different Indo-European religious concept can be seen in the many cognates for the English word "sacred," which is derived from the Indo-European root sak- ("to sanctify"). The similarities among the English "saint," Spanish "santo," French "saint," and Italian "san" reflect their common derivation from the Latin term sanctus ("sacred"). Other Indo-European languages have similar terms. Sak- is also the root for the word "sacrament" (as well as "sacrifice"). Today, the word "sacrament" is commonly used to refer to certain Christian (especially Roman Catholic) rituals. In Latin, sacramentum originally referred to the oath that Roman soldiers would speak as part of their initiation to military service. Here again, we can observe similarities in the meanings of the root of this term and the way in which it came to be used in different religious traditions. Although today's sacraments are very different, the idea of initiation and the practice of oath-taking is still a part of such Christian rituals as baptism, confirmation, and marriage.

Biological Anthropology

The fourth field of anthropology is **biological anthropology**. Also known as physical anthropology, this is the branch of anthropology that explicitly focuses on humans as *animals*. Biological anthropologists investigate an extraordinarily wide variety of phenomena. For example, molecular anthropologists compare samples of DNA collected from people around the world to develop a more comprehensive understanding of the ways in which humans differ from one another as individuals and the ways in which we are the same. Primatologists observe the behavior of monkeys and apes in the wild and study the cognitive and linguistic abilities of primates in laboratory settings. Paleoanthropologists use fossil remains and the artifacts found with them to reconstruct the sequence of events that led to the appearance of modern humans. These and other lines of evidence enable us to distinguish the traits and abilities that humans share with other animals from those that are unique to our species. They also enable us to consider the sequence in which we acquired our uniquely human abilities, including the human propensity for religiosity and the ways this finds expression in spirituality and religion.

Biological anthropology offers two important perspectives for looking at religiosity. First, the study of *human evolution* provides us with a "deep time" perspective for exploring why religiosity first appeared and how it became established in every culture in the world. The evidence contained in the fossil record, and comparative studies of the behaviors and other abilities of different animals, indicate that religiosity did not appear all at once at some moment in the past, but developed gradually over time. (We will consider this development further in Chapters 4 and 5). Second, the study of *human variation* makes it possible for us to understand how and why people differ from one another, both in terms of physical traits such as our hair color and in the expression of our religious impulses. Why do some people readily hear and see spirits, while others never have a religious experience? Biological anthropological research suggests that these differences are not due solely to differences in our cultural or personal upbringing, but are also the result of differences in our biological makeup.

How Humans Differ. Humans differ from one another in many ways. Many of the ways in which we differ are the results of **mutations**, random changes in a sequence of DNA known as a **gene**. Genes code for proteins, so a change in a gene may produce an altered version of the protein for which it codes. If the new version of the protein provides the individual who possesses it with an advantage over the other members of its population who do not possess it, then that individual may produce more offspring than the other members of the population. An individual might possess such an advantage because he or she can metabolize some food item more efficiently, can see more effectively at night, or can hear voices that others cannot.

It is important to note that mutations do not occur just because they are "needed"; they are random events, and most are actually deleterious to reproduction and survival. There is no intention or direction to evolution. However, once a mutation does arise, it can be subjected to selective pressures coming from the environment, and it can provide the basis for new traits and future adaptations.

Some human characteristics are the product of a single gene; they are **monogenic**. Your ABO blood type, for example, is determined solely by the two copies of the ABO gene that you have inherited from your parent. Such traits do not change over our lifetimes, making them very useful for assessing the relationships between both individuals (paternity tests) and groups (see Box 1.3: The Mystery of the "Black Jews"). Other traits are the result of the interactions between numerous genes; they are **polygenic**. Your hair color is one example. In contrast to monogenic traits,

Box 1.3 THE MYSTERY OF THE "BLACK JEWS"

According to their oral tradition, the Lemba, a southern African tribe of some 50,000 people, are descended from Jews who traveled south by boat from their homeland. Interestingly, the Lemba practice circumcision and follow certain dietary restrictions resembling Jewish customs. An examination of the Y chromosomes of Lemba males, neighboring Bantu (African) males, and several Semitic (Jewish) groups found that the Lemba males have features in common with both, but are more closely related to the non-African groups. Moreover, the Lemba clan (known as the Buba) that is said to be the oldest of all Lemba kinship groups—and which plays the most significant role in the performance of many rituals—was found to possess a relatively high frequency of a particular version of the Y chromosome that is also found among members of the Jewish priesthood. These findings suggest that the Lemba—who are often referred to as "black Jews"—are indeed genetically related to non-African Jews and that the Buba are related to a high-ranking Jewish lineage. This discovery is particularly interesting in light of the Jewish belief that "lost tribes" of Jews were scattered throughout the world as a result of numerous historical events.

Such studies indicate that the traditional knowledge of a group can tell us something about events that occurred in the past. But because these traditions change over time, it is important that we use outside sources of information to assess their validity. In this case, further studies of chromosomal markers and other genetic data may shed more light on the identity of the Lemba and their relationships with other Jewish groups.

polygenic traits are open to influences from the environment. Consequently, your hair color will change throughout your life as a result of environmental factors such as sunlight, diet, and the changes in the types of hormones you produce as you age.

Genes and Religiosity. The fact that the major features of religiosity are found primarily in *Homo sapiens*, but not in other animals, suggests that humans acquired some unique mutations since the time our common ancestors split with the modern apes. What might these mutations be, and is religiosity a monogenic or polygenic trait? Given the complexity of the behaviors and other characteristics involved in religious thought and behavior, we can expect that religiosity is the product of both. Thus, the many features of human religiosity arose as a consequence of numerous different evolutionary events, not a single adaptation.

Some of these events may have been relatively simple changes in monogenic traits. In his book *The God Gene*, Dean Hamer (2004) rather provocatively suggested that a single mutation may be responsible for at least one aspect of religiosity. Hamer found that a gene known as VMAT2 (from "vesicular monoamine transporter"), which produces a protein that plays a role in transporting certain neurotransmitters across neuronal membranes, is statistically associated with scores on a psychological assessment of self-transcendence. There are two versions (or "alleles") of the gene for VMAT2, and the protein that each codes for differs in its abilities to transport the neurotransmitters dopamine, noradrenaline, and serotonin. People who possess a copy of

one of the alleles are more likely to score higher on the self-transcendence scale. This may be due to the different levels of these neurotransmitters—all of which are involved in mood regulation—in their cells. This study, however, explains very little about differences in religiosity, for the gene explains less than 1% of the variance in the self-transcendence scale. Moreover, this gene has been found in people who do not have notable spiritual experiences and is often absent in people who do. If VMAT2 is indeed a "God gene," it is not the only one, nor is it a very powerful one.

It has long been known that differences in certain proteins affect the abilities of specific cells to pass materials into and out of themselves. But it is extremely doubtful that the many forms and expressions of religiosity could be the product of just a single genetic mutation. It is much more likely that religiosity has arisen as a result of a large number of mutations and that most of the genetic differences in individual predilections to religiosity are due to a number of genes operating in tandem. Consequently, these traits are open to the effects of the environment.

One intriguing study which suggests that at least some aspects of religiosity are the product of polygenic traits was carried out by Laura Koenig and Thomas Bouchard (2006), who compared twins raised apart to determine the possible genetic bases of the psychological traits of "religiousness," "authoritarianism," and "conservatism," which tend to occur together. Koenig and Bouchard found that these traits changed over the course of an individual's lifetime as the person's social status changed (reflecting new environments). Individuals who scored high on standard psychological measurements of these traits before starting college showed changed scores as their college careers progressed, indicating that they were becoming less religious, authoritarian, and conservative. But when these same individuals were retested years later—after they had become parents— their scores had reverted to their precollege levels. This study demonstrates that certain measures of psychological rigidity and control—which are related to attitudes about traditional moral values—can change throughout an individual's lifetime, thereby suggesting that these traits are the product of both genes and the environment.

It is likely that the tendencies of some people to "hear voices" or to intuit the solutions to problems are due to both genetic and environmental influences as well. Human intelligence, which varies over time and even throughout the day (try taking an exam after a large meal!), is made possible by the "**mental hardware**" that enables us to perform tasks such as recognizing faces, distinguishing living beings from nonliving things, and understanding logical and mathematical reasoning. All of these are polygenic traits. Consequently, we can expect that some people will tend to "see faces" in abstract images more often than others, that some individuals will be more likely to experience a feeling they describe as the unity of all things than others, and that some people will be periodically and spontaneously presented with solutions to problems they are facing—an excellent quality for a religious leader or prophet— while other people may have a difficult time "connecting the dots" to find a way out of difficulties. Because of environmental factors (which can include diet and the hormonal changes that take place during our lifetimes), we can also expect that an individual's ability to see faces, experience mystical union, or receive revelations can change over that person's lifetime and can be affected by changing social and family status, altered religious affiliation, increased commitment to a belief system, and even variation in diet and exercise patterns.

Religious traits that are the result of interactions between many genes and the environment tend to occur "more" in some people and "less" in others. Because they are open to environmental influences, they are also expressed differently at different stages of an individual's life. In other words, it is biologically reasonable for us to assume that individuals will exhibit significant differences in their religious abilities and sensitivities.

Because religious institutions and spiritual experiences are a part of every culture in the world, we can conclude that the genetic traits responsible for religiosity have been present in the human line for hundreds of generations or more. But since they are the result of

mutations—random changes that have occurred in our genetic makeup—we should not expect specific traits to be equally present in all populations. We can also expect that different cultures will have different understandings of what these traits mean, what they can be used for, and how to train people to make the most effective use of them. The insights of modern biology clearly suggest that religiosity is a product of our biology and that it will be expressed differently from one person and society to the next.

Key Evolutionary Concepts. The biological process by which populations of organisms change over time is known as **evolution**. Modern evolutionary thinking is based on several core concepts.

Natural Selection. The principle process through which evolution occurs is **natural selection**. Discovered independently by Charles Darwin (1809–1882) and Alfred Russel Wallace (1823–1913), natural selection is based on the insight that the members of a species all differ from one another and that these differences may affect their individual abilities to survive and reproduce. Darwin and Wallace developed the concept of natural selection to explain their observations of differences in plants and animals living on neighboring islands. Noticing that species differed from one island to the next in ways related to the conditions in which they lived, both realized that the variation among members of a population gave some individuals advantages over the others. Those with the advantages—speed, intelligence, or whatever other feature made them better adapted to their environment—were more likely to survive and hence produce more offspring than the individuals who did not possess these characteristics. Consequently, the next generation of organisms exhibited a higher frequency of the advantageous characteristics. Over time, the process of natural selection can lead to significant changes within a species and even give rise to new species.

Adaptation. An **adaptation** is an inherited feature acquired through natural selection that enables a plant or animal to survive—and, most important, reproduce—in its environment. The leaves of a plant are adaptations for collecting sunlight, which is essential for photosynthesis. Its roots are adaptations that enable it to obtain water and nutrients and to store the products of photosynthesis. Adaptations can also be behaviors. The instinctual ability of a frog to turn toward small moving objects and flee from large moving objects is one type of adaptive behavior; another is the tendency of mammalian babies to observe their mothers and, from them, to learn the kinds of foods to eat. From a traditional evolutionary point of view, a trait or behavior can be considered an adaptation only if it is genetically encoded in DNA and thus is capable of being passed down to the next generation. Although we do not yet fully understand the ways in which our genes are related to our cultural abilities, culture—including religion—has become one of the most important of all the adaptations that enable humans to survive and reproduce.

Fitness. The measure of an organism's evolutionary success in passing on its genes is known as its **fitness**. The most direct measure of an individual's fitness is the number of reproductively capable offspring it contributes to the next generation. Thus, fitness is a relative or comparative concept that refers to the reproductive advantage that one individual has over another member of the same species who occupies the same ecological niche. Because members of a group always possess some different genetic traits, individuals will always differ from one another in terms of their fitness. Consequently, some members of a group will be more fit in a particular environment than others.

Environment. Whether a particular trait offers an advantage or not depends on the **environment** in which it occurs. The environment of an organism is composed of the physical features in which it lives (climate, geography, etc.), the other species (plants, animals, fungi) that live around it, and the other members of its own species. These members not only compete for resources, but also create other environmental demands as well. For in highly social species—especially mammals—individuals must also be able to respond to the interpersonal demands of their group, and these demands become greater as social groups increase in size and complexity.

When the environment changes, the advantage or disadvantage offered by a trait may change as well, or it may be neutral in the new environment. In a cold climate, for example, a wolf with long, thick fur will have an advantage over another wolf with short, sparse fur because the animal with the thicker fur will conserve its energy better and have a lower risk of freezing. But if the climate changes and becomes warmer, the advantage will shift to the wolf with the thinner fur, because it is able to cool itself more efficiently. In this example, the temperature of the environment exerts a **selective pressure** on the individuals with different types of fur. An environment offers many selective pressures for and against particular traits, and as the environment changes, these selective pressures change as well. It is important to note that it is not the environment in total that determines whether a trait offers an advantage,

but the **ecological niche**—the specific aspects of the environment that affect the survival and reproduction of the species. For example, although the high-pitched sounds of bats are important aspects of the ecological niche in which bats (and their prey) live, humans cannot hear these sounds, and they have played no role that we are aware of in the evolution of humans.

Environment of Evolutionary Adaptedness. If we wish to assess the evolutionary events that led to the adaptations found in modern humans, we must consider the ancient environment, and the selective pressures it presented. For it was these selective pressures that led to different adaptations becoming more common among our ancestors. Because that environment differs in many important ways from the environments in which we now live, we refer to it as the **environment of evolutionary adaptedness**. Archaeological evidence and ethnological analogy both indicate that our ancestors exploited this ancient environment by living in small groups and practicing a hunter–gatherer lifestyle. Consequently, to understand the selective forces that favored the biological adaptations involved in religiosity, we need to think in terms of the advantages that these traits might have offered in the ancestral natural and social environment that existed after our ancestors had split from the lines leading to the modern apes (especially chimpanzees). For such purposes, it is more fruitful to examine the environments of premodern hunter–gatherers than the physical and social environments in which most people now live. Unlike our ancestors, most modern humans now depend on specialists to grow our food and produce the other material objects we need and desire, and we live in groups far larger than at any other time in our history or prehistory. Our environment is very different from the environment of evolutionary adaptedness, a fact that raises two questions crucial for understanding religiosity: Did environmental conditions provide selective pressures that produced religious adaptations across evolutionary time? Is religion adaptive in the environments of today?

Side-Effects of Evolution. The theory of natural selection is based on the insight that organisms possess certain traits because these traits contributed to their ancestors' reproductive fitness. However, these traits—called *adaptations*—often bring with them other traits and abilities that are neutral with respect to any selective pressure. For example, the white color of our bones is not the result of direct selection (so that bones that are white would offer a reproductive advantage over bones that are different in color). Rather, they are white because they contain calcium, which itself is white. Thus, the whiteness of our bones "came along" with the calcium that was selected for other reasons. There are several types of evolutionary "side-effects".

Exaptations. An **exaptation** is a trait that was originally selected because it was adaptive for one function and subsequently was selected for a new function and began to serve a new purpose. For example, paleontologists believe that properties of feathers were originally selected because they kept the early birds that possessed them warm. Once present, however, feathers could be useful for a different purpose: flight. Here, feathers were originally an *adaptation* that enabled early birds to stay warm. Later, they became an *exaptation* when they were further selected because of their ability to enhance the capacity for flight. Similarly, mammary glands are thought to be an exaptation that appeared when some of the sweat glands that secreted oil and water (and that enabled early mammals to control their body temperature) were subsequently co-opted to produce milk—a different type of "sweat" that contains proteins as well as fat.

Spandrels. A **spandrel** is a trait that originally served no function at all but simply "came along" (was inherited) with a trait that was being selected. Once a spandrel becomes established, it can subsequently come to play a new role in a different environment, where it may or may not be adaptive. Spandrels may serve certain purposes or be functional for some activities, but their presence is not a direct product of selection. For instance, our chins are useful for strapping on helmets, and helmets can definitely enhance our survival, but our chin did not evolve to enhance our ability to wear helmets. Many biologists have considered religion to have the same status, at best a lucky accidental by-product of evolution.

Evolutionary By-Products. The term **evolutionary by-product** is used to refer to a new trait that does not directly serve a biological function or enhance an individual's reproductive fitness but that is a side-effect of a feature or features that were selected for because they served other purposes. For example, our ability to fold our hands when we pray is an evolutionary by-product of the grasping abilities of the primate hand. During the course of human evolution, many evolutionary by-products have presumably been selected for *culturally* because they were useful for psychological, cognitive, or other purposes rather than survival and reproduction. The idea of a by-product is that it serves no useful function, but establishing that something is

actually completely useless is also a challenge. Indeed, when we examine religious activities and beliefs, it is easy to find how they enhance survival and reproduction. (Think of the injunction to "Go forth and multiply.") However, the question remains as to whether these features of religion that facilitate adaptation were the products of natural selection for religion, or whether their religious use is a by-product of other selection events.

Evaluating Adaptations, Exaptations, and Spandrels. Just because a behavior is a religious universal or cultural universal, or involves an adaptation, does not mean that the behavior is a product of natural selection. Adaptations may be used for novel behaviors without having any functional relevance for survival, as is exemplified in humans' use of the hands for playing tennis. Human adaptations can be co-opted by other motivational mechanisms and combined with other cognitive and physical capacities in order to produce behaviors that are "universal," such as soccer, but that are not products of natural selection (Buss et al. 1998).

Evolutionary frameworks provide criteria that we can use to assess whether something is an adaptation, exaptation, spandrel, or functionless by-product. These concepts differ in the role of selection in contributing to the manifestation of the associated feature. In the case of adaptations, these traits derived from new mutations that were selected for and that became established as universal features of the species. While the term *exaptation* is often used to imply that it is not an adaptation (for example, Kirkpatrick 2005), exaptations are, in fact, adaptations as well. These original adaptations, their selected and nonselected features, are the basis for exaptations and spandrels. Exaptations are co-opted adaptations that involved an original selection for an adaptive mechanism which was later involved in a subsequent selection, where it was co-opted for a new function, such as the aerodynamic properties of feathers. Similarly, spandrels, features that were by-products associated with an adaptation, may eventually be co-opted for adaptive functions in a new environment. With co-opted spandrels, properties that were coupled with selected features were the focus of an additional selective pressure that reshaped the potentials of a by-product to serve a new function.

To determine whether a trait involves a co-opted exaptation or a co-opted spandrel, we need to establish evidence that the later co-opted functions are distinct from the original functionality. However, we must follow the same logical procedure we used to establish that the original adaptation had an adaptive function, first specifying causal processes recognized by evolutionary biology and then determining that an adaptive problem can be solved by the psychological mechanisms that have been proposed (Buss et al. 1998). Common features shared by adaptations and exaptations are specialized functions for solving a specific adaptive problem and are characteristics of special design. According to Buss et al., an adaptation has "features that define special design—complexity, economy, efficiency, reliability, precision, and functionality" (citing Williams 1966). Alleging that something is an adaptation is an assertion that it has functional aspects involving a special design that could not have arisen by chance because of its complex features.

Buss et al. note that establishing religion as a functionless by-product also requires an evolutionary analysis to establish, first, the evolved mechanisms underlying the particular religious capability or behavior, and second, the cognitive and motivational mechanisms that allow humans and religions to co-opt and exploit those capabilities. By-products do not solve adaptive problems; on the other hand, a feature that can enhance survival and be transmitted to the subsequent generation is an adaptation. "Natural selection plays a key role in both adaptations and exaptations" (Buss et al. 1998). New adaptations and their new functions are always superimposed to varying degrees on a predecessor structure that constituted a preadaptation for the new ability.

The Importance of Evolutionary Side-Effects for Understanding Religiosity. Evolutionary side-effects occur when traits that were established in a population of organisms because they served one purpose begin to be used for another purpose or give rise to new traits that can be used for new purposes. During the development of a phenomenon as complex as the human propensity for religiosity, evolutionary side-effects may have played an even larger role than features that arose as a direct result of selection in a particular environment.

For example, many humans believe in a caring, benevolent God that watches over them and protects them from harm. It is not likely that our ancestors survived as a direct result of one of them acquiring a mutation which caused that individual to believe in such a God, after which that mutation was subjected to natural selection. Rather, our belief in a more powerful being that will nurture and protect us is likely an exaptation of the normal mammalian tendency to expect that our parents will feed and look after us (Kirkpatrick 2004). In other words, the selective pressures that directly favored those of our mammalian ancestors who were

able to develop a caring relationship with their parents—a relationship which increased the likelihood that the offspring would survive and reproduce—indirectly created the possibility for humans to develop caring relationships with distant spirit caretakers. But is this the entire story? Or do benevolent God concepts involve more than simply our mammalian attachment system? And if so, did this new belief in an all-knowing God with extensive supernatural powers in turn lead to something novel that could contribute to human survival and reproduction in a new way?

Understanding the distinctions among these various types of evolutionary sources and effects is essential to understanding religiosity and to considering the general sequence of steps that led to the emergence of religiosity. If we can identify traits that were adaptations at one time and then became exaptations later, it may be possible to reconstruct the sequences of evolutionary events and consider the ways in which previously existing functions continued. By identifying traits that have no parallels among animals, we can also gain a greater understanding of the uniquely human aspects of religiosity.

Whether they initially arose as exaptations, spandrels, or evolutionary by-products, the traits responsible for religiosity all involve aspects of human biology that helped our ancestors to survive and reproduce. They are all products of evolution and natural selection. Thus, even if they serve no adaptive function today, they should be evaluated in the environment of evolutionary adaptedness to determine the possible effects they had on fitness in that context. These and other factors make any attempts to assess the evolutionary status of religious features challenging.

Conclusions: The Biocultural Approach to the Study of Religion

In this chapter, we briefly examined the history of different Western approaches to understanding religion and how these led to the development of the anthropological biocultural perspectives. Anthropology considers religious beliefs from the insider (emic) perspective, as well as from a scientific, or outsider (etic), perspective. Anthropology's four-field approach (cultural, archaeological, linguistic, and biological anthropology) illustrates how these diverse perspectives can contribute to our understanding of religiosity. Evolutionary principles provide an essential framework for evaluating the factors that are responsible for the emergence of religiosity. The biocultural perspective provided by anthropology gives us a comprehensive tool for addressing both the humanistic and scientific perspectives on religion and integrating them in a holistic, interdisciplinary synthesis.

The biocultural perspective is based on the explicit recognition that humans are biological organisms whose primary means of adapting to the world is culture. Some of the most important—and most fascinating—ways that humans now adapt to the world are made possible by the human propensity for religiosity. As a human universal, religiosity is rooted in our biology and given expression by our culture. In ways we are only beginning to understand, religiosity is made possible by features that are coded into our DNA and expressed as we develop and build the **mental hardware** that we use to understand the world. As we grow up, this mental hardware is shaped and programmed by the cultural software that we acquire from the other members of our society. In this way, the propensity for religiosity that we share with the other members of our species is channeled and shaped into a uniquely individual experience.

Today, religiosity finds expression in every human society, and it plays numerous important roles in our social and cultural life. The many and varied manifestations of religiosity in cultures throughout time and across the globe clearly demonstrate that religiosity is a product of a variety of features that helped our ancient ancestors adapt to their world. In this book, we will examine these features and consider the role that they played in shaping human evolution.

We will also explore some of the many ways that religiosity finds expression in both individuals and societies today, and we will consider whether religiosity is a human trait that arose as a direct product of events in the past or whether it is a side-effect of features that arose to serve one function but could then be used for others. However religiosity arose, it now represents an evolved aspect of our biology that serves many adaptive functions. We will consider both these adaptive functions and some of the maladaptive features of religiosity as well.

To better understand the ways that religiosity continues to affect us today, in the next chapter we will step back and take a broad look at the place of humans in the natural world and the ways in which we—as societies and as individuals—are able to develop an understanding of that world. We will explore how we gain information about our world and how we structure that information into a coherent worldview. And although we now often think of science and religion as opposing ways of understanding the world, we will see that the two share many features in common.

Questions for Discussion

- What problems can result when people interpret another person's religion using the standards provided by their own?
- When considering the reasons behind any religious belief or behavior, why is it important to consider the insider's (emic) view as well as the outsider's (etic) view?
- What is the relationship between language and religiosity?
- Is religiosity a direct product or a side-effect of human evolution?

Glossary

adaptation a feature of an organism that enables it to survive in a particular environment

anima the nonmaterial aspect of a living being, typically conceived of as a spirit or soul

animism the belief in the existence of spirits

anthropology the scholarly discipline that studies humans

archaeology the field of anthropology that reconstructs cultures of the past, primarily by studying the material evidence left by a culture

behavioral component culture in action; culture as expressed through human activity

biocultural approach an anthropological perspective which recognizes that humans are biological organisms whose primary means of adapting to their environment is culture

biological anthropology the field of anthropology that studies human evolution and variation (also known as physical anthropology)

closed systems of language systems of communication in which sounds always mean the same things

cognates words that have similar sounds and meanings in different languages

comparative the use of descriptions of different cultures to determine the basic principles of culture

cross-cultural the comparative perspective of anthropology

cultural anthropology the field of anthropology that focuses on those aspects of human life that we learn from other members of our society and in turn pass on to others (culture)

cultural relativism a methodological strategy that reminds us that we should always strive to study other cultures objectively and not see them through the lens of our own culture

cultural universals of religion features of religiosity that are present in all cultures but not in every ritual of a culture

culture the knowledge, behaviors, and objects shared by the members of a group and passed down from generation to generation within the group

deism a belief system that asserts that there is a God but that rejects all religious dogma

displacement the ability, thought to be unique to humans, to use language to discuss things that are not happening right now in the immediate environment

ecological niche the specific aspects of any environment that affect the survival and reproduction of a particular species

emic the point of view of someone who lives within a culture; the "native" perspective

environment the context in which an organism exists, including the physical features of the landscape, the climate, and other organisms

environment of evolutionary adaptedness the environment in which the vast majority of hominid evolution is thought to have taken place

ethnocentrism the tendency to view other cultures through the framework of one's own culture

ethnographic analogy a method of comparing a culture known from the archaeological record with other cultures studied by ethnographers to determine the general features of the past culture

ethnography a description of a particular culture (or some aspect of one)

ethnological analogy a method of using insights obtained through cross-cultural studies to interpret the archaeological record

ethnology the comparative study of different cultures with the intent to develop general theories of culture

etic the point of view of someone outside a culture; the "scientific" perspective

etymology the study of the derivation of words

evolution a biological theory that explains how and why species change through time in response to changes in their environments

evolutionary by-product a trait that did not arise as an adaptation itself but as a side-effect of an adaptation

exaptation a feature of a species that is used for something for which it did not directly evolve

exclusivism a point of view that holds that only one religion (usually one's own) is true

fieldwork a research method that involves living with people to study their lives and the ways they understand the world

fitness a measure of an organism's evolutionary success, usually measured by the number of reproductively capable (fertile) offspring it produces

gene a sequence of DNA that codes for a particular protein

historical linguistics a subfield of anthropological linguistics that studies the origins of words and the ways in which languages change over time

historical particularism a relativistic way of looking at cultures and societies which recognizes that each is the product of a unique constellation of environmental and historical factors, and which advocates studying each on its own terms rather than comparing it with a supposedly superior culture

holistic looking at the "big picture"; using all relevant data when considering questions

ideational component the mental aspect of a culture; culture expressed through concepts, emotions, and values

linguistic anthropology the field of anthropology that focuses on the role of language in human life

linguistic determinism the "hard" form of the Sapir–Whorf hypothesis which argues that language *creates* the way we view reality

linguistic relativism the "soft" form of the Sapir–Whorf hypothesis which argues that language *shapes* the way we view reality

material component the physical manifestation of culture; the objects people make and use in a society

mental hardware the biological structures of our brains that shape how we experience and understand the world

monogenic a genetic characteristic that is produced by a single gene and that is not open to environmental influences

mutation a random change in a sequence of DNA

natural selection the process by which species adapt over time in response to pressures from the environment

open systems of language systems of communication in which a finite number of sounds can be combined to produce an infinite number of utterances

participant-observation a research method in which a fieldworker lives with a group of people and takes part in their activities to understand the group's culture from the insider's perspective

polygenic a genetic characteristic that is produced by the interaction of multiple genes and that is open to environmental influences

rationalist a religious philosophy that emphasizes reason over revelation and that argues for a universal understanding of religion

religious universals manifestations of religiosity that are found in all aspects of all religions

Sapir–Whorf hypothesis the idea that language shapes or creates the way that we view reality

selective pressure an aspect of an environment that makes a trait advantageous or disadvantageous, in response to which the frequency of the trait in a population tends to increase or decrease

social universals of religion manifestations of religiosity that are found only in certain kinds of societies, such as agricultural or foraging societies

society a group of people that is organized together or structured in some way by a shared culture

spandrel a trait that originally served no adaptive function but that "came along" (was genetically inherited) with a trait that did

symbol an object that stands for or signifies something else

temporal a way of looking at cultures across time, especially "deep-time"

unilineal evolution the outdated theory that all societies develop following essentially the same sequence over time

universalism an approach to religion that recognizes the common themes in different religions and views all religions as paths to the same end

variation the ways in which individual organisms within a population differ from one another

Our World and How We Know It

CHAPTER OBJECTIVES

- Illustrate the processes through which we come to know the Universe.
- Examine how our biological capacities for knowing the Universe are affected by culture.
- Illustrate how our knowledge of anything is always mediated by some type of symbolic model.
- Demonstrate that "spirits" are a natural product of human cognition.
- Explore the differences between religious and scientific ways of knowing the Universe.

The old man had been sick for some time. Some days, he found it difficult to get out of bed. He was consumed with grief over his dead niece, and fretted about the witches who had killed her. He was worried about his people as well. To escape from their despair, some of them had given themselves over to promiscuity and used love charms to seduce one another. If a woman became pregnant, she often aborted the unwanted child. The people drank heavily when whiskey was available, and he himself often drank himself into a stupor. As he was falling asleep, he would sing the sacred songs he had learned as a boy. When he woke up, he would be filled with regret and vow never to drink again.

One morning, he collapsed as he was leaving his house. His daughter, who had seen his uncertain steps, rushed to his side and quickly summoned their relatives. Finding no signs of life, they feared the worst. But then, some two hours later, the old man awoke and told the people gathered around him about the vision he had received. As he was falling, three angels had reached out

to catch him. They comforted him and told him that the Creator had sent them with a simple message: the Creator disapproved of whiskey, witchcraft, love magic, and abortion and sterility medicine. The angels told him that if he passed this message on to the others, then he would recover and they would visit him again.

* * *

The man turned the crown over and over in his hands, wondering what to tell the king. He knew that he would need to give the king an answer soon. Had the goldsmith made the crown of pure gold as he had been bidden, or had he taken some of the gold and replaced it with something else? The man knew that he couldn't melt the crown down or cut it apart, for it was intended for the Gods. How could he solve this riddle?

The answer came when he was least expecting it. Taking a break from his labors, the man went to visit the local bath house. As he entered his bath, he watched with fascination as the water level rose. The more deeply he immersed himself, the higher the water climbed, until it finally flowed over the rim of the tub. Suddenly, he realized he had found the solution to his problem. In his excitement, he climbed out of the bath and ran home naked, shouting "I have it!"

Introduction: Science and Religion as Ways of Knowing

As these stories remind us, people often come up with intuitive "inspirational" solutions to practical problems. The first story describes how Handsome Lake, an Iroquois Indian who watched as his people were confined to reservations following the American Revolutionary War, received a vision in which he was told to abandon a number of practices that were harming him and his people. Because the contents of this vision related to problems facing many of his fellows, they eagerly accepted the message he related. The resulting movement soon grew into a new religion, and its teachings led to a renaissance in Iroquois culture.

The second story tells how the Greek mathematician Archimedes discovered a way to determine whether a crown that his king had commissioned as a gift for the Gods was made of pure gold or whether some of it had been replaced by another metal. This insight also proved to have wider applications, for shipbuilders and others still use the principle of liquid displacement to solve the problems they face today.

Although Handsome Lake and Archimedes were facing quite different types of problems, each found the answer in a moment of inspiration. Inspiration is one of the most important sources of human knowledge, but it is not our only source. We learn about the world in many ways. We may have a flash of insight, or we may learn by asking questions, devising experiments, and checking our results. We can ask our elders how they have dealt with issues they faced in the past. In reading this book, you are learning about the world in yet another way.

Although often thought to be at odds, religion and science both represent attempts to understand ourselves and the Universe. In this chapter, we will explore some of the similarities between the ways that science and religion provide answers to the questions we face and point out several of the important ways in which the two differ. Because the biocultural approach is rooted in the natural sciences, we will begin by providing a brief overview of the scientific understanding of the Universe. We will then examine the biological and cultural processes that enable us to create an understanding of reality by making "models"—both scientific and religious—for understanding the world. These models, which are made possible by the human capacity for symbolic thought, enable us to function within the world by extending what we already know to new domains of knowledge. But as we will see, these models also limit our thinking.

A Very Short History of the Universe

Science has revealed that the Universe is not static, but dynamic. Since it originated, it has been changing and giving rise to new types of phenomena and new levels of complexity. Subatomic particles combined to produce the first atoms, and atoms subsequently combined to produce the first molecules. Eventually, molecules emerged that were able to make copies of themselves, to store information, and to break chemical bonds to release energy. When these various types of molecules began to function together, an even more complex phenomenon emerged: life.

Each of the first living organisms consisted of just a single cell, but eventually animals composed of groups of cells appeared. Such colonies of organisms still exist today (corals and sponges). But in one lineage of organisms, some cells began to specialize in function. Some of the cells extracted nutrients from the environment, while others carried these nutrients to other members of the group, and still others disposed of the waste produced by the group. Yet other cells specialized in passing on the information needed to produce the next generation. These increases in cellular specialization occurred in both plants and animals. But in contrast to plants, animals also developed unique groups of cells whose primary task was to collect information about the world—the first receptors—and other specialized cells that enabled the animal to move—the first muscles. In between these cells were others that connected them and regulated their activities, an "intermediate network" of cells that received messages from the receptors and then instructed the muscles what to do. Eventually, these systems for integrating and processing information would give rise to the first brains.

Today, the most complex brains known are found inside our own heads. In humans, several million neurons transmit information from our receptors to our brains, and several million other neurons carry messages from our brains to our muscles. The control center is our brain, with its estimated 100 billion neurons and 60 trillion (!) interconnections.

Our brains process the information coming in from our senses by comparing our current perceptions with our memories, and in noting differences between present experiences and previous ones. Using these observations, it is able to develop increasingly complex models for interpreting future events. The brain is also the seat of our emotions, a type of information processing that tells us what our perceptions mean and the value they hold for us (which we might label as "attractive," "repulsive," or "scary").

As the increasingly sophisticated features of our brain emerged over evolutionary time, its more primitive features did not simply disappear. Instead, these newer brain structures literally grew around the older ones, altering and adapting the neural structures that our ancestors used to comprehend and function within the world. As a result, many of the ways that we understand and respond to the world are still profoundly affected by the ancient parts of our brains (we will look at this in more detail in Chapter 4). But these ancient parts are now linked to newer parts that enable us to learn from one another through observation and through elaborate systems of communication. This has led to the emergence of a number of new phenomena that were essential to the evolution of humans and to the development of both religion and science. One of the most important of these phenomena is the use of symbols, which have unleashed the representational powers of our minds.

The Mind: How We Know the World

The **mind** is a high-level function of the brain that receives information that has already been filtered, structured, and categorized to a very high degree. By the time it arrives at the level of the mind, information about both the world outside and inside our bodies has been linked with our personal and cultural ideas to produce the global "picture" that is the reality we experience.

That aspect of our brains that we typically regard as "most human"—our minds—is really just the tip of a huge mental "iceberg" composed of numerous neural circuits that work to produce the comprehensive picture presented to the mind. To understand this more fully, consider this book. It was not written for the receptor cells in your retina, or your optic nerves, or even your visual cortex, but for the part of you that receives the finished products of all of their efforts: your mind. To achieve this, an enormous amount of information must be processed, categorized, and prioritized into something relevant. We don't experience this process, only its products.

As you are reading this, you are probably paying no attention to the various curves that make up the shapes of the letters on this page, the sensations of

pressure that your chair is generating in your legs, or the background sounds around you. Although readily accessible, all this information is generally outside your awareness, especially if the meaning that the letters and words are communicating is engrossing enough (which we hope it is!). You can easily shift the focus of your attention to these other sensations, and indeed, you may not be able to avoid doing so when we mention them. But as you can see, most of the information coming into your body through your senses is processed at a level below consciousness, and it is often filtered out before it ever reaches the level of the mind. Thus, many of the mental processes that allow us to survive and act within the world are running more or less automatically in the background, based on models embedded in our subconscious. Because of our reliance on these models, much of what we do, and many of the ways in which we experience the world, are *habitual* and *stereotyped* (that is, we perceive that things tend to occur repeatedly, and in essentially the same way every time).

This system has the advantage of enabling speedy responses, but it also means that these responses will not always be entirely appropriate to the present moment. Only a small portion of the information flowing through your nervous system ever becomes available to your mind as "completed" perceptions (such as words with meanings) and "finished" images that have already been linked to sounds (such as when the signals from your eyes, ears, and nose are merged into the comprehensive "picture" of your friend looking at you as she bites into an apple). The mind receives this picture from the various sensory modalities, as well as the interpreted sensations from your body that require your attention ("I'm hungry," "I need some sleep"), and links these together into a coherent whole that can be assessed against your previous experiences as well as your plans for the future. The emergence of the human mind has given our species an unprecedented degree of autonomy to act within the world and the power to create the realities that are taught to us by both science and religion.

We can gain a greater understanding of the ways in which our mental hardware and cultural software enable us to know the world by examining how these compare with the ways in which other animals know it. Like all animals, we work to find food, mates, and shelter, and to avoid obstacles and predators. Most animals know about their world and how to act within it largely because of properties that are "wired" right into their nervous systems. They have inherited these instinctual, essentially fixed ways of understanding and acting. A bee does not have to be taught how to fly; it does so automatically. A frog does not have to be taught how to catch an insect; it knows how to do this instinctively.

In contrast, higher animals such as birds, and even more so mammals, are less fixed in their responses to the world because the ways that they know about and act within the world are much more open to being shaped by learning. Like other animals, we humans know about the world and how to act within it partly because of features that are wired right into us. But more than any other animal, we are also able to *learn* about the world, both on our own and from the other members of our species. This ability to adapt using the knowledge you acquire during your own lifetime is very useful if you live in an environment that is changing rapidly, or if you move into an environment that is not familiar. In such a case, any ability to modify your behaviors on the basis of things you experience in your own lifetime would bring obvious advantages. Culture emerged when this ability to learn became coupled with the ability to communicate what we learned to other members of our species and to learn in turn from them.

The view of the world that we humans ultimately develop is thus a product of both our biological hardwiring and our cultural programming. The cultural processes through which each of us comes to know the world occur so automatically that, as adults, we believe that the way we experience the world is the way it really is. But it is not, for the world in which each of us spends our entire life is actually a learned abstraction, a constructed reality. On this, both scientists and religious mystics agree. The process of manufacturing this abstraction has three basic steps—sensation, perception, and cognition—each of which yields an increasingly complex and ever more condensed and abstract view of the world. An organism acquires its "raw data" about the world in the form of stimuli or sensations. If a particular stimulus is found to be relevant, the organism recognizes it as a perception. The organism then interprets these perceptions by using cognitive processes to determine the categories they fit into and their meanings. In other words, we do not experience the world the way that it really is, but the way that our mental hardware filters and structures the world and the way that our cultural software categorizes and evaluates the results. Because the present discussion is concerned with two things—how we obtain information about the world and how we interpret that information—we will discuss sensation and perception together before turning to the process of cognition.

> All the mind's arbitrary conceptions of matter, phenomena, and of all conditioning factors and all conceptions and ideas relating thereto are like a dream, a phantasm, a bubble, a shadow.
>
> Buddha
>
> (Cited in Thomas J. McFarlane [ed.], *Einstein and Buddha: The Parallel Sayings,* Berkeley: Seastone, p.11—original in Dwight Goddard, ed. *A Buddhist Bible* [Beacon Press: Boston: 1970])

> Excepting immediate sensations and, more generally, the content of my consciousness, everything is a construct.
>
> Eugene P. Wigner
> 1963 Nobel Prize Laureate in Physics
>
> (Cited in Thomas J. McFarlane [ed.], *Einstein and Buddha: The Parallel Sayings,* Berkeley: Seastone, p.111—original in *Symmetries & Reflections,* Bloomington, IN: Indiana University Press, 1967, p. 189)

Sensation and Perception: Our Windows on the World

The first step of acquiring information about the world is **sensation**, which occurs when a stimulus is detected by a specialized neuron called a **receptor**. The receptor produces an electrical signal that it then passes on to the next neuron. Our brains do not have direct access to information about the Universe. Instead, they receive information that is filtered through and augmented by specialized systems of receptors. Intriguingly, most of the sensations that an organism is receiving at any one moment through its sensory receptors will not be experienced in any way.

Any neuron along the pathway between your receptors and your mind will only pass information on to the next receptor if it is also receiving similar signals from other neurons. When several signals reinforce one another, the neuron that is receiving them will generate a signal. In this way, information about our sensations is bundled and combined into patterns that are sorted for relevance as they move "up" through the nervous system (see Fig. 2.1). The "windows" through which we humans are able to perceive what is going on "out there" in the world are our five senses. Each is sensitive to a particular

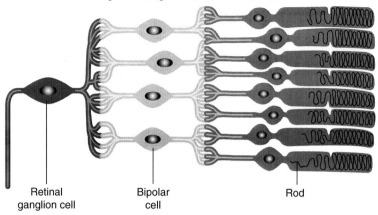

High Convergence in Rod-Fed Circuits

Retinal ganglion cell   Bipolar cell   Rod

Figure 2.1 This schematic representation of the interconnections between rods (the light-sensitive cells in our eye), bipolar cells, and retinal ganglion cells illustrates how sensory information from multiple neurons is "bundled" together as the information passes up to the higher levels of the nervous system.

type of stimulus. Our eyes are sensitive to electromagnetic energy, our ears detect vibrations, and our nose and taste buds react to the presence of specific molecules.

While our senses tell us that something is going on "out there," they do not tell us what it is. **Perception** takes place when higher-level neural structures within the central nervous system recognize sensations. These mental structures categorize the sensations, looking for recognizable patterns in memory. A great deal of filtering and condensing occurs during the process of perception, as well as during sensation. Two of the most important criteria used to assess the potential usefulness of perceptual information are novelty (is this something that has not yet been encountered and, hence, cannot be categorized?) and the significance of the information (how important is this information compared with the other things that are being perceived?).

During the evolution from lower to higher animals, a shift occurred so that perception was no longer primarily the product of an animal's genetically programmed "mental hardware," but was increasingly shaped by the actual experiences the animal had during its own lifetime. Consequently, the instinctual responses that play such an important role in, for example, fish perception have been replaced by the learned responses that are so typical of mammalian perception (we will explore this in more detail in Chapter 4).

As our nervous system develops both in utero and following birth, it is shaped by experience. In other words, the biological "hardware" used to recognize patterns and understand the world is "plastic," or malleable, and is formed and entrained by the things it is exposed to. As the nervous system of any complex animal grows and matures, it develops networks of neurons that specialize in handling repetitive—and, therefore, predictable—information. These neural networks then generate the hardwired "models" that make it possible for that organism to respond to regularly occurring stimuli in programmed ways without having to focus attention or bring the response into consciousness. This process occurs in all animals with complex nervous systems, but is most pronounced in our own species. As a result, the human nervous system is more "plastic"—more malleable— than that of any other species. In a very real way, our culture and our individual experiences shape the development of our nervous systems.

Cognition: Making Sense of the View

To survive and function in any environment, it is not enough to simply perceive that something is going on. These perceptions must *mean* something. **Cognition,** the process by which perceptions are interpreted, provides that meaning, and in doing so it creates the reality within which an animal lives. We assess the significance of the information we are perceiving by comparing it with models of previous experiences of similar information. If the current information is novel and hence unknown (*what is that?*), we may pay additional attention until it can be understood in a way that makes sense. When the current information is evaluated as being significantly important (*that's a lion!*), it is given a high priority and will override less important information. In both of these cases, it is the process of cognition that provides the interpretation.

Human perception, like that of other animals, is a product both of our biology and our experience. But in our case, the term *experience* refers to more than just the things each of us encounters in our own lives; it also refers to the things our ancestors learned as well, and, thus, to our culture.

The repetitive stimuli to which a growing child is exposed are produced not only by the other animals around the child and the physical environment in which he or she lives, but also by the cultural behaviors of the child's family and friends. As soon as we are born, we begin to hear the sounds of a language being spoken around us, we smell the foods that others eat, and we see how the people around us move and interact with one another. These patterns of behavior affect our development during a period of great neural plasticity. As a result, our nervous systems literally reshape themselves in response to these behaviors.

Becoming encultured into a group "tunes" our bodies—including our muscles, organs, and nervous system—to that group, creating specific patterns that we will then use to understand and respond to our perceptions of the world. As we grow older, we acquire a language that provides us with words to describe the things our nervous system already knows how to experience.

The fact that we carry our culture in our bodies as well as in our minds helps to explain why we feel so much "at home" when we are around people who speak the same dialect as we do, why we continue to enjoy the same kinds of foods throughout our lives, and why we can even recognize where a person comes from by simply watching that person walk or sit. It also helps us to understand why so many people continue to practice the same religious behaviors and beliefs throughout their lives: they literally are "wired" for it.

Cognition classifies perceptions into categories, and an animal's responses to its perceptions are determined by the categories they fall into. A simple example can demonstrate this. To communicate with other members of their species—and, in particular, to announce their position to prospective mates—Polynesian field crickets (*Teleogryllus oceanicus*) produce sounds between 4,000 to 5,000 Hz (Hertz = cycles per second) in frequency. The bats that live in their environment use extremely high-pitched sounds (over 30,000 Hz) to hunt the crickets, and the crickets are able to hear these sounds as well. It is understandably vital for a flying cricket to be able to make an immediate and correct assessment of the sounds it is perceiving, and it does so by basically dividing these sounds into one of two groups: sounds with a frequency less than 16,000 Hz (= mates?) and those with a frequency greater than 16,000 Hz (= bats!). Based on the category a sound falls into, the cricket will then either fly towards or away from the source (Wyttenbach, Michael, and Ronald 1996).

Although our cognitive skills are obviously much greater than a cricket's, and the meanings we assign to our perceptions are much richer, we humans interpret our perceptions in essentially the same way as all other animals. Some perceptions, such as a sharp stabbing pain in the sole of the foot, will be categorized (pain!) and responded to very quickly ("ouch!") by lifting the foot up. And we will do this without thinking about it. Only afterwards will we look to see what we stepped on. Such rapid assessments enable us to respond al-

most instantaneously to things that are happening in the environment. Individuals who are able to quickly and correctly respond to such perceptions of danger enjoy a clear selective advantage over individuals who cannot do so.

Most cognition occurs on a subconscious level; that is, we interpret most of our perceptions without ever being aware that we are doing so. We see an object and immediately know whether it is red or blue. We can tell the direction from which a sound is coming without even turning our heads. We can recognize that a face is familiar long before we recall the name that goes with the face. We are able to do these things so quickly because our ancestors needed to do these things "without thinking" to survive, and those who were able to do this lived long enough to pass this capacity down to their offspring.

The outcome of the process of cognition is an **inference** about what we are perceiving. This inference is a "best guess" interpretation of our perceptions that is derived from models that are based on past experiences (whether one's own experiences or the experiences of one's ancestors that have been passed down in the form of instincts). To persist, an inference must facilitate the survival and reproduction of that species.

The Limitations of Our View of the World

There is an economy to the way we encounter the world that is necessitated by the fact that we receive only a very limited amount of information about the world and have only a finite amount of brain power for processing this information. The cognitive inferences we make about our perceptions are *models of the world* that suggest certain strategies for acting. Although these models make it possible for an animal to act effectively in the world, they are never a completely accurate description of the world, for no animal is capable of perceiving everything that is occurring in its environment.

Because we are continually making inferences about the world—many of them subconscious and based on only a few cues—we occasionally act on the basis of a model that yields an incorrect assessment about the world. For example, you might conclude that something coiled up on the ground is a "snake" (especially if you live in an area where snakes are a problem or if you have a fear of snakes). Only upon closer inspection will you realize that it is just a piece of rope. The inferences we make about the world can be wrong for a number of reasons: because they are based on insufficient information, because we are not paying enough attention to the right things, or because our emotions cause us to jump to conclusions. Some kinds of "overactive" models—such as "snake"—may be adaptations that we still use today because they were so clearly helpful to our ancestors.

The emotions that we attach to our perceptions and cognitions play a key role in determining how the information received by our senses and processed by our brain engages our attention and responses. If you are walking through a swamp and a hanging vine brushes across the back of your neck, the sensation will likely evoke a variety of involuntary responses—shock, fear, anger. But in a different context, such as the presence of a loved one, the very same sensation will likely produce different responses—trust, reassurance, arousal. While the stimulation on your skin and your automatic responses (e.g., a tickle and a shiver) are the same, the different contexts will lead you to interpret—that is, perceive and understand—the raw sensations in very different ways. In the same way, the context in which a person perceives a flash of light in the periphery of the visual field can affect the person's interpretation in many different ways. Some people may understand the flash as nothing more than a product of random activity within the visual system, while others might attribute it to an outside agent, such as the reflection of a car's lights. In certain contexts, people may even interpret these same flashes of lights as a sign of the presence of spirits. In other words, *the meaning of any experience is derived from the model that is used to interpret it, and identical experiences can be interpreted in very different ways.*

The models we humans use are a product of both our biology and our culture. Although all of the organisms that live in a particular environment are exposed to essentially the same things, they do not experience or relate to that environment in precisely the same way. The filters and models used by animals that rely primarily on instincts to evaluate their perceptions are "hardwired" right into their nervous systems and largely determine their experiences and reactions. As the most malleable of all animals, we humans use both hardwired and culturally learned filters and models to interpret our perceptions of the world. Because of the differences in our filters, we can say that we humans actually live in five different kinds of reality.

Five Kinds of Human Reality

Our brief survey of the history of the Universe noted how the complex phenomena of the mind are made possible by simpler processes. Thus, being human involves a large number of dimensions, from the strictly physical (the atoms and molecules that compose our bodies) to the abstract levels of mind, culture, and language. Thinking of humans as living in five different kinds of realities provides us with a useful framework for understanding science, religion, and spirituality.

The Universe. The primary reality of all organisms is what we call the **Universe** (with a capital U). The Universe is **objective reality**, all that exists, in all of its forms, including both the things of which we are aware and the things of which we are not. The Universe operates according to certain principles and exhibits patterns, and humans study these patterns in our attempts to discern its principles ("laws"). All animals—including humans—need to develop some understanding of the Universe.

The Species World. Each species is capable of perceiving only a small portion of the Universe. The receptors of different species are sensitive to different types of stimuli, leading each to experience the world differently. Dogs have a sense of smell just as we do, but their abilities to perceive the Universe are different from ours. For one thing, humans have only about 12 million olfactory receptor cells in our nose, while most dogs have about 1 billion (and a bloodhound may have as many as 4 billion!). Because of this, dogs can detect scents that humans cannot. Dogs also see and hear differently than humans. Dogs are exquisitely sensitive to low levels of light, which is why we often say that dogs can see "in the dark." Humans can hear only sounds whose frequencies lie between about 20 and 20,000 Hz, but

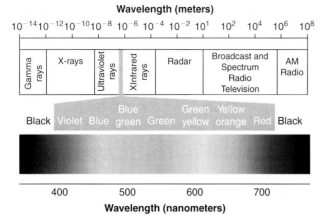

Wavelength (meters)

10^{-14} 10^{-12} 10^{-10} 10^{-8} 10^{-6} 10^{-4} 10^{-2} 10^1 10^2 10^4 10^6 10^8

| Gamma rays | X-rays | Ultraviolet rays | X Infrared rays | Radar | Broadcast and Spectrum Radio Television | AM Radio |

Black | Violet | Blue | Blue green | Green | Green yellow | Yellow orange | Red | Black

400   500   600   700

Wavelength (nanometers)

Figure 2.2 Humans are capable of perceiving only a small portion of the electromagnetic spectrum. For the cells in the retina of our eye to be stimulated—for us to see—these cells must be exposed to electromagnetic energy with wavelengths between about 380 and 760 nm (1 nanometer = one-millionth of a millimeter). If they are, then the cells produce electrical signals that subsequent neurons may perceive as colors, shapes, or movements. If the light is of a different wavelength, the cells in our retina will not respond, and the absence of signals from the retina will be perceived as "dark."

dogs can hear frequencies of 45,000 Hz or more. In a certain sense, dogs have "supernatural" abilities, for they perceive things that humans do not (see Fig. 2.2).

You may be wondering why a book about religion is discussing dogs. The reason is that the differences between our two species can help us to understand a fundamental and crucial fact of existence: Although there are a lot of things going on "out there" in the Universe, the members of any particular species are aware only of a small portion of the events around them. All animals, including humans, are literally blind to things that other animals can sense. Our perceptions are rooted in our biological structures—our mental hardware—and the mental hardware of a human is different from the mental hardware of a dog. Consequently, while humans and dogs live in the same Universe, the way that humans experience the Universe is different from the way that dogs experience it, and even more different from the ways that frogs or fish experience it. Each species—including *Homo sapiens*—lives in its own **species world** that is a product of its evolutionary past.

The Perceptual World. A third variety of human reality results from the fact that no two individuals of a species can ever perceive the Universe in exactly the same way. Color-blindness provides a simple example. Most humans can perceive colors, but some cannot.

People who cannot are characterized as "colorblind." Some people have 20/20 ("perfect") vision, while others cannot see objects clearly unless they are wearing corrective lenses. Clearly, while all humans live in the same Universe, our abilities to perceive it visually differ.

We differ in our perceptual abilities in many ways, including our ability to hear sounds and our sensitivities to taste, touch, and smell. (Only a very few people have such sensitive noses that they could ever hope to find work developing perfumes.) Some people can sense electrical and magnetic fields that most can't. Some people have a capacity for **synaesthesia**, a type of perception that enables them to "hear" colors and "taste" sounds. These and other kinds of "sensitive" perceptual capacities are found in spiritual people around the world.

Our senses and the other features of our nervous systems are based on genetic programs that are expressed as we develop. Yet, since even identical twins (whose genetic make-up is the same) cannot avoid following somewhat different developmental paths, there will always be subtle individual differences in the distribution of sensory receptor cells, the lengths and the thicknesses of individual neurons (which influence their transmission speed), and every other trait that is open to the influence of environmental factors. These differences are a part of what it means to be an individual.

Each individual also changes throughout his or her lifetime. These changes affect the sensory apparatus and the structures we use to produce our perceptions and to evaluate what they mean. As we age, the clear fluid in the lenses of our eyes thickens, making it increasingly difficult for the muscles that control these lenses to change their shape so that they can focus on very close objects. Even people who grew up with "perfect" vision often find themselves in need of glasses by middle age. As a result of these differences in our perceptual apparatus, each of us perceives the Universe somewhat differently, meaning that each of us lives in an individually unique **perceptual world**. Because of the changes that take place during our lifetimes, the world also changes around us. The implications of this fact are profound: *No one has ever perceived the Universe exactly the way you are perceiving it right now, and you, too, will never perceive it again in precisely this way.* Each person unavoidably lives behind his or her own limited, idiosyncratic, and everchanging windows on the world. But because our genetic programs are so similar, two human beings experience the Universe in more similar ways than the members of two different species do. Our common biological heritage ensures that we will perceive the Universe in ways that are more alike than different.

The Cultural World. All animals live in three kinds of reality: the *Universe*, the *species world*, and the *perceptual world*. Humans also live in two other kinds of reality. The first is based on the fact that humans are less dependent on instinct and more able to learn about the world than any other species of animal. This ability to learn from other members of the group led to the emergence of the **cultural world**. The cultural world that we grow up in provides us with models of reality that are much more relevant to current conditions than the models provided by instinct alone. The cultural models that we use to interpret the Universe can be rapidly modified or replaced, enabling more dynamic, varied, innovative, and ultimately relevant interactions with the world. It is our ability to change our minds faster than we can change our bodies that has made humans, arguably, the dominant species on the planet.

Our cultural world is made possible by group living, which provides opportunities to learn by observing others. Most of us begin our learning by observing and then mimicking our mothers and other members of our groups. Observation-based learning and mimicry are soon supplemented by language, the most important tool that we have for learning and transmitting culture. Our language provides us with labels for the categories that our culture teaches us to use to evaluate our perceptions ("blue," "flower"). As we learn these labels, we learn the assumptions that our culture makes about the Universe, the *models* that our culture provides us for constructing our world.

The vocabulary of our language provides us with terms to discern culturally relevant features in the environment that we might otherwise overlook. (Recall our discussion of the Sapir–Whorf hypothesis in Chapter 1.) Because we share a common vocabulary, we can communicate with others involved in the same types of activities, thereby creating an **intersubjective reality** that we can all more or less agree on. For example, Americans label many things "bugs," a term that obscures the differences between worms and spiders while suggesting that there are similarities between ants and viruses. Our use of this term effectively creates a category or model for looking at the world that many Americans share, but that the speakers of other languages may not.

Thus far, the examples we have used all pertain to things outside our bodies. It is relatively easy to understand the items or qualities to which these words refer because we can use our senses to detect the qualities that allow a particular word to be applied. (That "flower" is "blue.") But cultures also offer their members a vocabulary for referring to our inner worlds. For example, the labels that English provides for our subjective states range from the common ("happy," "bored") to the more unusual ("ecstasy," "despair").

Because human language is an open system, the same language that permits us to easily speak of things "out there" also makes it possible to refer to things "in here," the subjective experiences known only to an individual self. As we have seen, language also enables us to speak about things ("angels," "titans," "deities"), and places ("heaven," "Olympus," "Asgard") that do not exist within the Universe at all and whose existence is, consequently, not open to any type of consensual validation. Perhaps not surprisingly, the existence of these beings and places must be taken "on faith," and they are said to exist in realms where the laws and properties of this Universe do not apply. In addition, religions provide terms for exceptional kinds of experiences ("agape," *moksha*), and their followers learn these terms during their religious training. Outsiders unfamiliar with such terms will be unable to understand the types of experiences they refer to. But insiders will understand. In this way, a religion can provide its followers with opportunities for extraordinary experiences that will then be interpreted as confirmation of these esoteric aspects of reality.

The effect of the confluence of culture, language, and individual experience is that different cultural worlds provide their members with different models of reality. Some of these models pertain to phenomena in the consensual domain ("out there"), some to nonconsensual experiences that are available only to an individual self ("in here"), and some to notions about reality that can be expressed through language but cannot be directly experienced and must be accepted on faith ("nowhere"). Because of our linguistic abilities, we tend to treat all three of these domains as if they are equally "real." This has important implications for both religious and scientific pursuits, and we shall consider these implications in a moment. But first we must address that most profound of all human worlds: your own.

The Personal World. Just as no two people have exactly the same perceptual apparatus, no two people will ever acquire the same understanding of their culture. It is unavoidable that we will all learn a somewhat different version of our culture. One reason is that all cultures have rules governing which members can learn what knowledge. The most common distinction—and one that is found in every society—is made between the things that men learn and the things that women learn. Later in this book, in the course of examining different religions, we will also encounter religious rules that stipulate which individuals may work in certain occupations, which ones may carry out particular rituals, and even which ones may use specific forms of language.

Our personal interests and predilections also affect which of the bodies of knowledge that our culture offers to us we will actually learn. You may decide to become an artist, an accountant, or even an anthropologist! As you learn the knowledge of your chosen field, you will also be exposed to the language of that field (its **jargon**). Physicians acquire a body of knowledge and a jargon that is so specialized that outsiders often have no idea what they are talking about. As a result, it is very easy for physicians to speak with one another, but it is difficult for those of us who do not understand medical jargon. But even two physicians who take the same classes at the same medical school cannot help learning their subject somewhat differently (one reason why it is often helpful to get a "second opinion"). Even if it were possible for two individuals to receive exactly the same training, they would still learn and understand the concepts and practices of their discipline differently because of dissimilarities in their biological and psychological make-ups and in their social environments. Just as the differences in our sensory apparatus mean that each of us lives in a unique perceptual world, the differences in our cultural training, our social settings, our personal experiences, and our biological and psychological makeups mean that each of us also lives in our own **personal world**.

Your personal world is unique, and it is accessible to no one but you. Just as no two members of the same species can ever live in the same perceptual world, no two members of the same culture can ever share the same personal world. Each of us unavoidably lives within our own private **subjective reality**, a reality that changes throughout our lives. The implications of this fact are also profound: *No one will ever understand the Universe exactly the way that you do now, and the ways in which you understand the Universe will change as you grow and learn.* The biocultural perspective makes it very clear that not only is each of us a unique and dynamic part of an ever-changing Universe, but also that each of us spends our entire existence in perceptual and cognitive isolation, making inferences about the Universe "out there" on the basis of limited and personally unique models.

Summary: Our Knowledge of the Universe

Although the Universe is ultimately beyond comprehension, we humans try to comprehend it anyway. To do so, we make use of very limited models of the world, some of which reflect things going on in the Universe and some of which do not. Our desire to understand the Universe is rooted in our ability—indeed, our need—to make sensible inferences about the world. The limitations of our senses and conceptual capacities restrict our attempts to understand both the world outside and the world inside ourselves. This restriction has several important implications. Notably, the view of the world that any culture posits—and the idiosyncratic version of the cultural world that any individual learns and develops—is limited and in many ways inadequate for understanding the Universe. Just as no species is capable of perceiving the entire Universe, no culture has models for everything in the Universe. All cultures (including our own) have no models at all for most of what is going on both "out there" and "in here." At the same time, all cultures also provide numerous models for things that are occurring "nowhere" at all.

As we learn cultural models for such everyday verifiable qualities or objects as "blue" and "flower," we are simultaneously exposed to other cultural models that provide explanations for aspects of reality that are not as easily accessible to perceptual validation and to models that have nothing at all to do with reality as we experience it through our senses. All cultures offer their members models about such basic concerns as the origins of humans and the world, the proper ways to live, and what happens after we die. Most of us unquestioningly accept these models because they are taught to us by persons of authority (such as parents, teachers, and priests) and because other members of our society also accept them. Our tendency to more or less uncritically adopt the models used by the people around us is a reflection of our "culture instinct." In the same way that our biological propensity to acquire a language as we grow up leads us to adopt the dialect of the language being spoken around us without consciously thinking about it, our biological propensity for culture leads us to adopt the models offered by our culture without a great deal of critical analysis.

Science, Religion, and the Universe

Our discussion of the different kinds of human realities and of the ways in which we construct our models of the Universe provides us with a useful starting point for considering how both science and religion help humans to understand ourselves and our place in the world. Although it is widely thought that science and religion focus on different aspects of the Universe, both science and religion depend on models that are culturally inherited. Some of these models are derived through observation of the world. Other models are obtained through spontaneous flashes of inspiration. In other words, the explanations that both science and religion develop to interpret the Universe have their roots in the same types of perceptual and cognitive processes. But the attitudes that scientific researchers and religious believers take toward their models differ, as do the procedures that each group uses to "verify" the correctness of its models. Thus, while science and religion share significant features in common, they also differ in important ways.

Analogies and Metaphors as Models for Thought

Both science and religion use models to understand the Universe. As we have seen, we are constantly interpreting what is going on "right now" by unconsciously comparing our current experiences to models we acquired in the past. We also use the models we already possess to help us comprehend the things we do not yet understand. Thus, our learned models often function as *analogies* or *metaphors*, through which one "thing" is explained and understood in relationship to some other "thing."

We make sense of the unknown, the distant, and even the unfathomable by making analogies to the things that are known, nearby, and comprehensible. When we say that electricity is a "current" that runs through the wires, we are using our knowledge of how water flows as a metaphor to understand the less comprehensible properties of electricity. In the same way, when a deity is referred to as "God the Father" or "Mother Earth," we are using commonly known familial relationships to help us conceptualize our relationship with a supernatural being. Throughout this book, we use the metaphors of "mental hardware" and "cultural software" to enable you to more easily grasp certain aspects of our biology and culture by comparing them to aspects of computers.

Everything that humans know is understood through metaphors, through models of the world that mediate between sensation and perception, and between perception and cognition. This cognitive process of seeing the unknown through the models of more familiar phenomena helps us to incorporate the unknown into our existing conceptual categories. Yet while metaphors make the unknown more intelligible, they can also lead us to make assumptions that are not accurate and cause us to overlook some significant features of the unknown.

The specific metaphors and models people use are not permanent—"engraved in stone"—to use a metaphor. From time to time, cultures may abandon one metaphoric model in favor of another. For example, atoms were once conceptualized as particles, indivisible "building blocks" of matter; later they were conceptualized as having a core and revolving particles, much like the solar system. Now atoms are understood as probabilistic fields of energy.

Humans often replace an inadequate model with a new model that provides a more comprehensive view of some aspect of the Universe. This process of shifting metaphors—of replacing one model of the Universe with another—occurs in science, religion, and all other aspects of human cognition. Both theoretical breakthroughs in science and religious conversions involve abandoning one set of metaphors and adopting another set for understanding the Universe and guiding our behavior within it. But while science makes it a priority to develop new models, religions generally do not.

Is Science Rational and Religion Irrational?

It is commonly thought that scientific advancement occurs through an empirical and rational process in which new "facts" about reality are discovered. The common conception is that scientific knowledge is a large collection of "truths," to which individual scientists are constantly adding more knowledge. Scientists often reinforce this view when they acknowledge their debt to their predecessors. We can call this the "perspiration" view of how we acquire new knowledge, in reference to the hard work that it requires. In contrast, many people regard religious knowledge as the product of a nonrational process known as "inspiration." According to religious traditions, Gautama attained enlightenment while meditating, Jesus realized his purpose after having a series of visions in the desert, and Muhammad received the entire Qu'ran from the Angel Jibril.

Although it is easy to describe science as the product of "rational" thinking and religion as the product of "irrational" inspiration, both science and religion actually involve both ways of knowing. Many religious statements represent rational attempts to explain things that people have observed. Not all religious taboos

If I have seen further it is by standing on the shoulders of giants.

Isaac Newton, in a letter to Robert Hooke dated February 5, 1676 about food and sex, for example, are arbitrary rules intended to keep people from enjoying themselves. They also serve practical purposes related to hygiene and safety. The Hindu proscription against eating cows has long helped to ensure that Hindus would have cows (for milk and for their dung) even during times of food shortages. In Europe, medieval Catholic rules against premarital sex and adultery helped to insulate lower-class Christians from syphilis and the other sexually transmitted diseases that were spreading across Europe as travelers returned from overseas bringing these previously unknown afflictions.

Other empirical and rational aspects of religions concern the events recorded in many myths. The widespread occurrence of "flood myths" in the Gilgamesh epic, the Old Testament, and Greek legend (the lost continent of Atlantis) suggests that some type of major flood took place in ancient times. And indeed, we know now that the Greek island of Santorini is all that remains of a volcano that exploded around 1650 B.C.E., creating a tidal wave that is thought to have destroyed the ancient Minoan culture (see Fig. 2.3). Thus, while the accounts passed down by any particular version of a myth may not be completely accurate, at least some of the seemingly arbitrary and "irrational" aspects of religious myths may be based on actual events.

In the same way, many of the facts of science are actually the product of inspiration that comes from nonrational thought processes. This "aha" effect is well recognized in science, and the story of Archimedes that opened this chapter is one of the best-known examples. Another example concerns Friedrich August Kekulé (1825–1896), one of the founders of structural organic chemistry, who discovered the chemical structure known as the benzene ring while dozing at home in front of a fire. For years, Kekulé had been working on questions about how carbon atoms bond. One evening, he dreamed of a figure of a snake that was holding its own tail in its mouth, forming a circle. When he awoke, he jotted down the notes that would ultimately lead to his breakthrough discovery.

New scientific discoveries often entail such sudden shifts in the ways that a scientist looks at the world (see Box 2.1: The Revolutionary Nature of Science). But is religion so different? By all accounts, the Buddha, the Christ, and the Prophet all made heroic efforts in their quests to find meaning, which appeared to them in visions. If their insights had no "real world" applications, why would billions of people now follow their teachings? The visions of Gautama, Jesus, and Muhammad have given rise to some of the most powerful and successful organizations on the planet; clear evidence of the adaptive abilities of these belief systems. For this reason, it may be more appropriate to regard such spontaneous insights as *nonrational* (instead of irrational).

Inspiration does not occur in a vacuum, and it is typically not accepted on "blind faith" alone. Both scientific and religious organizations have procedures for validating claims. In the scientific world, new ideas are typically subjected to peer review before they are published in journals. Scientific researchers investigating such unusual phenomena as "out of body" experiences or clairvoyance may find themselves outside the mainstream of science, unable to obtain funding for their research or publish their studies in an established journal. To remedy this problem, they may seek private funding and may establish journals and professional organizations that are more open to such studies. Similarly, many established religions have committees or groups of clergy that evaluate claims about miracles or revelations. Disagreements about the merits of such claims may result in schisms and cause the birth of new religious movements. To the followers of Joseph Smith, the golden tablets that the Angel Moroni revealed to him were genuine, the latest revelation from God. To Christians who believe that the birth and death of Jesus was the fulfillment of *all* revelation, Joseph Smith and his followers are heretics.

The Nature of Scientific and Religious Assumptions

While both science and religion make use of metaphors to understand the world, they differ in the nature of the assumptions they make about reality, the sources of their metaphors, and the methods they use to evaluate their statements. To understand these differences, we need to step back from both science and religion and consider the philosophical bases of each.

Metaphysics is the branch of philosophy that deals with the most basic assumptions about reality. One assumption is **monism**, the notion that the Universe is comprised of only one basic substance or principle. To science, that one substance is physical: matter (or energy). The notion that only physical "things" exist is a metaphysical assumption, not a scientific fact. In contrast to science, most religious systems accept **dualism**, the idea that the Universe is composed of two fundamentally different types of substances or principles, often referred to as matter and spirit. Although different religions define matter and spirit in different ways, and also differ in their ideas about how matter and spirit interact, they tend to agree that matter and spirit can affect one another. In other words, these religions are

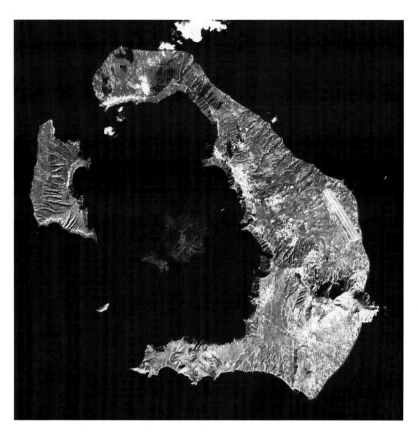

Figure 2.3 This satellite image (above) of the Greek island of Santorini (known in ancient times as Thera) shows the flooded center of what was once a single island. A volcanic eruption that occurred around 1650 B.C.E. destroyed much of the island, and the resulting tsunami is thought to have triggered a series of events that led to the collapse of the Minoan culture of Crete, located only 150 kilometers from Santorini (see map below). This event may have influenced numerous ancient myths from the eastern Mediterranean.

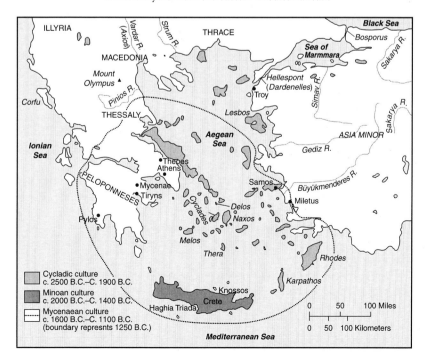

Box 2.1 THE REVOLUTIONARY NATURE OF SCIENCE

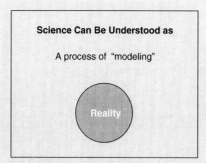

Science Can Be Understood as

A process of "modeling"

Reality

Figure 2.4

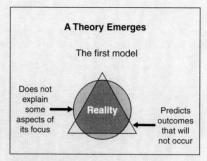

A Theory Emerges

The first model

Does not explain some aspects of its focus

Reality

Predicts outcomes that will not occur

Figure 2.5

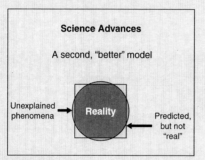

Science Advances

A second, "better" model

Unexplained phenomena

Reality

Predicted, but not "real"

Figure 2.6

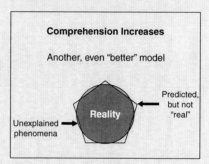

Comprehension Increases

Another, even "better" model

Predicted, but not "real"

Unexplained phenomena

Reality

Figure 2.7

Science textbooks often portray science as a cumulative process through which scientists are constantly adding to our knowledge. The sequence in which topics are presented in these textbooks is frequently thought to reflect the sequence in which scientists come to understand a particular area of inquiry. While part of this picture is true, there is another side to science as well—its revolutionary side.

This aspect of science was the subject of *The Structure of Scientific Revolutions*, a highly influential work in which Thomas Kuhn (1970) examined the history of theoretical progress in several fields, especially astronomy, physics, and chemistry. Kuhn characterized the basic framework that guides research in a field at any time as the "paradigm" of that field. A paradigm defines the theoretical assumptions of the field, describes the means by which research should be conducted, and stipulates the types of problems on which scientists working in the field will focus. Scientific paradigms help scientists to frame problems and evaluate the accuracy of their conceptions of the world. The adequacy of any particular paradigm is assessed by the extent to which it explains and makes successful predictions about some aspect of reality.

A scientific revolution—or "paradigm shift"—occurs when an existing paradigm is found to be inadequate and a new, more powerful paradigm is developed to replace it. We can understand this process by using a circle (labeled "reality" in Figure 2.4) to represent some aspect of the Universe. The first scientists who investigate this aspect of the Universe will develop a number of competing and sometimes contradictory models to explain the feature in question. It is only when one of these models proves to be sufficiently coherent and powerful that the other scientists in that field will agree to focus on that model. This step gives rise to the first paradigm for that aspect of reality, and it marks an important turning point for the field that studies it.

The explanations provided by this initial paradigm are shown in Figure 2.5 as a triangle laid over the circle that represents reality. The triangle covers (explains) most of reality, but it leaves some areas inside the circle uncovered (unexplained), and it extends beyond the circle in other places (predicting things that will not occur). As research based on this initial paradigm continues, the scientists who use it become increasingly aware of its shortcomings (see Fig. 2.6). Eventually, a new and more powerful model that provides a more comprehensive set of explanations for reality will be proposed. But this model will also leave some aspects of reality unexplained, and it, too, will predict things that will not occur (see Fig. 2.7).

Is there such a thing as a "perfect" paradigm, a model of reality which explains everything that exists and predicts nothing that does not exist? Not yet. No field of science has yet succeeded on developing a perfect theoretical model. This situation is one reason scientists continue to search for new "facts" and to propose new theories to explain them.

based on a set of metaphysical assumptions that assert that nonmaterial forces are capable of acting on physical matter, and vice versa.

It would be incorrect to conclude that the monist focus of science *proves* a monist **ontology** (origin) of the Universe, just as it would be mistaken to think that the dualist premises of most religions *prove* that spirits exist. There is no way to test the assertion that *only* matter and energy exist, and there is no way to test the assertion that God exists. The monist perspective of science is based on practical considerations and methodological principles. While the Universe certainly contains things that we currently cannot even imagine, science will not progress if it assumes that interventions which momentarily suspend the laws of nature or even come from outside the known Universe—miracles—are responsible for every phenomenon that it cannot yet fully explain. To avoid the pitfalls of using miraculous claims to explain the physical world, scientists apply the principle of **methodological materialism**, a pragmatic position which argues that natural phenomena should be explained only through other natural phenomena. It is important to note that this is not the same as **philosophical materialism**, the nonfalsifiable position that matter (and energy) is all that exists.

Another key difference between science and religion concerns the **epistemology** (from the Greek *epistēm(ē)*, meaning "knowledge") of each, the methods that each considers valid for knowing about the Universe. Because science investigates phenomena in the Universe that can be observed by our senses (or with instruments such as microscopes and thermal imagers, which are extensions of our senses), science has a strong **empirical** (from the Greek *empeirikós*, meaning "experienced") focus in which shared sensory experiences or "observations" are used to establish facts. Consequently, the phenomena that science investigates are all understood to be forms of matter or energy, which is all that our senses or machines are capable of detecting. These phenomena are then evaluated through the experimental method and mathematical analysis (more on this follows). In contrast, religious ideas are generally regarded as deriving from **revealed truth**, which is typically understood as coming from a spirit being. While such inspirational events are experiences, they occur "in here," and hence are not open to the same degree of intersubjective validation as experiences "out there." Thus, in contrast to the explicit language of a scientific statement, which is formulated to explain the relationships between observable phenomena in a way that can be tested, religious statements often point to a reality that is beyond words, cannot be tested, and is accessible only through direct personal experience or faith.

Although clearly different in these regards, science and religion are similar in the sense that both represent attempts to understand a Universe that is ultimately beyond our comprehension. As a result, we ultimately base all our conceptions—both scientific and religious—on assumptions derived from our prior experiences, especially our culture. And herein we find another important distinction between science and religion: how each treats the assumptions upon which it rests. While scientists actively search for evidence to confirm or disconfirm their ideas, religious ideas tend to be accepted on the basis of tradition and faith, and there is little effort to find evidence against them.

Religious assumptions typically take the form of **dogma**, statements that must be accepted on the basis of religious authority (from the Greek *dogma*, meaning "opinion," from *dokein*, meaning "to seem good, think"). Science also builds its models on the basis of assumptions. But in science, a statement about how some aspect of the world works is known as an **axiom** (from the Greek, *axiōma*, from *axios*, meaning "worthy"). Like dogmatic statements, axiomatic statements are initially accepted; then a system of explanations is built upon their foundation. But in contrast to the process in religion, the accepted scientific procedure is to abandon axiomatic statements when consistent research findings reveal that they are false and then to adopt new sets of axioms that yield better theories than their predecessors. In science, the criteria that are used to determine whether one set of axiomatic statements is superior to another are not statements of faith or traditions of received wisdom, but the degree to which the axioms explain and predict observable phenomena of key importance (see Box 2.2: Spirits and the "Species World" of *Homo sapiens*).

Analyzing Scientific and Religious Models of Reality

Earlier, we painted in broad strokes the story that science tells us about the history of the Universe and how humans came to be a part of it. This story involves origins and outcomes, and describes the sequence in which different phenomena emerged (e.g., atoms came before molecules, not vice versa). Religions also tell stories about origins, outcomes, and sequences of events. In some ways, the explanations that science has developed of the Universe resemble the accounts that different religious systems provide their adherents to help them comprehend the world, how it came to be, and their place within it. For instance, one can find parallels between the general sequence of events in the Genesis accounts of creation and the models that

Box 2.2 SPIRITS AND THE "SPECIES WORLD" OF *HOMO SAPIENS*

Because it is rooted in the biological sciences, you may think that the biocultural perspective would regard spirits as illusions, erroneous by-products of the ways our brains and minds provide structure to our perceptions. But this conclusion would not be correct. Although their explanations differ widely, all cultures have models—concepts—about spirits, entities with some kind of nonphysical presence that can nonetheless affect humans and the physical world. And people in every culture have experiences they interpret as involving contact with a **spirit**. This universality of spirit beliefs indicates that the basic perceptual and conceptual frameworks positing the existence of spirits are a part of human nature. But the cultural universality of spirit beliefs does not establish that spirits are "real" in an ontological sense (i.e., that they exist in and of themselves). Indeed, many spirit concepts in different cultures contradict one another. But the cultural universality of spirits does suggest that they are real in a **phenomenological** sense; that is, that there are real *experiences* that people have which they interpret as spirits.. Thus, while spirits may not be real from the etic or scientific perspective, they are certainly real from the emic perspectives of most if not all cultures. Moreover, the universality of these emic realities indicates that spirit perceptions are the product of more than just cultural beliefs, and that they constitute a transcendental, culture-independent aspect of *Homo sapiens*' species world.

In other words, although spirit perceptions are interpreted in ways that are specific to particular cultures, the tendency to have spirit experiences appears to be an aspect of human biology. So whether or not Spirits are real in a scientific sense, spirit beliefs are real in terms of their personal and social consequences. Spirit beliefs can affect our behavior and, consequently, our reproduction and survival. Consequently, they have adaptive implications that can be considered independently of the question of whether spirits objectively exist.

The insight that spirit concepts are products of the adaptations that enable humans to construct our understanding of the Universe provides a deeper perspective for understanding the phenomenological reality of spirits. Consider the phenomenon that we call "blue." The wavelengths of light that strike the receptor cells of our retinas really do exist, but not as we perceive them. We do not perceive the color that the object *is* (or, more accurately, the wavelengths of light that it absorbs), but the color that it reflects. An object appears "blue" because it absorbs all of the wavelengths of light except for the ones that our eyes interpret as "blue," which it reflects. What we "see" is actually the color that the object is *not*. But this does not mean that our perception of "blue" is not real; it just means that the object is not what we perceive it to be.

The situation may be similar with regard to "spirits." There may indeed be something "out there" that we first perceive using our mental hardware and then interpret using the software we were programmed with as we grew up in our culture. These models may explain our experiences by attributing them to a supernatural domain or by classifying them as hallucinations, the products of "an overly active imagination," or as random visual activity. But just because a culture uses a certain type of model to explain—or explain away—the experience of "spirits" does not mean that those models are true. None of our models can demonstrate whether "spirits" do or do not actually exist in the Universe.

Thus, the answer to the question "Are spirits real?" depends on our perspective and our understanding of the term *real*. Most followers of a particular religion are likely to say "yes," at least with regard to the spirits their own beliefs allow. Philosophical materialists would tend to say "no." From the biocultural perspective, the most appropriate way to "deal" with spirits is, first, to accept the reality of the spiritual experiences of people who have them by giving credence to their emic cultural descriptions of their experiences; and, second, to use cross-cultural, biological, and interdisciplinary data to develop etic, scientific explanations of both the commonalities and variations in peoples' experiences of spirits. Thus, the biocultural perspective takes an **agnostic** position toward spirits, which is to say that we do not (yet) have the evidence that would enable us to clearly determine whether spirits do or do not exist and, if they do exist, what their nature is.

science uses to explain the origin and evolution of the Universe. But still there are significant differences in scientific and religious explanations.

Consider the fact that there are two basic types of humans: male and female. The scientific story explains the two sexes by pointing out that numerous species have male and female forms and that the model of two sexes is well documented in the fossil record, indicating that humans and other animals have inherited our sexual features from our ancestors. It also notes that sexual reproduction results in genetically unique individuals. The implication is that the great diversity of complex plants and animals in the world today is a result of the great diversity that is continually being produced within any sexually reproducing species. The scientific story accounts for the two sexes by relating this fact to other phenomena in the natural world and by explaining the advantages of sexual reproduction.

Religions also provide stories that acknowledge the existence of the two sexes, offer explanations for their differences, and consider the implications of these differences. One of the best-known religious stories of this type in American society is the account related in Genesis (2:7, 21–22) that tells how God formed the first man "of the dust of the ground" and then removed a rib from the man to make the first woman. The different origins of the first man (dust) and the first woman (bone) suggests that men and women differ in fundamental ways, and in some religious groups these differences have been used to explain why men are more "god-like" than women and to justify why men should have authority over women.

The Yanomamö, a people who live in the rain forests of Venezuela and Brazil, also have stories explaining how men and women came to be and why they are different. According to the Yanomamö, men arose after one of their early ancestors shot the Moon in its belly with an arrow. The blood that fell onto the ground became the first men. In contrast, the first woman arose from a *wabu* fruit that grew on a vine. The men (who had been created first) copulated with the woman, and the daughters of these unions were the first Yanomamö women (Chagnon 1997, pp. 104–5). Because of their different origins (men from blood and women from fruit), the sexes have different temperaments and different physical characteristics.

These scientific and religious stories all refer to the past to understand the present nature of men and women, and they all provide explanations for the fundamental differences between the two sexes. But there is a crucial difference between the scientific and the religious accounts: The scientific stories are explicitly meant to be scrutinized and criticized so that they can be improved, while the religious stories are not. Indeed, it is considered one mark of a good scientist to constantly expose his or her ideas to rigorous scrutiny.

In contrast, persons who accept religious stories as literally true accounts of events generally do not subject these stories to scrutiny or criticism and may even risk being ostracized from their communities if they do question the stories. Even today, some believers in a literal interpretation of Genesis think that human males have more ribs than females and overlook the fact that males have an X and a Y chromosome while females have two X chromosomes. (If Eve was cloned from

God creating Eve from Adam's rib. (From the Souvigny Bible, 12th century.)

Adam's rib, shouldn't she and all other women have the same set of sex chromosomes as he?) Religious stories are passed down from one generation to the next and, like so many other aspects of a culture, are typically accepted "on faith."

This more or less uncritical acceptance of received wisdom is a key characteristic that distinguishes religion from science (Elfstrom 2002). Perhaps the first people to systematically espouse the idea that the wisdom of the elders *should* be exposed to critical analysis were the ancient Greeks. Their skepticism may have been a result of their geographical location. Standing at the crossroads of Asia, Africa, and Europe, the Greeks were exposed to beliefs and customs from throughout the region, many of them contradictory. Religious notions were used to explain many observable events, but were the Gods truly responsible for *everything*, including the storms that raged across the Mediterranean, the falling of the autumn leaves, and the quickened pulse of a person in love?

Some Greek thinkers began to challenge such supernatural explanations, for they noticed rhythms and patterns in the *kósmos* (their word for the order, form, or arrangement of the Universe), and they became convinced that it was possible to comprehend the causes of events. Nature, they argued, could and should be understood on its own terms, without reference to *any* Gods. But they realized that this understanding could be achieved only if the student of nature stood apart from that which he was observing (i.e., adopted an objective point of view). Realizing that even objective observers could still arrive at alternative explanations of the same event, they began to expose their explanations to criticism from other thinkers who exerted themselves to point out the shortcomings and contradictions in these ideas.

The implications of this shift in perspective and analysis were profound. In the course of their attempts to understand the workings of nature, the Greeks learned to avoid projecting qualities onto the world, whether those qualities be animal, human, or divine. They felt that the world, in other words, should be understood how it is, not how we would like it to be. These ancient ideas of critical evaluation and objectivity are hallmarks of modern science as well. But science still shares many of the same patterns of thinking and acting with other systems for explaining the world. After all, science is conducted by scientists, who have inherited the same mental hardware as nonscientists. Both science and religion have their roots in the ways we experience the world and interpret our experiences by means of models passed on as part of our culture.

Scientists understand that their frameworks will change as they gain a greater knowledge of the world. As one **paradigm** replaces another, scientists accept a new set of assumptions about the nature of the Universe that explains many of the significant factors that were unaccounted for by the old theory. In the process of adopting a new paradigm, many of the facts and data produced by the old paradigm become irrelevant. In contrast, religions seldom abandon their root explanations. Rather, they seek explanations for why their expectations were not fulfilled.

Science and Religion as Open and Closed Systems of Thought

This openness to change is a key distinction between scientific and religious (traditional) thought. Religious thought emphasizes the maintenance of established tenets, whereas scientific traditions are strongly oriented toward an awareness of alternatives. Horton (1967a, 1967b) characterizes these as "closed" and "open" orientations, respectively. Closed orientations such as religion do not lack rationality, for they engage in logical deduction and inferences within their system of beliefs. However, people who internalize these traditional orientations are not well prepared to think outside of their system, which is why it may be described as a **closed system of thought**. In contrast, scientific thinking is aware of and actively engaged in searching for alternative explanations, making it an **open system of thought**.

This lack of awareness of alternative explanations eliminates the possibility of questioning the established tenets on which the system rests. As a result, the traditional system of ideas is accepted as the only reality. Nonetheless, traditional thought is very much concerned with explanation and prediction. It uses a variety of safeguards to account for cases in which a prediction or magical action fails to yield the desired outcome. Such failures do not discredit the foundations of the system of thought, but discount or excuse the specific failures of the system.

These defenses are secondary elaborations, or "blocks to falsifiability," a form of explanation that accounts for specific instances of failures without questioning the system as a whole. For instance, when a diviner utters a prophecy that does not come true, the failure does not discount the entire system of divination, but only that specific act. The members of the community may continue to see the diviner as generally effective. They may assume that in this specific instance, the diviner was fooled by the powerful countersorcery of the witch whom he was trying to reveal. Or the diviner may have failed to correctly carry out all of the ritual preparations or did not make an offering that was suitable to the spirit that aided him in his divinations. By using such rationalizations, believers avoid attributing the failures of a traditional system to the system itself, attributing them instead to the shortcomings of individual practitioners and their specific efforts to use the system.

When we come to understand the important influences that supernatural beliefs can exert on daily life in traditional cultures, it becomes apparent that the people who share these beliefs are not mentally defective. The beliefs that the members of a traditional culture hold about invisible spirits and undetectably small influences are typically held on the same grounds as the beliefs that members of scientific societies hold about atoms and subatomic particles. Most modern people who adhere to "scientific beliefs" about atoms or the sun's revolutions around the sun do not do so because they have conducted their own scientific investigations into atoms or planetary orbits. While the ideas they believe in may be scientific, the process by which most people acquire these beliefs is not. In both traditional and modern societies, people accept what they are taught because they have *faith* in their teachers and other authorities.

While we often believe that the members of modern scientific cultures think and behave in rational and empirical ways, our self-congratulatory assurances of superiority are easily dashed by evidence to the contrary. Even in the United States, the majority of the populace still unquestioningly accepts many of the traditional assumptions of their religious systems. They believe in spirits that survive bodily death, the power of intercessory prayer, and the existence of angels. As Horton (1967a, 1967b) points out, this important difference between open and closed systems of thought reminds us that traditional religious thinking is primarily a theory about society and human relationships, rather than a set of guidelines for exerting influences on the physical Universe.

Science and the Experimental Method

The modern scientific method involves the critical evaluation of assertions about the physical world using the experimental method to test hypotheses, which are statements developed to explain the relationships between different phenomena. A scientific **hypothesis** is a special kind of inference about the world that states its assumptions in terms that are as explicit as possible and that predict outcomes in formal terms. Newton's first "law"—which states that a body (object) at rest will tend to stay at rest, while a body that is moving will continue to move with a constant velocity unless it is acted upon by an external force—is an example of such a statement. Since it describes phenomena that can be observed, it is possible to set up controlled conditions to test Newton's statement. Scientists can conduct experiments that vary both the masses of the objects involved and the forces acting upon them, thereby obtaining results the scientists can use to derive the general principles that are involved. An adequate understanding of the phenomena that have already been observed makes it possible to predict what will be observed in future experiments. If these predictions are borne out, then the hypotheses that generated them receive additional support. The observations and experiments that have been performed to test Newton's statements have produced such highly consistent results that these statements are considered universally valid when the appropriate conditions are met. Thus, they are known as "laws."

A key word in this discussion is "support." Tests of scientific statements cannot ever provide proof of a model. To *prove* a scientific statement such as Newton's first law, you would need to observe every possible occurrence of the events it intends to explain (including the situation where no forces act on the object—a

physical impossibility in our Universe) and show that, in every case, the expected effect is valid. This is clearly impossible. Instead, scientists attempt to demonstrate that their statements are *false* by performing experiments under as wide a variety of conditions as possible, each experiment designed to generate findings that may or may not support the predictions of the hypothesis. In the case of Newton's laws, continued experimentation has demonstrated that they apply only within certain boundary conditions. If these conditions are exceeded (for example, when an object moves at a speed close to that of light, or under conditions of extreme heat and pressure), these laws are no longer valid. It was partly the recognition of these limitations that inspired the development of relativity theory and quantum mechanics. But within the "normal" conditions of our everyday experience, Newton's laws continue to provide very useful predictions and explanations of events.

Because even a large number of positive observations cannot suffice to prove that a hypothesis is true, scientists focus on trying to demonstrate that their hypotheses are false. This is an essential feature of scientific work: For a statement to be a *scientific* statement, it must be open to **falsifiability**. In other words, there should be at least one experiment that can be conducted in the attempt to disprove or falsify the statement (Popper 1959). For example, the statement "the moon is made of green cheese" *is* a scientific statement, because there are ways to show that it is false, and indeed this has been done. In contrast, both the statements "God cures cancer" and "God causes cancer" are *not* scientific statements, because there is no way to demonstrate that either of these statements is false. (There are no experiments that we can perform to falsify it.) Since there is no way to even attempt to disprove such statements, science is not in a position to evaluate any claims concerning their truth or falsehood. When discussing things that are not open to falsifiability, the scientific position is agnostic, for science is unable to make any kind of definitive statement about such things (including the existence of God). In other words, the requirement that scientists make an effort to disprove their theories means that there are limitations to what science is able to study.

Although the testing of hypotheses is central to science, many disciplines of science rely on *observations* of natural events rather than experiments. Meteorology, geology, and astronomy all test their hypotheses against systematic observations of the weather, the earth, or celestial bodies. But like the more experimentally oriented sciences, these fields also make use of the other major tool of modern science—mathematics—to frame their

Box 2.3 MATHEMATICS AND SCIENCE

As we have seen, one of the most important distinctions between scientific and religious models of the Universe is that scientists actively attempt to improve their models, while religious believers do not. One of the tools that scientists use as they attempt to falsify their old models and develop new ones is mathematics. Mathematics is a useful tool because it generates predictions scientists may then test experimentally.

Different systems of mathematics (such as algebra and geometry) are based on different sets of axioms. For example, Euclidean geometry is based on five axioms, the best-known of which is the "parallel postulate," which states that two parallel lines can never meet. Although many people consider the parallel postulate so obviously "true" that they think it is a property of the Universe, it is not. Euclid's five axioms are, in a very real sense, simply rules that are used for "playing" with a particular type of geometry. Other types of geometry are played with different rules. Commonly referred to as non-Euclidean geometries, these systems usually adhere to most, but not all, the rules of Euclidean geometry. Probably the best known example of these is Riemannian geometry, named after its developer, Bernhard Riemann (1826–1866). His system of geometry retains all of Euclid's axioms except for one: the parallel postulate. Riemann replaced Euclid's postulate with a postulate which says that all parallel lines do eventually meet.

Riemannian geometry gained fame because Albert Einstein used it when he was developing his General Theory of Relativity. Euclidean geometry was inadequate for his purposes, so Einstein turned to Riemannian geometry as an alternative. But when he decided to use this geometry, he had to accept every one of its assumptions, including the axiomatic statement that all parallel lines eventually meet. Because, on the "game board" Einstein was now playing with, parallel lines always met, the board appeared curved rather than flat. For Einstein, this meant that space-time had to be curved, and he concluded that mass causes the curvature. Discussions about how extreme this curvature could become soon led to questions of whether there might exist objects that are so massive that nothing which comes close to them can ever escape their gravitational pull. These were the first conjectures about black holes, a concept initially thought to be so absurd that even Einstein himself was unable to accept the possibility of their existence. Today, astronomers estimate that our galaxy alone contains hundreds of these strange objects.

This example illustrates the ways in which mathematical models can predict scenarios that were previously unimaginable. Indeed, one way to test a new theory is to conduct experiments to see if the predictions of mathematical models are borne out. These new predictions often take science in entirely new directions. Mathematics is a powerful tool of science precisely because it can both explain our current observations and enable us to predict what we might find in the future—predictions that occasionally force us to rethink what we know about the Universe. The combination of the experimental method and mathematical description has provided us with such powerful tools for making models of reality that we are able, for example, to calculate where and when the sun's shadow will next touch the earth (allowing us to make travel plans to view a solar eclipse) and to send a spacecraft on a journey that may last for years (to arrive at a destination that was in a different location when the spacecraft was launched).

Mathematics does not provide a single system for describing reality, but offers many different systems, each with its own axioms, rules, and implications. As scientists shift from one mathematical description of the world to another, they change their assumptions about the world. Since none of our current scientific theories provides a perfect description of the aspect of the Universe it is designed to explain, scientists fully expect to develop new and more comprehensive theoretical models that better explain the structure of atoms, the movement of the planets, or the origin of life. Developing these new models will require new systems of mathematics.

hypotheses and determine whether they are correct (see Box 2.3: Mathematics and Science).

Mysticism as Science

While mysticism is often considered to be the spiritual side of religion, it is also a science of human psychology and the mind. As an effort to understand the nature of the Universe, mysticism addresses metaphysical (ontological) issues, while, in its efforts to understand how we know what we know, it deals with epistemological concerns. Mystical experiences are typically characterized as "incomprehensible," "beyond words," and "transcending all description." What is the biocultural perspective on mysticism? One aim of the mystical disciplines is to achieve a condition in which the individual merges with something greater than him- or herself, and a person has no words to describe that state even after it has been attained. Thus we may hypothesize that this mystical practice bypasses or "short-circuits" the features of our mental hardware that make use of language and directly affect the nonverbal cognitive processes of more primitive brain systems.

How may we understand the subjective experiences of mystics? Can their visions provide a basis for valid knowledge? Mystical experiences, like all experiences, are personal, and yet in numerous cultures mystical experiences are corroborated in much the same manner that scientific ideas are in our own society. Both mystical experiences and scientific ideas are reported to recognized and trained authorities whom society views as qualified to interpret and validate the primary personal experiences. In other words, the reports of these intensely subjective experiences are subject to the scrutiny of the larger community of other mystics or scientists, who may intersubjectively affirm the validity of the personal experiences.

Mystical traditions reject the notion that subjective experiences should be accepted as empirical reality or truth. Mystical traditions typically view our everyday experiences of reality as illusory, and emphasize that even mystical experiences must be critically evaluated to determine their validity and value. The idea that a person must undergo a specific type of training in order to have valid experiences is important, as it provides a basis for developing a science of subjectivity or a science of consciousness that informs us about how to make systematic observations of religious experiences.

Philosophers have questioned whether or not it is possible to apply the rigor of science to mysticism. Some suggest that the perceptions of mystical states are a result of conditioning, a kind of self-fulfilling prophecy derived from training. In many ways, the experiences reported by mystics are shaped by their cultural traditions, mystical theories, and personal experiences, just like any other experiences. But one of the primary objectives of mystical techniques such as meditation is to limit the extent to which our memories of past experiences can affect our interpretations of our present experiences.

Mystical techniques that are intended to eliminate the influence of the past on the perception of the present are often characterized as an effort to achieve an *unconditioned* state. Mystical traditions teach their followers to attain modes of consciousness that differ from ordinary perception and religious perceptions, both of which are based on understandings learned in the past. In mysticism, a current experience is understood in its present context alone, thereby suspending the influences of past learning of cultural categories and forestalling evaluation through personal experiences. Mysticism recognizes that perception requires a perceiver, making the qualities and conditions of the self central to the nature of the perception and knowledge obtained. The self must be developed through the honing of skills of detached evaluation.

Another way to understand the nature of mystical perception is to examine the assumptions, discriminations, and mental activity that characterize *different* forms of awareness. Our subjective experiences are a consequence of our **enculturation**, the process of growing up within a culture and learning how to interpret reality. Due to enculturation, in many ways the world we think we are experiencing is, in fact, an *illusion*, for instead of perceiving the world as it is, we constantly interpret it in terms of the mental models we have acquired in the past. Thus, mystical traditions aim at suspending both the mental hardware and the cultural software that we use to interpret our experiences and understand the Universe.

The development of mystical forms of consciousness permitted the emergence of a *spiritual* awareness, an awareness of a wider range of human needs beyond the physical that could arise only when humans became capable of transcending self-centered awareness and its personal and culturally defined needs. When this occurred, human minds became capable of directing their development towards fulfilling interpersonal, transpersonal, and spiritual needs. Moreover, this new ability to have a "present-centered consciousness," to be completely in the "here and now" and thus to suspend the use of our previously acquired models, also contributed to the emergence of scientific thought (McNamara 2004).

But not all science is present-centered, for the thinking, observing, and experimentation that make up such a large part of the scientist's work are based on assumptions that were learned in the past, during the scientist's training. In this sense, the everyday activities of "normal science" are much like the everyday activities of religion. Of course, the distinction between the scientific reliance on axioms and the religious adherence to dogmas sets the two apart. Nevertheless, science and religion—like most other human activities—are made possible by models we acquire as we learn a particular culture, and it is often difficult to separate ourselves and our observations from our models of the Universe. The intention of mystical experience is to remind ourselves of this fact, and to learn how to experience the Universe as we did before we acquired the many layers of culture that filter our thoughts and perceptions (see Box 2.4: Mystical Participation).

Neurophenomenological Perspectives on Transpersonal Development

Laughlin, McManus, and d'Aquili (1992) characterize the meditative traditions' higher phases of consciousness as involving a maturational process reflecting the development of structural features of human neurophysiology. These features are produced by entraining neural networks through the conscious application of the individual's will and by the individual's attention to his or her own development. By focusing their attention, meditators create new patterns of neuronal association, literally rewiring their brains.

These advanced stages of meditative and mystical development are relatively rare. This is because the retuning of the autonomic nervous system requires both considerable effort and supportive social institutions, such as the monasteries. Meditative traditions provide both the social support for study and the "technologies" designed to produce a fundamental transformation of the relation of the physical substratum of the brain with the mental realm. According to Laughlin, McManus, and d'Aquili (p. 336), "Transcendence is a

Box 2.4 MYSTICAL PARTICIPATION

Anthropologist E. E. Evans-Pritchard provided support for a different view of magical thought, one also expressed in the oft-rejected ideas of Lucien Lèvy-Brühl (1857–1939) about how primitive peoples viewed the world. Lèvy-Brühl (1926) had introduced a view of primitive thought that he characterized as "mystical participation," an understanding of the world in which logical contradiction was not an important criterion for evaluating ideas. Instead, emphasis was placed on notions of mystical forces and influences that were capable of producing the changes desired by the magical act or religious petition. Cultures that followed this way of thinking believed that the Universe was pervaded with powerful, but unseen, influences that could be used to achieve practical ends. Evans-Pritchard agreed with Lèvy-Brühl's argument that the "primitive" person was not a mental imbecile, but merely someone who viewed the world differently from the way Western science and empiricism viewed the world, because of his or her cultural system and socialization. Rather than being irrational or childish, magical and religious thinking was a product of a cultural system that instilled certain ways of understanding the world. Within these cultural assumptions about the world, mystical religious beliefs were normal and made sense. Understanding religious practices in the context of how people came to believe in and practice them illustrated how religion fits together with the other patterns of the culture. From Evans-Pritchard's perspective, primitive people's belief structures were both scientific and mystical, and they saw no contradiction between the two ways of thinking. Mystical thinking pervaded every aspect of life, including the practical and technical domains.

Evans-Pritchard emphasized the importance of treating religious beliefs as symbolic expressions rather than literal statements. The Azande people of north-central Africa held what might be viewed as logical contradictions. They characterized themselves as "red parakeets," regarded twins as "birds," and considered oxen and cucumbers equivalent for the purposes of sacrifice. By analyzing each of these aspects of Azande thought in the broader context of their culture, Evans-Pritchard was able to illustrate that these beliefs were analogies and metaphors, symbolic statements about their beliefs rather than mistaken ideas about the physical world. For example, their consideration of twins as birds reflected their concepts of spirits, while their identification of people as animals was a product of their totemic thinking. They did not actually confuse the different entities, but thought of human differences in these terms. In effect, these were not beliefs about the nature of the physical world, but rather beliefs regarding their mythological system.

Evans-Pritchard rejected many of the previous characterizations of primitive religions as failures to understand the worldview and beliefs of different people. He felt that these characterizations made the mistake of evaluating them using Western criteria of rationality. His studies of the Azande oracles (divination processes) illustrated the skepticism and rationality often embodied in religious thought. The oracular mechanisms employed by the Azande involved critical thinking processes. Consultation with the oracles involved feeding a mild poison to a chicken while asking a question. If the chicken died, the answer to the question was considered to be yes. A second chicken was selected and the question was reversed. This time, if the answer was yes, the chicken was expected *not* to die from the poison. This skeptical attitude of the Azande expressed a need to seek both confirmatory and contrary evidence related to the revelation from the initial consultation with the oracle.

process of extraordinary neural development. . . . The ego is the maturation of adaptation, mature contemplation is the maturation of reflection. Both are mediated by the same neurobiological processes."

Laughlin et al. formulate a model of contemplative experiences and higher phases of consciousness based on manipulations of the autonomic nervous system (see Chapter 3). They hypothesize that the experiences of centering and movement of psychic energy (especially ascending and descending) are a result of sensing activity in the autonomic nervous system and endocrine system. Psychic energy experiences involve homologous representations of the perceptual and bodily senses with physiological processes. For instance, many mystical traditions speak of the experience of unity, connection, integration, and understanding. In Chapter 3 we will discuss the **neurophenomenology** of these experiences, in the sense that the neurological or physiological effects of altered states of consciousness (ASC) are directly related to the phenomenological characteristics of the experiences. These ASC involve patterns of brain wave synchronization and brain system integration that are correlated with the phenomenological experiences of unity and integration, and that produce insight through the integration of different brain processes.

In sum, mysticism is often used as a pejorative term, a put-down in contrast to the presumed empiricism of science. But mysticism also has empirical content, providing traditions spanning thousands of years and using rigorous methods to study the mechanisms that underlie the processes of the mind. These contemplative mystical traditions can thus be understood as a science of the mind and consciousness, turning trained attention and observational processes toward a systematic examination of mental processes.

Neurotheology: Looking for God in the Brain

The idea that all experiences—even those we call religious—are the result of brain processes is one of the foundations of the modern neurosciences. Today, sophisticated methods of seeing into the brain and recording its activity are providing new understandings of consciousness that reveal how our brains create our personal consciousness through interaction with our cultural beliefs. If our "God experiences" are functions of our brains, can we determine the particular brain areas that produce these "God experiences"? These are complex questions involving not only scientific methodology but also epistemology and metaphysics.

The conceptual framework that underlies this work is known as the **neural correlates of consciousness**. It postulates that every conscious experience we have is correlated with some type of activity within the brain. Researchers are careful to use the expression "correlated with" and not "caused by," for the precise relationship between what we are experiencing and what is happening in the brain is unclear. While recent advances in science allow us to observe the brain's activities during religious experiences, what those data mean and what they tell us about the nature of religious experiences and reality remain contentious.

To answer questions about the brain states associated with mystical experiences, researchers use techniques that measure the activity levels of different parts of our brains. The first important technique for measuring brain activity—electroencephalography (EEG)—was invented in the 1920s. EEGs measure "brain waves" via a number of electrodes attached to the surface of the head. Unfortunately, this method has two major limitations. First, the electrodes can only record the activity patterns in millions of neurons that are in close proximity to one another. Second, an EEG cannot measure what is occurring in areas of the brain that lie further below the surface. In spite of these limitations, EEG measurements have provided important insights into the different patterns of brain activity associated with religious and scientific thought and experiences.

In recent years, new noninvasive methods of measuring the activity levels *inside* the brain have been developed. These techniques have given us amazing insights into how the functioning of our brains correlates with our experiences. Single photon emission computed tomography (SPECT) uses radioactively tagged chemicals ("radiotracers") that are injected into the bloodstream and then accumulate in the areas of the brain that are most active when a person is performing a particular task. The amount of radiation being emitted from these regions is then read and assembled into an image of the brain.

Functional Magnetic Resonance Imaging (fMRI) allows researchers to make real-time measurements of the changing amounts of blood flowing through the different regions of the brain over time. The relatively high resolution of fMRI devices (which are able to detect changes in activity in regions as small as 2–3 millimeters) allows researchers to localize which parts of the brain are receiving more or less oxygen at a given moment. Thus, the technique can be used to indicate the parts of the brain that are more or less active while a person is performing a certain type of task, such as reading a book or looking at photographs of faces or buildings.

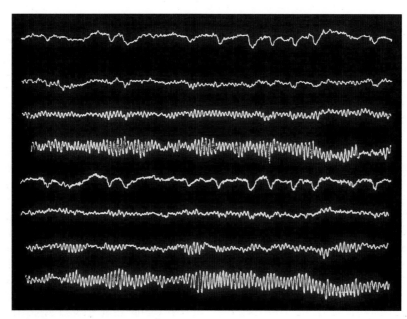

An EEG recording shows patterns in the activity of large numbers of neurons in the upper layers of the brain.

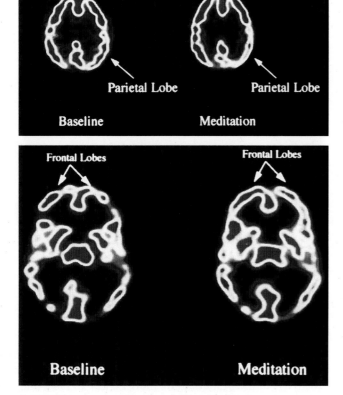

A SPECT image can show much blood is flowing to a particular region of the brain while a person is carrying out a task.

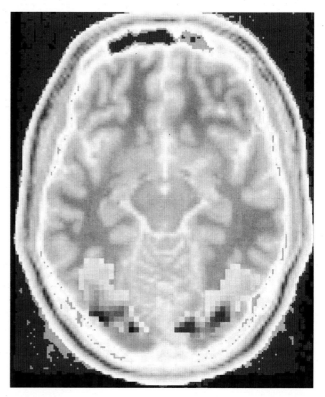

An fMRI image depicts the relative amount of blood flowing to different areas of the brain. This technique can pinpoint areas that are active with much more precision than EEGs or SPECT scans.

These new technologies have led to the emergence of a new field of study known as **neurotheology,** which attempts to discern the parts of the brain that are involved in religious activities such as meditation and prayer. One of the first neurotheology studies to gain widespread notice used SPECT scans with eight experienced Tibetan meditators (Newberg et al. 2001). This study found that there were noticeable differences in the flow of blood to different regions of the subjects' brains before and after meditation. One area that attracted particular attention, the superior parietal lobe, is responsible for our sense of being in a distinct space. Blood flow to this area decreased during meditation, a finding which suggests that limiting the flow of blood to this region may be responsible for the sense of "merging" (*unio mystica*) with something greater than themselves that is often reported by mystics from different traditions.

A recent study (Beauregard and Paquette 2006) examined fifteen Carmelite nuns who were asked to "relive" a mystical experience while their brain activity was measured using the fMRI technique. The investigators found that brain activity increased in numerous different regions of the brain, including areas involved in perceptual, emotional, and cognitive processing, particularly in the temporal lobe, an area implicated in many studies of altered states of consciousness. They also noted significant increases in activation in areas of the brain which are involved in the processing of positive emotions. This increased activity correlated with the joy the nuns related that they had experienced as they meditated.

These studies indicate that different techniques for inducing mystical experiences each affect different constellations of brain regions. Given that the subjective reports about the experiences produced by each technique differ, these findings are no surprise. However, it should be emphasized that these findings are very preliminary. The small sample sizes of the mystical practitioners, the fact that they were "self-selected" for mysticism because they actively pursued their mystical paths, the fact that the practitioners were studied under laboratory rather than "natural" conditions (such as meditating in their normal locations), and the use of different methods for measuring brain activity all make it difficult to generalize these findings and develop a comprehensive model of what is happening in the brain during a "spiritual" experience. In any case, it is becoming clear that there is no one "God spot" in our brains and that religiosity not only includes a variety of different kinds of spiritual experiences, but also activates a number of different brain regions.

Although these experiments demonstrate that we have entered an entirely new period in the scientific study of religiosity, they have not yet produced answers to some of our age-old questions. Since the brain activity of mystical experiences is "real," are the experiences themselves similarly "real"? Or conversely, does the fact that we can capture an image of a brain during a spiritual experience mean that spiritual experiences involve nothing more than brain activity? While some reductionistic approaches might argue this case, science cannot substantiate such conclusions.

As an analogy, consider the TV programs you watch. We can monitor your TV set to establish the fact that *The Colbert Report* is on, and we can measure the electrical activity that produces your experiences of the program. To a person who does not understand how television works, the appearance of Stephen Colbert on the TV set may seem magical: No matter how much they examine the TV set, they will never find Stephen Colbert inside it. But this does not mean that he doesn't exist, or that his program isn't "real." In the same way, we are limited in the inferences that we can draw from neurological research into spiritual experiences. Whether or not there is a physical brain phenomenon that can be measured during a spiritual experience has no bearing on whether or not the experience reflects something true about the ultimate reality of the Universe (see Box 2.5: The Universe from Multiple Perspectives: A Parable).

Conclusions: Comparing Science and Religion

This chapter examined the ways that humans come to know about the Universe, and we discussed different types of animal and human realities. Insights from both biological and cultural studies indicate that each person lives in a unique perceptual and cultural reality shaped by biology and the socialization experiences provided by culture. Religious and scientific models of the Universe are also shaped by the culture we experience as we grow. Although religious and scientific models are often thought to compete with one another, they are both made possible by our symbolic capacity for thought.

Science, religion, and myth are all made possible by the mental hardware that humans use to understand the world. The fact that all known cultures have spirit beliefs, origin mythologies, and other supernatural explanations of the Universe strongly suggests that the underlying traits that are responsible for this behavior are part of

Box 2.5 THE UNIVERSE FROM MULTIPLE PERSPECTIVES: A PARABLE

An ancient Asian parable tells of a group of four blind men who were told that a circus was coming to their village, and that its main attraction was an elephant. The blind men were curious, for they had never heard of an elephant, and they were eager to find out more about it. So when the circus arrived, they asked the elephant handler if they could approach and touch the elephant so that they could learn about this wondrous animal.

The elephant handler agreed. He led the first man to the front of the elephant and placed the blind man's hands on its trunk. He watched as the blind man slowly felt his way up the trunk, marveling at the elephant's tusks.

The handler then led the second blind man to the back of the elephant. The blind man felt the tuft of hair at the end of its tail, and then worked his hands up until he reached the elephant's enormous backside.

The handler took the third man to one side of the elephant and placed his hands on one of the elephant's legs. The blind man moved his hands across the leg and then onto the elephant's belly. Continuing on, he soon came to a second leg, and then a third and a fourth.

The elephant handler led the fourth blind man to a ladder and helped him climb onto the elephant's back. He then handed the blind man some leaves. The blind man knew that he was far off the ground, but the gentle demeanor of the elephant put him at ease. He was amazed when the elephant reached its trunk back and took the leaves from his hand. The blind man felt the elephant's large ears, and then its large head.

After their experiences, the blind men thanked and blessed the handler and the elephant and set off for home. On their way, they discussed what they had discovered.

The first blind man said, "The elephant is like a long snake protected by two great spears. Clearly, the elephant is an animal that can defend itself against any threat."

The second blind man said, "I, too, felt what I thought was a snake, but then I realized that it was really just a swatter for keeping the flies away from an enormous wall. It seems to me that the elephant is like a large building."

The third blind man told the others, "I felt four great pillars, each larger than myself. They were connected by a roof whose sides seemed to reach up forever. I think that the elephant is like the sky that connects together everything on earth."

The fourth man was silent for a bit. When the others pressed him for his thoughts, he told them, "I think the elephant is many things. It is very large, and it has a very big head. So it must be very intelligent. It takes food from above, and it has large ears that it can use to hear everything. In my opinion, the elephant is one of the most remarkable things I have ever encountered."

A parable is a simple tale that makes a profound point. In the parable just discussed, the elephant represents religiosity, and the four blind men represent our various efforts to understand our human capacity for religiosity. Each of the blind men is trying to understand religiosity using the insights that he acquired from his own perspective. Each has developed a partial picture of the elephant that, while true in its own way, does not recognize the true appearance and the many features of the elephant.

Metaphorically, the different ideas that these blind men developed about the elephant are similar to the many views about religiosity. Like the experiences of the first three blind men, who were only able to see the elephant from a limited perspective, most approaches to understanding religion are incomplete. The fourth blind man, who experienced the elephant from a loftier perspective, was able to realize that the elephant has many qualities that it uses for a variety of purposes. This man represents the biocultural approach, which tells us that we can develop a truly adequate understanding of the elephant only if we examine as many of its features as possible and only if we consider what the purposes of those features might be. Like the others, the fourth man will always have an incomplete understanding of the elephant, but his broader outlook will enable him to arrive at a much fuller understanding of the elephant than theirs. We, too, will explore a variety of perspectives to understand more about the nature and purpose of our capacity for religiosity.

the "hardwiring" of the brain and are manifestations of our species' need to understand and explain the Universe.

Although the explanations offered by mystical and scientific thinking share similarities in their reliance on our symbolic capacities, brain studies of their physical correlates indicate that these forms of thinking are different. Many religious experiences involve slow wave brain patterns (so-called theta and alpha waves) in the limbic system (the "emotional brain"), ideas that we will discuss in Chapters 3 and 4. In contrast, scientific thinking is primarily associated with activity in the frontal cortex and, in particular, the left hemisphere, the seat of our linguistic and conceptual abilities. The brain-wave patterns typical of such thought (e.g., beta waves) are faster. These findings suggest that religion and science are different, yet complementary ways of thinking. Religious experiences tend to involve the more ancient, lower brain systems that generate our self-concept and enable us to bond with others. Scientific thinking, on the other hand, emphasizes our knowledge of the external world and is mediated by the high-level sensory processing areas of the brain. Understanding the relationships between what is occurring in the brain and what we are experiencing can shed much light on the differences between religious and scientific thought, allowing us to gain a greater appreciation of the important role that each plays in human life and culture.

It is our ability to perceive things that are happening in the world and to make inferences regarding the meanings of these things that lies at the basis of both religion and science. The recognition that our assumptions—our models—about the Universe could be evaluated on the basis of the descriptive power they provided and the predictions they made possible provided a way to distinguish between the axiomatic statements of science and the dogmatic statements of religion. The shift from dogmas to axioms moved us from an intersubjective understanding of reality based simply on accepted cultural tradition to an understanding of reality that could be challenged by anyone with the appropriate training.

Both science and religion are based on assumptions about the world. Religious assumptions about the existence of Gods and spirits, and about the locations where souls spend the afterlife, are dogmatic statements that must be accepted or rejected "on faith." When scientists are conducting their everyday research activities, they generally accept without question the axiomatic statements that provide the basis for their paradigms. But the predictions that are derived from them are based on empirical evidence and are evaluated by considering the explanatory and predictive power they provide. The history of Western science contains numerous examples of dogmatic religious statements about the Universe that have been challenged and falsified by science. The idea that our earth was the center of the Universe has given way to a view in which our sun is but one of many stars in our galaxy. The idea that both our solar system and humans exist in the same forms now as when we first appeared has been replaced by a more dynamic understanding of the Universe in which the physical Universe changes over time and simpler forms of life give rise to more complex forms. The idea that men and women were created directly out of dust and bone (or blood and fruit) has been superseded by a view of the two human sexes as evolutionary products of sexual reproduction, a strategy that is adaptive for many species.

Although we have been speaking of science and religion as if all scientists and religionists think the same way, both science and religion are practiced by individuals. We can thus observe the same spectrum of differences among these individuals that we find with regard to other cultural domains of knowledge. Some scientists are "true believers" who become so attached to a particular theoretical conception of the world that they refuse to abandon it even when the other members of the scientific community shift to a more powerful paradigm. Others believe that the assumption of methodological materialism that guides scientific research necessarily implies an ontological materialism (that is, that matter truly is all that exists). This can lead to **scientism**, the attitude that only scientific assumptions and methods matter. There are also religionists who are very skeptical about some of the dogmatic statements of their religions and yet manage to maintain their overall faith.

In this chapter, we have considered some of the ways in which we obtain and evaluate our knowledge about the Universe, and the ways in which the worlds that humans experience differ from the "objective" features of the Universe. The models through which we understand the Universe are products of both the special biological features of our species and the cultural tradition in which we are raised.

Science and religion make use of many of the same features of our mental hardware, and consequently have many features in common. But there are also important distinctions between the two, especially with regard to the types of evidence for the models each uses and the ways in which this evidence is collected and evaluated. One of the most important differences between the two is that scientists work to test and improve their models, while religions often attempt to maintain beliefs even in the face of contradictory evidence. But as we shall see in later chapters, this conservative aspect of religion can have important adaptive effects.

Questions for Discussion

- Why will we never be able to know the world as it really is?
- Given that each of us lives in a different world, what can we do to minimize misunderstandings?

- If spirits are a natural product of human cognition, why do some people experience them while others do not?
- If science and religion are based on similar ways of understanding the world, why do they so often appear to be in conflict?

Glossary

agnostic having the attitude that there is not enough evidence to justify favoring or opposing a particular assumption; a person who holds this attitude

axiom a statement that is accepted on the basis of its ability to contribute to an explanation of an observable phenomenon and that can be abandoned when found to be false

closed system of thought a system of thought that does not offer its members alternative ideas that would enable people to think outside the system

cognition the mental process by which perceptions are interpreted

cultural world the sum of the ways in which a culture teaches its members to interpret the Universe

dogma a statement that is accepted solely on the basis of religious authority and that members of the society in question are discouraged from challenging

dualism a conception of reality that posits the existence of two fundamentally different types of substances or principles in the Universe (typically construed as the physical and the spiritual worlds)

empirical the use of shared sensory observations of natural phenomena to establish facts about the Universe

enculturation the process by which a person grows up within a culture and learns its concepts and values

epistemology the branch of philosophy that considers the methods that humans use to understand the Universe, as well as the limits of our knowledge

falsifiability the quality of a statement about some aspect of reality such that the statement may be shown to be incorrect

hypothesis an inference about the world that explains the relationships between observable phenomena and that is open to being falsified

inference an interpretation of the products of perception that is based on past experience

intersubjective reality the view of reality that is agreed upon by individuals who share a common vocabulary for speaking about that reality

jargon the specialized language specific to a particular domain of cultural knowledge

metaphysics the branch of philosophy that deals with the most basic assumptions about reality

methodological materialism the scientific position that natural phenomena can be explained only by referring to other natural phenomena

mind a high-level function of the brain that receives the integrated products of perception and cognition in the form of a global "picture" of the world

monism a conception of reality that posits the existence of only one basic substance or principle in the Universe

neural correlates of consciousness the idea that every conscious experience we have is correlated with some type of activity within the brain

neurophenomenology relationships between the neurological or physiological aspects of brain function and the phenomenological characteristics of experiences

neurotheology a field of study that attempts to determine which parts of the brain are involved in religious activities

objective reality all that exists, in all of its forms, including both the things we are aware of and the things we are not. See **Universe**.

ontology the branch of philosophy that considers the nature of existence

open system of thought a system of thought that offers its members alternative ideas and encourages people to think outside the system

paradigm a framework that guides scientific research by stating a set of theoretical assumptions about reality and stipulating the types of problems to be studied

perception the recognition of a sensation by a higher-level neural structure that contrasts and categorizes sensations

perceptual world the way that an individual organism perceives the Universe

personal world the view of the Universe that humans create individually by using their own interpretation of their cultural world and their own personal experiences to interpret the products of their unique perceptual apparatus.

phenomenological the ways and means by which reality is experienced

philosophical materialism the nonfalsifiable assertion that only matter and energy exist

receptor a neuron that is specialized to detect sensory stimuli

revealed truth knowledge obtained through communication with a spirit being

scientism the attitude that science is the only valid means for determining what is true

sensation a product of neural stimulation that provides some type of information about the world

species world the way that a particular species of organism is able to perceive the Universe

spirit a supernatural being that possesses some qualities of humans while also having other qualities not shared by humans

subjective reality the world as an individual perceives and understands it

synaesthesia a rare type of perception in which normally distinct sensory modalities blend together, allowing a person to "hear" colors or "taste" sounds

Universe all that exists, in all of its forms, including both the things we are aware of and the things we are not. See **objective reality**.

CHAPTER

Consciousness and Spiritual Experiences

CHAPTER OUTLINE

Introduction: The Experience of Religion
What Is Consciousness?
The Biological Bases of Spiritual Consciousness: The Integrative Mode of Consciousness
Origins of Religious Experiences: Natural Induction of the Integrative Mode of Consciousness
Adaptive Aspects of the Integrative Mode of Consciousness
Conclusions: Religious Experience as Personal Experience of Biology

CHAPTER OBJECTIVES

- Introduce the role of extraordinary experiences in religions.
- Understand religious experiences in the context of consciousness and altered states of consciousness and as a natural feature of the human brain.
- Provide a biological framework for understanding the special qualities of religious states of consciousness.
- Examine some of the different types of religious states of consciousness.
- Examine the origins of religion from the perspectives of the biological factors involved in altered states of consciousness.
- Illustrate the adaptive functions of religious states of consciousness.

ONE DAY, SIDDHARTHA GAUTAMA SAT DOWN BENEATH A tree and swore an oath to meditate until he either attained realization or died. He meditated for weeks. During this time, he was visited by a great demon, Mara, who tried to distract Siddhartha by appealing to his sense of family, his ego, and his desires. But Siddhartha's concentration could not be broken. After weeks of meditation, Siddhartha had a vision. He saw his life before him, and then all of the lives he had lived before. He saw how all of these lives were connected by karma, and how the deeds of his past lives had caused him to be born into his subsequent lives. It was then that he realized how he could break the chain of karma that caused him to be continually reborn. It was then that Gautama became a Buddha, an "enlightened one."

* * *

Shortly after his encounter with John the Baptist, Jesus went into the desert to pray and seek answers concerning his identity and his purpose. For forty days and nights, he ate no food, and he remained alone. While he was in the desert, the devil came and tempted him three times. Once he offered Jesus food, and another time wealth and power. He also challenged Jesus's faith in God by asking him to jump from the temple roof. After resisting each of these temptations, Jesus left the desert and began teaching. He now knew who he was, and he knew his purpose. He was the Messiah (in Greek, Christos) that had been predicted in earlier Jewish scriptures, and his purpose was to teach others how to resist temptation and enter the Kingdom of God.

* * *

Muhammad had often gone into the cave near Mecca to pray and contemplate for days at a time. Once, when he was about forty, he had a vision of a blinding light. The angel Jibril (Gabriel) appeared in the cave and commanded him to read. Muhammad told the angel that he could not read, but Jibril would not let up. He embraced Muhammad and squeezed his chest as if to press out the words. Muhammad then asked Jibril what he should read, and words poured from Muhammad's mouth. From that time forth, Jibril visited Muhammad, revealing messages from Allah. Muhammad was able to remember all the messages, and these were compiled into the Qur'an. Soon, Muhammad was recognized as the Prophet of Allah, the last of a line of prophets that extended all the way back to the time of Adam.

Three of today's major world religions (Buddhism, Christianity, and Islam) trace their origins to a specific individual who had a visionary spiritual experience in the course of his formative development. These three founders formed offshoot religions from other religions—Gautama the Buddha from Hinduism, and Jesus the Christ and Muhammad the Prophet from Judaic roots. Each religious leader took an established religious belief system and transformed it into a new religion as a consequence of his dramatic spiritual experiences. The belief systems they replaced were rigid in some ways, limiting the freedom to worship a particular God and practice certain rituals to certain castes or kin groups. Thus, there was little possibility for an outsider to become a member of a religion, and access to religious knowledge and power was restricted to certain lineages. Although their messages differed in significant ways, all three of these religious reformers opened up and universalized the teachings that were inherent to their traditions. Today, over 4 billion people follow the teachings that these three men received while they were having a profound mystical experience.

Research has shown that sensory deprivation (from meditating, sitting in the dark, and staying awake throughout the night) and fasting alters the body chemistry in ways that affect brain functioning. Under such conditions, hearing voices and seeing visions is, in fact, quite common. Thus, the visions and other experiences that Gautama, Jesus, and Muhammad had while they were in solitude and actively seeking answers and practicing the religious techniques they had learned appear to be very normal outcomes under these conditions.

Introduction: The Experience of Religion

While the variation in religious beliefs and practices around the world is staggering, they share similarities in the notion of a special realm of *experiences* of a religious and spiritual nature. We consider these *religious* experiences because they are represented in traditions, but they also represent *spiritual* experiences because they occur to individuals.

Religious experiences may occur spontaneously—unexpectedly and "out of the blue"—or as the expected outcomes of ordinary or special socialization processes. The extraordinary experiences that are the focus of this chapter present several paradoxes for our understanding of religiosity. On the one hand, these spiritual experiences are extremely personal and often solitary, and on the other hand, they often show cross-cultural similarities exemplified by the universal features of mystical experience. Another paradox presented by these experiences is that while their spiritual nature suggests that they are nonphysical, they are often induced by physical means such as trauma and drugs. Furthermore, the mystical experiences that these activities can induce are quite different from the experiences of most religious people and churchgoers today, who may never have a mystical experience.

For instance, most religious people in Western societies personally experience their religious beliefs in connection with a community of others during group rituals or in moments of solitary prayer. These rituals may provide an opportunity for the individual to reflect on his or her beliefs and hopes, and they often help the person figure out how to deal with a complicated life situation. During religious experiences, people may feel the presence of their God, or the love and support of a spiritual figure. These religious experiences are not what mystics consider to be the true nature of spiritual experiences.

More profound spiritual experiences are generally achieved through extended periods of silence, meditation, solitary contemplation, severe fasting, and other practices that produce visionary experiences, including encounters with the Gods and other beings of myths. These mystical encounters are generally experienced in a deeply personal way, such as an intimate conversation with God. Usually experienced as visions, spiritual experiences can profoundly shape a person's life and can even lead to changes of entire cultures and broad swaths of humanity. The examples of the Buddha, the Christ, and the Prophet demonstrate that a profoundly individual spiritual experience can affect people born centuries later.

What is it about human nature that produces the extraordinary experiences of the founders of many religions? During the course of human evolution, our ancestors not only acquired abilities to think about and act on the world in ways that no other animals could, but also abilities to experience the world in unusual ways. At first glance, these extraordinary religious perceptions, feelings, and understandings of the world might seem to be maladaptive, for what possible benefit could be attained from spending time in a condition in which one is unable to interact with the environment in a "reality-based" manner? Yet there exists a wide variety of cultural practices around the world for inducing religious states of consciousness. The benefits such experiences might provide that exceed their costs lie in their numerous physiological, psychological, social, cognitive, and therapeutic properties (Winkelman 2000). The universality of religious healing beliefs and practices illustrates how our ability to experience the world in religious, spiritual, or mystical ways could have benefited our ancestors and constituted an adaptation that enhanced human survival. The ability of religious experiences to change the course of lives, cultures, nations, and world society suggests that they have powerful adaptive consequences.

In this chapter, we will look at a range of religious and spiritual experiences and the different ways in which religions make use of these unusual human capacities. Societies around the world utilize a number of methods for producing religious experiences, including singing, praying, dancing, fasting, various austerities, and powerful sacred medicines. Some cultures seek profound spiritual experiences as a part of every person's life, while other cultures leave spiritual experiences to the few who dedicate their lives to religious service or the search for enlightenment.

In spite of these differences, cross-cultural studies (Winkelman 1986, 1997) suggest some basic similarities in religious experiences. These similarities in religious experiences indicate that they are rooted in our biology and may have been selected for over the course of our evolution. Some of the potential adaptive benefits of the capacity for religiosity include the enhancement of our ability to integrate information, improved synchronization of separate brain activities, better conceptualization of personal and social dynamics, improved coordination of social groups, and enhanced integration and release of emotions.

In order to understand what is special about religious experiences or states of consciousness, we will consider some of the common ideas that scientists, religious experts, and mystics share about the nature of mystical experiences. There is a perennial psychology of mysticism that involves universal beliefs about the nature of mystical experiences and realities. These cross-cultural similarities in mystical and other profound religious experiences illustrate that they are based in components of our mental hardware and represent fundamental aspects of human consciousness.

We will examine these **altered states of consciousness (ASC)** in the context of different forms and functions of consciousness in general and with regard to how the major patterns of variation in consciousness are related to our brain functions. This will provide a framework for understanding what is similar about different religious experiences and about the roles they have played in human evolution. The framework illustrates that the biological origins of religious experiences are related to a variety of natural physical procedures that induce ASC, and demonstrates that religious experiences are both personal and part of our nature as a species. Their variability comes from the influences of culture on religious experiences, which may either pathologize them or support them as potentials for personal transformation, giving one person a distressful encounter with the eternal void of darkness and another person a blissful experience of nothingness and eternity.

The biocultural perspective offers approaches to understanding both the diversity and the similarities that exist in religious experiences. First, it provides a cross-cultural approach to determining the similarities in religious experiences, as well as a basis for explaining cross-cultural differences in religious experiences as a function of cultural differences. Secondly, anthropology's biocultural approach unites the cross-cultural data with an interdisciplinary approach that links these universals of religious experiences to the biological functioning of our brain and the innate principles of the human mind.

Understanding Religion as Experiences: The Universality of Mysticism

What *is* a religious experience? What makes an experience "religious"? Is there something similar that underlies all religious experience? Or are there different forms of religious experience? One way to approach these questions is by asking people if they have ever had a "religious" experience and, if so, what it was like. Most contemporary Americans who report that they have had a religious experience describe it in terms of perceptions and sensations of contact with some kind of supernatural presence and the feeling of a personal relationship with this "divine other" (Stark 1997). The descriptions provided by these individuals indicate that they felt themselves to be in the presence of some being that had intentional, moral, and social characteristics much like their own. These findings suggest that the experiences that most Americans characterize as "religious" typically entail some sense of a "spirit other." But is a religious experience nothing more than an experience of a spirit?

In many societies, the experiences of religious practitioners are described in quite different terms. Mystical traditions, such as some schools of Buddhism, characterize religious experiences as consciousness of "void," or "nothingness." Some traditions emphasize a sense of feeling of being at one with nature and connected with the entire Universe, while others describe religious experiences as involving a sense of peace, tranquility, bliss, or ecstasy. These experiences generally do not involve a spirit or a relationship with a spirit.

These differences may lead us to conclude that the only thing that links together the diversity of experiences that are called "religious" is that the person who has the experience *considers* it a religious experience. But when we examine the wide diversity of religious experiences more closely, we find that there are many cross-cultural similarities. Often, religious experiences are described in very similar terms. Common descriptors include an experience of oneness or unity, a connection with the entire Universe; a sense of loss of self and a merging into something greater than oneself; a visionary or hallucinatory experience of profound significance about the ultimate nature of the Universe; an awareness of an all-knowing and powerful entity; and a feeling that words cannot adequately convey the experience. These commonalities underlie a longstanding tradition of understanding religion in terms of a particular class of experiences.

The idea of defining religion as a kind of experience is not new. Friedrich Schleiermacher (1768–1834), a Protestant theologian, considered the rites, rituals, and doctrines of religious traditions to be secondary to the experiences, the *feeling* of faith. Schleiermacher lived during the Romantic period in Europe, an era that was a reaction to the Enlightenment and its emphasis on the primacy of reason. Inspired by the Romantic emphasis on passion and emotion, Schleiermacher argued that the core of religious experience involves feelings of piety and an irreducible, distinct, and uniquely religious feeling of absolute dependence on God. In his eyes, our awareness of this dependence derives from our recognition of the finitude of our lives and our ultimate death. Schleiermacher was convinced that this experience of dependence on a great power was the foundation of faith. Given his Christian background, it is easy to understand why he thought this way. But not all religious experiences involve a concept of God or feelings of dependence.

Rudolf Otto (1869–1937), a German Lutheran theologian, attempted to provide a broader view of religious experience by emphasizing its **numinous** qualities, a term he used to refer to any experience of spirit and the sacred that was outside our normal rational categories of thought. For Otto, the most important feature of these numinous experiences was the sense of a *mysterium tremendum et fascinans*—something completely beyond our normal range of experiences (*mysterium*) that is awe-inspiring, overpowering, and completely separate from our selves (*tremendum*) and to which we are drawn with feelings of both curiosity and trust (*fascinans*). Otto's concept of the numinous, however, also has its limitations, for not all religious experiences involve a sense of excitement or awe. Some religious experiences involve feelings of absolute tranquility, a blissful sense of unity with a sacred other, or a peaceful connectedness with the divine Universe.

Another scholar who grappled with the nature of religious experience was the American psychologist William James (1842–1920). James also believed that the experience of religion was much more important than the institutions of religion (such as churches). He listed four principal indicators of mystical experiences:

1. They are *ineffable*. They cannot be expressed in words or communicated by any other means, but must be experienced to be known.
2. They have a *noetic* quality. They are special states of knowledge apprehended by the mind or intellect.
3. They are *transient*. They do not persist.
4. People are *passive* with respect to them. They cannot control when they occur or end.

While most scholars and religious practitioners would agree with James's first three indicators, his description of mystical states as "passive" overlooks the fact that many religious traditions have specific techniques that enable practitioners to deliberately enter these mystical states. Walter Stace (1961), a British civil servant and writer, attempted to encompass the experience of all of the mystical traditions in the concept that at the core of mystical experience, there is some apprehension of the "One" or "oneness" that transcends both our senses and our intellect. He also listed other characteristics of mystical experiences, such as the following:

- a perception of experiencing an ultimate truth
- a sense that the experience was ineffable
- a sense that the experience had a sacred quality
- profoundly positive emotions, such as joy and bliss

Stace further distinguished two different types of mystical experience: introvertive and extrovertive. During an **extrovertive mystical experience**, a person remains aware of the outside world while simultaneously perceiving the oneness and the unity of the Universe, in connection with everything. During **introvertive mystical experiences**, the person transcends all of his or her immediately present sensations of the world and their conceptual frameworks—including the sense of place, self, time, and space—and experiences a state of consciousness that is beyond the person's comprehension.

Because extrovertive mysticism still involves sensations of the outside world, Stace (1960) saw it as a step along the path to introvertive mysticism. He thus proposed a continuum in experiences that culminated in what he called "mystical consciousness." Stace viewed the introvertive mystical experience as the more important aspect of mysticism because of its impact on the history of human thought.

Philosophers and comparative religion scholars have debated extensively the idea that there are universal principles of mysticism and cross-cultural similarities in mystical experience. Some have contended that the similarities are so obvious that anyone can understand and recognize the universals of mysticism. Others have questioned how such comparisons are even possible, asking, for instance, how we can be sure that one person's view of "nothingness" is really the same as another person's view of "void," especially if they are about nothing at all anyway.

The religious sociologist Ralph Hood has helped us answer these questions by studying reports of mystical experiences from many different cultures. In doing so, he has shown the similarities and differences in mystical experiences and their universality across cultures. By demonstrating that mystical experiences in different cultures share similar features, Hood's research attests to the universalities in mystical experiences and the cross-cultural validity of the concepts. Using a questionnaire that asked people about the variety of their experiences, Hood studied mystical experiences in different cultures and developed an overall measure of mysticism (the Mysticism Scale [Hood et al., 2001]; see the Appendix) that measures three different specific aspects of mystical experience:

1. extrovertive mysticism, characterized by a sense of unity with the whole Universe. Extrovertive mysticism was measured using questions that assess people's prior experiences such as "feeling absorbed as one with all of the Universe . . . a sense that all things are alive and aware . . . a sense of a oneness of one's self and all of the Universe, a merger of the self with the Universe . . . with all of the Universe part of the same whole . . . a sense of the unity of all things."

2. introvertive mysticism, characterized by an experience of the transcendence of time and space, as well as a sense of ineffability. Introvertive mysticism involved "a sense of timelessness and spacelessness . . . an experience of a void or total absence of anything . . . an absorption into something greater than the self . . . an experience that was incapable of expression in words or language or other forms of communication."

3. noetic experience, characterized by a positive mood and a sense of sacredness.

From the biocultural perspective, the distinction between these types of religious experiences is important because it underscores several key points: (1) there are different *types* of religious experiences; (2) there are phenomenological or experiential similarities in religious experiences in different cultures; and (3) in order to understand why religious experiences occur at all, we need to step back from the interpretations or explanations that a particular tradition provides for these experiences. Instead we ought to focus on their underlying features, regardless of the means by which they are produced or the context in which they are experienced.

This leads to several interesting questions. How are people from diverse cultures able to have quite similar experiences? What do the similarities in these experiences across cultures tell us about the reality of these experiences? Are these mystical experiences simply constructions of the mind or do they offer a perception of something real, a different but legitimate understanding of the nature of the Universe?

The answers to these questions have great implications for our understanding of religion. For if fundamentally similar religious experiences do indeed occur across cultures and time, they are not completely arbitrary constructions of the mind. A believer might argue that these similarities demonstrate that the worlds they encounter in their experiences are real, thereby "proving" their religious beliefs are valid. But there are other interpretations. The many cross-cultural similarities in mystical and other religious experiences suggest that our biology is partially responsible for producing these experiences, while our culture and religion tell us how to achieve them and how to interpret them.

To address these questions of the altered experiences of consciousness involved in religious experiences, we must first address the fundamental question of "what is consciousness?" How do our ordinary consciousness and experiences of the world relate to the activity within our nervous system, and what kind of changes in this activity occur during unusual religious

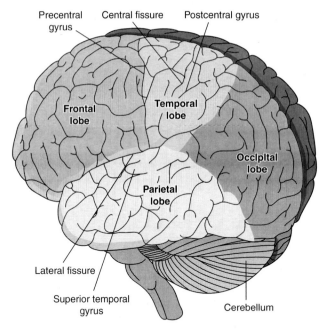

Precentral gyrus
Central fissure
Postcentral gyrus
Frontal lobe
Temporal lobe
Occipital lobe
Parietal lobe
Lateral fissure
Superior temporal gyrus
Cerebellum

Figure 3.1 This lateral view of the surface of the human brain indicates the positions of the four major lobes.

of uses of the term *consciousness* indicates that it refers to an epistemological relationship between a knower and something known—a relationship that is mediated by the physical brain and by our personal, social, and cultural filters. There are many different forms of consciousness involving many different ways of knowing the Universe.

A moment's self-reflection will remind us that the brain and the mind do not continuously and constantly interact with each other in the same manner. From instant to instant, both brain activities and the focus of our minds can change. While reading this text, you might shift your focus to the sound of a bird singing outside your window and then remember that you have not yet had lunch. At times, you may be able to stay focused on the single task of reading for hours, while at other times you may find your mind wandering off and worrying about personal problems or remembering what happened last night. Other times, your mind may seem to jump from one thought to another, and you may be unable to focus no matter how hard you try. After a heavy meal, you may not want to think of anything but taking a nap.

Consciousness is clearly a dynamic process, and yet there are specific patterns and tendencies in the interaction between our brains and our minds. This leads us to understand that religious experiences are correlated with, and at times are clearly caused by, very specific changes in the overall dynamics of the different subsystems of the brain.

The Four Basic Modes of Human Consciousness

Many mystical traditions concur with Western science in considering humans to function in four basic modes of consciousness: waking; deep sleep; dreaming (the condition of REM, or "rapid eye movement," sleep); and a fourth mode referred to here as integrative and more widely known as mystical, transcendental, and transpersonal. All of these have clear biological bases, provide functional adaptations, and constitute unique experiences.

It is safe to assume that if you are reading this text, then you are in a **waking mode of consciousness**. This waking mode is a product of strong selective pressures, for its focus on the world "out there" is what allows us to find our food, our enemies, and our mates. When we consider the enormous evolutionary benefits of being able to pay attention to our environment, it seems strange that we spend so much of our time in the sleep mode. Sleep cannot be avoided, nor should it be. For it is during this time that we restore the energy

experiences? And given that religious and mystical traditions use specific techniques to produce religious experiences, what are the effects of these techniques on the brain and consciousness? In addition, what are the different major types of religious experiences, and how are they correlated with different kinds of changes in the nervous system? Together, these questions help to identify both the biological and the cultural bases of religious experiences, as well as their similarities and differences. But to understand what is involved in a religious experience, we first need to know how they differ from ordinary experiences and everyday consciousness (see Fig. 3.1).

What Is Consciousness?

The word "conscious" is derived from the Latin word *conscius*, meaning "knowing with others, participating in knowledge, aware of" (Morris 1981, p. 283); it implies a sharing in some type of knowledge. It is related to the Latin word *scire*, meaning "to know," which is the root of our modern word "science." The presence of the prefix *con* ("with") and the suffix *ness* (which makes an adjective into a noun) suggests that consciousness is a condition in which we acquire knowledge about the Universe through sharing with others. An interdisciplinary consideration (Winkelman 1994) of the entire range we expended during our waking exertions and also process and integrate information about the things we have experienced.

During the waking mode, our brains exhibit a pattern of activity characterized by a predominance of high-amplitude and high-frequency brain waves (beta waves, 8–13 cycles per second). When we relax or fall asleep, the frequency and the amplitude of our brain waves progressively slow down until, after about one hour, we enter **deep sleep**. In this stage, our muscles and eyes relax, and our blood pressure, heart rate, and body temperature fall. Our brains function at a very low level (e.g., delta, 1–3 cycles per second), and as far as we can tell, our minds are dormant. While we are in deep sleep, information actually ceases to flow between the different parts of the brain for a time (Massimini et al. 2005).

After we have experienced a period of deep sleep, brain activity begins to increase again until it comes to resemble the activity levels of waking. Yet most of our body's muscles remain inactive, with the exception of the muscles of the eyes, which become very active. An observer can see the dreamer's eyes moving behind their closed eyelids. (This is why this phase is known as **rapid eye movement [REM] sleep**). In this **dream mode**, many of the brain's functions resemble those of the waking mode, but the brain does not normally register external events, nor do the muscles of the body respond to the brain's signals for activity. The brain is active, but the body is paralyzed, while our unconscious mind engages with an internal visual world of events and scenarios that are experienced as real—even when they involve fantastic visions and contradictions to the principles of the physical world that we experience during ordinary consciousness.

Normal sleep consists of alternating periods of the generally dreamless deep sleep mode and the REM sleep mode; a person needs to experience both modes in order to function optimally in the waking mode. The reduced brain activity of deep sleep is thought to give the neural circuits that process information and that create and sustain our personal world a chance to rest, recover, and "rewire" their connections with one another, enabling them to optimize their functioning for the next day's activity. Growth, recuperation, regeneration, and healing of the physical body occur primarily during deep sleep. The heightened activity of REM sleep is thought to be involved in forming memories of the significant experiences that occur while a person is awake, and the psychodynamic processes of dreams illustrate their adaptive roles in managing our interpersonal life and emotions.

In addition to the role of sleep in maintaining normal brain functioning, it also benefits other parts of the body. Hormonal changes occur while we are sleeping that help restore our energy levels, repair the body, and prepare us for the activities of the next day. Both the regularity with which we shift between the waking, deep sleep, and REM sleep modes and the evidence that indicates that we require all three to function optimally tell us that all three of these basic modes of brain activity represent normal conditions of human consciousness. These brain wave states are characteristic of virtually all mammals, but there is another mode of experiences that is unique to humans, one that involves theta and alpha waves (3–6 and 6–8 cycles per second, respectively). It is these brain wave frequencies of the integrative mode of consciousness (especially theta) that typify religious altered states of consciousness.

The Waking Mode as "Baseline" Consciousness

Our need to receive and process information about the external world makes the waking mode the **baseline consciousness** condition against which all other modes of consciousness should be compared. Even deep sleep and REM sleep serve at least in part to prepare us for functioning effectively while awake. The waking mode enables us to carry out the tasks necessary for our physical survival. It is also the mode of consciousness in which we are capable of interacting with the other members of our society, developing a consensus about the meanings of our shared experiences and thereby learning our culture. The baseline mode thus has a degree of primacy over all other states of consciousness. The fact that we learn about most "normal" aspects of consciousness in part from the other members of our culture implies that even our individual baseline consciousness has been shaped and affected by our culture's attitudes and values.

The experiences we have while in the baseline state are correlated with particular patterns of activity within the nervous system. As these patterns change and become less like those of the baseline, the mind experiences an alteration of consciousness. To better understand this special mode of altered consciousness, we need to first consider some basic features of our nervous system.

The Autonomic Nervous System and the Continuum of Consciousness

The major differences in our various modes of consciousness are related to the functional division of our autonomic nervous system. The **autonomic nervous system** is composed of neurons that enable the **central** nervous system (which consists of the brain and the spinal cord) to communicate with and control our internal organs (including those responsible for digestion, regulation of blood pressure, and production of hormones). The autonomic nervous system is responsible for causing the alternating periods of activity and relaxation by regulating the balance between its two principal divisions:

1. the sympathetic or ergotropic system, which provides adaptive responses to the external environment; and

2. the parasympathetic or trophotropic system, which maintains internal operation and balance of the organism.

These two divisions of the autonomic nervous system—sympathetic and parasympathetic—are central to the induction of ASC.

The Sympathetic and Parasympathetic Nervous Systems. When activated, our **sympathetic nervous system** provides us with energy for our muscles and controls alertness, arousal, strength, and vitality. The sympathetic nervous system achieves this by stimulating the adrenal medulla to release adrenalin and other hormones that prepare the body for action. These hormones channel blood to the muscles and relax the smooth muscles that ring our bronchial passages, making it possible for us to take in more oxygen. Because it is associated with activity, the sympathetic nervous system is part of the "ergotrophic" system (from the Greek term *ergon*, meaning "work"); it drives the waking mode of consciousness. Activation of the sympathetic nervous system is associated with EEG readings that feature high-frequency beta waves whose strength and duration vary widely across the neocortex, indicating that the different areas of the neocortex are working more or less independently of one another.

In contrast, activation of the **parasympathetic nervous system** causes us to relax and enter a restful state in which our body can regenerate and repair itself. It does this by shifting the flow of blood from the muscles to the stomach and intestines (facilitating digestion) and by tightening the muscles ringing the bronchial passages. The parasympathetic nervous system operates primarily through the serotonergic and cholinergic groups of neurotransmitters. The parasympathetic system is part of the "trophotropic" system (from the Greek term *trophē*, meaning "nourishment"), which regulates the vegetative nervous system, controlling tasks ranging from cellular activity through digestive functions and sleep. It is responsible for synchronization of the cortical EEG patterns, relaxation, control of somatic func-

tions, and physical repair and development, especially during undisturbed sleep. The parasympathetic trophotropic systems are associated with rest, sleep, and restoration of the body after periods of exertion. Even the simple act of closing our eyes increases the activity of our parasympathetic system and produces a slowing and increase in synchronization of the brain wave patterns across the different areas of the brain.

Thus, the sympathetic and parasympathetic branches of the peripheral nervous system complement each other to enable us to alternate between periods of activity and periods of rest. Our health and well-being depend on maintaining a proper balance between our need to be active in our physical and social environments and our need to rest and recuperate from this activity. In Chapter 6, we will consider some of the health problems that can arise when the balance between these two systems is disrupted for prolonged periods, and we will examine how religious healing methods help to restore this balance. Here, we will see how interrupting this balance and provoking the sympathetic and parasympathetic nervous systems to their extremes induces religious ASC.

In contrast to the shift to sleep that occurs during the normal cycles of the autonomic nervous system, an extreme overactivation of the sympathetic system may cause exhaustion and a rapid collapse. When this occurs, our nervous system may respond differently from normal. Instead of the normal unconsciousness of deep sleep and REM sleep that occurs during the period when the parasympathetic system is dominant, a person who has just experienced an overactive sympathetic system may have a conscious awareness of vivid experiences while he or she appears to be completely asleep. A variety of techniques induces states in which an individual appears to lose unconsciousness while actually retaining some special form of awareness of him- or herself and of the outside world. The EEGs of people in these parasympathetic dominant states exhibit slow and synchronized brain waves, particularly in the theta range, and constitute a core aspect of the biological bases of spiritual experiences.

Altered States of Consciousness as Extreme Variation in the Autonomic Nervous System

The psychologist Roland Fischer (1992) developed a model that places different altered states of consciousness along a continuum of experiences, from those dominated by the sympathetic nervous system to those dominated by the parasympathetic nervous system. In the center of this continuum is the normal (or baseline)

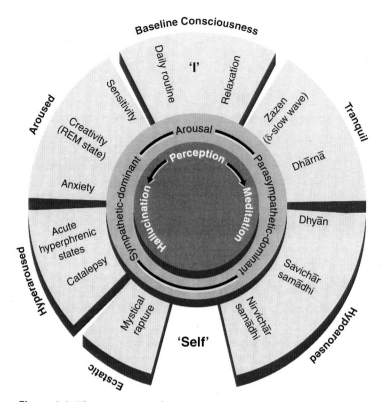

Figure 3.2 The continuum of consciousness states. Baseline consciousness is the normal waking mode in which a person is aware of the distinction between the individual (experienced as the "I") and the rest of the Universe. Both increasing sympathetic nervous system activity and increasing parasympathetic nervous system activity lead to a loss of this distinction between the individual and the Universe. When this occurs, the individual experiences a state of being ("Self") in which the distinction between the individual and the Universe is no longer perceived.

Adaptation of Figure 1, "States of Consciousness", p. 7 from "A Cartography of Cognitive and Non-Cognitive States of Consciousness" by Roland Fisher, Anthropology of Consciousness, July/December 1992/Vol. 3, Nos. 3 & 4, pp. 3–13. Copyright © 1992 by American Anthropological Association. Reprinted by permission of Wiley-Blackwell.

state, a condition in which we are able to use our cultural models to interact with the Universe (see Fig. 3.2). In this state, consciousness helps us to work at finding food, to avoid becoming food, and to speak to and interact with members of our group. These perceptions of reality are characterized by a particular constellation of sensory and motor activity.

Changing sensory and motor activity consequently affects our consciousness. Fischer suggests that this happens in one of two basic ways: either increasing or decreasing the activity of the nervous system. Increasing the activity of the sympathetic nervous system and the amount of sensory input coming into the brain can eventually exceed our ability to handle information. This situation can induce conditions ranging from rela-

tively common feelings such as anxiety, in which a person may find his or her mind racing in an effort to deal with an apparently overwhelming situation, to mystical rapture, as exemplified by the famous Sufi "whirling dervishes," who spin around for hours while listening to a "trance" music of which the tempo gradually accelerates.

On the other end of the continuum of consciousness are states produced by a reduction of nervous system activity, typified by conditions in which a person is quiet and not moving. In such a state, the sensory input coming into the brain is either reduced or extremely repetitive, and the brain "tunes out" the repetitive input because it has no informational value. For example, consider how you learn "not" to hear the sound of an air conditioner that is running all the time or the sounds of traffic on the street where you live. Because of the lack of motor activity, there are also fewer signals leaving the brain, and this, too, contributes to these states of quietude.

If you look at the two arms of the continuum in Figure 3.2 closely, you will notice that the emic names for the states on the sympathetic arm are Western (English) terms, while the names on the parasympathetic arm are taken from Eastern (Hindu and Buddhist) terms. Fischer suggests that the methods that have traditionally been used to induce ASC in the religious systems of the West have emphasized activity and emotion, whereas the techniques used in the East have stressed withdrawal from the world of activity. For this reason, he characterizes the sympathetic-dominant states as "hallucination" and the parasympathetic-dominant states as "meditation."

Fischer's model makes several points that are important for our discussion. He emphasizes that (1) different cultural traditions use very different methods to induce altered states of consciousness; (2) these methods are consequently defined by a specific tradition, and both the procedures for inducing a particular method and the models that are used to interpret what the experiences mean are learned within that tradition; and (3) as a person moves further along the ergotropic or the trophotropic continuum, the person becomes increasingly removed from baseline consciousness and therewith from the possibility of verifying whether his or her internal thoughts and experiences are reflecting actual events in the external world. When the alteration of consciousness is powerful enough, it produces a condition in which the "I" is no longer experienced. This religious consciousness is reflected in the liminal state encountered in rites of passage during which an individual exists in a state of consciousness between the various types of status that make up his or her social and personal identity. When this occurs, a powerful ASC may be experienced as the individual feels detached from any kind of cultural status, from any sense of personal history, and even from the feeling of being an individual. In this state, a person experiences a different higher aspect of identity: the "Self."

For Fischer, the "I" identity experienced in the baseline state involves awareness that the individual is distinct from the rest of the Universe. It is this sense of separateness that allows us to see ourselves as something different from the things we can eat and the things that can eat us. In humans, this is also the state in which we learn our culture, understand our statuses, and acquire our memories. As we move away from this state, we become progressively less aware of our "I"-ness—our sense of being distinct from everything and everyone else—and more aware of simply being. This experience of "Self" is the most subjective nonconsensual experience that a person can have. In contrast, the "I" is the closest we can come to objectivity. As Fischer (1971) characterized the two, "the 'Self' of exalted states is that which sees and knows, while the 'I' is the interpretation, that which is seen and known in the physical space time of the world 'out there'" (p. 902). Alterations of this experience of the self can be produced by provoking the autonomic nervous system to either extreme, providing a variety of natural methods for ritual induction of the integrative mode of consciousness.

The distinction between the ergotropic (sympathetic) and the trophotropic (parasympathetic) states recalls the words of Walter Stace cited earlier, in which he suggested that "introvertive mysticism"—the state in which an individual completely transcends all sensations and concepts—represented the culmination of the historically most important type of mystical experience. As we will see, the experiences associated with these states of personal transcendence have profoundly shaped the development of religious thought.

The Biological Bases of Spiritual Consciousness: The Integrative Mode of Consciousness

The alterations of consciousness induced through such diverse means as fasting, pain induction, sleep deprivation and ritualized sleep, drumming, chanting, singing, dancing, stimulants, hallucinogens, alcohol, sensory stimulation and deprivation, exposure to extremes of heat and cold, and exhausting exercise all produce similar effects in the brain: synchronized slow brain wave patterns. These are typified in theta waves (3–6 cycles per second) that originate in the serotonergic circuitry linking the lower regions of the brain (Mandell 1980). These theta-wave patterns ascend in integrated brain-wave discharges that synchronize the frontal cortex with slow-wave patterns (see Winkelman 1986, 1992, 2000 for studies). The common physiological effects of many rituals involve activation of the sympathetic nervous system to the point of exhaustion, causing collapse, and a rebound in the parasympathetic nervous system. Other techniques for inducing altered states of consciousness (meditation, relaxation) lead directly to a parasympathetic dominant condition with relaxed skeletal muscles and synchronized cortical rhythms.

Central to most ASC is the activation of the brain areas that regulate emotions, control the balance between the sympathetic and parasympathetic divisions of the autonomic nervous system, and integrate current information with our memories. Mandell (1980) suggests that the specific physiological mechanisms underlying the regularities in "transcendent states" involve a temporal lobe limbic circuitry based in serotonergic pathways. These pathways extend upwards from the basal areas of the brain in the hippocampal–septal–reticular–raphe circuit that produces powerful coherent theta waves that synchronize the hemispheres of the frontal cortex.

That this response is basic to our human nature is illustrated by our ability to induce and access this integrative mode of consciousness with a variety of agents and procedures, including chemicals that a person might ingest, as well as activities such as long-distance running that stimulate the production of their analogs in our own bodies (neurotransmitters and hormones). Many agents and conditions (such as thirst, hunger, and lack of sleep) have similar effects on serotonergic mechanisms in disinhibiting temporal lobe structures and producing synchronous discharges that release ecstatic affectual and cognitive processes. The loss of inhibitory regulation by serotonin results in a reduction in the "gating" or control of emotional responses. This reduction in control results in the emotional flooding experienced as ecstasy and experiences dominated by visions from the "inner world." The many different agents and activities that can all produce this pattern indicate that it is a fundamental aspect of human neurology and consciousness.

Cognitive neuroscientist Arne Dietrich (2003) proposes that a wide variety of ASC shares characteristics caused by a temporary deregulation of the higher order information and cognitive functions associated with the prefrontal cortex and the frontal lobes. This allows the emergence of the lower brain functions and their effects in producing an integration of consciousness. Mandell's model of ASC indicates that it is the blocking of normal serotonin effects on the temporal lobes—an inhibitory effect—that results in the increased temporal lobe activity and the resultant experiences. The disinhibition of the temporal lobes releases their emotional processes and the associated experiences. The effects of activation of the hippocampal–septal system illustrates why this is an *integrative* mode of consciousness. The hippocampal–septal circuits form part of an extensive system of innervation connecting areas of the brain—somatic and autonomic nervous systems—and linking the frontal cortex with the lower brain. The limbic system (the paleomam-

malian brain) is the part of the brain where emotions are integrated with memories (see Fig. 3.3). The limbic cortex receives all of the brain's internal (interoceptive) and external (exteroceptive) information, with the hippocampus, amygdala, and related structures serving as the point of information convergence en route to the frontal cortex. The hippocampal–septal system functions as an association area and is central to learning, memory, recall, memory processing, orienting, and attention (MacLean 1990; Mandell 1980).

Religious experiences have been characterized in terms of understanding, enlightenment, integration, awareness, and connectedness. These experiences reflect the psychophysiological dynamics of the integrative mode of consciousness. Religious experiences are integrative, enlightening, and meaningful because they stimulate the centers of the brain where information integration and a sense of certainty about the truth of what we know are produced.

Religious States in the Integrative Mode of Consciousness

The ubiquity of religious experiences such as possession and soul flight in cultures around the world suggests that these different experiences reflect stable adaptations to the potentials of the integrative mode of consciousness and that they are in some fundamental sense rooted in the nervous system of our species.

Although these experiences reflect something fundamental about our human nature, cultures differ considerably in how they view and relate to these manifestations of human consciousness; some cultures provoke them, while others repress or ignore them. In the West, profound religious experiences have often been defined as either delusional (hence, pathological) or demonic (hence, evil). These experiences are vilified, repressed, and, if possible, eliminated by medication, therapy, or exorcism. The mystical traditions of the West have often been forced underground, and the knowledge of their practices has been restricted. The Sufis of Islam and many of the great mystics of medieval Christianity—such as Hildegard of Bingen and St. John of the Cross—lived relatively solitary lives apart from most believers. It is ironic that the Western tradition would repress such spiritual experiences, for the founders of many Western religious traditions—such as Jesus, Muhammad, and Joseph Smith—had profound religious experiences involving visions, voices, and contact with the spirit world. Yet their modern-day followers often experience their faith solely through praying, singing, or attending religious services, and few expect,

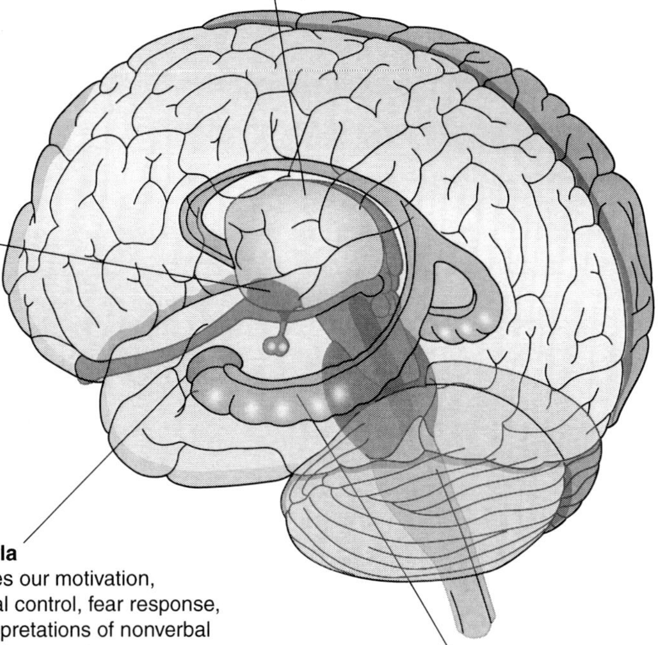

Thalamus
Part of the forebrain that relays information from sensory organs to the cerebral cortex

Hypothalamus
Part of the forebrain that regulates the amount of fear, thirst, sexual drive, and aggression we feel

Amygdala
Influences our motivation, emotional control, fear response, and interpretations of nonverbal emotional expressions

Hippocampus
Plays a role in our emotions, ability to remember, and ability to compare sensory information to expectations

Figure 3.3 The limbic system is that part of the brain that regulates our emotions.

pursue, or even desire visionary revelations like those experienced by the founders of their religion.

Within the integrative mode of consciousness, the means by which ASC is induced is quite varied and includes piercing the body with objects; walking over hot coals; holding particular body postures; ingesting various plant, animal, fungi, and mineral substances; and remaining in quiet, long-term solitude. Consequently, the states produced by these techniques are quite varied. Terms such as *shamanic journey, possession, vision quest, mystical union*, and many others have been used to label these different experiences. These terms refer to distinctly different forms of religious experience, each with its own set of unique physiological and phenomenological affects.

Cross-cultural studies of the altered states of consciousness (Winkelman 1986, 1992, 1997; see Winkelman and White [1985] for data)—reported among more than 100 religious practitioners around the world—identified three major types of altered states of consciousness: the *shamanic, meditative*, and *possession* states (Winkelman 1986, 1992, 2000). These three types differ primarily in terms of how each type is induced. The shamanic states exhibit both ergotropic excitation and trophotropic responses, meditative states exemplify trophotropic relaxation, and possession states are characterized primarily by ergotropic excitation.

The Shamanic State. The **shamanic state** is typically produced by intense motor behavior (such as dancing, chanting, and drumming), causing a state of exhaustion leading to sleep and what appears to be unconsciousness. A persistent awareness remains however; a primary experiential feature of this state is a soul flight or out-of-body experience, during which the shaman perceives his or her soul leaving the body and traveling to other worlds. This experience of the spirit or soul separating from the body and traveling to the spirit world is not associated with shamanism alone, but may also be reported by mystics, induced by near-death experiences, or sought by modern psychics.

These kinds of experiences are culturally interpreted as "soul journey" in shamanic practices. During these experiences, the shaman may relate the experiences as they occur by whispering to an assistant or by telling about it afterwards. The shaman's ability to recall the details of the soul journey is one of the distinguishing features of this state. Also common to shamanic soul flight experiences is the sense of being transformed into an animal. In this form, the shaman is able to enter into a nonordinary experiential world and interact with spirit entities. A wide range of emotions—from terror to bliss—are associated with shamanic experiences.

Shamans utilize a variety of practices to induce these experiences. The use of drumming and other percussive sounds, singing, and chanting are universal features of shamanistic healing practices. This repeated rhythmic stimulation produces a phenomenon known as **auditory driving**, which can induce brain wave patterns characterized by both alpha and theta waves; visual sensations of color, pattern, and movement; and hallucinations, seizures, and general emotional and abstract experiences. Another universal type of shamanic behavior—dancing and other movements—can lead to hyperventilation, oxygen depletion, and a drop in blood-sugar levels. These effects together induce slow brain-wave activity (theta and alpha), hallucinatory experiences, and a parasympathetic dominant state. When these intense movements continue for a prolonged period of time, the shaman's body also begins to release endogenous opiates. These natural neurotransmitters mitigate the perception of pain and induce a feeling of "letting go," creating a profound sense of calm similar to that achieved in deep meditative states (Hunt 1995). Vision quests, for example, include procedures such as fasting and water deprivation, exposure to temperature extremes, and austerities like sleep deprivation, prolonged exposure to monotonous auditory stimuli (including drumming and chanting), and dancing. In some cultures, shamans may also ingest psychoactive substances. Many South American shamans use particularly potent forms of tobacco—which they may smoke, eat, or drink—to enter a shamanic state. The amounts they ingest would kill a normal person, and part of the shaman's training involves learning to tolerate these dosages.

The likely role of the brain in the shamans' out-of-body experiences is suggested by a research paper published in *The New England Journal of Medicine*. De Ridder and colleagues (2007) discovered that sensations like out-of-body experiences can be produced by activity in specific brain regions. These experiences result from interference with the integration of sensory information, caused experimentally by electrical stimulation of areas in the temporoparietal junction. The researchers noted that abnormal brain activity occurs in two brain areas during these experiences. One area was around the juncture of the angular and supramarginal gyri, which are responsible for the integration of sensory stimuli to provide an orientation for the body. The other area of unusual activity was in the right superior temporal cortex, which plays a key role in mapping self-perception. These two brain areas do not normally function together, and their joint activation is apparently responsible for these experiences. We do not know, however, if this is what produces shamanic soul flight, nor how shamanic ASC induction activities might stimulate these areas. Soul flight involves much more than the sense of a displacement of the body. The studies do show, however, that such experiences can be produced by special operations of our brains.

The Meditative State. The history of meditative (or mystical) traditions spans thousands of years and cultures around the world. Although most people associate meditation with the religious traditions of Asia (e.g., Hinduism, Buddhism, Taoism), the Jewish, Christian, and Islamic traditions also have meditative or contemplative traditions (Walsh 1983; West 1987).

Today, many meditation practices are also utilized in the course of secular activities (West 1987). The **meditative state** can be induced through mental focus, chanting, fasting, and such austerities as sleep or sensory deprivation. Although the term **meditation** is applied to a wide variety of practices, certain features are common to most of them. Compared with the shamanic state, the meditative state is characterized by greater self-control and concentration, lower arousal, a sense of calm and emotional detachment, a loss of the sense of self, greater awareness, and experiences devoid of content (Walsh 1990). Meditative states are also characterized by the presence of emotional control and equanimity, as well as ecstatic bliss.

Meditative states exhibit many characteristics that have also been observed in conjunction with other types of altered states, such as theta and alpha wave coherence, parasympathetic dominance, and an internal focus of attention. Research on hemispheric and EEG activation in meditators (see Winkelman [1997] for a review of such research) illustrates that certain physiological parameters correlate with particular descriptions that meditators provide of their experiences, especially control, focus, coordination, integration, and insight. Other qualities commonly attributed to meditation include insights into the constructed nature of perception and into the nature of consciousness and reality, as well as the development of increased control over attention, a new sense of self and identity, and more profound concentration in contemplative states.

Meditative traditions aim at effecting dramatic changes in the meditator's sense of identity. The meditative focus on internal experiences and self-evaluation often leads the meditator to the realization that there is no fixed and permanent self. Accordingly, the meditative disciplines emphasize that many of our beliefs about the nature of our selves are derived from the "mindless"—that is, unconscious and automatic—information processing that is characteristic of most of our waking baseline consciousness, behavior, and thought. Meditation helps a person "unlearn" the conditioning that causes automatic identification with the content of consciousness. By disrupting the conditioning that causes us to identify with our thoughts and behaviors, meditation practices can provide a person with an expanded understanding of who he or she is. Thus, meditation is often viewed as a technique for revealing the illusory nature of our usual sense of self and consciousness.

As meditators advance in their practice, they often begin to have experiences of pure awareness or of being a detached observer. The members of one group of Hindu meditators (yogis) studied by Castillo (1991), for example, were trained to recognize the distinction between two co-conscious selves: one that participates in the world and another that observes the world without becoming involved in it. Castillo referred to the active participator as the "personal self" and the observer as the "transpersonal self." For these yogis, the initial goal of meditation is to learn how to separate the two aspects of self and consciousness. They learn to focus so narrowly that they eliminate all other aspects of consciousness, conquering their tendency to be distracted by sensory input and developing their attention to the point where all that they experience is attention itself. A later goal is to develop a permanent state of meditation attention that exists alongside the more habitual focus on everyday activities. This enables practitioners to experience both aspects of consciousness simultaneously: the participating and observing selves. The ultimate goal of this meditation tradition is

to attain *moksha*, or liberation, which occurs when the observing or true self (called the *atman*) separates from the participating or false self (*jiva*). A person who achieves the transpersonal self—which witnesses events but does not participate in them—is freed from the pain and suffering that come from the identification with the personal self.

A variety of physiological changes are associated with meditative states, although their specific parameters may differ, reflecting the specific intents of the meditators. Some forms of meditation have been shown to increase dopamine levels in the brain, while others have been associated with increased levels of serotonin (Kjaer et al. 2002; Meyer and Quenzer 2005; Walton and Levitsky 1994). These neurotransmitters have specific effects within the temporal lobes, enhancing emotional processes and input into the frontal cortex.

The Possession State. Cross-culturally, the **possession state** is typically characterized by amnesia, convulsions, and spontaneous seizures. As the name indicates, these experiences are often interpreted as a spirit taking possession of a person's body. The term *possession* has been used to refer to a wide variety of phenomena—trance, dissociation, hysteria, spirit domination, displacement of personality, obsession, mental illness, and other states of consciousness and conditions. Neurologically, possession states are associated with excessive activity in the temporal lobe of the brain. Socially, they are most commonly found in societies in which local communities are integrated into higher level political systems. Here, the stress and deprivation associated with oppressive political conditions may help to trigger possession states. Because possession encompasses a wide range of phenomena—including pathological, communicative, and normative behaviors for transformation of self and others (see Winkelman 2008)—a wide range of emotions may be expressed in possession states.

When possessed, an individual typically exhibits such a dramatic transformation—changes in personality, behavior, voice, expressions, movements, and identity are common—that he or she seems to have become another person. Although the phenomenon of spirit possession in different cultures appears very similar, closer examination reveals that there is actually substantial variation. Consequently, it is problematic to regard possession as a unitary phenomenon. Some cultural traditions recognize this fact; Brazilian spiritists, for example, distinguish among several different forms or degrees of possession (Krippner 1987). A person may be possessed by the influences of a spirit while retaining a basic sense of self and identity. Other times,

Box 3.1 ARE SPIRITUAL EXPERIENCES FORMS OF PSYCHOPATHOLOGY?

The concept of "divine madness" has long been associated with illness and religiosity. Many cultures have interpreted religious experiences as forms of psychopathology. Joan of Arc heard voices; whether they came from God or from the devil depended on whether you were her French countryman or her English enemy. Are religious experiences just psychiatric disturbances? Many cultures around the world see a relationship between the spirits and illness, and believe that some health conditions may be resolved only by answering the call of the spiritual path. Possession reflects an illness that is resolved in many cultures by becoming an initiate medium and developing one's ability to communicate with the spirits. Whether episodes of possession are religious experiences that enhance health or signs of disturbing psychopathologies may depend on how the individual and the culture respond to them.

Although many early Westerners viewed the shamans they encountered as crazy, there is abundant evidence demonstrating that shamans are not pathological from their own culture's point of view, nor from the perspective of descriptive clinical diagnostic criteria (Noll 1983; Walsh 1990; Winkelman 2000). While religious practitioners may manifest behaviors similar to symptoms of psychological or nervous system disorders, the conditions may not be pathological. Shamanistic practitioners enter and leave ASC at will, have control over their extraordinary experiences, and are functional in their societies. These features distinguish religious experiences from psychotic episodes, which are characterized by lack of control, are terrifying, and are overwhelming.

more powerful influences appear to be at play, causing a split in the psyche, a dissociation experienced as the reemergence of past-life personalities, or the development of a hysterical personality syndrome with a negative alter personality. Sometimes possession takes complete control of the individual; spiritual healers and mediums, for example, experience possession by spirits who temporarily inhabit their bodies and direct their behavior.

An especially significant link exists between possession and political integration beyond the level of the local community; that is, a political hierarchy in which a distant government exercises sovereignty over local communities (Winkelman 1986, 1992). In these societies, the religious leaders who experience possession are known as *mediums*. A medium receives a "call" spontaneously as a type of seizure thought to be outside his or her control or intentions. The medium's convulsions are taken as evidence that something else has taken control of the body. Because the medium is unable to control what happens—and cannot afterward recall what transpired while he or she was possessed—it is believed that the medium's actions are guided by the spirit world.

The predominance of women in possession cults often occurs in societies in which cultural rules restrict women from adequate nutrition. Possession episodes may be exacerbated by general nutritional deficiencies (especially calcium and protein) that contribute to changes in the central nervous system, resulting in emotional disturbances, changes in cognitive and emotional

functioning, and in some cases, the production of seizure symptoms interpreted as possession. Thus, social conditions of inequality that create dietary deficiencies among women may be partially responsible for their physiological conditions which produce dissociation and predispose them to seizures that are interpreted as possession. Malnutrition may also cause physiological effects which predispose them to have a religious personality (see Box 3.1: Are Spiritual Experiences Forms of Psychopathology?).

Is Possession Pathological?

In cultures around the world, the concept of possession generally invokes the idea of an illness caused by a relationship with a spirit. Possession is generally conceptualized as a condition in which an individual's body and mind are taken over (possessed) by a spirit. Possession conditions suggest psychological disorders because the person may have glazed eyes or appear oblivious to the immediate context. The person often has disturbed behavior, disoriented actions, and unusual facial expressions, emotions, and voice quality. These conditions and other symptoms, such as anxiety, sleep disturbances, depression, and panic attacks, led psychiatrists to characterize possession as a form of **dissociative disorder**, where a split-off part of the personality temporarily controls the person (Castillo 1997). There is not, however, a simple congruence between the possession experiences of professional mediums and the diagnostic criteria of dissociative disorders (Castillo 1995).

Possession has symptoms associated with dissociative disorders (for example, memory loss), but the memory loss is only for the possession episode, not a general amnesia or inability to recall personal information. Dissociative fugue states, in which a person acquires a new identity with no awareness of any past identity, are also distinct from possession cases, because the religious specialist returns to his or her normal personal identity following the possession episode.

Another diagnosis associated with possession is multiple personality disorder (MPD) or, as it is known currently, dissociative identity disorder (DID), in which separate personalities have developed that are dissociated from the ego. A person with DID/MPD has two or more distinct personalities or identities that exercise different periods of control over the person's experiences and behavior. In this dissociative reaction, major aspects of the psyche, emotions, and behaviors acquire autonomy from the ego and control the individual's intentions and behavior. When the alternate personality is dominant, the ego goes unconscious. When the normal ego is in control, it is generally unaware of its secondary identities, but secondary identities may be aware of one another and of the primary identity. Behavioral similarities between possession and MPD indicate that they are two different manifestations of the same human capacity.

Cultural differences in interpretation of the experiences produce cross-cultural differences in the experiences of people who suffer from these dissociative reactions. In cultures where possession is accepted, dissociation can provide relief from distress. In modern cultures where such spirit possession is not normative, the dissociative experiences can increase distress. Western cultures produce greater difficulties for the patient by pathologizing the occurrences, which compounds the negative experiences and limits therapeutic success, in contrast to those cultures where the possession is accepted.

Whether a possession episode should even be subjected to psychiatric classification depends on the cultural interpretation. Religious experiences may or may not produce psychopathology, depending on how they are managed by culture and how other members of the social group respond. If the experiences are understood to provide an important communication with the divine, the person may receive many social benefits from the association with divinity. If the culture considers them to be evidence that the devil is inside the person, he or she may be killed for having the experiences.

Spirituality and DSM-IV "Spiritual Emergencies"

The Diagnostic and Statistical Manual of Mental Disorders (DSM-IV) of the American Psychiatric Association includes the categories of "spiritual emergence" and "spiritual emergencies." These categories apply to experiences that are natural and that may be either inspiring or pathological, depending on the cultural response. The contemporary manifestations of these ancient biological capacities are reflected in the enumerations of the DSM-IV category "spiritual emergencies," which includes

- mystical experiences;
- spirit communications;
- psychic energies;
- extrasensory perceptions (e.g., clairvoyance, telepathy);
- spontaneous shamanic journeys or out-of-body experiences;
- past-life memories;
- possession, a domination by spirits expressed in archetypal patterns;
- the death and rebirth experience; and
- "psychic opening," an experience of psychic abilities.

Addressing religious and spiritual experience in psychiatric care is important because people who have overwhelming spiritual experiences risk being treated as mentally ill and hospitalized or medicated. The response of others to the episodes may either contribute to distress and pathologization or provide models and support for integrative growth experiences. Religious institutions have been much more successful than organized medicine in addressing these maladies because religion provides frameworks for addressing such experiences as natural manifestations of consciousness and as developmental opportunities rather than pathologies. This reformulation permits people to address these powerful unconscious forces as opportunities for transformation to greater health and for transformational development. By presenting information to consciousness, the experiences serve an adaptive purpose. The symptoms of personality disorders, emotional disturbances, hallucinations, traumatic experiences, and communication with spirits can be interpreted as processes of the unconscious and symbolic communications that provide direction for personal growth. With the correct approaches, these experiences can be normalized as growth experiences because they provide the opportunity for new dynamics of psychological integration.

Temporal Lobe Syndromes: A Religious Personality?

Another reason for the association of pathology with spiritual experiences is the worldwide use of these spiritual beliefs in interpretations of epilepsy, dissociative disorders, and various personality syndromes associated with hyperactivity in the temporal lobe regions. The temporal lobes are directly adjacent to regions of the limbic brain that are central to induction of ASC.

The presumption of pathology in possession states is often derived from the superficial similarities that these states share with epilepsy and dissociative disorders. The physical control of the body by something other than the person's own intentions, as is exemplified in epileptic seizures, clearly contributes to the spirit possession belief that the person is being controlled by something else. The convulsions, twitching, and compulsive behaviors of epilepsy are due to electrical discharge patterns produced in any of the lobes of the cortex, but most frequently the temporal lobe. Epileptic electrical discharges are manifested as a slow wave pattern in EEGs, including theta waves. Epilepsy is not a disease, but a manifestation of a synchronized brain discharge deriving from a specific region. Like religious ASC, epilepsy involves synchronized brain discharges from a specific brain region that dominates the entire cortex, but it differs in that the discharges of ASC are coordinated along the neuraxis, the main nerve bundle running through the center of the brain.

The physiological basis for the similarities between religious ASC and pathophysiological symptomology is explained by Mandell's (1980) model of transcendent states. The central nervous system disinhibitions that occur in epilepsy, other temporal lobe discharges, and brain responses to trauma, malnutrition, and toxicity all involve the same basic pattern of brain changes outlined above for the integrative mode of consciousness—hyperactivation of the limbic brain's serotonergic circuitry that stimulates theta wave production and synchronization in the brain.

A "temporal lobe" personality syndrome has been long recognized in psychiatry. The unusual activity in the temporal lobes and underlying limbic brain structures are associated with a range of personality characteristics that reinforce religiosity and spirituality, such as increased emotionality, with enhanced tendency to feel euphoria, ecstasy, anger, and aggression; obsessive tendencies and a tendency to heightened moral judgment; and a sense of personal religious destiny. Persinger (2003) has carried out a range of studies that indicate the stimulation of the temporal lobes and underlying limbic structures (hippocampal and amygdaloid) can produce intense emotional experiences. Another link of psychopathology with religious experiences and practices involving the temporal lobe is the ictal personality syndrome. This syndrome is characterized by emotional deepening, preoccupation with philosophical and religious interests, hyposexuality, hypergraphia (automatic writing), and an increased need for social affiliation (Waxman and Geschwind 1974). The ictal personality syndrome changes the personality and deepens affective response in a way that may be experienced as fear, panic, and terror or as feelings of religious ecstasy. Persinger characterizes the temporal lobe transient states as intrinsically pleasurable and rewarding, resulting in reduction of anxiety.

Origins of Religious Experiences: Natural Induction of the Integrative Mode of Consciousness

Because our mode of consciousness is correlated with the interplay between the sympathetic and parasympathetic nervous systems, techniques for altering consciousness affect this interaction. There are five basic techniques (Ludwig 1966):

1. increase sensory stimulation, motor activity, and/or emotion (dancing, drumming, chanting, temperature extremes of hot or cold, panic, mob activity)

2. reduce sensory stimulation, motor activity, and/or emotion (withdrawal into a dark room, physical immobility, mantra meditation)

3. increase alertness or mental involvement (mental absorption in a task, praying, meditation focused on an object)

4. decrease alertness or relax critical faculties (daydreaming, free association, meditation with no object of focus)

5. directly change the body's chemistry or neurological functioning (fasting, dehydration, hyperventilation, psychoactive drugs)

However, in spite of the divergent methods used, the consequences for the brain are remarkably similar. This is because the production of spiritual experiences is a natural response to a variety of natural conditions. Altered states of consciousness are, by necessity, part of human nature. The innate source of these experiences is illustrated in their universality, in the worldwide distribution of many similar features, and in the manifestation of their characteristics in response to diverse circumstances. We will examine the specific characteristics of near-death experiences; starvation, trauma, and injuries; dreams, particularly lucid dreams; hypnotic susceptibility; and the effects of natural substances such as the psychedelic *Psilocybe* mushrooms.

Trauma and Near-Death Experiences

Features of the natural transformations of consciousness are illustrated in the widely studied near-death or clinical death experiences (Greyson 2000; Moody 1975; Ring 1981, 1986). In these cases, a person is clinically dead, but he or she is eventually resuscitated and returns to life with an incredible story. Near-death experiences (NDEs) generally involve a number of common features, including

- a sense of the soul separating from the body and moving upward;
- an observation of the person's physical body in a different location than his or her point of view;
- movement toward a hole, tunnel, and, eventually, another world; and
- encountering a bright light, spiritual beings, and perhaps God and deceased relatives.

NDEs are generally experienced as profoundly positive emotions, a joyous entry into the afterlife. The person is, however, told to return to the physical world, where he or she then reenters the body and returns to life. Alive again, the person remains convinced of the reality of the death experience, of the eternal immortality of the soul, and of his or her eventual return to the afterlife.

In addition to these features, there are a variety of common mystical themes that may occur in NDEs, including

- ineffability, a sense of an inability to explain the experience in words;
- feelings of peace, tranquility, calm, and joy;
- a panoramic review of one's life and other dramatic visual images and memories;
- an experience of being all-knowing or experiencing the realm of universal knowledge;
- a sense of hyperalertness or awareness;

- a deep depersonalization, including a sense of complete separation from the body, accompanied by detachment and lack of emotion;
- a sense of cosmic unity;
- transcendence of the physical world and an engagement with supernatural realities; and
- an experience of a void, or nothingness, a realm of total nonexistence.

In the modern world, these near-death experiences typically have a profound and beneficial psychological impact on the person, transforming his or her personality to one with an increased concern with spirituality. They often manifest dramatic increases in selfless behaviors, focusing on the importance of personal relationships, helping others, and experiencing a profound engagement with spirituality and the afterlife. The person almost awaits death, but engages vigorously with life in overcoming challenges and exhibiting a spiritual purpose in his or her compassionate behavior toward others (Greyson 2000).

NDEs are not merely a product of the ability of modern medicine to bring people back from the brink of death. The NDE was a well-described clinical phenomenon in the nineteenth century provided by people who had recovered from drowning, accidents, war wounds, and other traumas. NDEs are also reported by a large percentage of contemporary people who nearly die, including about half of all children who survive a potentially fatal illness (Greyson 2000). While severe health problems may provoke these experiences, a fear of death rather than actual physical threat or debilitation may also cause them; NDEs have been reported by individuals who do not have any trauma or organic brain malfunctions (Greyson 2000).

Mystical experiences may also be induced by deliberate wounding of the body. Kroll and Backrach (2005) note that self-wounding, a frequent activity in heroic asceticism, can be understood in the broader context of its effects in eliciting healing and care responses from others. Ritual activities that induce the release of endogenous opiates—including self-mutilation and emotionally painful experiences—can be intrinsically rewarding. They not only reduce the firing of pain networks, leading to a reduction in pain, but they also directly stimulate areas of the brain involved with reward functions and pleasure. Although the reward pathways are separate from the pain pathways, they utilize the same opiate peptides as neurotransmitters, enabling stimulation in one area (pain) to produce rewards in another (pleasure and bonding).

NDEs are a natural part of our biology, a response of the organism to threats to its well-being. This same pattern of experience appears in other natural sources of mystical ASC—those associated with fasting, self-mortification, drug-induced ASC, and induced sleeplessness. The NDE provides an important point of reference for understanding a variety of features of mystical experiences.

Fasting as a Natural Inducer of Altered States of Consciousness

The mystical traditions are well known for inducing altered states of consciousness through the reduction of nutrition (fasting), self-mortification (intentionally inducing pain and wounding), and prolonged sleeplessness through the use of pain and prayers. These three mystical activities—fasting, pain, and sleep deprivation—are also natural consequences of food scarcity, physical trauma, and the need for prolonged vigilance in the interest of survival. They also have physiological effects with direct consequences for the induction of ASC. Fasting and nutritional restrictions increase slow wave brain discharges through indirect effects on the hypothalamus and hippocampal–septal system. These physiological effects are independent of cultural expectations, as illustrated in the worldwide use of such activities for inducing a spiritual consciousness. Activities ritually used to induce ASC, such as fasting, pain, and sleep deprivation, all occur as natural consequences of human adaptation.

Anthropologist Daniel Fessler (2002) reviews a variety of studies that illustrate the effects of semi-starvation in producing ASC, neurosis, hysteria, dissociation, and hypochondria (a paranoid belief that one is ill). Other associated features of extreme food reduction include auditory hallucinations, paranoia, and megalomania. Fessler suggests that evolutionary perspectives can help us understand the occasional human propensity toward voluntary restriction of diet. He proposes that severe dietary restriction results in an adaptive reduction of serotonin activity in order to promote increased risk-taking that could improve current circumstances and future survival. Reduced serotonin levels, which are associated with anorexia nervosa, obsessive–compulsive disorder, and self-mutilation, result in enhanced impulsivity. It is well established that food deprivation produces depersonalization experiences, dissociation, and sleep disruption due to reduced levels of melatonin precursors and serotonin and to

effects on serotonin synthesis (Fessler 2002). These disruptions can produce the visionary experiences associated with mystical and shamanistic ASC.

The Roles of Dreams in Religious Experiences

The role of sleep deprivation in inducing ASC is well known; a direct consequence of both short-term and long-term sleep deprivation is the spontaneous induction of REM or dream sleep, which is normally experienced in a more dramatic visionary manner than ordinary dreams. Why are dreams viewed as a fundamental aspect of religious reality in cultures around the world? What relationship do dreams have to religious experiences and the origins of religion? Dreams have been the context for the appearance of visions, encounters with spiritual messengers, and many other experiences of a spiritual reality. Humans' efforts to interpret dreams may not necessarily have led to the development of religion, but the widespread association of dreams with the supernatural points to their intrinsic linkages. Dreams are necessarily linked to supernatural concepts because they give us experiences of immaterial entities with active agency, "others" without substance but with profound impacts on our emotional reality. Dream processes represent unconscious structures and functions of our personalities and selves, relatively autonomous systems that can impose themselves on consciousness and behavior even while we are awake. We can slip into daydreaming while driving or trying to work, and if we go too long without sleeping, we will have spontaneous "waking dreams."

In addition to ordinary dreams that color our nightly experiences and occasionally slip into our waking reality, there are deliberately induced dreams that are provoked by rituals. Cultures around the world have institutionalized practices for inducing dream experiences to provide access to spiritual experiences. These practices of "dream incubation" induce ASC by linking the potentials of the dreaming to the waking mode of consciousness. The overnight activities of shamanic ritual necessarily engage the automatic cycles of dream processes, a deliberate intent of shamanism reflected in concepts of "dream time." Dream incubation uses ritual practices and meditative techniques to blend waking and dreaming processes, engaging the ability to maintain self-consciousness during dream experiences. The ritual elicitation of these natural visual and symbolic processes of dreams provides a basis for many religious experiences.

The Psychobiology of Dreaming. The mode of consciousness called dreaming involves high levels of activation of the physiological and visual systems combined with a decoupling of the brain from the body, producing a paralyzed hallucinatory state in which one's brain acts without producing movement in the body. Dreams are a biological process for managing emotional life and memory formation, an adaptation for learning during sleep by producing associations "off-line," using the frontal cortex as a working space for memory consolidation (Winson 1985, 1990). The universality of dreaming in mammals indicates that it constituted a preadaptation for uniquely human forms of consciousness (Brereton 2000).

Dream information processing and consolidation use innate cognitive systems involving visual or presentational symbolism (Hunt 1995). Dreams are primarily visual, as opposed to verbal, reflecting a process of preverbal representation and unconscious representations of the various structures of the brain, mind, and personal and social consciousness. Dream memories involve the closest engagement of the structures of ordinary ego awareness with the structures of the unconsciousness (Laughlin et al. 1992), reflecting an "unconscious personality." The preegoic level of self is reflected in the typical lack of self-consciousness of ourselves and the reality that we are dreaming (a lack of awareness of the source of the dream experiences). Dreaming involves processes for expressing, adjusting, and consolidating emotional life through meeting the expressive needs of the unconscious, our unfulfilled desires and frustrations. Some of the most important aspects of dream representation are related to aspects of self and our relations with others, particularly the emotional aspects of those relationships.

Brereton (2000) has characterized the adaptive aspects of dreams as a process of "virtual scenario construction" that provides processes for risk-free examination of social and cognitive options. Dreams provide scenario-building processes that engage opportunities for model construction related to issues of social adaptation, using this visual symbolic modality as a workspace for exploring the implications of different scenarios. Laughlin et al. (1992) suggest that dreaming should be viewed as a form of "play" in which the neurocognitive systems operate independently of the outer environment. Hunt suggests that dreams are based in a visual–spatial image-focused intelligence that integrates memory and imagination in an abstract form of visual representation. Religious and mythological impulses have often emerged from these pre-egoic integrative processes to give a sense of the unconscious levels of reality that underlie our lives.

Artists and others have long been fascinated with dreaming.
("The Nightmare" by John Henry Fuseli.)

Lucid Dreaming. The ritualistic use of dreams for religious purposes produces experiences similar to the phenomenon of lucid dreaming, in which the person is aware that he or she is dreaming. While lucid dreams are generally considered an ASC, LaBerge and Gackenbach (2000) note that there are few differences between ordinary dreams and lucid dreams. The few differences there are, however, are significant: lucid dreams offer the dreamer greater auditory and kinesthetic sensations; a greater sense of control; a greater ability to confront the threatening persons or situations encountered in dreams; an ability to deliberately manipulate the dream to enter into contact with specific persons or situations; and an identification of one's own personality dynamics and the ability to change them through dream encounters. Normal REM sleep characteristics reflect a lack of input from the prefrontal cortex that is manifested

Box 3.2 SPIRITUAL EXPERIENCE AND SOCIETAL CHANGE: MAZEWAY RESYNTHESIS

Religious ASC can produce experiences that convert an individual to a radically new way of religious life or even a new religion. Anthropologist Anthony F. C. Wallace (1956) referred to these processes as "mazeway resynthesis," a reformulation of the ordinary habitual ways of understanding the Universe. Wallace developed this concept while he was part of a team of scientists sent to study the responses of individuals to disasters. In one small town that had been destroyed by a tornado, he observed an elderly woman sweeping the concrete porch of a house that no longer existed. Interviewing the woman, he realized that she had not yet accepted the events that had transpired, and so she simply continued the cycle of chores that she had practiced for years. It took the woman several days before she overcame her denial and accepted the evidence that her house had been destroyed.

His research led Wallace to develop the concept of the **mazeway,** the individual's internalized map of the "routes" he or she must take to obtain gratification and avoid problems. Wallace compared this to the internalized model that a laboratory rat develops when it is introduced into a maze in which food rewards wait around some corners, while dead ends and even punishments (such as mild electrical shocks) are located around others. Rats typically explore the entire maze when they are first introduced to it, but later they run only along the pathway that takes them to the rewards. When researchers used the same maze layout, but moved the rewards and punishments around, the rats continued to follow their accustomed path long after it was obvious that it was no longer rewarded.

Wallace suggested that humans do essentially the same thing, although, of course, on a much larger and more complicated scale. That is, we each develop an internalized map of the world that we use to reach the rewards and avoid the punishments of our culture. Then we automatically run our "mazeway" every time we encounter prompts to perform some culturally accepted behavior.

But what happens when the mazeway we have acquired is no longer able to satisfy our needs? What happens when the world around us has changed so drastically that we can no longer find the rewards we seek, and punishments and setbacks await around every turn in the labyrinth?

This is the situation faced by people whose cultures are changing rapidly, usually in the face of environmental collapse, disease, famine, or contact with an outside culture that is able to overwhelm their traditional ways of living. In such cases, we are all like the old woman who continued to sweep her porch even though she no longer had a house. People attempt to continue their lives until they finally realize that it is no longer possible. Then depression, antisocial behavior, and other individual and social pathologies become common and society faces disintegration.

People who live during such times often resort to behaviors that would have been unthinkable just a few years before. Many begin to abuse alcohol or other drugs, suffer from depression, or even commit suicide. But some find a different way out through a process of **mazeway resynthesis,** a sudden "cognitive and affective" restructuring of the concepts and values held by a person. Similar to a scientific paradigm shift, the process can result in an entirely new way of approaching the problems that the individual was facing. If one individual's solution appeals to others, a new set of cultural rules and expectations can emerge that can restore society, not to its old ways, but to a new pattern of beliefs and behaviors. This can lead to a **revitalization movement** that can produce profound and beneficial changes to the society, and may even result in a new religious movement.

in dream features such as the absence of self-reflection, limited attentional control, lack of active decision-making, and a limited theory of mind. Dietrich (2003) proposes that it is the engagement of the prefrontal cortex in lucid dreams which produces the capacities that are normally absent in dreams—willful action, self-awareness, the deliberate direction of attention, abstract and creative thought, and planning. This can be seen in the story of Handsome Lake and the impact of his spiritual

dream (see Box 3.2: Spiritual Experience and Societal Change: Mazeway Resynthesis).

The Handsome Lake Revitalization Movement

The prototype of all revitalization movements is the religion established by Handsome Lake, a Seneca Indian whose visions and teachings literally saved his people from cultural collapse. Handsome Lake was born in 1735, at a time when the Seneca Indians were at the peak of their prosperity. A vision by the legendary Hiawatha some two hundred years earlier had led the Seneca to cease their centuries of feuding and warfare with the Mohawk, Oneida, Onondaga, and Cayuga, their most important and deadly enemies. Hiawatha, who had lost his wife and children during the fighting and had withdrawn into the wilderness, had been visited by a God who urged him to unite the five nations to fight their common enemies. The resulting League of the Iroquois became the greatest and most important association of Indian peoples north of the Valley of Mexico. While each nation was essentially autonomous in its internal affairs, the nations were required to unanimously agree to any declaration of war or peace. This seldom proved to be a problem, and the Iroquois eventually controlled or intimidated most of the Indian peoples between New York and Tennessee and from Maryland to Ohio. Iroquois war parties were often sent to resolve disputes among their neighboring tribes, and they hunted and traded where they wished.

As a boy, Handsome Lake had experienced the prosperity of the Iroquois, and he had acquired prestige and renown as a hunter, warrior, and leader. But things were changing. The Iroquois had banded together with the English to fight the French (and their traditional enemies, the Huron) during the French and Indian War of 1754–1763. The English wished to continue this alliance when the American colonists began asserting their claims to independence, but many Iroquois were friends of the colonists, and the League was unable to decide which side to support. The tradition of unanimity was broken, and each of the separate nations was forced to decide its own course of action.

When the Revolutionary War ended, the Iroquois were forced onto ever smaller reservations, too small to support hunting. Their traditional way of life was gone, and Christian missionaries began to appear who urged the Iroquois to abandon the remnants of their traditional lives. Faced with the destruction of their way of life, Handsome Lake and many of his fellows began to lead dissolute lives of drinking, gambling, and sexual promiscuity. They used "love magic" to seduce the wives of others, and "sterility magic" and abortions to avoid bringing any children into a world that was clearly disintegrating. Debates raged as to whether the Indians should resist change or whether they should abandon their old way of life entirely and adopt American beliefs and values.

Handsome Lake, who was now in his sixties, was becoming ill. He brooded on his impending death and

tried to soothe the pain by drinking and singing the old sacred songs he had learned as a boy. In the morning, he would feel bad for singing the songs outside their ritual context. He had lost a niece—allegedly to witchcraft—as well as one of his sons, while his other son showed little concern about the fate of his father.

Then, over the course of several months, Handsome Lake had three visions that would help both him and his society. In the first (described at the beginning of Chapter 2) he was greeted by three angels who assured him that his time to die had not yet come. He was also told that God wanted the Iroquois to abandon their destructive habits. In his second vision, Handsome Lake was taken on a "sky journey" in which he was shown the punishments that awaited Indians who did not abandon their destructive ways as well as the rewards that awaited Iroquois who reformed their ways. When Handsome Lake awoke and reported what he had seen, the Seneca began to consider the wisdom of his messages.

In his third vision, Handsome Lake was told to write down what he had seen and to spread the word to the other Iroquois. His message contained three principle themes: (1) the world was facing imminent destruction, (2) the sins that the Creator found offensive were clearly defined, and (3) the course of action for averting catastrophe and reinvigorating society was open to all.

The fact that the Iroquois had always placed great emphasis on visions led them to seriously contemplate the message of Handsome Lake and to introduce numerous changes in society. There was no way of turning back the clock to an earlier time, but Handsome Lake offered several pragmatic solutions to the problems the entire Iroquois Nation was facing. He restated the obligations of kinship and reaffirmed the idea that young people should take care of the aged. Because men could no longer hunt in the small areas of land available to them, he redefined a man's tasks to include farming, a domain that had previously been women's work. This restored the men's sense of contributing to the well-being of society and gave them a task in which they could once again acquire prestige as providers. He mixed several traditional Iroquois religious concepts with ideas that had been introduced by the missionaries and made a clear distinction between the fates of those who continued to practice antisocial behavior and those who worked to restore Iroquois society. He also encouraged the Iroquois to resume their discussions and debates about the best ways to deal with outsiders. He told the Iroquois that they needed to decide as a group how they would deal with the forces of change, thereby reaffirming their common bond and giving them all voices in the decisions that were to shape their future.

Today, the religion that Handsome Lake started, which became known as the Gaiwiio ("the good word"), is still practiced in many Iroquois communities. What was once a radical revisioning of a way out of a cultural impasse that threatened to destroy the Iroquois has now become a force of conservatism, and the Iroquois have regained their sense of tribal identity and the tools they need to face the challenges of the future as a cohesive group.

The concept of mazeway resynthesis explains a variety of adaptive features of religious experiences and movements and how they arise in the face of perceived threats to the cultural order. Each individual is a source of potential solutions to the problems facing our culture because the problems we as individuals face are likely shared by others, and solutions that one person develops may resonate with others as well. Ultimately, the leaders of new religious movements were attempting to find their own way and to resolve personal issues as to their identity and place in society. But the insights they achieved clearly resonated with others around them, and they continue to resonate today.

Of course, as a religion becomes established, it is reinterpreted by later followers and adapted to fit local traditions. What was once a force for radical change may become a force for cultural continuity and may lead to new social institutions and structures against which later visionaries may react. The history of religions is filled with examples of reformers who found fault with the established religions of their time, and many of them paid the price of challenging authority.

Psychoactive Substances and Spiritual Experiences

A wide variety of drugs induce dreamlike experiences and ASC. While they differ in specific effects, enhanced coherence of theta brain waves is a typical feature of the natural psychoactive substances called psychedelics and hallucinogens. These substances also produce a number of typical features of mystical experiences.

Drugs that induce mystical states are derived from substances produced by thousands of plants, fungi, and animals. As our foraging ancestors explored the possible food items in their environments, they encountered these substances, particularly mushrooms. When psychedelic experiences were produced by these substances, how did early humans interpret these unusual experiences? Could the human encounter with such substances have contributed to the development of religiosity? There is good evidence that such substances induced spiritual experiences and contributed directly to the development of religious explanations and activities. They also affected selection for humans' more elaborate serotonergic receptor system (see Chapter 5).

Hundreds of cultures have used psychoactive substances in religion, particularly shamanistic traditions (Rätsch 2005; Schultes and Hofmann 1979). The religious implications of these substances are evident in some of the names they have been given: "voices of the Gods," "plants of the Gods," "saintly children," "flesh of the Gods," and "plant teachers." These names reflect cultural beliefs that their religious traditions originated in the spirits revealed by ingesting these plants. Anthropologist Weston LaBarre (1972) noted that many cultures believed that the roots of their religions lay in vision-inducing substances. He suggested that psychedelic substances stimulate aspects of the subconscious mind, provoke visual representations of supernatural and mythological beings, and contribute to the formation of spiritual beliefs.

The objective ability of the psychedelic drugs to induce mystical and spiritual experiences is attested to not only by cultural traditions around the world, but also by carefully controlled clinical studies. In the classic "Good Friday" experiment that took place in 1962, seminary students at Harvard Divinity School took psilocybin mushrooms or a placebo control (Pahnke 1966). Most of the seminary students who received psilocybin had an experience that they described even decades later as the most profound spiritual experience of their religious lives.

This chemical basis of these spiritual experiences was recently confirmed in a replication study carried out at Johns Hopkins University and published in the prestigious journal *Pharmacology* (Griffiths et al. 2006). A carefully designed double-blind study with hallucinogen-naïve participants showed that psilocybin has the ability to induce mystical experiences, as measured by a formal assessment of mystical experiences (Hood et al. 2001). Of the 36 participants receiving psilocybin, 22 of them had a complete mystical experience, a phenomenon almost completely lacking in the control group, which received the nonpsychedelic psychoactive drug methylphenidate and lay in the dark for eight hours. Only 4 of the 36 control subjects reported a complete mystical experience. Two-thirds of the psilocybin group rated the experience to be among the most meaningful and spiritual experiences of their entire lives, and one-third of the individuals in the psilocybin group considered the experience to be the single most significant spiritual experience of their lives. Many of the subjects who received psilocybin reported spiritual and mystical experiences that affected their attitudes, their moods, and their own experience of spirituality for months afterwards.

Objective third-party community observers noted substantial changes in participants' behavior and attitudes in the weeks following the administration of psilocybin. Compared with the controls, psilocybin ingesters had significantly higher ratings on the scales used to assess mysticism and altered states of consciousness, including introvertive mysticism, extrovertive mysticism, internal and external unity, sacredness, intuitive knowledge, transcendence of time and space, ineffability, positive mood, and experiences of oceanic boundlessness and visionary structuralization. They also experienced greater fear of ego dissolution and other dysphoric moods during the psilocybin episode, but did not show any increases in negative attitudes, moods, or antisocial behaviors. Instead, the psilocybin participants showed significantly higher levels of peace, harmony, joy, and intense happiness. In addition, individuals who took psilocybin noticed persistent long-term effects in their lives, including an enhanced positive attitude about life and themselves, positive mood changes, and positive altruistic social behaviors.

These kinds of effects illustrate that the content of psilocybin-induced mystical experiences is due more to the ways that psilocybin affects our mental hardware than to the cultural programming that is used to interpret the experiences. This hardwired ability to enter into a positive and affirming altered state of consciousness is reflected in a variety of nondrug mechanisms that induce the same kind of experiences.

Neurotransmitter Bases of Psychedelic Effects. Although the psychedelic substances are characterized by a number of different chemical structures and modes of action, they produce a number of common physiological effects through their effects on the serotonergic neurotransmitter system. The major naturally occurring psychedelics (such as peyote cactus, psilocybin mushrooms, and ayahuasca) contain phenylalkylamine and indole alkaloids, whose chemical structures are similar to the neurotransmitter serotonin, and they affect consciousness and induce spiritual experiences through their interaction with serotonergic receptors. The role of serotonin as a neuromodulator, the structural similarity of psychedelics and serotonin, and the specific effects of the psychedelics on serotonergic transmis-

sion provide a basis for characterization of these substances as "psychointegrators."

Psychointegrators enhance the integration of information in the brain by stimulating areas that are central to managing processes related to fundamental aspects of self, emotions, memories, and attachments. The coherent theta wave synchronization along the neuraxis (the nerve bundle linking the structural levels of the brain) that these substances induce may be experienced as feelings of healing, wholeness, interconnectedness, and cosmic consciousness.

These effects of psychointegrators have an important adaptive advantage: enhanced consciousness. Consciousness is improved by increasing the integrative information-processing capacity of the brain. Psychointegrative effects derive from the disinhibition of emotional and social processes and the systemic integration of emotional and cognitive brain functions. The increased hyperactivity of the visual regions of the brain is experienced as visions.

The worldwide association of psychedelics with the origins of religious traditions, together with the ability of these substances to produce profound spiritual experiences, gives strong support to the hypotheses that religious traditions may have arisen because of the profound effects of these substances on consciousness. The original spiritual experiences and the impulses underlying shamanism may have been provoked by these substances in plants and fungi that early humans ingested. Why would these experiences have been adaptive? The adaptive effects appear to involve the general adaptive functions of the serotonergic nervous system, a neuromodulatory system involved in many brain and bodily functions, including the regulation of other neurotransmitter systems.

Hypnosis and Mystical Experience

Hypnosis induces a variety of features that are associated with mystical experiences (Dietrich 2003):

- a sense of detachment of the self
- experiences of timelessness
- a divided stream of consciousness, often experienced as being a separate observer of the self
- vivid images and sensory hallucinations
- a high degree of alertness with a narrow focus of attention or awareness

Hypnosis has been one of the primary areas of study of the psychological phenomena associated with ASC. Hypnotic susceptibility involves a variety of physiological changes, but it is defined primarily in terms of the person's tendency to comply with the suggestions of others while in the hypnotic state. Hypnosis has effects on particularly susceptible people that are similar to the powerful effects of religion. Under hypnosis, people can be convinced to act as if something were real when it is apparent to the external observer that the beliefs are false or delusional. Why are people who are more susceptible to hypnosis more likely to believe in Gods and accept the dogmatic assumptions of religious systems?

McClenon (1997, 2002) has proposed that religion emerged out of the capacity for being hypnotized, a hypothesis we examine further in Chapter 6. Being hypnotized involves having experiences similar to dreaming and engages the ability to become deeply engrossed in an internal mental focus, an alternate reality that generally excludes awareness of the external world.

Hypnotic susceptibility is an innate capacity that enables hypnotized people to sustain inner attention with better focus and to ignore environmental stimuli. Individuals who are highly susceptible to hypnosis can give up reality testing which enables them to become deeply engrossed in imaginative activities in vivid imagery. They also engage a holistic information-processing style and an enhanced cognitive flexibility that together involve an ability to change their cognitive strategies and focus of awareness. This reflects the enhanced interaction between subcortical and cortical levels of the brain.

Enhanced theta brain waves are associated with right hemisphere activity among highly susceptible individuals, as well as with the quiescent periods of meditation. Graffin, Ray, and Lundy (1995) found that highly susceptible subjects had an EEG pattern characterized by greater levels of theta activity, particularly in the frontal regions of the cerebral cortex. During hypnosis, both in individuals who were highly susceptible and in those who were not, theta activity increased in the posterior areas of the cortex, specifically the occipital region where visual processing occurs. The enhanced limbic–frontal interaction characteristic of highly hypnotizable individuals reflects an enhanced interaction between the limbic and frontal brain, an increase in the integration of brain wave patterns across the different brain levels and regions. While the experiences of hypnosis generally lack the ecstatic engagement of religious experiences, they manifest the key aspect of visionary engagement, the ability to enter into an imaginary reality. Hypnosis therefore points to origins of some religious experience and capacity (see Chapter 6).

Adaptive Aspects of the Integrative Mode of Consciousness

The striking similarities in religious experiences from cultures around the world provide strong evidence that these experiences reflect biological capacities that were selected for in the course of human evolution. But did some specific capacity evolve to provide us with these experiences, or are they functionless by-products? Can there be something adaptive about these experiences or the behaviors that produce them?

The universality of institutionalized ASC and the many ritual practices used to induce them indicates that across cultures, if not universally, humans have found it useful to induce these experiences. Ritual techniques for altering consciousness are found in more than 90% of world cultures (Bourguignon 1968; see also Bourguignon and Evascu 1977). Furthermore, it appears that all intact cultures have institutionalized in their religious activities some ritual processes for inducing ASC (Winkelman 1992). These worldwide patterns support the conclusion that altered states of consciousness are natural products of our mental hardware.

These experiences are manifested in very similar ways across cultures and even in young children who have never been told that such experiences are possible. Our biological propensity to experience altered states of consciousness thus raises an important question: Is there something adaptive about these experiences?

The NDE experience of oneself as a "soul" has led many scholars to postulate that it provides an engagement with a fantasy world that protects a person from the emotional shock of reality: imminent death. The dissociation of NDEs provides emotional tranquility, an engagement with a pleasant afterlife that allows one to remain calm and to preserve one's energies while awaiting assistance from others. This engagement with an alternative reality, referred to in the psychological literature by terms such as fantasy proneness and absorption, is intimately related to other aspects of human consciousness such as hypnotic susceptibility and dissociation.

A general adaptive aspect of religious ASC involves their ability to enhance access to information that is normally unconscious and to integrate it into conscious thought processes. Highly hypnotizable people, for example, have thin cognitive boundaries that enable greater access to the information from the unconscious. When they are hypnotized, they experience focused attention, reduced peripheral awareness, and an abeyance of critical thought that facilitates concentration on internal imagetic representations from the unconscious. This condition provides survival advantages by facilitating the development of innovative and creative strategies.

These innate propensities of ASC integrate different brain systems, enhance learning, and promote behavioral, emotional, and cognitive integration. The integration of information from the unconscious is exemplified in religious visions, in which the symbolic imagery system underlying the dream mode of consciousness is stimulated through ritual practices to provide dramatic visual displays of information. Religious ASC brings the body-level awareness of the preverbal mind into consciousness. The functions of the dream capacity are elicited, or co-opted, by religious ritual and integrated into new functions in expanded forms of consciousness and social planning capabilities of the waking mode of consciousness.

The role of ASC in human evolution must be understood in relation to the role of the serotonergic system in the overall brain. Anthropologist Michele Ernandes and Marco Giammanco (1998) propose that the evolution of the serotonergic system reflects the evolution of the brain according to MacLean's model of triune or three brain subsystems. In the reptilian part of the brain, serotonin functions as a regulator system. In the paleomammalian brain, serotonin controls the R-complex, excites limbic brain emotional functions, and distributes information through connections with the prefrontal and neocortex. Ernandes notes that the serotonergic system is the most central and powerful system of integration and coordination among the three brain subsystems. ASC stimulates this serotonergic system and produces other effects that enhance integration of brain functions.

We can find evidence for a variety of ways in which religious ASC may be adaptive today. In the subsequent chapters, we will consider the roles of ASC in healing, cognitive conceptualization, emotional management, healing, socialization, and other cultural processes. However, the really relevant question in understanding the potential evolutionary implications of religious ASC is not what they are "good for" now, but how they might have enhanced survival in the past in the environment of evolutionary adaptation. Did religious ASC first develop in humans out of distinctly human adaptations, or did religious ASC derive from something that was part of our animal heritage? Given the activation of the ancient reptilian and paleomammalian brain structures caused by religious ASC, and the notable loss during ASC of the uniquely human higher cognitive functions of the prefrontal and frontal cortex, it seems reasonable that religious ASC had some preadaptations in the animal world. Because rituals are used by humans to induce these religious ASC, the ritualized behaviors of animals are an obvious place to start our inquiry into the deep biological roots of religiosity and spiritual experiences.

Conclusions: Religious Experience as Personal Experience of Biology

This chapter has addressed one of the key questions in understanding religiosity in general and spirituality in particular: What is special about religious consciousness? The approach presented here provides the important understanding that there are universals of religious consciousness manifested in the many features associated with mystical states, and that these experiences involve special patterns of brain function. The patterns of the brain during mystical states and other spiritual experiences do vary, but they tend to share specific characteristics that help us understand their special nature. These spiritual experiences manifest an "integrative" mode of consciousness in which the enhanced activities of the lower brain structures create a highly synchronized slow brain wave pattern. By making information that is normally stored in the unconscious mind accessible to consciousness, spiritual experiences can offer significant adaptive advantages to both the individual accessing that information and the group to which they belong.

Religious altered states of consciousness have a biological basis in the overall dynamics of our nervous system and consciousness. Spiritual experiences reflect the enhanced operation of areas of the brain that developed earlier in our evolutionary history, called the reptilian complex and paleomammalian brain. Understanding these bases of religious experience requires that we examine the functions of these brain systems in other animals.

Religious experiences are natural. The frequency with which these experiences occur and the diverse ways in which they can be induced suggest that each of us has within us a potential source of religious experience, insight, and renewal. Individuals who enter a religious ASC leave behind the baseline reference of waking consciousness and the cultural models they have learned in the baseline state; consequently, they may then better perceive the tensions and fractures in the models of reality that were acquired from their culture.

Religious ASC may show us that our cultural models are ultimately inadequate for truly grasping the Universe. This can lead us to question our sense of personal and cultural identity and to develop new ways to resolve the inconsistencies between what we have been taught and what we experience, leading to a new religion or culture. For this reason, many religious traditions do not encourage their members to enter into these profound experiences and may question and condemn as heresy the insights reported by people who do.

Of course, the fact that some ASC inspire cultural and religious reformation does not imply that all knowledge obtained during an ASC will be personally or culturally valuable. Just as the insights that scientists gain while taking a bath or falling asleep in front of a fire must subsequently be examined in the cold light of empirical analysis, the insights gained through religious experiences must be viewed in relationship to the cultural context in which they occur.

In this chapter, we have considered how religious altered states of consciousness can be adaptive. The cultural universality of institutionalized altered states of consciousness and their inherent basis in our mental hardware suggest that they confer advantages and survival benefits. The general tendencies for animals to withdraw in the face of stress, starvation, shock, inebriation, and a variety of other natural and ritual procedures help them to preserve their physical resources and conserve their bodies' energies by reducing exertion. In addition, the novel mental functions of ASC can produce intuitive visions that can help us cope with or resolve a crisis. Religious experiences can also provide a sense of (re)orientation in an ever-changing world. Sometimes, these experiences can lead to improved health and functioning for the individual; other times, they can result in profound crises that can threaten a person's well-being.

While these are personal experiences, when shared they can become the bases of religions that affect the lives of billions. In the chapters to come, we will consider how these experiences play a role in health and healing and in creating a sense of group—and national—identity, and we shall consider what types of religious movements are developing today and what types may arise in the future.

Questions for Discussion

- Is it appropriate to speak of "states" of consciousness? Can you think of any terms that may be more accurate?
- Why would a religious explanation help a person understand an altered state of consciousness?
- How can an altered state of consciousness lead to a new way of looking at the Universe?

Glossary

altered state of consciousness (ASC) a modification of consciousness from baseline consciousness

auditory driving the use of repetitive stimuli (e.g., drumming, chanting) to induce changes in consciousness

autonomic nervous system the sensory and motor neurons that connect to the central nervous system

baseline consciousness the state of consciousness in which the individual is able to actively engage with the external world; see **waking mode of consciousness**

central nervous system the brain and the spinal cord

deep sleep a state of consciousness in which the body functions at a very low level and the mind is dormant

dissociative disorder condition where a split-off part of the personality temporarily controls the person

dream mode a period of sleep in which the unconscious mind is engaged with an inner world of sights and experiences; see **rapid eye movement (REM) sleep**

extrovertive mystical experience an experience in which a person perceives a sense of unity with the Universe while remaining aware of the external world

introvertive mystical experience an experience in which a person loses all sense of self and the Universe and enters a state of consciousness beyond comprehension

mazeway the internalized "map" an individual develops in the course of growing up and uses to avoid punishments and obtain rewards

mazeway resynthesis the sudden shift in a mazeway that can occur when a person is confronted with evidence that his or her existing mazeway is no longer appropriate for avoiding punishments and obtaining rewards

meditation a term used to refer to a variety of techniques that lower arousal levels and produce emotional detachment and experiences devoid of content

meditative state an integrative state of consciousness produced by concentration and low levels of arousal

numinous an experience that cannot be explained by rational categories of thinking and hence that may be interpreted as sacred in nature

parasympathetic nervous system the portion of the autonomic nervous system that enables an individual to rest and regenerate

possession state an integrative state of consciousness characterized by amnesia and by physical and emotional excitation

rapid eye movement (REM) sleep a period of sleep during which the body is largely inactive but the eyes move behind closed eyelids; see **dream mode**

revitalization movement a social movement that may develop when an individual experiences a mazeway resynthesis that offers solutions to shared community problems and that leads to a regeneration of that person's society

shamanic state an integrative state of consciousness produced by intense motor behavior

sympathetic nervous system the portion of the autonomic nervous system that enables an individual to be active and alert

waking mode of consciousness a state of consciousness that enables an individual to actively engage with the world; see **baseline consciousness**

Ritualized Animal Behaviors and the Roots of Religiosity

CHAPTER OUTLINE

Introduction: Ritualized Behavior in the Animal World
What Are Rituals?
The Triune Brain and Ritualized Behavior
Ritualized Animal Behavior
The Evolution of Ritual Behaviors
Conclusion: The Animal Roots of Human Ritual Activity

CHAPTER OBJECTIVES

- Explain why studying animal behavior is important to understanding the origins of human religiosity.
- Describe the basic forms of ritualized behavior found in the animal world.
- Illustrate the relationship between brain systems and ritualized behaviors.
- Describe the ritualized behaviors of reptiles and mammals and their functions.
- Illustrate the preadaptations for human ritual capacities indicated by commonalities in the ritualized behaviors of the great apes, particularly chimpanzees.

SHE SPOTTED THE STRANGERS AS SHE WAS COMING *around the hill. Aware of the threat they posed, she hurried back to inform her family. As soon as she arrived home, her sisters began to gather around her. They watched as she began to dance excitedly, swaying back and forth, toward and then away from them. Soon, many of them had joined in the dance as well. Then they rushed off to search for the intruders.*

It seemed like the rain would never end. Suddenly, a sharp clap of thunder rolled across the skies. Startled, one of the leaders jumped up and cried out. Rocking from side to side, he roared his challenge to the sky. Then he ran to the top of the hill, followed by the other males. Together, they shook trees and ripped off branches, flailing them about. Some charged back down and then up the hill again. From a safe distance, the females and the youngsters watched attentively.

A member of the group began to stomp first one foot and then the other, while another began to slowly spring from foot to foot. A third individual began spinning in a circle with arms extended; then, joined by the others, he began moving in a circle around the post, all of them wagging their heads in rhythm. Trading friendly expressions with one another, the group members engaged in the swaggering movement together with an eager enjoyment.

Introduction: Ritualized Behavior in the Animal World

How did we humans develop the capacity to build a mental world that included assumptions about a supernatural reality? When did our ancestors start to believe in spirits and Gods, and use rituals to try to affect them? What led us to live in complex societies with elaborate moral rules for interacting among ourselves and with the Gods and spirits? In short, what led to the emergence of religiosity?

While we may never definitively know the answers to all of these questions, we may be able to determine the broad details of such developments. The presence of religiosity in every culture demonstrates that its roots are in our biology. But what are the biological bases of religiosity? And if religiosity is indeed rooted in our biology, is it a uniquely human capacity, or does it have precursors in other animals? The biocultural perspective suggests that even if religion is uniquely human, we should find at least some preadaptations for religion in other animals, especially those to whom we are most closely related. What might these animal precursors to religion be?

Although other animals do not (as far as we can tell) contemplate their mortality or worry about religious issues of good and evil, they do exhibit some behaviors that are strikingly like our own: the complex displays that make up their ritualized behaviors. The similarities in ritualized behaviors across different species indicate that they are rooted in common adaptations. Just as we can compare the physical features of bodies to determine evolutionary relationships between species, we can study ritualized animal behaviors to help us understand the origins of humans' ritual behaviors.

This does not mean that human religious behavior is "nothing more" than ritualized animal behavior, for, clearly, humans do and think things that other animals do not. We are the only animals that pay homage to unseen Gods, dance throughout the night to cure a sick relative, and undertake long journeys to recreate events in the life of the founder of a religion. But we also engage in ritual behaviors similar to those of other animals, such as acting out our intentions, displaying to "unseen others," and vocalizing to express our emotions. Identifying the specific behaviors in the animal kingdom that resemble human rituals can help us glimpse the roots of our own religious behaviors.

Why Study Ritualized Animal Behaviors?

The idea of looking at other animals to understand religiosity may seem odd—even disturbing—for we normally consider religion to be a uniquely human trait. However, our desire to draw a line between ourselves and all other animals has been challenged before. Language was long regarded as the key trait that separated humans from the "dumb beasts." Yet, over the past several decades, studies of animal communication in the wild and in captivity have led both scientists and philosophers to reassess their definitions of language and to recognize that the gulf between humans and other animals is not as great as we once wanted to believe. Indeed, our studies of animal languages have revealed a great deal about our own attitudes about ourselves. Could the situation be similar with regard to our capacity for religiosity?

Studies of ritualized animal behaviors indicate that they have adaptive roles in social life. A **ritualized behavior** is a complex sequence of animal displays that helps to coordinate social life. The ritualized behaviors performed by animals function as communication and social signaling mechanisms that reduce ambiguity (and consequently reduce stress), contributing to the structuring of individual and group behaviors. These genetically based behaviors facilitate interactions among the members of a species by providing information that allows individuals to synchronize and coordinate their activities. For example, "mating dances" bring a male and female into contact for purposes of reproduction, and dominance/submission displays make it possible for animals to live in complex and dynamic societies by minimizing conflict.

Because the human capacity for religiosity is often expressed in the form of ritual behavior, examining the ritualized behaviors of other animals can help us identify the adaptive functions of the ancient biological systems that underlie religiosity. The similarities between ritualized animal behaviors and human ritual behavior—and the ways in which each fulfills these functions—provide a necessary starting point for considering the origins of religiosity. We cannot determine the origins of religiosity by looking at beliefs, for it is difficult to know what animals believe, and their known cognitive capacities suggest that most human religious beliefs are beyond the conceptual capacity of other animals. We do share observable behaviors with other animals, however, and the use of ritualized behaviors to coordinate animal groups suggests that these played a role in the emergence of religiosity.

Examining ritualized behaviors in the light of models of brain functioning and cognitive processing can help us understand how our mental hardware is related to particular types of religious behaviors. Since the nineteenth century, we have known that the most significant observable difference between the brain of a human and the brain of a chimpanzee or gorilla is size, both overall and with regard to specific regions of the brain. There are no great differences in their anatomical structures or organization. Microscopic studies have even revealed that the arrangement of cells within a human brain is virtually indistinguishable from that in a chimpanzee or even a rabbit brain. Overall, the most basic structures of all land-living vertebrates are quite similar, although more complex species have elaborated on these structures. This observation suggests that the behaviors that these brains control will also be similar.

A basic rule of thumb for understanding the potential complexity of a particular species' behaviors is to consider the relative size of its brain: the larger the size of the brain in proportion to the rest of the body, the greater is the number of neurons and interconnections that stand between the senses and the muscles, and thus, the more complex is the behavior. Of all living organisms, the species with the largest relative brain size is *Homo sapiens*. It is no coincidence that of all animals, we humans exhibit the greatest variety and flexibility in our behavior. But our brains contain many of the same ancient structures found in other animals. Just as our brains have elaborated on the basic brain structures we inherited from our primitive ancestors, our ritual activities have elaborated on the ritualized behaviors of those ancestral animals as well.

When comparing species of animals, we often look at **homologous traits**, characteristics (such as anatomical features) that are similar in different species because they have been inherited from those species' common ancestors. Humans, chimpanzees, and orangutans, for example, all have flattened fingernails instead of curved claws on the digits of their hands and feet, because fingernails were present in the common ancestors of all three species (and, indeed, of all primates; all monkeys and apes have fingernails). All three species have five digits (fingers or toes) on each hand or foot because our reptilian ancestors had five, as both the fossil record and studies of living species demonstrate.

Species can also be compared on the basis of homologous behaviors. The different degrees of homologies among species reflect the degree to which they are related. For example, newborn cats and humans have a similar suckling response because *all* mammals need to feed on their mother's milk as soon as they are born. Mammals share this homologous instinctual behavior because all mammals inherited it from our common mammalian ancestors. Reptiles have no such suckling instinct. But reptiles do engage in other ritualized behaviors.

Some ritualized behaviors help an animal to fulfill its individual needs, such as locating food, establishing a territory, finding a mate, and avoiding predators.

Other behaviors enable group activities, allowing the individual to join with others to defend the group's territory against intruders by communicating its intentions to the other members of the group. Behaviors that communicate information are known as **displays**, and you have probably witnessed many. A dog that rolls onto its back and presents its belly is displaying its submission. A peacock that fans its tail feathers is signaling its desirability as a mate. A baboon male that flashes its eyebrows at another male is communicating a threat.

Chimpanzees have numerous ways of displaying their intentions to other chimps. When they are challenging each other, their hair may bristle, and they often stand upright and wave their arms. Male chimps may shake trees, throw rocks, and even bang kerosene cans (which make a tremendous amount of noise) in their efforts to assert their dominance over other males. All of these displays make them appear larger and more powerful than they really are and reinforce their position in the social hierarchy. During these displays, the lower-status males often bow down before their superiors, a display which signals that they recognize and accept the dominant chimpanzees' higher rank. Subordinates extend their arms to seek assurances from dominant animals. In return, the dominant male may reach out and grasp a submissive animal's hand, a display of reconciliation and friendship.

Humans also display to one another, and we do it so "naturally" that we often do not even realize that we are doing so. Around the world, people smile or grin when faced with an awkward situation, raise their heads or eyebrows in greeting, and lower their heads or avert their eyes when they encounter someone of higher social rank. The unconscious and near-universal nature of human displays—and their obvious resemblances to the behaviors of many other types of animals—clearly indicates that these are a part of our own instinctual repertoire of behaviors. As we saw in Chapter 2, instinctual behaviors are a double-edged adaptation. Their automatic nature saves time, enabling us to rapidly respond to stimuli that are also easy for the other members of a species to understand. But their hardwired nature also means that these responses cannot easily be modified. Of all animals, humans have the greatest ability to modify their behaviors through individual experience and cultural learning, and this flexibility is the source of much of their success. The wide diversity of religious beliefs bears witness to the creativity and flexibility of humans when it comes to developing *concepts* about the supernatural. In contrast, much about our religious *behavior* appears to be rather conservative. These conservative aspects can be

Reconciliation among chimpanzees. The outstretched hand represents a request for reassurance.

seen in the similarities of the behaviors of humans to those of other species, particularly the great apes. Just as we can study the physical features of bodies to help us determine the evolutionary relationships between species, we can study animals' ritualized behaviors to understand the antecedents of our own religious behaviors. We have identified many of the brain systems involved in the ritualized behaviors of other animals and are coming to understand the adaptive roles that these behaviors play. These similarities in animal and human behaviors help illuminate the origins of human religiosity.

The Animal Roots of Human Religiosity: Ritualized Behaviors

One of the primary reasons why we must focus on the ritualized behaviors of other animals in order to explore the roots of human religiosity concerns the fact that animals cannot tell us why they do what they do. Consequently, it may be impossible to detect any religious *beliefs* in animals. For this reason, it is more relevant to examine those animal *behaviors* that are also found in human religious expressions. But what are religious behaviors? The anthropologist Anthony F. C. Wallace (1966) has identified thirteen "minimal categories" of religious behaviors. These categories, the basic "building blocks" of religious ritual behavior, will be discussed near the end of this chapter.

Do ritualized animal behaviors express the same elements as human rituals? If we define religious behaviors as activities that involve some concept of a relationship with the supernatural, then we are presuming that we know something about the intentions of the one performing those behaviors. But how could we ever determine whether an animal is behaving in a certain way because it believes that it is interacting with spirits? By narrowing our focus to observable ritualized behaviors, we can identify some of the precursors of human religious behavior without making presumptions about supernatural beliefs.

Ritualized behaviors are relevant for understanding the evolutionary roots of religiosity because ritual is part of human religion, and ritualized behaviors provide specific adaptive advantages in animals. Ritualized behaviors occur in a variety of contexts, particularly within the context of courtship and mating, but also in aggression, submission, and dominance displays while establishing hierarchies and alliances; in activities like grooming that help establish social bonds; when communicating with one another (especially when separated); and in collective behaviors. As we will see, ritualized behaviors integrate animal groups in ways that are important for survival and that illustrate the adaptive bases of human religion.

What Are Rituals?

The word "ritual" can be applied to many types of human activities, from a ceremony that may take place just once in a person's lifetime to the way that a person ties his or her shoes every morning. What these behaviors share in common is their routinized nature, their occurrence as part of a habitual pattern. **Routinization** is the process by which specific behaviors come to be repeated at certain places and times. Although individual routinized behaviors, such as the habits you have every morning when you get up, appear similar to other kinds of collective rituals, they differ from the rituals that coordinate the behavior of members of a group. As we will see, this distinction is found among other animals as well.

A human **ritual** is a stereotyped, repetitive set of behaviors aimed at achieving a particular goal or purpose. A ritual can be conducted to serve an individual's purpose or to fulfill the needs of a group. Often, they do both at the same time. The *stereotyped* nature of rituals means that the behaviors occur in essentially the same form and sequence every time they take place. The *repetitive* nature of rituals means that they occur with regularity.

Human life is filled with rituals. Across the globe, people conduct rituals to greet the day, bless their food, and prepare themselves for the night. We use rituals to chase away the winter, ask the plants and animals to grow, and thank the spirits for their gifts. Rituals welcome newborns into our communities, mark the change from childhood to adulthood, and send the deceased on to the next life. They join people together into families, and separate them when they do not get along.

One of the most widespread human rituals is the marriage ceremony. Because marriage ceremonies in different societies fulfill similar functions—to alter the status of the individuals being married from unrelated to related in a way that is officially recognized by society—the ceremonies themselves tend to exhibit similarities across cultures. For example, the people to be married usually stand or sit in a position of prominence where they are joined by an "officiant," a person of authority. They may dress in a special way or wear new garments that signal the special nature of the occasion. The families of the marriage partners give one another presents, and feasting is common. Such similarities in marriage ceremonies throughout the world reflect their common function in fulfilling the universal human need to establish socially recognized groups that can act as economic units and can raise and teach the next generation.

Humans differ from other animals in the complexity of our rituals and the reasons we give to justify them. But other species do have their own stereotyped and repetitive behaviors. The "dance of the sisters" that opened this chapter is actually one way that ants communicate with one another. The unusual "rain dance" was observed among a group of wild chimpanzees.

Many of the ritualized behaviors of other species are similar to one another because they serve similar functions. Just as our marriage ceremonies announce to society and to the people being married that they are bonding together to establish a new family, the ritualized courtship and mating behaviors of other animals help them to overcome their tendency to act independently so that they can achieve something together that they cannot do on their own. Animal courtship behaviors signal a male's readiness to mate and a female's receptivity to his advances.

By recognizing that many of the basic features of ritualized behavior are common throughout the animal kingdom and play fundamental roles in animal social behavior, we can understand why these behaviors are so important for all animals, including ourselves. Human rituals are more complex than ritualized animal behaviors, for we attribute multiple layers of personal and cultural meaning to our rituals and use them to communicate much more than animals do. But many of our rituals ultimately fulfill the same purposes as those of other animals, such as mating, signaling social status and group membership, and defending a territory.

Basic Elements of Ritualized Animal Behaviors

The similarities between animal and human behaviors derive in part from certain basic patterns of activity that are present in all vertebrate species. The most basic form of ritualized behavior that occurs between the members of a species is **isopraxic behavior**, which occurs when two or more animals perform the same action. The identical head-bobbing behavior of two male lizards as they approach one another is an example. Isopraxic behavior coordinates movements of two or more members of the same species, providing an important mechanism for group recognition and for initiating group activity. In primates, including humans, isopraxic behaviors are facilitated by "mirror neurons"; the nerve impulses that fire your arm muscles to raise your arm are triggered in an identical way when you watch another person move his or her arm. Consequently, when one animal performs an action, another animal may be induced to perform the same action.

Repetitious behavior involves the repeated performance of a specific act, such as the push-ups and head bobbing of a lizard. Many challenges between animals are not resolved by body size, but determined by which animal performs its signature display the most. The process of routinization that turns a specific behavior into a habit is essential for creating order in an animal's world. Although born with instincts, animals are not born with a map of their territory in their heads. An animal must learn its territory and determine where it will shelter, locate food, and defecate. As an animal becomes familiar with its surroundings, its behaviors become routinized, following essentially the same sequence and occurring at more or less the same time every day.

Once routines are learned, their **reenactment** causes the animal to repeat a series of actions in essentially the same form. For example, a lizard will typically follow the same path home every day, even if it is not the quickest or most direct route. It may have learned the route by following another lizard, or it may have taken it once to avoid a threat. In either case, the initial experience becomes a template for future behavior.

Tropistic behavior occurs when an animal automatically reacts to a stimulus (e.g., scent or color) on the basis of its instincts. The stimulus evokes a particular hard-wired interpretation or model of the event, and the animal then acts as it has been programmed to do. **Deception** is another animal behavior that has obvious survival value. Hunting requires a predator to act like an inanimate object, remaining motionless for long periods of time so that its prey will overlook it. An animal that "freezes" when threatened is also exhibiting deceptive behavior. Other deceptive behaviors may make an animal appear larger (to assert dominance) or smaller (to signal submission) than it really is.

Sequences of Ritualized Behavior. A ritualized animal behavior typically begins with an **intention movement** that signals that an animal is ready to engage in some type of activity. The fanning of a peacock's tail is an intention movement that communicates to others that he is sexually mature and is ready to mate. However, it does not guarantee that mating will take place. In fact, much of the male's posturing will come to naught. It is only when an intention movement triggers an appropriate response from another animal that the sequence of behaviors culminating in a specific outcome (such as a successful mating) can occur.

Such a sequence of behaviors is known as a **fixed action pattern**. Fixed action patterns have several common features: they are shared by all the members of a species; they appear spontaneously (that is, they are not learned) when an animal reaches a certain stage of its development; they cannot be unlearned; they involve a particular group of muscles moving in a particular way; and they are elicited by a specific stimulus, which might come from within the animal (hormones, hunger) or from outside (the sight of a potential mate or a predator). Fixed action patterns are much like the subroutines of a computer program, for once they have been initiated, they either continue until they have run their course or until they are interrupted, usually by an inappropriate response from another animal.

The specific sequences of fixed action patterns impart a rather rigid structure to the ritualized behaviors that animals use for purposes such as courtship, territorial defense, and challenges to the social order. The specific sequence of behaviors provides a series of checkpoints and filters which help ensure that all of the participants are indeed members of the same species sharing the same intentions. It is the hard-wired nature of a fixed action pattern that enables an individual to automatically understand the behaviors of other members of its species. Through these channels of communication, animals can coordinate their behavior so that they can avoid predators, find food or shelter, attract mates, and determine their place in the "pecking order" (a term based on the instinctual behaviors used by domesticated chickens to establish the social hierarchy of their flock).

Just as related animals tend to have similar perceptions of the Universe, they also tend to have similar reactions to events in their environment. Under the proper conditions, a spontaneous intention movement by one animal automatically elicits an appropriate response from another animal. The complexity of these movements and the amount of information they can convey are related to the complexity of the animal's brain.

There are many differences between the relatively rigid sequences of ritualized animal behaviors and the more flexible sequences of human rituals. The use of symbols and displacement means that human rituals can serve functions that go far beyond the "here and now" purposes of ritualized animal behaviors. But human rituals are rooted in abilities that are also found in other animals. To understand both why human rituals are so similar to the ritualized behaviors of other animals and how we are different, we need to more clearly understand the relationship between our brains and our behavior (see Box 4.1: The Ritualized Courtship Behavior of the Stickleback).

Box 4.1 THE RITUALIZED COURTSHIP BEHAVIOR OF THE STICKLEBACK

The ways in which intention movements and rigid fixed action patterns combine to form a ritualized behavior can be most easily understood by considering animals with comparatively simple brains and highly stereotyped behaviors. One animal that has been studied extensively for this purpose is the three-spined stickleback (*Gasterosteus aculeatus*), a small freshwater fish. Its rigid courtship behavior consists of several discrete and easily observable events.

A male stickleback (above) invites a female (below) into his nest to spawn. The female's abdomen is swollen with eggs, and the two sexes differ in their coloration. Sticklebacks make use of these physical cues during their mating behavior.

Stickleback courtship begins when a mature male leaves the school in which he has been living to establish a territory. Then he builds a nest consisting of a shallow pit covered by a mound of algae and other plants, through which he creates a tunnel. Once the nest is completed, the hormones in the male's body change his color from blandly gray (a color that allows him to blend into his environment) to bright red and blue, making him readily apparent to any passing female. For his part, the male can recognize the females because their normally slender bodies become shiny and swollen with unfertilized eggs.

When a female comes into his territory, the male first swims toward his nest and then turns and charges the female. He repeats this zigzag pattern until the female either leaves his territory or follows the male to the nest. If she follows him, the male then pokes his head into the nest, showing her the way. After she has entered, he induces her to release her eggs. The female then swims out of the nest, and the male enters to fertilize the eggs. He then chases the female away and begins looking for another partner. With luck, he may coax as many as five females to lay their eggs in his nest.

The male then loses his mating drive, changes colors once more, and becomes increasingly hostile to any fish that enter his territory, including females of his own species. He protects the eggs for a few days until they hatch, after which the young fish soon swim off to form new schools. The male's behavior is instinctually programmed and invariably follows the same sequence. Each step in the process begins only after the previous one has been completed. Males do not build nests until they have defended their territory for a time. If a researcher disturbs the pit the male has dug, he will dig a new pit before he builds the mound.

The ritualized courtship behavior of the male stickleback is composed of several behaviors that he also uses for other purposes, particularly in defense of his territory. The zigzag movement of the male toward and away from the female is an expression of both invitation and aggression. Research has found that a nesting male will attack *any* red object, and a male will begin to court another male that enters its territory if the interloper is not red and has a swollen body because it has just eaten.

Studies of the stickleback and other animals reveal the extent to which instinctually programmed ritualized behaviors rely on individuals recognizing specific signals and completing certain tasks before the next step can begin. One important difference between the ritualized behaviors of fish and reptiles, on one hand, and those of mammals, on the other, is the degree of flexibility or "plasticity" that an animal has. The great variation in human courtship behavior is a result of this flexibility and the cultural learning it enables, while the underlying similarities found throughout the world—including the culmination of courtship behavior in some types of marriage ceremonies—are evidence of our more inflexible instinctual drive to mate.

The Triune Brain and Ritualized Behavior

The architecture of our bodies and the processes by which they develop reflect our species' evolutionary past. As embryos, we briefly had tails and gill arches, just like fish. As adults, we retain many similarities with amphibians, reptiles, and other mammals because many of the genes that coded for our ancestors' bodies are still present within us (although other genes often modify how these ancestral genes are expressed). Consequently, all vertebrate bodies pass through similar stages of development, and our adult bodies exhibit the same basic plan (two eyes and an olfactory bulb located near our brains, an internal skeleton, external bilateral symmetry, etc.).

Our brains also resemble the brains of other animals. These resemblances provide insights into the role that our brains play in our behaviors and experiences. Similarities in the brains of humans and other animals are the basis of the model of the "triune brain" proposed by the neurologist Paul MacLean (1990). The model helps see similarities in brains across species. According to this model, the human brain is composed of three relatively distinct layers (see Fig. 4.1). Each layer is responsible primarily for a specific set of capabilities—behaviors, emotions, and thinking—that emerged in this sequence as each part evolved. Although the three layers are intimately interconnected in humans, they continue to operate in relatively autonomous ways. This is why it is possible for us to drive home while worrying about being late and simultaneously plan what we need to do the following day.

The most primitive part of our brain is the R-complex (the R is for "reptilian"). This **reptilian brain** is the "behavioral brain" that controls the various routines that an animal follows throughout its day. It also regulates internal, automatic processes (such as respiration, digestion, and circulation) and enables the animal to establish and defend a territory, hunt, mate, and assert its dominance over other animals. The reptilian brain manages many of the nonverbal communicative behaviors (displays) that are the building blocks of ritualized animal behaviors.

The next layer of our brain is the **paleomammalian brain** (*paleo* means "old"). Also known as the limbic system, this "emotional brain" literally surrounds the reptilian brain, which it regulates by reducing or amplifying the intensity of the signals it receives from

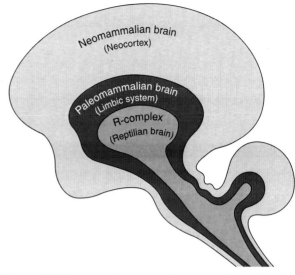

Figure 4.1 The triune brain. Over the course of vertebrate evolution, the newer parts literally grew on top of the older parts.

(Frontispiece from *The Triune Brain in Evolution: Role in Paleocerebral Functions* by Paul D. MacLean. Copyright © 1990. Reprinted by permission of Springer Publishing.)

the reptilian brain. The paleomammalian brain controls and coordinates the information coming via the five classic senses with information emanating from within the body. This process enables an animal to remember its experiences, develop more elaborate models of the environment, and participate in more complex social interactions. Nursing and maternal care (including the auditory and vocal communication that takes place between a mother and her offspring) are products of the paleomammalian brain. Hardwired to provide the individual with a sense of belonging, the paleomammalian brain is the foundation of the mammalian proclivity to live in social groups (such as herds, packs, and families) and generates the emotions mammals attach to these groups (affection, respect, love, and a sense of belonging).

The paleomammalian brain also mediates the emotions mammals feel as they are participating in ritualized behaviors. The evolution of this level of the brain allowed for emergence of new, more flexible forms of group behavior and learning, in particular, **play**. During play activity, young mammals are able to develop their instinctual capacities (such as pouncing on objects or wrestling with one another) to practice behaviors they will need in the "real world" when they are adults (for example, when they will need to hunt for food and fight one another as they attempt to move up the social hierarchy). The ability to play allows learning to modify instinctual behaviors, and it is no coincidence that play activity occurs during periods of rapid brain growth and development.

The outermost layer of our brain is the neomammalian brain, or **neocortex** (the "new covering"). The most recent part to evolve, this "thinking brain" provides symbolic learning and memory capabilities, enabling a much more comprehensive understanding of the external world. The neocortex makes it possible to understand cause-and-effect relationships and to plan for the future. Two of our most important problem-solving capabilities—**analysis** (the ability to discern the various parts that make up a whole) and **synthesis** (the ability to generate a big picture out of small parts)—are products of the neocortex. Human language, which enables us to share our knowledge and subjective experiences with others, is also produced in the neocortex. In humans, the neocortex provides the explanations—the myths—that tell us what our rituals mean.

Although it is convenient to think of these layers as three distinct brains, they are intensely interconnected, each layer communicating with the others through numerous nerve fibers. As a result, each is able to influence and sometimes even "seize control" over the others. When strongly stimulated by pain or danger, for example, our survival-oriented reptilian brain often overrides the normal functioning of our paleomammalian brain and our neocortex through its instinctual "fight or flight" response. Meanwhile, the emotional paleomammalian brain often usurps control when we fall in love, making us inattentive to things going on around us and leading us to ignore signs of hunger and tiredness, as well as rational thoughts that the object of our affections isn't really the right person for us. Certain religious practices (meditation, chanting, prayer) that are initiated in the neocortex can produce changes both in the emotional state of the practitioner (calmness, love, bliss) and in the physiological functions controlled by the reptilian brain (heart rate, breathing, and even the electrical resistance of our skin).

Other times, our different brains may "compete" with one another, while none of them will be able to completely override the others. When this occurs, a person may literally be paralyzed by indecision. Think about the ambivalence and uncertainty you may feel when the rational part of your brain determines that your best opportunity for career advancement is to move to a new city, while the emotional part of your brain urges you to stay near your loved ones, and the reptilian part of your brain makes you nervous about leaving your familiar surroundings.

In humans, each of the three parts of the triune brain plays a role in our conduct and our ritual behavior. Put simply, our reptilian brain controls the muscles we use in rituals and our automatic responses to cues contained in rituals, our paleomammalian brain generates the feelings we experience during (and because of) rituals, and our neocortex tells us why we are doing these movements and how to interpret the emotions they engender. But how do these capacities combine to produce religious experiences?

Animal Brains and Ritualized Animal Behaviors

Thinking of our brains as composed of three distinct layers allows us to examine how the "older" parts of our brains create the many similarities between human and nonhuman behavior, and how the newer parts contribute to the unique religious experiences of humans. The reptilian brain has a central role in submissive behaviors, and Ernandes and Giammanco (1998) have suggested that it is the source of the "immense power being" concept (see Box 4.2: The Triune Brain and the "Immense Power Being" Concept). Altered states of consciousness and the awe and ecstasy associated with religious experiences are correlated with certain patterns of neural activity in the paleomammalian brain. This layer controls the emotional responses of bonding that are involved in our sense of oneness and unity. The integrative experiences associated with mysticism also involve the paleomammalian brain, which produces brain wave patterns that cause neurons in all three levels of the brain to fire in synchronized patterns.

Although specific aspects of religious behavior may be controlled by a particular part of the brain, religious experiences in general appear to involve many parts and may actually integrate the activities of different brain areas. Consequently, different areas and functions of the brain may be activated in different ways, contributing to different kinds of religious experiences. By examining the ritualized behaviors of animals with less complex brains, we can learn about the behaviors we share with these animals and better understand what makes human ritual behavior so unique.

Ritualized Animal Behaviors

All reptiles and mammals use ritualized behaviors to maintain their societies and regulate the interactions between members of the group. These behaviors are

Box 4.2 THE TRIUNE BRAIN AND THE "IMMENSE POWER BEING" CONCEPT

The idea of an unseen yet powerful force that affects our lives appears to be a cultural universal. Ernandes and Giammanco (1998) have suggested that this concept of an "immense power being" is related to the brain activities associated with dominance and submission behaviors. This concept finds expression in many human religious rituals in which the participants often prostrate themselves, bow, or lower their heads before an image or symbol of a superior being. Ernandes and Giammanco consider these religious activities to be the human equivalents of the submissive behaviors of other animals, who lower their heads or lie down on the ground before dominant individuals. Some acts of religious submission also emulate the behaviors of nonhuman females when they present to males for copulation. One notable difference between humans and other animals is that we lower our heads before our Gods, not our posteriors.

Ernandes and Giammanco suggest that these human rituals of homage—and the recognition of dominance that they express—are rooted in the brain dynamics of the hierarchy forming structures of the reptilian brain. The "immense power being" concept originates subconsciously within the reptilian brain and causes us to project an image of a dominant individual into what the neocortex conceptualizes to be the spiritual world.

How did the social behaviors associated with submission come to be used in a religious setting? Because the paleomammalian brain serves to inhibit the functions of the reptilian brain, Ernandes and Giammanco suggest that our notions of a transcendent hierarchical being are the result of an ancient trauma that reduced the inhibitory effects that the paleomammalian brain and neocortex normally exert over the reptilian brain. This trauma occurred when the neocortex became aware of mortality, a perception of an existential threat that was transmitted to the emotional centers of the paleomammalian brain. The shock resulted in a loss of inhibition of the reptilian brain. Because the reptilian brain tends to interpret violence as a result of the actions of dominant individuals, it projected that an "immense power being" was the "cause" of our inevitable death.

The reptilian brain automatically assumes that dominance threats come from another member of the same species; therefore, the "immense power being" was conceived in human terms. Once these concepts became established in ancient societies, it was only natural that humans would relate to this being by turning to the stereotyped and repetitive actions we also use to communicate our understanding of rank to other members of our own species. In the face of a supremely dominant individual, prostration and other acts of submission became normal parts of our religious rituals.

97

fundamental to their ability to maintain predictable relations and establish a social order that permits them to function effectively as groups and reproduce as individuals. As the triune brain evolved, the newer structures added nuance and flexibility to the basic ritualized behaviors controlled by the reptilian brain. This evolution can be traced through the ritualized behaviors of three increasingly complex groups of animals: reptiles, mammals, and primates.

Reptiles

A reptile such as a lizard exhibits a variety of repetitive behaviors, some of them routines and some ritualized interactions. Some of these behaviors enable it to establish and defend its domain, which consists of its homesite (such as a sleeping nest), a larger area that it usually defends (its territory), and an even larger area that it traverses in search of food and water but does not defend (its home range). A lizard moves in a habitual (routinized) way throughout its domain as it per-

forms its various individual daily activities: foraging, hunting, defecating, and more.

When one lizard encounters another member of its species, ritualized behaviors guide their interactions. Territorial displays help the lizard defend its territory, while greeting, courtship, and mating displays help it to relate to other members of its species. To communicate, lizards use four basic types of ritualized displays (signature, territorial, submissive, and courting) in their body language.

As its **signature display**, the blue spiny lizard (*Sceloporus cyanogenys*) performs a single "push-up" followed by two head bobs (or nods) whenever it moves into a new area, even if there are no other lizards around. Blue spiny lizards perform this same sequence when two or more lizards meet (as a kind of greeting), when a male perceives that another lizard has entered its territory (as a threat), and during courtship. Signature displays involve isopraxic behaviors—identical behaviors by two or more members of a species. These behaviors are the basic way that members

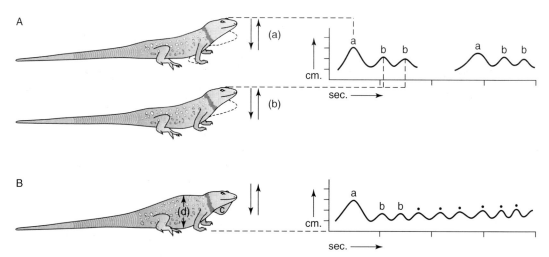

Figure 4.2 The signature and territorial displays of the blue spiny lizard. In A, a lizard performs a single push-up followed by two head bobs. This indicates that it has seen another lizard. In B, the lizard extends the fold of skin under its chin and puffs its body up. These gestures make it appear larger and better able to defend its territory.

(Figure 6.5, p. 108 from *The Triune Brain in Evolution: Role in Paleocerebral Functions* by Paul D. MacLean. Copyright © 1990. Reprinted by permission of Springer Publishing.)

of the same species are able to recognize one another and are the starting point for territorial and courtship displays (see Fig. 4.2).

If an initial signature display does not convince an intruder to leave, a male blue spiny lizard will put on a **territorial display** in which he challenges the new-comer by doing one push-up and then repeatedly bobbing his head. He may make himself appear larger by extending the fold of skin under his throat and changing his posture to a broad exposure, revealing the blue coloration of his underside. If the intruder still does not leave, then the defender charges toward him and, as he gets close, turns his body sideways to show his size. If this does not cause the intruder to withdraw, then the two males nudge and push one another and lash out with their tails as each tries to move close enough to bite the other. The fight continues until one of the animals either retreats or performs a submissive display in which it bows its head and lowers its body with respect to the other.

A **submissive display** is an important part of any animal's behavior because it helps the animal to avoid more dangerous interactions with the other members of its species. A blue spiny lizard signals its submission by pulling its legs close to its body and lowering its head and body so that they rest directly on the ground. These movements make the lizard appear small. An attacking lizard usually ceases its aggressive behavior when it sees these submissive gestures.

Female blue spiny lizards act in much the same way during a **courtship display**. But the female also holds her head up, sending a "mixed message" that entices the male to continue his advances while par-tially defusing his aggression. A reproductive female first signals her status by swishing her tail. The male answers with his standard signature display (one push-up, two head bobs) and then advances toward her as if to attack, while he continues to perform push-ups and numerous head bobs. When he has gotten close enough, he nudges and attempts to bite the neck of the female. He then wraps one leg around her tail in preparation for copulation. After copulating, the male may mark his territory and groom himself.

In all of these displays, an initial intention move-ment (a spontaneous signature display) triggers one of a series of fixed action patterns that lead to a spe-cific outcome. Each step of the process can be thought of as a gateway or filter, beyond which lies a variety of different pathways. An animal's response to a given cue determines the next step in the ritual series. For example, an animal that makes itself appear smaller by pulling its legs in and lying close to the ground is signaling the end to a territo-rial dispute, whereas an animal that swishes its tail at the proper moment is opening a pathway toward mating.

Although the elements of different reptiles' dis-plays do differ, the overall pattern does not. Reptile ritualized behaviors structure the basic relationships among members of the species, enabling them to protect their territories, avoid unnecessary conflicts, and perform the tasks necessary for survival. These behaviors also allow them to overcome their individualistic tendencies so that they can interact with others, both to defend territory and to mate. These capacities for ritualized behavior are dramatically expanded in the more social mammals.

Mammals

One of the primary features that distinguishes the mammalian brain from that of reptiles is the large "paleomammalian brain," also referred to as the "emotional brain." This layer of the brain provides the foundation for mammalian social groups, mother–infant bonding, and play—a type of activity that has parallels in ritualized behavior. Mammals have more complex ritualized behaviors than reptiles, reflecting both their more complex brains and their social nature. In contrast to the generally solitary nature of reptiles, mammals tend to live in groups whose members continuously interact, and ritualized behaviors are fundamental to keeping social life peaceful and organized. To illustrate how the evolution of the brain provided new communicative and interactive potentials, we will briefly consider some ritualized behaviors found in two mammalian species: wolves and chimpanzees.

Wolves. The wolf (*Canis lupus*) is an extremely successful carnivore species. Until it was pushed to the verge of extinction by humans, it was *the* major predator species of large mammals in the northern hemisphere, a fact that owes much to its sociability and intelligence. The basic social unit is the pack, which may consist of twenty or more animals, but is usually composed of ten or fewer. The members of a pack normally travel, hunt, feed, and rest together, but they occasionally break up into smaller groups or even travel alone for a time. A pack typically consists of an adult breeding pair and their offspring, together with any outsiders that may have joined. Some of the young leave the pack as they are approaching sexual maturity (at about twenty-two months of age), but many remain with a pack for life, and some even mate with members of their own litter. Because of the pack's stable membership, the relatedness of its members, and the extensive ritual interactions between them, wolves are generally on very friendly terms with the other wolves in their pack.

Packs are typically led by the original male and female that founded the pack. They may also include mature, but subordinate, animals; "outcasts," who rank so low that they avoid most of the other members of the pack; and juveniles and pups. Among young (immature) wolves, dominance crosses sex lines, but as they mature, wolves tend to divide into male and female orders. (However, the original dominant female retains her dominance over most of the males.) The dominant **alpha male** has the privilege of eating first at a fresh kill, and he also leads the group in deciding when and where to hunt and when to rest.

In an established pack, dominant individuals often assert their control over subordinates through the simple display of raising their tails and staring at the subordinate wolves. They can also assert their superior status by standing across the body of a subordinate who is lying down or by placing their forelegs over the shoulder of a less dominant individual, either from the side or from behind (a position similar to copulation).

Wolves generally avoid aggression within the pack through two types of submissive displays. A low-ranking individual signals "active submission" by approaching a dominant animal with its head, tail, and ears lowered, while the higher-ranking animal keeps its tail up, its head raised, and its ears erect. When approached in this manner, the dominant wolf usually tolerates and exhibits friendliness toward its subordinate. "Passive submission," in which an individual rolls onto its back to reveal its underside, occurs as a response to a show of dominance from a higher-ranking individual or when an individual is surrounded by several higher-ranking wolves. Except for the alpha male and female, all the members of the pack occasionally display some type of submissive behavior toward other pack members who are higher in the social order. This recognition of the social hierarchy allows the animals to avoid conflict and potential injury. Conflict within the pack arises primarily during the excitement of mating season and when the established leader dies or otherwise becomes unable to exercise dominance over the pack.

Wolf courtship is in some ways a continuous affair. Even before the estrus period, both sexes often snuffle each other and rub their heads together. During estrus, a male may court a female by dancing around her and lowering the front of his body while wagging his tail. He may nip at the female and mount her from the side, after which he mounts her from the rear. A

A subordinate wolf (the "underdog") signals its submission to its superior (the "top dog") by turning on its back and exposing its vulnerable underside.

female can initiate courtship by assuming a dominant position in which she places her front paws, neck, or head on a male's shoulders. She may also adopt a submissive pose and back up to the male as she lifts her tail or turns it to the side to display her genitals.

When her pups are due, the female retreats to a den, where she gives birth to four to seven blind and helpless pups. The mother often licks the pups' bellies, prompting them to urinate and defecate. This is an important step in developing the passive submission response they will use as adults, when they will lie on their backs in the presence of a superior, who may also lick their bellies.

The pups begin to spend time outside the den when they are about three weeks old. They begin to play and "play fight," a behavior that helps determine their position in the hierarchy of their littermates. When the pups are six to eight weeks old, their mother begins weaning them by standing up when they attempt to suckle, forcing them to follow her around for food. Now, when the pups approach and sniff or nuzzle their mother's mouth, she regurgitates semidigested food, which the pups eagerly lap up. They can also obtain such food from the other members of the pack. The begging behavior of the pups at this stage is the basis for the active submission behavior they will display throughout their lives whenever they approach a dominant individual.

Three significant aspects of wolf ritual behavior illustrate the adaptive aspects of ritualized behavior: play, group howling, and the practice of "baring one's neck" in fights.

Play. As we have seen, playing enables young mammals to hone and practice the inherited behavioral capacities in a context that shapes them for actual use. Play activity in wolves and other mammals has significant ritualized components. In essence, play involves activities that are like the lethal fighting and hunting activities the animals will use to survive in life, but the actions are carried out in a context in which participants know that the intentions are not serious, and the acts (such as biting) are "soft" rather than injurious. Play is primarily an activity of juveniles that involves activities relevant to their overall fitness in both the short and the long term. Play is a form of physical exercise that stimulates development and provides training in skills related to hunting and defense. Play offers a context for establishing social relations and role-taking—for instance, when a dominant individual plays a submissive role to allow a smaller animal to dominate. If play gets too rough, signals enable the participants to know that the intentions are not real, that they are "just playing." They nonetheless learn and perfect skills that they will use "for real" when they are hunting or fighting for dominance later in life.

Howling. Wolves may howl at any time throughout the year (although females with pups usually avoid howling until their pups are several weeks old). When one wolf begins to howl, the other members of the pack typically join in. This chorus can last for up to ninety seconds and may be followed by a second chorus.

Afterwards, none of the members of the pack will usually howl for the next ten to twenty minutes. Each animal has its own distinctive howl, and pack members can identify one another on this basis. Howling is often used to assemble the pack. When a solitary individual begins to howl, other members of the pack will quickly show up. Wolves rarely howl when hunting, but do howl afterwards to help individuals who have become separated find one another. Howling also occurs spontaneously. Wolves often stand shoulder to shoulder or face to face when they howl, and a howling session is accompanied by a great deal of excitement, tail wagging, and friendliness. Howling serves both the practical purpose of bringing the pack together physically and the emotional purpose of intensifying the bonds between the members of the group.

Baring the Neck. The neck-baring behavior of wolves appears to present a paradox. This behavior generally occurs in the context of mortal combat between two wolves engaged in a struggle for dominance. When, in the course of combat, one of the wolves becomes seriously disadvantaged in its defense, instead of seeking to defend itself, it does the opposite: the disadvantaged individual exposes its vulnerable neck and throat to the dominant individual. This exposure leaves the "underdog" literally at death's door, its vulnerable jugular vein exposed to the aggressor's fangs. The "top dog" maintains an aggressive demeanor, growling and appearing barely able to restrain itself from the attack that would end its opponent's life. But the attack does not happen as long as the subordinated individual remains in the same position, exposed and vulnerable. If he tries to run, the other will set upon him in a vicious attack. As long as he continues to bare his neck, the attacker will remain at bay, deterred by a deeply embedded adaptive mechanism that keeps him from destroying a member of his pack that he will rely on at other times. The function of this ritualized behavior is to balance aggressive rage and submissive fear, precluding fatal combat in a tolerable relationship of submission.

Chimpanzees

The living species thought to be most closely related to humans is the common chimpanzee (*Pan troglodytes*). Found in the rainforests and woodlands of Central Africa, this great ape has been the object of extensive studies both in captivity and in the wild. Indeed, the longest field study of any animal group ever carried out (which continues to this day) is that of Jane Goodall and her colleagues at Gombe National Park (Tanzania). The group rituals of chimpanzees are the most complex of any of the great apes, a reflection of their large groups and the alliances that hold them together.

A chimpanzee community typically consists of around fifty individuals, with more adult females than adult males. Chimpanzees live in a "fusion–fission" society in which the members of the group generally travel and feed in smaller groups for much of the day; however, some of the dispersed groups will reunite at night. In the evening, they call and drum to locate one another and engage in ritualized displays as they congregate into larger groups in the trees for protection while they sleep at night. Because of their freedom to come and go essentially as they wish, chimpanzees have a more fluid social life than perhaps any other animal except humans. Ritualized behaviors are an essential way that they establish sociality and maintain alliances and group structure. The fusion–fission arrangement also allows the chimps to maximize their abilities to find food (when researchers provision groups with food to observe them, chimps tend to travel in larger groups because they no longer need to "spread out" to maximize food acquisition).

In chimpanzee society, males stay in the area in which they were born, while females migrate out to join another group or wander between groups. This creates a society in which males must maintain lifelong relationships with other males. While there is a great deal of interaction between the sexes, both males and females have more interactions and much stronger bonds with members of their own sex. These relations are established, expressed, and maintained through a variety of interactions, particularly grooming and displays (see the discussion that follows). Chimpanzees express recognition of, and respect for, the social hierarchy and their own place within it through ritualized behaviors. By grooming one another, lower-ranking males may build relationships that allow them to form alliances with one another to resist or even depose an alpha male. They may spend years cultivating the friendships that will help them improve their status through strategic alliances. In addition to grooming, males establish and maintain these alliances through meat sharing, cooperative hunting, and territorial patrols.

Grooming. Chimpanzee females usually give birth to a single infant at a time, which they then nurse until the

Grooming is a favorite pastime for chimps that reduces conflict and promotes bonding.

young chimp is three to four years old. A mother grooms her infant intensively throughout this time and carries it around as she moves, further strengthening the bonds between the two and facilitating the transmission of learned behaviors. Even after they are grown, mothers and their offspring often spend considerable time grooming one another. Even a twelve-year-old will sometimes return to his mother for grooming and reassurance, especially if he has been injured in a fight or suffered some other setback.

The grooming sessions for which chimps are so famous generally involve same-sex grooming partners and may include several individuals. Grooming sessions usually last longer when they occur between members of the same sex; males will often decline to groom a female, even if she has just groomed them. Mothers groom their own offspring more than they groom others, a practice that helps bond the family and teaches child-rearing behaviors to their daughters. These sessions may go on for as long as two hours, during which time the chimps will alternate between grooming and being groomed. A session typically ends when the individual who was being groomed does not reciprocate by grooming the other.

Grooming has a hygienic function, as partners remove ticks, other parasites, dirt, and dead skin. But chimps also appear to receive a great deal of pleasure from grooming. As a grooming session progresses and the individuals relax, the body language of dominance and submission temporarily vanishes. Each groomer (regardless of rank) will gently move the other's body

around to facilitate grooming, while a groomee will direct the groomer toward parts of the body that he or she would like to have groomed (usually places that the groomee cannot see). Grooming is a state of interpersonal accord, the antithesis of aggression and conflict between individuals (see Box 4.3: Primate Belongingness as a Preadaptation for Religiosity).

Mating Behavior. Chimps exhibit a wide degree of mating behavior. Females in estrus develop a pronounced sexual swelling, a condition that lasts some seventeen days. Copulation is usually preceded by some type of male courtship display, which often takes the form of a direct gaze, a waving of branches, stretching out of one or both arms, swaggering on two legs, or stomping on the ground. These behaviors resemble the purely aggressive displays described later, but the female is able to distinguish them as courtship displays because courtship behavior is *always* accompanied by an erect penis. Upon noticing the courtship display, an interested female will approach the male and crouch in front of him, presenting her backside. Although copulation usually takes place with the male squatting behind the female as she crouches, chimps also use a variety of other positions.

There are two primary patterns of mating. Promiscuous mating patterns, in which a female copulates with several males, are common during the initial period of the female's sexual swelling. The high-ranking males show little aggression toward one another at this time and willingly share the female. Low-ranking males

Box 4.3 PRIMATE BELONGINGNESS AS A PREADAPTATION FOR RELIGIOSITY

In her book *Evolving God: A Provocative View of the Origins of Religion*, Barbara King (2007) suggests that the evolutionary origins of religion are found in the primate desire to belong, a craving and a need for emotional connection with another. The ritualized and emotional interactions among primates are of a different quality than the one-on-one interactions that are typical of the ritualized behaviors of other mammals. King suggests that the ways in which the great apes experience "belongingness" to a group and express their emotional attachments directly indicate how our own **hominin** ancestors lived and on what basis they developed religion.

King proposes that this need for belongingness that was the basis for religion emerged from a need for, and dependence on, mothers that was extended to spirits and Gods. King considers this belongingness to be "a necessary condition for the evolution of religion" (p. 8); today it is reflected in a characteristic feature of modern human religions: our deep emotional engagement with others in sacred realms. King proposes that this hominid need for belongingness was extended to new functions of religious imagination.

It is clear that the human line's diversion from the common ancestors that we share with apes involved an intensification in emotional relationships and empathy that reflects the importance of individuals acting together across their entire lifespans. King suggests that the mammalian capacity for empathy and emotional contagion that derived from the emotional ties with other members of the group was the basis of religion. It was the increasing cognitive abilities of our ancestors that allowed them to channel their emotions in ways that also considered the needs of the other members of their group. This involves our cognitive capacity to use the self and project it into the other's circumstances as a frame of reference for understanding the other. The social capacities for reading the behavior of others is an adaptive skill that allows animals to function in coordinated ways in larger groups. Thus, the social cognitive ability of the self—the ability to place oneself in another's circumstances and to use the self model as a framework for understanding the other—is another preadaptation on which the human religious capacity ultimately depended and exapted for new purposes.

King proposes that these communications, along with cognitive empathy and capacities for following rules, using the imagination, and having special forms of self-consciousness, provided the evolutionary platform for complex social behaviors in primates. Ape communication is first developed in the connection between the infant and its mother and other social partners. In humans, these behaviors extended to the religious imagination and meaning-making processes. They enable us to use our imaginations to engage in thoughts, feelings, and behaviors that refer to contexts other than the current physical reality. We can observe this engagement with the "make-believe" in "human enculturated" chimpanzees that imitate playing with toys, for instance, acting as if they are dragging an object on a string. This chimpanzee capacity for imagined interactions indicates a precursor to the capacity for human religious beliefs and practices. This is a capacity for an imagined reality, not physically, but nonetheless real for purposes of interactions with others. The capacity for engaging in make-believe is an extension of capacities manifested in mammalian play and is further developed in humans by linking that imagined reality into meeting our personal and social needs.

The foundation of spirituality in an expansion of belongingness and emotional engagement with others is why there are deep positive emotions at the origins of religion. The social and emotional bonding and other processes characteristic of belongingness in mammals and primates are developed to a far greater extreme among humans. The human need for belongingness, and our intense desire for emotional relationships, is a reflection of how our brains are wired to feel empathy for others. As humans evolved in social complexity, this need was expressed in symbols of body decoration, burial, music and dance, and art. The powerful intrinsic rewards that come from meeting our needs for belongingness in communal experiences can even be achieved with thousands of anonymous others. This is attested to in the cosmic and spiritual experiences reported by many who today attend not only group religious ceremonies, but also secular concerts or sporting events.

(From *Evolving God: A Provocative View of the Origins of Religion* by Barbara King, Doubleday, 2007.)

and adolescents may also copulate with the female during this phase, but often do so furtively. As the female's cycle progresses, one of the males may become more possessive of her. If the male is low-ranking, he usually still stands aside when a higher-ranking male approaches

to copulate. Dominant males, on the other hand, may monopolize the female. Often, the mere presence of a dominant male is sufficient to keep other males away. This is a consequence of ritualized behaviors that previously established these males' dominant status.

A male chimpanzee strikes a threatening pose.

Dominance and Aggression. Both sexes use aggressive displays to establish social ranking. Simple displays convey the mildest threats when an individual raises its head or arm slightly or gestures as if preparing to throw something. When threats are serious, a chimp's hair will stand on end. This alone is often enough to provoke a submissive individual to leave the area. A chimp expresses a more serious threat by standing up and swaying from foot to foot or by running toward an opponent on two legs (often while waving its arms). Threats often involve combinations of these, usually building in the sequence described. Chimps also shake the branches of nearby trees, throw rocks and other objects, and flail with sticks or branches. The most dramatic and serious type of aggressive or dominant behavior is the charging display, during which a chimp (usually a male), may shake, drag, or flail branches, throw objects, slap the ground with its hands and stomp with its feet, leap and swing through

trees, vocalize, and even drum on tree trunks. Chimpanzee displays involve a lot of noise (made by vocalizing, stamping, and drumming) but are not always directed at a particular individual.

Most direct attacks within a group are over within a few seconds and are followed by "peace-making" activities, such as embracing, hand-holding, and especially grooming. Although attacks occasionally result in serious injury, ritualized behaviors generally eliminate direct within-group aggression because displays communicate dominance or submission. More serious bouts of aggression occur when an adolescent male is attempting to establish his position with the adult males or when other males are challenging an alpha male. The female members of the community generally play no role in such displays, but they often do exhibit considerable aggression toward other females that have recently migrated into their group.

The situation is very different with regard to outside groups. Chimps from one group sometimes engage in prolonged attacks on chimps from another group when they encounter them alone, wounding and even killing them. However, relations among separate groups of chimpanzees generally are maintained through physical separation that is mediated by vocalizations and drumming incorporated into aggressive displays.

Communication Mechanisms: Vocalizations and Drumming. Van Lawick-Goodall (1968) observed that expressive movements are generally combined with vocalizations. These serve important communicative functions in chimpanzee societies because they structure the interpersonal relationships among the members of the group. Chimps vocalize a great deal within their own territory to communicate specific information, such as the presence of predators, the discovery of a food source, and feelings of aggression or interest in mating. After vocalizing, chimps often listen, as if waiting to hear how others will respond. On some occasions, chimps vocalize together without attempting to convey any specific type of information. These "singing" episodes are usually initiated by males, and females and youngsters may enthusiastically join in. Once the chorus has ended, the participants resume feeding without waiting for any type of response.

In general, vocalizations provide information to members of the community and to members of other chimpanzee communities; they are particularly important for maintaining contact among members of the dispersed group during daily foraging. These vocalizations communicate hierarchical order, enjoyment of food, fear, and a variety of other concepts related to context. They also play an important role in the expression of emotions. Chimpanzee calls, particularly long-distance pant–hoots, also communicate individual identity that is recognizable to both chimpanzees and human observers.

Pant–Hoots. The pant–hoot is a loud and complex call that includes an introductory phase, a buildup to a climax, and a let-down phase (Reynolds 2005, pp. 134–35). Pant–hoots may be performed individually or by a number of animals who join together in a chorus. "Pant–hoot choruses may break out during the night, especially when two groups are sleeping within earshot, in which case the calls pass back and forth, or when a large number of chimpanzees are nesting together" (Goodall 1986, p. 134). Male chimpanzees perform loud calls predominantly, with the pant–hooting peak phase followed by charging displays. Pant–hooting is one of the most important forms of chimpanzee auditory communication, providing crucial information to others regarding personal identity and emotional state. Pant–hoots are expressed primarily in the context of social excitement (for example, pant–hoots signifying arrival), as well as to express enjoyment when there is abundant food. Pant–hoots also allow members of the group to locate one another when they are out of sight, are used to call attention to predators and food sources, and may be cries for help. They are particularly important in the evening, when they are used to collect the dispersed group back together at a central location for nesting. Another function is manifested in the inquiring pant–hoot, a sociable call that is generally used to locate alliance partners. An inquiring pant–hoot may include tree drumming to determine the location of individuals and their identity. Roaring pant–hoots are produced during a state of high arousal and during intense social excitement. The roaring pant–hoots are also used during travel and tend to elicit responses from others, providing information about the location of other members of the group. Pant–roars are more typically used during a variety of display activities.

Chimpanzee vocalizations (and drumming patterns) are distinctly unique, and both other chimpanzees and humans are able to identify the individuals who make them. Within each population, individuals show a range of variation in terms of fundamental characteristics of pant–hoots, such as the frequency of the calls, the length of the buildup phase, and the rate of hoots (Reynolds 2005). Arcadi (1996) suggests that the members of a single community modify their pant–hoots to resemble more closely the patterns of their alpha male. This imitation leads to the development of a unique community pattern or "accent" that facilitates the recognition of one's own group members and avoidance of outsiders.

Drumming. Wild chimpanzees (*Pan troglodytes*) incorporate a variety of acoustic signals into their aggressive charging displays, including drumming, which is typically performed by males (although females and young chimps occasionally join in). Drumming is produced mostly by striking the hands and feet against the ground and trees. This action generates low-frequency sounds that provide a system of long-distance communication; the sounds are audible to humans at a distance of up to 1 kilometer. While these acoustic exchanges serve a practical purpose, they are performed spontaneously, and the performers take evident satisfaction in them. The drumming sessions are usually accompanied by choruses of pant–hoots, and the combination of drumming and vocalizations may provide a variety of contextual information.

Drumming activities serve several purposes. First, like vocalizations, drumming provides an auditory signal that allows dispersed groups to remain in contact with one another as they forage in separate areas. Drumming displays usually occur during travel and between individuals who are not in visual contact. Each individual has a distinctive pattern that is recognizable by the rate of drumming, the length of episodes, the number of distinctive beats, and the volume of sound.

Chimps may use drumming to protect their territory against other groups. When they are defending their territory, bonobos (*Pan paniscus*) often engage in group shouting, vocalizations, and aggressive displays with fast and loud "drumming" that they produce by beating and jumping up and down on tree buttresses (De Waal 1997). These acoustic signals call on the other members of the group for support during confrontations with chimpanzees from other communities (Arcadi, Robert, and Boesch 1998). When the group is near the limits of its range, however, and neighboring groups are likely to be near, chimps may drum but they will not vocalize.

Threat Displays as Graded and Maximal Chimpanzee Ritualized Behaviors. The social order and hierarchy within chimpanzee groups is maintained through a graded hierarchy of threat behaviors that assert relative social status; the maximum threatening behavior is the bipedal charging display. Meanwhile, the peace and tranquility of society are based on grooming behaviors that establish relaxed relationships and attitudes.

Aggressive behaviors are central to establishing and maintaining the dominance hierarchy within the chimpanzee community (Goodall 1986). The basic features of this signaling begin with hair bristling, glaring, and a bipedal posture that makes the animal appear larger and more dangerous. Extended features of the display, such as leaping, hurling rocks and branches, and beating on the ground, can escalate to intimidating charging display—stamping the feet, slapping hands and feet against the ground, beating branches, throwing rocks and sticks, waving arms, and drumming on the trunks or buttresses of trees with the feet, combined with upright running toward the threat while screaming and pant–hooting. Much of the display may be quadrupedal, but in its maximal form it involves a vigorous bipedal charge that enables the chimpanzee to wave and beat its arms, grasp branches, wave them from side to side, and beat them on the ground.

The charging displays, including the charging run toward another, the erect posture attained by rising up on the hind legs, the shaking of branches, and other aggressive gestures and vocalizations, are ritualized aggressive behaviors observed among other primates as well.

The power derived from these "noisy displays" is illustrated by the case of a chimpanzee called Mike. Mike was a low-ranking male when he began using empty kerosene cans in his displays. He would bounce and hit the cans in front of him while making aggressive charges. These displays quickly catapulted him to alpha male status, a bluff that he was able to maintain in the face of thirteen other adult males within the community (also see Goodall 1986, pp. 426–27).

The charging display involves an integrated manifestation of behaviors, body postures, gestures, and mobilizations that generally elicit a submissive response from the animal to which they are directed. Submissive responses usually prevent a physical attack. The types of threat behaviors that are designed to elicit submissive responses range from subtle signals, such as glaring or tipping the head upward and backward, to more obvious behaviors, such as swinging the hand toward the threatened animal. If such threats fail to elicit the appropriate submissive response, the aggressor may escalate its behavior into a direct physical attack that involves the above elements, as well as stomping, biting, and beating the victim with hands and sticks. Threat displays have different adaptive functions, depending on the context. For example, threat displays also occur when separated individuals greet one another when they rejoin the larger group. Threat displays also play a role in relations between different troops and in the release of tension.

Greetings. When individuals or groups that have been separated for a time rejoin one another, there are often aggressive displays as the chimps excitedly reassert their positions within the hierarchy. Males (but usually not females) initiate greetings with ritualized aggressive behaviors, typified in a bipedal swagger and stamping of the feet. Other significant greeting behaviors include "bobbing, bowing and crouching, touching, kissing, embracing, grooming, presenting, mounting, inspecting of the genital area, and occasionally hand-holding . . . Greeting behavior, comprising, as it does, elements of submissive, aggressive, and reassurance behavior, may be considered adaptive in relations to the specialized social structure of the chimpanzee community" (van Lawick-Goodall 1968, p. 284).

Intergroup Relations. Chimpanzee groups generally avoid other groups, but when they do come into close contact, aggressive behavior displays are likely from members of the dominant groups in the exchange. The organized call and drumming patterns characteristic of individuals and communities serve important roles in maintaining territorial boundaries. When chimpanzee patrols approach the boundary of their area and hear calls and drumming from a neighboring community, they will move away from the boundary. Once they are back in their own territory, the calls and drumming from the neighboring community will be aggressively met with loud calls and drumming (Reynolds 2005). Van Lawick-Goodall observed that particular drumming trees were preferred locations for group displays, which were generally only performed by males.

Release of Tension. Charging displays also have the function of releasing pent-up emotions. Sometimes chimpanzees make charging displays that are not directed at any other individuals, allowing these aggressive outbursts to release repressed emotions generated by social tensions. "The minor attacks and the wild charging displays with all their elements of aggression function to relieve social tensions and function to minimize the physiologically undesirable components of stress" (Goodall 1986, p. 356). A similar emotional release may underlie these dramatic displays when they are performed simultaneously by the dominant males in response to thunderstorms. Williams (1980) notes that the violent impersonal forces of thunder and lightning, together with the accompanying wind and rain, have direct implications for the apes' survival, threatening their security by neutralizing the scent and muffling the noises of other animals. Being in the rain also causes discomfort and prevents the apes from foraging as usual. Thus, rainstorms are sensed as threats, and chimps respond with charging displays to these powerful forces of nature

Luit, a male chimpanzee, "nearly in a trance."

that both threaten their practical well-being and manifest a mysterious powerful force. "Such instinctive and passionate action is the only defense they have against the invasion of a force that both terrifies and excites them" (Williams 1980, p. 79). The alterations of consciousness that are universals of human religion may not seem apparent in chimpanzee behaviors. Yet we have to ask about the effects of the exhausting physical displays, both the drumming and the vocalizations. In his book *Chimpanzee Politics*, primatologist Frans De Waal (1997) noted that these activities appeared to cause a "trance" in one chimpanzee: "Luit, nearly in a trance, with his eyes closed, displays a rhythmic stamping dance and crows during the climax of a ventilating [pant–hoot] display" (p. 182).

Managing Frustration. Van Lawick-Goodall groups together a number of chimpanzee behaviors that she characterized as manifesting frustration. These behaviors are a response to internal or external conflict, fear, an inability to achieve goals, and difficulties in communication with other members of the species. Frustration is manifested in displacement activities, such as scratching, yawning, grooming, masturbating, throwing temper tantrums, rocking, shaking and swaying branches, and "charging, slapping, stamping,

dragging, throwing and drumming" (van Lawick-Goodall 1968, p. 273). Particularly notable are rocking activities, which range from a slight movement of the head to more violent manifestations, including a vigorous bipedal "dance" from foot to foot.

Reassurance Behaviors: Grooming and Reconciliation. The counterparts to aggressive behaviors involve submissive behaviors and a variety of actions that provide reassurance to subordinate animals. Submission rituals reduce aggression. "Particularly between adult males, one male will literally grovel in the dust, uttering pant grunts, while the other stands bipedally performing a mild intimidation display to make clear who ranks above whom" (De Waal 1997, p. 30). Among the predominant patterns of submission behavior are grooming, sexual presenting and mounting, crouching and bowing, bobbing, kissing, and embracing. Submissive behaviors directed toward dominant individuals help meet the subordinate individuals' need for reassurance contact. After a subordinate animal is attacked, it often makes an indirect approach to the aggressor. A variety of "reassurance behaviors" will be used to calm both the threatened individual and the aggressor. When subordinate animals seek reassurance from dominant animals, the most frequent responses of the superiors are to initiate grooming. It is also common for chimpanzees to extend a hand to another chimp. When animals that are generally friendly have a confrontation and then show submission and reassurance behaviors, the behaviors have been referred to as reconciliation.

Victims of aggression and subordinates also may be reassured through behaviors such as touching, patting movements and contact with the body, embraces, and kissing. This reassuring contact may be provided by aggressors or allies. A subordinate individual may even throw a temper tantrum if a dominant animal fails to provide it with some sign of reassurance. These temper tantrums may also include behaviors involved in the threat displays. Responses to requests for reassurance, such as touching, embracing, or engaging in other contact with the individual, clearly reduce stress in subordinate individuals. Van Lawick-Goodall notes that the use of touch as a gesture of reassurance is displayed in many primates and that similar touching or patting also may be used to calm aggressive individuals following charging displays. In addition, self-calming may be achieved by an animal's holding its own hand or embracing or grooming itself.

The ability of grooming to reduce stress is generalized from the roles of grooming in chimpanzee relations from earliest infancy; being in contact with mother and being groomed by her is one of the most basic ways that young animals can resolve their fear or anxiety. Grooming relationships that begin in the affiliative behaviors between mothers and their offspring are generalized to the whole community in the formation and maintenance of personal relations. The use of grooming for reassurance may continue through adulthood. Adolescent males who are engaged in moving up the dominance hierarchy by engaging in threats and attacks will frequently seek out their mothers for grooming, which provides relaxation and stress reduction.

In general, grooming is focused upward in the hierarchy; subordinates initiate grooming and do so more extensively to please and appease dominant animals than they do to animals ranking below them. Grooming is a subtle and strategic approach to acquiring power by building strength through alliances and coalitions, rather than applying direct aggression. Grooming is an essential way that the males of a group cooperate and form alliances. Grooming is also used by subordinate animals to reduce the arousal of dominant animals. In addition, grooming is vital in restoring relationships between allies after temporary conflicts and is "essential to the maintenance of harmony within the community as a whole" (Goodall 1986, p. 402). "Chimpanzees, without doubt, gradually learn the calming effect that their own grooming behavior is likely to have on others. Grooming can then be used with *intent* as a manipulative tool" (p. 406).

The Evolution of Ritual Behaviors

Most mammals are highly social species and have numerous ritualized ways of establishing relations and communicating within their group. These begin with the interactions between a mother and her infant, which are extensive and long-lasting. Other members of the group may also contribute to the feeding, care, and protection of the young. **Reciprocity** (food sharing, help with child care, cooperative hunting, and grooming) helps to avoid or defuse aggression while expressing and strengthening the bonds between individuals. Reciprocity is based at least in part on the original mother–infant relationship, in which the mother provides the infant with milk and protection. Later in life, chimpanzees establish reciprocal relationships with other members of the social group, especially close kin, but may also extend them to a wider circle by exchanging a variety of resources or services (food, sex, grooming, support in aggressive displays). These exchanges are important in the development of alliances between unrelated individuals.

The high degree of social intelligence possessed by mammals enables them to live together in large numbers (which affords protection) and to function as groups rather than simply as numerous individuals living independent lives in close proximity to one another (as reptiles do). In mammals, the more recently evolved parts of the brain provide nuance and flexibility to the repertoire of behaviors that are hard-wired into the reptilian brain. The important roles played by ritualized behaviors can be seen in the ways that aggression is ritualized to maintain dominance hierarchies while avoiding physical conflict and its attendant risks. By communicating an individual's social position with respect to the other members of its group, ritualized behaviors actually reduce the need for violence and harm to group members. Submissive movements (such as when an animal lowers its head and body while remaining quiet) also reduce violence; they are essential to the self-protection and survival of low-ranking animals.

Mammalian aggression and courtship displays are similar in many ways, and elements of the two are often intermingled. The submissive displays exhibited by both sexes are similar to the posture adopted by a female when she (the subordinate individual) presents herself to a male for mounting. The ways in which ritualized behaviors serve to coordinate the behavior of members of a species—as seen in courtship behaviors—provide a clear example of their fundamental functions. These conspicuous series of fixed action patterns synchronize the individuals' emotional states and behaviors in ways that lead directly to reproductive behaviors (copulation).

Although mammals face the same basic challenges as reptiles (acquiring food, avoiding predators, protecting resources against outsiders), the emergence of groups whose members have emotional attachments with one another and practice reciprocity has made social living one of the most important of all mammalian adaptations. It has been suggested that it was these group dynamics that gave rise to religiosity (see Box 4.3: Primate Belongingness as a Preadaptation for Religiosity).

The demands of group living have profoundly affected humans' emotional and cognitive evolution and have made ritualized behavior even more important to group coordination. The differences between reptilian and mammalian ritualized behaviors provide insights into the roles that the paleomammalian brain plays in generating the awareness that an individual belongs to a group and in creating the emotional bonds between the various members of the group.

Mammals use many of their ritualized behaviors to integrate members of the group into relatively stable hierarchies. For example, the mother–infant bond provides a context for grooming that will teach the infant an important mechanism for reducing aggression and maintaining friendships and alliances later in life. The ritualized play activities of young mammals enable them to practice adult behaviors and skills in a safe environment. The intensive social grooming found among primates serves a variety of biological, personal, and social purposes. The primitive emotional value of grooming becomes apparent when an animal grooms itself, for this behavior often occurs when the animal is in a state of conflict. In sum, ritualized behaviors enable individuals to coexist in large, emotionally stable, and hierarchically integrated groups.

Group and Intergroup Ritualized Behaviors in the Great Apes

The commonalities found in great apes' displays indicate the presence of similar behaviors in **hominins,** the common ancestors that humans share with chimpanzees. Group singing, chanting, drumming, and dancing are all aspects of religious rituals found in human cultures throughout the world because they have a biological basis and deep evolutionary roots in the same functions of the ritual behaviors found in other primates and our hominin ancestors. Such behaviors have their roots in the calls and hoots that primates use for a variety of social purposes, and that our hominan ancestors developed as excited synchronous singing and dancing among members of a group.

Emotional Vocalizations. The songs and vocalizations of chimpanzees are affective displays made during conditions of high arousal for purposes of making social contact and regulating interpersonal spacing. These calls facilitate communication between individuals and groups, and provide information about location, spacing, food sources, danger, group cohesion, and group unity. Pant–hooting also occurs when members rejoin the community after an absence or when they make contact with strange members of the species. Their structural and behavioral similarities indicate that loud calls are the communicative precursors of human singing and musical abilities. Among primates, natural selection has favored the abilities to use verbal aggression, exemplified in screaming and shouting, as part of intimidation displays used both within the group and to threaten other species, particularly predators. These vocalizations are a precursor to the singing and other forms of musicality that eventually allowed for the more nuanced expression of human emotions. Williams (1980) has characterized the cries of rage and anger—the passionate outbursts in both vocalization and behavior that exhibits the tension of the individual—as the pathogenic side of music. While it is present in all the apes and in most monkeys, humans epitomize this capability for passionate and emotional outburst (p. 73). Primate calls are emotive vocalizations that communicate to other members of the species and have motivational effects on them. Today's fight songs, battle songs, and national anthems, as well as babies' lullabies, children's medleys, and love songs, indicate that song and music have similar functions in human groups.

Alpha Male Displays. Aggressive displays such as bipedal charges and the shaking of branches are widespread behaviors among primates. Gorilla calls often incorporate chest-beating, running through the foliage, and breaking branches. Among chimpanzees, males predominantly perform loud calls, with the pant–hooting peak phase followed by bipedal charging displays. Most great apes have displays involving kicking; stomping; shaking branches; beating on the chest, ground, or vegetation; and jumping and running (Geissmann 2000). Both chimps and bonobos engage in vocalizations, drumming, and charging displays when defending their territory (De Waal 1997). These activities are a manifestation of the primate dominance drive, the need to exhibit superior power and receive deference from subordinates. This integrating mechanism is the basis of some of the most dramatic chimpanzee displays, which occur in the evening as the dispersed subgroups of the troop come together around a specific tree. The loud vocalizations as they gather in the protective branches of the trees and the dramatic charging displays in and around the trees provide an auditory beacon for dispersed members. The aggressive displays, which can continue as darkness settles, serve to intimidate the "others" who are out there in the darkness. They also help to reaffirm the existing social structure, as even chimpanzees that are not the objects of aggression can observe the dominant displays of the alpha males. These dramatic ritual expressions are an important tool for reintegrating the dispersed society into a single group.

Primate Preadaptations for Human Religiosity

Jane Goodall has documented a type of chimpanzee behavior that she describes as a "rain dance." During a heavy rain, Goodall watched as chimpanzees left the trees and moved to the top of a ridge. In response to a thunder burst, a big male stood up and began to stagger rhythmically, swaying from one foot to the other and producing pant–hoots. He then ran back to the trees, followed by other males who entered the trees and began to sway the branches. Others broke branches from the trees and dragged them along. They then ran back up the slope to the ridge and made repeated charges up and down the hill, often gesturing at the sky. The other chimps (females and youngsters) took up positions in trees on the ridge and watched the display.

The German psychologist Wolfgang Köhler frequently observed patterns of "dancing" in captive chimps. One chimp climbed onto a box and began to stomp from one foot to the other, shaking the box, while another began to slowly revolve around, springing clumsily from foot to foot. Sometimes this motion would develop into revolving around in a circle like a "spinning top," occasionally with arms extended. In a way, the gyrations resembled human dances. Sometimes a pair would play around a post, moving around it in a regular circular movement. Others would join in, trotting in single file around the post with an uneven rhythmic gait to which they would wag their heads in time. These behaviors expressed friendliness and amicability and were engaged in by the chimps with an eager enjoyment.

This is not human dance. But there is a distant connection between human and chimp displays. Drumming is at the root of the human ability to produce rhythmic sound and is the foundation of music. "Music began with rhythm. It began with the beating of sticks and logs and the stamping of feet, with shouts, cries, wailing, hand-claps, thigh-slaps and lip smacking, with the whole body moving and working in rhythmic action" (Williams 1980, p. 53).

While chimpanzees are capable of engaging in rhythmic body movements, including using their feet, legs, hands, and arms, their capabilities do not include a real sense of rhythm, such as an ability to keep time to music or a beat. Chimpanzees' ability to keep rhythm is limited, mechanical, and not based on a feeling of the rhythm itself. Nor do they appear to respond to sustained rhythmic beats or to be motivated by rhythmic tempo. The noise of a drum may excite them, but the rhythm does not drive them the way it causes humans to respond. "[T]he chimpanzee has enjoyed the reputation of being a natural performer. But dancing and singing spring from a stranger impulse and a harder discipline that any he can know" (Williams 1980, p. 57). "The ape has no feeling for the unifying power of rhythmic sound. In the vocalizing

and rhythmic action of apes we do not find the elements, nor even the beginnings of the chant and dance ritual of primitive man, even though such action may be regarded as a precursor to primitive mimetic ritual" (p. 70).

Jane Goodall's remarks about the chimpanzee "rain dance" included the comment: "With a display of strength and vigor such as this, primitive man himself might have challenged the elements" (van Lawick-Goodall 1968, p. 53). This comment underscores the perceptions of Goodall and other primate researchers that some of the behaviors typically associated with religiosity were already present in our prehuman ancestors.

Clearly, though, these behaviors are social and emotional expressions rather than the worship of distant Gods or expressions of gratitude toward dead ancestors. For this reason, it is more appropriate to regard these aspects of animal—and especially primate—behavior as preadaptations for religion, not actual evidence of religion. A **preadaptation** is a trait that serves an adaptive function in a species in a particular environment and that, with only minor modifications, can be used by later generations in substantially different ways to survive in other environments. For example, the lobed fins of certain types of fish could, with only minimal changes, evolve into the early limbs of the first terrestrial vertebrates. Some humans appear to be resistant to the virus that causes AIDS because their ancestors were exposed to and survived bubonic plague. A difference in a protein found on the cell membranes of people whose ancestors were plague survivors inhibits the ability of HIV to penetrate into their cells so that it can reproduce. These individuals are *preadapted* to resist HIV.

A number of aspects of chimpanzee rituals—such as charging displays; stomping and drumming; shaking branches; beating on the chest, ground, or vegetation; and jumping and running—can be regarded as preadaptations for human religious activities—in particular, shamanism (which we will discuss in Chapter 5). Notably, chimpanzees often direct these activities not toward the nearby members of their own group, but toward *unseen* others. Drumming on trees signals an individual's presence both to the unseen members of its own group and to members of other groups. Thus, drumming is both a means to join individuals scattered over a distance and a way to signal boundaries by representing the presence of self to others.

Group vocalizations provide an emotional communication system that promotes social well-being, empathy, and social and cognitive integration. The call

Box 4.4 RITUAL DISPLAYS AS COSTLY SIGNALING MECHANISMS

Many aspects of ritualized behaviors are clearly self-serving. Dominant animals do not need to risk injury to receive respect and deference, and lower-ranking animals can avoid injury by displaying subordinance. Many aspects of sexual displays are designed to call attention to unusual or dramatic features, such as the extensive plumage displayed by the male peacock. While such eye-catching large feathers attract females as mates, they also have a certain cost in making the peacock a larger and more visible target for predators. The increased risk of exposure that results from the prominence the individual has because of such selected features has led some researchers to regard rituals as "costly signaling mechanisms." This notion is based on the idea that an individual that can survive in spite of the costs associated with specific features is displaying "excessive fitness."

For instance, the individual in a flock of birds or troop of baboons that first sounds the alarm when a predator is present seems to be calling additional attention to itself. During a ritual warning, an animal may engage in such conspicuous behaviors as jumping and hopping. Although calling attention to the individual, these visible behaviors reveal a disposition to act, a preparedness that may dissuade a potential predator to look for less active, robust, and vigilant prey. As a result, an animal that gives a ritual signal warning to its kin may also dissuade predators and reduce the need to flee. The signaling benefits both signaler and kin.

episodes of the great apes facilitate communication both within the group and toward outsiders. They provide information about the group's location, spacing, food sources, and danger, and enhance group cohesion and unity. But in humans, vocalizations took on an additional role in religiosity. Now primate call and vocalization systems are viewed as preadaptations that underlie the human capacities of song, music, and chanting, all of them activities that play an important role in religious ceremonies.

The group vocalizations observed in many mammalian species have their closest human parallels in the ritualized synchronous group singing that is at the core of humans' shamanic rituals. As in nonhuman primates, group vocalizations such as chanting and singing serve as an expressive system for communicating emotional states, motivating other members of the species, and managing social contact and mate attraction. Drumming and dancing, which are universally associated with shamanism, also have deep evolutionary roots as mammalian signaling mechanisms. Such vigorous activity signals one's location to others—both allies and potential enemies—and is an important indicator of fitness because it communicates vigilance and a readiness to act. "An amazing variety of mammals produce seismic vibrations by drumming a part of their body on a substrate. The drumming can communicate multiple messages to conspecifics about territorial ownership, competitive superiority, submission, readiness to mate, or the presence of predators.

Drumming also functions in interspecies communication when prey animals drum to communicate to predators that they are too alert for a successful ambush" (Randall 2001, p. 1). Drumming is widespread among mammals to convey information, a so-called costly signaling mechanism that displays fitness and reduces the need for action (see Box 4.4: Ritual Displays as Costly Signaling Mechanisms).

The related display and vocalization activities that have been observed among the great apes and among chimpanzees in particular indicate that our hominin ancestors, as well as the early **hominans**—ancestors of the uniquely human line—also participated in excited synchronous singing and dancing among members of a territorial group. The singing, chanting, and dancing characteristic of human rituals have a biological basis and deep evolutionary roots in the ritualized calls, hoots, and group enactments that animals use for a variety of social purposes. The functional effects of chimpanzee ritualized behaviors indicate the adaptive bases from which the human religious capacities evolved. It is not just the need for a sense of belongingness that provides us with the basis for the human capacity for religiosity, but rather these dramatic multifunctional threat displays.

Activities found among chimpanzees indicate that our hominin ancestors had developed social adaptations involving excited synchronous singing and dancing among members of a territorial group. These activities united and integrated the group each evening. Vocalizations that were the precursors of singing and chanting were part of affective displays made during conditions of high arousal that helped to maintain social contact and that signaled each performer's presence and emotional state to other members of the group. The pant–hooting served as a mechanism that helped individuals who had strayed to relocate the group. This example illustrates a basic adaptive mechanism of ritual. Pant–hooting and drumming provide both a system of long-distance communication and a reinforcement of the functions of threat and dominance displays. The role of ritual in the intimidation of both the immediately present "others" and the unseen "others" is illustrated in the use of dominance displays, which are dramatic enough that they intimidate other members of an individual's group, members of other groups that may be nearby, and even predators. The noise and drumming of these rituals also help to establish the group's home territory vis-à-vis the territories of neighboring groups of the species. This most complex chimpanzee ritual involves a communal activity that both unites the group and sets it in contrast with other groups, and involves many homologies with the shamanistic rituals found cross-culturally among technologically simple human societies.

Adaptive Features of Chimpanzee Threat Displays. The threat displays of chimpanzees include a wide range of behaviors that provide a variety of functional adaptations:

- establishing and maintaining status and order in society
- protecting the group and the individual from the physical harm of fighting
- establishing and maintaining boundaries among groups
- producing emotional synchrony within the group
- releasing tension and frustration
- protecting the group members from predators
- providing a group identity, exemplified in the shaping of vocalizations to mimic dominant group males
- creating an auditory beacon for group fusion, facilitating the reintegration of individuals into the protective community

Together, these illustrate a variety of common preadaptations for uniquely human rituals. So how close are chimpanzees to humans, and what is the gap between their behaviors and human religiosity?

Identifying the Roots of Human Religiosity in Ritualized Behaviors

The anthropologist Anthony F. C. Wallace (1966) has identified thirteen basic elements of human religious behavior. Religious rituals are composed of specific constellations and sequences of these behaviors:

1. prayer, which incorporates specific body postures and gestures used to petition or thank supernatural beings
2. activities such as music, dancing, and singing
3. induction of ecstatic spiritual states (altered states of consciousness)
4. exhortation, addressing supernatural entities for their intercession
5. recitation of a code, a succinct statement of core beliefs
6. simulation, a symbolic representation of one thing with another
7. mana, an impersonal supernatural power that can be transferred
8. taboo, a prohibited power
9. feasts, the sharing of food
10. sacrifice, giving up something desirable to achieve a supernatural goal
11. congregation, a gathering of individuals
12. inspiration, the experience of supernatural intervention in life
13. symbolic expressions of supernatural beliefs

Can we find equivalent ritualized behaviors in chimpanzees and other animals? If we reconceptualize the spirit relationships typical of religious rituals in a more general way that emphasizes relationships to "others," then we find that many aspects of ritualized animal behaviors are homologous to human behaviors:

1. postures of submission to dominant animals or for making requests
2. activities of chanting and dancing, particularly in a group
3. activities that can alter consciousness (in humans), such as drumming
4. vocal challenges to unseen others
5. repeated vocalizations that express intentions
6. reading signs of other animals' intentions
7. wanting to touch powerful others

8. avoidance of contaminated areas

9. sharing of food

10. sacrificing body parts to escape

11. group congregation with performances by alpha males

12. sensing the presence of unseen others

13. symbolic representations of dominance and submission

Of Wallace's thirteen ritual elements, the animal homologies that appear to have the greatest relevance for understanding the roots of religiosity include

- ritualized postures that show submission to dominant animals or that attempt to gain their support;
- collective group rituals involving vocal performances;
- ritual acts where alpha males direct aggression toward unseen others;
- activities involving singing, dancing, and drumming;
- behaviors for challenging powerful others, particularly postures and vocalizations;
- vocalizations that express desires and intentions;
- behaviors related to sensing and responding to unseen others;
- contexts in which food is shared with others; and
- symbolic representations, including social status, misdirections, and deceit.

Comparing the Minimal Elements of Chimpanzee Ritualized Behaviors and Human Rituals. There are clear similarities between certain elements of ritualized animal behaviors and human religious rituals (see Table 4.1). The ways that animals and humans signal submission are strikingly similar. Both humans and animals engage in ritual activities that deliberately attempt to affect consciousness in themselves and other members of the group. Both manifest "superstitious" attractions to, avoidances of, and behavioral responses to items in their environment. Although the sacrifices that humans make are far more extensive, animals do make sacrifices. They may give up their lives to protect their offspring or another member of their group, and they may sacrifice a body part to escape danger. Human religious congregations are more extensive than animal groups, but produce the same unifying effects. Humans' trance behaviors share underlying similarities with animal hypnotizability and appear to serve similar functions in the management of stress.

There are also, of course, obvious differences between animal and human rituals. Animals signal submission more frequently than humans, and they submit to the more powerful members of their groups, not to any Gods. The chanting and "dancing" of animals represents some of their most complex behaviors, whereas chanting and dancing are some of our most "primitive" human behaviors. Most ritualized animal behaviors have communication as the primary goal. The screams and aggressive displays of chimpanzees are more dramatic than the exhortations of humans, while the latter refer to a much more extensive network of beings and a much more complex mythological system. Humans' magical rituals embody a high degree of imitation, a behavioral capacity that is very limited in animals. Similarly our human concepts of mana, taboo, and supernatural power are much more developed than animals' sense of the power of others. The religious feasting of humans bears little resemblance to the sharing of food found in chimpanzees and is a behavior that is virtually nonexistent in other animals (except for parent–infant feeding). Although human religious symbolism is virtually lacking in animals, ritualized behaviors themselves are forms of primitive symbolization that provide the most complex communicative behaviors of animal species. How close do these behaviors come to human ritual and religion?

Is There a "Family of Resemblances" Link with Chimpanzee Ritualized Behaviors? Recalling that we have conceptualized religions as a "family of resemblances" sharing common features, we can see that while some of these features are found in animal rituals, others are not. The shared "family of resemblances" found in chimpanzee's ritualized behaviors include

- ritualized activities and ceremonies,
- activities and relationships that organize a socially defined community,
- ritualized behaviors for communicating with and influencing "other" beings, and
- ritualized behaviors that evoke personal experiences and emotions.

Some of the notably absent elements of the "family of resemblances" in chimpanzees' ritualized behaviors are

- a worldview that organizes both personal and group life;
- supernatural beings, such as spirits, Gods, demons, and ghosts;
- a cosmology and mythology that explains the origins of the world and beings;

Table 4-1 A Comparison of the Human Ritual Activities with Behaviors Exhibited by Chimpanzees

Wallace's Categories	Human Ritual Activities	Chimpanzee Ritualized Behaviors
Prayer	Addressing the supernatural	Postures of submission to dominant animals and gestures for making requests
Music	Dancing, singing, and playing instruments	Group vocalizations, particularly chorusing in group activities
Physiological exercise	Physical manipulation of psychological states	Extreme displays and activities that are known to alter consciousness when humans perform them, such as drumming
Exhortation	An intermediary addressing the supernatural	Alpha displays that address "unseen others" with vocal challenges
Reciting the code	Mythology, morality, and other aspects of the belief system	Vocal performances that express intentions or challenge others
Simulation	Imitating things	Imitation of possible actions; threatening but not attacking
Mana	Touching things	Wanting to touch or be near powerful others or be touched by them (e.g., through grooming)
Taboo	Avoiding touching things	Avoidance of contaminated objects and of powerful individuals
Feasts	Eating and drinking	Sharing of food; cannibalism
Sacrifice	Giving something of value to a supernatural power	Giving food or mating partners to others; sacrificing body parts to escape
Congregation	Processions, meetings, and convocations	Group gatherings with performances by alpha males; chorusing and "concerts"
Inspiration	Sudden acquisition of knowledge from supernatural forces	Trance-like behaviors, hypnotizability
Symbolism	Manufacture and use of objects with meaning and power	Symbolic representation of dominance and submission, as well as deceit

- a domain regarded as sacred—distinct from the ordinary profane world; and
- a moral or ethical system.

The similarities indicate the roots of religion in communal rituals and their emotional effects, while the uniquely human dynamics of religion involve the development of supernatural concepts, moral systems, and mythical explanations.

Conclusions: The Animal Roots of Human Ritual Activity

Displays and other ritualized behaviors represent the most complex behaviors of which animals are capable. These provide systems for communication that unite social groups and organize the behavior of the members. This chapter examined a range of ritualized behaviors, beginning with reptiles and continuing through mammals, primates, and, finally, the chimpanzees. Chimpanzee displays provide important adaptations for their societies and presumably played similar roles early in human evolution. Although the similarities between the ritualized behaviors of chimpanzee and human rituals illustrate our common hominin heritage and capacities, the differences or "gap" between them provides a framework for identifying the evolutionary developments of hominans that produced uniquely human religiosity.

Of all animals, humans are the most flexible in their behavior and thinking. Because we are able to rely on learned rather than innate models of interpreting and acting within the Universe, we have flexible methods for fulfilling both individual and group needs. Although we now have a wider range of responses to the world than any other animal that has ever lived, much of our behavior still reflects the basic biological drives that are hard-wired into the more primitive parts of our brains and expressed through routinization and ritualized behavior.

Reptilian behaviors continue to find expression in human life. We establish homesites, patrol and defend territories, perform courtship displays, and demonstrate submission before our superiors. We often find ourselves doing the same thing at the same time as others (isopraxis), such as when one person yawns and others immediately do as well or when we find our footsteps matching those of the person walking next to us. We have "instinctual" (tropistic) aversions to certain tastes and smells, and an entire industry has developed around the idea of using different colors and scents to produce specific moods. And we continue to act in (deceptive) manners that mislead others, although we now have a new tool to help us in this purpose: language. But while these behaviors bear witness to the continued role of the "reptilian" part of our brain in our lives, our behaviors are also now controlled by the other two parts of our brains.

As mammals, social living is programmed into our brains. But our complex brains now produce a wider range of emotional responses to our groups, while our behavioral and cognitive plasticity have given rise to new groups for us to identify with (country, profession, political party, church) and new ways to ritually display and communicate both our individual and our group identity (clothing, adornment, salutes, religious symbols). We now identify with many more people than we can ever know, and our notions of territoriality are no longer restricted to the actual space in which we pursue our daily activities. Language allows us to create new worlds of meaning and labels for our inner experiences, as well as elaborate systems of rules for behavior.

But once again, the centrality of our basic drives is illustrated in the focus of many of these rules, which aim at controlling or modifying our "baser instincts" (i.e., sex, aggression). Different religious groups now champion nonaggression (for example, the Hindu concept of *ahimsa,* or nonviolence), practice voluntary dietary restrictions (abstinence from pork, beef, or shellfish), and pledge themselves to lives of sexual abstinence (priests, monks, and nuns). The reptilian brain nonetheless continues to regulate our internal processes, and it controls many of our motor responses to the world and to each other. The information it sends to the paleomammalian brain and the neocortex is also processed by both of these. This arrangement permits a kind of "parallel processing" so that the brain can deal with two sets of information simultaneously, but in different "programming languages" (emotional versus conceptual).

Rituals represent an important method for simultaneously engaging all three parts of the brain. Many human religious rituals intentionally aim at coordinating our behaviors, emotions, and thoughts by using a stereotyped set of sounds, movements, and other sensory and motor input to produce emotions that intensify the bonds within the group while validating our culturally learned ideas about the Universe.

The ritualized behaviors that are important adaptations in the animal world do not exemplify the "family of resemblance" definition we considered earlier or the features of religiosity as we know it today. Religion seems to be a uniquely human practice. But the idea of looking at nonhuman animals for insights into the roots of religiosity is a scientific approach based on evolutionary theory. A chimpanzee's DNA is more like our own than it is like even a gorilla's. Consequently, our two species exhibit numerous similarities in our bodies, our societies, and our behaviors. In both size and structure, chimpanzee societies resemble the human hunter–gatherer societies in which all humans are thought to have lived until perhaps 15,000 years ago. In both societies, the size of the group varies throughout the day as activity patterns change. In both groups, males typically remain in the group into which they were born, whereas females leave to mate with the members of other groups. Faced with many easily observable similarities, we can expect that there are other similarities we cannot directly observe, such as how group conflict and aggression were managed in chimpanzees and in humans' ancestral past. But since the great apes share a common heritage of ritualized behaviors, we can assume that similar behaviors were manifested by our common hominin ancestor with chimpanzees that lived perhaps 5–7 million years ago.

What happened in the millions of years of evolution between our hominin ancestors and the emergence of the hominan ancestors who showed the first clear expressions of religious behavior? Our quest to understand how religiosity has evolved must now turn to the archaeological evidence and cross-cultural data that illuminate the patterns of religiosity found in ancient human societies. The next chapter will take the baseline of hominin ritual established in this chapter and examine various forms of evidence regarding the appearance of new religious features in human evolution. Something happened to our newly evolved hominan ancestors that brought a range of features together and sparked the emergence of a uniquely human religiosity. Its first expression was shamanism, a cross-cultural form of religiosity that was central to the modern humans' cultural explosion that emerged around 45,000 years ago.

Questions for Discussion

- What are some of your behaviors that reptiles also do? What are some that other mammals also do?
- How do the ways that humans signal dominance and submission differ from the ways that chimps do? How are they similar?
- What types of nonverbal behaviors are uniquely human?

Glossary

alpha male the dominant member of a mammalian social group

analysis a cognitive ability that identifies the various parts that make up a whole and their relationships and effects

courtship display a behavior that indicates that an individual is ready to mate

deception a type of display in which an animal communicates an "erroneous" message that helps it to survive

displays behaviors that serve to communicate information from one member of a species to another

fixed action pattern a species-specific sequence of behaviors that leads to a particular outcome

hominans ancestors of the uniquely human line of hominids

hominins the common ancestors that humans share with chimpanzees

homologous traits features that are similar in related species because they have been inherited from a common ancestor

intention movement a behavior which signals that an animal is ready to engage in some type of behavior

isopraxic behavior a type of animal ritual behavior in which two or more individuals simultaneously perform the same action

neocortex the most recently evolved portion of the triune brain; the part that is responsible for cognition

paleomammalian brain the part of the triune brain that is responsible for emotions

play an activity in which young mammals refine their instinctual abilities by practicing the behaviors they will need as adults

preadaptation a trait that serves an adaptive purpose in one environment but that may become useful for a different purpose in another environment

reciprocity the act of giving one service or resource in exchange for another

reenactment the process of repeating a number of activities in essentially the same sequence at different times

repetitious behavior a type of display in which an animal repeatedly performs a specific act

reptilian brain the most primitive layer of the triune brain, primarily responsible for behavior

ritualized behavior a sequence of animal displays

ritual a stereotyped and repetitive set of behaviors that coordinate a social group in order to achieve a common goal or purpose

routinization the process by which an animal comes to perform specific behaviors at certain places and times

signature display a behavior that enables one member of a species to recognize another

submissive display a behavior in which one animal makes itself appear smaller, thereby signaling that it recognizes another animal's dominance

synthesis a cognitive ability in which different components are linked together to produce a large-scale idea

territorial display a demonstration to an intruder that the resident is ready to defend an area

tropistic behavior an instinctual, automatic response to a stimulus

The Origins of Shamanism and the Flowering of Religiosity

CHAPTER OUTLINE

CHAPTER OBJECTIVES

- Characterize the primordial form of human religiosity involving shamanism
- Contrast shamanic rituals and chimpanzee ritualized behaviors to characterize the gap with respect to human religiosity
- Examine the evolution of capacities for spiritual experiences
- Analyze Paleolithic cave art as evidence of shamanism and new forms of representation
- Illustrate the role of shamanic practices in the emergence of modern culture and illustrate the adaptive features of these practices
- Examine the prehistoric emergence of new forms of religious activity in fertility and ancestor cults

THE FEMALES BUILT THE FIRE NEAR WHERE THEY would spend the night. When it was ready, they gathered around it and began to sing. At first, just one or two of them could be heard, but soon others joined in a loud chorus. The young boys began to dance in a circle around the group, practicing their steps. As more people arrived, the women pressed closer together, swaying in unison to the rhythm of their song. The dancers' excitement increased, and their feet pounded out a powerful rhythm that vibrated through the ground. Some of the dancers joined in the song, their loud voices pushing it into a new direction. Suddenly, one of the dancers fell to the ground, and others rushed over to watch over him. Then another man broke off his dance and ran off into the darkness.

Several other males chased after him and guided him back to the circle as he continued to shout threats at the spirits. They rubbed him to calm him down. A third male looked into the darkness surrounding the dancers and yelled challenges to the spirits. Such incidents occurred throughout the night.

Introduction: Evidence for the Emergence of New Forms of Ritual

This passage describes a healing dance ritual of the Dobe area !Kung, a nomadic group of African foragers studied by anthropologist Richard Katz (Katz 1982).

A Dobe !Kung healing circle.

For the !Kung, the most powerful force that exists is *num*. By dancing and singing, the !Kung can activate the *num* and enter *kia*, an extraordinary state in which they can heal themselves and one another.

The Dobe !Kung live in the desert region that straddles the border between Botswana and Namibia. The border in that area is a straight line that has nothing to do with the geography of the land or the ways the !Kung live on it (see Fig. 5.1). But it splits their territory in two, a poignant symbol of the changes being imposed upon the !Kung and thousands of other societies around the world as forces beyond their control sweep aside their ancient ways. And yet, in spite of seemingly unstoppable change, the ancient ways live on in us all. For, like the !Kung, people everywhere continue to perform rituals that include percussion and singing, rhythmic movements, group vocalizations, and calls to unseen forces.

To understand the reasons why this is, we now need to consider the continuities and the differences between the largely instinctual patterns of ritualized animal behavior and the primarily acquired patterns of human religious behavior. Although we now learn our religious behaviors as we grow up within a culture, many features of human religious practice still echo the largely instinctual patterns of ritualized animal behaviors. But there are also many important differences: Our rituals are more nuanced, more complex, and more easily changed. And they involve

more than just behavior, for the other two components of culture—material objects and ideational concepts and values—are now interwoven into them. As a result, humans now use rituals not only to assert dominance, defend a territory, or find mates, but also to combat diseases, contact spirits, and pay homage to our ancestors.

The evidence contained in the archaeological record suggests that the full flowering of religiosity did not occur until around 30,000–40,000 years ago. What happened? What evolutionary events led to the emergence of religiosity? Was there one watershed genetic change that caused the "religious switch" to be thrown? Or were there distinct stages in the development of religiosity, small incremental steps toward its final appearance in modern forms? The evidence suggests that the second view is more accurate.

To consider this evidence, we need to expand our discussions beyond the biological framework provided by evolutionary theory. A biocultural model, the **shamanic paradigm**, will help us link human and animal behaviors in order to identify their homologies and the preadaptations that gave rise to the first expressions of human religiosity. The shamanic paradigm also enables us to identify the universals of premodern religions and, using these, to infer the religious practices of the distant past. This provides us with a perspective for considering the changes produced in human society and religion as cultures evolved.

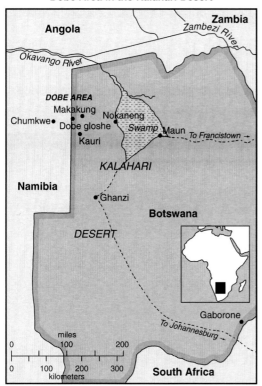

Dobe Area in the Kalahari Desert

Figure 5.1 Colonial-era surveyors drew a national border line (between Namibia and Botswana) directly through the territory in which the Dobe !Kung have long lived.

("Dobe Area in the Kalahari Desert" reprinted by permission of the publisher from *Boiling Energy: Community Healing Among the Kalahari Kung* by Richard Katz, p. xvi, Cambridge, Mass.: Harvard University Press, Copyright © 1982 by the President and Fellows of Harvard College.)

Interpretation in Archaeology: Ethnographic and Ethnological Analogy

It is archaeology that provides us with our most important window on early religiosity. The artifacts left behind by our hominan ancestors are the only material evidence we have that documents the emergence of human culture. But what does this evidence mean? To answer this, archaeologists use ethnographic analogy (see Chapter 1), which provides insights from specific cultures) and ethnological analogy, which tells us about the universal features of different types of societies today. Together, these enable us to make general statements about societies of the past.

For instance, studies of foraging (hunter–gatherer) societies around the world allow us to safely infer that men have been the primary hunters in all foraging societies that have ever existed. Similarly, the common

patterns in the religious practices of foraging societies permit us to make inferences about the religious behaviors of foragers in the past and to contemplate the origins of religiosity. It is important to note that contemporary foragers are not living examples of our ancient human ancestors. But the common patterns of subsistence, social organization, and ideology found among all foraging groups provide us with useful guidelines for making inferences about the ritual behaviors of the prehistoric past.

What types of behaviors were occurring before religious rituals first emerged? As we saw in Chapter 4, our hominin ancestors were likely performing ritualized behaviors directed toward "unseen others." Alpha males were performing dramatic and public displays that included vocalizations and rhythmic drumming. As with modern chimpanzees, these activities would have played important roles during territorial disputes, when predators were encountered, and in the nocturnal activities that brought the group together. Gradually, over the course of hominan evolution, the expressions and structures of these rituals became more elaborate. At some point, our ancestors acquired an ability to experience a spiritual world and an ability to express those conceptions in a mythic world by acting it out, an ability known as **mimesis**. These early rituals, which built on the preadaptations provided by chimpanzee ritualized behaviors, provided the basis for shamanism.

Shamanism is thought to have emerged as an adaptive response to inhospitable environments that favored those who were able to forge close bonds with outside groups that could provide the assistance—particularly the food resources—to deal with temporary shortages (Hayden 2003). Ritual activities were particularly valuable in enhancing emotional bonding and establishing alliances that lasted across time. This helped to override the typical mammalian tendency to identify with one's own group and exclude outsiders. Group rituals that helped to forge bonds between individuals of different groups created a larger community with greater access to resources. Shamans were the key actors in these integrative rituals.

What Are Shamans?

The word **shaman** was derived from European contact with the Tungusic language of Central Asia. Today, it is used as a comparative (etic) term to refer to a religious practitioner found in foraging and many other small-scale societies around the world. The original Tungusic term, *šaman*, means "one who shakes," and refers to the shaman's agitated condition as he enters into an "ecstatic" state of consciousness. Cross-cultural research shows that both shamans and the states of ritual ecstasy that are induced in group ceremonies are found in societies around the world and share many features in common (Winkelman 1992, 2000).

Although both men and women can be shamans, the shamans of foraging societies are predominantly males. Shamans are charismatic figures who provide leadership to their groups by conducting the central community rituals, especially those intended to heal and protect members of the community. Shamanic rituals are unparalleled in the life of a community. No other activity has greater public importance or participation. In contemporary foraging societies, these rituals are typically nocturnal events in which the entire local community congregates around a fire, often forming a circle. The shaman generally dances around the group while drumming, shaking a rattle, or clapping, and exhorting the spirits through ancient songs and chants. Often, other members of the community join in. The shaman communicates with the spirits, and asks his personal spirits to come and assist him while exhorting evil spirits to leave and cease their afflictions. The shaman may mimic or act out his struggles with the spirits, the behaviors of the animals whose powers he has summoned, and his journey through the spirit realms.

The key to the ritual performance of the shaman is his ability to enter into an "ecstatic" state (from *ec*, "out of" and *stasis*, "the state of standing," hence to be outside of a "normal" mode of functioning, or "standing outside of one's self," as in an "out-of-the-body" experience). Often accompanied by assistants and the community, the shaman may spend hours dancing, drumming, and chanting to deliberately induce this state in himself and other members of the community. (The description of the !Kung healing ritual that opened this chapter provides an example.) A shaman experiences these profound experiences as a "soul journey" or "magical flight" in which he leaves his body and travels to the spirit world. There the shaman appeals for help in healing, divination, communicating with the dead, recovering lost souls, protecting against other spirits and sorcerers, and finding animals (see Box 5.1: Hunting in Human Evolution).

The animal and plant spirits that the shaman acquires provide him with numerous powers and abilities, including the potential to transform into animals (the shaman's spirit allies). When a shaman transforms into one of his spirit allies, he temporarily acquires that animal's capabilities. For example, if a shaman's spirit ally is a bear, he can learn to travel like a bear and to have the strength, ferocity, and endurance of his spirit ally. If his spirit ally is an eagle, the shaman will learn to fly like the eagle and use its keen eyesight to see what is transpiring below.

The shaman typically first encounters these spirits during a "vision quest" that is part of his training and development. During this quest, initiates are expected to encounter spirit allies who will teach them the powers that they will develop during their lives. Although older shamans sometimes supervise and guide the initiates during their vision quests, a shaman usually encounters the spirit powers alone, and he must confront them in an attempt to dominate and control them. Shamanic initiations typically involve experiences of one's own death and subsequent rebirth. This experience often occurs in conjunction with visions in which the shaman is torn apart by the spirit beings. The spirits then reassemble the shaman into a stronger and more knowledgeable person with powers to enter the invisible worlds and perceive things that other people cannot. It is because of the shaman's personal experience of death and his knowledge of the spirits and the ways to control them that he is able to find lost souls and to guide the souls of the deceased to their destination in the afterlife.

The shamanic worldview is multidimensional and takes different forms in different cultures. In general, shamanic cultures view the world as consisting of at least three distinct realms. Humans occupy the middle world, while spirits and other supernatural beings are found in both this world and in the upper and lower worlds. These different realms are connected by an *axis mundi* or world tree. The beings found in these different realms have different powers that they use to keep the Universe functioning and in balance. Shamans can learn many things from these beings, such as how to travel along the paths that connect the worlds and how to acquire and use the powers of the spirit beings. This knowledge allows them to journey throughout the Universe in quest of the knowledge they need to help their community. Because the shaman regularly travels into these realms, he is able to develop a "map" of these worlds and of the paths between them. As a consequence, shamans are able to help others to navigate between and within these realms. Experienced shamans will often teach initiates to find their way around the spirit worlds and help the souls of the dead to make their way to the next world.

Some anthropologists have disputed the universality and cross-cultural nature of shamans and have questioned

Box 5.1 HUNTING IN HUMAN EVOLUTION

The highly skilled hunting behaviors of chimpanzees strongly indicate that our common hominid ancestor was also a skilled hunter. A significant part of human evolution involves enhanced cultural skills that aided humans in their transformation from prey for other animals into hunters. A key element of hunting involves the adoption of various animals' behaviors, which grew into imitation and disguise of hunters as animals. Hunting activities contributed to a conceptualization of self in terms of the ability to acquire power over animals, based in the knowledge of their habits, behaviors, and strengths. This power began through deception and imitation, mimicking the vocal calls of animals to attract them or to cover the hunter's own noise. The emergence of this imitative capacity from the disguise and concealment practices of hunters is directly linked to the roots of one aspect of shamanism, the role as master of the animals.

Hunting likely engaged and selected for the mimetic capacity, the ability to imitate, which would have directly enhanced hunting success through the ability to engage in deception through imitation. Imitation also played a role in teaching about hunting and animal behaviors. The imitation used by early humans to facilitate concealment while hunting must have produced through association a greater sense of identification with the animal. This enactment of the "other as animal" must have been part of the evolution of public ritual as successful hunters re-enacted their exploits. Such enactment was also likely training and psychotherapeutic adjustment. Many animals—not just predators, but also game animals such as deer, caribou, boar, and buffalo—posed a serious risk of death to hunters; their knowledge of possible death undoubtedly induced fear. Hodgson and Helvenston (2006) suggest that the common practice of imitating predatory animals during rituals may reflect "a compensatory strategy for gaining some 'control' over their most feared predator by means of ritual dancing and singing that deliberately induces a trance" (p. 8). They propose that the behavioral paralysis and the nonresponsive attitude typified by humans in trances are homologous to the freezing response exhibited by most mammals and primates when they are in the presence of dangerous predators. Because predators respond to movement, such freezing is adaptive.

Hunting in Limbic and Emotional Evolution

Hodgson and Helvenston (2006) propose that hunting directly stimulated the evolution of the limbic system (the paleomammalian brain), which is central to primate emotions, learning, and memory, and which is the anatomical basis of the reward system related to hunting behavior in carnivores. This reward system is elicited by a direct neural pathway linking the limbic system with input from the retinal–thalamic pathways, providing input for dealing with potentially threatening environmental features. As the primate limbic system evolved, the connections among the principal cortices of the brain (limbic, frontal, and motor) became enhanced. These enhanced connections provided a basis for greater emotional and behavioral responses, guided by an enhanced cognitive capacity. There were also increases in the limbic system and components such as the hippocampus and amygdala; Hodgson and Helvenston (2006) suggest that hunting played a role in selection for enhancement of these areas.

Hunting dangerous animals can evoke a variety of emotions. Hunting stimulates feelings not only of fear, dread, and horror, but also wonder, veneration, and the anticipation of a good meal. Hunting must be seen as a central feature enhancing consciousness and awareness of death, as hunting kills animals and exposes oneself to the risk of death as well. Ritual encounters were used to prepare hunters for these life-threatening activities. These adaptive complexes related to animals and death are core features of shamanism.

whether shamans were indeed the "original" religious specialists. Winkelman's (1992) cross-cultural study demonstrates that shamans represent a universal type of religious figure in both ancient and near-contemporary foraging societies. The universal presence of shamans in these societies points to a biological basis for features associated with shamanism and provides a shamanic paradigm for assessing when features of religiosity first appeared.

Shamanic Universals in Biological Perspective

Winkelman (2000) has proposed that the cross-cultural manifestations of shamanism are the result of our evolved psychology—a pattern of ritual adaptations derived from our ability to enter into altered states of consciousness that provide spiritual experiences and access aspects of our mental hardware to produce integrative experiences. Shamanism combines primate ritual capacities with uniquely human cognitive hardware capacities—**innate modules**—to enhance social and psychological integration (Winkelman 2000). Shamanism provided an adaptive strategy for integrating a variety of capacities—biological, social, and cognitive—that contributed to human evolution, adaptation, and survival.

The uniformities in shamanic practitioners and practices worldwide reflect biological bases involving

1. brain processes related to the biological roots and functions of ritual involving dominance displays that serve as a social communication and coordination system;

2. community bonding rituals that manipulate mammalian opioid-attachment mechanisms to help assure well-being through enhanced access to resources and social support;

3. altered states of consciousness that produce an integrative mode of consciousness characterized by cognitive integration;

4. shamanic soul flight and visionary experiences, which reflect the informational capacity for dreaming known as presentational symbolism;

5. manipulation of innate mental hardware, or cognitive operators, using our innate animal representation system as a model for personal and social identification; and

6. integrative forms of thought manifested in visions produced through blending or integration of various innate representational systems (Winkelman 2000, 2002b).

Shamanic rituals involve group activities, vocalizations, ritual dancing, and the imitation of desired goals. These activities are derived from the same biological structures and functions that help animals to communicate with one another and coordinate their behavior. These enactment and communicative activities involve the reptilian brain and paleomammalian brain, which provide systems of meaning in behavior and emotional vocalizations, respectively. Human rituals elaborate on these communicative and integrative functions, first by using mimesis as a system to expand expression of intentions and later by using symbolic systems. These symbolic systems are produced by the integration of the representational functions of humans' mental hardware. By using ritual ASC to integrate the processes of the specialized components of the mental hardware, shamanic practices

produce symbolic thought, represented in the shamanic metaphors of soul flight, animal allies, spirits, and death-and-rebirth experiences.

The relationships between the physiological foundations of ritual and the psychological aspects of shamanism can be seen when we examine the biological and evolutionary roots for community rituals, healing activities, spirit concepts, and integrative altered states of consciousness. The retention of prior adaptations in processes of biological evolution is illustrated in the preservation in shamanism of the previous adaptive structures found in ritual activities of other animals. Shamanism incorporates the mammalian ritual processes that facilitate community bonding and attachment. The uniquely human foundations of shamanism are found in the adaptive functions produced by the creation of new forms of cognition and symbolic healing processes. These are manifested in the roles of animal spirit concepts in the formation of personal and social identities, and in the information processing and integration provided in the visionary images of shamanic states of consciousness. These images provide information for personal development (individuation), social integration, cognitive and emotional integration, and symbolic healing.

The biological bases and adaptive aspects underlying the core aspects of shamanism involve its ritual nature as a social communication system, the adaptive mechanisms involved in community rituals (which have a variety of healing effects), the altered states of consciousness central to shamanic experiences and healing practices, the spirit relations that involve forms of self and other representations, and the metaphoric systems of thought produced by integration of different innate representational systems.

Shamanic Continuities with and Differences from Chimpanzee Ritualized Behaviors

The similarities of shamanic rituals to chimpanzee ritualized behaviors include a number of features that indicate their evolutionary continuity:

1. the most dramatic ritual activity of the community, involving an upright posture and charging displays;

2. an aggressive display by a charismatic alpha male asserting dominance over unseen "others";

3. drumming and vocalizations;

4. nighttime activities that unite and protect the entire group; and

5. elicitation of opioid bonding mechanisms and a sense of community connectedness.

The rituals of shamans incorporate many more of the minimal ritual behaviors identified by Wallace (see Chapter 4) than do the ritualized behaviors of chimpanzees. Especially notable in shamanism are the symbolic dimensions of prayers, exhortations, and myths, as well as the expanded ritual activities of music and dance, feasting, sacrifices, and many associated beliefs and taboos. The ancient phylogenetic bases of ritual capacities found in primates and hominins provided many basic aspects of shamanism, but these were also expanded into much more prolonged display activities involving extensive drumming, dancing, and music. Because the shamanic audience is often engaged throughout the night, these rituals could exploit the cognitive processes involved in dreaming, producing integrative visionary experiences, including experiences of the soul and the soul journey. Music and singing by shamans and the community expanded the expressive repertoire. Capacities for mimetic enactment expanded symbolic enactment and permitted expressive dance. The induction of ecstatic altered states of consciousness and otherworldly spirit experiences has become a central feature of shamanic rituals. Among the main functions of these rituals are divination (a means of acquiring hidden information) and healing (a dramatic and symbol-laden expansion of grooming activities). Another central feature of these ritual practices pertains to the management of death, for the death-and-rebirth experience that transforms the shaman into a superhuman enables him to interact with the spirits of dead individuals and guide them on their journey after death. Animals have emerged as central symbols of religious beliefs and powers, suggesting that something about animal nature has a central role in the fundamental conceptions of religiosity.

These are the aspects of shamanic ritual that presumably have significant biological bases and which were part of the repertoire of abilities that were selected for in hominan populations. From these emerged the more extensive ritual practices that characterize shamanism. These religious features of humans evolved in the context of a wide range of other cognitive and behavioral adaptations of our hominan ancestors.

On what factors could selective influences have acted to produce shamanism? There are several likely candidates, beginning with the use of drumming and other ritual procedures to produce ASC and spirit experiences. In the following sections we will explore additional mechanisms that produce ASC. To understand the emergence of these new potentials and processes further, we will also consider hominan evolution, the archaeological record, and human prehistory to understand the adaptations and cultural changes that led to modern humans and their religiosity.

The Evolutionary Origins of Spiritual Experiences

Where do we look for something unique in our hominin ancestry that establishes exactly when a new form of religiosity had first emerged? The differences between chimpanzee and shamanic behaviors provide clues to the factors that we should examine. There are several reasons we should look for evidence of the emergence of religiosity in new behaviors that produce spiritual *experiences*, rather than *beliefs*. First, there is no need for a religious explanation (belief) until there is a religious experience to be explained. As we saw in Chapter 3, a variety of natural processes—starvation, pain, injury, and sleeplessness—induce mystical experiences and the integrative mode of consciousness. Other means for producing altered states of consciousness have appeared during hominan evolution, specifically bipedalism and long-distance running, enhanced opioid systems, and enzymes for processing psychedelic plants and fungi. These areas are linked to unique human features that contributed to the evolution of our capacity for spiritual experiences.

Bipedalism and Mystical Experience: The Runner's High

One of the most significant features that distinguishes humans from apes is our habitual upright posture. As we saw in Chapter 4, chimpanzees can move bipedally and will often do so during their charging displays. But their skeletons differ from ours in important ways, and chimpanzeess prefer to knuckle-walk on all fours. Although some fossil evidence suggests that bipedalism may have emerged shortly after the split of the chimpanzee–human lines some 7 million years ago, the first unequivocally bipedal species was *Australopithecus anamensis*, which, according to the fossil record, existed about 4.2 million years ago. However, the full capacities of upright posture and running did not emerge until around 1.5 million years ago with *Homo erectus*. This species had a body that was proportioned similarly to our own and shared many other features of our postcranial skeletal structure. With *Homo erectus*, we see the emergence of a new potential: long-distance running.

While humans are not as swift as many other mammals, humans are remarkably effective at endurance running, a uniquely human capability: This human capacity for long-distance running significantly affected the course of human evolution (see Bramble and Lieberman 2004). Running is more than just a by-product of the ability to walk upright. *Homo*'s abilities to run for long distances were made possible by new adaptations, including structural adaptations for weight distribution and impact, and thermoregulation and dissipation of the heat generated by intense activity.

Running offers a variety of possible adaptive advantages in predator–prey relationships and scavenging of carcasses that may have helped offset the higher costs of running in unstable bipedal human bodies (Bramble and Lieberman 2004). Long-distance running undoubtedly improves the ability to escape predators; it also provides physical capabilities that underlie another unique human ability: dance (see later). Most significant for our purposes is the ability of long-distance running to produce mystical experiences.

This mystical experience goes beyond the classic "runner's high" produced by long-running distance due to the release of endorphins (see Noakes 1991). Ultrarunning marathons of thirty or more miles can induce profound feelings similar to what mystics have described—a sense of peace, connection, and knowing—a rare experience of the "zone," a mystical state referred to by d'Aquili and Newburg (1999) as "Absolute Unitary Being." The state is associated with

- positive emotions such as happiness, joy, and elation;
- a sense of inner peacefulness and harmony;
- connection with the ineffable aspects of the Universe;
- an experience of energy and flow;
- a sense of timelessness and cosmic unity; and
- a feeling that one is connected with nature and the Universe (Dietrich, 2003).

Why does running induce mystical experiences? Jones (2005)places the ultrarunning high in the context of the extreme activation of the autonomic nervous system. In addition to the activation produced in many body systems by exercise, the prolonged activity forces a kind of meditative breathing with regular methodic inhalation and exhalation. Physical stress activated by long-distance running provokes the release of the opioid, adrenaline, and noradrenaline neurotransmitters, as well as elevated body temperatures, oxygen depletion, and chemical and neuronal imbalances that can create unusual states of awareness. Endurance running leads to a saturation of the sympathetic nervous system and asso-

ciated structures of the hypothalamus and amygdala (particularly in the left hemisphere)—a "spillover" effect that leads to the simultaneous activation of the parasympathetic nervous system and the amygdala and hippocampus areas of the right hemisphere. This results in the simultaneous activation of what are usually separate functions and areas of the brain, and a saturation of both sides of the brain that overloads the sympathetic and parasympathetic nervous systems and normal attention, emotional processing, and comprehension. The cessation of these processes causes a shutdown of the normal processes of the mind, leading to a sense of ineffability and a disintegration of the self.

Opioids in Human Evolution

Opium-like substances are found in our bodies (endogenous) as well as in nature (exogenous). Why do we seek to use exogenous sources of opiates, and in the context of ritual, engage procedures to increase the release of endogenous opiates? The dominant neurobiological approaches to the use of opiates and other drugs has focused on the reward and reinforcement effects that they have on the mesolimbic dopamine system, involving the limbic brain concentrations of the dopaminergic neurons projecting from the lower brain areas. Virtually all classes of drugs (including alcohol, nicotine, stimulants, and THC) have effects on these opiate systems and dopamine transmission in the limbic system, and typically produce unconditioned pleasurable responses.

Sullivan, Hagen, and Hammerstein (2008) point to the paradox in this concept of hedonistic drug rewards. The substances in plants that cause pleasurable responses in humans' reward systems are generally characterized as toxins that evolved because they deterred consumption by animals. Why, then, do our brains view these same substances as rewards? Since animals do not evolve genetic capacities or neural circuitry that rewards non-adaptive fitness-reducing behaviors (such as the consumption of dangerous neurotoxins), we must conclude that humans evolved capacities to metabolize these substances in order to make use of them. Features of the neural circuitry in our brains involved in reward and/or reinforcement were selected for in order to take advantage of their effects.

Sullivan and Hagen (2002) point out that there is good evidence of a long-term evolutionary relationship between psychotropic plant substances and humans' cognitive capacities that indicate the selective benefits of substance use. They characterize these benefits in terms of the ability of plants to provide neurotransmitter analogues that serve as substitutes for endogenous transmitters that are rare or otherwise limited by dietary constraints. These are primarily the monoamine neurotransmitters (such as serotonin) as well as acetylcholine. Both are crucial for normal functioning, and both require dietary precursors, as do norepinephrine and dopamine. These neurotransmitters are central to managing stress and inducing ASC, making cultural practices that encourage their consumption or production adaptive.

Opioid Evolution in Humans

Significant differences exist between human and chimpanzee genome sequences (Chimpanzee Sequencing and Analysis Consortium 2005). Rapid evolutionary divergence in the human line involved selection for genes that produced proteins that could metabolize frequently encountered xenobiotics, plant substances that are foreign to our system (Sullivan, Hagen, and Hammerstein 2008). Sullivan et al. contend that the mammalian xenobiotic-metabolizing enzyme cytochrome P450 provides evidence of a deep evolutionary history of adaptation to plant toxins that resulted in a positive selection for the CYP2D gene, which produces enzymes that enable the body to metabolize opiates, amphetamines, and other drugs.

During the divergence of hominans from our hominin ancestors, the selection for other polypeptide precursors and genes involved in opioid regulation accelerated in the human line (see Wang et al. 2005; Rockman et al. 2005). Wang et al. report that the uniquely human pituitary cyclase-activating polypeptide precursor (PACAP) underwent accelerated evolution since the time of separation from our common ancestor with chimpanzees. The significance of the selection for PACAP involves the neuropeptides' roles in the central nervous system as both a neurohormone and a neurotransmitter. This rapid evolution of the PACAP precursor gene in humans had the direct consequence of promoting the development of uniquely human cognitive capacities, enhancing the biological activity of neuropeptides by protecting them from enzymatic degradation and increasing their affinity for receptor binding (Wang et al. 2005).

Rockman et al. (2005) note that there have been waves of selective effects in the hominid line for genes associated with opioid *cis*-regulation. Natural selection increased the expression of human prodynorphin, a precursor molecule for endogenous opioids and neuropeptides. This selection for expression of prodynorphin contributed in significant ways to the evolution of human capabilities in perception, emotion, and learning. The prodynorphin gene is found in chimpanzees as well, but it is expressed to a far greater extent in humans.

Genes that control protein sequences have evolved much more quickly in humans than in chimpanzees (Shi, Bakewell, and Zhang 2006). Consequently, some of the most significant differences between chimpanzees and humans are the segmental duplication of genes—their repetition in specific areas of the genome. These gene duplications produce changes in the onset and extent of gene expressions and also facilitate the diversification of genes, which can provide a basis for novel functions (Wooding and Jorde 2006). The human CYP2D6 gene resulted from segmental duplication, producing the enzyme (cytochrome P450) involved in the metabolism of drugs and natural toxins.

Human evolutionary divergence from chimpanzees involved many subtle changes in the extent to which gene features were expressed. Oldham, Horvath, and Geschwind (2006) suggest that chimp–human differences involve increased connectivity in the frontal brain networks of humans. In human brains, the genes associated with the central nervous system and the frontal cortex innervations underlying higher cognitive processes are expressed more intensely. This enhanced human capacity for neural transmission principally involves the opioids and serotonin. Both of these classes of neurotransmitters have exogenous sources as well and physiological effects that produce what are interpreted as spiritual experiences.

Adaptive Advantages of Opioid Systems. So why has the presence and use of opioid receptors been selected for in humans? The stimulation of the mesolimbic dopamine system by these substances suggests that we direct our attention to its broader functions in the regulation of attention, sensorimotor integration, and the modification of behavioral programs (Sullivan et al. 2008). Opioid effects are part of our mammalian heritage, responsible for bonding in mammalian species. Endorphins are a mammalian adaptation that promotes social bonding, reduces pain and stress, and enhances learning and memory. Humans may have enhanced opioid systems because opioids have many functions in the body, and their presence enhances many aspects of human functioning. Long-distance running enhances the release of endorphins; the ability to engage in such extended physical activity could have been adaptive in flight from predators or hunting activities, and the pain-numbing effects of opioids may facilitate the ability to continue to run rather than succumb to muscle cramps, shortness of breath, and so on.

This image of a "bee shaman" covered in mushrooms was found in a cave in the Tassili region of southeastern Algeria.

The placebo effect also can elicit the endogenous opioids. Religious rituals use many mechanisms for eliciting the opioid system, including extensive drumming and exercise, pain, fatigue, fear, positive emotions, overnight displays, and other stressors (Winkelman 1998). A selective influence for the extended capacities for ritual—drumming, physical endurance, pain resistance, and overnight displays—could have occurred because of the ability of these rituals to release endogenous opioids. Opioids may also play a central role in dancing (see shortly).

Psilocybin-Containing Mushrooms as Sources of Spiritual Experiences

Because foraging groups acquire a detailed knowledge of the resources available in their environments, it seems likely that hominans would have discovered the profound psychoactive effects of many plants, animals, minerals, and fungi early in their evolution. Fungi, especially toxic species of mushrooms, were a significant feature affecting hominan evolution. Many mushroom species have fatal effects; many others produce mystical experiences. Species containing the psychoactive substance psilocybin have been found in most ecozones around the world, indicating that humans may have been exposed to this substance for millions of years (Guzman, Allen, and Gartz 1998).

The premodern consumption of these psychedelic fungi is supported by several lines of converging evidence, namely (1) species unique to specific areas of the world and (2) indigenous traditions of sacred use of these substances that have great antiquity, as attested to in language, art, and physical residues. Prehistoric ritual mushroom use is attested to in rock art from cultures around the world, including Africa, Europe, and the Americas (Rätsch 2005).

The adaptive advantages of consuming these substances are suggested by the use of the hallucinogenic *Boletus* species among the Kuma and Kaimbi cultures of New Guinea (Dobkin de Rios 1984). Rather than shamanistic use, these cultures employ mushrooms for a variety of individual needs, including the reduction of intragroup tension and conflict. The mushrooms were used individually to deal with bereavement and sorrow, as well as to induce anger or excitement. The mushrooms may produce in the user a frenzied state of temporary insanity, a hyperexcited state of "mushroom madness." In this excited condition, affected people sing, dance, yell, and engage in a variety of uninhibited and drunken behaviors, including feigned attacks with spears, as well as real attacks in which others are injured by spears or arrows. Under the influence of the mushrooms, the men take up their weapons and run around terrorizing whomever they encounter. The stimulant effects of the mushrooms give the men great endurance, allowing them to engage in physical activity far beyond their normal limits. They often attack members of their own families and communities, as well as people in nearby communities. The dynamic displays associated with the stimulation produced by the *Boletus* mushrooms have substantial similarities to the typical chimpanzee display—the rushing around, brandishing objects in a threatening manner, fierce vocalizing, feigning attacks on others, and even occasionally injuring them. This suggests that one adaptive effect produced by the ability to metabolize these substances is a dramatic elicitation of the hominin alpha male displays epitomized in chimpanzees and shamanism.

Features of Mushroom Uses and Effects. A number of features are associated with the use of psychedelic substances in cultures around the world (Dobkin de Rios

1984; Shanon 2002; Winkelman 1996, 2007b). These cultures have beliefs that these substances

- provide access to a spirit world and bring the mythical world to life;
- separate one's soul or spirit from the body and allow it to travel to the supernatural world;
- produce a dramatic encounter with the personal unconscious experienced as the spirit world;
- activate powers within and outside the person, including the sense of the presence of spirits and their incorporation into the person's body;
- establish relationships with animals, especially felines and serpents;
- induce an experience of transformation into an animal;
- provoke a death of the ego and its transformation or rebirth;
- provide information through visions;
- provide healing, especially through emotional experiences and release (catharsis); and
- induce an integration of the group and enhancement of social cohesion.

These features of psilocybin-induced experiences are also central to shamanism. Consequently, we have to consider the possibility that these fungi may have played a role in the emergence of religiosity. The likelihood of this is increased because these psychotropic substances also offer a variety of other adaptive advantages.

In addition to their integrative and informational properties discussed in Chapter 3, psychotropic plants and fungi are toxic to parasites, particularly a wide range of intestinal worms. The consumption of toxins that destroyed parasites would have contributed to human health, and perhaps a ubiquitous sense that these plants are in some way "cleansing." There are also a range of physiological effects that differ with dose (Winkelman 1996). Although large doses of psychedelic substances can be temporarily debilitating, low dosages can produce increased awareness and attention, enhanced visual acuity, and excitement (including erection and sexual arousal).

Visual Evolution. The human visual system underwent a significant expansion across human evolution (Hodgson and Helvenston 2006); this would have permitted the capacities of vision-inducing plants to extend exploitation of the visual associational cortex and its ability to manage visual and other information. The visual association areas came to dominate our per-ceptions of the environment, giving predominance to visual forms by integrating input from other sensory cortical areas within the visual cortex. This expanded associational area improved the brain's capacity for learning, problem-solving, and memory formation. The visual system became the basis for the representation of information in multiple ways, a re-representation process that is the basis for symbolism. This enhanced cognitive capacity represented in the role of this region of the brain in presenting internal representations includes the visionary experiences that were considered to be evidence of a spiritual realm.

Human–Chimpanzee Divergences in Serotonergic Binding. A wide range of evidence indicates that the human serotonin (5-HT) system was modified in the course of human evolution and contributed to our cognitive specializations (Raghanti et al. 2008). The principal effects of psilocybin and similar substances on 5-HT receptors indicate that these exerted selective pressures on our capacity to benefit from the experiences they produce. This selective influence is manifested in the human–chimpanzee differences in the 5-HT$_{1D}$ receptor amino acid sequences. Human and chimpanzee serotonergic ligands, including several LSD-like indoles and ergots, have comparable low-binding affinities (Pregenzer et al. 1997) and a remarkable degree of similarity in their binding with other ligands (agents that will bind to receptor sites). Nonetheless, there are differences that reflect evolutionary divergences in 5-HT$_{1D}$ receptor systems of humans and chimpanzees.

Pregenzer et al. (1997) examined the displacement of serotonin by various drugs in humans, chimpanzees, other primates, and other mammals. Their findings indicate that humans have significantly greater displacement (2.5 to 4 times greater) than chimpanzees on the binding of LSD and other ergots (metergoline, dihydroergotamine). This provides direct evidence that humans evolved to more efficiently process what are generally considered hallucinogenic or psychedelic drugs, the vision-inducing substances that produce psychointegration (Winkelman 2007a).

What transformation of consciousness and mystical experiences can animals other than humans experience? Because young children with preoperational cognitive development can have mystical near-death experiences, we can assume that some form of these experiences were also available to other hominins, including our distant ancestors who lacked our contemporary adult cognitive skills. The basic biological nature of the effects of both endogenous and exogenous sources of opioids is illustrated in the virtually identical descriptions of the experiences of ecstatic visions of monks and those of writers who experimented with drugs (see Smith 2000). Furthermore, these opioid effects are part of our animal heritage; exogenous sources of opioids induce similar patterns of behavior in humans and rats. We cannot infer with certainty what other animals experience; however, there are good reasons to believe they do *not* involve the same experiential qualities of humans' spiritual experiences because of many aspects of the personal manifestations, particularly the representational capacities linked to the exclusively *Homo* capacities for mimesis (imitation) discussed later in this chapter.

Toolmaking and the Emergence of Hominan Culture

We do not know when our hominan ancestors first began to fashion tools, but given the many different "tool traditions" among diverse groups of chimpanzees, it is certain that our common ancestor possessed similar abilities. Unfortunately, like the tools of modern chimpanzees, the objects crafted by our ancestors must have been made of either perishable objects that were not preserved in the archaeological record (sticks, shafts of grass, or leaves) or only modified in minor ways and hence barely recognizable as tools (nut-cracking stones).

The lack of preservation of ancient tools made from sticks and leaves is one reason why stone tools are so important. Stone tools do not decay, and they retain their shape over long periods of time. Stone tools are by definition a hallmark of hominans, and they provide significant evidence about ancient behaviors and cognitive processes. Stone tools are so significant that paleoanthropologists and archaeologists use them to mark a new era of prehistory: the Paleolithic (Old Stone Age).

The Paleolithic began with the appearance of the first stone tools in Africa about 2.5 million years ago. These "Olduwan industry" tools were made by striking two rocks together so that a fragment or flake with a sharp cutting edge broke off (see Fig. 5.2). This advance was so momentous that Louis and Mary Leakey, their discoverers, named the makers of these tools *Homo habilis* (literally, "handy man").

Stone tools changed little over the next million years, but by about 1.4 million years ago, a new hominan named *Homo erectus* was producing a new type of tool. Known as the Acheulean industry, these "bifacial" tools stayed sharper for a longer period of time and could be used for multiple purposes (see Fig. 5.3).

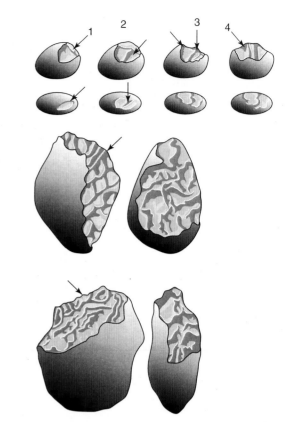

Figure 5.2 The earliest tools, known as the Olduwan industry, had edges that could cut through animal skins and remove tissues from bones quickly and efficiently. They were produced by striking two small rocks together in such a way that flakes of stone were dislodged from one of the rock surfaces. The resulting sharp edge was used as a cutting surface.

They were also much more complicated to make and required improved motor skills, greater hand–eye coordination, and a "vision" of the future tool. Because none of the original surface of the stone remained in the finished tool, bifacial tools demonstrate that these ancestors had become capable of "seeing" a finished tool inside a raw piece of rock. The striking uniformity in these stone tools across a million years demonstrates that the hominans who made them had acquired the ability of "mimesis," which has important implications for culture and other cognitive skills.

The Implications of Mimesis for Religion

The psychologist Merlin Donald (1991) argues that the fundamental similarities of the tools of the Acheulean tradition indicate that *Homo erectus* had achieved a new level of cognitive development that he termed "mimetic consciousness." This cognitive ability expanded the capacity for culture and human consciousness. Given

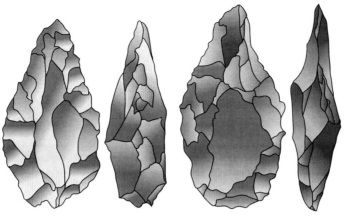

Figure 5.3 Acheulean tools were made by removing flakes from both sides of a stone, producing a tool that was flat, elongated, and often symmetrical in all three dimensions. When finished, none of the original surface of the stone remained.

the tool evidence for the emergence of the symbolic capacity for mimesis, it likely expanded the capacity for ritual expression as well. Mimesis is a uniquely human capacity that provides us with the ability to symbolize events or ideas by means of actions. This enables humans to consciously produce representations through metaphors conveyed by behaviors such as mime, imitation, and gesture. These enactments use our bodies' actions to represent perceptions, such as through mime and dance, and logically and necessarily preceded the ability to use language.

Mime is an extension of the capacity to represent information through ritual and provides strong evidence of the capacity of *Homo erectus* to engage in a new level of religiosity. These early forms of symbolic communication, exemplified in the expressive modalities of rhythm and melody, enhance social bonding and emotional communication (Molino 2000). Mimesis enhanced group coordination by expanding on isopraxis. As we saw in Chapter 4, isopraxis helps the members of a species to identify one another; its further development in mimesis led to more elaborate ways for individuals to recognize other members of their group.

Donald (1991) suggests that the first human mimetic activities were ritual dances that groups performed with vocalizations to imitate the sounds of animals. This mimetic capacity made possible the development of cultural expressions based on imitation and provided the foundation for customs, rituals, gestures, and skilled behaviors. Mimetic traditions enabled a collective expressive system that produced a shared group consciousness and culture. Mimesis also provided a more general expressive medium for letting others know about their inner states, past experiences, and future plans. The capacity for symbolization with the body expanded the capacity for spirituality as well, manifested in the capacities associated with dance.

Dance. The drama of chimpanzee charging displays obscures their limited capacities for running and dance. While chimpanzee displays are the closest to human dance of all of their behaviors, they are not human dance. Chimpanzees do not have the rhythmic capabilities—the ability to keep time to a beat—that humans do (Williams 1980). These differences reflect specific genes that emerged during hominan evolution. Bachner-Melman et al. (2005) found specific gene polymorphisms associated with people who are engaged intensively with creative dance performance. While all humans have common genetic features that give us a uniquely human capacity for mimesis and dance, professional dancers are significantly more likely to possess expanded expressions of these genes and gene interactions that enhance their dance capacity. The widespread distribution of complex dance forms in cultures around the world indicates that these special polymorphisms occurred before the human exodus from Africa.

The study by Bachner-Melman et al. found that professional dancers, in comparison with normal controls and professional athletes, had expanded expression of a genotype associated with serotonin transporters (SLC6A4) and an arginine vasopressin receptor (AVPR1a) that is an opioid. Furthermore, higher levels of expression of these features were significantly associated with a measure of spirituality and altered states of consciousness (the Tellegren Absorption Scale). They hypothesize that the association of AVPR1a and SLC6A4 is a reflection of the linkages among communication, courtship, and spiritual aspects of the dancing phenotype involving mediating personality factors.

The SLC6A4 allele is a more efficient serotonin transporter and is considered to be more effective in the removal of serotonin from the synapses. The AVPR1a gene is widely associated with social communication and affiliative behavior in primates. Bachner-Melman et al. propose that the association between dance and the AVPR1a gene reflects the central role of communication and social relations in dance. They hypothesize an evolutionary basis for the linkages of the AVPR1a gene and dance, reflected in the role of vasopressin in vertebrates' courtship behavior. Vasopressin is a peptide hormone similar to oxytocin; both are well recognized for their functions in human bonding, in both maternal behavior and romantic attachment. Thus, they propose that the interaction of these genes and human dance involves an engagement with the emotionality of dance experiences. Human dancing is involved in both courtship and social communication, and manifests many features that illustrate that human dance shares a conservative evolutionary history with other primates, such as manifested in common neurochemical mechanisms involved in mating displays and other affiliative behaviors.

The association of serotonin and the opioid system (vasopressin) with ASC and mystical experiences, as well as enhanced dance propensities among those with greater expression of these genes, suggest that these capacities of dance and ASC co-evolved. Clearly, dance has the capacity to induce ASC through a variety of mechanisms (such as stimulating the release of opioids), producing rhythmic stimulation of the brain, and inducing exhaustion and collapse.

The Domestication of Fire

Most animals have a profound fear of fire. For our ancestors to overcome their own fears and begin to use fire for constructive purposes demonstrates an enormous increase in their understanding of the natural world. Fire offers many practical advantages. It kills the parasites present in meat and breaks down the toxins in many plants. It can be used to preserve food, fashion weapons and other tools, ward off predators, and keep a shelter warm. Fire brings light into darkness and provides a focal point for nocturnal group activities, including all-night shamanic rituals. Today, fire is universally associated with sacred powers and is used as a religious symbol in cultures throughout the world.

Archaeological sites in Africa suggest that our ancestors may have been using fire as early as 1.6 million years ago. Naturally occurring brush fires are common in dry grasslands around the world, and early humans would have had ample opportunities to observe how fires drove away or killed animals and charred and roasted plant material. At some point our ancestors learned to "collect" and then maintain fire, and ultimately to produce it. Hearths were found at numerous archaeological sites, demonstrating that fire had become a common feature of human life, by around 100,000 years ago.

The domestication of fire likely affected the development of early religious thinking. Fire reduces solid objects to smoke and ash while giving off light, a transformation of the solid into the immaterial and energetic. Fire also expanded opportunities for ritual activities into the night, enhancing the processes through which dream states could be incorporated into consciousness through ritual.

Cannibalism

Many mammals, including lions, jackals, bears, and chimpanzees, occasionally cannibalize one another. Their teeth leave marks on the bones that are preserved as the bones fossilize. Archaeologists can distinguish these teeth marks from the cut marks that tell us that a hominid had removed the flesh from a bone with a tool. The presence of broken arm and leg bones (which contain a large amount of marrow) may also point to cannibalism. This evidence of cannibalism can be rather straightforward, but it does not tell us whether the cannibalism was performed strictly for nourishment or whether there were religious reasons for the practice.

Although there is considerable controversy about the accuracy of reports of cannibalism in both the historical and the ethnographic literature, reports of cannibalism come from prehistorical, historical, and near-contemporary societies around the world, which appear to have practiced cannibalism as a part of religious rituals. Thus, ethnographic analogy suggests that the ancient evidence of cannibalism—especially when found in association with deliberate burials—indicate that the society held religious beliefs regarding deceased individuals. An alternate hypothesis that explains the cut marks on bones would be the de-fleshing of the skeletons of ancestors in ancestor worship, an activity noted in the funerary rituals of some cultures. In contrast, strictly culinary uses would not exhibit religious elements, which would explain why some skeletons were simply discarded with other refuse rather than placed with special care in protected areas.

The evidence of cannibalism thought to be present in several skulls found at Choukoutien (China) in the 1920s and 1930s illustrates the difficulties in reconstructing the past. Franz Weidenreich, the anatomist who first studied the finds, noted that many of the skulls had been broken in a way that suggested the brains had been removed for consumption. Moreover, the Choukoutien site contained many more skulls than it did other bones. If these had been burials, we would expect to find numerous other bones in addition to the skulls. Unfortunately, the original fossils were lost during the Japanese invasion of China in 1941, so it is no longer possible to examine them for cut marks or other signs of how they were handled. And there is another, equally plausible explanation for the presence of the skulls: The bodies may have been scavenged by hyenas, which often break open skulls to eat the brains and which carry off other parts of the body for later consumption.

In contrast, the evidence of cannibalism found at Atapuerca Cave (Spain) is unambiguous. Cut marks found on the fossilized bones of at least six individuals reveal that the bodies were de-fleshed by stone tools about 800,000 years ago. After use, the bones (many of which were also broken) were unceremoniously dumped into a refuse pit. Although these finds do indicate that cannibalism was occurring, the site does not suggest that the practice had any ritual or symbolic significance. Many of the animal bones found at the same site had been worked over, broken, and discarded in the same way. On the other hand, the twenty-five cut marks that were made on the cheekbone, forehead, bone of the eye socket, and other parts of a 600,000-year-old skull found at Bodo (Ethiopia) demonstrate that the skull had been purposefully de-fleshed, but the small amount of meat on the skull and face suggests that this may have been done for either symbolic purposes or to more easily get at the brain.

What is the meaning of these finds suggesting cannibalistic practices? We know from historical documents and ethnographic studies that cannibalism was sometimes practiced to allow the eater to acquire the strength and life force of the victim, notions that clearly fall within the scope of religiosity. But the archaeological evidence does not allow us to conclude whether similar beliefs lay behind the cannibalism of the Paleolithic, and it is possible that the cannibalism was motivated by simple hunger. In any case, what may have originated as a dietary practice eventually became overlaid with symbolic significance as the concepts and values associated with religiosity appeared.

Early Hominan Ritual and Spirituality

Although the hominans of the early Paleolithic have left us with evidence clearly demonstrating that their mental life was richer and more varied that that of their hominin ancestors, any attempts to understand their rituals and religious life must depend on inference and analogy. For instance, the new tool traditions—characterized by a long-term consistency in the types and shapes of tools—indicate that they had developed the capacity for mimesis. This capacity, combined with their upright postures and ability for long-distance running, suggests that *Homo erectus* engaged in ritual dances. These dances likely took place primarily at night while the group was gathered around the safety of a fire. These new rituals likely engaged percussion instruments, perhaps expanding the banging of branches observed in chimpanzees into using spear shafts pounded defiantly against the ground. These developments, however, were likely driven by the need to enhance community cohesiveness rather than the specific desire to produce spiritual experiences. Natural selection for increased opioid receptors enhanced capacities for this social bonding; combined with other ritual effects, they undoubtedly contributed to inducing mystical experiences.

By the time of *Homo erectus*, our ancestors had an enhanced set of capacities and technologies for spiritual experiences and understandings. We have already identified several possible sources for early spiritual experiences: long-distance running; psychoactive mushrooms; and starvation, pain, and stress. The capacity for shamanic soul flight (or "out-of-body-experience") also must have been in place by this time. The concept of an embodied self which allowed one to communicate through bodily imitation also allowed people to conceive of the transcendence of that bodily-based form of the self. The basis of mimesis—the ability to experience and express self-as-body—provided a concrete operational level of mental development that was a necessary preadaptation and precursor for out-of-body experiences. You must be able to identify with your body before you can get "out" of it. Spiritual experiences involved the use of techniques that took the person to a level of self experience beyond the physical body and self, exemplified in the "soul flight" or "out of body experience."

The capacity of mimesis and the use of imitation in hunting, disguise, and reenactment mean that humans also began to see themselves in terms of animal identities and to see animals as "others"—significant forces of nature. Group rituals and mimesis provide additional ways for individuals to communicate their past experiences and dream visions to one another. Enactment permits participants to feel greater empathy as they understand one another's experiences and also allows rituals to transform those emotional states. The evolutionary drive for transcendence may derive from the desire to overcome the emotions of grief and loss (Oubré 1997). Ritual was a preadapted process for engaging in behaviors that helped restore optimal opioid and serotonergic functioning. This deliberate ritual engagement permitted a linkage of biological and cultural self, engaging an integration of the behavioral, emotional, and cognitive identities.

The Expansion of Religiosity Among the Later Hominans

Much of the next evidence documenting the emergence of religiosity comes from one of the most famous of all hominans—the Neanderthals. Neanderthals entered popular lore as "cave men" who were bigger and stronger than most modern humans and whose average brain size (over 1500 cc) was even larger than our own (around 1350 cc). They survived in the cold, harsh climate of Ice Age Europe. True to their popular image as "cave men," the Neanderthals did occupy caves, at least during the cold season. They had a detailed knowledge of animals and plants, and the ability to manufacture specialized tools for specific purposes. Neanderthal tools were more sophisticated than any previously made and include the first tools that were made with more than one component (such as a spear with a wooden shaft and a stone tip held in place by sinew or fiber).

Paleoanthropologists debate whether the Neanderthals were simply a regional subspecies of *Homo sapiens* or a different species (*Homo neandertalensis*). Whichever view is correct, the Neanderthals were more like us than any hominan that had lived before, and their sites provide the first direct evidence of religion in the archaeological record. The ways in which they treated dead humans and animals suggest that they believed in the continued qualities of life and power of a person after death. This supernatural premise, the belief in a soul that survives bodily death, can be inferred from the appearance of Neanderthal burials and, perhaps in some cases, of cannibalism. Burial activities and physical objects left in graves also indicate that a new level of cognitive representation and religiosity had emerged.

The central role of issues related to death in the emergence of religiosity is indicated by many of the shaman's central concerns that revolve around issues of death. These concerns include the shaman's "death-and-rebirth" experience and the ritual role of the shaman in helping the deceased person's soul on its journey to the next world. Such features of shamanism indicate that signs of the early manifestations of religiosity can be found in the archaeological evidence of death practices and in objects that were used for symbolic depictions rather than practical purposes.

Burial and Death Rituals. One task that is universally associated with religious ideas is the disposal of human remains. Decaying bodies attract scavengers and predators and pose additional health threats from contamination. For most of hominan prehistory, our nomadic ancestors dealt with corpses by simply leaving them behind when they moved. Eventually, however, they began to protect their dead from scavengers and leave "grave goods"—useful objects that the people would have needed if they were still alive—with the bodies. From time to time, they also ate the corpses in ways that suggest ritual purposes rather than a need for nutrition. In societies around the world today, burials are associated with belief in a spiritual world and in personal souls that somehow survive bodily death. When did such beliefs first appear?

Only a few intentional burials from the period between 35,000 and 150,000 years ago are known. In the early twentieth century, the fossilized remains of two adults, four children, and two fetuses were recovered at La Ferrassie (France). The bodies had been buried in six graves in close proximity to one another. The male and female were buried head to head, and one of the children's skulls had been removed from its body and buried separately underneath a stone slab. The remains are thought to be around 70,000 years old.

The site of Shanidar cave (northern Iraq) has yielded several well-preserved Neanderthal burials. One of the most dramatic is Shanidar 4, the 60,000 year-old "flower burial." This adult male skeleton was buried together with two female skeletons and the skeleton of a baby, and pollen was found in clusters around the male's remains. No similar clusters were found in any other place in the cave, suggesting that the flowers that were the source of the pollen were intentionally placed by the body. The pollen is derived from at least seven different kinds of flowers. Intriguingly, much of the pollen that has been identified came from plants with known medicinal properties (see Table 5.1). It is likely that the people of

Table 5.1 Medicinal Plants Found in Association with the Shanidar 4 Specimen.

Species	Medicinal Uses
Achillea sp.	A panacea used to treat inflammations, lower fevers, and promote blood clotting
Althea sp.	Wound treatment
Centaurea solstitiali	Diuretic, antiseptic
Ephedra altissima	Potent stimulant; also used to suppress coughing and to treat inflammations
Muscari sp.	Diuretic, stimulant
Senecio sp.	Used in childbirth to control pain and hasten labor; tonic, stimulant

Shanidar were aware of these effects. One of the archaeologists who excavated the site speculated that "Shanidar IV was not only a very important man, a leader, but also may have been a kind of medicine man or shaman in his group" (Solecki 1975, p. 881). As is so often the case, however, there are also alternative explanations: The pollen may have been tracked in by modern-day workmen, or deposited near the remains by burrowing animals.

One of the most spectacular of all Neanderthal burials was found in a cave at Régourdou (France), where the 60,000–70,000-year-old skeleton of an adult Neanderthal was found lying on a bed of flat rocks (see Fig. 5.4). A slab of stone covered the rib cage of the body, and upon this lay several stone tools and the split arm bone of a bear. Two bear leg bones were found near the feet of the Neanderthal skeleton. The skeleton and the other objects had been covered over by a mound of rocks, and a deer antler had been placed on the mound. Ash and charcoal found over the antler indicate that a fire had been made on top. Less than two meters away, the remains of most of a brown bear were found beneath a flat stone weighing some 800 kilograms. The bones of the bear appear to have first been de-fleshed with tools, then laid out in a specific pattern: The skull was placed to the north, the shoulder blades were placed to the south, and the long bones of the arms and legs were placed at the sides.

These findings demonstrate that our Neanderthal relatives were intentionally burying at least some of their dead. The positions of the bodies suggest that the survivors mourned at least some of their fellows and prepared their bodies for some afterlife purpose. The presence of the animal bones points to an early "animal cult" and to beliefs that animals also had spirits.

Art and Adornment. People create art and adorn themselves for a variety of social and religious reasons. For example, a shaman's cloak is often adorned with shiny and rattling objects. The archaeological evidence of adornment indicates a greater degree of "humanness" than does tool production, for it represents a kind of symbolic social signaling related to personal and social group identity.

The most significant early evidence of adornment is found in ochre, a naturally occurring soft iron oxide (Fe_2O_3) mineral used as a pigment in paints in cultures around the world. Ochre is often employed to paint the body for a variety of religious activities. Ochre

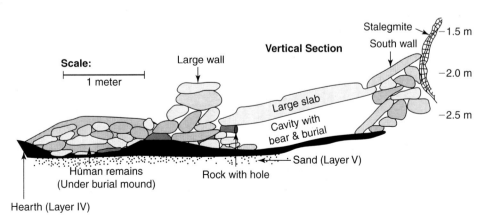

Figure 5.4 This Neanderthal grave in Régourdou, France, included the remains of a human and a bear skeleton, with a large wall of rocks separating the two.

The Origins of Shamanism

133

The Berekhat Ram figurine may be the earliest known representation of the human form.

may be ground and rubbed onto the body or an object to color it. It can be used to preserve animal skins and may be added to plant fibers and other material to create an adhesive to haft stone points and other tools to wooden handles. Depending on what other minerals are present, ochre may be yellow, brown, black, orange, or violet, but it is most commonly red.

Ochre is found at many early hominan sites. The first pieces of ochre at archaeological sites from almost one million years ago exhibit few signs of wear or modification; perhaps the early humans who collected them were simply interested in the color. Evidence that *Homo sapiens* was grinding and using ochre for symbolic purposes appears in layers from Qafzeh Cave (Israel) dating to about 92,000 years ago. The people who lived at the site consistently used only certain colors and textures of *red* ochre over a period of several thousand years (even though other colors and textures were available at the same deposits). The fact that there was no evidence of hafting or other practical uses of ochre at this site has been interpreted as an indication that these pieces of ochre had symbolic signifi-

cance for their users, although it is not possible to reconstruct their meaning. Many researchers have suggested that red ochre—which has a color quite similar to that of dried blood—was sought after for its symbolic significance.

Two pieces of ochre from the South African site of Blombos Cave provide even clearer evidence of the symbolic use of ochre. These pieces, which date to about 77,000 years ago, exhibit a series of crosshatches and other lines that were made in a deliberate sequence. Once again, we cannot know what meanings these designs held for their makers, but the consistency in their production and the similarity in their design strongly suggest that they held some sort of symbolic meaning.

What may be the earliest known representation of the human form is a small figurine found at Berekhat Ram (Golan Heights, in the Middle East) that dates to between 250,000 and 280,000 years ago. Although it appears to be nothing more than a small and unusually shaped pebble, microscopic analysis has revealed that the stone was in fact intentionally scraped and cut to make it more similar in form to a human female. Alexander Marshack (1997), who carried out the analysis, has even suggested that the shape of the "hair" on the figure's head indicates that it was managed (cut or tied back), a clear sign of an increasing sense of self and of the cultural shaping of our human nature. We do not know how extensive symbolic expressions were at this time or whether they had a relationship to ritual practices. As we will see, however, by around 40,000 years ago humans had begun to engage in new symbolic forms and religious expressions.

Cave Rituals. The artifacts and ritual activities of Neanderthals provide direct evidence that they had religion. The fact that the Neanderthals treated certain items, such as bear skulls and teeth, with special ritual attention attests to the emotional nature of Neanderthal religious development (King 2007). The focus of their rituals relating to aggression is reflected in their elevation of the bear to a sacred symbolic status. Did early humans bow in submission to what was their largest land predator, or did they aggressively challenge it, mounting a threat display and attack? The idea that the bear effigies in caves were ritually killed suggests the latter, a ferocious attack against a mortal enemy of "man the hunted." Thus, our ritual practices engage our emotions through behaviors that put our fears to rest and our desires into action.

To the Neanderthals, caves were also special places for burying their dead and engaging in rituals with the most powerful and feared of their natural enemies, the cave bears, whose habitat they now invaded and dominated. The imaginative capacities of ritual were dramatically expanded in caves, where the physical properties of the environment contributed to the induction of altered states of consciousness. King (2007) has suggested that these Neanderthal activities in caves were forms of prayer in which our ape sense of belongingness was extended to the spiritual world. These social and emotional bonding processes are characteristic of other mammals and primates but are developed to a far greater extent among humans. These are the underpinnings of the human need for belongingness—intensely felt emotional relationships with others for which spirits ("others") become perfect sources.

Summary: Religiosity Among the Late Hominans

Although the archaeological evidence for ritual developments and religious activities among the Neanderthals and early *Homo sapiens* is sparse, it clearly indicates that these hominans had become aware of the inevitability of their own deaths and had developed notions about the soul and its survival of death. They intentionally buried some of their fellows, providing them with the things that they had needed in their own lifetimes. Intentional burials with practical items is generally interpreted as conclusive evidence of a belief in an afterlife and, consequently, in souls, spirits, and the efficacy of ritual to influence those souls and spirits. They may have even had some type of spiritual conceptions of animals as powers or spirits. Their use of controlled fires suggests that they were engaging in all-night ritual activities. They appear to have been decorating themselves and their tools with ochre and may have been modifying objects to produce art.

The archaeological evidence we have surveyed demonstrates that *Homo erectus* likely took the first true steps toward religiosity. Their ritual behaviors went far beyond the simple ritualized behaviors of chimpanzees, and their artifacts demonstrate that their intelligence and muscle control was more sophisticated than that of any animal that had lived before them. The groups that succeeded them—the Neanderthals and early *Homo sapiens*—greatly expanded these capacities by intentionally burying their dead, creating the first pieces of art and adorn-

ment, and conducting rituals in caves. With these activities, our late hominan ancestors had reached the threshold of modern human religiosity, which began with the explosion of symbolic consciousness associated with the emergence of culturally modern humans.

Shamanism and Human Cultural Evolution

The emergence of modern humans, *Homo sapiens*, is still something of a mystery. Anatomically modern humans appeared some 200,000 years ago or more, but the manifestation of modern symbolic culture—the signature of modern humans—did not occur on a substantial scale until about 40,000 years ago. Why did the cultural evolution of modern humans lag so far behind their physical evolution? And why did it announce its dramatic arrival in art that is intimately tied to shamanic themes?

Cave Art as Evidence of Shamanism

The most spectacular evidence of the emergence of the newly modern mind and its concerns with religion is found in the dramatic paintings discovered in the hidden caves of Europe. Although such astonishing renderings of animals, humans, and other forms were also produced in rock shelters and on cliff walls, it is the tens of thousands of images found on the walls and ceilings of deep caves that have been preserved until the present day.

Over the years, a number of ideas have been put forth to explain this art. One of the most influential was proposed by the Abbé Henri Breuil (1877–1961), a French prehistorian who dominated thinking about European cave art during the first half of the twentieth century. Breuil regarded the many images of animals portrayed on the walls and ceilings of European caves as expressions of sympathetic magic. Their makers, he argued, painted bison, horses, and ibex to ensure that there would always be animals to hunt. He interpreted the images of more dangerous animals (such as bears, felines, and mammoths) as attempts by the painters to acquire the strength and power of these animals.

A second school of thought favored a much simpler explanation for these images: They were the expression of early man's artistic impulses and were illustrations of what their painters saw around them. They were, in other words, essentially "art for art's sake." According to this view, the best way to appreciate and understand the images would be to gaze upon them the same way one would contemplate any other art, from any place and from any time.

For decades, these two attitudes shaped the ways that archaeologists and others looked at cave art. But they left many questions unanswered. Why were horses the most commonly depicted animals, even though the butchered bones recovered from sites from the time clearly demonstrate that other animals, such as reindeer and bison, were eaten more often? What were the meanings of the many red dots, parallel lines, and other abstract images? Why were some of the figures made deep in the recesses, on the ceilings, and even in pits found far inside of the caves? And what did the images of human hands, and of half-human, half-animal figures, mean? These strange images had often been lumped into the category of "mythical images," but little more was said about them, for the myths seemed to be forever lost.

Then, in the late 1970s, a new way of looking at this art emerged. David Lewis-Williams, a cognitive archaeologist and rock art researcher who had spent years cataloging and studying thousands of rock art sites found throughout Southern Africa, suggested that these images represented spirit animals, experiences of altered states of consciousness, and transformations into animals. They were, in other words, depictions of shamanic events. Lewis-Williams arrived at this conclusion by comparing the myths, personal stories, and descriptions of other aspects of San (South African Bushmen) culture that had been recorded in the 1870s. He felt that these accounts could provide some insights into the cave paintings, but was not certain how the details they related applied to specific images. Coincidentally, ethnographic research in the 1960s and 1970s revealed that the San and other Bushmen still had an oral tradition which shared many of the same myths, and that these living peoples understood the meanings of the cave paintings. As a result, Lewis-Williams was able to relate these narratives to specific images and groups of images, and to determine how the various elements of San mythology had been translated into the signs and images found on the walls and ceilings of these caves.

Another framework for interpreting this cave art was emerging from neuropsychological research, which found that specific forms of visual experience called entoptic phenomena (or "phosphenes") are produced by both hallucinogenic substances and natural altered states of consciousness. Humans around the world experience the same types of phosphenes, an indication that these are a product of our mental hardware for vision. Assuming that early *Homo sapiens* were capable of the same experiences of altered states as modern humans, some of the images found in caves may have been representations of the visual phenomena that are experienced in these states. The many dots, squiggly lines, and other geometric and abstract designs found in rock art are typical of phosphenes, which often appear as a person begins to enter into an altered state (these can also be seen by gently pressing your fingers against your closed eyes).

Many archaeologists and anthropologists (e.g., Lewis-Williams, Dawson, Clottes, Winkelman, Whitley) now agree that these caves and the images they contain are best interpreted as expressions of a shamanistic tradition. The images found on the walls and ceilings of the caves depict different aspects of shamanism, including visionary experiences, the merging of human with animal identities, and the powers of different animals. This shamanic interpretation of cave art suggests that the walls and ceilings of the caves were conceived as a layer or membrane which separated the world of everyday human reality from the world of spirits and that the images which humans painted or carved into the walls were records of the spirits that had crossed between these worlds.

The cave sites also provide evidence of shamanic behaviors. Many of the human footprints found at these sites differ from normal footprints; they consist primarily of heel or toe marks rather than prints of the entire foot, an indication that ritual dances may have occurred at the sites. The acoustic properties of the caves are ideal for inducing ecstatic states. Within a cave, the normal sound of the human voice is affected as it echoes through the chambers. In addition, striking or drumming on the stalactites produces low-frequency sounds that resonate throughout the cave, and other percussion and musical instruments (such as flutes) have been found at some sites. And of course, the darkness and isolation inside the caves would have also affected the people inside.

The Cave as the Shamanic Lower World. In cultures throughout the world, caves are seen as the entrance to the lower (or under) world. As people journey into a cave, they leave the everyday world of openness and light and enter a region of darkness, quiet, and restricted space. In many cultures today, this transition is regarded as a movement into the unconsciousness and lower (under) world, a symbol of the shaman's inward journey. The presence and location of the art found in these caves suggests that they were associated with shamanic activities and reflected visionary experiences. The natural features of the caves also contributed to altered states of consciousness, and the suggestibility typical of people experiencing these states would have been useful as the people were introduced to spirit beliefs and concepts.

Animal Representations. As we have seen, foraging societies around the world have many features in common, including a preoccupation with locating game animals, a desire to increase both animal and human fertility and to heal individuals and the community, and the need to maintain a balance with nature. The images found within caves clearly suggest that these concerns were also central to the people who made them. Although some early scholars of cave art suggested that the animal images were evidence of hunting magic, less than 10% of the animal images appear "wounded" or "killed." Moreover, many of the animals depicted (particularly those found in the depths of the caves) were species that were not often eaten, but were rare and dangerous animals with little importance as food sources (e.g., cougars, lions, bears). A shamanic interpretation is that the people who produced these images were trying to evoke or acquire the powers of these animals. In addition, the bear's habit of hibernating through the winter may have also provided a symbol of the death-and-rebirth experiences that are typical parts of the process of becoming a shaman.

Human Representations. Human images are much less common in the caves of Europe than are animals. These images occasionally combine human and animal features (such as a human torso with an animal head), a combination that can be seen as an expression of the shaman's animal spirits and role as master of the animals. Moreover, these images also evoke notions of animal spirit allies and symbolize the belief that shamans transform into these animals. These human–animal images were often placed in very significant positions. (The "Sorcerer of Les Trois-Fréres" is located high above a cave floor.) These humanoid forms may be the earliest representations of shamans, the "Masters of Animals," who are responsible for human–animal relationships and for controlling animal spirits and life forces. Another human image is the "wounded man" (often shown speared or knocked down), reflecting the death-and-rebirth experience of shamanism. Images of "bird-men" recall the shaman's soul flight, while reclining human–animal forms (many of them with erections) are evocative of the dream state, a shamanic altered

The "Sorcerer of Les Trois-Fréres" is a composite human–animal figure found in a cave near the village of Montesquieu-Avantès (Southern France). Located 5 meters (15 feet) above the cave floor, this is the only figure in this cave that appears to be looking directly at the observer.

state of consciousness and one in which males often develop an erection.

Cave Art and Shamanic Consciousness

Because many of the cave art images represent shamanic activities and altered states, it is likely that subterranean rock art sites were used to induce altered states of consciousness for shamanic vision quests. Symbols of initiatory death, self-transformation, and animal empowerment are consistent with the patterns of shamanic cave initiations found in contemporary cultures. The heightened emotions of being in this unfamiliar environment, together with the harrowing and difficult experiences of entering the caves and crawling through the dark passageways and the sensory deprivation produced by being in the dark and quiet—where the only light is produced by one's own torch, and the only sounds are the echoes of one's own progress—even today induce an altered state in most people.

The manner in which much of the art seems to jump out of cracks and holes in the cave's structures, the organization of the animal motifs, and the sequences of movement from one chamber to the next all suggest that they were used in shamanic alterations of consciousness. Many of the most detailed images were found near the entryways and in the first series of chambers or in other large rooms within a cave, suggesting that these rooms were used repeatedly and by many people. In contrast, people often had to travel single-file and on their backs or stomachs to get to some of the deeper chambers, where many of the images found in pits, near narrow ledges, and in other inaccessible places tend to consist of just a few lines. This pattern suggests that as people entered the underground world, they first saw these impressive images of powerful animals from the world they knew and subsequently made their own images while they were having visions much further from the entrance. This interpretation is supported by the fact that the "nonsymbolic" representations found on cave walls are strikingly similar to entoptic phenomena, which often appear in conjunction with sensory deprivation and in other states.

The shamanic paradigm provides a comprehensive model for interpreting both the images of this cave art and their location deep within dark, quiet, and relatively inaccessible underground chambers. For example, the "wounded man" motif is difficult to explain without reference to the classic shamanic experience of death and rebirth. Furthermore, the experiences produced in caves contribute to the transformation of consciousness associated with shamanism.

Of all the explanations that have been proposed to explain the various types of images and their placement deep within caves, the shamanic interpretation provides the most comprehensive framework. Not only does this tie together the many types of images and the reasons for their positions deep within the caves, but it also suggests that certain core elements of religious thought and behavior were already present at the dawn of the Upper Paleolithic.

The presence of these same elements in premodern societies that practiced shamanism provide the ethnological and ethnographic analogies that indicate the involvement of Shamanism in ancient practices and that shamanism was the ancient religion of all hunter-gatherer groups. These religious features of shamanism were at the forefront of the wave of new cultural developments that emerged approximately 40,000 years ago. Why is religion central to this new mindset and to the emergence of modern human culture? To consider the roles of religious practices in the evolution of human culture, we must first understand the broader evolution of the brain and mind, the challenges faced by the developing intellect, and how religiosity provided solutions.

Human Cognitive Evolution: The Emergence of Specialized Intelligences

In Chapter 4 we illustrated how the triune brain model provides a framework for considering the evolution of the brain from reptiles through our hominin ancestors. Subsequent changes over the course of hominan evolution involved both the expansion of the neocortex (especially the prefrontal cortex) and the development of specialized human intelligences. These capacities provided improved abilities to make tools, to manage larger social groups, and to more effectively exploit animals. They also led to artistic activity, adornment, and, ultimately, language and religion.

Throughout this text, we have been referring to the biological structures that construct and shape the ways in which we experience, comprehend, and act within the Universe as our "mental hardware." If we extend this computer analogy, we can see that our mental hardware actually consists of numerous components, each of which contributes to specific functions. For example, a computer can support a monitor because it has a "video card"; it can generate sounds because it has an "audio card"; and it can interact with other computers because it has a "communications device." It is both the specialized architecture of the various subsystems and the integrated functioning of these component parts that create the abilities of computers—and of our brains.

The idea that our various mental abilities are products of different brain components or innate modules has had a profound effect on how we look at human intelligence. Today, most scientists who study the brain and its workings do not view it as relying on a single, all-purpose general intelligence that is devoid of content when we are born and that is then trained and "filled up" by the culture into which we are born. A general intelligence of this type would need to learn everything through trial and error and by comparison with the things it has already learned. This would make it slow and prone to mistakes.

Instead, the human brain is believed to have evolved many different kinds of specialized intelligences, each of which is a complex problem-solving component that processes information about a specific domain of importance to humans. For example, speech and musical ability are autonomous systems of information expression; while they share some human capacities in common (exhalation of air from the lungs), they are otherwise so autonomous that one can lose language abilities without losing musical abilities, and vice versa. These modular intelligences have been compared to the different blades and tools on a Swiss Army knife, each useful for a particular purpose. Specialized intelligences process information much more rapidly than any generalized intelligence could, but they do so at a cost: they cannot process information that lies outside the domain of their functioning. Understanding how these components of our mental hardware came to function together in an integrated fashion can shed light on the emergence of modern culture in general and the emergence of religious beliefs and practices in particular.

Steven Mithen is an archaeologist who has applied this insight to interpret the stages of human evolution on the basis of the evidence in the archaeological record. Mithen has proposed (1996) that our specialized intelligences were once closed off from one another, functioning as separate and independent modules. Eventually, the barriers between these intelligences were overcome by new processes that integrated the contents and processing capacities of each of these specialized domains of knowledge into other domains. The resulting "cognitive fluidity" involved a re-representation of information that gave rise to the explosion of symbolic thinking that characterizes the modern mind and modern culture that emerged some 40,000 years ago (see Box 5.2: Humans' Innate Modular Intelligences). What caused this integration? What new capacities emerged in humans?

The Emergence of Cognitive Fluidity

The archaeological record allows us to reconstruct the emergence of our specialized intelligences. The changes from the simple Olduwan stone tools of *Homo habilis* to the sophisticated Acheulean tools of *Homo erectus* illustrate the emergence of technical intelligence. The increasing consumption of meat and the migration of human populations into new environments illustrate the emergence of natural history intelligence. The evidence that such large animals as elephants and rhinoceroses were being hunted by groups indicates a coordination that suggests that our social intelligence was improving. In contrast, the evidence of linguistic intelligence, which required humans to develop the anatomical features that make speech possible, did not appear until much later; exactly *when* it emerged remains a topic of debate.

The specialized nature of each of these intelligences means that each can do only the things for which it was selected during evolution. Technical intelligence allowed our ancestors to make tools and to manipulate physical objects, social intelligence enabled them to keep track of other group members and understand their intentions, and natural history intelligence improved their abilities to track and hunt animals. Although these abilities greatly facilitated the survival of early hominans, they were not integrated; in other words, the products of each type of intelligence were not accessible to the others. Consequently, early hominans exhibited a "fragmented" consciousness. Modern humans do not face this limitation, for we possess a cognitive fluidity that allows us to do things such as think of animals as people and people as animals, manipulate both animals and people the way we do tools (and even discard them!), and classify human groups the way we do animal species.

Mithen had argued that it was the emergence of fully modern language, which allows for symbolic representation, that broke down the barriers among the other three types of intelligence, allowing each of the intelligences to be applied to other areas. Language did not start out with this capability. Mithen contends that our ancestors' linguistic intelligence was initially related solely to their social intelligence and involved limited vocalizations that were primarily for social purposes, as exemplified in the functions of primate vocalizations. Comparative studies of brain size and group size among primates indicate that as group size increases, the relative size of the brain increases as well, apparently due to the need to keep track of social relationships. In small groups, grooming helps to maintain these relationships, but groups eventually became too large for each individual to groom all the others. One hypothesis is that early language evolved as a form of "long-distance grooming," enabling individuals to remain in contact and reassure one another as they foraged. Early language made it possible for people to maintain connections with larger "circles" and integrate the social group. One relic of this function today is gossip, a group-bonding activity that has been observed in every human society (Dunbar 1997).

Eventually, the linguistic intelligence that evolved to help our ancestors maintain their social relationships began to be applied to other activities. Instead of just speaking to relatives and friends, our ancestors also became able to speak about themselves and about animals and stones. As language created connections among all of these specialized intelligences, it produced the "cognitive fluidity" that forms the basis of symbolism

Box 5.2 HUMANS' INNATE MODULAR INTELLIGENCES

Mithen suggests that several types of specialized intelligence were key to the evolution of the modern human mind. He focuses on four: a technical intelligence that allowed for toolmaking; a natural history or animal intelligence for making inferences about animal behavior; various forms of social intelligence, including "mind reading" of others' intentions; and language. Other researchers have identified a number of other specialized modular structures as well. These include modules for mathematics—manifested in "idiot savants" (who are otherwise mentally and socially inept)—and music—an expressive capacity that can function completely independently of language capabilities.

Social Intelligence

According to Mithen, the most ancient of our innate modules produces our **social intelligence**, which originated early in primate evolution and enabled our ancestors to manage information about large social groups. Social intelligence makes it possible to understand different social positions as well as the hierarchical relationships within a group. It is clear that many primates possess this type of knowledge, for their actions clearly demonstrate that they are aware of the hierarchy of their group and of their own place within it.

A second, more complex aspect of social intelligence, which appears to be present only in the hominids (great apes and humans), involves the ability to make inferences about another animal's mental state and, on this basis, to predict how that animal will behave. To do this, an animal must possess a "theory of mind" that allows it to use its experience of its own self and its motivations as a model for understanding the inner motivations of the other members of its group. The political maneuvering and alliance-building observed among chimpanzees indicate that they possess this type of social intelligence to some degree. But a chimp's awareness of others' minds is limited to its dealings within the social domain. There is little evidence to suggest that chimpanzees are able, for instance, to actively teach one another (e.g., how to use stones to break nuts). Instead, chimpanzees learn to fish for termites and crack open nuts solely through trial-and-error, an indication that they acquire these behaviors through a more general type of intelligence.

Technical Intelligence

It is our specialized **technical intelligence** that gives us the ability to make and use tools. Technical intelligence allows even young children to quickly comprehend that physical objects behave in different ways than living beings. Unlike a cat, a box does not grow, and it cannot move on its own. Our innate understanding of the properties of physical objects enables us to make tools, to know which materials to make them from, and to understand what type of tools a particular task requires. Although they are able to make tools for specific purposes (such as stripping leaves from a twig to produce a termite fishing stick), chimpanzees have virtually no technical intelligence; their manufacture of tools is a rare, rather than a regular, activity. Moreover, chimpanzees have never been observed to use one tool to make another. One of their most sophisticated tool uses, the hammer-and-anvil techniques that some chimpanzees use to break open nuts, is a simple task for a human child, but it requires years for chimpanzees to learn. Apparently, there is an enormous technical intelligence gap between using two stones to crack open nuts and striking two stones together to produce a sharp cutting edge.

Natural History or "Animal" Intelligence

Our **natural history intelligence** enables us to quickly recognize similarities and differences in the natural world. Children quickly grasp the essence of a cat or dog and understand that a cat that is missing its tail or one leg is still a cat. Cross-cultural studies have shown that every known culture classifies plants and animals in similar ways on the basis of various salient features. (This type of classification ability also finds expression in the Linnaean classification system used in biology and the natural sciences.) Our natural history intelligence enables us to readily distinguish among animal species, understand their behaviors and cycles of movement, read animal tracks in pursuit of game, and understand the similarities and differences among species of animals. Chimpanzees display only a little of this intelligence. They do return to termite mounds and ant nests to fish for insects that they know are present because they previously encountered them at the site. They are limited, however, in their abilities to apply what they know. Their knowledge of food is based on their prior experience of where food was found, and they find new sources of food primarily through chance encounters. They do not appear to be capable of understanding that certain kinds of plants grow under specific ecological conditions, which would enable them to systematically seek out new sources of food.

Linguistic Intelligence

One of the most remarkable domains of specialized human intelligence is our **linguistic intelligence**, a capability that is generally thought to define *Homo sapiens* itself. We acquire language as children, and we do so without any formal training in grammar or pronunciation. Mere exposure to spoken language is sufficient to trigger this linguistic intelligence and elicit its learning capabilities. Some children can even learn to speak a foreign language primarily by watching television programs. A six-year-old child knows hundreds of words (or more), and can use them appropriately without reflection. Although each language organizes words into sentences in its own specific ways, all languages follow certain universal rules, such as the distinction between the subject and the verb in a sentence. The many common features of languages around the world as well as the many similarities in the stages of language acquisition indicate that language is based on features that are hard-wired into us.

Music as an Innate Modular Capability

While language and music are closely related and share some of the same basic brain capacities, particularly an overlap in the processing of syntactic relations, music and language nonetheless have capabilities that may be completely dissociated from one another and function as autonomous systems (Aniruddh 2003). The modular basis of music processing involves a range of neural components specialized for processing music (Peretz and Coltheart (2003). The separate modular basis of music from language is illustrated in its persistence in people in whom brain damage has interfered with the language capacity. Similarly, localized brain trauma may lead to the loss of musical ability even when spoken language functions persist. There is reason to believe that music capacity developed before language did. The continuity with primate vocalizations suggests that music was a more ancient communicative capacity. But human auditory processing of music is distinct from that in animals. Humans have a musical sensitivity to harmony and a dislike for dissonant chords. Music appears to affect emotions in ways that are transcultural, and humans show innate capacities for music processing and perception (Hauser and McDermott 2003). Consequently, music may have been a catalyst for brain development, selecting for individuals with a greater capacity for expressive vocalization because they were able to play more powerful roles within the group (Wallin, Merker, and Brown 2000).

(in which one thing "stands" for another) and unleashed an unprecedented period of cultural innovation.

Mithen suggests that the barriers between our specialized intelligences began to break down around 100,000 years ago. As this occurred, knowledge was able to flow from one domain of intelligence to another, creating new ways of thinking. Sophisticated harpoons dating to at least 90,000 years ago provide clear evidence that bones were being made into tools, a sign that natural history intelligence and technical intelligence were becoming integrated. Animal concepts were integrated with personal and social identities in the anthropomorphic and totemic ideas that constituted some of the early religious conceptions and practices. People produced beads and other objects of personal adornment with distinctive styles, indicating that they were seeing themselves as members of groups and using their technical intelligence to distinguish these groups from one another.

Although language could have provided this kind of integration, did it? Language is thought to have emerged during the explosion of cultural representation that occurred approximately 40,000 years ago. But if language is taken as evidence of this transformation of humans, how could it also have caused it? What else might have produced these changes in human cognitive capacities? The shamanic paradigm suggests an answer.

Cognitive Fluidity and Shamanism

In many ways, shamanism integrates our representational capabilities. Shamans blended social and personal identities with the animal world, integrating natural history intelligence into personal and social identity in animal powers. Shamans were experts in the use of social intelligence, which enabled them to become charismatic group leaders. Their natural history intelligence enabled them to be the "master of the animals" and direct hunting activities. Shamans use music and other integrative processes, including drumming, that produce ASC, which have integrative effects on consciousness, identity, emotions, attachments, social bonds, and even sense of self. These cognitive capacities are all involved in the cultural explosion of 40,000 years ago and suggest that shamanism had a previous functional role in the evolution of modern human consciousness and culture. These integrated forms of thinking produced the universal abilities of shamans, which can be seen in their use of the various specialized intelligences to produce the modern mind. The ASC of shamans have the capacity to produce this kind of cross-modular blending through synesthesia, a mixing of sensory modalities in which one can "see" sounds and "feel" colors. The visionary experiences of shamanism also reflect a blending of human capacities, illustrated in lucid dreaming, which blends the capabilities of the dream mode of consciousness with the waking mode; animal powers, which blend human and animal representation systems; and views of the Universe as an interconnected and interdependent system.

Ritual Displays and the Dream World: Accessing Presentational Symbolism. A key aspect of shamanic practice is the integration of dream cycles within ritual altered states of consciousness. Shamanic rituals are typically performed overnight, so it is inevitable that they will incorporate the dream cycle. Not only would drumming displays have the adaptive advantage of deterring predators; these vigorous nighttime activities would have likely induced unusually intense and conscious episodes of dreaming, which could have naturally led to the experiences of soul flight and out-of-body experience. Shamans may also engage in dream incubation to integrate intentions into subsequent dream and visionary experiences. As the widespread concept of the "Dream Time" makes clear, many shamanic cultures explicitly acknowledge the role of dreaming in their practices. Shamanic visionary experiences engage the same self-representation and symbolic capacities that underlie the mammalian capacities of dreaming (Hunt 1995).

Dreaming constitutes a mammalian adaptation for learning by producing memory associations during sleep by using the "off-line" frontal cortex (Winson 1985). The universality of dreaming in mammals indicates that this form of consciousness constituted a preadaptation for uniquely human forms of consciousness (Brereton 2000). Dreams are a manifestation of an "unconscious personality" (Winson 1985) that shamanism manages through ritual. Brereton (2000) characterizes dreams as a representation of self in emotionally salient space, a process of "virtual scenario construction" that provides a mechanism for a risk-free construction and examination of personal options. This scenario-building process provides an opportunity for developing plans related to issues of social relations and personal adaptations. Through rit-

ually induced dreams, shamanism was able to use this scenario construction capacity, exapting the functional processes of dreaming to other domains.

Shamanic Flight as Neurognostic and Symbolic Reference. A fundamental characteristic of the shamanic spirit world encounter is exemplified in the visionary experiences of the shamanic "flight," "journey," out-of-body experience, or astral projection. These experiences are manifested cross-culturally and across diverse situations because they are based in innate structures (Hunt 1995; Laughlin 1997; Winkelman 2000). Hunt suggested that these innate capacities involve *presentational* symbolism, an imagistic symbolic modality involving body sensations and images that is different from our *representational* (word) symbolism.

The images of shamanic experience reflect structures of the nonverbal mind and manifestations of self, emotions, and repressed memories. The expressions in visions provide new perspectives for developing self-awareness and increasing the capacity for rapid transmission of information. This capacity of the presentational modality is expressed in the saying "A picture is worth a thousand words" and in the rich levels of meaning that can be derived from a single dream image. Mental imagery has adaptive advantages in analysis, synthesis, diagnosis, planning, and psychological manipulations. Internal images reflect an innate cognitive capacity for producing representations from the mind's own materials. They are also forms of biological communication reflecting basic principles of neural organization and involve a preverbal symbol system that can act directly on the body (Achterberg 1985). Images play a central role in coordinating a wide range of unconscious biological systems. The shamans' visionary experiences engage this imagistic capacity, using the symbolic potential of body-based representations to address the dynamics of emotional and social life.

Why should the shamanic experience be out of a *body*? Soul flight is a symbolic representation of the shaman's transcendence of the physical body. Body-based principles are the foundation of all knowing, and the body image is a natural symbol system for knowing the Universe through our actions in and on the world. Our bodies are natural symbols—models for organizing both our internal and our external experiences. Body metaphors provide a natural symbolic system for all levels of representation, from organization at metabolic levels through self-representation, social relations, and advanced conceptual functions (Laughlin 1997). These roles of the body are exemplified in common metaphors such as "He's the *head* of the group" and "Give me a *hand* with this."

This body-based foundation for knowledge is superseded in the shamans' out-of-body-experiences, reflecting a transcendence of consciousness beyond the framework of the body. Hunt proposes that this aspect of shamanic consciousness engages the human capacity to "take the role of the other," constructing a new model of the self derived from externalized perceptions of self. This perspective on self from the perspective of the "other" is the same process by which we learn to see ourselves as other members of the social group do. So, too, can we distance our perception of our own body, taking the perspective of the "other," developing greater contextual awareness by separating our perceptual capacities from body-based awareness to allow them to operate in the symbolic domains of presentational visions.

Animal Powers as Personal and Social Identities. One of the key adaptive components of shamanism is its integration of animal and human characteristics, which occurred when the barriers broke down between our social intelligence (which allows us to "think about people") and our natural history intelligence (which allows us to "think about animals"). This gave rise to new ways of thinking that people still use to make sense of their place in the world. **Totemism** ("thinking about social groups as animal species") considers human societies to be analogous to animal species. Totemistic ideas are common among modern hunter–gatherer groups, which often organize their societies into different descent groups, each identified with a different animal (we will discuss this in more detail in Chapters 6 and 7). Totemism applies our natural history intelligence to the social realm, employing capacities for understanding differences in animal species to understand and form social identities. The notion that the shaman is the "master of the animals" who can visit the "mother of the animals," the shifts in personal identities that occur when animal familiars and guardian spirits appear, and the shaman's role as the most important charismatic group leader all reflect an expansion of the capacity for social intelligence based on the ability to understand others by using these innate modules in novel ways. This capacity for identification with the animal world likely emerged millions of years ago when hominans began to use animal disguises to hunt.

Shamanism involves an engagement with an animistic world pervaded by unseen but causal agents. Animals play a central role in shamanic thought because they express and engage the mental hardware of our "animal" brains (i.e., the reptilian and paleo-mammalian brains). These animal-like aspects of ourselves allow the use of animal concepts to connect us with more basic "animal-like" cognitive processes. This connection enhances self-awareness of information relevant to environmental adaptation, hunting and food procurement, and protection.

Human Identity in Nature. Animism involves social intelligence, especially the "theory of mind." Humans naturally view the world in human terms, and spirits are typically seen as possessing many of the same qualities as humans while differing in significant ways (such as lacking bodies). **Anthropomorphism** ("thinking about animals as people") attributes human characteristics to animals. This tendency to see animals in human terms provided a great advantage in hunting, for hunters could now apply the "theory of mind" that they used to understand their fellow hunters to understand the animals they were pursuing. In shamanic "animal powers," humans acquired the powers of animals. By seeing lions as "brave," foxes as "cunning," and rabbits as "shy," humans had a shorthand description of the qualities of these animals that they considered worthy of emulating. Our ability to attribute our own qualities to others also allows us to conceive of animals as allies and guardian spirits. Animal qualities became models for human development. Animals came to represent the internal characteristics of shamans and other people, a cognizing of psychological characteristics (e.g., powerful, timid, quick) in terms of the qualities of the animals people are thought to possess.

The Networks of Perception and Consciousness. Shamanic cognition produces special attributes of human consciousness of the environment that result from the projection of meaning and intentionality onto elements of the natural world (Hubbard 2002). This projection of "intentional stance" involves the attribution of our mental states, desires, and beliefs to nature, producing an understanding of phenomena in the natural world in terms of the dynamics of people. Hubbard notes that shamanism's extension of intentionality into the natural world expands the "in-group," considering nature to be basically like the self. The result is a greater sense of connection with the Universe.

This shamanic projection engages generic structures and processes of human thought that are recognized in contemporary cognitive science's connectionist models (Hubbard 2002). These connectionist models see memories as part of networks, a perspective reflected in the shamanic "web of life" model of the interconnectedness and interdependence of all life forms. Human self-awareness and psychological integration are enhanced by this view of complex linkages among all aspects of the natural world, including humans. The environment has contributed to the formation of the structures of the neural networks of our memory, making the structures of the natural world similar to human conceptual structures. These similarities are reflected in shamanic visions, which transfer information to conscious awareness via images that emerge from the unconscious structures of the brain by virtue of their iconic similarity. This process provides the conscious mind with information it does not ordinarily have.

Summary: Cognitive Adaptation in Shamanism

Many of the key features of shamanism illustrate that religious beliefs and behaviors are the products of the integration of the different modalities of thinking that gave rise to the modern symbolic capacities. Shamanism appears as an expression of our ancestors' increasing cognitive sophistication derived from the internal visionary experiences of the dream world, our primordial symbolic substrate. Shamanism provided the context within which the further developments of our ritual capacities developed into symbolic religious beliefs and behaviors. Shamanic practices provide activities that enhanced human adaptation, well-being, and reproductive success by permitting the expansion of our symbolic capacities to enhance group inclusion, coordination, and communication and to elevate unconscious information into conscious awareness.

New forms of cognition and symbolic processes were manifested in animal spirit concepts that defined personal and social identities, and in the information-acquiring capabilities associated with the visionary images of shamanic ecstasy (which occurs in divination, healing, and other practices). These processes provided mechanisms for healing, personal individuation, social integration, cognitive and emotional integration, and symbolic expressions, all of which we will examine in subsequent chapters. Shamanic cognition extended the use of the mental hardware that originally evolved to help us respond to the social and natural environments—such as the brain structures underlying attachment and bonding, kinship, altruism and coalitional thinking, and ordinary unconscious intuitive thought processes—and used these structures to serve other psychological and social functions. Shamanic rituals offered our ancestors adaptive advantages, helping them manage their emotions and social interactions in ways that aided survival. These brain features also have adaptive qualities in themselves. Because they were necessary preadaptations for shamanism, it seems that shamanism exapted a number of functional systems and integrated them in ways that provided a new level of human symbolic adaptation.

"Complex Hunter–Gatherer Religions": The Rise of Ancestor Cults and Priests

The spectacular religious developments that began about 40,000 years ago ultimately led to new forms of ritual activity that transcended the activities of the shamans. This occurred when food-gathering societies increased in complexity and began to produce food surpluses.

Anthropologists have long attributed the religious changes associated with the rise of priesthoods to the emergence of agriculture and the increased resources that resulted from the domestication of plants and animals, which freed many of the members of society to specialize in other tasks. However, this explanation overlooks a basic fact: People in most food-producing societies actually spend *more* time working to obtain the essentials of life than they do in most foraging societies. Why would people around the world abandon the rich, varied, and generally leisurely life of foraging and adopt the more labor-intensive ways of life involved with plant and animal domestication?

An alternative explanation for these changes and the evolution of more complex societies is the desire to accumulate and store large amounts of food for prolonged periods. Such food surpluses could support not only a more sedentary and complex society, but also extravagant ritual displays. This resulted in what archaeologist Brian Hayden (2003) calls a "complex hunter–gatherer" type of religion characterized by unequal social statuses. This occurred as small, elite groups began to control both the resources of key areas and the labor to exploit these resources. These elite groups then used art and dramatic public rituals to express their control and influence through public displays that demonstrated prestige and success. This gave rise to several new expressions of religion.

Fertility Cults

The public cult activities of these new religions were focused on fertility. Fertility cults helped the elite lineages compete with one another for the wives who

The Venus of Willendorf, the most famous of the "Venus figurines," was discovered in 1908 during excavations near the city of Vienna. The figurine, which was originally painted red, clearly shows female features. It is estimated to be around 25,000 years old. European sites have yielded over two hundred similar figurines dating to between 30,000 and 12,000 years ago.

would produce the children who would continue the lineage. Fertility cults, animal cults, ancestor worship, and feasting were all part of a system in which the production of food surpluses improved the likelihood that elites would have large numbers of offspring and that these offspring would have a greater chance of survival.

The rise of fertility cults is epitomized in the "Venus figurines," the most famous examples of early "portable art." The exaggerated female features of many of these pieces (broad hips, large breasts and buttocks, and prominent genitalia) have been taken as signs that these figurines represented pregnant women and reflected their adoration in a fertility cult. Although the true meaning and use of these statues may be unknown, their presence over a large region and across thousands of years of time indicates that the ideas that lay behind these figurines were part of a widespread tradition that adored the ample female body as a natural sign of health and fertility. Their

high quality, the extensive work involved in their production, and the standardization of their features suggests that these were produced by specialists and were items of prestige that only the elites possessed.

Animal Cults and Ancestor Worship

The early phase of these new religions appeared to focus on animal cults, with groups glorifying and worshiping specific species. Ethnographic analogy indicates that religious activities involving animals were related to the type of social group known as a **clan.** These animals represented the lineage groups or kinship systems that constituted the most important social organization of society (see further discussion in Chapter 9). The extensive collection and ritual treatment of the skulls of fierce animals such as bears also attest to the linkages between hunting animals and human ritual activities. Just as shamans acquire animal powers, so too do more complex societies link their powers to the concepts of fierce animals.

Animal cults were eventually refined and subordinated to ancestor cults. The dramatic burials of leaders with elaborate jewelry and grave goods suggest that specific ancestors were taking precedence over group totemic symbols. Nonetheless, animals (including some newly domesticated species) continued to play important roles in numerous ritual activities. For example, bulls became central features of many ritual complexes (the minotaur of ancient Crete was half man, half bull, and the God Mithras was sacrificed in the form of a bull before returning in human form). Bulls were central symbols of fertility and military power, of force and violence, and of masculine sun powers. Animal symbols were associated with ritual burials of high-status individuals. While some of the honored dead were likely shamans, others were probably important social leaders such as the heads of clans. Ancestor cults are suggested by the special care given to the burial of a few elderly men, interred with elaborate grave goods and offerings that indicated their elevated status. Their skulls were often removed and used as ritual objects, reflecting the special importance of these individuals in their afterlife roles—the kinds of practices that ethnographic analogy suggests are involved in ancestor worship and totemism.

Commodity Items

Jewelry, figurines, and other "cult" items are an outgrowth of the activities of the rulers who exchanged them to extract further surpluses from the common people. Ritual objects that reflect status allowed these commodities to become a source of social identification for the masses and power and riches for the elites that produced them. These durable, attractive, and artistic objects served as symbols of success; ethnographic analogy suggests that they may have been used as a currency in bridal payments, as compensation for death, and as gifts or tribute to produce political alliances. Symbols of power and authority are also prominent in objects such as axes, shields, crooks and staffs, suns, boats, and bulls. These objects played prominent roles in the public feasts that cemented social alliances.

Public Feasting

In these emerging complex societies, the sharing of food took on a new dimension. The males of elite groups used the large and public ritual feasts that food surpluses made possible to increase their own prestige, power, and wealth, and to promote bonding and solidarity. These activities have their precursors in the meat-sharing behavior of male chimpanzees. But in contrast to both this chimpanzee behavior and the local and in-group bonding provided by shamanism, the public feasts of these complex societies linked the males of *different* communities together. Feasting also provided a basis for extending the veneration of the elite groups' ancestors into a broad community practice in which the entire society worshiped these ancestors as Gods.

Megalithic Architecture

The most conspicuous of all the objects produced by these new hierarchical societies were megalithic architectural works. While these enormous structures (such as the henge monuments and the pyramids) were erected to honor the dead, spirits, and supernatural forces, they also symbolized the economic, political, and reproductive success of the groups that sponsored their construction. They were public statements of the power of the leaders, and their size emphasized their elevated status in the hierarchy. Many megalithic structures were seen as reaching to the heavens, the abode of the Gods. The association of ancestor objects (bodies, skulls, etc.) with this monumental architecture illustrates the role these structures played in both honoring the ancestors and elevating the status of the living descendants. Some structures had lower-level shrine areas that were accessible only from the upper-level residence of the elite rulers, suggesting that these areas were intended for special cult ritual activities. Cult activities provided a basis for the initiation of the

youth into power structures, for building alliances between elite members, and for providing a point of assembly for public rituals.

Elite Initiation

The new strata of elites used the ancient shamanic practices of ecstasy to socialize their offspring into cult groups. They likely began to enhance their own privileges in society by restricting most peoples' access to ecstatic states and asserting that they alone had access to the divine. Their rituals may have included special initiatory ceremonies held in caves for the children of the leaders of these societies. A range of evidence supports this interpretation: the presence of the footprints of children in these sites; the intermittent and rare use of caves that suggests that they were utilized by a small elite; the depiction of animals that have symbolic social implications rather than nutritional importance; the location of these sites in areas of rich food resources; and the evidence that feasting took place at these sites.

Summary of "Feasting Religions"

The emergence of elite cults represents a turning point in the evolution of religions. The shift from popular to elite cults made it possible for members of elite groups to use religious symbols to manipulate and control their communities to serve their own ambitions. Shamans undoubtedly played a significant role in these initiations, using their power and position to form important alliances with the elites of these emerging complex societies, and reinforcing hierarchies within shamanic practitioners and the society in general.

In modern chiefdoms, the leaders of resource-rich societies rule by virtue of their position in kinship systems, and they may exert control over thousands of people. Rituals to honor the ancestors of the chiefs often provide the focus for public religiosity. Wealth exchanges and prestige competitions are central economic and political processes, and slaves, captives, human sacrifices, and ritual and actual combat are prominent features of society. Prestige items are important markers differentiating elites from others and play a role in ancestor worship activities that promote the ancestors of current leaders as Gods. The major features of such societies include wealth exchanges, bride exchanges, arranged marriages, social alliances, debts and fines, and the allocation of resources in times of scarcity. Groups express their superiority through warfare, human sacrifices, and megalithic architecture, and these features reflect a strata of religious practices that eventually become dominated by priests rather than by shamans.

Table 5.2 Magico-Religious Practitioner Types, Social Conditions, and Biosocial Functions

	Magico–Religious Practitioners Types and Societal Configurations				Biosocial Functions
		Priest	Priest	Priest	Social control
			Sorcerer/witch	Sorcerer/witch	Social conflict
			or		
			Medium	Medium	Altered states of consciousness
	Shaman	Shaman/healer	Healer	Healer	Altered states of consciousness
Socioeconomic Conditions	Hunting/ gathering	Agriculture	Political integration	Social classes	

The Socioeconomic Transformation of Shamans and Shamanistic Healers

As human societies increased in population and developed more complex political structures, their ritual practices also became more complex. One of the most important results of the **Neolithic Revolution** (also often referred to as the "agricultural revolution") was an increasing specialization in the roles of men and women. As societies shifted from foraging to agriculture, the resulting increases in food allowed large numbers of people to engage in other activities not directly related to food production. These changes also affected the roles and duties of the shamans.

The emergence of sedentary agricultural societies with more complex political and class structures changed the context within which religiosity was both defined and expressed. As a consequence, the various tasks and capabilities that had previously been the domain of the *generalized* shaman were split among a number of culturally defined religious *specialists*. Cross-cultural data (Winkelman 1990, 1992) illustrates how sociocultural evolution produced changes in the shaman, which evolved into other types of magico-religious practitioners as socioeconomic conditions changed. The factors that led to the transformation of shamanic practices to other types of religious practitioners included (1) the emergence of agriculture; (2) the transition from a nomadic to a sedentary lifestyle; (3) the political integration of small, local communities into larger, hierarchical societies; and (4) the stratification of society into distinct classes. The relationships of these socioeconomic conditions to religious practitioner types can be seen in Table 5.2. These practitioner–societal configurations reflect a correspondence between the practitioners' selection procedures and their professional functions, providing the basis for a model of the evolution of magico-religious functions.

The social evolution of cultures divided three of the major aspects of shamanism: altered states of consciousness and healing; social power; and malevolent or evil potentials. The shaman's role as the social leader was superseded by the role of the priest as a social–political and religious leader that emerged from fertility cults. The leaders of this new hierarchical power structure eventually challenged the local power of the shaman, repressing and distorting shamanism into a strictly negative profile manifested in the role of the sorcerer/witch. The roles of shamanism in healing and divination through altered states persisted, however, and was transformed into the new manifestations of **shamanistic healers**—ritual leaders who use ASC to interact with spirits on behalf of the community to heal and acquire information.

Priests. Priests emerged as the preeminent religious specialists in the "public feasting" rites of more complex societies. This new level of religious leader did not completely replace the shamanistic level, but did result in new religious practices and powers. The role of priests is based on their position in the kinship system that defines the ruling power for society. These kinship foundations provide the basis for ancestor worship, a form of religion that links secular and sacred power into one system. These economic, political, and social leaders generally directed the agricultural cycle by determining the timing of planting and harvesting, and by conducting the calendrical rituals that celebrated the major phases of the agricultural cycle. We examine priests in more detail in Chapter 9.

Witches and Sorcerers. The beliefs about the negative supernatural abilities of shamans was retained in complex societies in the **sorcerer/witch**, who was thought to perform only harmful and evil acts. These sorcerer/witches also maintain many other features associated with shamans. They obtain their powers from animal familiars, and are often thought to be able to transform into animals and to fly about at night. Concerns about evil are central to religious systems and are examined in Chapter 10.

Shaman/Healers. In agricultural societies, **shaman/healers** perform healing, divination, and agricultural rituals for the community. Shaman/healers differ from shamans in a number of important ways. They constitute a professional group that provides instruction and training to initiates who, when their training is complete, are ceremonially recognized as healers. Shaman/healers specialize in their roles. Some make diagnoses or perform agricultural rituals, but do not heal. Others work only as healers or treat only specific kinds of illnesses. Although shaman/healers enter ecstatic states and interact with the spirit world, they generally do not experience soul journeys. Instead, many use meditative states. Their powers are derived from both spirits and impersonal sources, and they use rituals and techniques learned from other professionals. We discuss shaman/healers in Chapter 6.

Mediums. In societies with complex political hierarchies, **mediums** serve as diviners, healers, and mediators of relations with the supernatural. Mediums are predominantly women of low social and economic status. It is generally believed that they do not engage in malevolent acts but work to counteract the influences of sorcerers, witches, and evil spirits. They worship and propitiate their possessing spirits and make sacrifices to them. The altered states that mediums experience generally begin as spontaneous possession episodes that occur in late adolescence or early adulthood. As part of their training, mediums learn how to deliberately induce these altered states. This enables them to gain control over when, where, and why they occur, and to integrate these events into their lives. We discussed mediums in Chapter 3.

Healers. Healers are found in agricultural societies that are politically integrated beyond the level of the local community. Almost exclusively male, healers generally enjoy a high social and economic status that is reflected in their political, legislative, and judicial powers and their position as officiant at group ceremonial activities. They are full-time specialists who belong to powerful professional organizations with formal political power. Although healers use a variety of specialized techniques to diagnose and treat disease, they do not perform the ecstatic activities that are the defining characteristics of shamans. We discuss healers in Chapter 6.

Shamanistic Healers. The persistence of shamanic healing practices in the transformed practices of mediums, healers, and shaman healers reflects a universal of religion: healing. All societies have religious healing practices that involve the use of ritual, altered states of consciousness, and an engagement with the spirit world to diagnose illness and treat it. These universal cultural traditions reflect biological bases and point to another area of the potential of religion to provide adaptations through healing, which is the topic of Chapter 6.

Conclusions: The Evolutionary Origins of Religion

In this chapter, we examined evidence for the origins of human religiosity in shamanism, a spiritual practice found worldwide in foraging societies. The practices of shamans are intimately tied to some of the central features in the evolution of modern human cognition and the evolution of new human symbolic, social, and personal capacities. Central features of shamanism reflect the utilization of these innate modules of our mental hardware that enable us to understand and adapt to specific features of our environment. The underlying biological features of human shamanism persisted, while aspects of their manifestations changed as more complex societies with different types of religious specialists evolved; consequently, many of the core concepts and behaviors associated with shamanism can still be found in more complex societies, although in modified forms.

Like biological evolution, cultural evolution is a process by which new forms develop on top of older ones and give the old forms new expression. Thus, shamanic elements persisted in the shamanistic practices of more complex societies. These elements include a persistent feature of religiosity—healing. This topic leads us to the next chapter, which explores how these capacities for enhancing human well-being also evolved in the context of shamanism. We will see how the capabilities that appeared with the first shamans continue to underlie the religious practices that shape both individuals and societies, and we will seek explanations for religious healing practices in terms of their relationships to our biological nature.

Questions for Discussion

- In what ways are the behaviors exhibited by shamans similar to those of chimpanzees? How are they different?
- What explanation for the origin of religiosity makes the most sense to you? Why?
- Did religiosity appear suddenly or emerge gradually?

Glossary

anthropomorphism the practice of ascribing human characteristics to nonhuman beings and objects

clan a type of kinship group, usually organized according to either the male's or the female's lineage

module = independent units

innate modules the components of our mental hardware, each of which is responsible for a specific capability.

linguistic intelligence a specialized type of intelligence that makes it possible for a person to learn and use language

medium a religious practitioner found primarily in agricultural societies, often a woman of low socioeconomic status who enters possession states to communicate with spirits and obtain answers from them to the questions posed by her clients

mimesis the ability to learn by imitating others

natural history intelligence a specialized intelligence that enables an individual to similarities and differences among liv

new stone

Neolithic Revolution the period (around 10,000 years ago) during which humans began to actively grow their food rather than just hunt and collect it; also known as the "agricultural revolution"

shaman a part-time general-purpose religious specialist found in foraging societies

shaman/healer in agricultural societies, a religious specialist who performs healing and divination

shamanic paradigm the theory, based upon cross-cultural and biological data, that shamanism best typifies humankind's first religious practices

shamanistic healer a religious practitioner that reflects the shamanic roots of ASC, spirit engagement, and healing, but which is found in complex societies

social intelligence a specialized type of intelligence that enables an individual to manage his or her knowledge of large social groups

sorcerer/witch a religious practitioner who is credited with performing harmful or evil acts

technical intelligence a specialized type of intelligence that gives an individual the ability to make and use tools

totemism a practice in which a human group is defined or organized through reference to an animal species

totem pole (high to low)

The Origins and Functions of Religious Healing

CHAPTER OUTLINE

Introduction: Religious Healing as a Cultural Universal
The Co-evolution of Community Healing and Religiosity
Spirit Beings as a Mechanism for Coping with Stress
Music and Healing
Hypnosis and Placebo Effects as a Foundation for Religious Healing
Adaptive Mechanisms in Pre-shamanic Healing Systems
Shamanistic Religious Rituals as Self- and Emotional Healing
Conclusions: Shamanic Healing Process

CHAPTER OBJECTIVES

- Describe the universal associations of religious concepts with healing and illness, and provide evidence that explains their interrelationships.
- Illustrate the positive effects of religion on health and some of the mechanisms through which religion can affect health.
- Examine the co-evolution of healing and sickness responses and religiosity.
- Describe the evolutionary origins of healing responses in hypnotic and placebo responses.
- Describe the special roles of religious coping in the autonomic nervous system.
- Examine the pre-adaptations for shamanic healing and the additional adaptations and exaptations of shamanic and religious healing.
- Illustrate the adaptive role of spirit assumptions in the social and psychological processes of individual and group integration.

THE JUVENILE HAD BEEN WEAKENED BY THE WOUNDS he had received in the vicious attack by the males of the neighboring group. Now running for his life, he stumbled through the bushes toward the excited cries of his relatives in the distance. Those shrieking from the treetop on the adjacent hill guided him towards the safety of the group. He arrived, collapsing in exhaustion against the tree trunk. The group gathered around him, grooming his bruised body and carefully wiping dirt from his wounds with leaves. Their cooing voices combined with the sounds

of the evening in an envelope of warmth and security. As he relaxed, he fell into a vivid hypnogogic dream in which he saw once more his close encounter with death at the hands of the neighboring tribe. His spirit soared above his body, which he saw running on the trail below. In the distance he heard his family singing their power songs to the night, defying their foes, both natural and supernatural.

* * *

The journey had been long and arduous, and it had been expensive. But they had no remaining alternatives.

They had already consulted with their local healers, who had asked the woman questions, looked into her eyes, felt her pulse, and subjected her to a host of other tests. But all were at a loss as to what was wrong with her and how to heal her. So her family had decided to take her to the place of miracles, renowned for its healers and its special powers. It was said that people without hope could find hope there.

Introduction: Religious Healing as a Cultural Universal

These opening vignettes illustrate a central aspect of human nature: our reliance on supernatural and religious remedies for addressing our health concerns. These special concerns with health are an outcome of hominan evolution. "Care of the sick is not a helping behavior commonly found among unrelated chimpanzees at Gombe. . . . Indeed, the ill and wounded may be shunned by other members of the group who often appear fearful of the sick, injured, and those with infections. Among captive chimpanzees, however, there may be a very different response, including cleansing of wounds and extraction of diseased teeth. These behaviors reflect the chimpanzee's cognitive abilities, including the capacity to empathize with others, understanding their needs" (Goodall 1986, p. 385). Under the influence of domestication, chimpanzees also begin to express concerns about the well-being of others. But it takes humans to heal.

Because sickness and injury are unavoidable aspects of life, every society has specialized individuals who work to help cure people of their diseases and restore health. Although the ways that cultures conceive of illness and treat it vary greatly, there are many common features of the "healing arts." For example, for people everywhere, religion is an important aspect of the healing process. These common features point to the biological origins and evolved features of religious healing.

It is of special significance that one of the universal functions of religion is to heal, and every culture has its religious healing practices. What is the basis for the central role that religion plays in healing beliefs and practices? All cultures believe that there are supernatural causes of illness originating from the spirit world and from humans with supernatural power. These common concerns of health, illness, and religiosity have deep roots in our prehistory, a reflection of the intimate connection between well-being and spiritual concerns in human nature.

Throughout the world, supernatural concerns have been the most important determinants of health, even more so than physical factors. In many societies, even physical illness is thought to be a consequence of the actions of evil spirits, ghosts, and sorcerers, or a punishment from the Gods. Supernatural agents play a central role in most theories of illness, and cultures everywhere believe that people can become ill because they have lost their souls or have been possessed by spirits.

The universal belief that religious activities can play a central role in human health and healing is supported by contemporary scientific studies that have demonstrated a causal relationship between religion and health. Virtually every scientific study of the relationship between health and religion finds religious people are more likely to be healthy and recover more quickly. This holds true no matter what religion a person might adhere to. Given the many recognized ways in which religion has effects on health through influences on behavior (e.g., drug use, sex), this association of religion and health is not surprising. One widely noted religious healing mechanism involves a medical phenomenon known as the "placebo effect," where positive expectations, confidence, and belief produce physical changes in the body. But how do placebos produce the perception—and the reality—of healing?

By providing meaning and a sense of ultimate protection, religion has the power to affect and control the physiological changes that result from the deadly stress response. There are a range of religious healing mechanisms, from the physiological effects of rituals, evaluations, and worldviews to various psychosocial effects of the group on the psychological and physiological conditions of the participants. Religions produce this broad range of effects because they can affect the physiological responses of our opioid and autonomic nervous systems, enhancing bonding relationships with significant others that can reduce anxiety and stress.

All healing systems derive effects from the authoritative and charismatic characteristics of the healer, the trusting relationship between the healer and patient, and the expectations for a successful healing process. These dynamics can engage the body's placebo response and induce the release of opioids, our natural pain-killers that evoke immune system responses. These endogenous healing processes involve mechanisms that can be elicited by religious healing. Rituals may heal through their effects on social bonding and through charismatic ritual performances and other aspects of ritual processes that evoke a range of responses. The effects of rituals are expanded by socialization of associations of symbols with physiological processes, allowing religious meanings to

Box 6.1 THE ETYMOLOGICAL ROOTS OF RELIGION, HEALING, AND ILLNESS

The idea of a common biological foundation for both religion and healing finds linguistic support in ancient English and in the roots of the Indo-European languages, which has a common linguistic root—*kailo*—for heal, holy, and whole. Religious concerns with health are also reflected in the broader ancient root meanings of the English terms "cure," "sick," and "illness." *Heal* also means "To rid of sin, anxiety. . . . To become whole and sound" (Morris 1981, *American Heritage Dictionary* [*AHD*], p. 607). Spiritual implications are found in the root meanings of *cure;* the Indo-European root *cûra* also has religious significance, referring to the "spiritual charge or care of souls, as of a priest for his congregation." The words *ill* and *sick*, the opposite of *healthy*, also have spiritual meanings. *Ill* has linguistic roots in the Middle English *ill(e)*, meaning "sickness of body or mind," evil and wickedness (*AHD*, pp. 655–56). *Sick*, derived from the Indo-European root *seug-*, means suffering or deeply affected by emotions, as well as "corruption."

evoke the body's healing responses. These learned associations and the linkages of rituals with cultural beliefs are important aspects of the religious healing processes involved in making a person "whole."

This chapter explores the evolutionary origins of the relationship between healing and religion. We identify the pre-adaptations and exaptations on which religious healing is based and the uniquely human religious healing adaptations associated with shamanism. Pre-adaptations for core aspects of shamanic healing involve dominance and submission relations, reflected in primate grooming and its role in eliciting the relaxation response and opioids. The evolution of hominan ritual healing capacities expanded pre-adaptations involving the investments that mammals make in their offspring and relatives, assisting them in the basic tasks of survival. The mammalian bonding capacities were extended to healing through enhanced abilities to elicit our opioid system through a variety of mechanisms, including ritual. Religious adaptations involving healing also provide enhanced coping strategies for the management of emotions, particularly the processes of stress reduction. We examine other pre-adaptations for shamanic healing found in hypnotic susceptibility and placebo mechanisms and consider how they were extended in ritual dynamics that used spirit concepts for purposes of healing. Religious healing provided a variety of adaptive advantages through producing a psychological system for a variety of intrapersonal and interpersonal functions, using spirit concepts in the processes of emotional modulation and self-development and management.

Spirit theories of illness such as "soul loss" and "spirit possession" provide mechanisms through which religious healing makes the self "whole." Religions provide personal and social representations that heal by shaping the self and its emotions through encounters with the sacred self and others. Emotional transactions and transformations of the self are produced by ritual enactments and spirit interactions. The opioid-mediated healing produced through ritual group bonding and the positive emotional states are expanded by ritual enactments and mythological drama. Religions' symbolic effects also heal (make whole) through the models and metaphors embodied in the myths that provide models for understanding our selves, our emotions, and our interpersonal relations with others. Because religious concepts expand the elicitation of endogenous healing processes, religious healing constitutes one of the most important adaptive functions of religion that is still manifested in the modern world in a universal feature of religion: shamanistic healing (see Box 6.1: The Etymological Roots of Religion, Healing, and Illness).

Universals of Religious Healing: Shamanistic Healers

Winkelman's (1992) cross-cultural research found a cultural universal of religion: all cultures have religious activities for healing, and use altered states of consciousness to heal in communal rituals involving interactions with the spirits. These shamanistic healers enter into altered states of consciousness (ASC) so that they may contact spirits who will help them to diagnosis diseases and heal their group. Why should the belief that humans can enhance their health through interactions with supernatural powers be found in all cultures? A key feature of shamanistic healing activities involves a communal dimension, sometimes the entire local community, or a smaller more intimate group such as a family. Particularly in premodern cultures, religious healers occupy important leadership roles associated with their supernatural powers. These religious healers attempt to enhance health by engaging the beneficial effects of spirits and supernatural power or by removing their malevolent supernatural effects.

Every year, Roman Catholics and others journey to the French city of Lourdes in the hope that they will be cured of their afflictions.

A central feature of religious healing systems is the faith that both the healers and patients have in the system by eliciting positive expectations. Traditional healers are often feared for their power, but many have a warm, caring, personal style that encourages their patients to feel confident that they will recover. The high prestige that healers typically hold within their cultures further helps to reinforce the positive expectations of patients. The social group also plays an important part in the therapeutic process, helping to reinforce both parties' emotional commitment to the effectiveness of the therapy. Universal aspects of the therapeutic process include the power of faith, providing patient and healer with a sense of control and mastery over the illness episode. Religious convictions are particularly effective ways to engage belief and produce healing.

These features of successful healing encounters are engaged by religious expectations regarding powerful supernatural others who can assist by using powers that exceed the human capacity. Religious healing is generally provided by a powerful, esteemed individual who mediates this relationship with the supernatural power and engages the power in ways that restore the patient's health. But the supernatural may also be thought to produce the opposite effect—illness and death. All cultures have healing practices involving actions to remove harmful spirit influences, as well as to counter the effects of humans' malevolent supernatural actions (e.g., sorcery or witchcraft). Although cultures differ with regard to the spiritual diseases they recognize, the types of spirit interactions used for healing, and the rituals

and magical techniques they employ, the belief that spirits are key agents in both illness and healing are central to all these practices. The belief that religion can enhance health is not merely a product of superstition or supernatural fallacy, but reflects scientifically established effects of religion on health.

Scientific Evidence of the Effects of Religion on Health

The evidence that religion can enhance health is literally overwhelming. First, there are many accounts of people who claim to have been healed of a variety of conditions, including recognized medical diseases. In addition, hundreds of epidemiological studies show a statistically significant relationship between religious participation and lower morbidity and mortality rates for virtually all diseases (Koenig, McCullough, and Larson 2001; Levin 1994). Almost every measure of religion is associated with more favorable health outcomes for nearly all groups, independently of the type of religion or disease. The risks for morbidity and mortality from most diseases are lower among religions that are stricter, suggesting that religions with higher levels of religiosity have enhanced effects on health. The impact of religion on mental health is particularly well noted, and most studies have indicated that people with greater religious involvement are more likely to express happiness, optimism, and satisfaction with their lives; experience higher self-esteem; adapt better to loss and grief; have lower rates of anxiety, depression, and loneliness;

have lower levels of suicide, psychosis, and drug abuse; and, in general, experience greater marital and life satisfaction.

But some people have pointed to possible flaws in such studies. For instance, do healthier people simply feel well enough to go to church more often than sick people, leading to a false indication that religion enhances health? There are also questions about the possible health effects of associated factors such as the economic status; education; age; health status; smoking and alcohol consumption; and dietary, sexual, and social activities of religious people. The recognized behavioral, psychological, and social effects on health are part of religion's effects in enhancing health, but religion also has positive health effects independently of these factors.

As Sloan, Bagiella, and Powell (1999) point out, some of the well-publicized associations between religion and health were no longer statistically significant once controls for other social and behavioral variables were introduced. This does not disprove that religion enhances health, but does illustrate the need to explain how religion interacts with the recognized mediating psychosocial mechanisms that affect health, such as restrictions on diet, drug use, and sex (Koenig et al. 1999). The larger social network and support systems of frequent church attendees provide these people with greater surveillance for health problems and a network of resources that helps them to cope with problems, reducing stress, depression, and self-destructive behaviors. Religion also has psychodynamic effects through beliefs that can help reduce stress and anxiety, creating emotionally tranquil states that may facilitate placebo effects.

But is there something more? These recognized health mechanisms do not appear to explain all of religion's effects on mortality; Strawbridge et al. (1997) show that the relationship between health practices and preventive behaviors constitutes only part of the causal pathway through which religion affects health. The analyses and controls involved in research by Strawbridge et al. established that more religious people had lower mortality rates independent of initial health and established risk factors found in social conditions. Nonetheless, social conditions do act both as intervening variables and as causes of the relation between religion and mortality.

Although these intervening variables are the stronger predictors of health (for example, those who frequently attended church were less likely to use drugs, more likely to reduce their smoking and drinking, and more likely to remain married), there is still a remaining religious effect on health. The effects of religious attendance on survival persist when controlling for demographic conditions, mental and physical health, health behaviors, social support networks and confidantes, and drug use (Koenig et al. 1999). This indicates the need for studies to determine the specific behavioral or psychosocial mechanisms that produce these differences, particularly religion's broad effects on attitudes and coping responses.

Religion as a Natural Healing Mechanism. Religion seems to be a natural for healing. Why? A range of evidence illustrates the interrelationships of healing and religiosity and reflects the co-evolution of these adaptive responses. Innate healing capacities are derived from social bonding processes and they function more effectively when people make assumptions about the supernatural. Cognitive capacities derived from religious assumptions contributed to the expansion of the human healing capacities. To establish that religious healing constituted a human adaptation, we need more than just the overwhelming evidence that religious participation can produce healing effects. We must also identify the adaptive behaviors that produced these healing benefits and the mechanisms that were subject to natural selection in the environment of evolutionary adaptation. A principal mechanism involved expansions of the opioid systems that are mediated by social relations, both of which have positive effects on health. Other mechanisms of religious healing involve the ability of the associated meaning systems to manage the stress mechanisms and the modulation of emotions. McClenon (2002, 2006) has illustrated additional mechanisms of religious healing in the hypnotic and placebo capacities and their effects on health. We will examine these and other aspects of the evolution of humans' healing capacities to illustrate the pre-shamanic adaptations involving the effects of community ritual effects on health. These baselines clarify the distinctive religious adaptations that provided the basis for humans' shamanic healing practices based on spiritual assumptions.

The Co-evolution of Community Healing and Religiosity

In Chapter 5, we looked at the evidence for the origins of modern religiosity in shamanism. Shamanic healing practices provided the context for interrelationships between and the interdependent co-evolution of religion and healing. These were communal practices that built out of the common bases with our hominin relatives, expanding on capacities for altruism, reciprocity, bonding, and emotional communication.

Evolution of the "Sickness and Healing" Response

Evolutionary perspectives reveal that human adaptations to sickness and healing have a common basis tied to religious concerns. Psychiatrist Horacio Fábrega (1997) shows that humans have a "sickness and healing" response that is an integrated social and biological adaptation involved in helping others. Our innate healing responses are expansions of adaptations involving caring, altruism, and compassion for our offspring and relatives. This sickness and healing response expands assistance to others in ways that elicit natural recovery processes. When humans' biological systems are disturbed, they react adaptively and protectively; part of this reaction includes a psychosomatic mediation of physiological and hormonal changes, where beliefs, hopes, and social support can induce changes in physiological responses (such as a reduction of stress and increases in opioid levels).

Fábrega shows humans' innate sickness and healing adaptations are the result of an evolutionary trend involving care-giving. The tendencies for care-giving have ancient roots that are reflected in chimpanzee behaviors involving the care of infants, grooming, and other forms of reassuring touch. Such care is sometimes extended in response to the wounded members of their group, where some chimpanzees provide them with protection, caressing, and assistance. The dramatic expansion of sickness and healing responses in humans indicates that they were part of divergent human evolution from our common hominin ancestors with chimpanzees. Uniquely human sickness and healing practices reflect a hominan expansion of a biologically rooted care giving, sharing, and sociality. This expanded response reflects changes in social organization that occurred during human evolution that have extended social bonds beyond the family through collective ritual interactions.

The sickness and healing response involves an emotional awareness of another's situation, a capacity that is manifested in the primate tendency to respond to the emotional displays of others with expressions of empathy and sympathy. Some of the emotions that naturally elicit healing responses are states of pain, suffering, and distress in others, which can evoke responsive capacities of empathy, compassion, and altruism. The sickness and healing response represents a type of emotional communication based in the ability to take another organism's condition into consideration. This requires a theory of mind that enables the individual to infer that another is suffering and needs assistance that can be provided. Our awareness of the needs of "others" reflects the enhanced social awareness that underlies the religious belief in the supernatural "other." Fábrega proposes, however, that what links healing with religious concerns is death. Since sickness can result in death, healing is necessarily concerned with death as one of the possible outcomes. Consequently, efforts at healing direct attention to death and questions about the afterlife and, consequently, spirits. Spirit beliefs extend the care of the deceased into the spiritual domains. These beliefs provide particularly powerful coping mechanisms that enhance health and well-being, particularly emotions, which we examine below and in Chapter 8. There are even more ancient physiological adaptations involving our mammalian attachment system and the positive health effects of social integration. A key feature of hominan survival that was greatly expanded in hominans is the capacity to integrate larger groups into harmonious coordinated systems. Ritual is a fundamental tool of social integration that was expanded in human adaptation and evolution for enhanced healing functions.

Healing Through Community Ritual Bonding and Opioid Release

Eliade's (1964) classic conceptualization of shamanism emphasizes that the shaman acted on behalf of the community, and that shamanic ritual provided the most important reason for the community to gather. Religious healing generally occurs within a community. In small-scale societies, the entire local residential group may participate in the healing ceremony. This community presence enhances healing through many factors, including social—such as reintegrating the patient into the social group—and psychophysiological—where religious attitudes and activities produce effects on the person's body and physiological processes. The group participation associated with religious healing is a central source of the therapeutic effects, including psycho- and socio-physiological effects. Religious ritual groups can produce healing through evoking feelings of belongingness, euphoria, and omnipotence. These effects are not just psychological, but also manifested in physiological responses. These responses include activation of the body's attachment system and release of its own opiate-like substances, the opioids or endorphins.

Frecska and Kulcsar (1989) show how religious healing practices elicit psychobiologically mediated attachment based in opioid mechanisms. Mother-infant bonding in mammals is based in the opioid system. Community bonding rituals also elicit this biologically based mammalian attachment. Our basic patterns of mother–infant attachment and their physiological, emotional, and cognitive responses are exapted and extended by religion. This enables opioid release to be induced by the feelings of comfort and protection received from a powerful figure—spiritual or human—and for those feelings and associated physiological responses to become associated with religious symbols during socialization.

The community engagement by shamanic ritual has important social, psychological, and psychophysiological effects because it uses our mammalian attachment systems. The stimulation of feelings of attachment—a mechanism that evolved to ensure that infants and caregivers remained in close proximity to one another—make people feel secure and confident that they are being protected by a powerful figure (Kirkpatrick 1997, 2005). These mammalian capacities were enhanced in humans and extended to broader groups, meeting the need for group coordination which expanded in importance in hominans.

Humans' evolutionary context produced a neuropsychology for adaptation to a social world, a need for emotional life that is wired into the human nervous system. These opioid-mediated dynamics of health and well-being were greatly expanded in human evolution, as indicated in the studies reviewed in Chapter 5 regarding the enhancement of human opioid systems. Social life demands a capacity for emotional attachment and self-control based on internalizations of social identities developed in the symbiotic caregiver–child relationship and bonding experiences that engage the mammalian attachment dynamics. Social identity and personhood became a necessity, a reflection of social interdependency that coordinates individual neurological, emotional, and psychological development in relationships with social others. Shamanic ritual practices met humans' attachment needs and expanded them to a broader group through ritual social bonding and spiritual symbols.

Being involved in a group activity can elicit a variety of sociopsychological and sociophysiological responses. These range from crowd contagion, where mob behavior and psychology engulfs individuals, to a range of related sociophysiological effects produced by the presence of others (i.e., the elicitation of opioid responses). These psychological and physiological responses become associated with the religious symbols that are present, producing a cross-conditioning of the body and religious symbolism. This linkage of religious and physiological domains through the association of symbolic and emotional processes provides a basis for subsequent ritual elicitation of the opioid system through the manipulation of religious symbols.

Ritual also brings together a group of supportive others, a social network whose disposition to help has

long-term positive effects on health. Group rituals help to meet fundamental human needs for belonging, comfort, and attachment to others. Rituals integrate people, enhancing social support systems and group identity, and healing through providing supportive attachments. The individual's self and psychodynamics are constituted—created—within the social attachment relations that provide socialization experiences, which develop personal and social identification and self-models for internalization. Spiritual attachment relations contribute to emotional development by influencing personal and social identity through providing self-models for internalization. Rituals produce powerful physiological reactions through their deep phylogenetic roots in the mediation of our emotional states and social relations with others.

Hayden (2003) shows why these enhanced social ritual practices emerged very early in human evolution. These behaviors were not explicitly for healing, but used to help integrate different groups of people to create alliances that favored survival. Rossano (2006) suggests why we should consider these group rituals and their ecstatic states as the first stage of the evolution of religion that emerged prior to the Upper Paleolithic and the advent of shamanism. There was a significant dynamic of hominan healing that exceeded hominan ritual but did not involve the full dynamics of shamanic healing that emerged in full form in the Upper Paleolithic. Shamanic rituals expanded the healing capacity of these prior social bonding processes with the manipulation of spiritual symbols of self and other. Shamanistic practices also expanded prior dynamics of ritual, adopting practices that stimulated the release of opioids through a variety of physical and behavioral mechanisms, including extensive drumming, dancing, and clapping activities; repetitive physical activity; temperature extremes (e.g., sweat lodges); stressors such as fasting, flagellation, and self-inflicted wounds; emotional manipulations (e.g., fear and positive expectations); and nocturnal activities that occur at times when our endogenous opioid levels are naturally highest (see Winkelman 1997 for review and original research). There were also exaptations of prior opioid healing mechanisms in the expansions of hominin grooming practices into a specialization of shamanism: massage (see Box 6.2: Grooming as Healing).

The Health Effects of Social Support. There is much evidence that the dynamics of social rituals provide a variety of other health benefits. Contemporary research into the health effects of social networks illustrates that they not only provide material and interpersonal assistance

Box 6.2 GROOMING AS HEALING

One feature of hominin ritual that has virtually disappeared in modern humans is grooming. Grooming is a complement to the aggressive behaviors of dominant chimpanzees and is a peaceful action that provides reassurance to subordinate animals. Attacks are often followed by a variety of "reassurance behaviors" that calm both the threatened individual and the aggressor. When subordinate animals seek reassurance from dominant animals, their most frequent behaviors are to extend a hand to seek contact with the aggressor and to initiate grooming; the aggressor may respond with grooming, touching, patting movements, contact with the body, embraces, and kissing. Chimpanzees may also achieve self-calming by holding their own hands, embracing themselves, and grooming themselves. Goodall concludes that chimpanzees learn the calming effect of grooming on others and use it with the intent to manipulate. The ability of grooming to reduce stress is generalized from mother–infant contact and affiliative grooming relationships to the whole community in the formation and maintenance of personal relations.

Shamans inherited this complex of behaviors. With actions reminiscent of grooming, shamans often carefully inspect the body of the sick person—touching, examining, and prodding areas that appear unusual. Shamans often employ massage, the therapeutic behavior of modern humans that bears the greatest resemblance to primate grooming. Grooming and massage share characteristics of touching the body, and both elicit opioid responses. One of the primary reinforcers for grooming at the biological level is the release of endogenous opiates that help the groomers bond (Dunbar 2004). The laying on of hands and similar practices that resemble shamanic healing practices have been shown to enhance functioning of the opioid system in humans.

A female chimpanzee with an infant reaches out to a male for reassurance.

with health, but that they also have a variety of positive psychological and physiological effects. Religious rituals also have a capacity to enhance health through their many immediate and long-term effects. Religion can enhance personal well-being by maintaining a support system that provides material assistance and a sense of belonging and comfort. Religious participation can pro-vide immediate effects on health by meeting fundamental human emotional needs for attachment, emotional closeness, and a sense of belonging and comfort with others. Rituals integrate and bond people in long-term groups, enhancing social support systems. These social effects derive from rituals' ability to facilitate social integration and cohesion. Religion can affect health through its influences on a person's day-to-day social relations, providing assistance and support by creating social obligations that mobilize others to provide support, relief, comfort, and protection.

The positive effects of social support on health are illustrated by many contemporary studies (Berkman 1984, 1985; Berkman and Kawachi 2000; Heaney and Israel 2002; Kawachi and Berkman 2003). Social support networks can enhance health and recovery, implicating the community relations formed by religions as mechanisms by which religion influences health. Social networks involve a web of social ties that link people together through material assistance, assistance with daily living, social activities, and other interactions that meet basic needs. Social networks affect health by influencing people to take preventive measures, encouraging them to comply with treatments, and helping them to avoid risks. Religious participation may reduce risk behaviors such as malnutrition, inactivity, engaging in unhealthy activities, mishandling relationships, and excessive emotions such as grief that could provoke further health problems.

The association of social networks with a reduction in a wide range of diseases indicates that the health effects of social networks operate through a number of different pathways. Research on the positive health effects of social support have implicated the following mechanisms (Berkman 1984, 1985; Heaney and Israel 2002):

- intimacy, companionship, and sense of belonging
- opportunity for nurturing behavior and reassurance of personal worth
- assistance with the provision of tangible resources
- guidance and advice, particularly problem-solving
- enhanced disease surveillance and access to information and assistance
- reduction of risk behaviors and enhancement of preventive health measures
- positive interpretations of circumstances contributing to perceived control

Social support processes of religion can affect biological pathways through behavioral, psychological, and social responses. Central to religion's healing effects are the social relations that reduce the deleterious effects of stress from potential threats or problems. Religions offer a permanent sense of social and emotional support through assurances of God's protection and help, as well as the emotional and material assistance of other followers in the group. Religious groups offer various forms of assistance to their members, including significant

information and emotional moderation, relieving anxiety and the stress response. Social support may involve emotional, instrumental, material, financial, and informational dimensions that affect one's appraisal or assessment of circumstances and one's personal ability to cope with them (Heaney and Israel 1998). Appraisal emphasizes *perception* as the factor most strongly linked to the effects of social support on health outcomes. This suggests that perceptions regarding benevolent spiritual providers also have the potential to positively affect health.

The provision of social support, intimacy, nurturance, and reassurance, as well as the sense of belonging, can terminate stress responses. Social networks may inhibit an individual's stressful physiological responses associated with anger and depression by reinterpreting those responses or by changing behavioral or physiological responses that exacerbate the stress response. Social networks not only help people cope because they make it possible for them to share emotional and cognitive strategies for managing stress, but also may enhance their access to medical care or their capacity to make better health decisions. In short, social support enhances well-being by improving the individual's integration within social networks. Social integration in turn may enhance health by creating a positive self-evaluation that gives the individual a sense of mastery and purpose and that prevents despair and anxiety. Social relations may also induce the release of endogenous opioids, which enhance immune system responses. The social support generated by relationships with people may also be met by relationships with supernatural spirit others.

Spirit Beings as a Mechanism for Coping with Stress

Central healing processes of religion involve symbolic management of the physiological consequences of stress. By managing our emotional reactions of anxiety, religious interventions enhance many aspects of health, well-being, and, ultimately, survival. Social relations and symbols can evoke the relaxation response. By relieving anxiety and stress, religion provides believers with a sense of control and may evoke automatic—and autonomic—responses. Religious beliefs can inspire confidence and contribute to the mobilization of personal defenses and social resources. Religious healing provides a unified psycho-socio-physiological response in which personal meaning and social support instill a sense of serenity that may prevent activation of the general adaptation syndrome and can mediate the detrimental effects of stress. Ritual activities, religious symbols, and social processes can have direct physiological effects on the autonomic nervous system. Rituals can help to reduce high levels of stress hormones by creating positive hope and expectations, countering anxiety, altering our emotional responses, and, consequently, altering our stress responses. This reduction of stress and its physiological concomitants enhance the immune system and the body's capacity for recovery.

Religion involves an adaptive set of beliefs that have direct positive effects on survival and health that can be broadly characterized as coping. **Coping** refers to the ways in which human beings confront the difficulties that they face. Coping involves changing the environment, ourselves, or both. Religion plays a variety of powerful roles in coping and other healing processes (see Lee and Newberg [2005] for review). Religious coping is associated with more favorable outcomes in the face of negative events, indicating that belief in a benevolent deity is particularly adaptive when the demands we face exceed our capacities to cope (see Spilka and McIntosh [1997] for review). Spirit assumptions are adaptive because they provide positive hope and expectations about the adequacy of resources for managing our stress.

Coping begins with an appraisal process in which the individual assesses the significance or meaning of an event. For many people, religious ideas play an important role in this appraisal process, for they believe that a deity can have an influence on their situation and its remediation. During this process, the person attempts to interpret his or her personal situation within a broader framework of values, beliefs, and concepts about the Universe. Religious concepts are particularly effective for explaining unpredictable occurrences, helping us answer such personal questions as "Why me, God?" Because of the interpretive framework that a religion offers its adherents, even very tragic occurrences may come to be seen as part of a "plan." This can provide people with a sense of assurance in spite of the immediate tragedy.

During the second stage of the appraisal process, the individual evaluates the resources he or she possesses to address the threats to effective coping. Individuals must address both the threats presented by the situation and the emotions those threats are engendering. Many of the problems we face—such as death, natural disaster, and uncertainty about the future—are things that we cannot change. When circumstances cannot be altered, coping often focuses on changing our emotional responses to our problems. Religions often directly address the anxiety and stress associated with threats and challenges to our well-being.

People are especially likely to turn to religion to help them cope when they perceive that they or their significant others are threatened. Religion appears to be particularly useful for countering our negative emotions and refocusing our attention on more positive expectations. People's tendency to turn to religion when they face threats or challenges reflects religion's particularly effective role in producing positive and constructive emotional responses. When people are faced with tragedy, religion can provide meaning and contribute to their coping and adjustment processes (for example, attendance at religious services in the United States spiked dramatically for several months after September 11, 2001).

Because many religions teach their adherents that their God is able to overcome any circumstances, believers are able to maintain a sense of control, and this can play a significant role in the coping process. There are several ways that a religion can offer its followers this sense of control: It may teach that the deity is in complete control of events, that the individual is in control, or that control comes about through the relationship between the deity and the individual. Many people find it easier to face stressful and threatening life events when they believe in a God who is loving and supportive and who will assist them as long as they pray, have faith, or participate in religious activities.

There are also other ways that religions help to cope with stress. Simply being a member of a religious community or congregation may provide a person with access to additional resources in times of need. Religious faith often promotes an optimistic view of life, and participation in a religious ceremony can instill feelings of well-being and positive affect. These experiences provide an effective means of reducing stress at both the physiological and psychological levels. The ability of religious practices and beliefs to affect our physiological functioning through the use of symbols has made religion one of our most important means of cultural adaptation. Religions provide many symbols, meanings, and processes that affect the biological processes involved in our responses to stress.

Stress is not an automatic response to a particular type of event. As we saw in Chapter 2, all events are evaluated and understood within the context of each individual's personal world. When faced with a challenging or dangerous event, an individual will interpret that event using the models she has learned during experiences with earlier, similar events. Her own sense of how capable she is of responding to the current event (based on her previously acquired models) will determine whether or not stress results. Our models and assessments of our perceptions are linked to emotions and, consequently, to our physiological responses to perceived threats to our well-being. In other words, stress is not merely a product of the objective circumstances, but a product of our perceived ability or inability to effectively respond to those circumstances. Depending on the individual's assessment of the situation, he or she may experience fear and anxiety, or peace and serenity. Stress is managed through coping resources that mediate physiological responses by imbuing events with particular significance and meaning; religion is a particularly effective means of mediating potential threats by providing a variety of psychological, social, cognitive, and ultimate assurances.

Symbolic Effects on the Autonomic Nervous System and Stress Responses

To better understand what stress is and why we experience certain events as stressful, we need to look once more at our nervous system and how it functions. This time, we will focus on our "involuntary" responses, those actions and reactions of our body that we typically do not think about. You already know quite a bit about these involuntary responses. Perhaps you enjoy watching "scary" movies. If you do, then think about the way that your hair may stand on end during a particularly frightening scene or how you may start to fidget or close your eyes when you know that something scary is about to happen. Or think of the "butterflies" you get in your stomach, the prickly sensations that run up and down your skin, and the accelerated heart rate you may experience when you face such threatening moments as taking an exam, applying for a job, or meeting your new girlfriend's parents for the first time.

These responses are all part of the **general adaptation syndrome**, the hard-wired reaction that mammals experience to **stressors**. The general adaptation syndrome was discovered by Hans Seyle (1907–1982), an endocrinologist who studied how stress affects body chemistry. Our basic response to stress has become known as the "fight or flight" response. When an animal perceives a threat, numerous chemical changes occur in its body that help it prepare for the burst of activity that will allow it either to defend itself ("fight") or to quickly flee to safety ("flight").

These physiological responses to stress begin with an increase in activity in the sympathetic branch of the autonomic nervous system. Sympathetic activity involves the release of several hormones and neurotransmitters, especially epinephrine (adrenaline) and norepinephrine. These substances prepare us for action in the outside world by shifting blood to our muscles and mobilizing fatty acids for use as energy. They also accelerate our heart rate and raise our blood pressure. As you may know, this "adrenaline rush" can be quite exhilarating, and many people now pursue it for its own sake by engaging in dangerous activities such as racing cars, parachuting, hang gliding, or bungee jumping.

In the short term, the responses of the general adaptation syndrome can aid in survival by providing the bursts of energy animals or people need to get out of danger. But if the stress hormones our bodies produce when our brains perceive danger are not metabolized through muscle activity, they will continue to circulate throughout the body. Over the long term, this can cause such problems as arteriosclerosis (hardening of the arteries) and heart failure. Continued stress can also compromise the immune system, increasing a person's susceptibility to infection. Prolonged activation of the general stress response exhausts the resources of the body and makes it more susceptible to disease. Because stress results in increased brain activity, long-term stress can also exhaust neurotransmitter resources and affect normal brain functioning. The psychological effects of stress include depression and anxiety.

Unfortunately, these deep-rooted mammalian responses to danger are now evoked by situations in which "fighting" or "fleeing" are not good options. For too many people, a college exam, a job interview, or dinner with the parents are modern-day stressors that evoke these ancient responses. In cities, the constant background noise, the many sources of stimulation, and the need to commute to a job through crowded streets often evokes the general adaptation syndrome, and the "fight or flight" response can be expressed as "road rage" and other forms of aggression. Similarly, social situations and even symbols can activate and mobilize the body. But if a person has no appropriate way to respond to all these stressors, he or she may develop ulcers, hypertension, cardiovascular problems, and migraine headaches.

Even the mere thought of a particular situation can produce the same physiological responses as the actual situation if a person is fearful enough. That is, a symbolically threatening situation can produce the same general adaptation syndrome activation as an actual threat to physical survival. These and other physical problems are a consequence of a person's inability to respond adaptively to the psychological and emotional aspects of life. Instead debilitating emotions are experienced. For example, when you are walking alone late at night, shadows from a bush that you interpret as a hidden attacker provoke the same physiological reactions— fear, trembling, hair rising up on end, shortness of breath, and an elevated heart rate—as if a person had actually been standing there. But symbolic threats do not permit a physical struggle through which we would utilize the hormones released to address the threat and physically overcome it. Although our hard-wired responses ensure that our body is mobilized, the situation we face may not allow us to make use of our inherited responses, leaving us with residual long-term stress and its physiological consequences.

The Roles of Meaning in Coping and Stress Management

The symbolic management of these physiological consequences of our emotional reactions and the resultant stress is central to adaptations provided by religious healing rituals. Just as social relations and symbols can evoke stress, they can also evoke the **relaxation response**. The relaxation response activates the parasympathetic division of the nervous system, producing physiological changes that mediate rest, recuperation, sleep, and the maintenance of internal balance. When religious beliefs promote a sense of serenity and tranquility, a sense of assurance that everything is in the hands of a nurturing being that provides feelings of comfort and protection, these are not merely psychological effects. Such feelings induced by religious occurrences result in physiological effects on our bodies that prevent or minimize activation of the general adaptation syndrome and the detrimental effects of stress.

The anthropologist Bronislaw Malinowski (1954) attributed the origins of religion to the management of emotional life and its stress, anxieties, and frustrations. Stress and anxiety are contributory to illness and provide mechanisms through which religion and ritual can enhance health. Religion provides assurances as well as explanations that may relieve emotional conflicts and distress (for instance, by attributing impulses to possessing spirits). Religion provides a sense of control by providing its believers a domain of known possibilities and the appropriate behaviors that enhance coping and alleviation of distress.

Meaning is fundamental to stress mechanisms; consequently, religion can alleviate the potentially devastating physiological consequences of stress by providing meanings that give assurances and instill confidence, counteracting anxiety and its physiological effects. Religious healing provides a unified psycho-socio-physiological

response in which personal meanings from supernatural relations and the social support that comes from group membership counteract stress. Ritual healing is a dynamic function of the psyche that provides mechanisms for maintenance of autonomic balance (Valle and Prince 1989). Ritual symbols, social processes, and activities have direct physiological effects on the autonomic nervous system. Ritual can alleviate high levels of pituitary/adrenal activity of the resistance stage of the stress reaction through creating positive hope and expectations, countering anxiety, changing emotional responses, and altering autonomic balance. The altered states of consciousness induced by religious rituals lead directly to a parasympathetic activation and relief of stress and enhances the immune system and the body's capacity for recovery.

Religion's role in healing practices worldwide and the often-reported relief that people receive from these practices attest to the special role of religion in promoting well-being. People who cope with negative events by turning to religion have more favorable outcomes, suggesting that a framework based on benevolent principles is particularly important when the demands of life exceed personal coping capacities (Spilka and McIntosh 1997). Religion makes threats and tragedies meaningful by integrating them within a framework of beliefs, and it helps make them manageable by providing assurance that anything is possible with the assistance of a deity.

But how does meaning produce changes in one's experience and health? How are effects transmitted from the mind to the body? Religion's healing mechanisms are wide-ranging, from the personal worldview it provides to its psychosocial effects on the group and the physiological effects of rituals on the individual. The attachment of emotions to religious symbols is a fundamental part of a process that links meaning and the body's psychophysiological responses. Religious expectations reduce stressful life circumstances by managing perceptions of threats and the uncertainty, anxiety, and depression they can evoke.

The power of religion and myth to manage our emotions derives from their engagement of our prelinguistic structures of thought and phylogenetically ancient brain that manages unconscious representation and communication processes. Religious rituals can modify emotions by instilling attitudes that control autonomic processes so that the brain responds to challenges with positive emotional responses (God has given me another challenge to overcome) instead of stress (how am I going to deal with this?). Although higher cognitive processes have little control over our emotional reactions, the ritual manipulation of our lower brain structures (the paleomammalian brain and reptilian brain) can directly affect our emotions through manipulating elements of our previous socialization and attachments. The symbolic elements of a religion—pictures, crosses, and significant objects—may acquire associations that allow them to evoke automatic—and autonomic—consequences, inspiring confidence, allying fears, and contributing to the mobilization of our personal will.

Religion's supernatural assumptions provide a system of meaning that can alleviate the physiological consequences of stress by providing assurance and instilling confidence, counteracting anxiety and its physiological effects. Religious healing provides a unified psycho-socio-physiological response in which personal significance (meaningfulness) and social support manage stress. This reduction of stress and its physiological concomitants enhance the immune system and the body's capacity for recovery.

All of these effects of religion point to an adaptive set of beliefs and behaviors that have direct positive effects on survival. These may be some of the most basic adaptive functions of religion, for they have enabled religion to contribute to more effective mechanisms for individual and group survival. It is adaptive to believe that spirits can help you, especially if you also do whatever you can to help yourself. Religion offers not so much a way to engage with the practical demands of life such as protection from predators, but rather a coping strategy for management of the emotional aspects of life through beliefs about the spirit world.

Religious Production of Healing Emotions: "Psychophysiological Symbolism"

Religion's healing power derives in part from its roles in the developmental socialization of emotions and its consequent ability to elicit emotional responses with religious symbols. Religious socialization exploits human emotional plasticity, the tendency for biological responses to be shaped by the cultural environment. While our emotional potentials are based in our biology, they develop through interaction with physiological and sociocultural factors, producing associations that are embedded in the development of the neural structures (synaptic connections) that mediate emotional experiences. This developmental interaction produces "local biologies," reflecting a developmental indeterminacy in emotional potentials and a physiological plasticity that is structured through the cues provided by others in the social environment (Hinton 1999). Emotions are elicited and shaped by culture, and religious socialization can play a principal role in

this process of evaluating the physical and social environment. Consequently, our assumptions and values are literally wired into neural networks (Castillo 1997). Our perceptions of attachments, threats, primary relations, and the nature of the self all involve aspects of our biology that can be shaped by religious meanings, which can elicit and mediate their physiological activations.

Emotions are part of the cognitive evolution of our species. They promote personal and species survival by helping us become attuned to the perceptions of other members of the species. Religion has been one of the most important systems for communicating these codified perceptions of the group, instilling them in the next generation, using emotional excitement and contagion to bring the individual into emotional congruence with other members of the culture, and producing emotionally driven dispositions that respond to certain symbols and value particular behaviors. The religious values and priorities that are instilled through socialization and "emotional contagion" entrain the development of psychological processes and physiological structures in association with cultural symbols.

Religious socialization produces a psychophysiological symbolism (Averill 1996) and entrainment (Laughlin et al. 1992), forms of learning that shape emotions by integrating symbols of the spirit world into personal biological development. Religious processes associate socially valued meanings, symbols, emotional experiences, and physiological processes, developing neural network connections. Learning incorporates cultural programming, including religious beliefs and evaluations, into the responses of the emotional brain, allowing religion to guide us on how to feel about and respond to circumstances by engaging the emotionally driven paleomammalian brain in the decision process, allowing us to act "without thinking."

Religions produce interpenetrations of biological and mental processes, linking physiological processes to cognitive representations. Consequently, religiously evaluated emotions are part of the linkages of the organism with the social and physical environment that are mediated through physiological processes, behavioral activities, communicative interactions, and cognitive interpretations. These connections enable ritual and religious beliefs to affect emotions in a number of ways that are related to healing. Such connections

- elicit physiological responses (fear, anxiety, tranquility, peace, acceptance);
- structure the self and its emotional dynamics, modeling and instilling ideal emotional values and entraining appropriate personal responses; and

- conceptualize emotions and their causes, processes, and functions, often externalizing them in the form of spirits.

If we include human drives and needs—protection, food, sex, security, affiliation, and bonding—within the broader domain of emotions, it becomes apparent that religion is one of the basic tools of socialization through which these basic emotional needs are met. Religions and emotions interact in intimate ways by engaging

- neurophysiological structures, processes, and reactions,
- motivational dynamics and attachments,
- evaluation of environmental conditions and events,
- value orientations and cognitive appraisals,
- behavioral responses and communicational interactions,
- subjective and personal experiences, and
- self-regulation responses.

Our genetic bases for such human capacities as love, compassion, and empathy for others, as well as our altruistic behaviors, are engaged by ritual and religious beliefs. Religion is a powerful means of engaging and meeting those emotional drives through the mechanisms provided by a supernatural ideal other. The elements modeled in a supernatural spirit other ("God") provide important mechanisms for forming connections between individual emotions and collective psychology. The spirit as ideal "significant other" provides a basis for expansion of group identity, particularly in its ability to exceed the innate preference of people to engage in reciprocal altruism with closed kin alone.

Music and Healing

A universal of shamanistic healing is music; all cultures have shamanistic healers who use melodic sound and instrumentation as part of healing rituals. Music has ancient origins in the *Homo* lineage, evolving in hominans as a communicative and expressive function. Music enhances human functioning at a number of levels, particularly social, and in healing. Music engages an innate primal biological function of primates—the ability to express and moderate emotions through vocalizations. The effects of tone and sound on emotions allow music to have a number of adaptive effects on health. Crowe (2004) notes that throughout history music has been used as a curative agent and has been understood to promote health and wellness by restoring the natural balance and harmony in our emotional systems.

Music produces many levels of synchronization, from the physical vibratory effects on the body through synchronization of brain waves, coordination of emotions, and a common focus of intention. Music can enhance the power of a group, creating a sense of unity and connectedness and strengthening the emotional bonds among group members. The physical beat of music produces a synchronization that coordinates and organizes the group. Music has been considered the most effective device for group coordination, whether it involves coordination of movement, interpersonal entrainment, or the creation of a spirit of teamwork (Brown 2000).

Music and the Brain

The impacts of music on the brain begin with the direct auditory nerve connections into the reticular activating system. This area of the brain plays a key role in perceptual alertness, behavioral responses, and maintenance of homeostasis. The basic auditory processing areas in the medulla oblongata are located close to nuclei that control heart rate and respiration; music's physical effects on these areas mediating typical indicators of stress (increased heart rate and restoration) may underlie its noted ability to reduce anxiety and tension. The sound of music alone imposes a resonant pattern that can elicit a similar brain wave response across the brain. Crowe (2004) reviews a number of other mechanisms through which music may also induce relaxation and reduce stress. For example, music affects the autonomic nervous system. Crowe reviews evidence indicating that the sound input to the brain travels from the thalamus to the amygdala, carrying input from the reptilian brain. The amygdala combines this information with input from higher brain centers before diffusing sound information across the brain. Sound information received by the hypothalamus triggers the autonomic nervous system, producing a significant activation of the emotional processing centers.

Janata and Grafton (2003) propose that one of the central effects of the rhythmic properties of music is the entrainment of neural oscillations that synchronize perception and action to the beat of the music. The spatial and temporal sequencing in music has a broader impact on unifying perception, cognition, and behavior. Group experience of music, then, has the potential to unify the group's cognized and experienced Universe. Music can induce common emotions in a group and synchronize the group's responses to the environment. "Because music spans such a broad range of sensorimotor complexity, it provides a potential path for bridging the gap between abstract experimental task and real-world behavior" (Janata and Grafton 2003, p. 687).

Healing Processes in Music

Music can heal by eliciting emotions and providing a supportive context for cathartic expression that relieves troubled emotions. This capacity results from music's intrinsic abilities to evoke certain repressed emotions and to stimulate an intensive expression of both negative and positive emotional states. Crowe (2004) considers the ability of music to stimulate emotions to be the consequence of biologically determined neural responses. Music's direct impact on nonverbal communication processes demonstrates its operation through a "language of emotions." Like spoken language, music has the ability both to communicate something specific (an emotion) and to elicit that same experience in others. Crowe reviews a range of research which indicates that emotional expression induced by music is based on the elicitation of innate, biologically determined emotional states. Music can heal by eliciting those emotional states and by providing a mechanism for venting and constructive expression of repressed emotions. The subjective emotional experiences that are produced by music increase our emotional awareness, bringing emotional concerns to a level of consciousness where ritual processes can be reinforced by their connections with other meanings. Music can generate insight into our own feelings, elicit our emotions, and stimulate our personal development, values, and memories.

Through its effects on the hypothalamus, music may enhance immune system function. Some of the established effects include the ability of music to reduce cortisol and increase the secretion of IgA, both indicators of enhanced functioning of the immune system. Music can counter stress responses, reducing blood pressure, cardiac rate, and other ANS stress markers.

There is good evidence that music is an effective therapy in rehabilitating traumatic brain injury. Crowe (2004) summarizes the therapeutic effects of music in improving cognitive function: It stimulates the senses, provokes complex perceptions, enhances alertness and arousal, increases attention, and affects memory. Music can affect the function of the mind and the brain on every level. Music therapy has been used to address a wide range of health problems, both psychological and physical. Music has been shown to reduce the perception of pain, apparently interfering with the central nervous system transmission of pain stimuli. Positive effects of music on pain include its ability to stimulate the release of endorphins, the body's natural pain-killers.

Music can also induce positive responses in general emotional states, as well as in mental attitudes.

Perhaps the most general effect of music on health involves the broad principle of entrainment, epitomized in the general model of altered states of consciousness and the integrative mode of consciousness—the coherent theta wave brain discharges that synchronize the levels of the brain through the enhanced functioning of the serotonergic nerve networks. The vibroacoustic effects of musical sounds produce resonant patterns in the body structure that initiate the entrainment process. Sound vibrations establish resonant patterns across the body, including resonance in specific organs that vibrate in response. Crowe proposes that these vibratory frequencies of music give it the ability to change the resonant patterns that produce disease, replacing them with an energetic balance. Music appears to elicit responses from the energy fields of the body, ranging from the physical structure of organs, body tissues, and molecules to brain waves and the emergent experiences of consciousness. The ability of music to infuse this hierarchy of the body, brain, and mind with energetic vibratory patterns gives it the potential to carry emotional and subtle biogenetic energies from singer/healer to the patient and community. Crowe proposes that music can amplify the energy of the therapist's emotions and transfer them to the energy field of the patient.

Music appears to have a special connection with the strongest electromagnetic fields of the body—those produced by the heart. According to Crowe, music therapy research and practice confirms that music has the capacity to function as an energetic power that elicits manifestations of unconditional love. She considers this elicitation of love to be the most beneficial of all healing states. The activation of the heart through music and the resultant experiences of love and compassion appear to be universal responses to music that are extended in caring responses directed toward others. One of the effects of music is the induction of empathy—the ability to understand and identify with the experiences of others. Music produces empathy by synchronizing our experiences through rhythm, tone, melody, lyrics, and other dynamics that produce a common awareness. Music has also been widely considered to produce spiritual and transcendental experiences. Music may elicit ecstatic experiences or blissful peace, depending on form, structure, context, and the individual listener. Many different types of music are capable of eliciting emotional bliss and other euphoric states.

Music manifests the phenomenon of complexity, characterized by the emergent properties and novel features of a system that are not merely the sum of its components. These additional characteristics of complex systems reflect a higher level of organization than that manifested by the component parts. The communicative properties of music go beyond the nonverbal expression of basic emotions to the expression of more developed feelings.

Hypnosis and Placebo Effects as a Foundation for Religious Healing

The sociologist James McClenon (2002) proposes a common biological root for shamanism, religion, and ritual healing involving an inheritable quality that is manifested in hypnotic susceptibility and its associated placebo effects. **Hypnotizability** involves focused attention, reduced external awareness, and a reduction of critical thought processes that facilitate a focus on internal images. This ability to focus on inner worlds provides an engagement with the symbolic world of religious beliefs. Hypnotizability and increased suggestibility also provide a basis for cures that affect survival. The overlap in phenomena associated with hypnotizability and placebo effects includes healing responses reflecting a susceptibility to beliefs and expectations associated with spiritual phenomena. Because they were able to benefit more from healing practices that involved hypnosis, those humans who were disposed to hypnotizability enjoyed a survival advantage. Our capacities for hypnotic states are rooted in ancient primate mechanisms that reduce aggression and social stress and engage the relaxation response and dissociative processes. These ritual capacities and hypnotic tendencies were pre-adaptations for religious healing practices. Among humans, the repetitive behaviors associated with ritual and hypnotic behaviors produce classic aspects of religious and mystical experiences, an alteration of consciousness and a sense of intragroup cohesion experienced as "union" or "oneness."

The hypnotic capacity reflects a psychophysiological condition that creates a highly focused attention isolated from the actual environment and bodily awareness. These experiences reflect an engagement with an alternate reality that uses our increased susceptibility to the effects of suggestion to induce psychological and physiological changes. The supernatural dimensions of these experiences enhance their emotional impacts that can produce notable biological changes and significantly affect long-term motivational and behavioral dispositions.

McClenon (2002) proposes that religious healing capacities were selected through adaptive responses associated with hypnosis, dissociation, and the placebo effect. Because humans who were hypnotizable and prone to the anomalous experiences found in dissociative states had better healing responses, these dispositions conferred a survival advantage. The universality of dissociative-state experiences—such as soul flight, possession, mystical awareness, and ESP—indicates that they reflect an innate tendency derived from our mental hardware and the ways it shapes how we know the Universe. These same experiences are generally interpreted by people who have them as evidence of the spiritual world. Accessing these kinds of dissociative experiences is part of the normal cycle of daily consciousness in which we shift from awareness of the external world to an internal focus of attention and engagement with sleep and the experiences of dreams. Ritual activities can engage this same cycle of dissociation from ordinary reality to engage with the internal imagined worlds.

This hypnotic capacity enhances survival by increasing access to the unconscious mind and facilitating the development of creative strategies for personal development and psychological change. Because of their enhanced access to the unconscious mind and its emotional dynamics, humans susceptible to hypnosis can better discover the unconscious dynamics causing their illness. According to psychiatry, most psychological and emotional problems involve the repression of feelings and desires, as well as the conflicts that this repression produces in the self. Hypnosis and other ASC engage the emotional brain to elevate these repressed issues into consciousness where they can be addressed and resolved for healing.

McClenon (2002) contends that humans acquired their capacity for religiosity through the adaptations produced by the healing effects associated with hypnosis and placebo effects. The tendency to suggestibility contributed to a biological capacity for recovery from disease by engaging in alternate realities that were less stressful. Suggestibility enhances symbolically induced physiological changes that facilitate healing. Shamanistic healing practices appear capable of treating the same kinds of conditions for which hypnosis has been shown to have significant clinical effects: somatization, mild psychiatric disorders, simple gynecological conditions, gastrointestinal and respiratory disorders, self-limiting diseases, chronic pain, neurotic and hysterical conditions, and interpersonal, psychosocial, and cultural problems (see McClenon [2002] for review). The elicitation of the pain reduction mechanism is also part of the innate properties of hypnotic susceptibility, where mental expectations can result in a significant reduction in pain. This makes hypnosis adaptive in enabling people to continue to pursue survival-related activities in the face of significant pain. This suggests that the origin of human religiosity derived in part from the adaptive effects that are provided by the healing capacities derived from suggestibility and associated placebo effects.

Shamanic healing practices emerged from the therapeutic effects of ritual activities, social practices that provided selective pressure for genotypes related to various dissociative propensities for religiosity, including hypnotic susceptibility, dissociation, and placebo effects. By using the ritual process to induce ASC and access the emotional unconscious (i.e., through dreaming, activation of the paleomammalian and reptilian areas of the brain, and the visual imagistic processes), shamanism provided mechanisms for healing through integrating the aspects of the pre-symbolic self.

Dissociation is a central phenomenon of hypnosis, possession, anomalous experience, and shamanistic healing (McClenon 2002). Dissociation, broadly defined, is a state in which the person is disconnected from ordinary baseline consciousness and experience of the external world. In this condition, a person who is able to dissociate can be directed by suggestion and become hypnotized. McClenon points to many lines of evidence that indicate dissociation facilitated early humans' ability to cope more effectively with stressful experiences. Shamanic healing rituals contributed to selection for humans who could benefit from the dissociative experiences. Dissociation provides adaptive benefits as a defense mechanism, allowing humans who are traumatized, particularly abused children, to compartmentalize (repress) memories of these traumatic events; this allows them to experience higher levels of health by ignoring their unhealthy memories (McClenon 2006). A standard psychiatric interpretation of the adaptive advantages of dissociation involves its ability to reduce stress.

Dissociation was a necessary by-product of human modular evolution; separate processing modules allowed the brain to unconsciously process domain-specific information. This domain specificity of automatized modules meant not only that information was separated or compartmentalized, but that it was generally not available to consciousness. Dissociation from the ego was a way to access this information in the unconscious. Lynn (2005) proposes that adaptive dissociation derived from the brain's ability to by-pass ordinary self-related cognitive operations and instead develop alternate neural pathways that were not tied to awareness of self and others. In bypassing our ordinary ego states and their intimate linkages

to the desires of others, we are better positioned to act in our own self-interest. Dissociation with possession, in which a deity or spirit expresses one's personal demands, provides a further distancing from apparent self-interest.

Bulbulia (2006) characterizes humans as faith healing primates, reflecting the long connection between religion and healing responses. He suggests that self-deception can work to our advantage and sometimes make us better because religious beliefs have a "low error cost" in comparison to the benefits provided. The benefits of being "duped" are affirmed by a large body of literature that illustrates how self-deception serves self-interest by making it easier for us to deceive others about our true intents and interests. Self-deception gives us confidence and can be adaptive by helping to mitigate stress. "The world loses *real* stressors when supernatural understandings benefit religious agents" (Bulbulia 2006, p. 100).

Bulbulia concludes that religiosity has facilitated evolution through effects on our psychosomatic systems, which are optimized for social inputs, particularly for healing effects derived from provision of care and personal expressions of concern. Bulbulia emphasizes a "costly signaling" theory of the motivations for healers whose public expressions strengthen individual and group confidence and enhance health by mitigating the debilitating effects of stress. Thus, he ties healing capacities to the effects of the *group* context of religious healing rituals which signal a commitment to the group (see Chapter 9). This elicitation of healing by the presence of important social others is found in placebo responses.

Religious Healing as the Placebo Effect

Medicine generally has considered evidence of religious healing to reflect a **placebo effect**. Moerman (2000) defines placebo effects as "the desirable psychological and physiological effects of meaning in the treatment of illness" (p. 52). Doctors often misunderstand what placebos and placebo effects really are. Placebos are typically inert substances, "sugar pills" that do not have biological principles which can evoke a physiological response. Ingestion of the placebo nonetheless results in measurable physiological and/or psychological changes. The idea that the placebo is "all in your head" or is a "self-fulfilling expectation" misses the point that placebos can produce physiological responses that resolve health problems. Placebos elicit the release of endogenous opioids, the body's own natural opiate substances, as well as produce other effects (Benedetti and Amanzio 1997). Placebos reduce pain and psychosomatic conditions (asthma, hay fever, coughing, ulcers), as well as mental health problems (anxiety, depression, and schizophrenia). They also help alleviate some physical conditions, such as cardiovascular problems (hypertension and angina pectoris), multiple sclerosis, Parkinson's disease, and rheumatoid and degenerative arthritis.

Placebo effects are also produced by treatment processes, such as interactions with others who elevate expectations that the problems will be alleviated. Placebo effects are a part of all medical encounters that express support and concern, eliciting the patient's own body to respond in ways that processes a successful treatment. Placebo effects challenge the biomedical paradigm by illustrating that the person's subjective experiences and expectations can produce physiological responses. Belief and the social interactions that support positive expectations elicit healing responses. Placebo effects are central mechanisms of religious healing. While placebo effects originated independent of religiosity, the characteristics of placebo responders illustrate why religion is particularly well-suited for eliciting placebo effects.

Placebo Mechanisms. Placebos affect illness and disease through the individual characteristics of both doctor and patient and the effects of conditioning and meaning (Benedetti and Amanzio 1997). An individual is more likely to have a placebo response if he or she views the physician as competent and attractive, wants the physician to decide the choice of treatments, and has positive expectations regarding the outcome of the treatment. This reflects the patient's general acquiescence to authority and a reactivation of sense of security and trust that originated in mother–infant bonding (Helman 1994). Specific characteristics of healers, including symbols of high status such as a greater age, a prestigious appearance, and symbols of authority, often produce placebo responses because they enhance the patient's confidence in the healing process.

Placebo responders often have higher levels of anxiety than patients who do not respond to placebos, suggesting that the reduction of anxiety is one mechanism through which placebos act (Benedetti and Amanzio 1997). Pain intensity and stress also mediate the placebo response, with higher levels of discomfort eliciting stronger placebo responses. The desire for relief from pain elicits the expectation that pain will be reduced. Desire and expectation, like hope and faith, help to elicit placebo responses (Kirsch 1997).

Information and Meaning as Placebo Mechanisms. The effects of placebos are elicited by previous information and learning, particularly a memory of a previous incident in which drugs or treatments were associated with relief. Such a memory allows for unconditioned healing effects to be elicited by response expectancy (Montgomery and Kirsch 1997). For example, pills produce changes, so when a patient takes pills, he or she expects and experiences changes. By analogy, participants who

Healers often display attributes that indicate their status and abilities to others. The white coat and stethoscope of this Western physician are signs of his status, and the diplomas on the wall provide evidence of his training and abilities.
(Tomas del Amo/PacificStock.com)

167

The elaborate clothing worn by this Nepali healer also identify him as a practitioner of power and ability. His horn and drum are tools for diagnosis and treatment, and the ritual objects on the table in the rear remind the patient of the healer's contacts with the spirit world.

experienced emotional changes during prior religious activities learn an association and expectation of changes when they attend religious rituals. Expectancies produce physiological responses that are analogous to the ways in which our intentions elicit our voluntary behaviors. When we think we want to move, we move; when we think something will upset us, it generally can just by thinking about it without experiencing directly the upsetting stimuli. Similarly, placebo responses are based on our expectations of improvements that produce requisite responses in our bodies. One consequence of this learning effect is that placebos are resistant to extinction, the loss of a response effect. Instead, extinction is prevented because placebos confirm the expectancy that generated them, providing their own intrinsically-induced rewards. Montgomery and Kirsch (1997) conclude that effects of conditioning on the response to placebos is completely mediated by expectancy, showing that verbal information can be used to alter expectancy and obstruct the effect of conditioning. Their results show that it is the *interpretation* that produces the placebo response. It is "mind over matter"—placebo and drug effects are mediated by subjective information.

A fundamental mechanism of placebo activation involves the patient's attitudes and belief, expectancy effects that may produce even stronger effects than the specific drugs, and even physiological actions opposite to the active agents given to patients. This greater power of placebo expectancy over physical agents was found in a study by Flaten, Simonsen, and Olsen (1999). Patients responded more to the information provided (i.e., being told the effect was a stimulant or a relaxant) than the actual physiological properties of the drug taken. These effects were not only psychological, but also physiological, indicated by the differential absorption of the drug by the body; subjects given a relaxant had lower absorption when told they were receiving a stimulant. Moerman (2000) suggests that the effects of placebos are derived from a "meaning response," the attribution of meaning to the treatment by patients. These attributions are influenced by the physician's enthusiasm, the interaction between the physician and patient, and cultural influences such as the colors and forms of the pills.

The placebo response is a Darwinian adaptation that evolved to address disease, injury, and other threats to health. Humphrey (2002, p. 261) suggests that the placebo response is an emergent property of other adaptive features that involve "economic resource management" of our "natural health-care service." These adaptive responses exapted other human emotions, particularly those related to hope and despair, that have the capacity to act directly on our immune systems and healing processes. Humphrey proposes that placebo responses are generated by three general factors: past personal experiences, rational and logical arguments, and the power of respected external authorities. Our past experiences of positive outcomes with treatments engender our placebo responses. Having good reasons to believe in treatments also engenders responses; the most important way to generate placebo analgesia might be to do something that you think is effective. Perhaps the most effective of all placebo elicitation mechanisms is the power of external authorities. Humphrey notes that the placebo response cannot be "self-administered," but rather reflects the outcome of some powerful outside permission to engage in the process of self-cure. This feature suggests that pre-adaptations for placebo responses are manifested in chimpanzee submissive-reconciliation behaviors that are the complement to the aggression and dominance displays.

The placebo effect involves the physiological consequences of expectation mediated through hormones and neurotransmitters that meets our needs for care and concern. This elicitation of placebo responses by social and cultural conditions of meaningfulness is what makes religious healing so powerful. The dramatic symbolic influences of placebos on bodily functions reflect personal, social, and cultural processes that enable our beliefs, expectations, and the associated meanings to have causal effects on our bodies. Since placebo responses are found in animals as well, they emerged prior to shamanic healing practices.

Adaptive Mechanisms in Pre-shamanic Healing Systems

Shamanistic healing practices have pre-adaptations manifested in the following hominin activities:

1. rituals as a mechanism for group coordination and emotional regulation

2. community bonding processes involving elicitation of mammalian opioid-attachment systems

3. group night-time displays involving vocalization, drumming, and bipedal charges/dancing as social integration mechanisms

4. capacities of hypnotizability found in animals as a mechanism for stress management

These commonalities in chimpanzee and shamanic rituals and their functions point to the biological roots of religious healing practices. The primate and hominin biogenetic functions of ritual as a system of social coordination and communication underwent further evolution in hominans in collective ceremonies involving all-night rituals. These evolutionary adaptations are illustrated in the differences of shamanic rituals in comparison to our

closest relatives in the animal world, the chimpanzees (see Chapters 4 and 5). These include

- the expansion of the ancient phylogenetic bases of group rituals to involve all-night rituals with dramatic expressions in music and dance;
- the expansion of community bonding rituals with enhanced opioid capacities for social bonding;
- deliberate alterations of consciousness to produce intentional spirit-world voyages such as the soul flight or the "vision quest," which were natural outcomes of the nocturnal timing of the rituals, which integrated the cognitive processes involved in dreaming;
- use of animals as symbols of religious beliefs and powers, with animals' nature as central to conceptions of spirituality;
- elaborate mimetic enactments of engagement with the spirit world;
- the use of symbolic dimensions of prayers, exhortations, and systems of mythological explanation involving spirit worlds;
- the acquisition of information, as in divination of the causes of diseases;
- the creation of healing practices that engage a variety of social and symbolic processes that produce psychological well-being through expansion of hypnotic and placebo responses;
- the management of death fears;
- healing by using spirits for personal and social identity and self-transformation; and
- the creation of processes of personal integration through eliciting the innate modules.

These practices involved a variety of pre-adaptations in innate modules and cognitive capacities—mental hardware—that were exploited and integrated by shamanic ritual. The integration was a consequence of the physiological and psychological dynamics of altered states of consciousness that are expanded in the symbolic rituals. The forms of cognition associated with shamanism reflect the integration of major innate representational modules to produce new forms of thought—symbolism—through metaphoric processes, contributing to cognitive evolution (Winkelman 2002b). Shamanism expanded innate human cognitive representational processes by developing the fundamental metaphoric processes (using one thing to represent something else), manifested in shamanism in out-of-body experiences and the use of animals or animal spirits as self-representations.

Key aspects of these processes involved the expansions of representations of the self and others provided by the conceptual world of spirits.

There is also support for McClenon's hypothesis that individuals with high hypnotic susceptibility and responsiveness have genetic features that provided the basis for the evolution of the religious healing capacity. The hypnotic capacity for internal engagement with a visionary world was a preadaptation tied to the dream capacity that shamanic healing co-opted and exapted in the service of imagination and healing. The ability to undergo these dissociative cognitive processes contributed to a new function—that of representing the self within visually imagined spirit realms. This capacity of images and expectations to evoke physiological responses was a preadaptation that provided a basis for shamanic practices to apply human's symbolic capabilities to manipulate symbolic-physiological linkages to produce new healing functions.

Shamanic Expansion of Religious Healing Adaptations

The origin of the religious healing impulse involves many pre-adaptations that provided a basis for exaptations and new uniquely *Homo* adaptations for healing that emerged across hominin evolution. These enhanced adaptations included an expanded capacity for the hypnotic capacity in the placebo effect and the use of the symbolically mediated stress reduction and relaxation responses. Shamanism exapted these traits and extended their effectiveness by merging these prior adaptations with rituals and symbolic processes involving the supernatural world. This produced a new level of human adaptation in which religious concepts played a central role in healing.

These universal aspects of shamanic ritual reflect biological bases that contribute to human well-being as adaptations and exaptations (extensions of prior adaptations that constitute new adaptations). Shamanism extended the hominin ritual capacities for integrating new members into the group and to produce endogenous healing responses. Shamanism developed new healing features derived from the capacities of symbolism involved in the beliefs in the spirit world, and the roles of the shaman in managing the internal psychological dynamics and personal relations among members of society.

Ritually induced ASC are the basis for the shaman's engagement with the spirits and professional activities of healing. The typical shamanic state of con-

sciousness involves visionary experiences, exemplified in the "soul flight," where an aspect of the shaman departs the body and travels to spirit worlds. These soul flight experiences provide many adaptive potentials, including mechanisms for healing. Shamans heal by recovering patients' lost spirits and souls and reintegrating them into the patient during a community ritual. Many capacities contributed to these healing processes—hypnotic susceptibility, placebo effects, role enactment, and dissociation.

The new principles of shamanic cognition involved exaptations of prior cognitive systems that provide adaptive advantages in producing psychological change through spirit representations. The concept of spirits is key to the shamanic healing practices and involved exaptations of abilities for

- detecting animacy and agency, intentional causal agents with personalities;
- representing social others as ideal models;
- recognizing social others and making inferences about their mental states;
- distinguishing animal species and their natural characteristics and tendencies;
- representing concepts using the body and animals as metaphoric systems; and
- producing self-representations through internalization of the "other."

Shamanic ritual activities also engaged uniquely human innate representational modules, structures, and cognitive processes to facilitate social and psychological integration (Winkelman 2000). Shamanism provided adaptive strategies in integrating a variety of capacities—biological, social, and cognitive—that contributed to human evolution, adaptation, and survival.

The following sections address the expansion of ritual's adaptive roles in uniquely human healing practices of shamanism involved in the management and transformation of the capacities of self. Uniquely human mechanisms of healing are derived from the roles of symbolic spirit concepts in the formation of personal and social identities and in the information processing and integration provided by the visionary images of shamanic states of consciousness. These altered states provided mechanisms for personal individuation, social integration, cognitive and emotional integration, and symbolic healing, all of which can be seen as visual representations of the self-processes of the lower brain structures. Shamanism provided the mechanisms for shaping human's developmental capacities, linking the natural frameworks of our ancient animal brains and our more recently evolved cultural symbolic systems. Shamanic practices provided a variety of mechanisms for social integration and psychological healing through relationships with spirits, which involve forms of self and other representation that provide a basis for self-transformation. These self-transformation processes are guided by shamanic symbols that use myth and metaphoric thought to produce transformations in human identity and experience.

In subsequent chapters we elaborate on these aspects of shamanic healing adaptations such as those involving cognitive and mythological systems (Chapter 7), emotional socialization of structural features of humans' evolved innate psychology (Chapter 8), and the "period expectant" nature of religious socialization (Chapter 9).

Meaning and Metaphoric Processes in Religious Healing

The attachment of emotions to religious symbols is part of a process that links meaning with psychophysiological responses. The linkage is enhanced by metaphors, the symbolic models we use to understand the Universe. Kleinman (1973) called attention to the importance of the symbolic reality that connects the biological and the psychological levels of human existence. The linkages of symbols and physiology provide therapeutic effects in religious healing by aligning individuals with cultural expectations, values, and beliefs. Symbolic healing processes involve the use of metaphors—systems of analogy between the Universe and our own bodies and emotions that allow our beliefs to be manipulated to elicit physiological responses.

Religious healers' treatment activities create and interpret experience by dramatically manipulating the cultural worldview in ways that shape the patient's experiences. Dow (1986) notes that universally symbolic healing processes use symbols to affect the mind and, consequently, the body. These processes involve the religious practitioner presenting for the patient a general cultural mythic system and interpreting the patient's condition within that system. The attachment of a patient's emotions to mythic symbols during socialization allows the patient to undergo an emotional transformation through the manipulation of the religious symbols associated with aspects of the patient's personality, self, and identity (such as souls, spirits, and morals). Healing is produced by remodeling the self within the structure of the mythic world.

Dow suggests that symbolic healing is based on the human capacity for interpersonal communication, which is based on our ancient capacity to communicate with ourselves through emotion. Through evolution, this intrapersonal biological communication mechanism was extended into symbolic systems and religious language. But all these levels have remained linked, so that religious rituals and symbols are able to reciprocally affect biological processes and effect a cure through symbolically influencing unconscious and somatic processes (Dow 1986, p. 64).

These emotional healing mechanisms respond to suggestion by others, emotional restructuring from interpersonal influences, and the dramatic aspects of therapeutic rituals. The self and the body are linked through the emotions, and healing occurs when the ritual leads the patient to relieve emotional tensions.

The meanings of a metaphor are created in engagement of the self with the world and are manifested in feelings, imagination, thought, and social interactions. Metaphors derive their efficacy from ways in which analogy and metaphorical processes produce psychophysiological effects. These metaphorical effects are shaped by the expectations created through religious ritual, cultural traditions, and the associated feelings and images.

The basic mechanisms of symbolic healing involve the following processes:

- *establishment* of a generalized mythic world;

- *persuasion* of the patient to particularize his or her problems within that mythic world;

- *attachment of* the patient's emotions to symbols from the mythic world; and

- *manipulation of* those symbols to assist in emotional transactions.

Metaphors have power in the symbolic realm as well as in the physical body. Metaphors use mythic representations that link the body and cosmology, combining biological and experiential meanings and integrating objective conditions and subjective experiences. Kirmayer (1993) suggests that metaphor, myth, and archetype represent distinct levels of meaning—social, psychological, and bodily. Each level is associated with its own dynamics of meaning. Religion can integrate these different levels of meanings, affecting bodily, psychological, and social processes, and thereby providing mechanisms for healing.

Kirmayer (1993) suggests that metaphors provide healing by

- implicitly structuring conceptual domains through the logic of metaphoric implication,

Box 6.3 RELIGIOUS THEORIES OF ILLNESS

While modern biomedicine sees disease as a result of microbial activity or some type of organic defect, in most cultures and times the causes of illness have been attributed to the spirit world. Most cultures attribute illnesses to these "personalistic" factors, the consequence of the personal actions of humans or supernatural agents. In a cross-cultural study, anthropologist George Murdock (1981) found that most cultures' central concepts of illness causation included supernatural notions; that is, that a willful human or spiritual entity caused illness in the victim. These universal expressions of perceptions of willful actions by an "other" find their expression in theories of spirit aggression and in human supernatural aggression (e.g., sorcery or witchcraft). Murdock also found other supernatural causes as well, including those based on concepts of guilt and sin (e.g., taboo violation, mystical retribution). The universality of cultural beliefs about the roles of supernatural powers in causing illness suggests that these beliefs, too, have derived from biological influences.

The most generic form of supernatural health effects involves spirit aggression. Spirit aggression beliefs take many forms, including concepts of illness caused by ghosts or spirits inhabiting the person's body and taking over that person's will and behavior through possession. Spirits may also attack people by sending darts, worms, insects, or other entities into their bodies. One universal supernatural explanation of illness involves theories of human supernatural causation in which a malicious person—such as a sorcerer or witch—causes negative effects upon another person's health. These effects can result from overt actions—such as spells—and from the inadvertent effects of emotions, particularly envy or jealousy. In sorcery, illness is the result of an *intentional* and aggressive use of magic, whether a product of the individual's power alone or through assistance provided by a specialized sorcerer or spirits. (In later chapters we address questions regarding these assumptions of supernatural punishment as adaptive mechanisms that put into effect a moral order.) These are also potential functions of other supernatural theories of illnesses that involve forces other than humans and spirits, such as "mystical illnesses" that are thought to involve the "automatic consequence of some act or experience of the victim mediated by putative impersonal causal relationships rather than by the intervention of a human or supernatural being" (Murdock 1981, p. 17). These mystical illnesses may be the automatic consequences of taboo violations and other effects of impersonal forces. A principal form of mystical causation involves *mystical retribution*, in which illness is a consequence of a forbidden act that violates a taboo or moral injunction. In most cultures, the major taboos are prohibitions on food, drink, or sex, as well as etiquette, ritual, property, and verbal taboos. Some behaviors may cause illness directly (that is, illness is an automatic consequence of them), such as *contagion illness*, which results from contact with polluting objects such as menstrual blood, corpses, or some other defiling substance. In Chapter 7 we examine the adaptive functions of contamination beliefs.

- evoking strong sensory/affective associations, and
- bridging the archetypal and mythic levels of experience.

Metaphors provide new images with sensory and emotional qualities that extend the capacity for empathy. The healing efficacy of myths derives from their ability to unite disparate aspects of human experience, especially deep contradictions. Archaic myths still work today when they can be interpreted in ways that tap into the patient's archetypal structures and unite the abstract and concrete, the sensory and affective, and thoughts and feelings, into the same image, producing meaning and understanding (Kirmayer 1993). Religious therapy uses metaphors to evoke and bridge cultural models and bodily experiences. Metaphor is thus a tool that can provide meaning for our experiences of illness guided by the concepts of spirit and the explanation in the world of myth (see Box 6.3: Religious Theories of Illness).

Shamanistic Religious Rituals as Self- and Emotional Healing

A universal aspect of shamanistic healing is the use of ritual to cause dramatic effects on emotions. Shamanistic practices heal through many mechanisms, including manipulation of our emotions, identity affirmation or change, confession and forgiveness, the restructuring of painful memories, the resolution of conflicts, the alleviation of repressions, and the expression of unconscious concerns. Shamanic practices may evoke unpleasant emotions and painful memories, providing a basis for patients to confront their fears by focusing on vivid images of threatening objects and helping the patient confront them with the supportive assistance of the shaman, the community, and the spirits. The explanations provided by shamanistic healing processes typically minimize personal guilt and intrapsychic conflict by attributing the cause of a problem to external factors such as the spirits. Thus, religious healing can alter our emotional relationships, attachments, and sense of self. Religious states of consciousness also provide a variety of therapeutic mechanisms for altering emotions. These states of consciousness can activate the paleomammalian brain, which regulates our emotions and integrates them with our memories, self-concepts, and social attachments. By synchronizing the frontal cortex with theta brain waves, religious states of consciousness can produce an emotional flooding that can help us reevaluate memories and affective attachments. Religious healing practices produce a variety of emotional transformations, exemplified in the differences among shamanic soul recovery, mediumistic possession, and meditative emotional detachment. In shamanism we see a dramatic engagement with emotions, especially hope and fear. Possession practices have been characterized as practices that allow the "victims" of possession to engage in and express normally prohibited emotions. The meditative traditions have emphasized controlling the emotions and experiencing blissful emotions as a consequence of suspending one's ordinary attachments. All of these emotional transformations can provide therapeutic relief.

Soul Loss and Recovery.

The most central shamanic illness is **soul loss,** in which a person loses an aspect of his or her self or soul. The soul may leave during a dream or because of the soul's fright or capture by a spirit or act of sorcery. Achterberg (1985) characterizes soul loss as an injury to the core or essence of one's being that is manifested as despair, disharmony, and the inability to find meaning in life, belongingness, and a connection with others. Soul loss involves a loss of connection with those aspects of the self that provide vitality to life, our vital essence, and our emotions. Soul loss occurs because of a trauma that causes an aspect of one's self to dissociate. This separated aspect of the self carries with it the impact of the traumatic experiences that are dissociated from the rest of the self. If soul loss occurs early in life, it can arrest ego and emotional development at the time when the loss occurred. Reintegration of these dissociated aspects of self is central to shamanic healing.

Soul recovery involves a dramatic enactment of the shaman's encounters with the terrifying spirits he

battles to rescue the patient's soul. Threatening spirit images symbolize the repressed aspects of the self. Shamanic states of consciousness manage emotional trauma and the sense of self-loss by reintegrating those dissociated and repressed aspects of the past. Through soul recovery, one regains a valued sense of the social self that was alienated through trauma. Community participation in healing rituals underscores the importance of social relations in retrieval of the lost soul. Both the cross-cultural literature and contemporary shamanic work suggest that healing power is derived from others witnessing the return of the soul. The shaman's dramatic struggles with the spirit world engage a conceptual framework that provides a representation of the dissociated aspects of self and emotions. The attribution systems of shamanism provide a self-empowering system that exerts control over the spirits. Emotional healing through social bonding is also facilitated by release of the body's own opioids that produce a sense of well-being.

Possession.

Possession involves an experience of external control conceptualized as an invasion of spirits that act upon one's self, body, and consciousness. Possession involves dramatic changes in personal expression and, presumably, changes in emotions and self-dynamics as the possessing spirits engage the person in normally prohibited social roles and emotional expressions. During possession, responsibility for feelings and behaviors are attributed to a spirit entity that controls the body and mind. Possession produces a variety of psychodynamic processes, including dissociation, emotional transactions, and interpersonal and self-transformations. When possessed, a person may dramatically enact the situations that caused the conflict, expressing his or her repressed desires or performing prohibited behaviors. Because these acts are attributed to the "spirit other," the patient is not held responsible. Possession also provides a means to manage emotional problems related to social influence by having the spirits make demands—for instance, demanding that the patient be treated in certain ways or receive special privileges. Possession changes relations between individuals and groups through the incorporation of various "others" into self. By enabling people to transform the emotional dynamics that rule their lives and their personal identities, possession provides adaptive expressive functions.

Meditative Detachment.

Meditation integrates emotions and thoughts but generally suspends emotional attachments and reactions to achieve freedom from suffering. Meditative practices enhance one's control of attention in order to change mental processes and consequently affect the meditator's emotions by allowing him or her to develop a detached observational attitude involving the suspension of evaluative processes. Meditation provides a framework for developing an "observing self" or "witnessing consciousness" that is capable of observing without reacting. Enhanced awareness of unconscious emotional processes may lead to the compassion, charity, and service characteristic of meditative traditions. Alexander et al.'s (1990) analysis of Vedic psychology illustrates the notion that feelings have a role in interconnecting the levels of mind. Mature levels of emotional consciousness provide information to integrate the ego, self, intellect, and motivations in intuitive decision-making processes that transcend earlier stages of emotional development. These developments enable individuals to suspend the connection of evaluation and emotional processes and to release emotions. The result can be seen in common meditative experiences such as rapture, bliss, and overwhelming love and compassion. Meditation also affects emotions by inducing the relaxation response, which helps to reduce stresses, fears, and phobias. Meditation allows its practitioners to focus on the perceptions, memories, thoughts, sensations, and emotions that arise because of their psychodynamic energy, providing primary material for processing and emotional release.

Healing Through Ritual Transformation of the Self

Religious healing transforms how an individual experiences him- or herself and consequently can heal identity, attachments, and emotions. The ability of religious healing practices to transform the self is in part explained by role theory. Religious healing engages the human capacity for role interactions that are similar to the ones people use in interacting with one another. In the development of our personalities, we incorporate the "other" as a model for self and a source of feedback about the nature of self. Religious healing is derived from an expansion of the projective processes by widening these understandings of social "others." This expansion allows humans to exploit the influences of spiritual "super persons" in the development of personhood and identity (Pandian 1997). Normal human dynamics involve a social context that affects our self-development by providing perceptions regarding ourselves that are held by other people, the "generalized other." Humans are innately predisposed to "mind read" others' perceptions and incorporate them

into our self-perceptions. This adaptation to and integration of the social inferences of others orient us to the normative patterns of the world in which we live, in essence, providing mechanisms for enculturation.

Spirit assumptions also use our innate capacities for social intelligence, including the ability to infer the mental states of others. The attribution of mental states to others involves modeling others' likely thoughts and behaviors by using one's own mental states and feelings as models. This practice provides an intuitive "theory of mind" that allows us to perceive others' perspectives and use them. In the context of religious healing, the therapeutic processes engage the self in an intense emotional relationship with spirit others. Consequently, just as ordinary human roles are developed through internalizing the expectations of others with whom we have attachment relationships, one can modify one's self by internalizing the identity and expectations represented in the "divine other."

The "spirit other" is a key mechanism for managing the individual's emotional and psychological dynamics and coordinating those aspects of the self with other members of the group. The religious presumptions of a superior deity, a superordinate "social other" who models roles and expectations for individual behavior, provide an effective adaptation for a variety of human individual and social needs. This evolved capacity has preadaptations in a variety of previously evolved structures, including dominance and submission behaviors, dependency bonding on a nurturing "other," and the attribution of agency and intentionality to unseen others. It expands on these capacities by using a novel concept of a "super person" on which to model our behaviors.

Spirit concepts can represent these personal and social roles, emotions, attachments, and repressed complexes, as well as dissociated aspects of identity and significant social forces. Spiritual beliefs provide models of the self that link an individual's experiences and emotional processes with the expectations of that person's society. In shamanic healing, the shaman may engage in "role-taking" by modeling social roles derived from the spirit world and demonstrating alternative personalities to the patient. Rituals can transform the patient's identity through the modeling provided by role-taking, illustrated in the adoption of various personalities of the spirits that are performed by shamanistic healers. These performances give patients new roles that they may internalize and enact, affecting their psychodynamics.

As we will discuss further in the next chapter, the qualities of spirits also provide useful tools in personal identity formation and integration. Spirits have social psychology functions as representations of the structure of human psychology, providing a language of intrapsychic dynamics of the self and social relations with others. Spirit concepts can have therapeutic effects because they represent fundamental aspects of self and models of social others. Spirits represent generic aspects and structures of human thought and self, mediated by phylogenetically older forms of representation and communication that manage emotional well-being. Spirits provide symbolic systems that reflect these "complexes," unconscious but willful and integrated perceptual, behavioral, and personality dynamics that operate independently of ego control. Ritual manipulation of these complexes can heal by restructuring and integrating the unconscious personality dynamics with social models, uniting the unconscious and conscious mind. These processes involve significant emotional bonding dynamics that can promote healing.

Spirit beliefs also reflect the cultural dynamics of social and interpersonal relations and are used in shamanistic practices to manipulate the self and personal identity. Ritual interactions with spirits elicit, mediate, and transform these primordial psychological and cognitive processes related to well-being and attachment and align them with social models. Shamanistic ritual activities access psychological structures not normally accessible to the conscious ego and transform them. By altering the relationship of the self to the outside world, shamanistic ritual can help the individual to achieve a new psychological integration with the cultural models of the Universe. This effect is illustrated in a variety of healing processes: the roles of spirits in healthy attachment, in the dynamics of contemporary "Catholic charismatic healing," and in the processes of metaphoric healing.

Healing Through Spirit Attachment. The enhancement of the sense of secure attachment, even if it is only temporary, can prompt even severely insecure people to react more strongly to the needs of others with a style typical of those who have a more secure attachment style. The secure attachments provided by others—real or imagined—include a variety of consequences of having a positive self-concept and view of self, including the self-fulfilling outcomes of optimism, confidence, and enhanced skills in acquiring interpersonal support; increased coping ability; increased control of one's affective responses and one's expression of emotion to others, including the development of romantic relationships; and increased general capacities for empathic responses, compassion toward others, and altruistic tendencies, including a reduction in the innate bias against outsiders (Kirkpatrick 2005). These tendencies elicited by secure attachment illustrate the adaptive advantages provided by a personal attachment to a God with nurturing and loving representations. Such an image provides humans with a mechanism for enhancing the availability of the various benefits that are derived from a secure attachment dynamic. Even individuals who lack secure attachments can acquire their benefits by forming a secure attachment to the deity (see Box 6.4: Catholic Charismatic Healing).

Box 6.4 CATHOLIC CHARISMATIC HEALING

The Catholic charismatic healing movement makes use of shamanistic healing principles and other universals of religious healing involving self-processes, emotions, sacred others, and imaginal transformations (Csordas 1994, p. 100). Csordas has characterized Catholic charismatic healing as engaging themes central to North American culture and the self—personal control, intimacy, and spontaneity. One prominent feature of charismatic healing is falling into a sacred swoon. Known as "resting in the spirit," this occurs when a person falls backwards to the ground because he or she has been overpowered by a divine presence. A "catcher" helps to break the fall and allows the person to rest comfortably in an altered state that may last from a few seconds to several hours. The experience involves cultural issues of trust, intimacy, and spontaneity. The manifestation of the divine power engages the patient in a direct person-to-person relationship, but in keeping with Western cultural concerns about the integrity of the person, the Holy Spirit does not enter or possess the person, but instead hovers nearby. Csordas interprets this experience of the divine presence as an intimate preobjective relationship, a time of nurturing, healing communication and companionship that surpasses normal human relations. Cultural issues of intimacy can be dealt with through a personal relationship with Jesus, while spontaneous spiritual experiences enable the individual to overcome the normal cultural emphasis on control and surrender to the deity.

These charismatic healing processes change personal identity by linking the self, body, and social world with the personal unconscious. Csordas suggests that the bodily self-awareness produced through such ritual engagement is interpreted as an awareness of the divine. The "otherness" of the self that seems "not-me" is a consequence of the autonomic functioning of our bodies that produces an embodied hidden presence. As part of the healing process, this division between the true self and the false self is resolved. Attachment relations that are created during our development create a false self because we learn to identify with aspects of the self that please our parents and other caregivers and to dissociate ourselves from aspects of our true self of which they disapproved. Imagery reveals conflicts and dynamics of the true self that must be addressed to heal these earlier developmental traumas.

Divinities play a role as "internalized others" that facilitate resolution of developmental blockages produced by trauma. One predominant theme in charismatic healing is the lack of intimacy or failure in intimacy, often stemming from childhood trauma or problems with marital relations. The divine embrace with Jesus substitutes for absent or lost parental or spousal intimacy, providing an enduring relationship of interpersonal intimacy. Identity as a charismatic Catholic requires having a personal relationship with Jesus that involves experiences of power, spiritual gifts, and inspiration. These experiences produce a new sense of self that Csordas characterizes as the "real self," involving "genuine intimacy with a primordial aspect of the self" (p. 157). Development of the awareness of the power of Jesus in one's life leads to transformations of memory and self. Csordas characterizes the relationship with Jesus as a metaphor for selfhood, and the images of Jesus as a culturally specific manifestation of the ideal other.

In charismatic healing, images are deliberately evoked to transform orientations to others and self. Images are revelatory information and a sign of divine presence, a communication from the body that is embodied and reflected in a "presentational immediacy" in consciousness. The images involve a special relationship among memory and self that removes suffering by creating a positive sacred self. They link the past and present, self and other, and mind and body in ways that allow for the reconstruction of memories. The repressed dynamics created by trauma are revealed in these images. Retrieval of traumatic memories from the subconscious can release emotional blockages and generate healing, while evoking these memories in the presence of divinity can neutralize the emotions and provide them with new meanings.

Demons and the Self

Csordas also analyzed the charismatic movement's concern with demonology in terms of its implications for the nature of the self. Evil beings are conceptualized as "persons" and "intelligent entities" whose qualities are represented in their names, which reflect sins and negative emotions—greed, lust, anger, bitterness, and jealousy. These characteristics reveal the negative attributes of a person. The demonic spirits attach themselves to a person, producing undesirable behaviors and emotions that must be severed in order to be healed. This freedom from bondage also reflects cultural concerns with freedom and control. Demonic possession involves a loss of control that is compounded by the negative behaviors that the demonic entities produce in the person. These negative aspects are viewed as not-self, are dissociated, and are attributed to the demonic entity. Their effects on a person represent a crisis of control, a contested self. The nature of one's problems is manifested in the qualities of these demonic spirits, which are exhibited indirectly in the mannerisms and moods of the patient, including facial and eye expressions and bodily postures. Healing addresses these threats to the self by ritually eliciting emotional self-processes that engage body awareness. This is the existential ground of the self. Sacred healing addresses the physical body and its disabilities by changing a person's habitual modes of engaging the world.

Western psychology considers the elicitation and consciousness of repressed memories to be a significant opportunity for healing. To be healed in the Catholic charismatic healing movement, it is necessary for the victim to forgive the perpetrator of the trauma and engage in an imaginal reenactment of the traumatic event in a way that allows Jesus to heal the trauma. These practices help to heal emotional scars by promoting forgiveness and producing a growth toward maturity. Healing of the self has its basis in a conception of the person that involves body, mind, and spirit, and that is manifested in Jesus, God the Father, and the Holy Spirit. Charismatic healing addresses these three aspects of the person by healing the physical body, the emotional distress of memories, and the effects of evil spirits. These are not three separate dimensions, but relationships in which spiritual healing has dramatic effects on the mind and body.

Conclusions: Shamanic Healing Process

The human healing response is a biological adaptation that expanded on capacities for caring, altruism, and compassion. These hominin baselines of healing were expanded over hominan evolution to increase susceptibility to hypnotic engagement, suggestibility, and placebo responses. Shamanism integrated these and other qualities of a mammalian caring heritage into community ritual practices that provided healing and survival through a variety of mechanisms. These include:

- eliciting the visionary experiences as representations of the outcome of unconscious mental processes;
- bonding together different groups in alliances for food and protection;
- expanding the psychosomatic capacities for healing;
- engaging community participation to trigger self-development using the mammalian attachment dynamics;
- implementing psychological and self-therapies, engaging spirits as psychocultural systems, and representing innate psychological dynamics of the self as animal spirits; and
- developing symbolic psychophysiological dynamics from the ritual manipulation of emotions, self-structures, and the nervous system.

Shamanism reflects the evolution of human capacities for information integration. Religious ritual has a principal effect on our social relations. Religion meets attachment needs, enhancing personal well-being through a support system that provides material assistance and a sense of belonging and comfort. Religious healing practices can also transform a person's perspective on life by improving his or her emotional state. In doing so, they produce a sense of confidence in a more favorable outcome, a faith that is a vital part of healing the individual. Part of this assurance comes from the relationship the patient has with the healer, a powerful and prestigious individual who exudes emotional assurance, personal concern, confidence, and charisma, and these in turn initiate the patient's own placebo healing responses. By providing an explanatory framework for the patient, all types of healers help incorporate their patients into systems in which their medical conditions are understood and can be addressed. These "meaning-generating" practices are an important aspect of all healing systems and are an important part of generating the placebo effect, where suggestion and expectations mobilize the patient's own body to respond in ways that enhance health. Shamanism's extension of an adaptive ritual complex contributes to symbolic development by producing synesthesias in experiences, combining visions, sounds, memories, and bodily sensations in producing a new world of experience and new tools for affecting the body and physiological responses. This experiential reality enhances the capacities of hypnosis by the use of spirit concepts that provide a new level of symbolic adaptation to mold the self.

Questions for Discussion

- Have you ever used a "supernatural" means of healing? If so, for what condition did you use it? Was it effective?
- How do Western physicians attempt to create an aura of authority and knowledge in their interactions with their patients?
- How do religious healing methods treat the "whole person"?

Glossary

coping the process of appraising one's situation and developing strategies to deal with adversity

general adaptation syndrome a mammalian response to threats in which the body prepares itself for exertion; also known as the "fight or flight" response

hypnotizability the ability of an individual to be induced to reduce critical thinking and focus on internal imagery

placebo effect a process of healing that depends on belief in efficacy rather than any specific treatment method

relaxation response a physiological process in which changes occur in the body that promote rest, recuperation, and the restoration of internal balance

soul loss a shamanic conception by which a person becomes ill because his or her soul has been stolen or otherwise has left the body

stress physiological and psychological responses to perceived threats to well-being

stressors activities or events that elicit the general adaptation syndrome

Religion and Cognition: How Religion Shapes the Way We Think

CHAPTER OUTLINE

Introduction: Religious Ideas and the Structure of the Universe
Animism: The Belief in Spirit Beings
Myths and the Universe
Substantive Beliefs
Conclusions: Spirit Concepts as Indigenous Psychology

CHAPTER OBJECTIVES

- Examine how modern biocultural insights offer more comprehensive and less ethnocentric views about religious ideas than do earlier theories.
- Examine similarities in religious worldviews—cosmologies—embodied in spirit beliefs, myths, and substantive beliefs about the nature of the Universe.
- Consider the adaptive advantages offered by the belief in spirits.
- Illustrate the adaptive ways in which myths help regulate a society's interactions with its physical environment.
- Examine how a variety of substantive religious beliefs reflect principles of the Universe.

He who has seen everything, I will make known (?) to the lands.
I will teach (?) about him who experienced all things,
... alike,
Anu granted him the totality of knowledge of all.
He saw the Secret, discovered the Hidden,
he brought information of (the time) before the Flood.
He went on a distant journey, pushing himself to exhaustion,
but then was brought to peace.

(First eight lines of Tablet I, "The Legacy," p. 3 in *The Epic of Gilgamesh*, translated by Maureen Gallery Kovacs. Copyright ©1985, 1989 by the Board of Trustees of the Leland Stanford Jr. University. All rights reserved. Used with the permission of Stanford University Press, www.sup.org.)

Introduction: Religious Ideas and the Structure of the Universe

Thus begins the epic of Gilgamesh, the first story that humans are known to have recorded in written form. In this ancient myth, Gilgamesh, the greatest hero of his age, is described as two-thirds God and one-third human. As a young man, he was an arrogant and callous ruler who built the formidable walls of the city of Uruk but mistreated his subjects. In response to their pleas for help, Anu, the Lord of the Heavens, sent a wild creature named Enkidu to befriend Gilgamesh. Together, Gilgamesh and Enkidu undertook a series of great tasks, even slaying Humbaba, the powerful demon who guarded a sacred cedar forest. But killing Humbaba upset the order established by the Gods, so, as a punishment, the Gods caused Enkidu to fall sick and die.

Shocked by the death of his friend, Gilgamesh went on a quest to overcome his own mortality. Ultimately, his search would take him far from the realms of everyday reality and would introduce him to many strange beings. One was Utnapishtim, a human who had ruled the world prior to a great flood. Utnapishtim and his wife had been warned of the impending disaster and had survived by building a ship. After the waters receded, the Gods had made the two survivors immortal. Utnapishtim told Gilgamesh that he, too, could become immortal if he could but stay awake for six days and seven nights. Gilgamesh agreed but then fell asleep in spite of himself. To console Gilgamesh for this loss of his chance at immortality, Utnapishtim told him of a plant that would make him young again. Gilgamesh gathered the plant but was hesitant to use it, and a snake slithered up and ate it instead.

In the end, crushed by his failures, Gilgamesh could only fall on his knees and weep. His own human weaknesses had prevented him from achieving his goals. Ultimately, he realized that he—like all of us—must one day lose all that he had acquired. But he also found wisdom, for he recognized that he would live on through the deeds he had accomplished, the city he had built, and the stability he passed on to his people.

The oldest version of the epic of Gilgamesh that has come down to us is contained in cuneiform texts on clay tablets that date to around 1800 B.C.E. By that time, the events they described already lay far in the past, for the historical Gilgamesh was likely a king of the Mesopotamian kingdom of Uruk who lived sometime between 2750 and 2500 B.C.E. During the hundreds of years that had passed since his death, the figure of Gilgamesh had taken on superhuman quali-ties and had become associated with an incredible series of adventures, acquiring features from other tales from very different places and times.

The epic of Gilgamesh provides us with a glimpse into a worldview whose structure has endured far longer than the walls of Uruk and one that has left its mark on the religious conceptions of many cultures today. In the epic, Anu—the Leader of the Gods—dwells in the distant heavens. The underworld—which Enkidu sees in a dream—is an unappealing place populated with equally unappealing beings. And all humans live only a single life. These features are such ancient aspects of the Western religious worldview that you may think of them as entirely self-evident and present in every culture. But they are not. For the worldview that developed a few thousand miles to the East, in the plains and foothills of South Asia, was based on some rather different assumptions about the Universe (see Fig. 7.1).

The Rig Veda, the oldest known religious work of humankind, contains hymns to numerous Gods, most of whom are personifications of natural forces. But there are also passages that speak of a single creator or cause of the Universe. Over time, this idea of a single creator would develop into the concept of *Bráhman*, the impersonal, unmanifested, and Absolute Source that gave rise to everything that exists. Although the concept of *Bráhman* resembles the idea of the Supreme Creator that would evolve in the West, the two differ in important ways. The Supreme Creator of the West would eventually supplant the earlier Gods of the region, who would be redefined as devils and other forces of evil. Consequently, the One God of the Western religions is now usually seen as a force of good standing against the forces of evil. In contrast, as the Indian idea of *Bráhman* developed, the various other Gods came to be seen as existing within the manifested universe, meaning that they became subject to the same laws of impermanence as everything else that exists. Because good and evil exist within the manifested universe, they, too, are manifestations of *Bráhman*—which is beyond all qualities, including good and evil—and they, too, are impermanent. Because *Bráhman*, the Supreme Mystery, cannot be grasped in word or thought, most Hindus today prefer to venerate a personified form—usually a manifestation of Vishnu or Shiva—as the active agent that created, maintains, and will ultimately destroy the Universe. But no matter which particular manifestation of *Bráhman* a person might prefer, the idea that the Universe is repeatedly created and destroyed throughout eternity is fundamental to the Hindu worldview.

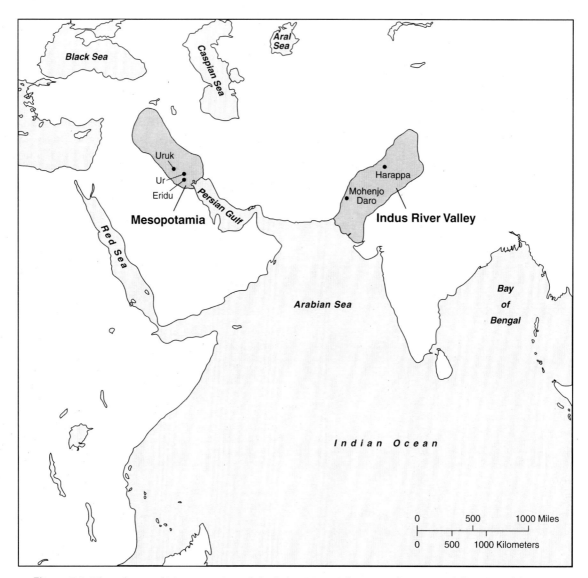

Figure 7.1 The cultures of Mesopotamia and the Indus River Valley created two very different world views.

Although they differ in important ways, both the Indian and the Mesopotamian worldviews—and the many variants to which each has given rise—also have many features in common. Each posits the existence of beings more powerful than ourselves, provides accounts of their deeds, and tells us how we should relate to them. Each provides a description of the Universe that includes an explanation of how it came to be, of what it consists, and how it operates. And each depicts the human condition in terms that acknowledge our mortality while positing that humans also have another, nonphysical self. These common features are, in fact, part of *every* religion.

Religious ideas provide answers to some of our most fundamental questions of meaning. What is the nature of the Universe? How did it—and we—come to be? Why do the seasons have cycles? Why do humans act in certain ways and animals in other ways? These questions reflect our deep-seated need to adapt to the world by making it into an understandable and predictable place. Religious ideas provide the framework for some of the fundamental questions humans seek to understand about the Universe.

All cultures provide their members with religious explanations for the observable phenomena of the Universe—such as the behaviors and effects of the sun and the moon. All cultures also tell their people about distant places, incredible beings, and primordial times that are beyond their immediate experiences. They also explain the nature of humans, couched in a language of relationships among our souls, spirits, ancestors, and other spiritual entities such as Gods. These ideas explain the Universe of our experience, communicating a framework within which societies adapt to their environment. Ideas about the seasons and the cycles of plants and animals help us to navigate our way through the Universe, and beliefs about the unseen agents and the actions of supernatural beings help us to orient the practical activities of everyday life.

The many universal features of religious conceptual frameworks indicate that they are products of the same brain structures and cognitive processes that help us to understand other aspects of our lives and the Universe. This chapter explores the idea that religion reflects a number of cognitive processes. These particular manifestations of the mind support a system of thought that guides behavior by providing:

- concepts of the Universe, nature, and ecological processes (cosmology);
- representations of persons, their internal dynamics, internal motivations, and processes (spirit concepts and mythology, constituting an indigenous psychology); and
- operating principles of the Universe and guidelines for behavior.

Irrespective of the scientific evaluation of religious claims, they orient humans in coordinated ways with respect to our personal experiences and the Universe.

Cosmology: Religious Models of the Universe

A **cosmology** is a model of the Universe that describes its structure, tells how it came to be, and explains the beings and forces that affect it. Anthropologist Anthony F. C. Wallace (1966) characterized religious cosmologies as involving several interrelated components: a pantheon of spirit entities, a mythology that describes the origins of the Universe and tells of the deeds of the spirits, and substantive beliefs regarding the way that the supernatural operates.

Pantheon. The **pantheon** (from the Greek term *pan*, meaning "all," and *theion*, meaning "holy") consists of the supernatural beings recognized by a religion. The variety of supernatural beings that people recognize is astonishing. There are omnipotent and omniscient Gods (such as the Jewish Yahweh and the Muslim Allah); nature deities (such as the Germanic Storm God Thor and the Hawaiian Earthquake Goddess Pele); forces of chaos or evil (such as jinn and demons); elemental spirits (nymphs, elves); and ghosts and the souls of human ancestors and other beings. A pantheon is a cultural expression of the universal animistic belief in spirit beings.

Myths. To anthropologists, **myths** are narratives that describe the origins and significant events of the Universe. Some myths describe how the Universe came into existence, while others tell of the deeds of various supernatural beings, especially those who interact with humans. In contrast to common usage, the anthropological view of myths does not differentiate between "correct" and "incorrect" (or "true" and "false") myths. Thus, the two ancient accounts in the Book of Genesis (1:1–26 and 2:4–22) and the modern scientific ideas about the "Big Bang" and subsequent organic evolution are all regarded as creation myths.

Clearly, the anthropological understanding of the term *myth* differs from the ways that the word is often used in everyday language, where you may hear such statements as "the myth of male superiority" or "the myth of global warming." In such cases, the word "myth" is generally used to refer to something that the speaker does not believe to be true. This is why some people refer to the sacred narratives of other religions as "myths," while referring to the sacred narratives that underlie their own religion as "truths." Regardless of what we might consider to be their "truth value," myths have powerful influences on behavior. Myths not only provide a rationale for rituals, they also justify behaviors with relationship to nature and other groups. Myths have a sacred quality, a charter that justifies and demands certain behaviors.

For example, the Hajj—the great annual pilgrimage of Muslims to Mecca—commemorates the time when the Prophet Mohammed and his followers migrated from Mecca to Yathrib (later renamed Medina). Prior to that time, the people of the Arabian Peninsula had generally traveled in groups joined by ties of kinship. In contrast, the group that traveled with Mohammed to Medina was composed of people from numerous different tribes. This was a watershed event, for what linked these travelers together was not their tribal identity, but a new, broader identity based on the Prophet's teachings. This first *hijra* (Arabic for "migration") is now seen as the beginning of the Islamic religion and marks Year One of the Islamic calendar. The Muslims of the world are still united by this ritual that obligates them to go to Mecca at least once in their lifetime.

Different religions populate the Universe with different pantheons. The pantheon of Roman Catholicism features an elaborate hierarchy of supernatural beings. Catholics believe in a Supreme God who is both a solitary deity and a trinity of deities (the Father, the Son, and the Holy Spirit). There are also "choirs" of angels divided into different orders (the seraphim, cherubim, and ophanim). While most angels are anonymous, some—such as the Archangels Gabriel and Michael—are known by name. Mary, the mortal woman who gave birth to the Son of God, was subsequently taken into heaven in her bodily form, and she now has the ability to intercede with God on behalf of mortals. The Roman Catholic pantheon also includes numerous saints, deceased humans who had extraordinary religious experiences or displayed great piety and devotion during their lives, and who were then ritually raised into sainthood after their deaths. These saints provide role models for the living and, like Mary, are able to intercede with God on a person's behalf. Souls of the dead comprise another class of supernatural beings and often referred to as "the departed." There are also evil beings (devils) led by Satan, a "fallen angel" who dared to challenge the authority of God.

The Christian trinity is depicted in this painting, *The Trinity Adored by the Heavenly Choir*, painted by Tintoretto around 1590. God the Father is shown holding the crucifix on which Jesus died. The Holy Spirit is shown as a dove under Jesus' feet.

(Studio of Tintoretto, The Trinity Adored by the Heavenly Choir, ca. 1590, Oil on canvas, The Collection of the Columbia Museum of Art, Gift of the Samuel H. Kress Foundation, CMA 1954.36.)

Substantive Beliefs. The **substantive beliefs** of a religion describe the natural and the supernatural domains, the phenomena within them, and the laws or principles that govern their functioning. Substantive beliefs include several central elements:

- a sacred geography of the Universe, including its natural and supernatural components,
- specific kinds of entities within the supernatural Universe, and
- operating principles that govern the Universe and its entities and define how humans are affected by them.

All cultures make statements about natural and supernatural places—the realm of supernatural beings and powers. This **sacred geography** provides a means to understand the nature of the Universe as well as providing a "map" that shamans and other religious figures can follow as they journey through the supernatural realms.

Human Supernatural Entities Cosmologies include ideas about the nature of the supernatural and natural entities of the Universe. Some of the most important of these concepts involve the natural and spiritual nature of human beings, manifested as souls, personal spirits,

The Hindu pantheon bears many similarities to the Catholic pantheon, in that it too consists of a multitude of supernatural beings. The principal Gods are Brahma, Vishnu, and Shiva, often referred to as the Creator, the Sustainer, and the Destroyer. (Brahma, as a manifested deity, is not to be confused with *Bráhman*, the unmanifested source.) In India, there are thousands of temples to Vishnu and Shiva, and devotees are free to worship both deities at any temple they choose. Images of Vishnu and Shiva figure prominently in both religious and nonreligious settings. In contrast, images of Brahma are relatively uncommon, and there are only a handful of temples dedicated to his worship. Some say that there is no need to worship Brahma, for his purpose—to create the world—has already been fulfilled. In addition to these principal deities, there are countless other minor deities. Several—such as Rama and Krishna—are avatars (incarnations) of Vishnu. Others are symbols of devotion who serve as role models for humans. Hanuman, the Monkey God, is venerated for his selfless devotion to the avatar Rama, while Sita—Rama's wife—is the model of the ideal spouse.

This nineteenth century engraving shows the Trimurti or "Hindu trinity." On the left is Brahma (the "creator"), whose four heads are an expression of his ability to watch over the Universe. He is shown holding a copy of the Vedas. In the center is Vishnu (the "sustainer"), who holds a discus that symbolizes the cosmic mind. On the right is Siva (or Shiva, the "destroyer"), whose trishula (trident) stands for the three Gods as well as the past, present, and future.

and ancestors' spirits. These conceptual frameworks inform us about the aspects of human nature, their principles of operation, and the factors that motivate human behavior (see Box 7.1: How Many Souls Do We Have?).

Operating Principles. Religious cosmologies make statements about the **operating principles** of the Universe—that is, the ways the Universe works, particularly its supernatural aspects, and the ways that humans can influence it. For example, Hindus believe that every sentient being takes part in *samsara*, the great cycle of life, death, and rebirth. The smooth functioning of society, and indeed of the Universe,

depends on each living being fulfilling its *dharma*, the duties and obligations associated with its current status in existence. Individual creatures who properly fulfill their *dharma* improve their *karma* and earn a future life in a higher status, while those who display negligence or self-indulgence violate their *dharma* and must be reborn into a lower state. For sentient beings of low status (such as a snake or a rabbit), it is difficult *not* to act in the proper manner and thus fulfill their *dharma*. In contrast, the many desires and the competing demands of our various social obligations make it extremely difficult for humans to fulfill our *dharma*. It is even more difficult for the Gods, who possess enormous power but experience little suffering—

Box 7.1 HOW MANY SOULS DO WE HAVE?

In the Hindu cosmology, a soul (*atman*) is said to be reborn a multitude of times before it can attain *moksha*, or liberation from *samsara*. In contrast, Jews and their religious descendents—Christians and Moslems—believe that a soul inhabits just one body and that it journeys to its reward (or punishment) after a single lifetime. In the Judeo-Christian-Islamic tradition, a soul is generally construed as the immortal and nonmaterial aspect of ourselves that exists eternally after our physical demise. This conception makes it possible for the religion to influence people during their lifetimes by proposing that their souls will spend the remainder of their eternal existence in a place ("heaven" or "hell") that directly reflects the rewards or punishments those people merit on the basis of their lives. In contrast, the "soul" (*atman*) of an individual Hindu is regarded as the counterpart of the great world soul (*Brahman*), and the relationship between the two is often compared to a bottle of water floating in the sea. The inside and the outside are the same, but they are cut off from one another by the bottle itself, which represents our physical nature. An atman is reincarnated into a variety of "bottles" (or forms), but its ultimate fate is to merge again with Brahman. In this system, both "heaven" and "hell" are temporary conditions that are experienced as the atman moves from one physical form to the next in its quest to attain liberation from samsara, the cycle of death and rebirth (Pandharipande 1996).

The Jívaro, a small group living in Eastern Ecuador, believe in the existence of three souls, known collectively as *wakanl*. Both men and women possess a "true" soul, a *nëkás wakanl*, which is born at the same time as their physical birth. After a person dies, the true soul leaves the body and begins an invisible life in which it recapitulates the entire life of its dead owner. This soul undergoes a series of transformations until it finally changes into water vapor. It exists forever as mist, and joins with all of the other dead "true" souls as clouds and fog. Of their three souls, the Jívaro are least interested in this "true" soul, which has little influence on them during their lifetimes and whose fate in the next life is also of little importance. In contrast, the other two souls are of great concern.

The second type of soul, the *arutam wakanl*, is that which gives a person *arutam*, or visions. This soul must be acquired, and possessing one is so important for a man that it is said that he will not live past puberty without one. (Although women occasionally obtain such a soul, it is not thought to be as important for them.) Boys begin to search for an arutam when they are around six years old. The process is arduous and usually involves making a pilgrimage to a sacred waterfall, fasting, drinking tobacco water, and waiting. When an arutam does appear, the boy is expected to approach and touch it. As the arutam enters into him, the boy feels a surge of power that gives him both intelligence and strength, and enables him to resist violence and sorcery. The other members of his tribe can tell when a boy has acquired an arutam, for it imparts his words and actions with much more power than they had previously. The arutam also motivates the boy to want to raid another village so that he may kill an enemy man and acquire the third soul.

This soul, the *muisak wakanl*, only comes into existence when a person who has already acquired an arutam is killed, and its sole purpose is to avenge that person's death. The easiest way for a Jívaro warrior to avoid such harm was to shrink the head of his victim, for this forced the muisak to remain within the head. Once back in his home village, the killer could then pass the power of the muisak to his female relatives, increasing their abilities to produce food for the tribe. But the muisak continued to pose a threat, so eventually it would be ritually expelled so that it would return to its home village. To further decrease the likelihood that the muisak would cause harm, the shrunken head was usually sold to an outsider who would carry it far from the area.

In former times, the Jívaro were involved in ongoing warfare with neighboring groups in which they would periodically raid neighboring tribes and would in turn be attacked by these tribes. The Jívaro believed that any man who possessed an arutam was protected from harm during these raids and would also feel the power he needed to kill one of his enemies. If he was successful, the killer would not only defeat his enemy, but would also take his muisak soul, acquiring additional power for himself and for his group. The muisak in his possession would serve as a reminder to the victor to exercise care when leaving his enemy's territory. The Jívaro system of three souls both explained a person's existence and embedded the long-standing tribal warfare of the area into a system of supernatural concepts that limited when attacks would take place and explained why some people had great power and others did not.

The Roman Catholic Universe consists of several domains. The realm of humans is thought to lie "below" heaven and "above" hell. God, the angels, the saints, and the souls of deceased good persons dwell in heaven. Some of these beings—such as guardian angels—occasionally travel to the realm of humans. Satan and the other devils, as well as the souls of deceased evil persons, dwell in hell, but some also occasionally travel to the realm of humans. Thus, humans occupy a middle world that is visited by both the forces of good and the forces of evil, and the world of humans is often construed as a field of battle between the two. Although both good and evil supernatural agents are thought to make journeys to the realm of humans, there are only a few mythic accounts of supernatural beings moving between heaven and hell. In one account, Satan and the other devils were banished from heaven and sent to hell after disobeying God (an event known as "the fall"). In another, Jesus descended from heaven to the middle world to be born as a human. Following his death, he briefly visited hell to atone for the sins of all humans. He then journeyed back to earth to live for a short time again among his disciples before returning to his home in heaven.

The Roman Catholic cosmology bears many similarities to the cosmologies of other religions. This reflects their shamanic roots, for most shamanic cosmologies posit three major tiers to the Universe: humans live in the middle world, while various supernatural beings live in all three worlds and are able to journey between them.

and yet will also die—to fulfill their *dharma* perfectly. Thus, some Hindu myths describe how once-powerful Gods were reincarnated as insects and other lowly creatures. In the Hindu world, every sentient being—including every spirit and other supernatural being—must adhere to the same basic laws of *dharma* and *karma*.

Other religious systems are concerned with different operating principles, some of which appear to be universal. Many rituals use the same operating principles—action through similarity and imitation, concern with contagious contact—that are basic principles of human thought. In this chapter, we will examine some of the universal features of religious cosmologies—spirits, myths, and substantive beliefs—and show how the biocultural perspective enables us to understand their origins and functions in human life.

Animism: The Belief in Spirit Beings

In Chapter 1, we considered Edward B. Tylor's hypothesis that religion began in early humans' belief that the world was populated by countless *anima,* or spirits. The anima was seen as representing some fundamental life force of the organism. Tylor thought that animistic ideas were the result of efforts to explain some of the most fundamental facts of our existence, including sleep, dreams, death, and visionary experiences. He suggested that the belief in the idea of spirits or personal souls was a result of the mistaken attempts of

our primitive ancestors to explain the differences between sleeping and being awake; the experiences a person has while dreaming; and a person dying for no apparent reason. The soul animates the body and makes it alive. The departure or loss of the soul results in unconsciousness and death. The soul also provides answers to questions regarding the nature of dreams and death.

Tylor suggested that primitive peoples had developed animistic concepts because they lacked the modern scientific insights to explain death, dreams, and altered states of consciousness. While Tylor regarded animism as a mistaken or false science, an early phase of human evolution, we can no longer assert that modern people are not animistic in their thinking. We know that notions about spirits and souls are central to all religions, and most people on the planet still believe that these entities are capable of affecting their lives and well-being, particularly their health here and their fate in an afterlife.

For this reason, Tylor's interest in explaining animism continues to engage anthropologists who are interested in understanding the human propensity for religiosity. The biocultural approach provides a platform both for investigating the biological bases of our universal tendency to believe in spirits and for examining how universal beliefs regarding the properties of spirits are manifested in personal and cultural life. In turn, this perspective allows us to consider the adaptive functions that animistic beliefs play in human life.

What Are Spirits?

All religious cosmologies include concepts about spirits, and people in every culture have experiences they interpret as contact with a spiritual reality. This emic universality of spirits clearly implies that beliefs about the existence of spirits are more than just arbitrary cultural constructs and reflect some fundamental biologically based aspects of the species world of *Homo sapiens*. Cross-culturally, humans conceptualize **spirits** as intentional agents that possess some—but not all—of the qualities of humans while simultaneously possessing other qualities humans do not have. When people perceive a spirit, they typically sense some type of contact with a presence that has characteristics very much like our own (Stark 1997). But while spirits and deities may be experienced or portrayed with human-like forms, most spirit beings have either no bodies at all or are part of an animal or plant. Most (if not all) spirits are also thought to have some superhuman qualities or behaviors. Often spirits are said to be able to fly, see through walls, read minds, speak to animals, or change shapes. Spirits may appear as ordinary humans, but they are generally not bound by human limitations; for example, the Gods of Hinduism differ from humans in that they do not sweat or blink (O'Flaherty 1975). Animal spirits around the world are believed to be able to perceive things humans cannot (in the same way that their "real" animal counterparts are able to perceive things we cannot).

Why Do Humans Believe in Spirits?

What is the basis for this human tendency to believe in spirits? Their universality in human cultures indicates that they are derived, not from culture, but from more basic aspects of human functioning. Could it possibly be adaptive to believe that spirits exist? In other words, could spirit beliefs have contributed to the survival and reproduction of our ancestors? Or are spirit beliefs some kind of by-product of evolution, derived from other adaptive human capabilities? The answer is both.

Although people's perceptions of spirits are interpreted in ways that are specific to particular cultures, several major themes appear repeatedly throughout the world. We have already encountered one principal theme in animism: the idea that there are intentional forces that are generally unseen, but that can be felt and perceived. A second theme of spirits is *personalism*, in which people attribute these forces with psychological, emotional, cognitive, and intentional qualities like our own. A third theme is *social reference*, which occurs when these forces are interpreted using cultural ideas about kinship obligations or other relationships (such as "God the Father," "Earth Mother," and "ancestor spirits"). A fourth theme of spirit beliefs involves their *counter-factual principles*, features that contradict the ordinary principles of our hard-wiring, making them appear to exceed our normal capabilities and limitations. These universal principles of spirits derive from several basic features of humans' mental hardware that enable us to respond effectively to contingencies in the Universe. These features include

1. an "animacy detection system" that causes us to interpret events in the Universe as a consequence of aware and intentional agents,

2. models of the internal dynamics of our "self" as an agent that can act within the world,

3. concepts of social "others" that we use to evaluate our selves and guide our behavior, and

4. intuitive integrative cognitive properties derived from suspending the ordinary limiting assumptions of our innate modules.

Animacy Detection. Humans, like other animals, need to respond without hesitation to the possibility of predators. Scott Atran (2006) has argued that our ancestors evolved mental hardware for "animacy detection" to respond to possible predators, and then automatically and unconsciously used this hardware to respond to all sorts of other phenomena. In other words, the basic concept of animism that underlies the properties of supernatural beings is a result of our normal cognitive processes for detecting animate agents. This is why we automatically attribute causal actors to all sorts of phenomena, particularly novel events of unknown origin and phenomena with complex designs.

We can see parallels to our animistic thinking in the behaviors of other animals. For example, a cat or a dog will often chase a ball—or even a moving light—as if it were a living, willful entity. Why? Anthropologist Stewart Guthrie (1993) has argued that the assumption of animism—that the world is populated by living beings—offers advantages even though this assumption may frequently be false. In evolutionary terms, the "costs" to an animal, which assumes that an inanimate object is alive, are minimal. In contrast, assuming the opposite—that something is inanimate when it is actually alive—could cost an animal its life. Consequently, animistic thinking is adaptive for all animals, whether predators or prey.

Spirits as Models of "Self" and "Mind." The qualities of spirits involve more than just animism—for spirits are much like ourselves. The spirit concepts around the world today indicate that people derived their ideas about spirits from the same types of mental models that they used for the domains of human activity. When our ancestors extended their understandings of the Universe to the unknown, they naturally attributed human properties to these unknown actors. This assumption of personal and cognitive similarity of unseen agents was an inevitable result of humans' use of their own self-model to understand the unknown other.

Our processes of understanding others produced the human-like characteristics of spirits; these qualities are derived from our adaptive ability to project our self into others to be able to predict their behaviors. Our universal human tendency to assume that other beings and objects are similar to ourselves offers important advantages, for it increases the likelihood that we will appropriately respond to human-like actors, the most important agents affecting our survival.

Bering (2006) notes that the supernatural agency concept depends on prior adaptations manifested in the concept of the "theory of mind" in which we use our own mental states and feelings in order to understand others' thoughts and likely behaviors. This enables us to conceive of supernatural beings by using as an exaptation our capacities for inferring how social others are thinking. It also results in the attribution of our own human-like characteristics to a wider group of "others," including spirits. Our projection of principles of animism onto the Universe is an inevitable consequence of our innate assumption that other beings operate mentally and emotionally the way we do. Consequently, spirits are understood in terms of our mental and personal capacities, as well as our social and interpersonal relations. Because of this, spirits also provide important models for both understanding ourselves and learning how to relate to others.

Concepts of "Others." Because our survival depends on our ability to cooperate with other humans, it is imperative that we develop an understanding of the mental states of others, their views of the Universe, and their expectations. The dynamics of self-development in a social context involve our ability to infer the perceptions and expectations of other social actors, an understanding of the views held by others in society (the "generalized other"). Religious beliefs about spirit "others" also provide models for human behavior, orienting us to the values and expectations of our culture. Spirits and myths provide models which we can apply to understand social situations and to guide our behaviors. Although the models that shape our development come from many sources, the most important are our primary social relations within our family. Unfortunately, the people around us do not always behave in a culturally ideal fashion. Our beliefs about how an ideal spirit "other" might behave can help to counteract the contradictory models we encounter ("what would Jesus do?"). People of a group learn how to appropriately interact with each other using models derived from spirit "others."

Are Spirits Just Exaptations?

The pre-adaptations and co-opted aspects of spirit beliefs involving animacy detection, self-projection, and social inference have contributed to the dominant view that religious assumptions are just complex side effects of other adaptations. In essence, the ways in which we ordinarily understand natural phenomena leads us to attribute agency and intentionality to natural, personal, and social events, thereby making them appear to be supernatural. But is there something more to the supernatural, an adaptive aspect of spirit beliefs that is more than "agency detection," "theory of mind," and the social reference capabilities also found among chimpanzees? Is it possible that these exaptations are used for new adaptive behaviors?

Human religious and spiritual beliefs are made possible by a variety of social, emotional, and cognitive preadaptations. Whether there was a new adaptation in spirit beliefs depends on whether these mechanisms perform the same functions in religiosity as they did in the context of their original selection. Spirit beliefs would be an adaptation if they provided a new set of adaptive capabilities beyond those provided by the preadaptations. When supernatural agent beliefs have effects on individual behavior toward others, encouraging people to adhere to established sanctified social norms, do they go beyond human's original functions? If people have experiences of supernatural agents leading them to engage in different patterns of behavior, it is possible that these experiences point us toward adaptive behaviors that affect survival. For example, Johnson and Bering (2006) link the belief in supernatural punishment to enhanced group cooperation; such a supernatural belief system reinforces moral behaviors, with the all-knowing capacities of the supernatural entity exceeding the human ability to police other humans' actual cooperation (also see Chapter 9).

Spirits as Counterintuitive Principles. One widely noted aspect of deity concepts is the notion that they are not limited by human constraints; spirits have characteristics that are counterintuitive to our normal assumptions about humans and the natural world (Boyer 2001). Atran (2006) proposes that these counterintuitive agents have adaptive value because these qualities are "cognitively optimal" in enhancing memory formation, communication, and intergenerational cultural transmission. One explanation for the existence of these counterintuitive properties and contradictions to our ordinary assumptions is that they make religious events more memorable. This is undoubtedly true, but what in the real world, physical or social, or in humans' previously acquired cognitive capacities, constitutes the basis for spirits' superhuman capabilities and qualities? Are these counterintuitive qualities based on some prior adaptation that was exapted to ascribe these counterintuitive and superhuman qualities to the supernatural? Or did a newly acquired trait permit counterintuitive thought? Religion may provide an adaptation in those aspects of the supernatural premise involving nonintuitive, contradictory, and superhuman capabilities.

The counterintuitive properties of spirit beliefs are adaptive in spite of their contradictions with factual knowledge because they provide possibilities that are not found in our innate capabilities and modules. Central counterintuitive features and violations of ordinary ontological categories and principles of the innate modules include the belief that spirits are omnipotent and omniscient, all-powerful and all-knowing. The adaptations that are derived from these properties have applications in decision making and social integration. Because human knowledge is limited, deity omniscience is a more effective deterrent against deceit and cheating, because there can be supernatural punishment for failure to conform to norms, even if other humans don't know about the transgression. These beliefs are not merely exaptations of humans' own self-qualities, but engage assumptions that explicitly supersede the human capacity. The omniscient deity concept promotes moral adaptations by extending the ordinary human capacity for cooperation that we examine further in Chapter 9.

Assumptions regarding entities who have powers greater than our own expand our own possibilities. Supernatural capabilities are available to humans under certain circumstances, making possibilities beyond the world of known human capabilities a potential reality. These possibilities are engaged in a universal of human religiosity—divination—the practice of seeking socially and ecologically relevant information from the divine or supernatural. Spirits open the possibility of unseen but intuited mechanisms and relationships; ritual engages processes to obtain information and answers that affect opportunities for successful action.

Spirit beliefs are adaptive because they provide additional ways for resolving the problems we face. The assumption that there are unseen mechanisms inherent in nature that have powers beyond our capabilities, but that nonetheless may be accessed or influenced, has led humans to attempt to access and harness this power through the arts of magic. Such "magical" procedures as prophecy, divination, soothsaying, mediumistic channeling, and prayer and other interactions with spirits utilize techniques to activate unconscious mental and behavioral processes that can then provide information to the conscious mind (see Box 7.2: Divination as Adaptive Exploration of the Universe Through Counterintuitive Solutions).

Summary: The Adaptive Advantages of Spirits.

The biocultural approach suggests that spirit beliefs combine innate inference systems with cultural beliefs to shape how we know ourselves, the Universe, and our interactions with others. Just as we project our own theory of mind onto the other people we engage with, we also project it onto the unseen beings that our religion teaches us inhabit the Universe. But since spirits are "unseen" and therefore different from us, they also deviate from many of the normal assumptions we make about humans. This offers several adaptive advantages. Religious conceptions of superior deities—powerful "social others" who model the roles and expectations for individual behavior—provide an important mechanism for shaping and managing the emotions and beliefs of individuals and for coordinating the members of the group into common patterns of social development. Assumptions about spirits are adaptive because they can provide a channel to obtain strategic knowledge from the implicit and unconscious cognitive processes that humans engage through divinatory practices. The belief that "unseen others" are able to act on their own and are not subject to the same limitations as humans permits outcomes different than those based on human knowledge. Our beliefs in spirits allow us to expand our abilities of **scenario building**, the practice of mentally examining alternative courses of action and considering the potential consequences of these actions. Divinatory practices can provide mechanisms for establishing consensus, maintaining cooperation, and reducing conflict.

The etymological roots of divination—a process of acquiring information—are found in the concept of the "divine," revealing the assumption that there is information available from the spirits. While "scientific" approaches have generally rejected the idea that divination provides information, Peek (1991) characterized divination systems as an "epistemology of a people," a system of assumptions about the nature of knowledge that engage nonrational processes and intuitive modes of cognition (Winkelman and Peek 2004). People's willingness to submit important questions to divination processes reveals a willingness to take information from sources beyond the direct control of their rational processes and accept possibilities other than the known ones.

Altered states of consciousness and spirit possession rituals associated with divination are manifestations of these alternative modes of cognition that access the nonverbal information channels of lower brain centers. These processes are symbolic, but they are experienced in systems that function without the mediation of language. Divination systems combine this intuitive–synthetical mode of thinking with logical–analytical thought, enabling the diviner to communicate unconscious processes to conscious social discourse. Diviners often provoke reactions in the patient's body, interpreting these and the patient's dreams to determine the cause of illness. Diagnosis may be made through the use of a system of songs, paying careful attention to the patient's emotional reactions. In these processes, divination seeks answers in the manifestations of the unconscious that are then translated into symbolic communication.

Divination processes also integrate other forms of information and perspectives elicited from the client's family and friends, combining it with sources of information acquired from the spirit world. This integrative process is central to the development of social consensus. Dilemmas are resolved by incorporating previously inaccessible information within broader, culturally meaningful frameworks provided by the divination system (see Colby 2004).

By defining the nature of one's circumstances, divination provides relief from the anxiety produced by uncertainty of the unknown. It also fosters social cohesion by providing mechanisms for developing agreement about plans of action. By clarifying the nature of opportunities, whether empirically right or wrong, divination makes immediate circumstances intelligible within the broader frameworks of the cultural world. Divination procedures can alleviate anxiety and doubt by removing uncertainty, providing a sense of security in "knowing," and imposing momentary order and stability on an unpredictable world. Divination procedures can be effective in resolving stress because their directives are framed in terms of traditional cultural myths, metaphors, and proverbs that integrate individual experience within the broader cultural beliefs and reasoning processes that people use to make sense of the world.

Religion and Cognition

189

Spirit beings not only shape individual and collective actions, they also affect us in ways that reflect the qualities we attribute to them. Thus, we are able to develop relationships with spirits that are very similar to the relationships we develop with the humans around us and use them to substitute for human relations. Principles from the spirit world help regulate the ways in which we relate to the Universe, particularly the environment and others. These principles for behavior are communicated through the teachings and stories we call myths.

Myths and the Universe

We can understand spirits as products of our need to explain unseen agents and their actions within the Universe. Myths are a product of our need to construct more complex stories about our experiences of the Universe and the processes and agents that are responsible for it. Just as our experiences of spirits are shaped by universal biological and psychological processes on the one hand, and specific historical and social events on the other, so too are our myths shaped by both innate and social needs for explanation. Myths provide society with some of its most important assumptions about the Universe. Anthropologists and other scholars have developed a variety of theories to explain the origins, nature, and functions of myth.

Just as our earlier ideas about spirits have been replaced by more modern views that see spirits as culturally shaped products of universal human biological and psychological processes, so too have Western ideas about myths evolved from a simplistic view of myths as essentially "just so" stories about powerful spirits. Scholars have discovered deeper functions of myths and realized how the many common features of myths in different cultures reflect fundamental aspects of the way that humans perceive and comprehend the Universe. We now recognize that myths address many of the ultimate questions that humans have about the Universe.

Early Ideas About Myths

Max Müller, one of the most influential early Western students of comparative mythology, pointed out that myths provide a way to understand natural phenomena such as the moon, the sun, the rain, and the wind. By associating these natural forces with deities that have both human and superhuman qualities, myths "explain" these powerful forces in terms that humans can comprehend; that is, as the actions of human-like entities.

Edward B. Tylor's views of societies as possessing "more" or "less" culture led him to devalue myths. To Tylor, myths were childlike notions about the world that were typical of people who had only attained his "savage" state of social evolution. Tylor regarded both myths and magic as products of a false primitive science, an opinion that was widely shared by most of his contemporaries. One of these, James Frazer (1854–1941), suggested that mythic thought represented a stage in the evolution of human thought from magic through religion to science. In Frazer's eyes, myths were misguided representations of natural events that resulted from a misunderstanding of the causes of these events. Frazer claimed that myths were rooted in peoples' primitive beliefs that they could magically control the processes of life and nature. Their perspectives assumed that myths were delusions rather than something useful.

The psychologist Sigmund Freud, who studied the role that dreams play in giving expression to a person's unconscious wishes, also depreciated the nature of myth. Freud suggested that our individual tendencies to project ourselves and our wishes onto others were mirrored at the societal level by myths. To Freud, myths were similar to dreams, manifestations of the unconscious, but reflections of unconscious group dynamics rather than the individual unconscious. Like dreams, myths were projections of unconscious fears that were imaginatively portrayed to make them accessible to, and manageable by, the conscious mind. Freud suggested that just as our dreams reveal normally unacceptable aspects of our unconscious selves, myths reveal these conflictive issues at a collective level.

Although descriptions of natural forces are indeed found in myths around the world, this topic is not the main focus of most myths. Nor are most myths nothing more than expressions of our fears. Many myths are concerned with social life, its conflicts and organization, the ways that people should (and should not) behave, and other rather mundane aspects of cultural life. But in spite of their differences, the myths of different cultures also share many features. These features are expressions of the universal human need for a world view, a system of explanation.

Functional Perspectives on Myths. One of the first anthropologists to offer a more nuanced perspective on myths was Bronislaw Malinowski (1884–1942). Malinowski examined the ways that the myths of a culture fulfill the biological and psychological needs of its members, making him one of the first scholars to apply a biocultural approach to the study of myths. His approach, **functionalism**, emphasizes the useful roles that myths play in fulfilling such fundamental societal needs as instilling a common identity and creating social solidarity. Malinowski viewed myths as a kind of "sacred charter" that provided societies with a system of belief, a code for morality, and a pragmatic system for guiding behavior.

We now understand that myths are explanatory frameworks that help us to understand ourselves and the Universe. The worldviews communicated through myths enable people to structure their perceptions of reality so that they can participate in their society and respond to the Universe. Malinowski emphasized that a myth must be understood in relation to the contexts and manners in which they are told and their impact on the listeners. The social performance of a myth is what gives it meaning and importance; therefore, the meaning of a myth is contained, not just within its words, but in the ways that the myth is actually given expression in real life. The sacred character of myths makes it possible for them to serve an indispensable social function in providing precepts that define morality and guide perceptions and social behavior.

Of course, myths also deal with natural phenomena such as the sun and moon, the winds and rains, and plants and animals. Myths often describe these phenomena and provide reasons for their behavior. Even if the descriptions and reasons are inaccurate, they still contain truths, for they provide a system of reference expressing information about the Universe. In this way, myths also help humans adapt to the natural world.

The yin–yang symbol is an ancient Chinese image that expresses both the duality and the unity of existence.

Symbolist Perspectives on Myth. One of anthropology's most influential perspectives on the nature of myth was developed by the French anthropologist Claude Lévi-Strauss (born 1908). Lévi-Strauss's view of myths, known as **structuralism**, sees myths as products of the "deep structures" of our brain, biological principles that shape how we perceive and understand the Universe. Myths reflect similar concerns in cultures around the world because they are based in the same principles of the brain and mind and share common concerns about regulating human relations with the environment, each other, and other social groups. One of the most basic principles of myths is **binary opposition**, our hard-wired tendency to view the world in terms of basic cognitive dichotomies. Oppositions such as male and female, light and dark, and right and left are reflected in the basic structures of mythic thought and the structural dynamics of the myths found around the world. These universal manifestations of myth reflect some of the basic structures of consciousness.

One fundamental universal problem addressed by myths concerns the differences between humans and animals and the processes involved in the human transition from nature to culture. In his book *The Raw and the Cooked* (1966), Lévi-Strauss discussed the dichotomy between natural (raw) and culturally transformed (cooked) substances. These oppositions are integrated within the fabric of society and represent the tensions that arise between our basic animal urges and the controlling effects of culture. By expressing these tensions in myths, religion is able to affect the emotions and consciousness of the participants.

The symbolist approach views myths as reflecting many influences, ranging from the underlying biological or archetypal structures of the collective unconscious to the repressed material and unconscious psychic structures of the individual produced by the organizational structures of society. Analyses of myths make it clear that their representations and structures reflect many aspects of humans: our innate and acquired characteristics; the principles, structures, and organizations of our groups; and our relations with nature.

Myth and Ecological Relations

Cosmologies include myths that stipulate how humans should act within the Universe. Myths describe the forces of nature, including plants and animals, and often name them as supernatural entities and describe the appropriate ways for humans to relate to them. For example, the Book of Genesis provides an account of the origins of the world in which it states that humans were given dominion over all the plants and animals. Although it has been suggested that this attitude directly led to the widespread destruction of the environment that we can observe today, this view is simplistic. In ancient Jewish traditions, the Torah glorified nature and prohibited its senseless destruction. Muslims recognize that animals exist for other reasons than simply to fulfill the needs of humans, for they also bear witness to the greatness of God.

Religious systems regulate many ways in which individuals and groups relate to their environment, especially through managing natural resources and incorporating certain plants and animals into their diet. Myths provide significant guidance for the ecological relations of the group through practical rules for when to hunt, when to slaughter animals, and when to irrigate the fields. In many cultures, rituals scheduled according to the solar and lunar cycles—particularly the phases of the new and full moon or the equinoxes and solstices—are used to organize other activities that have a direct effect on the natural resources available to a group. Agricultural cycles may be planned by religious rituals that are scheduled on the basis of astronomical events.

The religious practitioners of a society often play important roles in regulating that society's relationships with the natural world. Many shamans have a special relationship with a spirit power—a relationship in which the shaman is often referred to as "master of the animals" or "mother of the animals"—that controls the availability of the animal species (see Box 7.3: Hunting Taboos Among the Tukano). When the hunters are having difficulties locating food animals, the shaman may undertake a journey to confer with the spirit power and learn the reasons for their failure. Often, the shaman will return with the news that one of the hunters has broken a taboo or neglected to perform some type of ritual activity. Confronted with this information, the hunter may admit to the transgression.

Box 7.3 HUNTING TABOOS AMONG THE TUKANO

The Tukano are a small-scale society with a very low population density in the Northwest Amazon of Colombia. They live on the meat they acquire by hunting and fishing and the plants they both collect and grow. Their mythology and cosmology regulate their social and economic activities, helping them to live in equilibrium with the available resources in the environment.

Tukano mythology integrates knowledge of the natural environment with an understanding of the factors that affect the well-being of humans, plants, and animals. Ritual mechanisms balance the long-term relations between humans and their food sources. Shamanic beliefs and myths dictate the ways in which humans should interact with the animals, plants, and other aspects of the environment, conserving resources and maintaining the ecological balance. The shamans (payé) play an important role in maintaining the proper relationship with the natural world.

The Tukano cosmology includes a variety of ecological regulatory mechanisms. Hunters must ritually ask the spirit protector of the animals for permission to kill animals for food. As part of these rituals, hunters must avoid sexual activity and erotic thoughts at certain times and must fulfill other ritual obligations concerning diet, purification, and emetics. No female member of a hunter's household may be menstruating when he is hunting. A man is not allowed to hunt many types of animals while his wife is pregnant, and he must also avoid hunting the animals when they are breeding. Many aspects of the human life cycle, ranging from insemination through pregnancy and childbirth, as well as mourning, are associated with restrictions on hunting. These restrictions primarily pertain to those animals that are protein-rich resources. The cumulative effect of these apparently unrelated factors is to restrict the times when hunting can occur, helping the Tukano to avoid overhunting.

When the hunters fail to capture prey, a payé will journey to the master of animals and ask him to release the animals. During their conversation, the payé may learn of people who have violated taboos and incurred the anger of the spirits. The payé also directly regulate hunting, fishing, and gathering activities, for it is they who stipulate where fish poisons may be used, how many animals may be killed, and which areas wild plant foods can be gathered. They also control other activities that can dramatically affect the availability of plant materials, such as when and where to build communal houses and other buildings. In addition, the payé decide when the group should migrate to a new area. In doing so, the payé help the members of their group avoid epidemics and prevent the overexploitation of game animals in any one area.

Embedded in the Tukano mythological system is a set of concepts about the world system and its energy inputs and outputs, which must remain in balance. Human sexual energy plays a central role in this system. The Tukano believe that when they repress their own sexual behavior, the sexual energy they save will be invested into nature. By restricting sexual activity in relationship to food acquisition activities, the Tukano cosmology reduces reproduction precisely when there are difficulties in obtaining sufficient resources. Sexual abstinence is required before rituals, and rituals are necessary precursors to many subsistence activities, directly linking reproduction and the environment. When limited resources require frequent hunting trips, sexual behavior and, consequently, the reproductive potential are restricted.

These various prohibitions are tied to the belief that violating these taboos will disrupt the ecological balance and lead to human illness. Overhunting, the overexploitation of food resources, and a failure to maintain appropriate ritual relationships with the animals on which they depend can all lead to diseases. To heal these diseases, the Tukano use shamanic rituals and principles to reestablish the balance of nature. Shamanic rituals also play a central role in establishing and maintaining the alliances between groups. Neighboring groups exchange food during rituals to ensure amicable relations and create close bonds of social identity that link past and future generations. These intergenerational linkages provide incentives to act in an ecologically responsible manner that maintains a balance between the Tukano and the plants and animals on which they depend.

This worldview attributes the uneven availability of natural resources to mistakes made by humans. Because there are so many taboos surrounding their activities that people will always be violating them, often without realizing it, the shaman offers a comprehensible explanation for the hunters' misfortunes as well as a means to rectify the problem. The mythologies associated with shamanism—and the ways in which these are expressed through shamanic behavior—serve to regulate the impact of the population on their environmental niche.

As agricultural societies appeared and priests took over this role of shamans, new ways of regulating the use of natural resources emerged. Since priests are typically found in agricultural societies, they generally engage in rituals related to the agricultural cycle. These rituals may help to determine when crops should be planted, or how to organize and when to celebrate harvest festivals. In many cultures, priests are attributed with a supernatural ability to control the weather, particularly to ensure timely rainfall. While their primary role may be to ensure the well-being of the crops, they may also regulate domestic herds of animals (see Box 7.4: Feasting and Ritual Regulation Among the Tsembaga). Priests may also use rituals to address calamities that affect public health, such as epidemic diseases, droughts, or crop failures.

Food Taboos and Religion. One of the most important ways in which religion affects how a society interacts with its environment is by stipulating which foods may be eaten and which may not. Why would a religion want to restrict the diet of its adherents? We can consider this question by examining the Jewish prohibition on pork and the Hindu prohibition on beef.

Many reasons have been given for the Jewish dietary laws prohibiting the consumption of pork. Pigs are regarded as "unclean," and their cloven hooves and curly tails are said to resemble those of the devil. From an ecological perspective, however, these are mere rationalizations. The anthropologist Marvin Harris (1974) analyzed the prohibition on pork in terms of the negative consequences the animal has on the environment. He noted that those areas of the Middle East in which the prehistoric Jewish people lived had already been subjected to deforestation and desertification for thousands of years. In contrast to grazing animals such as sheep, goats, cows, and camels, which eat the grass above ground without destroying the root system, pigs root up plants as they

search for food. Thus, their foraging activities have the potential to accelerate the destruction of the topsoil and expand the desert. Realizing this, the ancient Hebrews came to regard pigs—and their flesh—as undesirable.

Another well-known religious dietary law involves the sacred cows of India. Many people have asked why this important source of protein is off-limits to Hindus, especially when we consider the large human population and frequent food shortages in many parts of India. The apparent paradox of prohibiting beef consumption in a starving nation disappears when we consider the overall consequences of this prohibition. The rules against killing and eating cows actually expand the food base for the human population and produce other benefits as well.

Archaeological evidence has shown that the people of India used cattle in a variety of ways in the prehistoric past, including offering them as sacrifices and consuming their flesh. It was only as cities appeared that religious taboos began to surround cattle. These taboos affected the consumption of meat, but not of milk products. Harris explains this prohibition in terms of the impact of cattle on food availability to the population as a whole. Prohibitions on consuming beef help to optimize the distribution of food resources. For humans to consume cattle meat, it is necessary to devote pasture or cropland to growing feed for the cattle. This is an extremely inefficient use of vegetable protein, as a cow must consume twelve or more units of vegetable protein to produce a single unit of meat protein. In a populous society with limited food resources, it is much more efficient to feed the vegetable protein directly to humans.

The Hindu prohibition on eating beef also has a number of secondary advantages. In traditional Indian agriculture, cows are the most important source of energy for plowing and other activities. The religious taboos ensure that the cows are not eaten during the winter periods when they are not being used for such work. If there were no prohibitions on eating beef, people might be tempted to consume their cows when they were hungry; a temporary solution to food shortages with long-term implications for food production.

The cows also serve one additional purpose. The owners of the cows often allow the cows to walk around and forage. In their search for food, the cows eat many grasses, weeds, and other high-fiber organic material that could never be eaten by humans. This high-fiber diet yields a dung that, when dried, is a very important fuel source—especially for the poor—in an area that has been deforested for thousands of years. Untreated, the grass and other vegetation that cows eat would not provide an effective fuel for cooking. But when it has been transformed through digestion and the collected dung is then dried in the sun, it becomes a good, inexpensive, and renewable source of fuel.

Although sacred, the cows are in fact eaten when they reach the end of their natural lives. Caste rules prohibit the Brahmans and other elite groups from consuming dead cows, but the lowest caste of society, the untouchables, has the right to eat these animals. In Hindu society, this group is the one most in need of protein, and they also make a variety of products from the cow, using the horns, hide, tallow, bones, and so forth. Thus, even in modern India, there are a variety of adaptive reasons for maintaining the long-standing taboos against the consumption of beef (see Box 7.4: Feasting and Ritual Regulation Among the Tsembaga).

Mircea Eliade and the Language of Myth

Mircea Eliade (1907–1986), often considered the world's premier scholar of comparative mythology, rejected the view that myths are about "something else" and argued instead that myths should be understood on their own terms. His approach to mythology emphasized the importance of the *experience* of these sacred narratives; he also borrowed ideas from Jung and others that saw myths as a language of the human psyche. In his view, mythic elements are a product of human compulsions to produce narratives and understandings of our condition.

One principal function of myth is to provide models for human behavior. Myths embody ideal values, give expression to the perfect cosmic order, and provide important models for human behavior. Because humans do not always act in accordance with the ideals of the mythic world, myths also serve another basic function: They provide a means through which people may orient their lives to achieve congruence with the cosmos and the patterns of sacred time. Myths thus provide a way to bring humans closer to perfection, back to those sacred origins in which the models for human life were first established.

Eliade's approach to myth focused on the emic, or insider's, perspective; that is, how myths are experienced, valued, and believed by the people themselves and how they provide an engaging and convincing worldview. However, Eliade did not rely solely on the interpretations provided by believers. He also examined the symbolic structures and meanings of myths.

Because he realized that the people who believe a particular myth might not be aware of all of these meanings, Eliade emphasized the importance of the unconscious manifestations of mythic symbols. Thus, myths are windows to the unconscious structures and needs of the human mind; they also reflect the societies in which they are told, believed, and enacted. Consequently, those who participate in retelling and enacting the myths will not consciously understand all of their meanings, origins, and implications. Myths represent an unconscious expressive level of the psyche and provide a vantage point for understanding the unconscious structures of the mind and human needs.

Eliade's views of myth were strongly influenced by the psychologist Carl Jung (1857–1961), who viewed myths as involving symbols that are products of the unconscious. Myths are a natural way to express the human condition, for they make use of a combined language of the sacred and unconscious that connects humans with transcendent levels of reality beyond the assumptions of culture. Myths embody these symbols of the unconscious and provide vehicles through which transpersonal values and understandings can be represented in human life. While all symbols point to a larger meaning, religious symbols point to universal aspects of human nature and thus to transcendent principles of human life that reflect the structures of the world in the human mind and nature. Consequently, the symbols contained in myths point to a level of reality and a plane of existence that lies beyond the direct grasp of human consciousness.

Because religious symbols are able to express many meanings, they have the power to simultaneously represent ideas that are in opposition. For example, a mythological moon is not merely a celestial body, but also a symbol of its effects on natural cycles of regeneration, the tides, fertility, the feminine principle, and many other associations found in nature. These meanings are not evident in the image of the moon itself, but reflect a cosmic order, the linkages of patterns across different aspects of nature. Because of this ability to invoke multiple natural meanings simultaneously, myths—and thus religion—are able to represent complex truths about the ways that humans comprehend the Universe. These manifestations of myth are tied to the deep structures of our unconscious minds, making their elements natural symbols for understanding human nature and the Universe.

Myths and Archetypes

The insight that myths around the world have many features in common led Carl Jung (1875–1961) to suggest that these cross-cultural resemblances reflect the

Box 7.4 FEASTING AND RITUAL REGULATION AMONG THE TSEMBAGA

The ritual system of the Tsembaga, a tribal group of New Guinea, serves a number of functions. Anthropologist Roy Rappaport explained how an elaborate ritual cycle helps to conserve natural resources, balance the human population with the productive capacity of the land, reduce warfare, and ensure that high-quality animal protein is available when most needed. Tsembaga religious rituals help to regulate the group's interaction with the environment. The ritual cycle imposes a number of restrictions on when warfare can occur, how large the pig herds can grow, when sexual intercourse is permitted, and when and how particular kinds of foods may be eaten. All of these restrictions help to maintain the balance of human activities within the environment.

The many rituals that govern how humans interact with the physical environment also affect how they relate to the other groups in their area. Ritual practices provide a mechanism for establishing and maintaining alliances in a society lacking a political hierarchy. The distribution of food resources, particularly surplus pigs, ensures the support of regional allies in warfare and guarantees that a supply of quality protein will be available at critical times. Rituals keep the pig populations from adversely affecting the environment and diminishing other resources that humans need; they are also used to build alliances and assure quality protein at critical periods of conflict.

The pigs have a major role in the overall Tsembaga balance with the environment. The pigs dispose of garbage and human waste and limit secondary growth in the garden areas. After the harvest, pigs are released into the gardens to eliminate weeds and work up the soil by digging up roots. The pigs feed themselves during the day, scavenging for garbage and other available foods. At night they return to their owners, where they are fed the substandard tubers (sweet potatoes) that are left over from the harvest of tubers humans grow for themselves. Because the pigs roam freely, they can cause a variety of problems, including invading people's gardens and generally damaging the environment.

When the number of pigs reaches a level at which they become a burden on the environment and on the human population that cares for them, they are ritually sacrificed to reduce their numbers to a level at which they will not compete with humans for food. The pigs are slaughtered during ceremonies attended by a group's regional allies. The ceremonies provide an opportunity for people from diverse localities in the region to congregate and to engage in a variety of activities directly related to making decisions about warfare and marriage. The vigorous and obligatory dances that the men perform provide an opportunity for the women to see which men are the most fit, while the shells and feathers that men wear embedded in their ritual clothing provide an indication of their wealth.

These ritual festivities also enable groups to assess the strength of their allies and the extent to which they are fit for the warfare that begins after the pig festivals have ended. The festivals provide an opportunity for the interpersonal interactions that are key to recruiting allies for warfare. Since there are no political authorities that can command groups and force men to engage in war, the ability of a group to wage warfare depends on attracting kinsmen in other groups to join them in their fight. An invitation to attend a dance is tantamount to a request for military support, and that support is solidified in the context of the festivals and feasting. The dance performances of the warriors are also a tool for evaluating their effectiveness in fighting. Both vigorous dancing and fighting require great physical stamina, and the number of dancers a group brings is directly related to the number of warriors it can send to assist its allies.

During these festivals, a group will normally slaughter all but its youngest pigs. This generates an enormous quantity of meat that will be used both to strengthen the alliance and to feed the warriors during combat. The distribution of the pork helps ensure that these allies will be available for the conflicts, and redistributes a large amount of protein from the local ecosystem to a regional population. Rappaport estimated that one pig slaughter yielded approximately 8,000 pounds of meat that was distributed to people in more than a dozen groups.

The Tsembaga and their allies eat large amounts of salted pig fat right before they go into battle. This highly salted food helps the warriors to maintain their blood volume and blood pressure as they fight, a time during which the warriors are prohibited from drinking water. Following the day's combat, the warriors then consume lean pork meat, which has the effect of offsetting the effects of stress on the body's nitrogen levels.

Once warfare has ceased, the group conducts a ritual that suspends hostilities by planting a particular plant known as rumbim. This plant has a special connotation relating to the group's ancestors, and planting it stops the pig slaughters until the animals become numerous enough to carry out a sacrifice for the ancestors. Until then, restrictions on sexual activity, on warfare, and on the eating of various foods serve to ensure that the human population does not grow significantly until there are new pig herds, that new hostilities are not initiated until the debts to allies are paid, and that certain animal species that might otherwise be hunted into extinction are conserved. The rumbim remains in the ground until the pig herds are of sufficient size, at which point it is uprooted and a new cycle of sacrifices and ceremonies begin.

innate ways in which our mental hardware perceives the Universe. Jung regarded the universal features of myths as manifestations of unconscious **archetypes**—aspects of human experience and representations of humans minds and needs that are so fundamental to human nature that we have acquired structures to represent our experiences of them. For example, the attachment and caring behaviors that exist between a mother and her child reflect both our basic biological needs and our innate psychological attachment dynamics. Because these needs and dynamics are so deeply wired into our brains, cultures throughout time and space have conceptualized them in similar terms.

Jung demonstrated that archetypes link together many dualities of human existence, including mental and behavioral forms, the unconscious and the conscious, the instinctive and the symbolic, the subjective and the objective, individual propensities and universal species patterns of behavior, and the material and spiritual. These dualities reflect the complementary aspects of human nature and different levels of human experience that are mediated by the archetypes. Archetypes are experienced internally in our minds and expressed externally in both the material symbols and the behaviors we use to represent our selves and others, our emotions, and our innate potentials for action.

For Jung, archetypes thus reflect innate dispositions of all normal human minds, dispositions that he referred to as the **collective unconscious**. The archetypes mediate between the potentials provided by our biology and our personal experiences. They provide organizational schemata that enable innate potentials to be experienced as personal qualities. Our personal encounters with these archetypes enable us to experience and develop the potentials present in our mental hardware. Our personal engagement with the symbolic representations of myth provides us with opportunities to activate these latent aspects of our psyche.

In Jung's eyes, archetypes represent enduring aspects of human nature and truths about the human condition. Archetypal structures and symbols reflect the structural organization of the brain and its information-processing capacities. These unconscious processes and structures of the organism are manifested visually in the iconic images and associated ideas that emerge from the unconscious. These images are an ancient visual mode of expression that modern humans can still access in their dreams. Archetypes produce psychological integration by linking the individual's instinctive experiences with external symbols.

Jung characterized this integration in the context of shamanism, in which processes of psychological development involve individuation. Enhancing the linkages between the conscious mind and its instinctual grounding allows organic potentials to unfold and become integrated into personal development and social context. This integration engages concepts of spirits as representations of the unconscious primordial capacities of the self. These unconscious representations provide an integrative wisdom that can move one beyond the current level of self and consciousness by linking the implicit understandings of the unconscious with the self-conscious mind.

These archetypal images can be intrinsically healing, eliciting a "whole-ing" produced by eliciting the unconscious mind and its intentions, dramatizing and effecting their integration through ritual. If the conscious mind resists and rejects these intrusions from the unconscious, then, according to shamanistic principles, illness results, manifested by a disintegration of the mind through dissociation and a further fragmentation of consciousness. Mythology and ritual are processes for triggering the integration, allowing for the manifestations of the unconscious to be assimilated into the structures of consciousness and self throughout the symbolic and emotional processes provided by mythic content and ritual processes. Rituals also elicit dissociated or repressed aspects of our identity, split-off complexes that can acquire autonomy and a purposeful character that is experienced in the phenomenon of possession. These autonomous complexes may also be experienced as a feeling of being a master or sage, discovering an ancient wisdom within ourselves that can guide our spiritual development and the integration of the psyche.

The modern scientific mind can still find meaningful engagement with archetypes and mythology by recognizing that they are part of our human nature. To Jung, modern people can not rediscover spirits or reconnect with our innate drives by returning to the church or the religions of our parents and forefathers. It is the spiritual traditions, embodied in contemplation and meditation, that engage this ancient substratum of human consciousness and provide a basis for modern humans to reconnect with this aspect of our psyche. The practices of spiritual disciplines and meditation are an expansion and development of human consciousness, a process of individuation that can produce experiences of transcendental meaning and connection.

Within shamanism, this psychic integration is achieved through the symbols of animal powers and guardians, reflections of our unconscious mind and our animal brain that still form parts of our psyche and personality. To Jung, this anthropoid psyche was not only a vital aspect of the human personality, but also the source of our experience of the divine beings that populate our mythologies. Animal images are reflections of our own internal psychological structures that, when rejected, can take on threatening and even demonic forms, attacking our selves and our consciousness. But if they can be integrated and accepted as a part of our self, they can be conceptualized as spirit guides that facilitate human endeavors, integrating aspects of our unconscious psyche and potentials into our conscious behavior. These animal representations, expressed around the world as the integration of human and animal features (anthropomorphisms), reflect the dynamics of some of the deepest layers of the human psyche in which humans are still animals and also symbolic. Engaging these deep structures of the unconscious—these archetypal symbols of our own innate powers and potentials—is one of the fundamental functions of myth.

Archetypes as Neurognostic Structures

Laughlin, McManus, and d'Aquili (1992) characterize the archetypes in terms of **neurognostic structures**, the neurological foundations of our innate mechanisms for knowing the world. The archetypes represent the unconscious structure of the psyche that provides the basis for the conscious mind. They also represent images of future possibilities, the potentials we have not yet developed. Archetypes are evolutionary adaptations to the Universe—the real conditions of our internal and external realities and of our subjective experiences of the physical world that we inhabit.

Anthony Stevens (2003), a Jungian analyst and evolutionary psychologist, has elaborated on the archetypal concept, linking it to human neurobiology and the psychobiological dynamics of religion. In his view, the expressive modalities of mythology and their representations of innate aspects of our psyche reflect aspects of our biological nature related to religion and religious adaptations. Stevens characterizes archetypes as innate psychic centers that carry out the basic behavioral patterns and experiences of the human species—aspects so intrinsic to our nature as humans that they have many fundamental similarities across cultures and religions.

These functional systems have the capacity to initiate and control the common behavioral routines of the human species. They are innate aspects of humans, natural features of the life cycle of the human species involving experiences such as being mothered, engaging with peer groups, making the transition from puberty to adulthood, participating in religious initiation, functioning within social hierarchies and dominance systems, contracting marriage and engaging in sex, and being integrated into society. For example, these innate human dispositions are reflected in the typical dynamics of the interaction between mother and child everywhere, reflected in the patterns of mutual smiling, attachment, and emotional engagement. These dynamics are universal in their form, transcending the individual and particular situation, but located and experienced within those contexts. This is what allows mythologies to fulfill the spiritual function of providing perceptions of transcendent meaning and the higher purpose embodied in human nature in culturally relevant symbol systems.

Key to understanding the functions of myths, rituals, and archetypes is examining their engagement with the hormonal complexes and emotions that relate to species preservation and self-development. Archetypes represent these needs and their dynamics, while myths provide tools for managing these human psychosocial and biological dynamics as they become molded into cultural systems across human development. The archetypes also elicit particular feelings that link the ideas embodied in the archetypes with the meanings they have for the individual—their implications for the individual's lived experience. Mythic processes of elicitation and management of universal aspects of human emotion provide a cultural face to our innate expression of such universal feelings as anger, fear, disgust, surprise, happiness, and grief. Culturally specific traditions address these innate human potentials by highlighting the role of emotion in mythic materials. The reenactment of the myths engages innate aspects of our species—for instance, using ritual dance as a mechanism to elicit emotions and promote group bonding. It is through ritual that the abstract potentials embodied in archetypes take on their cultural forms that are of emotional importance to the individual.

Stevens considers those aspects of human nature that are embodied in the archetypes to be biological entities (features of our mental hardware) produced through natural selection. Similarly, to Jung, archetypes are the foundation for a science of human psychology, one that is based on the recognition of the fundamental biological and psychological similarities among humans everywhere. One fundamental function that myths fulfill is to manage the universal psychosocial aspects of the human life cycle. The genetically programmed aspects of our life cycle are manifested through the transitions we undergo from birth to puberty, adulthood, and, ultimately, death. Although they are shaped in many ways by culture, the psychosocial aspects of the life cycle are clearly preordained by our human nature.

Archetypes and myths also fulfill other basic psychobiological functions. Stevens points to their explanatory function, providing a coherent framework that helps meet the human need to know and understand. Myths also help to sanctify a group's ethical code, creating a commitment to a particular moral order and instilling in individuals the willingness to sacrifice their personal self-interest in favor of the interests of the broader community. Myths help fulfill our human need for culture and our desire to share a collective sense of identity. By providing these collective scenarios, myths and religious rituals integrate the individual into the group, thereby incorporating the individual's life into the patterns of the collectivity.

Myths and archetypes achieve this integration because they are able to affect processes of human nature—our innate psychology—that lie beneath the level of culture. Engagement with these representational systems that are innate to our species enables myth, religion, and ritual to elicit and transform fundamental aspects of our personal, emotional, and social nature. Myths help to shape our needs for attachment, learning, explanation, and social interaction into the patterns of our culture. In these ways, myths facilitate our fundamental need to learn our culture, particularly the rules of our society and the expectations that others hold for our behavior.

Archetypes manifest an awareness of unfulfilled needs that, like the archetypes themselves, are produced by our encounters with nature and the social world. Archetypes are key aspects of the processes of individuation by which the individual undergoes development to higher levels of psychological integration. Jung viewed individuation (the self-realization of one's individual potential) as a universal evolutionary principle concerned with an organism's drive to engage self-regulating processes to move toward achievement of the goal of self-completion. These developmental trajectories are part of the innate patterns and potentials for individual personal development embedded in our biology and shaped by our evolutionary history. Archetypal awareness engages a nonintellectual perception of reality derived from a different state of consciousness and processing associated with the paleomammalian and reptilian brains. These sacred perceptions are an elevated level of experience, one in which humans move beyond the ordinary awareness of reality and perceive some broader significance of human action and its relationship to the patterns of nature.

Summary of Archetypes. Archetypes remain relevant to us because they give expression to the wisdom that is programmed into our mental hardware. Archetypes reflect a structural organization of the unconscious mind; they are systems of personal and social meaning that precede the development of consciousness and culture. The manifestations of these unconscious images provide a process of centering, an engagement with the integrative influences of visual symbols. Elevating these symbols into consciousness and the self engages processes of psychic transformation that provide therapeutic benefits. The principal aspects of the therapeutic processes and benefits are psychological integration and a meaningful alignment of our own individual unconscious psychological processes with the psychosocial dynamics of our cultural world. Mythology provides that link through a socially shared narrative, a metaphoric depiction of reality that resonates with our own unconscious thought in the manifestation of its internal structures in archetypal symbols found in mythology. When the individual's psychic structures are integrated with the internalized representations of the social structures embodied in myths, the individual experiences a sense of integration and harmony of self, the social world, and the Universe. It is through this production of a correspondence between our internal representations and our representations of the Universe that humans come to feel complete and at home in the Universe. Myths depict these universals of our innate psychological structures and meaningfully connect the self and the cosmos in a way that transports the individual beyond the self and generates a sense of connection with the transcendent and universal.

Myth-Telling as an Adaptive Feature of Human Nature

Myths reflect basic structures of our evolved psychology. Scholar Bruce MacLennan (2002) contends that there are direct links between Jungian psychology and evolutionary neuroscience, linkages involving human neurology that provide the bridge between psychic and material realities. MacLennan regards archetypes as human instincts and as innate structures of perception and behavior—what Laughlin et al. refer to as neurognostic structures or the neurological foundation for knowledge. These archetypes provide structures for manifesting the contents in consciousness, experience, and behavior. They reflect adaptations to the environment of evolutionary adaptation and constitute evolved mechanisms that provide vital information related to survival. Their role is to attune human behavior to adaptive purposes for the individual and species. Some of the basic archetypal structures include

- parent, mother, and father (with variant types such as "devouring mother");
- self, the totality of the archetypes;
- ego, the conscious self for organizing information;
- shadow, involving instinctive aversions that are maladaptive;
- anima, the female principle in males, and animus, the male principle in females;
- superego, a drive to acquire the rules of social behavior of those around us; and
- complexes developed around these archetypes through socialization.

The universal presence of myths in human culture is a reflection of our hard-wired drive to explain and understand the Universe. In this sense, our tendency to develop myths is based on an ancient evolutionary accomplishment, the embodiment and expression of an understanding that provides a framework to help both individuals and societies coordinate their understanding of the Universe. This tendency to provide an orderly system of explanation also serves a vital socialization function, allowing the manifestation of order in the outside world to be internalized in the individual psychology of the members of the culture. Through their explanations of human nature, myths provide a system within which individuals can understand and accept their unconscious and subconscious drives and desires and learn to live with them.

Myths convey a particular way of seeing the world in which powerful, often humanlike forces hold sway over significant aspects of human life. These authoritative systems meet our innate need to experience our world as orderly and dominated by hierarchical structures. Myths that focus on nature and natural processes help us adapt by providing a framework for understanding the environment as orderly and therefore capable of being communicated about and adapted to in a rational way. Although modern scientific insights suggest that the models communicated in religious myths are not always accurate descriptions of reality, myths nonetheless help humans adapt to the environment in rational ways, as illustrated in our earlier discussion of hunting and food taboos. Mythological models make it possible to convey knowledge about the natural world, including the tendencies and variations in natural phenomena. Although they might be ontologically incorrect in their assumptions about the facts of natural forces, they can nonetheless be empirically correct in predicting their patterns and cycles. Mythological systems provide conceptual frameworks within which humans can describe the world and plan with respect to its changing patterns. These frameworks obviously provide important and generally effective adaptations to the stable aspects of the environment in traditional cultures, embodied in their conceptualizations of the cycle of the seasons. The ecological adaptations expressed in myths can enhance the survival of a group because they provide the group members with stable and effective adaptations to their local environments and help them form a cognitive map within which other empirical, material, and ultimately scientific adaptations may be made.

Myths provide systems of understanding that represent an important adaptation to the Universe. The storytelling capacity reflected in myths represents a significant adaptive aspect of religion. Myths provide explanations that make the Universe coherent. One of the fundamental principles of myths is that they express a moral system, reinforced by the will of the deities, that is regarded as a set of guidelines for individual development and collective behavior. Myths depict our human and spiritual nature with an **indigenous psychology** that provides humans with necessary structures for accommodations to social reality.

Myths are one of the most important sources of information informing a culture's worldview. They provide a social charter—an expression of social expectations that guide the organization of society, express its values, and dictate the appropriate behavior of humans—as well as guidelines for dealing with aspects of life yet to be encountered. Myths also represent humans and their various natures, especially their internal dispositions and capabilities, giving each group an indigenous psychological framework, based on innate principles, for guiding the human understanding of self, others, and the culture's collective dispositions. Although many modern humans may reject myths in favor of science, science also provides myth-like explanations, a total system of understanding the Universe that goes beyond the known facts to provide a sense of certainty and control in a Universe that is ultimately unknowable.

Substantive Beliefs

All religious systems' ideas about the pantheon of spirit beings and the myths that describe these beings and their activities also provide information about how humans can interact with the spirits and influence the Universe. In addition, religious systems provide their adherents with a stable worldview related to the actual principles of the Universe, expressed in understandable and coherent laws. If religion did not express ideas about the laws of the Universe, people might not find it believable or compelling. For this reason, religious cosmologies include substantive beliefs about the nature of reality and the operating principles according to which the Universe functions. One of the most important of the operating principles that people have developed is the principle of magic, the notion that spirits and supernatural powers can actually be compelled to produce certain effects by rituals.

Sympathetic Magic as Substantive Belief

The anthropologist and scholar of comparative religion James Frazer (1890/1911/1929) contributed to the early intellectual approaches to understanding religiosity in his book *The Golden Bough*. Frazer proposed several general laws of magic embodied in the concept of **sympathetic magic**. Two of these are the **law of similarity** (also called imitative magic or homeopathic magic), according to which "like produces like," with the desired effects imitated in a ritual (e.g., the image of a person is destroyed to cause him harm); and the **law of contagion** (also called "exuvial magic"), whereby something from a person (such as hair or blood) or some personal object is used in a ritual to harm a person, on the basis of the assumption that the "part affects the whole." Any action that is performed on that object will then be transferred to the person from whom it came (e.g., burning a lock of hair will cause the person from which it came to be consumed with heat). Contagion is exemplified by beliefs regarding the transfer of some quality, essence, or effect from a source to a target. Contact with a powerful object transfers some of its qualities to the target. In the contact with a source, an object may acquire a positive or negative "charge," protecting it or making it ill, even to the point of death.

Following the law of similarity, magicians attempt to influence systems by enacting rituals in which the procedures imitate the desired outcome. For instance, a ritual to make it rain might generate clouds of smoke and steam to imitate the rain clouds the magician wishes to produce. A hunter might paint game animals pierced with spears on the walls of caves to improve the odds of success in the hunt. To do away with an enemy, a magician might construct an image of the intended victim and then subject the image to attacks

(e.g., piercing, burning, poisoning) with the intention to transfer the effects to the actual person. Imitative magic often incorporates the principles of contagion by using objects associated with the intended victim (e.g., hair, fingernails, feces ["exuvia"], or articles of clothing) to enhance the contact.

Frazer characterized these forms of magic as "sympathetic magic" because they are based on the principle that objects separated from one another can still affect one another through a special sympathy, a connection that allows some energy or cause to be transferred between them. **Mana,** an impersonal magical energy or force that is presumed by these principles, provides a "sympathetic" link or connection that allows for a continued transfer of power from the source to the target. These magical beliefs are based on the assumption that the "self" is permeable, or susceptible to outside influences that can enter the body through its apertures or through symbolic influences and imitation. Nemeroff and Rozin (2000) suggest that magical contagion and magical similarity involve the notion of a shared essence that produces the links between objects. Similarity is based on the presumption that things which resemble one another in superficial ways also share a deeper level of common identity, while contagion suggests that once there is a contact between objects, an influence remains even after they are separated.

Frazer suggested that these basic laws of magic originated in a mistaken extension of certain basic mental principles. He proposed that both contagion and similarity were based on the mistaken belief that similarity in actions or symbolic connections could transfer effects. Frazer contended that these principles of magic reflected the befuddled mind of a person who could not distinguish between ritual action and reality.

Sympathetic Magic as Adaptive Cognition with Survival Value. Anthropologists and psychologists have offered other explanations of Frazer's laws, ranging from notions that the laws of similarity are actual principles of the Universe to suggestions about how such beliefs can confer survival advantages. Nemeroff and Rozin (2000) point to a number of principles embodied in the underlying cognitive processes of magical thought that have adaptive advantages. They characterize magical thought as a reflection of intuitive thought processes that confuse the operations within one's own subjective, internal world with what happens in the external Universe. Magic is nonetheless based on the accurate intuition that there are powerful but imperceptible powers, and that our relations with them are mediated by emotional, mental, and symbolic processes. The beliefs regarding magical connections serve a variety of adaptive functions—physical, emotional, social, and cognitive—that enhance human survival and well-being.

Nemeroff and Rozin (2000) reviewed a wide range of psychological research which illustrates that the properties, origins, and functions of these aspects of magic are universal principles not just of primitive thought, but also of modern thought. In some cases these principles are manifested in intuitions or preferences, while in others they appear as well-developed and rationalized belief systems. For example, American college students exhibit disgust reactions based on the principles of similarity. In one study, students who willingly placed a piece of fudge or a rubber stopper in their mouths were generally unwilling to do so when the fudge or stopper resembled a disgusting object, such as a piece of fudge shaped like feces or rubber that looked like vomit. Laboratory studies have shown that the avoidance of objects which have been in physical contact with "contaminated" or "polluted" sources (e.g., clothes worn by AIDS patients) reflect contagion fears rather than any rationally held beliefs or empirical facts about HIV transmission.

Why should modern people behave in ways characteristic of the superstitions of primitive magic? The reason is that magical thinking is natural and intuitive to human thought. Our belief in contagious effects is not present from birth, but it begins to become an active principle affecting behavior and disgust reactions in children aged six to eight years. Nemeroff and Rozin provide an analysis of magical thought which illustrates that it is normal, and in some cases literally true, for it maps out the actual contingencies in the Universe. The magical and religious postulation of unseen determinant forces might in many ways be seen as validated by modern scientific concepts of gravitational, magnetic, and electrical fields: germs that are invisible to the naked eye; DNA traces from our fingerprints; vaccinations; the mind-over-matter effects found in psychoneuroimmunology and placebo effects; and interpersonal influences on perception, emotions, and behavior (Nemeroff and Rozin 2000).

Contagion is based on concerns about a connection to and separation from other influences in the Universe. Humans are hard-wired to avoid contact with a variety of potentially harmful influences, including strangers, bodily excretions, decaying and dead creatures, and other sources of potential harm. We also are predisposed to seek out contact with positive objects—family and kin, holy figures, and powerful leaders—in the hope that

their influences will be extended to ourselves, enhancing our protection, well-being, and self-esteem. Contagious aversion appears to be reversed among close kin and with those with whom we have love bonds, illustrated in food sharing and sexual intimacy. This suggests that the operation of the opposite principle of positive contagion cements close bonds and interpersonal commitments. Negative contagion fears are more developed than positive ones, probably reflecting the adaptive advantages of avoiding potentially contaminating objects.

Contagion beliefs have adaptive value in the domain of food. Food avoidances that are based on contamination fears can help reduce microbial infections, whereas interpersonal avoidances may reduce the transmission of disease. The principles of contagion are well manifested in food aversions, which cause humans to avoid food that has been in proximity to contaminated objects by reacting to it with powerful feelings of disgust. Humans have apparently acquired a genetic tendency to contagion avoidance; chimpanzees, on the other hand, will eat food such as undigested pieces of meat that they find in feces. Human contagion avoidance is expanded in ritual acts of cleanliness and hygiene that reduce the effects of germs on human health. Efforts to limit contagion are expressed in innate habits that limit contagious contact, for example, avoidance of the ill. Anthropologist Edward C. Green (1999) illustrates the implications of concepts of contagion for health. Green notes that African understandings of contagion, particularly with regard to the spread of disease, have many parallels to Western concepts of germ theory. Fear of contagion most frequently arises in the context of contact with the dead, with bodily excretions, and with decomposed and rotting materials. Contagion is often attributed to "invisible" or microscopic objects. Green notes that this supernatural . . . indigenous contagion theory reflects a naturalistic understanding of disease causation rather than a set of illusions. Green concludes that contagion beliefs reflect knowledge of an empirical cause-and-effect relationship between contamination and the spread of diseases, a real-world understanding that has survival value.

Similarity magic can also be seen as a natural product of our tendency to interpret our present perceptions by using categories we learned in the past. This way of understanding the world assigns entities to categories on the basis of shared similarities. The principle of similarity, in which appearance is treated as reality, is a generally useful principle that is manifested in the animal world in the phenomenon of mimicry. In humans, this conflation of representations with reality is hyperdeveloped as a consequence of our extensive reliance on symbols, which extends the possibilities for levels of similarity and connection between objects. The principles of similarity are, however, deeply embedded in our nature and that of other primates; when a monkey sees another monkey reach for food, both monkeys' brains send the same impulses through their motor neurons.

Cognitive anthropologist Richard Shweder (1977) asserts that it is a normal human tendency to make conclusions about associations and causes on the basis of correlations found in personal experience. The cognitive processing structures of the human mind lead us to seek meaningful connections and to presume that we have found them. Since humans are not disposed to accept or comprehend the concept of chance occurrences, we are inclined to insert causal mechanisms of explanation that give us a sense of personal relevance and control. Such beliefs in control, while false, may be adaptive responses that enable people to overcome stress, depression, and learned helplessness. Even the illusion of control can lead to an enhanced sense of well-being and personal control.

The basis for these meaningful connections is our embodied experience—our use of our own bodies as preconceptual structures of experience that underlie our ordinary inference processes and abstract reasoning. Because the body is used as a framework for our understanding of the physical world, there is a preexisting foundation for the transfer of actions on the world to our own bodies. The magical blurring of distinctions between the self and the external Universe allows rituals to generate a variety of personal and interpersonal influences. Religious belief systems provide a way of reducing personal resistance to social influences, allowing individuals to situate themselves and their personal circumstances and development within the context of cultural expectations and patterns. The reduction of our personal boundaries allows us to incorporate ourselves into the amorphous, but sensed, normative social expectations, enhancing the integration of the individual into the social body.

Empirical Approaches to Substantive Religious Beliefs and Experiences

The intellectualist theories of Tylor and Frazer focused on religion as a cognitive phenomenon. Their assumptions led them to view magic and religion as primitive and delusional. This way of thinking made it easier for them to contrast religion with science and to argue that religion was a mistaken enterprise. But what evidence is there to support the idea that religion originated in contemplative thinking and not in reality? If thought alone was the basis of religion, wouldn't people be "thinking up" religions with great regularity? New religious movements do occur, but generally as a result of profound religious experiences rather than contemplative insights. In contrast to the intellectualist approaches to the origins of religion, many people have pointed to the experiential origins of religious beliefs, derived from what people readily interpret as evidence of supernatural entities and powers.

The scientific assumptions of materialism and anti-idealism that have dominated Western discussions of magic and religion have generally not given any serious consideration to the emic cultural claims that one can actually encounter and experience spirits, ghosts, and powerful supernatural forces. The intellectualist approaches that view religion as the result of cognitive processes are antiempirical for they ignore the empirical evidence—data from the senses—from people around the world who have reported sensing, seeing, and even feeling spirits. The emic perspective reveals that to people worldwide, the experiences of spirits are real. A valid etic perspective would attempt to understand how these perceptions arise everywhere. The scientific perspective need not accept the emic *explanations* of these experiences, but it should take the emic data as real experiences. The many cross-cultural similarities in magical and religious beliefs means that science needs to explain them as something more than just arbitrary cultural beliefs.

The notion that religious ideas have natural foundations in human experiences has a long pedigree. As we saw in Chapter 3, Friedrich Schleiermacher (1799–1996) saw religion as emerging from humans' intuitions and feelings about the universe, a notion expanded in Rudolph Otto's (1958) concept of numinousness, the experience produced by the awareness of the overwhelming power of the Universe. More recent developments have considered the possibility that a variety of experiences attributed to religious phenomena are in some sense real and have contributed to the development of religious traditions. Some of these approaches consider the roots of religion to lie within humans. That is to say, they maintain that while spirits are experientially real, the experiences humans have of spirits are actually products of specific human capacities and not something in the external world. For instance, biologically based tendencies to hypnotic suggestibility associated with anomalous experiences, such as apparitions, provide "evidence" of the spirit world.

Other scholars have accepted the experiential reality of the experiences of spirits, but have attributed the source of these experiences to unusual human capacities of extrasensory perception (ESP), clairvoyance, and psychokinetic abilities, and the effects of mind over matter. Transpersonal psychology and transpersonal anthropology have provided an understanding of a variety of anomalous experiences—spirits, ghosts, out-of-body experiences—as unusual but normal aspects of human experience that provide a basis for beliefs in the spirit world.

Psychical Research: The Science of Spiritual Experiences

In the nineteenth century, Western researchers began a scientific study of religious and spiritual phenomena that eventually led to the development of "psychical research traditions" and **parapsychology**, the scientific study of psychic phenomena. Parapsychology is a scientific discipline that studies the claims for such unusual human abilities as ESP and psychokinesis ("mind over matter"). These research traditions used controlled observations and experimental studies of spirit communication and carried out systematic surveys in which they recorded the conditions surrounding people's spontaneous experiences of spirits. The investigations of peoples' experiences of ghosts and of communication with the spirits of the dead not only sought evidence to support the "spirit hypothesis"— the survival of the soul—but also considered the "psi hypothesis"—alternate explanations of the apparent reality of spirits that suggest they are the consequence of human psychic abilities.

The Society for Psychical Research was founded in London in 1882 by a distinguished group of Cambridge University scientists and scholars to engage in the scientific study of the survival of the soul and the bases for paranormal abilities such as telepathy and clairvoyance. They carried out scientific studies of spiritualist phenomena such as channeling (mediumship), levitation, telepathy, and other psychic phenomena. Among the society's presidents were the physicists William Crookes, William Barrett, Oliver Lodge, and Lord Rayleigh, and psychologists such as F. W. H. Myers and Harvard professor William James. Their purpose was to apply scientific research methods to investigate whether there was an empirical basis for psychic phenomena evidence supporting the belief in the survival of the soul. While their opinions differed on the best approaches to investigating the various phenomena and on the interpretation of some of the results, their general conclusion was that there was solid evidence for the existence of telepathy and clairvoyance, as well

as substantial verifiable information communicated by mediums, presumably from the dead. While many scientists then and today remain ignorant of these studies and summarily reject the findings and interpretations, what remains is a solid body of empirical evidence regarding the experiences, including studies that provided rigorous verification of the information provided (see *Journal of Psychical Research, Journal of the American Society for Psychical Research*, and *Journal of Parapsychology*).

Andrew Lang, a specialist in folklore, was the first anthropologist to reject the notion of magic as a mistaken science and instead to consider data that suggested magical beliefs were based in actual experiences, entities, and abilities. Lang pointed out that the claims to experiences of apparitions and other psychical phenomena were universal among humans and argued that this was relevant to anthropological considerations of the roots of religion, particularly notions of animism. Lang wrote several books (*The Book of Dreams and Ghosts* [1897], *Magic and Religion* [1901], and *The Secret of the Totem* [1905]) examining anthropological reports of supernatural phenomena in light of the studies carried out by the Society for Psychical Research. After studying the descriptions of encounters with what were considered spiritual entities and other unusual phenomena involving human psychic abilities, Lang contended that the incredible accounts of apparitions, fire-walking, clairvoyance, and paranormal phenomena should be understood in the context of the findings from the scientific research being carried out by the Society for Psychical Research. He suggested that psychical research and parapsychology demonstrated an empirical reality to spirit experiences, as well as the existence of psychic abilities that could produce the kinds of information putatively derived from interaction with the spirits (see Box 7.5: The Census of Hallucinations).

Anomalous Experiences as Substantive Religious Beliefs. **Anomalous experiences** are a range of phenomena, experienced by people in cultures around the world, that are associated with religious beliefs. Jim McClenon's book *Wondrous Healing* (2002) documents the importance of anomalous experiences in understanding the origins of religious beliefs. These experiences are private perceptions of phenomena interpreted as ghosts and apparitions, communication with the dead, near-death and out-of-body experiences, spontaneous remission of disease and miracle cures, extrasensory awareness such as clairvoyance and precognition, and other experiences that are generally

Box 7.5 THE CENSUS OF HALLUCINATIONS

A study known as the Census of Hallucinations[1] was conducted in England in the nineteenth century and replicated in the United States and other parts of Europe in the twentieth century. The study investigated people's experiences of the spirit world and contributed to an understanding of the factors that often predispose people to have such experiences. Even in modern scientific England, people were experiencing spirits under circumstances remarkably similar to those found in the so-called primitive cultures around the world. The study found that important emotional (rather than intellectual) factors were associated with spiritual experiences, perspectives that became central in later efforts to understand magic.

The study of thousands of people in the Census of Hallucinations discovered that people not only reported numerous experiences with spirits or ghosts, but that the conditions under which such experiences tended to occur were remarkably similar. The vast majority of the cases occurred during the nighttime hours and had dreamlike qualities. The typical spirit experience involved a visitation from a close friend or family member who conveyed the idea that he or she was in great danger or dying. This predominant pattern of a spirit encounter in the context of a nighttime, dreamlike experience of contact with a dying family member has been replicated in more modern contexts. Why are there such similarities in people's experiences of the spirit world? One possible explanation is that the similarities are due to properties of the spirit world itself. An alternative explanation is that they reflect the structures of human experience.

Even the proponents of modern psychical research—scientific investigations into the existence of spirits—have generally concluded that this research fails to provide conclusive evidence establishing the autonomous existence of spirits or life after death. The crucial evidence that undermined the spirit hypothesis was not the lack of verifiable data purportedly communicated from the dead. There were numerous studies which showed that mediums and psychics could provide precise information about deceased people, even under well-controlled conditions. Instead, the society members themselves concluded early on that the data could not be used to prove the existence of spirits or life after death because the evidence could not rule out the possibility that information was being conveyed, not by spirits, but by telepathy (mind-to-mind communication) and clairvoyance (extrasensory perception). The "psi hypothesis," as this alternate explanation is called, has remained a problem that plagues this research tradition's efforts to confirm the existence of spirits. The evidence for mediumistic communication from clairvoyance rather than from a dead person was illustrated by "drop-in" spirit communicators who appeared to speak from the dead to provide information about their "past" lives, but who were later encountered alive on the streets by the surprised investigators!

Today, people continue to report experiences with spirits. This leads us to inquire into the biological and cognitive bases of this universal human perception that modern science continues to characterize as an illusion. From what basis does this convincing, but illusory, perception arise? And why are mediumistic communications so convincing, conveying both the personality of the dead person and significant information about the individual's personal life?

[1] See *Proceedings of the Society for Psychical Research*, Vol. X, pp. 25–422. A detailed description of the Census of Hallucinations findings is contained in G. N. M. Tyrrell's *Apparitions* (Duckworth, 1953).

interpreted as refuting the scientific assumptions of materialism. You may note that this list of anomalous experiences is very similar to the "spiritual emergences" we discussed in Chapter 3, regarding whether or not spiritual experiences are pathological. As we noted then, these are normal experiences in some circumstances, and their effects are in part due to how others respond to them. While these personal subjective experiences are generally discounted as unreliable by scientists, those who have such experiences often take them as conclusive proof of the spirit world. In his book *Supernatural* (2006), Graham Hancock shows that the persistence of contemporary beliefs in

supernatural entities is often driven by the direct experiences that individuals have with what they conceptualize as many forms of supernatural entities and powers.

Anomalous experiences occur in cultures around the world, although more frequently in some places than others. McClenon (2002) points out that people who have anomalous experiences are more emotionally sensitive, have greater hypnotic susceptibility, are more fantasy prone and often experience a "calling" to provide healing services. Strong correlations exist among hypnotic susceptibility, dissociation, fantasy proneness, and thin cognitive boundaries, all involving enhanced connections between unconscious and conscious aspects of the mind and manifesting as a greater than normal susceptibility to suggestibility.

McClenon (2002) argues that anomalous experiences provide the origin for religious beliefs about spirits and may even have a genetic basis, as reflected in the inheritable quality of hypnotic susceptibility and its interaction with suggestibility and placebo effects. This hypnotic capacity has ancient roots in primate biology, where it provides mechanisms for reducing aggression and social stress and engaging the relaxation response. For humans, the repetitive behaviors associated with animals' hypnotic behaviors produce both an alteration of consciousness and a sense of intragroup cohesion experienced as "union" or "oneness," classic aspects of religious and mystical experiences. The hypnotic capacity enhances innovation derived from access to the unconscious mind, providing survival advantages by facilitating the development of creative strategies. The thin cognitive boundaries characteristic of highly hypnotizable people give them greater access to the information in their personal unconscious and help them communicate information to the conscious mind. Hypnotizability and increased suggestibility facilitate placebo effects as well, providing a basis for miraculous cures that enhance faith and survival (see Box 7.6: Magic and Psi: Are Religion and Science Converging?).

Box 7.6 MAGIC AND PSI: ARE RELIGION AND SCIENCE CONVERGING?

The laboratory experiments carried out by parapsychologists have provided an understanding of the principles surrounding the operation of psi, giving anthropologists additional data from which to assess the bases of magical beliefs and practices. In essence, parapsychology suggests that there might be an empirical basis for claims that magic can indeed affect the physical world. Parapsychological research has suggested that there are certain human abilities of extrasensory perception, such as telepathy, clairvoyance, precognition, and psychokinetic abilities of "mind over matter." Known as psi abilities, these appear to be normal human capabilities displayed in extraordinary occurrences, such as precognitive experiences of future disasters. These psi abilities occur under certain conditions and with certain characteristics that suggest they are related to magic. A number of anthropologists have examined how parapsychological research findings may help us understand aspects of magical beliefs and practices (see Long 1977; Winkelman 1982).

A variety of characteristics have been associated with magical practices around the world, including an altered state of consciousness often referred to as ecstasy, trance, or possession; the importance of belief and the exclusion of disbelievers; and the use of visualization procedures that often involve enacting the desired effects. The parapsychological evidence suggests that each of these principles of magic—altered states of consciousness, belief, and visualization—can be effective at achieving the desired goals. Altered states of consciousness are associated with more unusual ESP phenomena and possibly access to more information than was available to the conscious mind. Belief is positively associated with performance on ESP tests, with believers in ESP scoring higher. The visualization of desired results frequently found in magical practices has parallels in parapsychological research findings that visualizing a desired outcome is the most effective strategy in laboratory experiments on human psychokinetic ("mind over matter") effects on machines.

Mana and Psi. There are additional parallels between the principles of magic and the research findings and theories of parapsychology. One of the concepts associated with magic is "mana," considered to be the source of magical power and effectiveness. Mana is defined as a force distinct from physical power, but that is nonetheless capable of altering the forces of nature. Mana is conceptualized as a force acting at a distance, an impersonal and immanent milieu that connects the magician and that which he is affecting. Mana is even considered to be the power underlying the natural and supernatural Universe, an impersonal natural force that the magician can manipulate. Parapsychologists use the term *psi* to refer to what they perceive as the common principle or force underlying ESP, telepathy, psychokinesis, and other psychic phenomena. Psi is conceptualized as a nonphysical force that transcends the limitations of time and space and that can act on the physical world. Psi effects are thought not only to produce extraordinary psychic phenomena, but to also underlie ordinary cognitive processes such as memory and intention. Both mana and psi are conceptualized as nonphysical powers that operate in ways that transcend the laws of nature, but nonetheless can affect natural processes. Both are viewed as powers that operate within and on nature, connecting individuals and their intentions with the systems that they want to influence. The similar metaphors and conceptions used by magicians and parapsychologists to characterize this elusive power suggest that both may be addressing the same underlying domains.

Magic and Psychokinesis. Winkelman (1982) has also pointed out that the kinds of tasks attempted by magic are similar to the types of systems that are most readily affected by psychokinesis. Psi is more likely to affect systems that are "active" and "labile" and that have lots of "noise," randomness, and uncertainty in their outcomes. It is easier to affect active and noisy systems such as random subatomic events or marbles cascading down a set of baffles than to levitate a spoon resting on a table. Malinowski (1927/1954) also characterized magic as a set of techniques used to affect domains that are uncertain and unknown, where skill or labor alone will not suffice. Mauss (1950/1972) characterized magic as a system in which the magical acts are designed to place objects into a condition in which ordinary occurrences will happen to a specific entity at a specific place and time. Rain is going to fall; magic makes sure that it falls on my garden. Evans-Pritchard also characterized magic as being used to produce outcomes that are already likely to happen, involving contingencies that have a great likelihood of occurring. All of these parallels suggest that the foundation of magic may lie in the same basic human potentials that underlie other psychic abilities.

Similarity and Contagion as Cognitive Principles

Winkelman (1982) examined possible explanations of the laws of similarity from the perspective of parapsychology. The high level of correspondence of magical beliefs found around the world with the principles derived from laboratory and experimental studies carried out by parapsychologists suggest some empirical underlying features of the Universe.

The law of similarity is generally exemplified in magical acts that induce, through ritual, a set of relationships or enact events in some other aspect of the Universe (e.g., the ritual imitation of clouds to make clouds appear in the Universe). The description and enactment of desired goals in magical rituals has parallels in psychological findings about goal orientation and in parapsychological research on the role of visualization in producing **psychokinetic effects** ("mind over matter").

Many magical practices involve visualizing a desired outcome, including the rituals of imitative magic and the practices of "imagining" the desired outcomes in a mental picture. A review of parapsychological research findings (see Winkelman 1982) illustrates the positive effects of expectation and belief on the manifestation of psychic abilities. The activities of enactment and visualization have well-recognized effects in focusing attention and behavior, enhancing success in a variety of endeavors. Laboratory experiments have shown that visualizing the desired effects is one of the most successful strategies for inducing psychokinetic effects on machines designed to measure subtle variations in the behavior of subatomic particles. Other effects of visualization include positive expectation—the "power of belief" that is associated with extrasensory abilities. How do ritually altered states of consciousness and dreams reflect practices through which we can obtain information from the Universe? These ancient principles of magical enactment, the use of ritual to imitate what we want to achieve, reflect ways in which our minds can affect the material and social worlds, and still serve to orient our intentions today.

Conclusions: Spirit Concepts as Indigenous Psychology

Basic adaptations provided by religious systems are cognitive frameworks such as cosmologies and mythologies that provide their members with frameworks for understanding of the Universe and themselves. The biocultural approach provides insights into the adaptive advantages of religious beliefs and myths in the descriptions afforded about the invisible mechanisms, structures, and patterns of operation of the Universe. Animism, the basic postulation of spirit entities, is based on exaptations of agency detection and other innate projective mechanisms of humans. Animism also includes suprahuman capabilities and counterintuitive assumptions that extend human cognitive potentials beyond the capacities of the innate modules. Myths, broadly speaking, provide important revelations about the patterns of nature, seasonal cycles, ecological adaptations, human complexity and internal dynamics, and social relations. Religious systems also include substantive beliefs that reflect principles of operation of the Universe that can provide adaptive behavioral and cognitive orientations to important stimuli, exemplified in contagion beliefs. Together, cosmologies, mythologies, and the spiritual and substantive beliefs of religious systems provide a necessary element of human social life, an indigenous psychology that explains the nature of humans and their potentials and behaviors.

Although every culture has its own ideas about what it means to be a human being, and what it means to lead a "proper" human life, this regularity and predictability of behavior among people of a group derives from the effects of culture in patterning humans' biological capacities. These biological universals provide capabilities that are necessary for social life, for instance, awareness of and representations of self and others. Many of these ideas are derived from beliefs in spirit beings and myths about deities, souls, and humans' nature and dispositions. Normal human behavior requires individuals to construct mental models of the self and others, using our capacity for "theory of mind" that infers others' thoughts and intentions. Consequently, every culture provides its members with what is called a folk or indigenous psychology—that culture's conceptions about normal human capacities and the internal motivations and mechanisms that explain what humans do and why they do it (Heelas 1981; Lock 1981). Although each culture shapes its own indigenous psychology, all cultures must inform people how to understand and program their innate capacities for cognitive and social life. The human symbolic capacity requires some type of framework that informs us regarding what it means to be human, how we should relate to the Universe, and why people behave in predictable patterns (Heelas 1981). Religions have been some of the most prevalent and powerful symbol systems for informing our collective needs for an indigenous psychology.

Indigenous psychologies provide the necessary frameworks for understanding other human beings in personal interactions, providing a conceptual map of aspects of the inner self, our emotions, motives and drives, personal will, and sense of agency. The symbols and meanings offered by religion inform the indigenous psychologies, providing the systems of meaning that link the individual and his or her experiences to the sociocultural order. These myth systems provide models for self that guide social development of the individual and enable the smooth relationships of coordinated social life (Heelas 1981, Lock 1981). The conceptions of the nature of humans that are used in organizing collective social life in cultures around the world employ supernatural concepts of identity, self, behavior, emotions, and agency.

Spiritual beliefs inform our mythologies and indigenous psychologies because they represent natural—neurognostic—conceptions of the internal capacities of humans and their intentions. Spirit concepts reflect the principles of human **personality**, concepts of the overall dynamics of human psychological processes, including concepts of the normal person and their symbolic, mental, emotional, behavioral, and social capacities, as well as dispositions, drives, perceptions, cognition, and memory. Cultural concepts of the internal nature and the dynamics of the person are typically conceptualized in spirit terms during most of human existence because they reflected adaptive structures of perception modeled on human capabilities. Spirit beliefs guide personal identity formation, self-understanding, and social integration because, like humans, spirits too are believed to have thoughts, intentions, motives, and desires. Spirit beliefs function as fundamental representations of the structure of human psychology, constituting a language of intrapsychic dynamics of the self and the cultural dynamics of social and interpersonal relations.

All cultures have (had) spiritual personality theories that are intimately bound up with religious concepts that explain the capacities and experiences of persons and models regarding how individuals conduct themselves. These models generally postulate souls, spirits, ancestors, lustful beings, and possessing entities to explain behavior. Concepts of personality, inner self, emotions, consciousness, will, memories, and intentionality/agency, all exemplify nonmaterial concepts of human nature; consequently, spirits and their nonmaterial aspects make them a natural source for indigenous psychology.

Religious systems provide adaptive advantages in symbolic depictions of the ideal person, societal forces, interpersonal conflicts, and how to manage them. Religions illustrate ideals for individual behavior and rules for social behavior. Religion provides a social identity in a "sacred self" (Pandian 1997). The cosmology and myths of a particular religion describe both proper and improper behavior, thereby helping to ensure the continuity of the institutions in that society. The nonmaterial aspects of humans (souls or spirits) enable religious beliefs to create a network of relationships and responsibilities that extends beyond our lifetimes and our physical bodies, ensuring the continuity of culture.

Mythology and other aspects of expressive culture inform a group's indigenous psychology through its expression of group sentiments and psychosocial dynamics, illustrating moral and ethical problems and exemplifying ideal behavioral and emotional responses. The ideational component of a culture offers its members orientations to the affective values that people acquire, shaping their evaluation and experience of the world and eliciting the emotions that bond people together and make them feel alive. We address these emotional and social dynamics of religion next.

Questions for Discussion

1. Why do religious systems around the world have so many similar features?
2. How does a cosmological system help us to feel at home in the Universe?
3. How can religious beliefs help or harm the natural environment?

Glossary

anomalous experiences private perceptions that are interpreted as contact with a spirit or that in some other way do not conform with the scientific assumption of materialism

archetypes innate and universal aspects of human experience and representations of structural conditions of the mind and humans' needs that are fundamental to human nature; our preadaptations to experience and express archetypes in nonverbal symbolic understandings and in the verbal manifestations of myths

binary opposition the human tendency to see the world in terms of basic cognitive dichotomies

collective unconscious the innate dispositions of human minds that mediate between the potentials provided by our biology and our personal experiences

cosmology a model that describes the structure of the Universe, tells how it came to be, and names the beings and forces that affect it

functionalism the anthropological theory of the ways that cultures satisfy the biological and psychological needs of their members

indigenous psychology the worldview that a culture provides for its members, including its cosmological beliefs and its attitudes about what it means to be human

law of contagion the idea that an object that was once in contact with a particular person can be used to harm or otherwise influence that person

law of similarity the idea that objects that are similar to one another can produce similar effects

mana an impersonal magical energy or force inherent to certain objects, places, or persons

myths narratives that describe the Universe and explain the beings and events that occur within the Universe

neurognostic structures the neurological foundations of our innate mechanisms for knowing (gnosis) the world

operating principles statements about the laws that govern the functioning of the Universe

pantheon the set of supernatural beings recognized by a religion

parapsychology the scientific study of psychic phenomena

personality the long-term structure of an individual's psychological processes, many of which are shaped by culture

psychokinetic effects actions that are performed solely by willing them with the mind

sacred geography the "map" of the domains recognized by a religion, including the paths used to travel from one domain to another

scenario building the process of mentally examining alternative courses of action and considering the potential consequences of those actions

spirits agents that resemble humans in many ways, but that also possess extraordinary abilities and powers beyond our own

structuralism the anthropological theory that examines how the relationships among different cultural elements combine to produce psychological and social stability

substantive beliefs statements about the various domains recognized by a religion and the principles or laws that govern them

sympathetic magic the idea that objects that are separated from one another can still have effects on one another through a special sympathy

Religion and Emotions: How Religion Shapes How We Feel

CHAPTER OBJECTIVES

- Examine the relationships between religions and emotions.
- Introduce anthropological and psychological approaches to the roles of emotions in religious beliefs and practices.
- Show the value of the ritual management of sexuality.
- Illustrate the roles of religion in socializing emotions and life-cycle development.
- Consider the evolutionary psychology view that religion elaborates on basic mammalian attachment mechanisms.

THE BOY WAS BEGINNING TO STIR. THE DRINK THAT his grandmother had prepared for him had caused him to sleep for almost a full day. During that time, at least one of the five watchers had always been by his side, waiting for his return from the spirit world. The boy was on a quest. He had consumed the sacred drink so that he could find his spirit helper, the one who would aid him the rest of his life. This was an important time for the boy, for without a spirit helper, he would never have success in life.

Now the color was returning to his cheeks, and his lips were moving as if he was speaking to some unseen being. The old man next to him began to chant. His words told the boy that he was now a man, and that he would no longer be permitted to act like a boy. As the young man came back to the everyday world, the old man sang to him, telling him what it meant to be a man. Soon, all five of the watchers had returned, and they *asked the young man to tell them what he had seen. He was one of them now. He was a man who could take up a position of power and prestige among his people.*

Introduction: Religion and Socialization

As children grow up in a society, they spend much of their early lives learning about who they are, what they should do with their lives, and how they should understand and relate to the Universe. The passage above describes one of the methods that the Chumash, a Native American tribe from California, used to teach a boy how to be a man (Applegate 1975). Among the Chumash, a person's personal and social success depended on having spirit helpers. The only way that

These petroglyphs from a cave in Southern California illustrate some of the visions of the Chumash.

think, feel, and act in accordance with that culture's models of the Universe. In traditional societies, religious concepts and values generally provided a "total cultural system" that defined virtually every aspect of existence. As we saw in the last chapter, myths help people to understand and relate to the Universe by explaining the meaning of the sun, the moon, and the stars, as well as the more directly experienced "down-to-earth" processes of plant growth, sexual reproduction, and death.

In every culture, religious concepts provide elements for the indigenous psychology that shapes a person's personality and emotions. Socialization channels each person's innate drives and emotions into culturally acceptable forms that make that person's actions understandable and predictable to others, and it enables the person to understand and predict what the other members of his or her society are likely to think and do. It is the process of socialization that counterbalances our natural tendency to see things in our own individual ways; socialization provides the common channels of communication and understanding that coordinate a society.

In this chapter, we will consider some of the ways in which religious socialization helps us manage our emotions and organize our lives. Religion allows us to moderate and control anxiety, make sense of our feelings, understand our place in society and the Universe, and adjust to the emotions that inevitably occur across our life. To be effective, an indigenous psychology must explain human nature and produce feelings of belonging. Consequently, we now consider some of the ways that religions create and manipulate our emotions.

Religion as an Emotional Response

The "intellectualist" approaches discussed in Chapter 7 looked at how religious systems provide explanatory frameworks that allow their followers to understand and act within the world. But religion involves more than just ideas. Religious beliefs and activities often produce powerful emotions such as awe, bliss, and tranquility that are considered to be key features of some spiritual experiences.

Among those who developed theories regarding the emotional nature of religion are the early anthropologists Robert Marett and Bronislaw Malinowski, as well as the psychologist Sigmund Freud. Marett argued that religious experience is rooted in a sense of awe and wonder, while Malinowski saw magic and religion as products of the unconscious and emotional stress. In contrast to these anthropologists, who did not typically

a person could acquire a spirit helper was to consume a drink made from the plant (*Datura wrightii*) that the Chumash called Momoy.

Although a child's development is programmed by genetic factors, social and cultural conditions also exert crucial influences. They affect the types of food the child will eat, the ways the child will dress and adorn him- or herself, and the types of physical activities the child will perform. Culture—and especially religious beliefs—also exert a profound influence in channeling a child's development, defining what it means to be a human, the age at which the child will become an adult, and the tasks and responsibilities that will be expected at each stage of life. A central aspect of these shaping influences involves defining and eliciting emotional experiences.

One of the most important traditional functions of religion is **socialization**, the process that shapes the individual in a manner that ensures that he or she will regard the peoples and cultures they studied as "pathological," Freud proposed that religion is a delusional system, an illusion that is the product of wish-fulfilling fantasies emerging from the unconscious. These early "emotionalist" approaches recognized that our religious experiences were at least partially a product of biology. More recent developments have provided insights that allow us to associate certain religious behaviors with specific biological adaptations.

Many emotional aspects of religiosity involve the manipulation of features that initially evolved for different purposes. For example, Kirkpatrick (2005) shows how the features of the mammalian attachment system that evolved to bond mothers and infants underlies the more general ability of humans to bond to one another and to their Gods. This illustrates how religious beliefs and practices involve the use of prior adaptations for new purposes. If the new application is subject to selection and contributes to survival, it is an exaptation, a "second generation" adaptation with a new functional ability that enhances survival. This view of evolutionary adaptations suggests that religious practices may provide extensions of prior by-products and adaptations to new functions in the management of our emotions and consciousness.

Sacred Emotions. Psychologist Robert Emmons (2005) notes that religious activities are often associated with profound emotional experiences. But the effects of religion on emotions vary widely across traditions. For example, charismatic religious traditions' production of positive ecstatic emotions differs dramatically from the mystical and meditative traditions' emphasis on calming the emotions. Nonetheless, most religious traditions emphasize positive emotional states involving bliss and joy. Religions also can determine which emotions are appropriate and which are inappropriate; can generate specific emotions, including those which enhance human well-being; and can cause their followers to experience what some consider to be uniquely religious emotions.

Emmons notes that there are prototypical religious emotions such as a sense of awe and reverence, as well as other emotions frequently directed toward deities, such as love, joy, happiness, serenity, and contentment. While religious emotions are not exclusive to religious contexts, specific emotions are more likely to be evoked in religious practices. Emmons suggests that the specific sacred emotions of gratitude, awe, reverence, wonder, and hope are commonly experienced by religious individuals in cultures around the world.

Gratitude. Gratitude is an experience that has its basis in the receipt of altruism; it is a recognition of the beneficial acts of others. Such a sentiment expresses one's moral tendencies and demonstrates one's appreciation for the kindness of others. These emotions have a direct contribution to spiritual tendencies and prosocial behaviors. Spirituality appears to generate gratitude in daily life and contributes to enduring moods of gratitude.

Awe, Reverence, and Wonder. Emmons considers awe and reverence to be central features of religious experiences. Analyses of the roles of emotions in spiritual experience illustrate that a central feature involves a sense that something far greater and more powerful than us exists. The transpersonal psychologist Abraham Maslow considered such emotions to be key to "peak experiences" that are central to spiritual development. Wonder, like other positive emotions, produces a profound reorientation of the sense of self and its obligations.

Hope. Hope is a well-recognized central theological virtue, a vision of a future that embodies the perfect world of God. There are many benefits of hope on both physical and mental health. Religious hope engenders contentment, enabling people to accept and enjoy their current circumstances and to use their expectations of a positive future to transform their personal sense of self and the Universe. Through faith and acceptance, people with hope begin to experience a more perfect order promised by the cosmology and goals of their religion.

These emotions and their links to concepts of the sacred, as well as to health and well-being, attest to the power of religion to generate and modulate emotional experiences and, more significantly, to produce enduring emotional moods. The appraisals provided by religious traditions broaden the individual's horizon of possibilities and shape expectations and actions in ways that help to fulfill the positive aspects of these expectations. Thus, religion shapes coping responses, as we discussed in Chapter 6 on healing. What makes an emotion sacred is not necessarily something distinct from ordinary emotions, but the interpretation of the circumstances in terms of the involvement of a higher power. Religions have the power to evoke a range of adaptive emotions for the individual, as well as the group.

The Emotional Adaptiveness of Magic and Religion

The English anthropologist Robert R. Marett (1866–1943) offered an important corrective to the early intellectualist approaches to religion when he proposed that magic was not a primitive thought process, but an emotional response to stress. Marett emphasized the importance of religious experiences and the emotions they engender, such as awe and fear of the divine and the feelings of love that people feel toward their deities. Marett argued that magic and religion are products of the emotional tensions we experience when we realize that our technical knowledge and abilities are insufficient for solving problems of everyday life. Noting that many magical practices imitate the effects they are intended to produce, Marett suggested that magic provides a sense of emotional satisfaction because it offers people a way to project their frustrated desires into magical processes through which they can be symbolically and psychologically fulfilled. Marett proposed that religion exploited the power of suggestion, with rituals manipulating the unconscious in order to restore confidence. Rituals project the individual's will and personality onto the world and toward the goals that he or she wishes to achieve. Magic instills people with a contagious confidence that they will ultimately find success in their endeavors. In this way, magic focuses both personal and social resources on the desired goals.

These ideas contributed to a major anthropological approach to the intimate relationship between emotions and the origins of religion articulated by Bronislaw Malinowski (1884–1942), one of the most influential anthropologists of the first half of the twentieth century. Born in Poland, Malinowski was university trained in philosophy, physics, and mathematics. This broad educational background led Malinowski to look at cultures from a holistic perspective and to consider cultural practices and beliefs to be parts of interrelated systems that contributed to the fulfillment of individual needs within a society. Thus, for Malinowski, culture exists to serve humans. Because he directly associated cultural phenomena with the biological and psychological needs of individuals, Malinowski redefined the role that society plays in human life. Malinowski suggested that society—in the form of what he called "institutions"—channels how individuals learn to think and feel about the world.

His background in the natural sciences trained Malinowski to pay attention to minute details and to strive for objectivity in recording information about non-Western peoples and their cultures. Between 1915 and 1918, he conducted ethnographic fieldwork among the Trobriand Islanders off the east coast of New Guinea—a group of people who lived primarily from horticulture and fishing. Malinowski studied many aspects of Trobriand life, including the islanders' magical rituals and the relationship of magic to other aspects of their cultural life.

Malinowski's empirical orientation and extensive fieldwork helped him to discount the intellectualist theories of the evolution of human thought from magic through religion to science. He pointed out that although there were no cultures without religion or magic, there were also no cultures completely lacking a scientific attitude. Malinowski realized that the people of the Trobriand Islands (who Tylor would have considered "savages") were just as rational and empirical as most Westerners. Malinowski found that they had a detailed and practical knowledge of the natural laws of leverage, equilibrium, buoyancy, hydrodynamics, and other principles of the physical world. Indeed, their knowledge of plants, animals, the human body, weather, and the stars and planets was far more scientifically sophisticated than the beliefs of many "modern" people in the West.

The Domains of Magic

Malinowski saw both magic and religion as responses to emotional stresses and crises, when empirical knowledge was inadequate or when certain emotions were evoked. Among the Trobrianders, magic was chiefly directed toward human activities involving nature. Whether it was used in gardening, trading, fishing, hunting, or managing disease and death, magic was an expression of the way that humans perceived their relationship to the natural world. Malinowski found that the Trobrianders employed magic in situations when their ordinary knowledge and methods were insufficient for controlling all the factors that could affect the outcome of an activity. They never used magic alone, but always integrated it with practical techniques. For example, once they carried out all the practical preparations for gardening, fishing, or canoe construction, they conducted rituals to favorably influence the factors that were outside their direct control. When elements of luck and chance played an important role in the outcome, the Trobrianders used magic to help reduce danger and uncertainty. When practical and empirical methods were sufficient, however, magic and ritual were unimportant. Malinowski's classic example of this attitude contrasted the Trobrianders' behavior when fishing in the lagoon with their behavior when fishing on the open sea. Magic was not necessary when fishing in the inner lagoon because there were reliable mechanisms for success and there was very little danger. In contrast, they used a wide variety of magical practices to address the dangers and uncertainties associated with fishing on the open sea, where there was a risk of death.

Malinowski noted that the Trobrianders believed emotional gestures and expressions are essential for magic to be effective. Expressions of emotions, including dramatic displays of love or hate, were essential, for they provided the power that made the rituals effective. For example, if a man wished to magically harm or kill an enemy, he had to both physically act out the violent actions designed to cause harm *and* express and experience the passionate emotions that generally accompany such violence. In a sense, the magician's actions defined the desired course of action for the effects of ritual, while the emotions provided the power. For example, to kill an enemy, a man might angrily mutilate an image or object representing the enemy. To cast a spell of love, he might fondle and embrace an object representing the desired person. To make magic effective, it was necessary to feel the emotions associated with the goals.

While magic depends on dramatic enactment, emotional passion, and the manipulation of charmed objects, the most essential element of the magical ritual is the spell itself. Magical power is ultimately derived from words, and to achieve the desired effects, it is essential that a spell be uttered correctly, whether by imitating natural sounds or expressing emotions. Spells evoke images of the desired goals, stating the ends to be achieved. In other words, spells create word pictures that verbally express emotional longings and empower the desired actions. The power of magic is derived from the power of emotions, or more precisely, from emotional tension. It is our spontaneous reactions to events that give rise to our magic, our thwarted desires, fears, and anxieties that create the tensions that drive us to action. We obsess about a goal, encounter frustration when we are unable to achieve it, and then act out our desires in a passionate emotional expression of the goal. The realm of magic emerges wherever our desires are thwarted or our technical skills and knowledge reach their limits.

The Origins of Magic

Malinowski viewed magic as a timeless human activity that had been part of our primeval natural existence and had been practiced by our earliest ancestors as an adaptation to managing our emotions. Magic emerges when emotions are expressed through gesture, dramatic utterances, and the enactment of the desired ends. The image of the desired end supplies the motive, the visualization of the goal, and the behavior for enactment. Magical ritual builds on these foundations, codifying these dramatic emotional expressions of the desired ends. To Malinowski, the effectiveness of magic comes from its ability to release pent-up tension—to allow physiological balance and inner harmony to emerge once the obsessing visions have been expressed. The subjective expression of the emotional tension gives the magician a deep sense of the desired reality, and the enactment and images give the impression that he or she has taken a practical step toward achieving the goal. Magical efficacy may derive from subjective illusions, but those internal experiences are powerful and convincing because they express what we want.

Malinowski proposed that magical rituals and beliefs are based on actual experiences of success, when expression of our desires leads to desired ends. Because even an occasional success can leave an impression that will far outweigh the more frequent failures, magic offers an emotionally satisfying approach to desires that are beyond one's reach. The failures of magic, however frequent, may be easily attributed to the failure to precisely enact a ritual or spell, to the inadvertent violation of some taboo, or to counter-magic performed by a rival. For Malinowski, magic survived because the impact of a positive outcome is greater than the evidence of failure.

The Emotional Adaptiveness of Magic in Human Life

By emphasizing that culture exists for individuals, Malinowski focused attention on the physiological and psychological functions of magical and religious practices and the important role that religious beliefs and behaviors play in helping people manage their emotional lives. Magic and religion also have practical applications for managing the emotions and drives associated with the biological phases of human development—in particular, the critical phases associated with adolescence and the transition to adulthood, marriage, pregnancy, the birth of offspring, and death. The transition from childhood to adulthood is often marked with protracted rites of initiation that provide young people with the knowledge they need for adult life. The biological drives leading to the association of males and females for reproductive purposes are controlled and shaped by the supernatural sanctions created by ritual, producing a sacred bond that reinforces the practical restrictions that facilitate the functions of marriage. Because the outcome of any pregnancy is uncertain, expectant mothers often go through a variety of ceremonies and ritual restrictions. Before, during, and after the birth of babies, a variety of magical rites may be used both to prevent danger and to purify the participants. At some time following birth, communal ceremonies are enacted to present the newborn to the community.

Management of Death Anxiety. One of the most important functions of magic is dealing with the greatest fear of all: death. Malinowski argued that humans have an instinctual awareness of and fear of death. The possibility of our complete annihilation, the total end of our personal existence, can produce fear and even paralysis. Why do people die, and what happens to them—to us—after death? Because religious systems provide answers to these questions, they are able to help people manage their anxieties about death, and they play a significant role in the rites of passage that surround death. Many religions declare that the demise of the physical body does not mean the end of the individual. Their beliefs in the existence of a personal soul and an afterlife serve to repudiate death and allay fear. Funerary rituals enact and reaffirm these beliefs and mark a new stage in the relationship between the departed and the community of ancestral spirits. These ritual relationships established by religion help provide an emotional reality for people's beliefs in immortality. A firm belief in an afterlife and in the spiritual continuity of our personal identity is one of the few comforts that humans have in the face of death. Instead of facing extinction when we die, spiritual beliefs in an eternal soul provide us with the comfort and assurance that death is not the end. And instead of paralyzing fear of our demise, we engage life with vigor and purpose.

The general functions of **funerary rituals** are tied to the broader functional implications of animism, the belief in the spirit world and especially in the personal soul. Funerary rituals define death as one of the many transitions that humans go through during our lifetimes—albeit a major one—as a movement from one realm of existence to another that the survivors of the deceased will one day make as well. Ritual mourning provides a context not only for the expression of personal emotions, but also for the reunion and reintegration of a community that has been affected by the loss of one of its members. Death rituals are extremely important for the well-being of the living, for they provide those who survive the death of a loved one with ways to emotionally manage their grief and to adjust their network of social relations to reflect the loss. The dramatic displays of grief and loss that characterize most funerary rituals provide a channel for emotional release.

Death rituals help us cope with powerful emotions and underscore the fundamental role that religious rituals play in helping us to manage our emotional lives. They also provide a poignant reminder of the ways in which a culture conceives of the relationship between its members and the Universe. Funerary rituals express and affirm those beliefs and create a relationship between the departed and the community of ancestral spirits. The belief that "we'll all be together again someday" extends the social network of this life into the next, providing a sense of familiarity and comfort.

The idea that a nonphysical aspect of the self will survive a person's physical demise is one example of how religions help people manage their emotional needs regarding death. An important latent function is to address the dread that death instills in most humans and the implications of a death for the survivors. Rather than being paralyzed by the fear of our inevitable death, believers in religion feel confident that they will survive the physical deaths of their bodies. Religion also helps people overcome the revulsion they feel toward corpses. A spiritual orientation can induce them to rise above their natural impulses to flee death and to abandon the corpse and the community, which would contribute to the disintegration of the group. Funerary rituals create obligations—the moral compulsion to participate in collective activities that help ensure that the group will survive the death of any individual member. Here we see again how religion can help us to overcome and control our instinctive impulses in the interest of communal survival. Our belief in a soul may save us from the paralyzing fear of death and provide assurance of a reality that not only addresses our deep emotional needs and desire for life, but also provides a variety of other forms of emotional adaptation.

Sigmund Freud and the Roles of the Unconscious in Religion

The Viennese psychologist Sigmund Freud (1856–1939), known for his theories on personality development and for developing the therapeutic practice of psychoanalysis, also devoted a great deal of thought to religion. While Freud's ideas about the origins of religion were not well received in anthropology, they are worth examining both for their historical significance and his views of the relationship between emotions and religious ideas. Freud's view of the emotional foundations of religion was derived from his general model of the psychological and emotional development of the individual and the role that the unconscious plays in human behavior.

Although Freud is considered the most important figure in the history of psychology, many of his ideas were misunderstood in the English-speaking world because of the choice of terms used in the English translations of his work. Translation issues obscured much of what Freud was saying in his most famous terms, known in English as "id," "ego," and "superego."

"Id" is the translation of "das Es" ("the it"), the German expression Freud used to describe the emotional drives that seem to arise from outside ourselves, but that control much of what we do. In using the term "it," Freud wished to emphasize that these drives are distinct from our experience of ourselves. The "it" is an aspect of humans that has been inherited from our ancient ancestors and that is now hard-wired into our psychology, involving features of our unconscious (instinctual) drives and motivations. In contrast to the it/id, the "I" (the correct translation of "das Ich," which has become known in English as the "ego") is an aspect of ourselves that arose as the brain evolved. The "I" or ego tells us that we are both different from the outside world and from the "it." In doing so, it functions as the intermediary between our innate drives ("in here") and the exigencies of the outer world ("out there"). The "over-I" (the correct translation of "das Über-ich," or "superego") is that aspect of our personality that develops in response to our cultural training and represents the internalization of our cultural rules, especially religious rules that dictate how the needs and drives of the "it" may be fulfilled.

These animal drives of the "it" need to be met because they are essential for our survival, both as individuals and as a species. They also need to be controlled, lest they conflict with the needs of other people and the demands for an organized society. Freud saw religion as an important mechanism for controlling these emotional needs in the interest of societal needs.

Freud's Psychoanalytic Model: The Unconscious and Dreams

To Freud, our **unconscious**—the source of the "it" and its biological drives, emotions, and motivations—is the primary determinant of behavior. Expressions of the unconscious are manifestations of our instinctual, biological needs, such as the drive for sex, the desire for love, and our tendencies toward aggression to acquire and defend our needs. These innate and unconscious desires for the things that give us pleasure bring us into conflict with other people, both our own families as well as the broader society. In order for humans to live together in peace, it is imperative for us to control our unconscious needs.

The unconscious includes not only the aspects of human nature that emerged early in human evolution, but also information and emotions that the individual has repressed or forced down into the unconscious because it has produced conflicts at the level of consciousness. Freud argued that the conflicts between our natural desires and the demands of society repeatedly result in situations in which we cannot meet our immediate needs and desires. To defend our sense of self, we must repress these painful frustrations, forcing them out of conscious awareness and down into the unconscious. Although these thoughts and emotions are now "out of sight, out of mind," they continue to exert an influence on us, leading to irrational acts, unfounded fears, obsessive attachments, and neurotic behaviors. Because these repressed drives are powerful natural energies, they emerge in other forms. These **defense mechanisms** include the projection or displacement of unacceptable drives onto other people or aspects of the Universe and the sublimation of desires into socially acceptable substitute goals. Repressed drives also may be manifested in symbolic forms in dreams, artistic expression, and religion.

Dreams: The Royal Road to the Unconscious. A central feature of Freud's model was derived from his understanding of human dreams as manifestations of the tensions between an individual's unconscious needs and the social processes through which a culture allows those needs to be fulfilled. Freud accepted Tylor's notion that beliefs about the soul and spirits had their origins in the experiences people have while dreaming. He also considered dreams to have a far more important role than was generally believed at the time in managing the psychological conflicts that people experienced. Dreams are a mechanism through which we are able to fulfill our repressed needs, a form of "wish fulfillment" that meets our unconscious needs and satisfies the repressed aspects of the self. The idea that dreams meet the unconscious needs of the individual provided the model that Freud used for understanding how religion meets human needs. Unconscious human needs are reflected in folklore, legends, myths, literature, and other forms of expressive culture, including religion. The dynamics of the collective unconscious are manifested in this expressive material, much as a dream manifests the unconscious conflicts and repressed desires of individual people.

Misattributing Individual Dynamics to Society. Like so many others of his time, Freud was profoundly influenced by evolutionary thinking and the nineteenth-century notion of progress. Freud's ideas about religion were also heavily influenced by experiences with his patients and by his own personal background as an atheist. These factors led Freud to view religious beliefs as false, and to attempt to explain why people cling to irrational beliefs. His psychoanalytic model led Freud to characterize religion in terms of mental illness and to suggest that unconscious dynamics produced both.

The troublesome behaviors of his patients led Freud to conclude that much human behavior is the product of unconscious forces that act outside the control and awareness of the "I." These irrational unconscious forces have effects on our behavior, contributing to impulses that lead to religious ritual. Freud's explanation of religion was based on the similarities he noted between ritual behaviors and the behaviors of his patients, particularly his neurotic patients. Like participants in religious rituals, neurotics repeat their patterns of behavior without apparent reason or practical effect. Freud's analyses of neurosis led him to conclude that these patterns of behavior were the result of repressed human drives, particularly the sexual drive. Just as individual acts of repression result in individual neuroses, Freud argued that collective acts of repression led to the collective patterns of thought and behavior known as religion. Fundamental to Freud's explanation of the origins of religion was the concept that the individual dynamics of neurosis found in patients are mirrored in a society's collective religious beliefs and behaviors. This idea led to his view that religion is a collective mental illness of our species.

In Freud's eyes, the similarities between the collective rituals of religion and the individual rituals of his obsessive neurotic patients were due to the fact that both had their roots in the same basic psychological processes (see Box 8.1: Obsessive–Compulsive Disorder and Ritual). In other words, he saw the *neurotic symptoms* of a mentally ill person as analogous to the *cultural beliefs* (i.e., the religion) of a society. Freud unabashedly proposed that we view cultural behaviors as the symptoms of a neurotic patient—the patient being society! This analogy between individual behaviors and collective rituals gave Freud insights into the psychological and emotional dynamics of religion. It also earned him virtually universal condemnation. Nonscientists did not appreciate the recasting of religious sentiments as pathological holdovers from an earlier time. Anthropologists pointed out that the ways in which Freud applied the dynamics of individual psychology were inappropriate for explaining the collective behaviors of societies, which have different dynamics—and needs—than do individuals.

The Oedipal Complex: The Patricidal Origins of Religion and Society?

A key aspect of the repression of human sexual desires and aggressive tendencies can be seen in what Freud called the Oedipal complex, named after the legendary Greek king Oedipus, a tragic figure who unknowingly killed his own father and later married his mother. Freud viewed this myth, as well as many other aspects of individual and collective human behavior, as an expression of ordinary human desires. He argued that unconscious drives arising in the "it"/id cause young children to sexually desire their opposite-sex parent. A boy's desire for sex with his mother causes him to compete with and experience aggression and hatred toward his father. However, the boy's fear of his father's power leads him to repress his desire for his mother and submit to the father's domination. As the boy's personality develops, he ultimately comes to identify with the father (in the form of the "over-I"/superego). Freud considered these acts of repression a natural outcome of the need to subordinate our incestuous urges in order to prevent damage to the family and society. The vehicle through which our ancestors were able to achieve this was religion.

In his book *Totem and Taboo* (1913), Freud addresses an aspect of supposedly primitive religious behavior: totemic worship and sacrifice. These phenomena, found in cultures around the world, share the characteristics of involving a special animal species (the totem) that people are prohibited to kill (taboo) except in special circumstances when it may be consumed in a communal ritual. Freud used his model of the Oedipal complex and the idea of unconscious motivations for behavior to explain some of the key aspects of totemic ceremonies, which involve the worship of the animal that symbolizes society; the ceremonial sacrifice and consumption of this totem animal, which is normally prohibited; the period of mourning that follows this otherwise prohibited act; and the festive rejoicing and excessively licentious celebrations that follow this period of mourning.

Freud wished to understand why people engaged in this forbidden act—the "killing" of the symbol of society—and why they both mourned over and rejoiced in the transgression. He used both the perspectives of psychoanalysis and prevailing ideas about human prehistory to explain this collective ritual behavior. To understand the origins of totemism, Freud drew upon the common (but erroneous) conception of his time that the original human society was a "primordial horde" in which the father controlled all of the females

Box 8.1 OBSESSIVE–COMPULSIVE DISORDER AND RITUAL

When Freud suggested that the symptoms of some of his neurotic patients resembled ritual behaviors, he was not entirely wrong. We now know that many of the similarities in rituals around the world are due to the mental hardware that humans use to process information and respond to the world. The basic functions of the human brain provide not only the foundations for the similarity in ritual behavior in cultures around the world, but also the basis for a mental disorder known as **obsessive–compulsive disorder.** People suffering from obsessive–compulsive disorder exhibit overly obsessive concerns with appropriate behavior and have recurrent doubts about what they are doing. Because of their anxiety, they feel compelled to repeatedly verify that they have done something (such as continually checking to make sure that the stove is off). They often have to count or touch things a certain number of times, they arrange things in symmetrical patterns, and they may hoard items they feel they cannot do without. They often exhibit extreme anxiety about contamination and cleanliness (pollution and purity) and engage in repeated hand-washing, use of cleansers, and other behaviors to ward off "germs." People suffering from this disorder experience a powerful sense that they must perform rituals similar to imitative magic in order to avoid personal discomfort or danger.

What makes religious rituals both similar to one another and distinct from other kinds of stereotyped and routinized behaviors, such as the patterned routines many of us follow when we are preparing for school or work in the morning, or the repetitive nature of many work behaviors? How do the repetitive activities of work differ from religious rituals? Cross-cultural and interdisciplinary studies (Dulaney and Fiske 1994; Fiske and Haslam 1997; Rapoport and Fiske 1998) provide intriguing answers to these questions. These studies examine the differences between the rituals of work and the sacred rituals associated with collective religious activities, and compare both with characteristic symptoms of patients diagnosed with obsessive–compulsive disorder. They found that in cultures around the world, people recognize similar differences between the routine behaviors of ordinary work rituals and the special behaviors of sacred rituals.

Obsessive–compulsive behavior. In this scene from *Macbeth*, Lady Macbeth is tormented by the visions of blood that only she can see on her hands.

(Continued)

These cross-cultural similarities in the specific characteristics of *sacred* (versus work) rituals suggest that the structures of religious rituals are based on our mental hardware.

This neurological basis is revealed in the findings that the characteristics of obsessive–compulsive disorder are much more similar to sacred rituals than they are to work rituals. Both sacred rituals and obsessive–compulsive disorder address concerns related to our self-integrity; our relationships with our significant others; and our concerns with bodily processes, grooming, sexual impulses, and aggression. The behavior of persons performing sacred rituals (but not work rituals) resembles the behavior of obsessive–compulsive disorder patients in seven significant areas. Both religious participants and neurotic patients

- fear that something terrible is going to happen to them or to their significant others,
- fear that they may cause harm to themselves or others,
- engage in actions that they believe will prevent harm to themselves or to others,
- are overly concerned with or disgusted by bodily wastes or secretions,
- pay special attention to thresholds or entrances,
- attribute special significance to specific colors, and
- engage in numerous repetitive actions.

Sacred rituals also share similarities with the symptoms of obsessive–compulsive disorder related to certain physiological functions, including unusual bodily sensations (such as palpitations, sweating, or a feeling of cold in the extremities); experiences of fear and horror or expressions of loathing toward particular objects or situations; and a sense that someone or something is attempting to harm the individual or his or her significant other. Similarities between sacred rituals and obsessive–compulsive disorder suggest that both are tapping into the same underlying human disposition. This concept has led to the suggestion that the underlying psychophysiological mechanisms that provide the basis for the universal features of sacred rituals are the same as those affecting people suffering from obsessive–compulsive disorder. This foundation in our mental hardware is the source of the commonalities and the reasons that humans are so disposed to participate in rituals and find them to be powerful experiences.

The commonality in ritual and obsessive–compulsive disorder behaviors appears to be due to similar brain functions in the reptilian and paleomammalian brains. The reptilian brain manages the performance of the following behaviors, which have implications for both ritual and obsessive–compulsive disorder (MacLean 1990, pp. 142–43):

- routinized behavior and temporal sequencing of behavior into structured subroutines
- behaviors repeated in the same way or manner
- tropistic behaviors, innate responses manifested in unlearned motion and fixed action patterns
- preservative behaviors, repeated performances of meaningfully interrelated specific acts
- reenactment behavior, involving repeated actions
- deceptive behaviors

The paleomammalian brain is responsible for emotional mentation, modulating the intensity of feelings, and guiding the behavior required for self and species preservation. Specific to its functions are sexual feelings, compulsions, internally derived behaviors, automatisms, stereotypes, species preservation behaviors, and the emotional behaviors of displaying anger or aggression, providing protection, caressing, and searching. The paleomammalian brain's mediation of fear of harm to self or others is key to both obsessive–compulsive disorder and ritual experiences. The rituals of obsessive–compulsive disorder frequently take place during periods of increased stress, suggesting that people often unconsciously switch on an "automatic pilot" to guide them through stressful events.

These universal ritual behaviors are associated with the functions of the basal ganglia and other structures of the reptilian brain that are responsible for managing fixed action patterns and self-protective behaviors. When these structures overreact, the same behavioral microprograms run over and over again, much like the endless loops that sometimes occur in a subroutine of a computer program. The basal ganglia are central to motor control, and their circuitry extends to the thalamus and frontal cortex to coordinate complex motor acts. The basal ganglia also potentiate previously learned rules that are based on environment and context (Rapoport and Fiske 1998, p. 163); in obsessive–compulsive disorder, this function apparently contributes to inappropriate recognitions of context, or an excessive potentiation of rules.

Ritual activities engage the communicative processes of the reptilian and paleomammalian brains, integrating information from these lower systems into the operational activities of the frontal brain and imposing the intentions of ritual into behavioral programming. This entrainment permits the symbolic reprogramming of the emotional dynamics and behavioral repertoires of these lower centers of the brain through the "language" of ritual and its symbolic expressions. Rapoport and Fiske (1998) conclude that humans are driven to create culturally meaningful rituals to address situations that produce stress or ambiguity. Rituals provide processes for affirming meanings and coordinating action with other people. The behavioral sequences of the reptilian brain—routinization, repeated actions, reenactments, and preservative and other innate responses—counter ambiguity by engaging the familiar, constructing meaningful responses through eliciting habitual neural circuits and our basic neurognostic structures and processes. This resonance with our most basic behavioral programs is what makes rituals compelling and what makes people susceptible to their influences.

and excluded his sons from sexual access to any of them. The many brothers—all sons of this dominating and controlling father—eventually joined to oppose their father. They succeeded in killing him, ending his patriarchal control, and together they devoured him. To Freud, it was this act of collective patricide that provided the impetus both for the formation of society— in which men work together for common ends—and for the creation of religion in the act of cannibalism of their feared father, in which they ritually acquired his strength by consuming his body.

In Freud's view, this criminal and cannibalistic act— the original totemic meal—provided the foundation for society, morals, and religion. The murderous brothers were soon overwhelmed by their feelings of guilt and remorse about killing their father, a result of their ambivalent feelings toward him—feelings of both fear and hate, on one hand, and love and admiration, on the other. Their collective remorse and respect led them to develop rituals to address their emotional distress.

Freud argued that the fundamental taboos associated with totemism—including the prohibitions against eating the totem and against sexual activities with a man's mother and sisters—arose from the brothers' guilt over killing their father and their consequent desire to reestablish his moral order. Freud contended that the rituals they developed made the totemic animal into a symbolic representation of the "father." The brothers attempted to undo their murderous act against their father by instilling prohibitions on the killing of the totem. They reverted to their formerly obedient and respectful attitudes toward their father and developed systems of moral rules that essentially codified their father's expectations: the social control that their father had imposed that had forbidden them to have sexual access to the females of their own group.

Freud regarded these two features of totemism—the prohibition of aggression against the totem (father) and the prohibition of sex with the mother—as products of the same fundamental dynamics that underlie the Oedipal complex. Both the worship of the totem animal and the prohibitions against consuming its flesh grew out of the brothers' efforts to assuage their guilt over their patricide, to reconcile themselves with their father. Just as a child learns to resolve its own Oedipal complex, the brothers learned to resolve theirs by renouncing sex with their mother (and sisters).

The totemic ritual practices served a number of psychological and social functions. The brothers came to identify with the father by consuming his body, and they submitted to his authority by submitting to the rules of society. By instituting the practice of exogamy, they established obedience to the father's system of control over the females. The prohibitions on sex with the group's females—which caused the men to look for wives who were not related to them, and hence outside of their group—provided the basis for society. The rules against eating the totemic animal prohibited aggression toward the authority structures of society.

Freud postulated that the actions of the primordial horde in resolving collective guilt and setting up prohibitions to avoid future murderous acts gave rise to the first human social organization and religion. He pointed out that the totemic practices of exogamy, which require that men marry outside their group, serve to control the sexual desires that would otherwise place the men of the group in competition with one another, becoming rivals in an effort to obtain sexual control of women. The brothers agreed to forgo the women of their own group—to implement an incest taboo—so that they could live together in peace. To Freud, these totemic prohibitions were the original "social contract" and provided the foundation for society.

The renunciation of sex with the females of their own group is the collective enactment of the Oedipal complex, the repression of the sexual desire for the mother and the acceptance of social authority. The totemic sacrifice, the symbolic enactment of the original patricidal murder, provides a release of the frustration that derived from the repression of unconscious human drives. The periodic communal enactment of the sacrifice of the totem reflects these deep emotional conflicts and the enactment of the aggressive rage that led to the primordial murder of the father. The totemic rituals both reenact this primordial murder and reaffirm the obedience to the father figure/society. In Freud's view, totemism was the original religion, a product of the same dynamics as the Oedipal complex. Totemism both prohibits and celebrates the homicidal act, thereby giving expression to the ambivalent emotional drives of love and hate and the need to control sexual impulses. But as we will see in the next chapter, anthropologists came to very different understandings of what totemism tells us about the origins of religion and society.

Religion, Sex, and Gender

Sex is among the most important aspects of our biology that are shaped by religious culture. Anthropologists use the term **sex** to refer to our biological identity as male or female and **gender** to refer to the ways in which a particular culture defines what it means to occupy a particular sexual status ("masculine" or "feminine"). **Sexuality** refers to the sexual act of copulation and behaviors surrounding it. Religion is concerned with regulating all three—sex, gender, and sexuality. Genetics also plays an important role in these phenomena (see Box 8.2: The Genetics of Sex).

Sexual development is a complex process, and it does not always produce a clearly differentiated male or female. Individuals may have undeveloped or underdeveloped genitalia and in rare cases may even have a combination of both male and female genitalia. These physical intermediaries may not be able to fulfill either the male or the female gender roles of their society. In addition, other poorly understood factors play a role in the psychosocial development of our sexuality, with the result that many individuals are not comfortable living out the gender roles that a society proscribes for a person of their biological sex. In some societies, such persons may be feared or persecuted

because they are different. But other societies offer their members more than two genders to choose from.

The hijras of India, for example, represent a third gender that is "neither man nor woman" (Nanda 1998). Born as males, these individuals may have underdeveloped sexual organs or may otherwise be disinclined to act as "males" in Hindu society. The strong patrilineal orientation of the Hindu caste system means that these individuals will not be able to fulfill the male role of producing a male heir, with the result that they are often forced out of their families and must move to the anonymity of a large city. There, they may encounter other hijras who are members of a "family" led by an older hijra. These individuals' ambivalent status makes them both feared and respected by other Hindus. When a boy is born, his family may hire a group of hijras to perform a ritual act to ensure that their child will not become a hijra as well. Failure to hire the hijras or to pay them when they arrive unbidden can lead to them cursing the boy to become like them. The hijras also have their own Goddess who, like them, occupies an ambiguous sexual position among the supernatural beings.

Even though differences in the biological development of sex may result in people who are not completely one sex or the other, old cultural and religious notions about human sexual identity change slowly. Thus many societies, including our own, continue to grapple with issues of sexual identity and orientation.

The Religious Regulation of Sexual Behavior

Religious systems often impose constraints on sexuality and regulate fertility by restricting legitimate reproduction to those individuals whose marriage bond has been recognized by a public ritual. However, religions differ substantially in the way in which males and females are deemed suitable to marry one another. Religions generally enforce some variation of an incest taboo that prohibits sexual behavior among family members (e.g., brothers and sisters, or members of the same lineage); they also stipulate a variety of rules regarding who may marry whom. Some religious groups prescribe **endogamy**, the requirement to marry within one's own religious or caste group, while others promote **exogamy**, marriage outside one's own group. Each of these practices has biological as well as cultural implications.

Over many generations, endogamy limits gene flow within a small population of people, increasing the risks of genetic defects as recessive alleles have the chance to combine. Religious rules that promote endogamy can

Box 8.2 THE GENETICS OF SEX

Although we are accustomed to thinking that there are only two biological sexes—male and female—the situation is actually more complex. Both genetic and developmental factors can produce an individual who is neither male nor female or who has characteristics of both. Although the majority of individuals do fall into one of the two categories, it is more accurate to speak of them as relative rather than absolute. In many cultures, people who fall in between these categories or in special third genders are thought to have special spiritual powers.

Human sex is determined by a gene on the twenty-third pair of chromosomes. Females have two X chromosomes, whereas males have one X and one Y chromosome. In our species, the "default" sex is female. That is, if embryonic development is not affected by certain specific events that take place during the first weeks of pregnancy, the embryo will develop into a female. Most aspects of our embryonic development occur independently of sexual development, which is why, for example, both males and females (in humans as well as other mammalian species) have mammary glands and nipples. The key factor in shifting a human embryo onto the trajectory that will make it male is the presence of a functional SRY gene. (SRY stands for "Sex-determining Region Y.") During human development, the SRY gene "switches on" and induces a series of changes that transforms the hitherto undifferentiated gonads (which would otherwise become ovaries) into testes. Once they reach a certain stage of development, the testes in turn begin to produce testosterone and other hormones that circulate through the body and cause a number of other undifferentiated cell groups to become "male." (For example, what would have been the outer labia becomes the scrotum, while the glans of the clitoris becomes the glans of the penis.)

Females typically do not have an SRY gene, so they do not experience a sudden surge of male hormones during embryonic development. Instead, their undifferentiated gonads develop into ovaries. The ovaries produce estrogen and the other hormones that will create the ova and guide the development of the female genitalia.

Simply because an individual has an X and a Y chromosome—or possesses an SRY gene—does not mean that the person will become male. The individual may have a copy of the SRY gene that is nonfunctional due to mutation and that fails to "switch on" the development of the testes, and the (XY) individual will be female. Some XX individuals possess a functioning SRY gene and develop into males in appearance, but are infertile. In addition, other genes are needed for sexual development, such as the genes needed to produce the male sex hormones themselves, and if any of these genes fail to code for functioning proteins, there may be problems during sexual development.

therefore increase the frequency of genetically transmitted diseases, a phenomenon that is apparent in the unusually high frequencies of genetic diseases in certain religious groups. (Ashkenazi Jews, for example, have an increased likelihood of Tay–Sachs disease, a single-gene recessive metabolic disorder that is often fatal.) But endogamy also ensures that a group's resources (such as land or animals) remain within the group. Exogamy increases genetic diversity and decreases the likelihood of these genetic disorders, but it also necessitates elaborate cultural rules regarding marriage exchanges and inheritance and property rights.

Marriage Rituals: Controlling Sexuality and Reducing Aggression. In many cultures, religions attribute significant religious connotations to marriage. The biological drives that induce males and females to mate are shaped by the supernatural sanctions created by ritual. Ritual creates a sacred bond to reinforce the practical restrictions that facilitate the procreative, socialization, and economic functions of marriage.

We can better appreciate the reasons why religions place so much emphasis on defining our marriage partners and their sexual status and roles by reconsidering the functions that ritualized behaviors play in the animal world. As we saw in Chapter 4, one of the fundamental functions of reptilian mating displays is to coordinate the behavior of the male and female so that they can overcome their individual and separate tendencies in order to reproduce. In the animal kingdom, mating displays play important roles in managing reproductive behavior and in determining individual reproductive success. Whether it is the social coupling that enables the mating of lizards, or the unequal access to mates that is typical of hierarchical mammalian societies, these behaviors directly facilitate differential reproductive success within a group and promote the overall well-being of the group.

In most mammalian species, the highest levels of within-group conflict and aggression occur when the females are in **estrus**. During this period, the female is ovulating and can therefore become impregnated, a fact

s to the males of her species by giving off
nt, taking on a different physical appear-
ly behaving in a different way than she
s. In most species, males and females only
exhibit a tendency to mate when the female is in estrus,
and the competition for sexual access to the females
increases the antagonistic encounters among the males.
Dominance and submission displays allow an animal to
signal a dominant or a subordinate position and avoid
direct conflict. When a subordinate signals its position,
it allows a dominant male to control sexual access to
females without having to physically assert its dominance over rivals. These displays enable dominant individuals to mate more frequently while minimizing the
occurrence of fighting and the potential for harm
among other individuals in the group, who often
depend on one another for mutual protection against
outsiders and predators.

In contrast to other mammals, human females give
no clear signs when they are ovulating, and their physical
appearance remains unchanged throughout their entire
menstrual cycle. This important difference between
humans and other mammals means that human mating behavior is not restricted to a particular season,
but can occur year-round. Consequently, human males
and females can mate anytime during the female's
cycle, even when there is no possibility of conception.
This reflects the functions of human mating behavior
for purposes other than procreation, such as to lower
aggression and to bond individuals together. This proclivity of humans to mate throughout the year also
means that human societies have a great need to manage the sexual behavior of their members.

In human groups around the world, ritual practices join males and females into relatively stable and
exclusive sexual relationships. These marriage rituals
change the "unmarried" status of individuals to a
"married" status, using rites of passage to announce
the new status to the community. Marriage is a ritual
adaptation that meets many biological and social
needs of our species. Humans have another reason for
imbuing this pair-bond with a special status. The drive
to copulate is manifested more strongly in humans
than in almost any other animal. In most primate
groups, the highest levels of within-group aggression
occur during the mating season. The human sexual
drive can also be a very disruptive force, and competition for mates can have lethal consequences. Because
humans are the most sexual of all animals (except perhaps bonobos), we have a high need to manage our
sexual tendencies. Marriage rituals address what
would be a source of continuing friction and conflict

in human societies, competition among males for sexual access to females. Human quasi-monogamous
pair-bonding dramatically reduces ongoing and long-
term competition among males for sexual access to
females by assigning each male relatively exclusive
access to a female. Ritualized marriages that help
assure pair-bonding and fidelity are also adaptive
because they help to prevent the spread of sexually
transmitted diseases.

The rituals of marriage, which join males and
females together for sexual and reproductive behaviors, provide a socially validated ritual for controlling
sexual impulses and limiting the potential of these
impulses to produce aggressive behaviors. The rituals
of marriage typically delimit sexual activity by the pair
and prohibit sexual activity with others. Even in societies in which one person is allowed to marry more
than one individual of the opposite sex, religious rituals are used to legitimize these relations, and religious
rules define how property, labor, and other resources
will be shared among the cospouses. Similarly, in traditional societies that sanction marriages among members of the same sex, religious rules typically stipulate
the roles that each partner will assume.

Marriage and the sexual restrictions on partners are
further reinforced by religious rituals that socially recognize the bonds, moralize them, and establish sanctions
for transgressions. The significance of the social bond is
made notable and visible by the marriage ceremony and
the symbols of marriage (i.e., wedding rings). Respect
and privileges accorded to married pairs in society, and
the widespread punishment of adulterers, indicate that
marriage patterns are part of the society's moral code.
The penalties for transgressing the marriage bond are
also significant in many societies—punishments on earth
(whipping, banishment, fines, and even death) and after
death (eternal damnation, rebirth into a lesser status)
(see Box 8.3: Sexual Prohibitions in Religion).

How Religion Shapes Our Development

Our personal development is affected by both our
uniquely individual biological characteristics and the
collective influences of our culture. We humans are
"born to be programmed," to learn the concepts, values, behaviors, and objects that our culture considers
important and that have facilitated the survival and
reproduction of our group in the past. Our basic psychological processes—including perception, cognition,
memories, emotions, and behavior—develop in response

Box 8.3 SEXUAL PROHIBITIONS IN RELIGION

Religious rules may also affect sexual behavior by requiring individuals to adhere to celibacy at particular times (e.g., before certain festivals or ceremonies, or after giving birth) or even permanently restricting sexual activity (recall the discussion in Chapter 7 of the sexual restrictions placed on Tukano men before they went hunting). The priests, monks, and nuns of many major religious traditions are expected to take a vow of celibacy. This official renunciation of sex—and, consequently, of procreation—raises questions about the adaptive nature of these customs. After all, when a person renounces sexual activity, he or she also gives up the possibility of having offspring. From an evolutionary perspective, how can such a religious prohibition on reproduction be a successful adaptation? These behaviors become understandable when they are viewed within the broader context of **altruism,** which suggests that one person's sacrifice may enhance the reproductive capacity of others to whom that person is closely genetically related (for example, one's own brothers and sisters). In theory, a person who chooses a celibate religious life frees up resources that may be committed to the successful rearing of children by others in the person's family or immediate community. He or she may also provide service to the community in the form of teaching or guidance to the younger generation that also improves the youths' chances of long-term success.

In some cultural settings, religious practitioners may be expected to adhere to temporary sexual prohibitions rather than permanent celibacy. For example, shamans are often expected to remain celibate during their training periods as well as before and after their ceremonies. Although these periods may last for only a few days in the case of ceremonies, they may last for weeks or years during training. Why should such lengthy periods of celibacy be imposed on these religious practitioners?

The emic explanations offered by these cultures emphasize notions of purity, as well as the idea that spirits are attracted to the celibate individual. From the etic perspective, there may also be important reasons related to the physiological dynamics of both sexual orgasm and ecstatic altered states of consciousness. Sexual activity involves simultaneous increases in the activity of both the sympathetic and parasympathetic nervous systems (Davidson 1980). When the peak of excitement is reached, the sympathetic system collapses in exhaustion and the parasympathetic system becomes dominant. As we saw in Chapter 3, many altered states of consciousness are induced by this pattern of nervous system activity. Because altered states of consciousness are regarded as mechanisms for achieving contact with the spirit world, a person's ability to enter them for religious purposes would need to be protected. Sexual activity could lead to physiological responses that might induce a powerful collapse into a parasympathetic dominant state of consciousness. This line of thought suggests that prohibitions on sexual behavior may help to ensure that a religious practitioner is able to attain the powerful state of consciousness for which he or she is preparing (Winkelman 1992).

to the cultural programs to which we are exposed. This interplay of culture and biology gives rise to our personality. Religious concepts are often central to the development of personality.

Our personalities are thus the products of our hard-wired dispositions, drives, and mental abilities, as well as the models of our culture that teach us about what it means to be a person. Across cultures and throughout time, religions have been important sources of these cultural models that shape our personalities by teaching us what it means to be a good person. The diverse manners in which we adapt to both our physical and social environments create a variety of ways in which religions can affect development. Religious beliefs and values affect how people learn about and understand

- the history of their group,
- the nature of the environment,
- which tasks are appropriate for which people,
- how children should be raised,
- how society should be organized,
- how decisions should be made,
- what it means to be a member of that group, and
- how their existence fits into the "bigger picture" of the Universe.

Religions help humans adapt in other ways as well. Religious ideas about diet and medical treatments often play a role in maintaining and restoring health. By defining how we should and how we may not alter our bodies (through circumcision and other genital operations, tattooing and scarification, and particular types of hair style and dress), religions often provide visible symbols of our group membership and our position in society. By stipulating who may marry, religions generally help to channel reproduction in ways that link different groups together and help to avoid incest.

Thus, the process of religious socialization is important for several reasons. It addresses our personal need both to understand ourselves and to establish and maintain relationships with the other members of our group and with the Universe as our culture understands it. It also provides a set of generalized cultural expectations for behaving, enabling us to anticipate how others will respond to our actions. By utilizing rituals that engage our emotions and associating them with culturally recognized symbols, religions also help to mold our "plastic" nature into a particular configuration of habits, preferences, attitudes, and motivations. Religious socialization exploits our innate potential to learn any culture and teaches us the meanings that one particular culture—our own—assigns to experiences. Religions fulfill our need for conformity—to be an accepted and recognized member of a group—and exploit our psychological suggestibility, enabling us to accept the cultural teachings of our elders without much questioning. In this way, a culture's religious models about the Universe become incorporated into its members' personal beliefs, values, and behaviors. Through their assumptions about human nature and the ways in which we should relate to the spirit world, religions also program us to experience ourselves and the world in particular ways, giving us an "indigenous psychology" of human motivations and capacities.

The Human Life Cycle in Biological Perspective

The uniqueness of each individual human **genome** ensures that all of us vary in numerous ways, in traits such as blood type, hair color, and susceptibility to certain diseases. Our genetic makeup also plays an important role in less discernible traits, such as our basic personalities and our abilities to learn different types of things. In every society, there are people who are confident in their abilities and assured about the future, as well as others who are less confident and less certain. We also find individuals who more easily learn how to hunt or dance than their fellow humans and others who seem to be particularly susceptible to interactions with the spirit world. Obviously, a person's own biographical experiences (such as a strict upbringing or being raised by a shaman) have important effects on the ways that the person thinks, acts, and feels as an adult. And yet we all know of siblings who were raised in the same family, by the same parents, and under the

same rules, and who nevertheless turned out very differently from one another. Clearly, the interplay between genetics and culture—between our human nature and the way it is nurtured—is complex and at present only partially understood. Religion helps to coordinate these differences into common patterns of behavior.

The process by which any individual *Homo sapiens* is shaped into a recognized and accepted member of a particular culture is known as **socialization.** Socialization involves enculturation, a variety of processes through which an individual who has the potential to learn *any* culture is transformed into a member of a *specific* culture by absorbing the material, behavioral, and ideational aspects of that culture.

Biological anthropologists and psychologists who study human development have identified a number of distinct stages in the human life cycle. The moments at which some of these occur, such as birth and death, are rather easy to discern. Others, such as the moment of conception or the onset of senility, are more difficult to detect. Sexual differences also affect our development. **Puberty,** the stage in which our bodies undergo rapid growth and development as our genetic program prepares us for procreation, is marked by changes that are rather easily observed in females but are less obvious in males.

Because the changes we undergo as we age take place within our social group, we learn both the meaning of and the expectations for each stage of our life from people who have already undergone those changes. One of the reasons that religions are able to exert such an enormous effect on our lives is that religious ideas and values often stipulate the behaviors and explain the experiences of people who are moving from one stage of their life to another. Religion also tells the other members of society how to relate to and interact with these "new" individuals. In this way, religions play an important part in imposing collective and socially recognized patterns onto individual development.

The socialization of events such as birth, marriage, and death is important for societies because these events provoke profound emotional reactions. Because religious rituals often mark such events in order to manage the associated emotions and transitions, they are able to exert an enormous effect on our lives. Religious beliefs about the proper ways to think and act during the various stages of our life cycle help people to move from one life stage to another, and they tell the other members of society how to adjust to an individual who leaves one status and takes up a new one. In this way, religions play an important part in imposing socially recognized, collective patterns onto individual development. These processes of socialization associate cultural symbols with these biological processes of development, incorporating religious associations into the natural biological phases and the emotional experiences and expectations.

The Cultural Entrainment of Biology

An individual's cultural upbringing actually shapes the physical development of his or her nervous system. As we learn the behaviors that are appropriate to our culture and the meanings and values associated with these behaviors, the behaviors literally become "wired" into us. Because our nervous system originally developed in response to their influences, religious symbols are able to provoke specific physiological responses.

The process by which cultural—including religious—symbols come to both elicit and suppress specific biological activities of our brains is known as **entrainment** (Laughlin, McManus, and d'Aquili 1992). Entrainment occurs whenever we are exposed to a particular symbol at the same time that we are experiencing a specific physical and emotional state. Eventually, we can re-experience this state when we encounter the symbol. This process of association is fundamental to the ways in which all animals—including humans—learn.

The classic experiments of Ivan Pavlov (1849–1936) can help us to understand the basic process through which we learn to associate external stimuli with internal states. While studying the mechanisms of digestion, Pavlov noted that the dogs he was using in his experiments would salivate whenever they saw a person wearing a lab coat. Investigating this more closely, he found that the presence of food caused the dog to salivate, a normal physiological reaction (unconditioned response) that prepared it to digest its meal. Pavlov discovered he could train his dogs to salivate in response to any type of stimulus, such as a bell, as long as it was initially associated with the presence of food. After Pavlov's dogs had been simultaneously exposed to food and the sound of a ringing bell enough times, the dogs began to salivate whenever they heard a bell, even when no food was forthcoming—a behavior termed a *conditioned response*. This process by which an animal learns to associate a stimulus (bell) with a response (salivating) is known as **conditioning,** and it occurs in humans as well as other animals. It plays an important role in socialization, although the symbolic associations that humans make are obviously much richer and more complex than those of other animals, enabling us to refer to future possibilities as well as past events.

This same process of conditioning affects the development of a young person growing up in a religious environment. In many religious families, for example, small children are taught to bow their heads, hold their hands in a certain position, and speak to one or more spirit beings before going to sleep. The process often begins long before the children are able to comprehend the meanings of the words they are saying (or to even pronounce them correctly). Nonetheless, the children come to associate the practice of praying before bedtime with other important responses (such as the reward of seeing their parents' approval of their praying). Children may also associate prayer with the relaxation response, since they typically fall peacefully asleep afterwards. The network of associations that develops within the children's brains reinforces the praying behavior in such a way that praying may occur in other contexts as well, such as during any type of anxious moment in order to experience the associated comfort and relaxation.

Over time, the constant repetition of these activities links the activity of praying to the concepts of God, salvation, and security that the children are learning from their elders. Ultimately, it may become unthinkable for the children (and, later, the adults) to go to sleep before they complete this task. To fail to pray before bed would evoke anxiety.

The full power of this process of religious socialization becomes clear when it is considered in the light of our ability to create and manipulate symbols. For example, as a Christian child grows up, he or she may learn to pray before a cross located in the bedroom. At first, the cross will mean little to the child, but as the child is socialized into the religion, it will become associated with notions about Jesus, heaven, and beliefs that no real harm can ever come to the child because of his or her faith. As the child becomes an adult, merely glancing at or even thinking of a cross can evoke many associations that the child learned while growing up; these associations can then evoke the relaxed self-assured response derived from praying.

The process by which an entire constellation of associated physiological and emotional responses comes to be evoked by a particular religious symbol is known as **symbolic penetration.** Symbolic penetration makes it possible for religious meanings to evoke a wide range of biological processes, affecting our emotions, our thought processes, and even our posture and physical movements. These learned associations give religious symbols their great power to evoke such responses as love, awe, fear, and contentment. They also make it possible for individuals to surrender personal control and put themselves into the hands of the "spirits" and their deeply embedded directives derived from their religious socialization.

The process through which we learn to acquire and manipulate symbols is fundamental to the ways our brains learn to organize our experiences, develop models of the Universe, and respond to events. Symbols link together a person's responses as he or she learns to adapt to the social and physical environments through adaptations mediated by culture and language. The associations that we learn to make between the symbols we encounter and our experiences "tune" our bodies into the patterns of responding to the Universe that our society considers appropriate. What makes the religious beliefs and behaviors so compelling is that they are deliberately associated with powerful emotional experiences and often deliberately designed to trigger them.

How Religious Rituals "Work." To an outsider, it may appear that a religious ritual simply cannot achieve what it claims. How could a Celtic winter solstice ritual —ostensibly carried out to ensure that the sun will begin its journey back north, bringing with it light, warmth, and the rekindling of the plant and animal world—possibly produce the effects it intends? This is one reason why religious rituals are often denigrated as "superstitions." Anthropologists have addressed this dilemma by distinguishing between the **latent function** (the hidden psychological effects) of the ritual and its **manifest function** (the claims that it induces the sun to change its course). By viewing rituals in this way, we can see that the main purpose of rituals is not to affect the physical world, but to promote social coordination by communicating important cultural knowledge to the participants in the ritual.

The biocultural approach to rituals focuses on the effects that rituals have on the thoughts, emotions, and behaviors of the persons who take part in them. Thus, while a solstice ritual might not be able to change the movement of the sun, it can produce significant personal, emotional, and interpersonal effects in the people who participate in it. Solstice rituals remind their participants to pay attention to the cycles of nature and remind them that their own lives follow the same sequence of birth, growth, and decay as all other life. In this light, the changes a person experiences with age appear as part of the "normal" scheme of things that one cannot and should not resist. Solstice rituals may also have more concrete and empirically verifiable effects, such as when they provide the basis for planning agricultural activities.

Rituals use symbolic statements about a culture's basic values, especially its conception of a person's relationships to the other members of society, to nature, and to the supernatural. These statements communicate to the participants in the ritual their society's expectations for social behavior and the proper way for them to view themselves. This connection is one of the reasons for the great power of religious socialization and the power of rituals in teaching or learning a religion. Ritual activities associate the symbols, behaviors, and objects they involve, and the concepts and values they express, with various emotions. In this way, the emotions associated with the realm of the sacred and the expectations for behavior with which they are linked can be maintained even in the profane world of everyday life.

The Roles of Myth in Socialization. Humans are master storytellers. The universality of origin myths and other explanations for the Universe (see Chapter 7) suggest that the capability to produce such stories has been selected for in humans. In every culture, folktales, legends, and other oral traditions have been passed down from one generation to the next; in some cultures, the stories ultimately were written down and codified as sacred texts. These stories serve to integrate people into a community with shared concepts and values, and thus a common perspective on life, whether or not an outsider might consider such stories "right" or "wrong."

One of the most powerful ways in which people learn the religious stories of their culture is through religious rituals. As we saw in Chapter 4, a ritual essentially consists of a stereotyped sequence of events that leads to a particular outcome. In contrast to the ritualized behaviors of other animals, however, which focus on territory, aggression, and mating, human rituals often include enactments of important social and life-cycle events, such as birth, naming, marriage, and death ceremonies.

Rituals communicate a variety of messages through their actions or behaviors. Because they take place in social settings in which symbols are also featured, rituals may "say things" about the social and cosmological order that the participants may understand but outsiders may not. Because rituals may also attribute objects with extraordinary value, these objects can become cultural and religious symbols of great emotional importance. Consequently, these objects can acquire a power that persists beyond the context of the ritual itself.

Rituals integrate the messages from a culture's mythology and cosmology into social life and patterns of individual behavior. Religious rituals often produce powerful emotional experiences and link them with explanations of the meaning of those experiences. The involvement of emotion produces a powerful sense that both the behaviors and the meanings of the behaviors are "correct." A person's belief in a sacred reality that permeates the world of profane existence arises because the processes of religious socialization link the emotions we experience during rituals and ceremonies with the symbols of our religion. These powerful experiences—often referred to as trance, possession, ecstasy, dissociation, inspiration, or mystical experiences—reflect the power of ritual to induce profound physiological transformations of consciousness (see Chapter 3). Interpreted as contact with the spirit world, these experiences can dramatically reinforce a person's conviction in his or her religious beliefs.

Religion in Emotional Socialization

Malinowski focused on religion's role in meeting individual needs, but individual needs have implications for social needs as well. These dual functions of religious socialization—addressing both individual and collective consciousness—were also emphasized by Malinowski, who pointed to the importance of religion in linking individual emotions and impulses to social control and integration. The fear of death and the natural inclination to flee from a corpse could lead to a disintegration of the cultural group and community. The obligations of religious ritual overcome this impulse to flee, reinforcing social cohesion, solidarity, and the continuity of society. This also reflects a social function of religion, making individual emotions congruent with social expectations represented in religious and mythological systems.

In the course of eliciting and shaping humans' emotional potentials, religion manages many aspects of emotional life for individual and collective benefit. This includes

- creating a conceptual system for expressing emotional experiences and interpreting emotions,
- eliciting and producing emotional experiences,
- managing individual and collective responses to emotions, and
- imposing values on the expressions of certain emotions.

Religion often addresses the most important of our emotions, engaging feelings of wonder, awe, fear, terror, love and tenderness, and indignant anger and aggression. Many religions attribute the causes of our emotions to spirit protectors, possessing demons, or the properties of certain bodily organs.

Religious systems focus on emotions because humans have emotional needs for security and protection and a desire for comfort, love, and secure attachments. Humans also experience anger, greed, and lust, which can be socially destructive, as well as fears and anxieties that can undermine the ability to focus on achieving the important tasks of life. Religions address most emotional drives, often characterizing them in terms of a moral system and offering assurances that can calm emotions. This moral system often defines the appropriate manifestation of specific emotions and drives (for example, sex, obedience, and love). Religions also provide mechanisms to meet emotional needs, including a community that can protect the individual from fear and anxiety and that can bring about feelings of belonging and comfort. Religions are particularly effective ways of organizing people to direct their emotional motivations and behaviors toward a goal. Religions create powerful emotional linkages to stimuli, producing a kind of automatic response free of hesitation, an emotionally committed approach to the group.

Emotional Coherence. Religions can bring the individual's experience of emotions into agreement with the expectations of the culture. This produces an emotional coherence, an alignment of individual motivations with collective cultural goals (Thagard 2005). Emotional coherence results from emotional contagion, our tendency to automatically synchronize with others' facial expressions, mimic their postures, and adopt their patterns of vocalization. Emotional convergence with others in our immediate presence tends to replicate their emotions in our own experiences.

Rituals produce emotional coherence by manipulating attitudes and creating symbolic control of autonomic processes and emotional responses. Higher cognitive processes generally have limited control over emotional reactions (LeDoux 1995). In contrast, ritual processes—which are grounded in the paleomammalian and reptilian brains—have the power to control emotions. Because of this power, rituals can then socialize and resocialize the associations among emotional, cognitive, and behavioral processes.

The roles of emotion in religion reflect some of the general roles that emotions play in human cognition, including the use of affective associations to help decide among relevant actions and make inferences. Emotions play a central role in the creation of learned associations based on our own emotional experiences and the experiences of others. Religion's moral or evaluation systems play a central role in defining the world in "black and white terms," an absolute system that leaves no choices, only learned reactions. Religion engages this level of emotional cognition, encouraging reasoning processes that favor the goals of the group. This helps to explain the power of religious cognition—faith—and the ability of religions to produce a commitment to certain forms of behavior, such as self-sacrifice.

An examination of the relationships between emotions and rituals in many different cultures and contexts makes it apparent that religions can elicit the entire range of human emotions. From the grief of funerals to the joy of marriage, from the fear of taboos to the disgust of pollution, religions manipulate our basic emotions and tie them to our collective needs for attachment, emotional security, and understanding. But religious emotions are more than just intense ordinary emotions. Religions enhance their power by taking our basic emotional experiences, desires, and drives, and associating them with the collective symbols to which we are naturally attracted by virtue of our need to be social beings. Ritual and myth give specific religious meanings to the emotions elicited by religion.

Religious experiences often involve taking ordinary emotional and neurological systems to the extreme levels of their functioning. The extreme activation of emotional systems may be a principle that religious systems utilize because extreme emotions indicate that there is something particularly important about a situation, thereby increasing the likelihood that a person will remember it. The emotions of others are also an important part of our learning how to respond to the environment and to other people, enabling religious emotional coherence to shape our perceptions. The presence of behaviors reflecting emotional coherence in other animals, but the far greater complexity of these behaviors in human societies, suggests that religion exapted emotional contagion as a mechanism for enhanced learning to benefit from advantages derived from relying on the learned experiences of significant others. Religion has exploited this dynamic of learning through the associations produced by emotional contagion. Religion is particularly effective for aligning the individual with common group intentions. The expectations and directives of the Gods become tools for creating common behaviors, submission, and cooperation that enable people to achieve goals that would be unobtainable with individual action alone. In producing coherence between individuals and the collective needs of society, religion fulfills human species and individual needs for personal and social order.

Rites of Passage

Every society distinguishes its members in at least two ways: their status as children or adults, and their identity as males or females. In every culture, each of these social categories has its own status and role, and the smooth functioning of society depends on every member playing his or her appropriate part. Some rituals serve to clearly mark an individual as either a male or a female. Some rituals help us to move between the various stages of our biological life cycle (such as birth, adolescence, marriage, and death) and learn the social status associated with each ("child," "teenager," and "adult"). These rituals help individuals adjust to their new status and the changes in social relations that each status shift entails.

The aspects of the life cycle that are the most deeply rooted in our biological development (birth, puberty, marriage, and death) are particularly likely to be ritualized by religions, giving them culturally specific meanings and associations. Other socially defined stages of development may also be ritualized, such as the entry into a religious community or special group. All of these rituals serve to reduce the ambiguity that people may experience as a result of their uncertainty about their status in society and the roles expected of them. The clarification not only helps to mitigate the psychological stress that often comes with uncertainty, but also promotes the general health and well-being both of the individuals who are changing their status and of the other members of society, who understand that these individuals should now be treated in a different way.

Anthropologists Arnold Van Gennep (1873–1957) and Victor Turner (1920–1983) contributed great insights into the ways in which certain types of rituals are used to help people move from one status to another. Van Gennep (1960) characterized those rituals that specifically aim at assisting a person in moving from one stage of life to the next as **rites of passage**. He noted that such rituals guide their participants through a transition involving three phases. These three phases—known as separation, liminality, and incorporation—enable the individual to let go of one status in life and take up a new one. Many rites of passage also physically mark the persons who have undergone such a ritual in a way that other members of society are able to recognize, making it easier for the other members of society to interact with them in ways appropriate to their new status (see Fig. 8.1).

A rite of passage begins with the stage of **separation**, during which the initiates are removed from their existing status and the expectations associated with it.

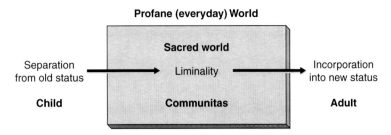

Figure 8.1 The basic structure of a rite of passage.

This stage often involves some type of physical seclusion from the other members of their society. After separation, the individual moves into a state of **liminality** (a word derived from the Latin term *limen,* meaning "threshold," or the space between two adjoining rooms). In this liminal state, the initiates no longer occupy their old status, but have not yet acquired a new status. As Turner noted, the initiates are now "betwixt and between" their old lives and their new lives. Old patterns of thinking and behaving are lifted from individuals who have reached this ambiguous state, producing feelings of autonomy or freedom from the expectations that have governed their lives up until that time. No longer bound to their old lives, and not yet occupying their future status, they are able to focus on learning the patterns of thought and behavior that are involved with their new position in society.

When individuals experience the liminal state along with other initiates, they also tend to bond with one another. Their shared freedom from prior social conventions enables them to see the world from a new perspective and to feel a sense of exhilaration as a consequence of their liberation from their previous roles, often causing them to interact with one another in spontaneous and uninhibited ways. Turner described this condition as **communitas** and noted that the special bonding that can occur among people undergoing a ritual transition together often creates lifelong relationships.

The rite of passage concludes with the **incorporation** of the initiates into their new status, one that all the members of the community will now recognize. The temporary freedom that came with the liminal phase is now replaced by a new set of social expectations and responsibilities. The new status is often signaled by having the initiates cross a symbolic threshold, by dressing or adorning themselves in a different manner, or by changing their names. In traditional societies, people typically go through a number of rites of passage as they move from one status to another throughout their lifetimes.

Welcoming a New Person into Society

Some religious rituals serve to welcome or incorporate a child into the community. At some time following birth, a newborn will be presented to the other members of the group and given a social identity, typically in the form of a name. The place of the child within the lineage of his or her ancestors may be recited, thereby describing the relationship that the child will have with various entities in the spirit world. Although these rituals may appear to focus on the child, they generally have little impact on the infant, who may be only days or weeks old and who consequently lacks the mental abilities to appreciate the implications of the ritual. Many Christian denominations baptize infants—a ritual that incorporates them into the community of believers—when they are only a few weeks or months of age.

Although it is the child who is actually changing status during the ritual, many aspects of these rituals are directed toward the people who are being affected by the child's entry into the community, particularly the parents. The parents and other people (such as godparents) also acquire a new status, and the ritual expresses this to the community.

Rituals of Social Identity. Many rituals of religious socialization address the basic human need to be a part of a group. These rituals provide a context in which the boundaries among individuals are broken down, allowing individuals to experience a sense of merging with a group. The integrative effects of such rituals promote social cohesion by resolving conflicts, helping to maintain group continuity in the face of loss, and modifying individual behavior to create group harmony. As we have already seen, many societies organize their members into totem groups that typically utilize animals as symbols of social membership.

The Maasai rite of passage known as *eunoto* changes the status of a group of adolescent "warriors" into "elders." As part of this ritual, a boy will shed his flamboyant warrior image and take on the appearance of an elder.

This image shows an adolescent soon to undergo *eunoto*. His long hair and necklaces are signs that mark his status as a warrior.

During *eunoto*, Maasai woman shave their sons' heads, an outward sign of the impending change in their status.

A group of newly shaven adolescents listens as the elders instruct them about their new responsibilities as adults.

Box 8.4 STATUSES AND ROLES

Anthropologists refer to a culturally defined position within a social network as a **status.** All societies recognize a number of statuses, and no person can ever occupy all of them. These positions are generally so important that they have cultural "names." You occupy a number of different statuses, such as "son" or "daughter," perhaps "employee," and, of course, "student." Each status is associated with a **role,** a set of culturally recognized attitudes and behaviors that is considered appropriate to that status. As a son or daughter, you may have learned that it is important to complete your chores before you go out with your friends. As an employee, you probably know that it is important to arrive at work on time and dressed in the attire appropriate to your job. As a student, you know that you should complete all of the readings and other work that you are assigned, prepare yourself for examinations, and attend class regularly.

Because statuses exist within a network of social relations, every cultural status is defined in part by the ways it relates to other statuses. Being a son or a daughter implies that there is a "parent," being an employee implies that there is an "employer," and being a student implies that there is a "teacher." Each status also has its associated roles. In American culture, parents are expected to provide for their offspring and to treat all of them equally. Employers are expected to give their employees breaks for meals after they have worked a certain number of hours. And teachers are expected to cover the material appropriate to their subject, grade and return their students' assignments in a timely manner, and not show favoritism to any particular student.

Every religious system also defines a number of statuses—such as "priest," "imam," "bishop," or "shaman"—and stipulates a set of expectations—the roles—that define how the people of each status should behave. As with our other statuses, religious statuses are also defined within a system of social relations consisting of many other statuses, such as "adherent," "acolyte," "initiate," or "pope."

Throughout the world, religions are an important means for defining and teaching normative expectations for behavior. Of course, people do not always fulfill the roles that their culture teaches them are appropriate for their statuses. Children, parents, students, teachers, initiates, and priests are all human, and they may prefer one individual over another, cut corners in their work, or overstep the boundaries of the behaviors that come along with their status. The "thou shalt nots" of a religion mark the limitations of culturally appropriate behavior, whereas other aspects of the belief system may even stipulate the punishments for violating these limitations (such as eternal damnation or rebirth in a lower caste).

We do not occupy a single status throughout our entire lifetime, or even a constant set of statuses. Each of us changes status at some time in our lives, and the sometimes contradictory expectations (roles) that come with our multiple positions (statuses) in society may lead to internal psychological conflicts that may require some type of healing. Moreover, not everyone attains a status in the same way. Some statuses, such as being born male or female, or into a particular kinship group (such as a patrilineal clan) are *ascribed* to an individual. Other statuses are *achieved* or acquired by virtue of attaining a certain age or learning and demonstrating certain skills. The processes by which people achieve and change statuses during their lifetimes are important both for personal development and for maintaining harmony and continuity in the group. Because our social statuses play such a significant part in telling us who we are and how to think and behave, it is no surprise that religions often play a central role in defining these statuses and in aiding us to shift from one status to another.

Religions make use of these innate symbolic systems (animal species distinctions and meanings) to define groups, emphasize their unique qualities, and socialize individuals into identifying with these groups. These nonhuman beings provide additional symbols for forming the character of the self by encouraging people to develop relationships with "sacred others." Identifying with spirit beings provides alternate role models for solving problems and dealing with personal and social conflicts (see Box 8.4: Statuses and Roles).

Rituals of Adult Transition: Becoming a Man or Woman

During personal development, it is necessary for all humans to move from one group or status to another. When we do so, we must learn the new attitudes and behaviors associated with the new status. These changes are often associated with uncertainty and trepidation, because it is not always easy to leave a status to which one has become accustomed and to take up a status that brings with it more responsibilities, less freedom, and the requirement of learning a new way of living. In most societies, the transformation from childhood to adulthood is marked by special rituals because it is vitally important for children to successfully become adults.

Adolescence as an "Experience Expectant" Period for Religious Transmission. Cultures around the world consider adolescence to be the most significant point in an individual's life for learning religious beliefs and behaviors. Anthropologist Candace Alcorta (2006) has suggested that it is natural for adolescents to learn about their religion at this time because it is an "experience expectant" period for learning. Alcorta points out that there are basic structural features found in all religions, such as community rituals that use music to elicit emotionally significant experiences of the sacred. The adolescent socialization features that have been noted in cultures around the world serve to redefine an initiate's social status and identity so that he or she will be able to take up positions of responsibility in society. Adolescence is a period of more intense emotional reactions and responses that must be organized and controlled within cultural patterns. Rites of passage fulfill this purpose by teaching both sacred and secular knowledge while the adolescent is being psychologically transformed into an adult. The great pain that is often inflicted during the intense and prolonged initiatory rites helps to produce a variety of changes in the individual that increase his or her commitment to the group, thereby promoting its long-term cohesion.

Adolescence is a period during which the individual is subjected to powerful shaping influences from the culture, social relations, and physical ecology. During adolescence, the prefrontal cortex and the frontal and temporal cortices of the brain undergo a period of continuous development. These regions play central roles in managing social behaviors. The role of the prefrontal cortex and its executive functions exemplifies this integration of a variety of emotional and social cues in the direction of appropriate behavior. The prefrontal cortex also plays an important role in impulse control, as well as in planning and social judgment that is based on the integration of social information with immediate context. Limbic structures also display significant growth during adolescence, particularly those areas involved in processing emotions and perceptions and in developing interconnections in areas related to elicitation of the "fight or flight" response and the brain's reward systems. Some of the crucial interconnections that are developed during adolescence engage the control of emotional inputs

and apply them in the management of personal and social life. Adolescent brain development involves the growth of nerve connections that play a central role in the integration of emotional capacities with socially mediated cognitive processes. This role of religious ritual in socialization for adulthood suggests that, in the environment of evolutionary adaptation, religious ritual was an adaptation to produce social solidarity and coherence. The association of religion with this expectant period of development provides essential models and identifications for collective identification in personality formation. The cultural assumptions regarding the nature of spirits enhances the transmission of cultural patterns by providing models for development in the roles of spirits.

This ritual recognition is an important part of the social changes that reinforce the new adult role. The religious transformation of a child into an adult often makes the person eligible for marriage and other adult rights. These ritual activities provide moral guidelines for behavior and explicitly teach the expectations of moral members of the adult community. In the Chumash ritual that opened this chapter, adult males utilized the receptive state that was produced by a boy's ingestion of a potent psychoactive drink to teach the boy about the proper ways to think and behave as an adult member of his community. Throughout the world, religious rites of passage are one of the most powerful and commonly used rituals for teaching adolescents the knowledge they will need to be successful adults in their society.

Gender-Specific Adolescent Socialization. The specific functions of ritual in integrating people into their appropriate roles in society require separate activities for males and females. While most of the important collective rituals of society involve the entire group, in general males and females undergo their initiation into adulthood separately and are prohibited from entering the areas where the opposite sex undergoes initiation. This practice underscores one of the fundamental functions of initiation rituals, which is to emphasize that the initiates are members of only one group and to distinguish their new status (and its associated roles) from the status and roles of the opposite sex.

There are, however, significant cross-cultural differences in the importance and focus of initiation ceremonies. Small-scale foraging societies place great emphasis on the initiation of girls. In contrast, societies with a middle range of social complexity emphasize male initiation ceremonies. Cross-cultural research has found that while both males and females undergo initiations, it appears more common for females to do so

(Schlegel and Berry 1980, 1991). Furthermore, females are generally initiated at or near the time of their first menses, whereas males are typically initiated in groups that may include pre- and post-pubertal boys. This indicates that female initiation is focused on managing issues related to human biology, and male initiation rituals are more concerned with social issues.

In foraging societies, female initiations focus on concerns about female "pollution," which is generally associated with menstruation. Menstrual blood is often believed to have a negative impact on the food supply and is sometimes thought to harm a male's ability to hunt effectively. Female initiation rituals teach the young girls about specific rules and restrictions (taboos) to which they must adhere, particularly during their menstrual periods. For example, in some societies a menstruating female is prohibited from preparing food for her husband or other males. During menstruation, and often in general, she may be prohibited from touching the tools used by the men, particularly those related to hunting. These taboos are not arbitrary, but are apparently related to empirical observations that the scent of a woman is more likely to attract predators and drive away the animals that men hunt (Dobkin de Rios and Hayden 1985).

Male initiation rituals are most likely to be found in societies in the middle range of social complexity. The extreme initiation rituals observed in many simple agricultural (horticultural) societies serve the purpose of cutting the ties between young boys and their mothers and incorporating the boys into the world of men. These ceremonies, which may last for weeks to months, generally involve a cohort or group of young men ranging in age from as young as six years to as old as about sixteen years. During the ritual process, the boys are often subjected to some form of genital operation (circumcision and/or subincision, where the penis is slit open through the urinary tract). This sexual surgery creates an obvious symbol of manhood, introduces the boy to adult society, and promotes solidarity with the other boys that are also undergoing the rite of passage.

The societies in which these practices are most common are typically found in tropical rainforests, where the ecological adaptations of horticultural subsistence limit the amount of protein in the diet. As a consequence, **kwashiorkor,** a disease caused by protein deficiencies, is often endemic in these cultures. The scarcity of protein has led to a pattern of infant care in which a child may be nursed for as long as five years. A woman can maintain such an extended period of lactation only if she does not become pregnant, so mothers are prohibited from having sex for several years after giving birth.

To compensate, males in these societies often practice **polygyny.** But although it is expected that each man will build and maintain a separate house and compound for each of his wives, he does not live with any of them. Instead, he spends his nights in a "men's house" that he shares with the other men of the village, all of whom were bonded together in their initiation.

The practice of long-term breastfeeding, combined with polygyny and the general absence of males, means that infants and children are generally raised apart from their fathers. Consequently, young boys grow up in a "women's world" that is isolated from the world of the adult men. Initiation is a process by which young boys are forcibly incorporated into the men's world and subordinated to the existing hierarchy of male cohorts in their society. The painful initiations not only serve to impress upon the young boys the power of the other men in their society, but also produce a dramatic alteration of consciousness that helps sever their connections to and identifications with the world of their mothers. During the process of initiation, they undergo fundamental personal and social changes. Once a boy undergoes initiation, he will never live with his mother again. Instead, he will become a member of an all-male group that lives in its own men's house, and he will be incorporated into a hierarchy of males that is headed by the elder males of the village.

These male initiation ceremonies provide a process for incorporating members into a coordinated group, one in which the hierarchy of power is clearly understood. The process of initiating young boys together as a group also bonds the members of this group into a cohort that will depend on one another for assistance throughout their lives. The young men's incorporation into the hierarchy not only organizes them as a group unto themselves, but also situates them within a hierarchy of power, incorporating them into a society with multiple levels that is dominated by the ancestor spirits. These initiation rituals reflect one of the fundamental functions of ritual in the animal world: the establishment and maintenance of dominance hierarchies (see Box 8.5: The Vision Quest as a Ritual of Adult Development).

Religion as an Evolutionary By-Product? Attachment Theory and Religion

The paradigm of evolutionary psychology considers many contemporary human behaviors and dispositions to be the consequences of adaptations that evolved

Box 8.5 THE VISION QUEST AS A RITUAL OF ADULT DEVELOPMENT

In many small-scale nomadic foraging societies, a vision quest is an important rite of passage for males and sometimes females. The initiates begin early in life to prepare for a direct encounter with a supernatural being that will provide them with the special powers they need to be successful adults. Before puberty, the youths may fast, engage in long prayers, undertake arduous activities, and retire in lonely vigils to prepare for a spirit encounter. These austerities are regarded as essential to attracting a spirit being that will become one's benefactor. When deemed ready by their elders, the youths generally go alone into the wilderness for a protracted period—which might last from a few days to several months—and fast and pray for a visit from a spirit being that will give them the personal power central to their adult skills and competencies. After days of prayer and many sleepless nights, the fortunate petitioner has a vision of a spirit being. The spirit (or spirits) encountered during the vision quest will serve as a role model for the initiate's adult identity and will help him make decisions about adult life.

During the vision quest, individuals may encounter animal spirits who bestow their qualities—such as strength, speed, visual acuity, or hunting prowess—upon the initiate. Acquiring these powers affects the seeker's personality, leading to changes in the person's personal powers and social identity. It may even provide him with the basis to develop into a shaman, who usually attempts to acquire the special qualities or identities of several animal spirits. From the perspective of contemporary psychology, these animal "familiars" may be seen as unconscious aspects of the self (e.g., unconscious motivations and drives). Expressed as animal spirits, these diverse aspects of the self help people to understand and effectively deal with different unconscious aspects of self and identity.

---

in the distant past. A wide variety of needs, ranging from the need to acquire food and guard against predators to the need to coordinate the group and understand the meaning of life, have all contributed to the evolution of specialized modules for managing these tasks. These physical traits supported certain behavioral adaptations that provided advantages to the individual who possessed them; for example, specific kinds of information processes and behaviors provided mechanisms that were able to recognize and quickly solve specific kinds of problems.

Many of these hard-wired thought mechanisms have been adopted—exapted—in the production of religious dispositions and thought. Many universal features of religion have biological bases that emerged as a consequence of evolutionary adaptations, but not because of religion or to produce religion. Kirkpatrick (2005) has argued that religion itself is not an adaptation, but rather an exaptation of innate mechanisms that evolved for other purposes. For instance, the game of soccer exists in many cultures, and one might call it a human universal; furthermore, playing soccer depends on several innate human capacities. But we did not evolve to play soccer, and we do not have a specific biological adaptation for playing soccer. Soccer is a by-product of evolution, and an **emergent phenomenon** made possible by other adaptations, but playing soccer is not the product of evolution nor adaptations.

For something to be an adaptation, it must involve more than being adaptive in just a psychological sense. To be an adaptation, it must provide a reproductive advantage, and it must have a genetic basis. Thus, to establish that some feature of religion is an evolutionary adaptation, we would have to identify specific adaptive mechanisms involved in an exclusively religious behavior, and then show that religion contributed to selecting for those traits that directly or indirectly enhanced reproduction.

Kirkpatrick (2005) has suggested that attachment theory helps to explain religion as the product of a variety of specialized psychological systems that evolved for nonreligious functions. **Attachment theory** is derived from studies of the factors in natural selection that lead to the emergence of a mammalian attachment system. In mammalian species, infants have an instinctual desire to remain in close proximity to, and even in direct physical contact with, their mothers. Virtually any threat to the infant activates this attachment system, leading the infant to seek physical contact with the caregiver or to vocalize distress to attract the caregiver. The attachment system is also an evolved mechanism for reducing fear and anxiety, inducing feelings of security, and providing a safe haven from which the infant can begin to master its environment. This system guides behavioral, affective, and social behaviors, feelings, and thoughts that have adaptive consequences in keeping a mother and infant together. This bonding with the caregiver is so fundamental to mammalian survival that a failure to bond may produce a "withering away" syndrome leading to death. The attachment mechanisms make it more likely that the infant will survive and the mother's genes will be passed on.

Kirkpatrick suggests that while the attachment capacity is the basis for religious behavior, religion involves co-opting those adaptive functions. Kirkpatrick proposes that many psychological mechanisms that were adaptive because they solved specific human problems were subsequently exapted or co-opted by religion. This is why religious ideas can seem so "natural." Kirkpatrick proposes that religion is a consequence of our need and ability to bond with our caregivers. Human emotional motivations and behaviors with respect to attachment mechanisms allow the psychology of religion to meet these human psychological needs. The existence of a mammalian attachment system reflects an innate need for protection that is not limited to the infant phase alone, but persists throughout adulthood. The attachment bond between an infant and its mother is the prototype for the bonds that the child will develop with others and play a significant role in emotional adjustment from birth through the end of life. Romantic love, for example, involves the integration of the attachment system with the caregiving and reproductive systems. The attachment system is also the basis for the relationship with that most important significant other—God—as Freud suggested (see Box 8.6: God as an Illusion).

Box 8.6 GOD AS AN ILLUSION

One of Freud's later works, *The Future of an Illusion* (1927), focused on the origin of the belief in God. Freud's atheistic and evolutionary perspectives led him to regard God as an illusion derived from our psychological weaknesses. He noted that even if we are able to repress our instinctual desires and conform to the demands of society, nature nonetheless brings destruction and ultimately death. These unhappy truths about life lead humans to an act of repression in which we desire to regain the reality we experienced as children when our powerful parents, and our fathers in particular, provided us with a sense of security and protection. Our need for a powerful figure who can protect us from the dangerous and capricious aspects of nature causes us to project a father image onto the Universe. Like a father who provides us with protection from our fears, God can provide us with a sense of protection in the face of the powers of nature, the terror of the unknown, and the inevitability of death. Religious faith provides the ultimate assurance of protection. To Freud, God was, in essence, a projection of our father figure onto the Universe in an effort to allay our deepest fears about personal death.

Freud characterized God as an illusion, in the sense of something that we wish to be true. This illusion fulfills our deepest need, the need to feel protected. This need may have been well served by religion in the context of primitive societies because it contributed to the establishment of a moral order. Freud felt that with the evolution of society and the emergence of science, religious superstitions had become unnecessary. Like the Oedipal complex of childhood, Freud regarded the human need for religion as a reflection of a primitive and simplistic mentality, a consequence of inappropriate emotional dependence, ignorance, and intellectual weakness. To Freud, the persistence of religion in advanced civilizations was like the continuation of childhood neuroses into adulthood. Freud saw the persistent practice of religion as a universal obsessive neurosis, and he argued that if humanity were to progress beyond its primitive roots, it would have to abandon the illusions of religion and replace them with the mature thought of science.

Although his schema of the personality and its development is overly simple, Freud exerted a significant influence on anthropology because he related the biological aspects of the individual to the cultural world into which that individual grows. The need for an orderly society that respects the rights and interests of all its members resulted in the development of another significant aspect of the human personality, the "over-I" (superego). The "over-I" reflects the influences of socialization, the moral expectations imposed upon the individual by society, and, in particular, by the institutions of religion. For humans, a specific aspect of our self, the "I" (ego) or "reality principle," was responsible for mediating these conflicts between the desires of the "it" and the demands of society as represented by the "over-I."

Freud's understanding of "primitive" religion was derived from his work with his patients and from reading the works of such anthropologists as Tylor and Frazer. He was clearly affected by the same sense of European superiority toward other societies as these early anthropologists. But his insight that individual humans somehow had to reconcile their biological and psychological needs with the needs of the social groups they lived within was an expression of a modern view of humans that would be echoed as anthropologists became more sophisticated in their thinking.

God as an Attachment Figure

Kirkpatrick (2005) points out that the range of attachment behaviors found in children reflects the range of relationships of people to their Gods. The major world religions generally portray the Gods as ideal attachment figures and as models for one's own caregiving and attachment behaviors. Many Christian attitudes toward their God, for example, emphasize the sense of safety and security that God provides. This demonstrates that the attachment relationships with God are "real" in the sense of functioning similarly to parent–child relations during childhood, even though the relationship is not with a real person.

Kirkpatrick illustrates a variety of ways in which God functions as a substitute attachment figure. The perceived relationships with God of people who have a deep religious commitment parallel the expressions of emotional love experienced in the attachment relationships with parents. These relationships reflect correspondence, in that our attachments to our Gods and to our fellow humans are similarly structured. The opposite pattern is compensation, in which those who lacked secure attachment relationships with their parents find such attachment in their relationships with God. This pattern of attachment relationship with God is often characterized as "falling in love" and may be manifested as a dramatic religious conversion. This latter pattern has generated theories that the origins of religion involve a dynamic in which a belief in God provides a substitute relationship for the caring power of a father or other caregiver.

Belief in God and other spirits provides a range of psychological benefits, in essence extending the range of personal social resources for psychodynamic management of the self and emotions. Being committed to a religion can directly contribute to a person's sense that he or she is personally competent to address the problems that lie ahead. Religious beliefs can help minimize feelings of anxiety and contribute to a sense of optimism about the future. People who sense that God is present during their prayers or other ritual experiences are likely to exhibit higher levels of well-being. This sense of intrinsic religious orientation, a genuine commitment to one's religious beliefs, is associated with a variety of measures of health, inducing a sense of personal competence and control and freedom from worry. Epidemiological studies have repeatedly found that religiosity is positively associated with a wide range of health measures (recall the discussions in Chapter 6). So are these feelings the same as mother–infant attachment dynamics, or do they involve something more?

Summary: The Adaptive Emotional and Socialization Practices of Religion

Religions are cultural institutions that co-opt the biological bases of attachment and its functional roles in social behavior, extending them for other purposes. Religions can meet our innate needs for secure attachment; they also have effects that extend far beyond those of the mother–infant attachment. They apply exaptations of the attachment mechanism that evolved to keep a mother close to her infant and to other functions, such as the bonding of members of a group into a cooperative entity. This cooperation enhances the reproduction of members of the group over that of groups that do not have similar mechanisms for cooperation. Kirkpatrick adamantly asserts that "religion is not an adaptation." Our attachments to Gods, however, involve a range of capacities that go beyond the evolved attachment mechanisms, providing further functional benefits different from those of the mother–infant bond.

Religious activities are predominantly communal activities, bonding not just individuals, but literally millions of people. The community engagement provided by religious rituals has well-recognized social, emotional, and psychological consequences. In many mammalian species, the attachment bonds between mother and infant are extended to a broader social group (think back to the wolves and chimpanzees of Chapter 3). But in no species is this ability as pronounced as it is in our own; humans extend an evolved capacity for adaptation to a social world and emotional life that is hard-wired into the human nervous system. Furthermore, as we reviewed in Chapter 5, humans evolved enhanced opioid systems, expanding our capacity for bonding with others. Religion utilizes the mammalian capacity for emotional attachment developed in the symbiotic caregiver–child relations and bonding not only to produce feelings of well-being, but also to generate physiological and social responses through social relations that enhance our individual and collective well-being, including opportunities for survival and reproduction.

These therapeutic effects also can be produced in communal ceremonies that integrate the social group and enhance group identity. Anthropologists refer to such events as **rites of solidarity** because they promote a sense that the individual is merging into a larger group. In communal rituals, individuals are often flooded with endogenous opiates (opioids), which promote these feelings of attachment and produce a kind of harmony within the group. You may have experienced the thrill of participating (even as a spectator) at such nonreligious activities as sporting events, school reunions, or concerts. This thrill occurs because we "naturally" feel good when we connect with a group of like-minded people. Communal rituals—which are extensions of the original processes designed to maintain mother–infant proximity through this attachment-based opioid release—are particularly effective at producing a variety of adaptive consequences. Religious rituals manipulate the symbols associated with social bonding processes to activate the opioid system. The release of these powerful substances stimulates our immune systems and produces many important effects, such as a sense of euphoria and feelings of certainty and belongingness. Opiates also increase our coping skills and our ability to maintain bodily homeostasis, and they enable us to more effectively tolerate stress and, consequently, to deal with situations occurring around us.

The practices of religion also engender a variety of adaptive benefits. They may in some cases involve new evolved adaptations, such as the enhanced opioid systems discussed in Chapter 5. The presence of a biological feature is not, however, necessary for a phenomenon to enhance reproduction and survival benefits. The creation of beliefs in a superordinate God provide benefits beyond those which we acquire from our mothers; they not only extend over a lifetime, longer than the benefits provided by attachment to a mother, but provide additional benefits—such as an omnipresent and eternal helping presence—which even a perfect mom cannot provide. The attachments to a superordinate being are also more complex than the attachments to our mothers. Mothers cannot allay our fear of death, only momentarily suspend it. Religions are capable of generating life-enhancing and prosocial emotional states that go beyond the dynamics of mother–infant attachment. Religious appraisals broaden a person's horizon of emotional and cognitive possibilities, integrate that person into a group, and can shape expectations and actions that help the person—and their cultural group—achieve specific goals.

Whether these dynamics involve unique biological capacities provided by genetic evolution or whether they are extensions of our cultural capacity is an important point for refining our understanding of the biological bases of religion. Irrespective of whether these aspects of religion can be considered strictly genetic products or cultural inventions, religious beliefs make a substantial contribution to human adaptation, survival, and reproduction. We note, furthermore, that while there is a prior biological basis for the attachment system, its use to promote bonding and cooperative behaviors among thousands and even millions of people involves an exapted adaptation. Its

genetic basis undoubtedly involved modifications in the mammalian attachment system over the course of human evolution.

Conclusions: The Religious Shaping of Our Emotions

The intimate connection of religion with emotions has led many to posit that religion has its origins in emotions. Although some early scholars of religion emphasized negative aspects of this religious manipulation of our emotional states, the biocultural approach views the religious use of emotions as a powerful technique for helping individuals acquire the knowledge they will need to be functioning and well-integrated members of their society. Religious rituals are well designed to evoke emotional responses, and religious traditions utilize these emotions in socialization processes. Attachment theory provides a basis for understanding how religion exapts prior adaptive functions for use in new functions that help to integrate human society. Religious belief systems program many aspects of our thoughts and emotions as they function to create an individual experience of the world that is consistent with the worldview and social needs of the culture. The linking of emotions and experience with personal and social expectations is one of the fundamental functions of religion.

Religions appear to be uniquely positioned to evoke adaptive emotional responses, although these responses are not uniquely religious. Across human history, and even in the current world, religion has shown itself to have an unparalleled power to shape and integrate emotions and the motivations of groups. Religion has swayed major transnational forces in human history, from the Crusades, the European Conquest of the Americas, Jihad, colonies, and missions, to wars and humanitarian efforts. Neither nationalism nor political ideologies (i.e., communism, socialism) have had the power to sway as many broad swaths of humanity as have the major religions. The social sciences have long recognized that religions serve adaptive purposes. While views about the bases of these adaptations have differed, it is clear that religion is an especially powerful set of institutions for creating unified social groups. These adaptive aspects of religion appear deeply rooted not only in humans' evolutionary history, but even deeper in the evolutionary past of the primates and other mammals where collective social rituals integrated the social hierarchy and group emotional life. New insights from biological anthropology and evolutionary psychology may help us to unravel which traits involved in religiosity represent uniquely new biological adaptations. Whatever their basis, religions clearly have been involved in enhancing human survival through organizing social groups, as we will see in the next chapter.

Questions for Discussion

- How do religious rituals manipulate emotions?
- How do extreme emotions help us to remember events?
- What types of rituals or other events have you experienced that caused you to lose your sense of personal identity and feel that you were part of something larger than yourself?

Glossary

altruism in biology, a behavior in which an individual sacrifices its life or its reproductive potential to promote the reproductive success of its kin

attachment theory the idea that the mammalian predisposition for infants to bond to their mothers has also led to a variety of other emotional bonds, including to spirits

communitas the psychological condition of liberation and bonding that is produced when multiple individuals pass through the liminal stage of a rite of passage together

conditioning the psychological process through which a specific stimulus comes to be associated with a certain response

defense mechanisms psychological responses that serve to lessen anxiety

emergent phenomenon a trait or ability made possible by a variety of other traits or behaviors, but whose appearance could not be predicted solely on the basis of these underlying traits or abilities.

endogamy the cultural requirement to marry within a particular group

entrainment the association among processes, such as the association of religious symbols with particular physical and emotional states induced by the religious rituals. Entrainment also refers to the synchronization of the brain waves to internal and external patterns.

estrus the period during which a female mammal is ovulating and is sending signals to the males of her species, notifying them of her condition

exogamy the cultural requirement to marry outside of a particular group

funerary rituals the religious and other activities associated with death

gender that aspect of human sexuality by which a particular culture defines what it means to be male, female, or a member of an alternate sex

genome the complete genetic makeup of an individual

incorporation the third stage of a rite of passage, during which an individual takes up his or her new social status

kwashiorkor malnutrition caused by protein deficiency, endemic among some groups living in the tropics

latent function the usually hidden psychological effects of a ritual

liminality the second stage of a rite of passage, during which an individual occupies an ambiguous state between the old status and the status that he or she is about to acquire

manifest function the purported effect of a ritual

menstrual cycle the reproductive cycle of the human female, characterized by a lack of overt signs that ovulation is occurring

obsessive–compulsive disorder a neurosis in which a person is overly concerned with cleanliness and proper behavior

polygyny a system of marriage that allows a man to have more than one wife

puberty the stage of the human life cycle at which a person becomes able to reproduce and generally assume the status of an adult member in society

rites of passage a ritual that is specifically designed to help a person to shift from one social status to another

rites of solidarity ceremonies that help to integrate the social group and enhance the sense of group identity

role the set of culturally recognized attitudes and behaviors associated with a particular status

separation the first stage of a rite of passage, during which an individual is removed from the social status that he or she has occupied until that point

sex the biological identity of an individual

sexuality the act of copulation and the sexual behaviors associated with it

socialization the process by which an individual is taught the concepts, values, and other aspects of a particular culture

status a culturally defined position within a social network

symbolic penetration the process through which a variety of physical and emotional responses come to be associated with a religious symbol

unconscious the part of our psychology that is the source of our innate biological drives, emotions, and motivations

Religion and Society: How Religion Shapes Our Relations with Others

CHAPTER OUTLINE

Introduction: The Social Bases of Religion

The Evolutionary Origins of Human Social Organization and Religion

Durkheim and the Social Symbolic Approaches to Religion

Religion and Social Control

The Social Origins of God-Concepts and Sacred Morality

Religion as an Adaptive Social Mechanism

Conclusions: Durkheim's Legacy in Understanding Religion as a Social Symbolic Phenomenon

CHAPTER OBJECTIVES

- Illustrate why religion has been intimately related to politics, and describe the evolution of religious political systems.
- Examine Durkheim's social symbolic approach, and explain why he considered totemism to constitute the foundations of society and the sacred.
- Illustrate the functional approach to religion, and consider how religion operates as a total cultural system, including as a system of social control.
- Show the variable roles of Gods in moral systems, and explain the emergence of morally concerned Gods in complex societies.
- Illustrate the relationships between concepts of deity and the structure of society, and the roles of concepts of superior Gods in the establishment and maintenance of moral systems.
- Examine how religion can be seen as an adaptive social mechanism that enhances in-group cohesion and success in intergroup competition.

When they divided Purusa how many portions did they make?
What do they call his mouth, his arms? What do they call his thighs and feet?
The Brahman was his mouth, of both his arms was the Rajanya made.
His thighs became the Vaisya, from his feet the Sudra was produced.
The Moon was gendered from his mind, and from his eye the Sun had birth;
Indra and Agni from his mouth were born, and Vayu from his breath.
Forth from his navel came mid-air the sky was fashioned from his head
Earth from his feet, and from his ear the regions. Thus they formed the worlds.

—(Rig Veda 10, 90, 11–14)

(Reprinted from *The Hymns of The* Rig Veda, translated by Ralph T. H. Griffith, 1896.)

Introduction: The Social Bases of Religion

This passage from the *Rig Veda*, perhaps the oldest religious text in the world, describes how Purusa, the primordial being, was sacrificed to create the world. This myth relates how the original unity of existence was destroyed in order to create the diversity that exists in the world, including the heavens, the earth, and the Gods. By dying, Purusa also gave birth to the caste system, and the relative positions and responsibilities of the various castes can be traced back to their original positions on his body.

Hindu society is divided into four principal castes, known as varnas. The highest are the Brahmans (or Brahmins), the priests and scholars of society. Because they arose from the mouth of Purusa, they are able to recite the sacred texts. The next highest are the Rajanyas (derived from *raj,* "to rule"), the warriors and rulers who are now referred to as the Kshatriyas. The Vaisyas, or merchants and craftsmen, are the third caste, while the Sudras are the laborers and farmers. People belonging to each of these varnas are attributed with certain qualities and a level of ritual purity corresponding to the position of the caste on the social body. The Brahmins are the most pure, which is why only they are able to perform the major religious rituals of society.

Each varna is subdivided into hundreds of subcastes. These subcastes are organized on the basis of occupation, meaning that the type of work a person is expected to perform is determined by his or her birth. This kinship-based division of labor assigns specific tasks to everyone in society, and the elaborate rules of dharma (derived from the Sanskrit term *dhr,* meaning "to uphold, sustain") stipulate how people should conduct their lives.

The myth of Purusa and others like it teach Hindus that society will remain stable and that their individual fates are best served if they adhere to the rules surrounding their positions in life; that is, by fulfilling the roles that are associated with their status. For example, any Sudra who attempts to learn Sanskrit and read the ancient scriptures is violating his dharma. Western critics who characterize the caste system as a hindrance to personal advancement usually fail to recognize that in the Hindu worldview, personal advancement takes place over multiple lifetimes.

The rules that govern the Hindu social order exemplify the ways in which a society can be organized according to religious principles. They also demonstrate how a religious group (the Brahmins) can provide justification for a political group (the Kshatriyas). Yet because these rules originated in ancient times, they often fail to account for features of our modern world. What, for example, is the dharma of non-Hindus? Ignorant of samsara and of their place within it, they are *mleccha* ("barbarians"), who are in no position to challenge the cosmic order.

Religion, Power, and Society

Many anthropologists have focused on religion as a social phenomenon involving beliefs and practices that both reflect the structure of society and provide symbolic meanings that organize the members of a group. These social approaches tend to regard religion as a central cultural practice with important functions for society as a whole. The social focus illustrates how religion and society are intimately intertwined and how religion provides norms, values, and collective activities that are essential for the functioning and survival of a group. The dominant role of religion in premodern societies is unmistakable, as religion defines and structures people's relationship to their environment as well as their marriage patterns, work activities and organization, cosmology, politics, and virtually all other aspects of their culture.

All societies must manage their internal affairs, set limits for acceptable behavior, and deal with outside groups. Because they help to organize people (as well as other beings) into social networks and cosmological systems, religions throughout history have been important sources of inspiration and justification for the cultural rules and models that societies use to define how to behave. Throughout the course of cultural evolution from small-scale egalitarian societies to large-scale stratified societies, religious beliefs, values, and behaviors have influenced the ways in which groups define, organize, govern, and identify themselves. Today, many people see religion and the supernatural as distant from the "practical world" of politics and economic power. But even in a nation like the United States, which explicitly separates church and state, there are still important relationships between religion and politics. Around the world, the integration of political and religious roles is the norm rather than the exception. Religion and politics are not strange bedfellows, but constant companions. Religious functionaries often serve as political leaders, and political leaders frequently justify their positions by citing religious beliefs.

Priests and other religious practitioners often play significant roles in groups' ecological relations, regulating foraging, agricultural activities, and food consumption. These relations between politics and religion

During a debate in the early stage of the 2000 U.S. presidential campaign, then-Governor George W. Bush answered the question of which "political philosopher or thinker" he identified with most: "Christ, because he changed my life." During that campaign and throughout his presidency, Bush often invoked associations with Jesus.

reflect the roles that ritualized behaviors play in the animal world. Other animals face many of the same challenges that humans do, including a need for social organization. Individualistic animals such as reptiles use ritualized behaviors to signal their presence to one another and to recognize whether another animal is a foe or a potential mate. Mammals, with their great proclivity for living in social groups, have elaborated on the elementary ways that reptiles communicate about dominance, territoriality, and mating. Mammals use numerous behaviors to identify one another, determine their relative social status, and integrate their groups in stable hierarchies. Consequently, given the importance of social life for humans, it is not surprising that humans have incorporated similar biological functions of ritual to organize our societies.

Even in modern societies, humans still need to establish relationships with strangers to achieve things we cannot accomplish on our own, such as irrigating crops, building cathedrals, or defending territory. Our societies—the most elaborate and complex ever known—are now held together by cultural rules that link millions of individuals together into nations led by relatively small numbers of people. Some rule systems associated with religions unite people across political nations, creating, for instance, the Muslim and Christian "worlds." While the rules and mechanisms that humans use are much more elaborate than those of

other animals, we find continuities of humans with other animals in terms of the roles of ritual in organizing life, and, in particular, in drawing boundaries that help to define "our group."

The ubiquitous role that religion plays in the cultural institutions of premodern societies has provided the basis for a functionalist view of religion, one that sees religion as a resource that maintains a variety of social institutions vital for the survival of a society. In this view, religion is a critical force for codifying the rules of society, with unique abilities to provide a moral system that regulates behavior and integrates the members of society into a coherent group. Functionalists view religion as one of the most important mechanisms for sustaining culture; it provides a world view in its cosmology and structures for maintaining the organization of society that regulate social life and enhance cooperation and maintenance of the status quo.

An alternative perspective on religion is the conflict approach, which emphasizes the role of religion as a tool that elite groups use to control other members of their society. This view characterizes religion as a source of conflict and a distracter that blinds people to the real conditions that affect their well-being, a tool of political control, and an ideological weapon that elite groups employ to subordinate the masses to accept exploitative conditions. Both the functional and conflict perspectives emphasize the broader social functions of religion that have continuities with the biogenetic bases of religion in ritual. These continuities between nonhuman ritualized behaviors and human religious rituals relate to the establishment of dominance and the control of aggression within groups, creating hierarchically organized and harmonious social groups. Why should religion have such a powerful role in the political organization of societies? A recent evolutionary perspective called **group selection** proposes that natural selection also operates at the level of the group, in addition to operating at the level of the individual, the traditional evolutionary focus. This idea links social functionalist perspectives with insights into the ways that evolutionary selection could affect the characteristics of groups, enabling them to compete more successfully with other groups.

A Sociobiology of Religion?

The importance of examining the evolutionary relationships among politics, religion, and morality was introduced to twentieth-century academic attention by the concept of "sociobiology" (see E. O. Wilson's *Sociobiology* [1975]). Sociobiologists applied approaches traditionally used to understand the behavioral adaptations of animals to the explanation of human behavior, hoping to illustrate the evolutionary bases of human behavior. The application of Darwin's ideas about evolution to understanding human behavior suggested answers to the questions of how natural selection led to the development of guilt, self-sacrifice, religion, and other human behaviors. The universality of such behaviors in cultures throughout the world attests to their biological bases and raises questions regarding their origins. Because religious systems and concepts have been central to premodern political organizations and developments, religion seems to have played a role in the evolution of political complexity and integration.

The idea that human biological evolution has implications for human social behavior—including political organization—is controversial for many reasons. Some of the initial developments of this "social Darwinism" are associated with the sociologist Herbert Spencer. His notions of "might makes right," "the law of tooth and fang," and "survival of the fittest" were used to justify human behaviors producing inequality, colonization, slavery, and the dominance of the weak and poor by the rich and powerful. The rejection of these racist ideologies by much of anthropology and the social sciences has made the ideas of sociobiology so contentious that many scientists have ignored or ridiculed these perspectives.

Yet if we fail to consider how evolution may have shaped our capacities for social behavior, we ignore an important perspective for scientific inquiry into our nature, dispositions, and constraints. Evolutionary thought has emphasized the importance of the environment and, in the context of evolutionary psychology, the "environment of evolutionary adaptation" (EEA). This environment includes the physical and social dynamics of early hominid groups, as well as selective factors operating across the Pleistocene (the period from about 1.8 million to 10,000 years ago). Such perspectives are important when we consider the many nonadaptive aspects of religious thought and behavior today, for we no longer exist in the EEA in which our innate psychologies developed. Recalling the EEA can help us assess the ways in which religious behaviors may have been adaptive. Just as our innate preference for sugars, which we acquired because it was adaptive in the EEA, no longer serves us well when a once-rare substance becomes overabundant, acquired religious dispositions may no longer serve us as well today.

The connections between morals and politics in the context of human evolution are an arena of intense debate and disagreement. Different views on the evolution of traits for dominance, cooperation, altruism, and other prosocial motivations are further complicated by questions regarding the precise nature of the "environment of evolutionary adaptation" that selected for these innate tendencies. Our tendencies for competition, aggression, and cooperation do not reflect unique human capacities, but reflect extensions of psychosocial and emotional dynamics that developed during mammalian, primate, and hominid evolution. Animals managed these dynamics through ritualized behaviors. These were expanded into the more complex behaviors of humans in response to the demands of increasingly complex social life.

The Evolutionary Origins of Human Social Organization and Religion

Both near-contemporary human foraging groups and chimpanzees live in fission–fusion societies that are generally no larger than about fifty individuals, an adaptation to the need to remain mobile in order to optimally exploit scattered and limited food resources. Rituals play an important role in the social life of even such small groups, where everyone knows everyone else and understands how to act. Thus, it is possible for mammals to live in large groups (herds, packs, bands) with clear distinctions in status and to coordinate their activities in ways that provide common protection and facilitate cooperation. This bonding provides the foundation for the often elaborate societies in which mammals live.

Like reptiles, mammals rely on ritualized expressions of dominance and submission to compete for territory, dominance, and mating partners. Occasional aggression within a group is unavoidable, but even chimpanzees, who are known for their outbursts of aggression, seldom have an aggressive encounter that lasts for more than a few minutes. If it does, the dominant alpha males tend to enforce "peace" on the others. The most serious aggressive displays typically occur within a chimpanzee troop when mature males rising in the hierarchy challenge one another for alpha status. In these situations, the same ritualized behaviors that maintain group harmony in general, such as grooming, diffuse the tensions generated by these political power struggles.

Humans use many of the same basic ritual mechanisms as other animals for organizing groups, maintaining peace and harmony within the group, and dealing with competing groups. As societies became larger, these mechanisms became more elaborate, but at their heart these new ways are extensions of the fundamental functions of ritualized behaviors found in animals.

The Emergence of Human Political Organization

In the course of hominan evolution, it became imperative for larger groups to function cooperatively. Religion was a tool for achieving this integration, building from the phylogenetic basis of ritual to develop more complex activities that still had the capacity to tap into the deep levels of the human unconscious and coordinate our behavior with others. Our hominid ancestors faced inhospitable environments that exerted important selective influences in the evolution of early modern humans. One adaptation to these hostile environments was forging close emotional bonds with members of other groups, people who could assist in providing them with food and protection when needed. Rituals are the ways in which highly social primates integrate members into their group. For example, chimpanzees use excited aggressive displays along with drumming and vocalizations to produce an excited group reunion. This hominid baseline was expanded in the course of human evolution into dramatic ritual enactments that included the production of profound altered states of consciousness that were adaptive in strengthening emotional bonds

among members of different groups and in fostering alliances that contributed to an expanded community. Through shared religious rituals and social exchanges, humans participating in religious ceremonies established bonds that were crucial for survival during difficult times. The human population collapsed in the face of extreme environmental conditions caused by an ice age and the massive expansions of glaciers. Now contacts with other groups became essential to avoid genetic bottlenecks and defects caused by inbreeding in small groups. Shamanic rituals provided many avenues for finding others, establishing contacts, and integrating them into a group of intimate "fictive kin." These shamanic aspects of religion can be seen as a fundamental adaptation for survival of small egalitarian foraging groups, which formed the dominant social feature of our evolutionary heritage.

Our Egalitarian Heritage

Human foragers, who live in the simplest and smallest of all human groups, are **egalitarian**. Everyone has essentially the same access to food, mates, and other resources, and political processes are flexible and inclusive, allowing considerable individual autonomy. Private possessions are minimal, and individuals who have shown themselves to be good at hunting, healing, or some other task valued by the group earn great prestige. Major decisions affecting the group are typically made by consensus, although high-ranking individuals can sometimes persuade others to their point of view. Tensions between individuals are often dealt with by having the persons concerned directly confront one another. Singing duels and name-calling contests in which the rivals attempt to outperform—or out-insult—one another in front of the assembled community are often sufficient to diffuse these tensions. The large territories in which foragers traditionally lived made it a relatively simple matter to avoid outsiders, while the shifting availability of resources meant that the group itself often split into smaller, nuclear-family-based units for part of the year. This, too, helped to minimize group tensions. These small groups, however, faced a number of challenges. They needed to have contact with other groups for survival activities related to food, protection, and finding mates. Shamans were responsible for meeting these needs.

Shamanistic Healers as Informal Political Leaders. In foraging societies, shamans are among the most respected members of the group. Shamanic ritual provides the most important collective rituals that produce social integration and a dramatic engagement with the culture's cosmology and religious practices. These dynamic ritual performances also cloak shamans with an aura of mystique. Their spiritual charisma often extends into other aspects of social life as well, so that many shamans are also the de facto leaders of their groups. This power is, however, *informal*, for a shaman's leadership— like that of the other highly respected members of the group, such as the good hunters—is accepted because he has shown himself to be "correct" in the past. If a shaman's actions or instructions repeatedly fail, the other members of society will begin to ignore him.

The informal political capacity of shamans was also manifested in other shamanistic healers. Although some are the children of religious figures, shamanistic healers can also be "called" to their vocations through dreams, encounters with spirits, or by surviving a disease or injury. As a result, these positions are potentially open to many members of society. During ritual activities, these individuals typically wear special objects that signify their special role, but once the rituals are concluded, they change their clothing and take up their usual statuses in society once more. These part-time religious specialists have limited political power. But as societies became more complex, a new class of ritual specialists, the priests, emerged. Initiates to the priesthood typically receive their training from groups of professionals who may charge for the training and decide when the initiate has completed training. Priests typically occupy permanent full-time positions in the political structures of the society.

The Rise of Inequality: Transegalitarian Political–Religious Evolution

During the early Upper Paleolithic some foragers were beginning to develop more complex **transegalitarian** societies, where the ability to accumulate and store large amounts of food that were used in rituals enabled the formation of elite groups with higher status.

These elite groups exercised control and influence through public displays of art and rituals that were intended to honor their ancestors and demonstrate their prestige and success. Archaeologist Brian Hayden (2003) sees the emergence of such cults as a turning point in the evolution of religion. Hayden interprets these new rituals with reference to activities found in near-modern chiefdoms, where leaders rule by virtue of their positions in kinship systems. They sometimes exercise control over tens of thousands of people. The public rituals of religiosity are oriented toward the ancestors of the chiefs, who used wealth exchanges and prestige competition as mechanisms for engaging economic and political processes. This wealth differentiated the elite chiefs from nonelites, but the ritual items of the elites were central to virtually all aspects of social life: wealth exchanges, bride exchanges, marriage arrangements, social alliances, debt payments, and allocation of resources in times of scarcity. Durable and attractive artistic objects also served as symbols of success and may have been used as a currency in bride payments, for death compensation, and in political alliances through gift-giving, exchange, and tribute.

Among the central features of this new "elitist" religion were warfare, human sacrifice, and megalithic architecture. These activities reflected a chief's ability to organize his group to achieve goals, which, while often viewed as collective (protecting the village), generally had dimensions that served to enhance the reproduction of the elites. These new religions had

- *fertility cults* that used animal figures to represent their clans and lineages;
- *ancestor cults* that transformed their ancestors into group Gods;
- *megalithic architecture* that provided public statements of power;
- *public feasting*, which supported alliance and kinship-based political systems;
- *commodity items* to reflect status in gift-giving, exchange, and tribute, and to increase wealth, power, and prestige; and
- *symbols of power and authority* such as axes, shields, staffs, suns, boats, and bulls.

Hayden has postulated that these more complex religions emerged as resources became more widely available and people began to compete for access to these resources. This led to social stratification as certain elite groups gained control of most of these resources, and these elite groups used these resources to increase their own prestige and power. Offerings to some of the dead indicated their roles as especially powerful individuals, people such as the heads of clans who held unusually important social positions. Ancestor cults and veneration are suggested by the special care given to the burial of a few elderly men, who were interred with elaborate grave goods and offerings that indicated their elevated status. Their skulls were often removed and used as ritual objects, reflecting the special importance of these individuals in their afterlife roles. The ancestors of the elite class were considered to be Gods (see below).

Among chimpanzees, meat-sharing among males serves to promote their common interest in defending

Box 9.1 ALCOHOL CULTS IN PREHISTORY

As we saw in Chapter 5, hallucinogenic substances from plants, fungi, and animals have probably been consumed in religious contexts since they were first discovered. But at some time in prehistory, the use of alcohol supplanted these more ancient techniques for altering consciousness. The states of consciousness induced by substances from plants, fungi, and animals tend to focus awareness on the inner world, which is why they are well-suited for initiation rituals in which individuals disengage themselves from one status and take on a new status. In contrast, the disinhibiting effects of alcohol make it very useful for communal rituals, where it functions as a social lubricant that produces feelings of euphoria and provides a "break" from work and anxiety.

The use of alcohol did not become common until the Neolithic Revolution, when agriculture made large amounts of sugar-producing plants available for fermentation. The spread of alcohol cults was related to the social and economic changes that occurred as political hierarchies emerged to meet the needs of these more complex agrarian societies. At the heart of both these political hierarchies and the alcohol cults were elite male warriors, whose central roles in society are evident from the many drinking vessels found in their graves (Rudgley 1993). Alcoholic beverages were used in multi-day rituals and festivals that reinforced community solidarity, social cohesion and rapport, and internal hierarchy.

Alcohol consumption played an important role in the religious and political life of Iron Age Europe. The Celtic kings of the British Isles gave feasts as expressions of their generosity, and the bonds of friendship between the king and his vassals were reinvigorated by the copious consumption of *cerevisia* (the *vis*, or "power" of Ceres, Goddess of the earth and grain). These often ostentatious public ceremonies provided a forum where the king could announce political decisions, hear complaints and adjudicate disputes, and sponsor competitions to assess the courage and strength of his supporters. They also provided an opportunity for the king's supporters to publicly declare their loyalty to the ruler.

The ritual consumption of alcohol became an even more elite activity when wine became the beverage of choice. Wine can be stored for much longer periods than beer and mead, which are easy to make but which must be used almost immediately to avoid spoilage. A drawback of wine was that while mead and beer could be made from local honey or grains, the grapes needed to grow wine required specific conditions. Consequently, wine was generally acquired through trade, a factor that promoted both commercial and political ties between groups. Political figures who were able to procure wine and store it for their rituals increased their prestige and influence as wine replaced beer in these important public religious feasts.

Alcohol played such an important role in the religious life of pre-Christian European societies that it was subsequently incorporated into the central sacrament of Christianity. This practice grew out of the ceremonial consumption of wine in Jewish religious celebrations, where it was used to promote solidarity with the community and with God. Several New Testament accounts note that Jesus consumed wine and once even transformed jars of water into wine for a feast. The communal role that wine plays in the Christian tradition is underscored by the accounts of Christ drinking wine with his disciples at the Last Supper, during which he instructed them to eat bread and drink wine in his remembrance. Eventually, wine became a symbol of Jesus's own blood and his sacrifice for humanity. This ritual consumption of alcohol is a classic rite of solidarity that helps to integrate the community and remind them of their core beliefs.

---

their home range. Human foragers also share meat and other resources to promote group bonding and solidarity. In the more complex transegalitarian societies, the sharing of meat took on a new dimension in the elaborate feasting rituals that became the central public rituals of those communities. These feasts provided a forum for public activities that linked together males of diverse communities in lavish bonding rituals that superseded the local community bonding provided by shamanism. These public rituals involved extending the elites' veneration of their own ancestors into a broad community practice in which all society members wor-shipped the elites' ancestors as Gods. Consequently, **social stratification** emerged, where a socially sanctioned system of inequality assures that some individuals and families had greater access to resources, power, and prestige. These led to new forms of social integration focused on the role of alcohol as a social lubricant (see Box 9.1: Alcohol Cults in Prehistory).

As societies became more complex, their concepts about the supernatural world became more complex as well. Just as some people became more important than others, some Gods became more important as well. People needed to develop relationships with these Gods, but in contrast to the egalitarian spirits of foraging groups, these new "High" Gods would not speak to just anyone, but only to their special representatives on Earth. It was no coincidence that these intermediaries, who were able to communicate the wishes of the people to the Gods and—more important—interpret the wishes of the Gods to the people, were usually the same people who occupied the other privileged statuses in society. Furthermore, the standards of morality that they set were often blatantly in their own self-interest (e.g., tithes and sacrifices to the priestly class), although they justified them as being the demands of the Gods. Here again, we see how religious concepts can play a central role in integrating larger groups of people and in enhancing the survival and reproduction of certain groups at the expense of others.

In these large groups, it was no longer possible for everyone to know everyone else or to predict how everyone else might act. New principles were needed to organize societies, to make decisions, and to determine whether people who did not know one another were related. These developments also led to the emergence of a new kind of religious leader, one who had a permanent grasp on political power: the **priest.**

Durkheim and the Social Symbolic Approaches to Religion

Émile Durkheim (1858–1917), one of the founders of modern sociology, also contributed to the development of the social and symbolic approaches in the anthropology of religion. Durkheim's classic book, *The Elementary Forms of Religious Life* (1964), emphasized the socially adaptive aspects of religion. Durkheim argued that if religion was nothing more than an intellectual adaptation to the environment, it would not have persisted for very long. It could not have functioned effectively in mediating our adaptations to the real world, and its failures would have far exceeded its successes. Durkheim argued that instead religion serves important functions as a symbolic system that plays a central role in the organization of social life.

In contrast to both the intellectualist and the emotional approaches to religion—which tend to focus on individuals and the ways in which they conceptualize and feel about the world—the sociological approach of Durkheim focused on the mechanisms that bind individuals together into groups. For Durkheim, the smallest unit of study is the **social fact,** which is a product of the *interaction* between individuals. An idea or emotion held by one person alone is not a social fact. It

becomes a social fact only after it has been communicated to another person, at which time it takes on a life of its own. Religious social facts include ideas about spirits and the rituals and other practices that are used to address the spirits and organize human activities.

Durkheim focused on the "collective representations" of religion, the symbolic systems that help individuals form moral communities. He regarded religion as a sacred system of rituals and beliefs distinct from the profane aspects of daily existence. The sacred involves collective representations that define the moral order of society, a framework that unites people together in a community. To Durkheim, religion and society are essentially synonymous, so much so that "religion is the worship of society." Each culture defines society through the demands of a sacred realm that provides important beliefs that affect virtually all aspects of life. These include norms for behavior, the values used to evaluate human conduct, and the beliefs that explain the phenomena of the natural world. In Durkheim's eyes, religion—and the moral community it makes possible—was the original cultural system that bound humans together into societies.

Durkheim felt that religion needed to be understood in terms of social relationships, structures, and institutions. He believed that society and religion are indispensable to one another, with religion serving as an adaptation to the human need for communal ties. In traditional societies, religion creates these ties by providing a "contract" that establishes morals and norms for behavior that are justified by the sacred realm. Durkheim embraced the scientific study of society and religion and regarded social norms and religious beliefs as social facts that could be studied in an objective and systematic fashion. These social facts are a product of the cultural context, a fundamentally moral context that produces an intimate interdependence and inseparability of social morals and religion. This moral system is defined by cultural concepts of the sacred, a special domain of concerns set apart from the profane experiences of everyday life.

Like many other thinkers of his time, Durkheim was interested in the distinction between religion and magic. He acknowledged that both involve myths, rituals, and sacred objects. But he distinguished between the two because of their focus. For Durkheim, magic is a private and individual activity. This sets it apart from religion, which relies on a group united by a common set of beliefs and practices provided by their shared conceptions of the sacred. These shared practices for relating to the sacred define the "church," which Durkheim regarded as the core aspect of the nature of religion, for it was the church that bound people together into a sacred community defined by religious rules.

Totemism as the Origin of Religion

To illustrate the basic functions of religion, Durkheim examined the phenomenon of totemism that we discussed in relation to Freud's theories in Chapter 8. Durkheim considered totemism to be the most basic form of religion, practiced by the simplest societies, and the form out of which other forms of religion developed. He derived his model from studies of Australian aborigines, whom Durkheim regarded as being one of the most primitive societies.

Totemism is a social and religious practice in which people are identified as members of different groups (generally kinship divisions known as clans). Clans typically include all of the members of one lineage or descent group. Because a person's clan does not change throughout that person's lifetime, the clan system provides a stable social reference point from which people can relate to others. Each clan is represented and conceptualized in the form of its **totem,** which is usually a class (species) of animal, although it may be a plant or natural object. Because the totem is also conceptualized as a spirit power, it represents both the power of the spirit and the power of the social group. Totems thus provide social groups with both their sacred deity and the emblem of their social identity.

This worship of the totem is the focus of the most important collective gatherings of the Australian aborigines. The members of a clan are prohibited from eating their totem except on special ritual ceremonies where it is sacrificed and consumed by the group. Because the congregation of society and the collective worship of the deity are the same event, and because both society and the deity are represented with the same symbols, Durkheim concluded that religion *is* the worship of society. This perspective was supported by the recognition that totemic worship had the latent function of creating society. Most of the year, the members of a clan are divided into smaller groups of people. The practice enables these foragers to effectively exploit the limited and patchy resources in their environment. But when food is plentiful, people from the same clan will congregate together for weeks of rituals—parties, festivals, initiations, and courtship—during which they will receive moral instruction from the elders. The women, who move away from their own clans and live with their husbands' groups after marriage, may also return to their clans of origin for these festivities. For the weeks that the festivals last, society—the clan—is physically and socially reconstituted by the ritual activities.

The central worship activities of the clan consist of totemic ritual ceremonies that are aimed at promoting the growth and well-being of the totem. Following these rites for enhancing the fecundity of the totem, a second phase of the ceremonies occurs, during which the normal prohibitions on the consumption of the totem are suspended. Now, the totem animal is ritually killed and consumed in a sacred meal. This meal allows the eaters to incorporate the power of the totem. During the annual gathering, the myths of the group are recounted, providing both entertainment and instruction in the basic values and beliefs of the society. The recital of myths also provides a dramatic expression of many other basic social expectations, including emotional communication and social roles. The incorporation of the totem within a mythological system extends its manifestation to virtually all aspects of life in an intricately interconnected system of meaning that links together the individual, the group, and the physical environment.

The ritual renewal of the totem is thus, in essence, a symbolic expression of the social function of the ritual to renew society. The totemic ritual provides the opportunity, and indeed the obligation, to renew one's commitment to the community. The ritual feast and ceremonies bring the symbol of commitment and identity—the totem—to a central place in everyone's consciousness. The awe-inspiring ceremonies—and the collective emotions they engender—help create a sense of commitment to the group. These intense ceremonial periods of collective emotional sentiments of enthusiasm, joy, and effervescence produce powerful feelings of contact with something beyond the self. For Durkheim, this experience of the sacred or spiritual was the origin of religion. Durkheim concluded that totemic religions demonstrate that religion is, in essence, the worship of society as embodied in the common symbol for the clan and the deity. Religion is a system designed to produce and ensure societal cohesion by providing rituals that help unify people into an integrated community that acts with a common purpose and set of moral orientations.

Animal Species in Human Thought and Social Classification

Durkheim noted that the use of animals as representations of society reflected their role as natural representations. His view of totemism as a system of social classification was expanded by the French anthropologist Claude Lévi-Strauss (*Totemism* 1962; see also Friedrich 1991). Lévi-Strauss identified commonalities underlying the many different belief systems in which human clans are associated with particular species.

In totemism, human kinship groups are identified in terms of animal species. By establishing a relationship between the natural domain of animals and the cultural domain of human social groups, totemism provides a metaphor for identifying human groups with the more easily noted and distinct characteristics derived from the animal world.

The biocultural perspective understands totemism as a natural product of the way humans think, structured by the mental hardware of the human brain. As we saw in Chapter 5, one of the components of our mental hardware is a specialized intelligence for classifying the natural world. Thus, the use of animals to represent clans is not entirely arbitrary, for it is based in this evolved aspect of human psychology. Evolutionary pressures selected for the capacity to recognize animal species on the basis of their unique characteristics. This deeply rooted adaptation was exapted into a natural metaphoric system that can be extended to many other areas of human thought. The use of animals in cognitive modeling is one of the most fundamental aspects of metaphoric and analogical thought (Friedrich 1991), providing a universal human system for expressing meaning and creating a person's social and personal identity.

Consequently, we can assert that the evolution of totemic classification systems exapted our systems for animal classification and applied them to the new functions of classifying social groups. These classifications facilitated in-group identification and regulation of relationships with out-groups, providing adaptations that facilitated humans' abilities to live in larger and more effectively integrated groups. These socially integrated groups enhanced individual and group survival. In this way, religious beliefs and practices contributed to human survival and reproduction. In this sense, totemism is an exaptation of an innate cognitive capacity that is extended to a new domain in the interest of promoting adaptive behaviors that enhance survival.

Functionalism: What Has Religion Done for You Lately?

Durkheim's view of the role of religion in social life introduced a new way of thinking about religion: examining the *functions* of religion in society. In other words, what do religious beliefs and practices do for the people and groups who hold and practice them? To Durkheim, religion is not born of some mistaken understanding of the world, but rather of a need to create a community or society. Durkheim's approach illustrates how certain cultural practices, including religion, function to maintain cultures as groups. Thus, the functions of religion

were to provide benefits for the group as a whole in the form of mechanisms that helped ensure the survival of the social group. The *manifest functions* of religious behaviors—the reasons that people give to explain the rituals—are not as important as the *latent functions*—the implicit (and perhaps unrecognized) effects that religious practices have on the society as a whole.

Durkheim conceived of a society as a kind of organism in which all the parts serve to maintain the operation of the body as a whole. Society functioned in an equilibrium or balance among its various parts, the institutions. This balance reflected the interdependence of all of the parts. While all institutions contribute to a well-functioning society, religion plays a special role in the process. Religion provides not only the norms that orient people's behavior, but also the culture's broader systems of explanation—its cosmology and worldview. The functionalist perspective emphasizes that society as a whole is more than the sum of its parts. This organismic view of society focuses on the functions that serve the collectivity rather than the individual. Durkheim proposed the most basic function of religion is to organize social life, to help overcome our individualistic tendencies and instill a sense of altruism.

A key aspect of this sense of commitment to the social group is mediated through symbolic processes. The integration of symbolic behavior and sacred representations allows those sacred symbols to organize behaviors, particularly behaviors that constitute the moral rules that bind people together in a community. Durkheim viewed religion as a symbolic system that reflects, and therefore supports, the social structure of the culture—the way in which social relations, class structures, and political hierarchies are organized. Religion is the force that unites individuals in ways that give societies their power. Religions elaborate on the power of rituals to provide signals, symbols, and social and interpersonal mechanisms to assure the tranquil persistence of the social hierarchy. While rituals are present in other groups of primates, in humans these dynamics have been expanded through the use of symbols as fundamental tools that are able to affect cognition, identity, and social relations through behaviors that influence survival and reproduction.

Structural Functionalism in the Anthropology of Religion. Durkheim drew on the research done by others, primarily anthropologists, when he developed his ideas about the nature of religion. When anthropologists influenced by Durkheim's theories began to investigate their relevance in the context of their own fieldwork, they both refined and qualified his ideas about the nature of magic and religion. One important result of this work was to undermine Durkheim's ideas about the differences between magic and religion and the distinction between the sacred and the profane. Anthropologists generally abandoned efforts to distinguish between magic and religion, and began to regard both as labels for a common category of activities. The anthropological focus on behavior led to an emphasis on rituals, which were interpreted as symbolic statements that expressed the concerns of the group and provided behavioral processes that integrated the society.

The English anthropologist A. R. Radcliffe-Brown (1881–1955) developed Durkheim's ideas of functionalism to illustrate how rituals affect the relationships among people in a society. Radcliffe-Brown (1965) points out that rituals create the "ritual value" that is attributed to objects that represent important common interests. The symbolic manipulations of these objects link together the members of a community within a common framework of assumptions. These frameworks are maintained by institutions (or structures), leading to the development of perspectives broadly characterized as structural–functional. Anthropologists investigated the structures of societies, including religious systems, and explained their functions within the broader cultural system.

The concept of taboo, derived from a Polynesian word that means "forbidden," illustrates how religious beliefs can play a fundamental role in creating the social and moral fabric of a society. Taboos are formal prohibitions of particular behaviors that carry a threat of punishment to any individual who violates them. The taboos of a society provide a set of values that guide human behavior. Violating a taboo may result in social punishments by the authorities, as well as supernatural punishments by spirits. Rituals provide a means for learning the taboos and for communicating information about social values and expected behaviors.

The relationship of rituals, ritual values, and ritual behaviors to the broader needs of a culture may not be directly apparent. The reasons that people use to justify their ritual behavior are often difficult for anthropologists to accept. For example, the reasons that people offer to explain why a ritual is performed to produce rain may not seem logical. Radcliffe-Brown (1965) rejects the notion that people engage in rituals such as rain-making ceremonies because of a faulty reasoning process. Instead, he emphasizes the need to understand rites in terms of their symbolic meanings, the implicit or latent functions that incorporate the individual within the cosmology of the culture. From these perspectives, rites are understood as a way of maintaining the cultural order and the place of humans within the Universe. A claim that a ritual has a technical effect

(its manifest function) must be placed in a broader context that considers other effects as well (its latent functions). Instead of emphasizing the apparent falsity of claims about the technical effects of the ritual, anthropologists try to discern the psychological and social effects of ritual performances—the symbolic effects on the behavior, motivation, and sentiments of the participants and the community. To explain individual psychological motives and functions, it is necessary to understand how a ritual functions within the cosmological system, in relationship to the social structure, and in terms of the control of human emotions.

The English anthropologist E. E. Evans-Pritchard (1902–1973) used his field work in Africa to illustrate the shortcomings of the intellectualist theories of religion and to show how religion functions to integrate society. Evans-Pritchard conducted extensive field work that enabled him to speak about the realities of cultural and religious life and their integration within a total system of meaning. His field work led him to live among other cultures for extensive periods of time, during which he learned their language, customs, and daily activities. This gave him insights into how religion functioned to provide an integrative framework for social life.

His field work enabled Evans-Pritchard to provide very elaborate descriptions of the Azande and Nuer concepts of the spiritual world and to show the errors in Tylor's evolutionary theories. The Azande and Nuer concepts of personal souls were quite different from the spirits of the dead that Tylor had regarded as the source of animistic beliefs. The Nuer also had totemic practices in which animal species were viewed as representatives of specific clans or tribes. While he criticizes some of Durkheim's ideas, Evans-Pritchard's work on the Nuer also demonstrates the usefulness of some of Durkheim's ideas about totemism.

The structural–functional approach of Evans-Pritchard does not fully embrace Durkheim's view that religion is defined by the sacred, nor does it completely reject the intellectualist view that religion is a belief in supernatural beings. His work shows how religious beliefs are related to the structures of society. He argues that this is the influence of social structure on religion, rather than a social determination of the beliefs and ideas regarding spirits.

Religion as a Cultural System

In his classic article "Religion as a Cultural System," Clifford Geertz (1966) integrates the intellectualist concern over the explanatory role of religion with the functionalist perspective. In doing so, Geertz provides a broad and all-encompassing definition of religion that incorporated the intellectual, emotional, symbolic, and social aspects of religion as part of the total worldview of a culture. Geertz's definition, which has resonated with many anthropologists, sees religion as "(1) a system of symbols which acts to (2) establish powerful, persuasive, and long-lasting moods and motivations in men by (3) formulating conceptions of a general order of existence and (4) clothing these conceptions with such an aura of actuality that (5) the moods and motivations seem uniquely realistic" (Geertz 1966).

A key aspect of Geertz's conception of religion is its role as a symbol system—a system of interconnected meanings that function to express the essence of a culture's worldview and ethos, encompassing such diverse domains as morals, character, values, aesthetics, and cosmology. The principal function of religion is to illustrate the conformance between everyday life and the ideal view of the Universe that is depicted in a culture's cosmology. Religious rituals provide mechanisms to make this connection emotionally convincing, giving people a certainty that the general principles in which they believe actually operate in the Universe. Religion projects a cosmic order that serves as a general model of the Universe, and then socializes human beings to help to ensure that people's morals, emotions, and judgments conform to these ideals.

Symbol System. Religion expands the functions of symbols beyond their ordinary capacities. Symbols normally refer to things that we can see and touch, but in the context of religion, symbols are used to refer to things that we may never see or touch and even to things that we may be unable to experience or conceptualize. The symbols of religion not only depict Gods as social beings, but also draws on an interrelated set of symbols—a model of the Universe—that provides explanations for many aspects of human existence. Religious beliefs embody models for psychological (personal) and social reality. The norms, values, beliefs, and requirements of religion play a fundamental role in shaping individual social and psychological development. Consequently, one fundamental effect of religion is to teach individuals to understand the Universe.

Moods and Motivations. Religion is one of the most significant cultural systems involved for socializing a person's "moods and motivations." Religion both shapes our innate emotional dispositions and elicits new emotional experiences and concerns. One fundamental function of religion is to channel the wide range of possible human developmental patterns into a particular configuration of dispositions involving habits, preferences, skills, attitudes, and motivations. Motivations are a particularly important aspect of religious socialization because they create a persistent tendency for humans to seek certain kinds of experiences and engage in certain kinds of behaviors. Religious socialization normally creates specific expectations regarding moods in different circumstances. A central aspect of religious socialization is to create a particular indigenous psychology, an understanding of the overall configuration of the cultural personality ideals that are used to guide human behavior. Religious socialization serves to make a person's moods and emotions meaningful both in terms of their personal experience and in terms of the broader cosmological frameworks of the culture. This use of religious beliefs and practices to assign specific meanings to particular experiences represents one of religion's central roles in human development.

Worldview: A General Conception of Existence. One of our basic human needs is to interpret or understand our experiences. Our need to explain our world is driven by our need to plan our behavior and escape from the anxiety produced by uncertainty. Conditions of inexplicable suffering pose a particular challenge to the human experience of meaningfulness in the Universe. Religious systems offer the ultimate explanation of suffering by providing a range of "reasons" for why it occurs. Suffering may be a punishment for a transgression—perhaps a failure to make an offering—or it simply may be a necessary aspect of God's "plan" for the Universe. While such explanations may do little to calm or relieve those who prefer more scientific explanations of phenomena, these "reasons" can make such events meaningful if they have been acquired as part of a learned worldview. Religious symbolism and meaning can help turn the inescapable suffering and incomprehensibility of the world into something that is conceivable and that is satisfactorily explained in mythic terms and frameworks.

Socialization: Giving Conceptions an Aura of Factuality. The fundamental processes by which religious explanations become believable are the processes by which humans accept authority, allowing the perspectives of powerful others to be internalized as one's own beliefs. Religious assumptions regarding the Universe provide a way for a person to understand the world. These religious perspectives are not the confused speculations of primitive or childlike believers, but accounts of the world whose authority is derived from the fact that they are learned from powerful elders. A common basis of religious engagement is the human need for faith, belief, and assurances in the received wisdom from others. In contrast to the detachment and inquiring attitude of the scientific approach, religion seeks to instill unquestioning acceptance and commitment. Religions provide rituals that help to mask the contradictions between a person's own experience of reality and the expectations provided by his or her cosmological system. One powerful tool of religious socialization is a public ritual demonstration that creates an association between certain moods and motivations and sacred symbols; for instance, joy when seeing a picture of a saint. These cultural performances simultaneously elicit emotions and link them to the explanation of their "meanings" within a cosmological framework, giving people a sense of certainty about their truthfulness. Through ritual socialization, the models of the Universe provided by a religion are incorporated into a person's own beliefs, expectations, roles, and motivations for behavior. These socialization experiences exploit the human need for psychological association, our deep human capacity to bond with and internalize within our self concept the "other" and generalized cultural expectations for human behavior.

Conviction: Making Religious Motivations Realistic. The effects of religious socialization are not noticed solely in the context of ritual, but throughout life. This continued certainty of a sacred reality in the context of profane everyday existence is a consequence of the power of religious experiences and socialization processes. This capacity of religious socialization to provide a more encompassing framework that includes profane reality is a direct consequence of the profound experiences induced by ritual. The power of a ritual to provide people with the experience of entering into the spirit world through trance, possession, ecstasy, dissociation, inspiration, and many other mystical and spiritual states produces a sense of conviction in the reality of religious beliefs.

Summary

Geertz's understanding of religion emphasizes its capacity to provide a framework for integrating and giving meaning to many aspects of human experience. The role of religious systems in socialization includes its ability to shape personal development. A key aspect of religion's ability to produce this structuring of indigenous psychology is its use of ritual to produce powerful emotional experiences and to associate particular meanings with these moods and motivations. Ritual makes these interpretations particularly "real" by associating them with powerful transcendent experiences.

Religion and Social Control

All societies must teach their members about acceptable and unacceptable behavior and exert some degree of control over the deviants who undermine the social order. Tensions are inevitable within any society, and people need ways to settle disputes, determine guilt or innocence, and punish transgressors. In small-scale societies, when problems arose, people looked to the group's elders, who provided answers on the basis of their own judgment in the matter, or to religious functionaries, who provided answers after consultation with the spirits.

The simplest principle that humans use to organize their societies is kinship. Unilineal kinship systems make it clear to whom a person is related and whom they can marry. Such kinship groups also regulate inheritance and provide a structure for dealing with conflict. Problems that arise between members of the same lineage are handled within the lineage, usually by the elders. Problems that occur between members of different lineages involve each lineage in its corporate or group form. If a member of one lineage kills a member of another, the offending lineage may be required to rectify the damage caused by providing a payment. If this payment is considered insufficient, if the harm is too grievous, or if the two lineages do not enjoy an otherwise peaceful relationship, a **feud** may erupt between them that may lead to low-level warfare lasting for years.

Some anthropologists have suggested that the **chiefdom**, a form of society in which the positions of leadership are inherited within the most important lineages, arose as a response to the need to control feuding between different lineages. In chiefdoms, one lineage is considered more important than the others, and the members of this lineage serve as mediators in disputes that involve two or more other lineages. In return, the members of the other lineages provide the chief and the other members of his lineage with extra resources, which they may allocate in times of hardship, offer as sacrifices to the Gods, or use in political exchanges with neighboring groups. Although chiefdoms do not have a formal court system, they do have established ways for settling disputes through recourse to the chief or other special designated judicial representatives. In some cases, these involve the use of special mechanisms to communicate with supernatural beings whose great powers enable them to see things that humans cannot and to provide justice. In complex agricultural societies, the role of judge is generally in the hands of the religious functionaries, such as priests.

The Formal Leadership of Priests

Although it is now common in our own society for a person to decide to become a priest (in the same way that he or she might decide to become a carpenter or a physician), the freedom to choose a religious occupation is a relatively recent phenomenon. In traditional societies, priests are generally born into their positions, and there is little possibility for others to become priests. In ancestor cults in which the reigning member of the lineage is also the chief priest, this position is normally passed on to his son upon his death. The elite nature of the priesthood is further assured in **ecclesiastical** organizations which stipulate the formal training period that priestly initiates must undergo, during which they are supervised by a group of religious leaders who test the initiates to ensure that they have learned the proper interpretations of tradition. Only after demonstrating a correct understanding of tradition will an initiate be judged worthy to enter the priesthood and wear the special garments or other insignia in public.

Priests are typically males. Females are usually only assistants. Those cases in which an Empress or Queen also acts as a priest are exceptions. Thus, the priest's position is an expression of male power. Although a priest is often considered the preeminent religious power in a society, he does not control the Gods or other spirits. Nor—in stark contrast to shamans—does he journey to their world to confer with them. Instead, he asks the Gods for assistance in this world and serves as an intermediary, petitioning the Gods on behalf of the people.

Just as the priests themselves mediate with the spirit world but do not normally enter it, priestly religions generally do not encourage people in society to experience altered states of consciousness for religious purposes. Religious states of consciousness generally produce a profound conviction that one has encountered the ultimate truth, and this can be difficult for a hierarchical organization to control. There is an old saying, "The bishop does not want to hear that there is a new saint in the parish."

A priest is typically in charge of an organized and permanent institution such as a church. Like the other specialized professions that are found in large-scale stratified societies, priests are organized hierarchically. The highest level of the priesthood may involve the king, emperor, chief, or other high-level ruler. In ancient Egypt, the Pharaohs were regarded as the direct descendents of Ra, the Sun God, and served to perpetuate the earthly order that he had established. In the Roman Catholic Church, the local priest is assigned to a local parish and serves under a bishop who administers a diocese consisting of numerous parishes. In turn, the bishops report to the Pope, who is also known as the Bishop of Rome. The Pope (a term derived from the Greek *papas*, meaning "patriarch" or "father") is the highest authority in the Church and answers directly to God. Although many of the statements made by a Pope can be amended by later Popes, any proclamation the Pope makes *ex cathedra* ("from the chair") is considered to come directly from God—the highest authority of all—and thus is considered to be infallible.

Priests often have formal judicial power and may be members of deliberative bodies that make laws affecting the populace. Generally regarded as the moral authorities of a society, priests—using the rules that the Gods have given them—determine who and what behavior is moral or immoral. The religious laws are often adopted as civil law, for example, where Islamic law (*sharia*) is imposed on a nation, or where Christians attempt to pass legislation that forces nonbelievers to conform to their Christian concepts of morality (e.g., prohibitions on abortion, same-sex marriages).

As we saw in Chapter 5, priests are found in sedentary agricultural societies (and some pastoral societies

Catholic priests often wear a white banded collar as an insignia of their office.

that depend on herd animals such as cows, camels, and reindeer). These societies have social classes and a political hierarchy that extends for several levels beyond the local community (i.e., villages are incorporated into districts, which in turn are controlled by states under the jurisdiction of a nation). Agriculture appears to be the main factor responsible for the rise of the priesthood, for while priests are sometimes found in societies without complex political hierarchies, in these societies they are associated with ritual activities intended to assure the success of agriculture. Even in these simple societies, priests often control considerable economic and natural resources and make decisions regarding their allocation. As a result, priests are able to exert control over many aspects of a society.

One important focus of priestly religious activities is the collective rites in which the Gods of the group are propitiated with sacrifices designed to ensure the general fertility of animals and crops and to thank the Gods for their past generosity. These **calendrical rites** generally occur at specific times of the year, particularly planting and harvest. While a portion of the harvest is sacrificed to the Gods, the offerings are often consumed by the priest and other people who participate in the rituals. The sacrificial offerings may include a wide variety of objects, but usually include domestic animals (cows, pigs, chickens, etc.). In many premodern societies, the majority of all the domestic animals that the people consume are sacrificed to the Gods before they are eaten by the community. While a variety of other foods is also consumed during these rituals, the ritual focus is on the major domestic animals, the principal sources of protein for the group. This pattern, in which the major protein resources of a society are consumed within a religious framework, underscores the importance of priests in controlling and maintaining a society's relationship with their resources (see Box 9.2: Priests as Programmers: The Water Temple System of Bali).

Conflict Perspectives: Religion as Social Control and the "Opiate of the Masses"

Religions do not always promote cooperation. They often exacerbate conflicts with outside groups and may promote the persecution of members of these groups. Religions may also create conflicts within a group. Witch hunts based on religious beliefs may turn neighbor against neighbor, and history has documented many instances of how witch "crazes" have led to the horrific torture of innocent people (we will examine some of these in Chapter 10). Religions have

been used to justify wars, human sacrifice, and cannibalism. Put simply, religion can produce conflict as well as harmony.

This insight greatly influenced the thinking of Karl Marx, who developed one of the earliest social science perspectives on the role of religion in society. Marx wrote his famous works on the evolution of economic systems and the nature of capitalism and classes during the mid-ninteenth century. In his time, just as in our own, the elite classes of capitalist societies controlled the economic systems of society—the means of production—and consequently the political systems as well. Marx viewed religion as an ideological tool that elite groups used to justify the subordination and exploitation of the working classes. In the Christian tradition, the humble and meek are promised the kingdom of heaven. Lower caste Hindus are promised a rebirth in a higher caste in a future lifetime if they act in the appropriate manner (adhere to their dharma) in this lifetime. Religious systems use values of obedience to ecclesiastical authority and the subordination of individual desires to group needs to indoctrinate the weak to accept their own exploitation. Instead of focusing on the social causes of inequality in this life, religion promises people that they will be rewarded in their future lives if they accept their positions in this life.

Marx regarded the "modes of production," the ways in which people produce the necessities of life, as the primary determinant of culture and society. These economic structures determine production and other social functions, and therewith the structure of a society. The economic base produces the ideologies, which, for Marx, included both the religious and political institutions of a society. The elite members of a society used an integrated set of beliefs (ideology) as a tool for oppressing others.

Adopting ideas from anthropologists of his time, Marx argued that the original mode of production was a kind of primitive communism in which everyone had collectively contributed to and shared in the goods produced by the group. These original, sharing societies disappeared with the rise of agriculture and ownership of land, and were replaced by a new system in which the wealthy owned the property on which the crops were produced and controlled the slaves and peasants, who worked in the fields. When industrialism and modern capitalism emerged, the control of agriculture became even more concentrated in the form of mechanized farm production. Consequently, the profits and power gained by the wealthy few became exceedingly large, leaving little for the impoverished masses of former peasants and factory workers.

Box 9.2 PRIESTS AS PROGRAMMERS: THE WATER TEMPLE SYSTEM OF BALI

The water temple system of Bali provides an example of the role that religion can play in economic and political activities (Lansing 1991). Although Bali is tropical, the extensive agriculture practiced on the island would not be possible if the available water were not apportioned in an appropriate manner. Rainwater is distributed via an irrigation system consisting of many lakes and canals that allow water to flow to the different areas below. A religious system involving temples, priests, mythological beliefs, and a ritual calendar regulates when the different canals are opened and closed, and thus when each of the fields receives water. The religious system not only controls the allocation of water and other agricultural activities, but also organizes the collective work for maintenance of the dams, canals, and supportive infrastructure.

A Balinese temple overlooks a lake. (William Waterfall/PacificStock.com)

Water use is coordinated over many square miles and by thousands of farmers on the basis of communities of people who live in an area fed by a branch of the irrigation system. These people share a temple at the branch of the irrigation system, and activities at that temple play a fundamental role in coordinating water use and resolving problems. At each level of the diversion of water, smaller temples serve to coordinate water use. In the local temples, different Gods with different requirements dictate how the water will be allocated. Meetings held in these ritual centers also coordinate the burning of fields to eliminate rodents and to set the dates for planting and use of water. The effective control of plant diseases, insects, and rodents requires a coordination of flooding and burning efforts on adjacent fields.

After World War II, outside aid workers persuaded the Balinese to abandon the water temple system and follow modern "scientific" ideas about how and when water should be distributed so that rice crops could be grown more frequently. The new schedule interfered with the natural cycle of plant growth and pest control and was soon abandoned in favor of a return to the traditional system. The Balinese temple religion provides powerful injunctions to ensure conformity with the established irrigation system and its rules, which provide a fair distribution of the water resources. The mythology dictates that the water and rice terraces belong to a sacred ruler associated with the Goddess of Water. Those who do not follow the rules will be cursed and their crops will fail. Sound scientific reasoning and social justice are incorporated in the rituals and beliefs, producing a kind of a secular utility of religion and pragmatic and well-adapted ecological and economic systems. In the Balinese water temple system, rituals integrate practical needs within a metaphysical system, providing a shared framework for the allocation of valuable water resources.

Marx predicted that this inequality would eventually lead to class warfare and that the proletariat—the workers who actually controlled the means of production—would rise up and overthrow the capitalist class. Society would then enter a transitional phase on its way to becoming a communist society in which social classes and private property would no longer exist, and humans would live in harmony and abundance. Many intellectuals, disturbed by the enormous inequities they saw in certain societies—especially Imperial Russia and China—took inspiration from Marx's ideas about the evolution of society from capitalism to communism and attempted to apply them to usher in dramatic social transformations of their societies. But because these societies had not reached the capitalist stage, the new, so-called "communist" societies they created were not able to realize Marx's vision that the workers would come to control the means of production. Instead, the leadership of the capitalist elite classes and foreigners was replaced by the leadership of the state and the elite communist party. Because of Marx's view that religion had helped to maintain a "false consciousness," the successes of the Communist revolutions led to the repression of numerous religious systems as the new leaders eradicated religious leaders and communities. They took special aim at the indigenous societies that still existed within their borders. As concepts of communism gained ideological control over the political and economic structures of these countries, communism came to control life so completely that some critics contended that communism itself had become a religion.

Thus, for Marx, religion was a product of material conditions. Religion is a tool used by those who control the material resources to reinforce their privileged social positions. Because religion can be used to justify oppression, Marx argued that the masses needed to be educated about how these false and arbitrary beliefs were being used against them. Religion was used directly to enforce acceptance of the system by demanding obedience to authority, prohibiting violence, and encouraging its followers to accept the status quo. For the communist revolution to be successful, Marx argued that the influence of religion on socialization needed to be overcome. The ordinary person suffers under the control exercised by religion as a tool of mystification, oppression, inducement of guilt, and exploitation. This use of religion to produce a "false consciousness" led Marx to famously describe religion as the "opiate of the masses." This view emphasized the ability of religion to confuse and delude, offering a fantasy world of future rewards that distracted people's attention from the actual circumstances of their lives.

Central to Marx's ideas was his claim that the material conditions of life, especially the control and distribution of economic resources and the means of production, impact all other aspects of life, including social and political systems and ideology—religion. Marx held an ideological view of religion, a perspective which held that religious beliefs could control what people thought and did. Although his ideas were expressed many decades before the work of Durkheim, in some ways they anticipated Durkheim's view of religion as a system for organizing social behavior. Marx's contributions lay in pointing out how different sectors of society use religious ideology as a resource, particularly in class conflict.

The Social Origins of God-Concepts and Sacred Morality

Durkheim was concerned with the social origins of religion in the practical needs of society. Although he did not think that a belief in supernatural beings was essential to the nature of religion, he did feel that a socially defined notion of the sacred was. To Durkheim, religion always involves a domain of special concerns conceptualized as sacred and distinguished from ordinary or profane concerns; an absolute distinction that defined a fundamental division in the Universe. The sacred refers to an ideal and transcendental realm distinct and apart from the material world. These two realms must be kept completely separate, and if they are not, contamination or death may result. Social rules tell people how they should relate to and honor the realm of the sacred. For Durkheim, this sacred domain is both characteristic of and constant in religious thought. It is embodied not only in myths and other beliefs, but also in symbols, relics, gestures, and even objects in the natural environment. The domain of the sacred is not constant from culture to culture, but is defined by culture, and it exhibits similarities across cultures in its concern with the interests and well-being of large groups of people.

In a totemic system, sacred qualities are ascribed not only to the species that is designated as the totem, but also to the clan that is associated with the totem and to the symbolic depiction that represents both the animal species and the social group. The source of the sacred qualities ascribed to these three aspects of totemism is not the species, objects, or groups themselves, but a common underlying principle manifested in impersonal forces. The beliefs expressed by religions are about social relations and dynamics—in essence—

society. In other words, the concept of the divine originates in society itself.

A totemic group exercises control over the individuals that comprise the group, dominating both individual and collective existence. When the group congregates to worship its totem, individuals may have profound experiences of a powerful external power (not unlike the communal spirit that may cause you to do the "wave" at a sporting event or to chant with the other attendees at a political rally). The sense of personal identity is both enhanced and transformed, particularly through the ritual participation and the masks and other adornments worn by the participants. By consuming the normally prohibited totem animal, the individual experiences the physical and spiritual incorporation of the sacred. This reinforces the individual's identity with the clan, with the sacred, and with the deity. The affirmation of collective identity produced by these rituals reinforces a person's sense that he or she has a special relationship with the divine and with society.

Totemism as a Source of Deity Concepts

One universal social experience for humans that helps to create our personal identity is our sense that we are part of a social group. In totemism, this social reference of personal identity is embodied in the clan and totem, essences that survive the death of any individual. As a result, social groups have continuity across time and are independent of the deaths of any of their members. Deity concepts are derived from these basic conceptions of totemism. Deities exhibit the same qualities that people associate with their clans, including their superior status and their immortality. Durkheim considered the belief in an immortal soul to be a natural consequence of totemism. Just as the totemic clan survives generation after generation, even as the individual members of the clan dies, the totem (as clan emblem) is also eternal. For Durkheim, the development of concepts of more powerful spirits, as well as souls, derived from this initial basis in the totemic principle and its immortal ancestral soul. The clan membership of each individual is also the source of that individual's sense of his or her own personal soul, a result of the incorporation and internalization of the clan identity within the individual.

The "Birth of the Gods" in Sovereign Groups

An important effort to confirm Durkheim's notion that "religion is the worship of society" was carried out by Guy Swanson in his 1960 book *The Birth of the Gods*. Using Durkheim's ideas as his starting point, Swanson hypothesized that people's concepts of the supernatural are derived from their experiences of living in a society. He carried out cross-cultural studies to demonstrate that different ideas about the supernatural are products of a particular type of society. The social experiences that produce supernatural concepts were attributed to specific groups that persist across generations and have a distinctive purpose, that of "sovereignty."

Sovereignty is the legitimate power to make decisions for a group. Societies differ in what they recognize as the sovereign group, from individuals or families through clans, chiefdoms, and a variety of regional and state-level organizations. Swanson proposed that these organizations of people provide a sense of purpose and create the structures of human life that people come to perceive as the supernatural. Consequently, each society's conception of the most significant spirits would be expected to reflect the principles of the sovereign groups that hold the supreme power in that society. In essence, supernatural beliefs are a reflection of social conditions and relations.

Swanson's cross-cultural study of the relationships between supernatural conceptions and the nature of sovereign groups has been criticized on a number of grounds and some of his initial findings have been called into question by more sophisticated cross-cultural studies (see Davis 1971, Peregrine 1996, Stark 2001). Nonetheless, some aspects of his research have been confirmed, with the general principles he identified also found in these other studies.

Band-level foraging societies generally have an egalitarian political organization. These societies have no permanent political leaders, and individuals have the right to go along with the group or go their own way. In essence, there is no sovereign group. In such societies, the principal form of deity is not a God who corresponds to the whole group, but a guardian spirit who is different for each individual. Just as each individual is sovereign in political life, the supernatural domain is conceived as containing an individual spirit for each person.

In societies with clan-level organizations, a typical form of religious practice is ancestor worship, often in the form of totemism. In these societies, the political system of the group is organized by the clan, a system in which the hierarchy of kinship relations provides the political structure of society. The head of the clan is regarded as both the supreme political authority and the principal mediator between the clan and the ancestor spirits. The clan leader holds his power by virtue of his relationship to the ancestor spirits, and he, too, will one day become an ancestor. In essence, when society is led by the elders of a kinship group (clan), the principal deities of that society mirror the political organization in the ancestor spirits that are worshipped. Swanson's research found such a relationship between kinship organization and ancestor worship. The belief that ancestral spirits actively intervene in human affairs is significantly related to the presence of sovereign kinship groups in society.

Another of Swanson's hypotheses was that monotheism, the belief in a single supreme supernatural being (High God), is found in societies in which there is a political hierarchy of at least three levels. Swanson found that High Gods are far more likely to be found in such societies and that they seldom occur in societies that lack a political hierarchy. In some societies (monarchies), the king or supreme leader is explicitly identified with the deity. The divine king is the embodiment of the power of God on Earth and is viewed as a living divinity.

Swanson contrasted monotheism with polytheism, in which society recognizes a number of important Gods, each specialized in a different area. A society might have a Goddess of agriculture, a God of war, a God of the seas, and so forth, all with their own power in their own areas of expertise. Polytheistic societies, according to Swanson, are associated with a variety of occupational specializations in which different adults do different jobs. He found that the great number of communal and noncommunal specialties is associated with a greater number of superior Gods. "As in heaven, so, too, on earth," or, as Durkheim might have stated it, "as in society, so, too, in heaven."

Many subsequent studies have followed Swanson's pioneering work in investigating the relationships between supernatural concepts and social systems. Peregrine (1996) found that the presence of a High God is correlated with increasing levels of sovereign social organization. But he was unable to replicate Swanson's hypotheses about a number of other relationships (e.g., hypotheses regarding polytheistic Gods, ancestral spirits, the immanence of the soul, witchcraft, and morality). However, Peregrine did obtain results that he interpreted as supportive of Swanson's overall theory regarding the origins of religious beliefs. He found that a number of religious variables are related to the nature of settlements and the ultimate sovereign kinship organizations. Large communities that have towns and cities tend to believe in High Gods, whereas smaller settlements such as villages and hamlets tend to believe in ancestor spirits. Peregrine suggests that when social relations are personal, the supernatural is believed to involve personal relations with ancestral spirits, whereas if social relations are impersonal, as in large communities, the supernatural is also conceptualized as impersonal.

This fifteenth-century painting by Jan van Eyck shows Jesus enthroned as the Divine King. The robes and insignia of office that he wears are similar to those worn by European kings of the time. (Jan van Eyck, "God," panel from the Ghent Altarpiece, c. 1432. St. Bavo's, Ghent. Scala/Art Resource, NY.)

Ancestor Worship: Kin as Gods. Steadman, Palmer, and Tilley (1996) argue that the origins of religion lie in ancestor worship. In many cultures, one's deceased ancestors are viewed as the most important spiritual beings. Collective and private rituals may frequently be carried out in order to honor these ancestors, who are thought to be able to affect the living directly and to influence the weather and other spiritual forces that affect the well-being of the living. Although they claim that ancestor worship practices are universal, they have taken a much looser definition than most studies. They suggest that any relationship to one's deceased ancestors or to the souls, spirits, and ghosts of the deceased constitutes ancestor worship.

With this very broad concept, Steadman, Palmer, and Tilley reviewed cross-cultural studies that came to the conclusion that ancestor worship is present in most but not all societies. They then examined those "missing" cases in which ancestor worship appeared to be absent, and searched for additional evidence that indicates a concern with the deceased, and, hence, ancestor worship. They found that all societies posit a relationship between the living and the dead, reflecting the importance of kinship relations in society. The important role of ancestors in religious beliefs is a reflection of their central role in the maintenance of a society and its cultural traditions. They point out that religious rituals that focus on ancestors provide mechanisms for strengthening kinship ties. A "family cult" provides rituals of intensification that help to maintain family bonds. The belief that the ancestors can continue to affect the lives of their living descendants provides mechanisms for strengthening the transmission of cultural traditions. The kinship traditions invoked by ancestor worship help to link together the many different descendants who claim a common ancestry, but may lack direct or recognizable kinship ties in their everyday lives. The linkages to ancestors provide a context within which their descendants can be compelled to accept common traditions of authority derived from the expectations expressed in life by their now-deceased kin. Those expectations are expressed in social norms that reinforce social solidarity, consensus, and conformity as living religious leaders communicate with the deceased ancestors and convey their expectations to their descendants.

We find evidence of the importance of kinship-like relations in religion in many cultures, including ones that do not explicitly worship ancestors. In addition, world religions evoke these kinship-related bonds, manifested in the widespread use of kinship terminology (e.g., "God the Father," "brothers and sisters") in religious discourse. This extension of kinship terminology to nonrelated others provides a significant adaptation for human communities, extending the kin-based altruistic tendencies to a broader group.

Gods and Morality

Durkheim's basic hypothesis—that religious rituals serve to maintain the social order—has been generally accepted by social scientists. Since the publication of Tylor's *Primitive Culture* (1871), however, evidence has been found that suggests that in many premodern societies religion is not linked to a moral system. Tylor points out that the animistic rituals of simple societies show little concern with ethical issues. It is not that morality is absent from these cultures, but rather that the ritual activities are not the source of morality and ethics. Durkheim's belief that the majority of religions dictated morality reflected his cultural background and biases and his selective use of case studies. In actuality,

systematic cross-cultural research indicates that religious rituals in general do not sustain a moral order. Swanson found that the presence of Gods who are concerned with morality and impose supernatural sanctions is a feature of complex societies, as indicated in correlations with such social conditions as the presence of personal debt, a system of social stratification (social classes), ownership of private property, and primogeniture (in which only the eldest son inherits).

Stark (2001) has also used cross-cultural analyses to assess Durkheim's hypothesis that the general function of religion is to sustain the moral order. Less than one quarter of the societies in a cross-cultural sample (*Atlas of World Cultures*) reported a belief in "High Gods," confirming Tylor's contention that religious ritual and morality are not linked in most premodern societies. A variety of measures of cultural complexity correlate with the presence of "moral gods," indicating that religious morality is primarily a characteristic of more complex societies.

Stark's research illustrates that it is particular conceptions of God that underlie the power of religions to sustain a moral order, those in which God is conceptualized as a conscious, active, and morally concerned being. Religious conceptions do not impact morality when God is conceptualized as being an unconscious essence or as having only a small scope of action. Religion appears to influence the moral behavior and commitment of individuals only in societies in which the dominant religious organizations have a conception of God that demands adherence to moral imperatives. Conceptions of the supernatural are irrelevant to morality unless God is conceptualized as a conscious, morally concerned being who is informed about humans, concerned about their situations, and willing to act on their behalf in imposing morality. In order for the Gods to enforce a moral system, they must have standards favoring good over evil and diverse powers that allow them to sustain moral precepts, derived from their power to exert the force of their rule over the entire Universe. The linkage of morality with participation in religious rituals is limited to more complex societies with these specific kinds of Gods. It is not the participation in collective religious rituals that sustains a commitment to a moral order, but rather particular kinds of ideas regarding God.

Roes and Raymond (2003) confirmed Stark's findings in their cross-cultural analyses showing that larger societies are more likely to have beliefs in "moralizing Gods" who establish rules for human conduct. In larger societies, the potential for conflict among members is obviously greater. Rules that regulate

Box 9.3 MORALITY INSPIRED BY ANCESTOR SPIRITS

Cross-cultural studies of the effects of social organization on supernatural beliefs have emphasized the notion that the High Gods are concerned with morality. Indeed, such relationships have been found in the research we have been considering. But are High Gods necessary for morality, or might other kinds of spirits also exert a moral influence?

In his analysis of a ghost cult among an East African people called the Nyoro, Beattie (1964) shows that other kinds of spirits may also be concerned with morality. Among the Nyoro, socially acceptable behavior is reinforced by beliefs regarding the roles of ghosts. A person who is mistreated in life has the power to return as a ghost and afflict those who injured him or her. This belief that ghosts have the power to take revenge on those who do them wrong plays a significant role in reinforcing social ideals about behavior toward other members of the society. When a person falls ill or suffers some other misfortune, the event is often attributed to the spirit of someone who has died. Ghosts may cause afflictions in a variety of ways. For example, a ghost can express its displeasure with the living by possessing a person. When a ghost is identified as the cause of a malady, it is typically the ghost of a person whom the patient—or one of the patient's family members—offended while the person was alive. That is, the victim of the illness may not be the transgressor; instead, a relative of the victim may be the transgressor, and the victim's weakness makes him or her susceptible to being entered by the possessing ghost. Children are especially vulnerable to the influences of ghosts, which makes them liable for the transgressions of their parents.

Beattie characterizes this belief in ghosts as a powerful set of social sanctions that encourages people to conform to accepted social norms. The power of these ghosts, however, is not tied to some ancestral cult and its existing social power among the descendants. Rather, social control and morality is exercised through the belief that the ghost can cause the living to become ill. While an illness-causing ghost may be ritually destroyed, another way of ending its destructive influence is to enter into a relationship with it by offering sacrifices. These ritual sacrifices provide relief from the stress and anxiety associated with the earlier misconduct and provide a visible social statement about the sanctions that may be imposed for socially unacceptable behavior. The sacrifices to the ghost remind the living members of the community that the people they torment can exact revenge on their tormentors when they die and also become ghosts. Consequently, if a person fails to maintain good relationships with neighbors, or if he or she is cruel or neglectful or fails to adhere to socially approved forms of behavior, then punishment may befall that person or the members of his or her family. In this sense, the ghost cults play an important role in healing rituals, and the ghosts serve as a traditional source of moral authority. Interestingly, among the Nyoro, the moral powers held by ghosts are not just derived from the members of one's own family clan and community, but may also be exercised by outsiders whose ghosts are thought to be particularly powerful and dangerous. Hence, the Nyoro believe that ghosts can exercise moral control within the group and also in relationships with outsiders.

behavior are more likely to be accepted if people believe that the rules were imposed by an external agent with no personal (material or reproductive) interests in the outcomes of the rules. Moral systems provide such rules, limiting the infringement of members on one another. This helps prevent the group from splitting apart and gives it advantages in the competition with other groups. Moralizing Gods are especially likely to be present when a caste system is also present, supporting a Marxist explanation of the role of religion as a mechanism for class/caste oppression. Moralizing Gods provide rules for regulating the behavior among diverse groups of people within a society and are particularly important when different groups (classes) have different interests (see Box 9.3: Morality Inspired by Ancestor Spirits).

Morality as an Evolved Capacity

Evolutionary theory can help explain moral behaviors, for morality provides the self-control that individuals use to resist animal urges and to conform to the expectations of social norms, legitimate authorities, and concepts of right and wrong. The role of morality—involving respect for authority—builds on older patterns of dominance and submission in social species. The behavior of subordinates to dominant animals is an action that weaker animals use to avoid being injured, allowing them to survive and reproduce. Deference behaviors are particularly adaptive in social species with strong dominance hierarchies. Behaviors of deference are clearly rooted in the dependency experiences of mammals with respect to their caregivers and contribute not only to the significant role of dominance and social status, but also to the dynamics of charismatic leadership and hero worship found cross-culturally.

Morality brings something more to the dynamic. Krebs (2005, 2008) places the evolution of moral values in the context of cooperation, specifically, mutualism and reciprocity. **Mutualism** is a system in which individual members of a species and group act in ways that are mutually beneficial, for instance, cooperating to protect themselves from predators. Throughout evolutionary history, there have been strong selective pressures for cooperation as well as awareness of identification with one's group. Some of the significant ways in which hominan evolution diverged from our hominin relatives include the creation of larger structural coalitions, particularly high degrees of male coalitional behavior to organize aggressive acts between groups. Because the power of groups and coalitions increases with their size, humans have been subjected to selective pressures to cooperate in increasingly large groups. Factors inducing individuals to cooperate involve a variety of forms of reciprocity, including direct and immediate payback, as well as delayed payback and indirect payback through intermediaries or third parties. These forms of indirect reciprocity appear to be a predominantly, if not exclusively, human characteristic.

Religion as Extensions of Ritualized Functions of Enhancing Cooperation

The roles of religion as adaptations must be assessed in terms of how well they facilitate the long-term survival of individuals and groups. Richard Sosis (2006) maintains that ecological conditions which selected for religious behaviors were the challenges of collective living. Religion has provided solutions to cooperative living that have their roots in the role of ritualized behaviors in maintaining cooperation and reducing conflict in animal society. These ancient phylogenetic origins of religion and ritual have been expanded as humans have acquired other needs and capacities as the members of larger and more complex social groups.

While evolutionary biology emphasizes the adaptive advantages provided by innate characteristics and dispositions of individuals, individuals live in a group context in which powerful collective forces can also affect an individual's reproductive success. These collective forces select for individuals who are capable of becoming well integrated into a collectivity, channeling individual development into collectively shared patterns and dispositions. Participation in religious groups enhances this social dynamic, contributing to individual survival and reproduction through adaptive advantages from being helped by other humans.

The patterns of cooperation among humans initially posed challenges to evolutionary theory: what benefit is obtained by self-sacrifices for others? The cooperation manifested in religion is part of broader altruistic behaviors involved in helping others. While it may appear that an individual is making a sacrifice for the benefit of others, the individual may nonetheless personally benefit from helping others. For example, performing an altruistic act for relatives can improve one's **inclusive fitness,** for an individual's kin share many of his or her own genes. Helping others incurs some reproductive costs, potentially decreasing the resources remaining for one's own offspring or increasing one's own risk of death, but the behaviors may nonetheless benefit one's own offspring. Helping others may also result in the receipt of support from others in the long run, a concept referred to as **reciprocal altruism.**

Reciprocal altruism provides a kind of opposite to the power of hierarchy and dominance, emphasizing that the actor is fair, even generous, and deserving of reciprocity. The evolutionary advantages of appearing to place other people's interests ahead of our own is a kind of self-promotion as a moral individual, but also a deceptive signal in that it implies that our behaviors are not in our self-interest. The modern view of the evolutionary advantages of deception involves the concept of "beneffectance," in which people attempt to make it look as though they are behaving in beneficial ways toward others and are being effective in the assistance they provide. Wright (1994) proposes that this beneffectance combines the advantages of reciprocal altruism and status from one's position in the dominance hierarchy.

Religion as "Family Values"

Many animals, including humans, exhibit altruism, the tendency to behave in a selfless (and sometimes dangerous) manner for the benefit of relatives and even nonrelatives. Many religions make use of altruism by inducing their followers to treat the other members of the religious community as if they were kin and by basing religious traditions on acts of altruism. The central premise of the Christian tradition is that Jesus allowed himself to be sacrificed for the salvation of all humanity. In some Buddhist traditions, *bodhisattvas* take vows to continue to be reborn even after they have attained enlightenment so that they may help other sentient beings to attain liberation as well.

Our proclivity not only to recognize, but also to give preferential treatment to, our own relatives is a product of the mammalian attachment system, our hard-wired tendency to emotionally bond with our offspring. Because the offspring of individuals who cared for and protected their offspring have a greater likelihood of surviving long enough to produce offspring of their own, the genetic basis for their abilities to care for others was passed down to future generations. The obvious selective advantages of good parental care have resulted in a "kinship psychology" that has also shown itself to be useful for religious purposes (Kirkpatrick 2005).

Once there is a basis for altruism within a population, additional selective forces will favor it. Behavioral mechanisms that increase such reciprocity include **kin-recognition mechanisms,** which involve both a disposition to identify kin and a behavioral tendency to engage in actions that favor those kin (Wright 1994). Kin-recognition mechanisms are expanded to include unfamiliar kin, as well as nonkin, as kin altruism biases are extended to other individuals by virtue of their identification as members of one's religion. In both human and nonhuman social groups, individuals that are related tend to act differently toward one another than they do toward nonrelatives. Nonhuman primates spend more time grooming relatives than nonrelatives, are more likely to share resources with relatives, and come to the aid of relatives more frequently.

The religious use of ideas and values about kinship is seen in the ways that members of religious communities address one another. Religious leaders, who are often referred to as "father" or "mother," may in turn address the other members of their community as "brothers," "sisters," or "children." Many cultural groups also conceptualize their deities in familial terms, such as "God the Father" or "Mother Earth." By tapping into the hard-wired brain mechanisms that induce us to trust our kin and give them preferential treatment, religion uses kinship language to help us expand our network of interpersonal relationships. Therefore, religion has been characterized as a "hypertrophied kin recognition process" (Kirkpatrick 2005) in which mechanisms that evolved to encourage adaptive behavior toward kin were subsequently expanded to create **fictive kinship** relationships within religious communities. Its use in forming communities allows religious identities to function as an adaptation meeting old and new needs through new mechanisms.

Although Kirkpatrick believes that our kinship psychology was exapted for this purpose, it is also possible to view "spiritual supreme fathers" as co-opted adaptations that expanded the application of humans' adaptive innate notions about the benefits given to kin. By expanding the group of people with whom they were able to identify—so that people could feel a sense of kinship with the deity and the community—humans were able to form even larger groups that were able to organize labor, exploit the environment, and compete more effectively with other groups.

Kirkpatrick shows that religions make use of our innate psychological mechanisms for showing preference to our kin to induce us to treat unrelated members of our group as if they were kin. This exaptation of kinship preferences enabled religions to motivate people to behave in ways that promote the overall welfare of a group. However, since no individual can possibly know all of the members of a large group, members need to be identified through symbols indicating group membership. This ability of religion to induce us to see and treat nonrelatives as if they were relatives is one of its most important functions, for it enables us to overcome our tendency to be altruistic only with those kin we know and recognize. In both human and nonhuman groups, it takes time and effort for unfamiliar outsiders to be accepted into the group. Eventually, the human use of kin terms to expand our notions of "family" was augmented by the use of garments, body ornamentation, and other insignia that provided a visual marker of identity that could be recognized even if a person's face or term of reference could not. It is likely that the articles of adornment—such as beads and other articles of jewelry—that begin to appear in the archaeological record almost 100,000 years ago functioned as identity markers that indicated a person's membership in a particular group. The same has been suggested as an explanation of the fifty-seven tattoos found on the still-preserved skin of "Oetzi," the famous iceman whose 5300-year-old frozen body was discovered in a glacial crevice near the border of Italy and Austria.

Religion as an Adaptive Social Mechanism

At the heart of Durkheim's functionalist perspective lies a fundamental insight: Religion is adaptive. David Sloan Wilson (2002) points out that both the functionalist and holistic perspectives imply that religions help not only *individuals* to adapt, but also *groups.* He suggests that three proximate mechanisms contribute to functionality in human life: unconscious psychological processes, unconscious group-level processes, and the processes of cultural evolution. All of these mechanisms can help to make religious belief systems adaptive. Evolutionary psychology has shown that our unconscious information processing systems—our mental hardware—play a significant role in organizing both individual and collective life. Numerous studies of social animals have demonstrated the existence of what has been called a "group mind," which enables social groups to be organized by unconscious processes. And within anthropology, cultural evolution has long been regarded as a consequence of cultural adaptations. Together, these three processes all contribute to latent functions that help groups to adapt.

The need to adaptively coordinate human behavior led to the emergence of specific social institutions that could function to resolve conflicts. These institutions became necessary as human societies increased their numbers, making the face-to-face interactions characteristic of foraging groups impossible. Wilson views the conflict-reduction mechanisms that evolved to deal with this increased social complexity as religious, for their power is derived from concepts of the sacred.

Wilson (2002) contends that the presence of a moral system for determining what kinds of phenotypic variation are allowed to exist within a group exerted influences on the genetic variation within the group. "By its very nature, morality shifts the balance between levels of selection in favor of group selection. In larger groups, which must become differentiated to function adaptively, the spirit of communitas serves as a kind of moral anchor" (p. 224). Group-level adaptations derive from our individual psychological mechanisms responding to what is adaptive for effective functioning in groups. This makes people feel that their needs are being met, no matter what position they hold in society. This ancient evolved psychology, however, is based on adaptations to human societies that probably numbered only about fifty or so individuals. Larger-sized human societies required mechanisms to integrate people at a level beyond the face-to-face bonding. Religion was the key institution that provided for this expanded identity, beginning with ancestor worship and continuing with moral Gods.

Religion as a Group Selection Mechanism

The concept of **group selection** is based on the premise that groups that are better adjusted internally and to their environments have an advantage when competing with other groups. As a result, selection favors groups that can work together more effectively as they compete with other groups. But the behaviors that promote group survival are nevertheless selected at the

level of the individual characteristics. These characteristics are a consequence of a selective process in which traits that may be disadvantageous to the individual (e.g., self-sacrifice) may contribute to the survival of other individuals, and thus to the group as a whole.

Religion is a powerful force for group selection. By offering people concepts like God and an afterlife, religions can motivate their members to engage in behaviors that may be disadvantageous for individual biological survival (e.g., dying in a holy war in defense of one's faith), but which can contribute to the overall success of their group. In essence, the supernatural conceptions of well-being in which a person believes (e.g., eternal paradise) can play a greater role in shaping behavior than issues related to the individual's own biological survival.

The behaviors that religion exapt, such as kin altruism and reciprocal altruism among members of a group, are selected for, not at the group level, but at the level of the individuals who live in the groups. Behaviors that provide evidence of a person's commitment toward his or her group also may be selected for at the level of the individual because the other members of the group will punish people who fail to exhibit behaviors that indicate commitment. Human emotions such as shame and guilt can motivate individuals to cooperate in achieving group well-being, suggesting that such mechanisms are involved in group selection processes (see Box 9.4: The Adaptive Benefits of Public Displays).

Group selection processes also help explain other unusual features of religion, namely, the commitment to what nonmembers consider to be irrational beliefs. Several anthropologists (Irons 2001, Sosis 2004) link the rationality of cooperating within a group with the irrational beliefs in supernatural entities that are part of a religious commitment. These "irrational" commitments are a mechanism for creating group trust and commitment. Trust between individuals is enhanced when they abandon their logical self-interest and make a commitment to a shared irrational belief. Sharing irrational beliefs signals trustworthiness and a willingness to cooperate with others. In this view, supernatural religious beliefs are a mechanism that provides for public displays of this commitment to group beliefs and needs, analogous to costly signaling behaviors in the animal world. Both "irrational" commitments, and the cost that religious groups often demand in terms of adherence to arbitrary beliefs and practices, reduce the impact of free riders, making it difficult for them to remain within the group when they are not committed to the group's beliefs or needs.

Wilson (2002) characterizes the adaptive nature of religion as a "unifying system." Religion is a special

Box 9.4 THE ADAPTIVE BENEFITS OF PUBLIC DISPLAYS

Religious rituals can be painfully costly activities. For instance, some religious initiations induce extreme pain in initiates, who are expected to endure their torture. Why do people invest so much in ritual activities that appear to have high personal costs? The concept of rituals as "costly signaling mechanisms" helps to explain these behaviors in both humans and other animals as forms of reciprocal altruism.

Sosis (2006) views religious rituals as costly signaling mechanisms, forms of communication that enhance an individual's own inclusive fitness by making public statements of commitment. By regarding religious behavior as communication, we can more clearly see its continuities with ritualized animal behaviors. Thus, human ritual communication may not be communication with deities as much as it is communication with other members of society that enhance social integration. Sosis analyzes ritual communication in terms of behaviors, badges, and bans—all features of religious devotion that can provide more compelling evidence of commitment than language alone. The behavioral ritual acts are signals that make the meaning of their messages intuitively clear by demonstration. The "badges" are evidence of religious participation (e.g., tattoos), and the bans—the taboos or prohibitions imposed on participants—make public commitments to moral orders, signaling a person's membership in a community and commitment to its rules. Arduous religious activities are "hard-to-fake" signs of commitment to the community and the beliefs that they endorse. Extreme risks and pain communicate commitment to the group, a willingness to sacrifice personal comfort for the collective well-being. Religion engages mechanisms that promote large-scale cooperation and establish onerous ordeals and restrictions that exhibit that commitment. These demanding ritual activities help to counter the problem of "free riders" who greedily benefit from others' cooperative behaviors.

William Irons (2001, 2005), a behavioral ecologist, addresses how religion provides a mechanism through which human groups can attain large-scale cooperation in ways that help prevent the individual "free rider" who benefits without contributing. How do humans achieve beneficial group cooperation when it is in each individual's interest to pursue individual benefits rather than cooperating? Sosis elaborates on Irons's perspectives, suggesting that we can understand religious behavior as signaling a form of dishonest communication—termed *dishonest* because it may be used to communicate something contrary to fact (e.g., greater strength, quickness, or fitness than perhaps the individual actually possesses). Signals are particularly valuable when they are difficult to fake. These "dishonest" signals, referred to as handicaps, are used by a variety of species, particularly when it is possible to send false signals by using behaviors that indicate a higher quality or capability than is the case. When deception can provide rewards, natural selection can favor it. Religious behaviors can signal commitments that exemplify one's willingness to sacrifice for the group, and reciprocally elicit support from other group members. Thus, behaviors, badges, and bans are arbitrary symbolic signals that morally oblige members of a community to provide assistance to one another.

case of a unifying system, and a particularly significant one for human societies. The ancient Latin root meaning of "religion" (*religio* means "to unite or bind together") emphasizes this role in producing an integrated and unified community. By examining some of the ways in which religions help to unite groups of individuals, we can see that the adaptive aspects of religious systems parallel the adaptive aspects of other animals' ritualized behaviors.

Judaic Adaptations: Group Exclusion Mechanisms. The group adaptation perspective helps to explain why a religious group may use one set of moral norms when dealing with people within the group and a different set when dealing with outside groups. This "double standard" has played a significant role in enhancing

the fitness of Jewish communities living in societies in which they were a minority and were subjected to persecution. Religious beliefs and practices have contributed to their cultural isolation and given Jewish communities advantages over other groups.

For example, Jewish marriage patterns and other cultural mechanisms have served to biologically isolate the Jewish community from other groups. This isolation has been well documented in studies of the genetic profiles of the Jewish populations around the world. Because they make no attempts to convert outsiders to their religion, the community of believers has remained genetically closed. The moral rules that regulate the interactions between members of the group have created a powerful set of in-group obligations, which has resulted in exceptionally cooperative communities whose cohesion is an advantage when they interact with other groups. Wilson illustrates how this unified community was more effective than other groups in regulating both internal and external social relations, creating cooperation in within-group interactions that enhance Jewish competition with other groups.

Christian Adaptations: Group Inclusion Mechanisms. Group adaptation also can be enhanced by mechanisms that open up a community to outsiders. The early Christian communities provide a stark contrast to the boundary-maintaining mechanisms characteristic of Judaism. The openness of these Christian groups allowed them to survive and expand during the early Christian era. Anyone may convert to Christianity. This open recruitment system has proven particularly attractive to marginalized people, including women without power, who were able to become full members of the community. Christianity not only welcomed women as members of the church, but also provided a social context in which Christian women were more likely to reproduce and have more children. In addition, Christianity offered a moral ethos that enhanced the survival of the community because members were encouraged to take care of one another. For example, Christians were encouraged to provide food, water, and other assistance to sick people, practices that contrasted starkly with the general Roman practice of abandoning such individuals. This care of the "other" produced a Christian society that mimicked a welfare state in a social context in which there was no safety net for the impoverished, the poor, or the abandoned. These in-group dynamics enhanced the survival of Christians and helped the Christian population to grow faster than that of other groups. The secular utility of Christian values coordinated the members of this group in ways that enabled them to thrive when other, less coordinated groups could not (see Box 9.5: The Protestant Ethic and the Spirit of Capitalism).

Religion's Effects on Survival

Religious systems can contribute to the overall survival of a group in a number of ways. Religions may be adaptive in facilitating the various tasks and needs of a group and in enhancing a group's ability to compete with other groups (recall the water temple system found on the island of Bali; see Box 9.2). To understand the role of religion in adaptation, we must consider both proximate mechanisms—genetic mechanisms involving variation in psychological and behavioral processes—and ultimate mechanisms—the ecological features that select adaptive features.

Sosis proposes that the challenges of collective action were the ecological conditions that selected for religious behaviors. Religious behaviors and badges facilitate group integration by allowing individuals to be identified as adherents to the group. The proximate mechanisms are concerned with the psychological factors that motivate adaptive behaviors. Proximate mechanisms include cultural capacities, acquiring cultural norms and habits, as well as the socialization of emotions and other psychological processes that are involved in coordinating members of a group to enhance their group adaptation.

Wilson (2002) points out that deity relationships provide proximate mechanisms for the group adaptive effects of religion. Deity concepts provide representations of positive, protective, and helpful entities that are consistent with secure attachments to a caregiver. Through the generalization of attachment dynamics, the supernatural representations provide to group members the recognized benefits of secure attachments and coordinated group behaviors. One of the mechanisms of religion used for this coordination involves the models of the Gods and their desires for human behavior. The emotionally charged relationships of humans with these dominant beings provide a mechanism for enhancing intragroup cooperation. Ritual relationships with a deity bring members of the group together, as we saw in the phenomenon of totemism. This enhanced within-group cooperation provides a process for cultural group selection. The extension of the attachment system dynamics affords additional bases for intragroup cooperation. This neurologically enhanced capability increased across human evolution, as illustrated by the new genes acquired by hominids, discussed in Chapter 5. Human evolution expanded the opioid-mediated bonding of the mammalian attachment system to enhance cooperation in larger groups through religious rituals. Rituals also provoked the release of opioids during experiences of pain or fear, providing mechanisms for selection for those with a greater potential for these healing and integrative biochemicals.

Religious beliefs, even if false or irrational, may still be adaptive if they orient human communities toward common purposes that help assure survival and reproduction. Religions may have a secular utility in spite of their logical inconsistency or factual inaccuracies. The power of a religious system comes from its ability to motivate behaviors. Among the advantages provided by religiosity are the abilities to imagine different conditions far better than those of the present and to project the means for creating new cultural structures that meet human needs.

Box 9.5 THE PROTESTANT ETHIC AND THE SPIRIT OF CAPITALISM

In his classic work *The Protestant Ethic and the Spirit of Capitalism* (1958), Max Weber examined the ways in which religious beliefs and practices can enhance or inhibit the economic development of a group and affect its ability to compete with other groups. Weber, a sociologist, asked why the Protestants, and especially the Puritans—but not Catholics or Jews—had played such a central role in the Industrial Revolution and the global spread of capitalism.

He noted that the long history of Catholic and Jewish economic interactions had led to established roles for each. Generally speaking, the rules of Catholicism were not conducive to creating a capitalist economy. For example, Catholics were taught that it was immoral for a person to charge interest on money that he or she loaned to *anyone*. Jews had a similar religious rule that applied to money loaned to other Jews, but not to outsiders. Because many activities required loans, Jews came to control this economic activity. Other economic practices—including brokering, financing state economies, conducting wholesale activities, and managing the commodity business—were also traditional forms of Jewish commerce. Because Catholics were not allowed to conduct such business, Jews had an effective monopoly on these essential economic practices. The tensions this created between the two groups led Catholics to mount frequent attacks on Jews, sometimes killing hundreds of Jews at a time.

Although these practices contributed greatly to Jewish prosperity, they were not the kinds of legal and economic processes necessary for the rise of modern capitalism. Because of the many prejudices against them and their need to relocate quickly if the local Catholic populace began to target them for attack, Jewish merchants had long preferred to keep their economic resources in "liquid" assets that were easy to move (such as gold and currency) rather than permanent structures such as factories.

In contrast to the long-standing roles of both Catholics and Jews, the emerging Protestant groups did not have an established economic position within European society. Puritan religious groups were able to take over different types of economic activities, both out of need and as a consequence of the types of organizations that the English created to colonize America. These economic organizations, known as joint stock companies, were the precursors of the modern corporation. These colonial companies gave all full members of the colony stock in the corporations and the right to vote on issues affecting the colony. Because many of the colonies were settled by breakaway religious groups, members of these religious communities had opportunities in the colonies that were unavailable to their brethren who remained in Europe.

The Puritan merchant classes that financed the colonies benefited from the economic system they helped to create. The poor of England were recruited to America as "indentured servants." In return for their passage to the colonies, they were required to work for one of the colonial companies for a period of seven years. After completing their service, they were given an allocation of land and became fully fledged members of the colonial company and the society. These practices provided a foundation for democracy in the colonies, in which ownership in the corporation became the basis for voting rights in society.

Thus, for the Puritans, business and other economic activities were not viewed as morally repugnant, but as their very salvation. The rationality with which the Puritans controlled their own sinful impulses to ensure their just rewards in the next life was generalized into the view that all activities in this life—including work and business—were part of God's plan. From this rationalistic perspective, a person's economic success—as measured by material well-being and belongings—provided evidence of that person's moral worth and was a sign of God's grace.

Catholicism was also capable of producing economic wealth. The colonial system that the Jesuit religious order established in the Spanish New World proved to be enormously profitable. The Spanish mission system organized and exploited the labor of their Indian converts to produce agricultural goods, other raw materials, jewelry, and a wide variety of manufactured goods. The colonial missions of the Jesuits were so extensive and powerful that they occupied most of the agricultural lands in New Spain (modern Mexico) by the middle of the eighteenth century.

Wilson emphasizes the importance of distinguishing between a "factual realism" concerned with a literal correspondence to the conditions of the real world, and a "practical realism" that is concerned with behavioral adaptedness. This distinction allows us to view religious beliefs in terms of how they contribute to the healthy functioning of cultural communities and their individual human members. Factual knowledge is not sufficient to motivate adaptive behavior. For instance, cigarette smokers know that smoking may harm them, but their knowledge does not stop them from smoking. Wilson points out that symbolic belief systems are far more powerful in motivating adaptive behavior (see John Calvin and the Salvation of Geneva).

Summary: The Adaptive Social Features of Religion

There are a number of ways that religions help to organize small-scale societies into larger groups. These adaptive features are based on such preadaptations as seen in the reptilian dominance and submission relations and mammalian attachment system. But they are used in novel ways, thus indicating that they are new functional adaptations, an exaptation or a co-opted adaptation. The ritualized community behaviors of primates attained a new level of integration in humans, for whom the spirit world provides a common identity, morals, and goals. These new levels of adaptation provide distinct functional advantages, employing symbols of group membership to expand our kin inclusion mechanisms to a broader group of people. Belief in spirits has given us bigger, better, more integrated groups with enhanced human survival and reproduction.

Moral deterrents are derived from concepts of impartial Gods who have the power to exert their rule over the entire Universe. These principles are not derived from the experience of being mothered. This suggests that God concepts involve more than the mammalian attachment mechanisms. Rather, High Gods represent social forces that exceed the dynamics of those mammalian attachment dynamics. High God concepts deflect perceptions of self-interested motivations in leaders' statements about morality, presenting them as the will of a higher power. This motivates conformance to general standards of behavior and reduces conflict in society. The ability of a religion to successfully integrate a particular group can offer that group a competitive advantage over other groups. But this adaptive feature of religion has its limits, for the same principles that foster cooperation among the members of one group can create conflict between members of different groups.

JOHN CALVIN AND THE SALVATION OF GENEVA

Born in France, John Calvin (1509–64) was forced to leave his homeland during the upheavals of the Protestant Reformation and the Catholic Church's response, the Counter-Reformation. Calvin was disillusioned with some aspects of the Catholic Church, but he did not become a reformer until he was asked to offer testimony in a discussion as to whether Lausanne, a traditionally Catholic city, should remain with the Church or join the growing reform movement. His comments earned him respect within the reform movement and eventually led to his being invited to settle in Geneva and help unify the competing groups within the city so that it could better withstand the pressures of neighboring Catholic groups.

Calvin began by writing a catechism, a book of religious tenets that everyone in the city was expected to learn. These tenets emphasized the need to live in accordance with God's law. Obedience became a prime virtue, whether it was to one's parents, the local authorities, the pastors, or God. Calvin reiterated the importance of adhering to the Ten Commandments and emphasized that every person—no matter what his or her occupation was—was important to the overall community. He also argued that every affliction is a part of God's plan and that, even though these afflictions might make no sense to us, faith demands that we accept them as part of this plan. Thus, even a poor and abusive leader must be obeyed until that leader can be replaced through lawful means. To ensure that everyone understood what this meant, Calvin also stated what was expected of a leader, the signs of a poor or abusive leader, and the process through which a leader could be replaced.

To achieve a stable society, it was important for individuals to submit their own wills to God's will and to allow Him to guide their every act and thought. Conformity became a virtue. There were several ways to deal with deviants, depending on the severity of their actions. All were designed to help deviants change their hearts and their behavior, after which they were welcomed back into the community of the faithful.

Calvin's catechism and the other steps he took to ensure the uniformity of thought and behavior did not meet with universal acceptance. The leaders of Geneva continued to reprimand miscreants—and mete out more serious punishments than Calvin advised—throughout Calvin's lifetime and thereafter. But his measures did succeed where they were most needed, for they united a city of some 13,000 people into a political unit that was able to resist outsiders and retain its autonomy.

Conclusions: Durkheim's Legacy in Understanding Religion as a Social and Symbolic Phenomenon

The interaction between religion and politics has its deep origins in the functional roles of ritualized behaviors in integrating hierarchies in animal societies. The common origins of society and religion have been a repeated theme, reflected in totemism, morality, and control of the social order. These relationships have spawned new views of religion that suggest that mechanisms are involved that provide for societal-level adaptations and that it is a functional system for uniting groups into moral communities with common goals, models, and beliefs. Recent models of group selection have expanded evolutionary assessments to consider more complex multilevel selection processes that include the roles of religion in intergroup competition.

Thus, although many of Durkheim's ideas have been criticized, they have long-term value. The validity of Durkheim's functional approach to religion, however, and its role in organizing cultural systems is challenged by the dysfunctional aspects of religion and its ability to produce conflicts. Yet the idea that religion is a powerful form of social and psychological organization for society remains a central tenet of the anthropology of religion.

Durkheim has left an enduring legacy for generations of anthropologists who have investigated the ways in which society helps to define the structure of religion and the ways in which religions reflect the organizational principles of their societies. This symbolic understanding of the bases of religion provided new ways of thinking about the important role that religion plays as a system for organizing social life. Religion is a significant force, and in some cases is the most powerful system for socialization, the process by which people acquire their cultural beliefs and practices. The focus of Durkheim and the anthropologists who followed him (such as Radcliffe-Brown and Evans-Pritchard) emphasized the manners in which religion served collective needs through their powerful effects on individuals, motivating them to meet group needs.

The biocultural perspective recognizes that both the group and the individual perspectives are important for understanding religion. Religions create groups, and use rituals to help people to feel that they are part of these groups. The process of religious socialization helps to ensure adherence to the standards of the group, and the symbols and other markers of one religion help to distinguish that group from all "other" groups.

The environments human groups live in today are very different from the environment of evolutionary adaptedness. We live in a global society that requires that we not only maintain the integrity of the groups we belong to, but also cooperate with other groups that are very different from our own. The adaptiveness of religion in maintaining in-group cohesion in contrast with outsiders now confronts us with the problem of the "excluded other," the demonized members that do not belong to our religious group. These ancient mechanisms for group coherence have also set us at odds with our neighbors, not only distant others, but those within our midst. The irony today is not just that religions put us in conflict with other religions, but that religious groups splinter and kill among themselves (as illustrated in the Sunni–Shiite conflicts around the world). What was once God's community is now a community of dissent. Defining something as "evil" is one of the most important means that religions use to ensure conformity within the group and to distinguish one's own group from other groups. It is to this concept that we now turn.

Questions for Discussion

- Humans often use animals as totems or symbols of their groups. Which animals do you think are most frequently used? Why?

- How does the pantheon of supernatural beings about which you learned as you grew up resemble the hierarchy of leaders in the society in which you grew up? How do they differ?

- What are the smallest and most narrowly defined religious groups with which you are the most familiar? What are the most broadly defined religious groups you know?

Glossary

calendrical rites rituals that take place regularly and in accordance with specific cycles of nature (solar, lunar, or others)

chiefdom a type of political system in which positions of leadership are passed down within specific lineages

ecclesiastical referring to a formal religious organization that prescribes the training necessary to become a full-time religious practitioner and that ensures the conformity of the religious tradition

egalitarian a society in which all of the members are essentially equal

feud a low-level form of warfare between two kinship groups that can persist for years

fictive kinship a social relationship in which genetically unrelated individuals treat one another as if they were related

group selection the idea that natural selection can operate at the level of the group by favoring traits that increase one group's fitness at other groups' expense

inclusive fitness a measure of the reproductive success of an individual which takes into consideration that individual's relatives, who share many of his or her genes

kin-recognition mechanisms behaviors that serve to identify relatives and to benefit those relatives

mutualism cooperative behaviors that help the members of a group

priest a full-time religious specialist, found in societies with social stratification

reciprocal altruism an altruistic behavior performed under the expectation that, in the future, the individuals who benefit from this behavior may repay the favor

social fact any idea, emotion, behavior, or object that is shared by more than one person in a society and that therefore creates ties between those people

social stratification the presence of different social levels, each with a differing degree of access to resources, power, and prestige

totem the symbol of a clan, usually an animal

transegalitarian a hunter–gatherer society in which some members are able to control resource surpluses and conduct rituals that show their superior social status

Supernatural Evil

CHAPTER OUTLINE

Introduction: Supernatural Evil as a Religious Universal
Anthropological Views of Sorcery and Witchcraft
The Sorcerer/Witch as a Social Universal of Religion
Witchcraft and Heresy in Europe
Human Sacrifice
Conclusions: The Limits of Religious Adaptations?

CHAPTER OBJECTIVES

- Illustrate the universal preoccupation with the negative use of supernatural power.
- Introduce anthropological perspectives on witchcraft and sorcery and present information on the relations of different forms of supernatural evil to social conditions.
- Illustrate mechanisms through which sorcery can kill through the effects on the general adaptation syndrome and the autonomic nervous system.
- Examine the deep roots of supernatural evil in the practices of shamanism.
- Present witchcraft trials in Europe as a process of social persecution of the marginalized classes.
- Examine the Salem witch trials as social phenomena that may have been partially motivated by the effects of hallucinogenic substances in food.
- Examine the phenomena of human sacrifice as a use of religious beliefs to reinforce the in-group versus out-group distinction.

IT WAS FIVE IN THE MORNING, AND THE SOLDIERS were gathering the prisoners together. The priests inspected the prisoners' garments to make sure that they were all wearing the cap and tunic appropriate to their crimes. When they were satisfied, they gave the prisoners each an unlit candle. Now they could begin the march to the city square.

A white cross made of wood was carried at the head of the procession, followed by the priests, then the condemned. Because it was important to remind the people that no one could escape the judgment of the Church, the procession included effigies of the people who had

managed to escape the city as well as the coffins of those who had died before they could be judged.

When they reached the square, the prisoners were led to a large platform overlooking the crowd. Across the square was another platform full of dignitaries and clergy. One of them began to speak, calling on the prisoners to repent their sins. The prisoners were then brought forward and their sentences were read aloud. Those who had committed lesser crimes were taken away to prison, or to be whipped. Those who had been condemned to death were led to a different spot, where piles of wood had been stacked around posts. As a sign of mercy, repentant heretics were strangled before they were burned; the unrepentant were burned alive. Some days there were so many prisoners to be burned that the Spanish sky was illuminated throughout the night.

Introduction: Supernatural Evil as a Religious Universal

Why do religions deem some people to be evil and kill, sacrifice, or otherwise abuse them? Are witch hunts, which are assumed to be a consequence of religion, good or bad for the group? Do witch hunts eliminate evil or give further advantage to the powerful?

Notions of witchcraft and other forms of supernatural evil powers may seem quaint or primitive to modern people, yet they remain an integral aspect of the way that people around the world interpret misfortunes. The universality of notions about evil supernatural powers suggests that they have played an essential role in explanations of the misfortunes in our lives. Our hard-wired tendencies to personalize causality and attribute responsibility for harm to others are embodied in beliefs about evil supernatural powers.

Concerns about supernatural evil, caused by humans or spirits, are found in all cultures. All cultures' indigenous psychologies include concepts about illnesses attributed to spirit entities and to humans who use supernatural power for evil ends. This universal tendency to attribute our misfortunes to malevolent humans and spirits reveals something about our innate attributional tendencies to blame "others" for our personal misfortunes. These "others" can be individuals, groups, or even nonliving objects. The belief that evil humans and spirits can utilize their supernatural powers to cause misfortune extends this common behavior into the spirit world. Evil—or sometimes just "upset"—supernatural entities are often invoked to explain hurricanes, earthquakes, and other disasters; misfortunes such as a bad relationship or failure in a certain endeavor; illness; and death.

People have long debated whether sorcery and witchcraft are real. In many ways, they are, for considerable evidence shows that such practices do exist and can indeed have their intended consequences of illness and death. Religious beliefs and practices are able to evoke and shape our emotions in profound ways, but these effects are not always benign or curative. Supernatural evil involves physical mechanisms, as well as psychological and social factors, that can lead to disease and death.

The universal beliefs in human and spiritual supernatural evil vary from culture to culture. In some cultures, the very same shamans and healers who help some people are also suspected of harming others. In other cultures, persons who do supernatural evil have no redeeming value whatsoever and may even be put to death. Concepts of supernatural evil can take on many forms, from the unseen witch who causes disease and death to the old, defenseless widow who is stoned to death in the streets of a village. This chapter explores concepts of supernatural evil to illustrate the roles that notions about evil can play in societies. We will see that what an outsider might consider evil may, from the perspective of an insider, be a protective or sacred act, or a victim's just punishment for their sins. We will see that the witches of the Inquisition, like the Wiccans of today, have little to do with the negative stereotypes often attributed to them. We will also see that many contemporary ideas about witchcraft are rooted in ancient social notions that were used to justify the persecution and eradication of shamanism. As priests and state religious systems expanded their domains of control and incorporated local communities, they often persecuted the local shamanistic healers and other religious practitioners.

Many lines of evidence show the relationship of shamanism to European sorcery and witchcraft. Cross-cultural research, historical analyses, and linguistic data all indicate that the shamanic practices of the past were eventually redefined as what the newly dominant Christian worldview called "witchcraft." This transformation was a consequence of the expansion of state-level political organizations, which used accusations of witchcraft as a tool to eradicate shamanistic practices from local communities and eliminate local-level political leaders. The "witchcraft" persecutions of local shamanistic healers by leaders of complex societies with priestly religions were so successful that the earlier practices often survive only in historical and linguistic evidence. This historical evidence includes references to flying witches and warlocks, the continued beliefs that certain plants and other substances can induce "demonic" visions, and the many place names that evoke themes from witchcraft ("Goat Mountain," "Devil's Leap"). The linguistic root of the term *witch* (*weik*) reveals many communal and shamanic referents, testifying to the ancient origins of these practices.

Anthropological Views of Sorcery and Witchcraft

Two classic ethnographic accounts of the practices of sorcery and witchcraft from different parts of the world demonstrate how anthropologists have long regarded those practices. Perhaps *the* classic anthropological discussion of witchcraft that distinguishes it from sorcery is by E. E. Evans-Pritchard, who conducted fieldwork among the Zande, an African pastoralist and tribal society, between 1926 and 1930. Another influential field study was carried out in the 1920s by the British anthropologist Reo Fortune (1903–1979), who studied the Dobu, a horticultural people who live on Dobu Island, one of the D'Entrecasteaux Islands that lie off the eastern coast of New Guinea.

Witchcraft and Sorcery Among the Zande

Evans-Pritchard (1937) reported that the Zande believed that witchcraft was the result of an inherited psychic power contained in the belly that could unconsciously and unintentionally cause illness or death as a result of jealousy and envy. Thus, "witchcraft" was inadvertent. Witches were thought to transform themselves into animals while they slept and then fly about with other witches and animals, eating the body organs and souls of their victims. In contrast, "sorcery" was believed to involve the deliberate ritual use of magical techniques to harm others through spells, poisons, and medicines.

Evans-Pritchard found that Zande witchcraft was a function of many factors. It was related to personal misfortunes and strained social relations, and was also a form of moral judgment regarding others' behavior. Witchcraft also provided a general explanation for misfortune. To the Zande, every misfortune was a consequence of witchcraft, even if there was a natural cause as well; they believed that the ill will of the witch caused the misfortunes to happen to a particular victim. For instance, the Zande would acknowledge that a granary had collapsed and crushed a person because termites had weakened the granary's supporting structure. But they would then ask, "Why that person?" "Why was that person under the granary when it collapsed?" Their answer would be that witchcraft had brought the person into the unfortunate situation.

To the Zande, witchcraft was a normal part of everyday life. Every member of the group expected that he or she would eventually suffer a bewitchment, so they often took steps to protect themselves. The Zande believed that witches lived among them in their villages and caused harm. People feared witches because they were thought to act out of anger, hatred, envy, or jealousy. Consequently, accusations of witchcraft arose primarily out of social conflicts, and when people felt that they were suffering from an attack by a witch, they would search for the culprit among their competitors, rivals, and enemies.

The Zande believed that power emanated from a witch because that person was feeling certain emotions toward the victim. The effects of the feelings traveled through social ties; witchcraft did not work between unrelated people. Feelings of hostility, grudges, jealousy, and spite were socially unacceptable behaviors thought to produce witchcraft. These negative emotions embittered people's hearts, causing them to focus their hostilities against those who had done them wrong.

The Zande expectation that people should behave in an appropriate, good-tempered, generous, and courteous manner was directly tied to their ideas about witchcraft. People who behaved inappropriately by violating expected social norms—particularly the norms that govern relations among friends and neighbors—were most frequently accused of being witches. The kind of person typically suspected of witchcraft was spiteful, ill-tempered, glum, greedy, offensive, or vulgar. Thus, even persons whose only offense was bad manners or poor hygiene were open to accusations of witchcraft.

The Zande also believed that a person might be born a witch, but that the witchcraft substance could remain inactive within that person's body. In such cases, a person could be a witch but do no harm to others, particularly if the person fulfilled the duties expected of a good citizen, neighbor, and family member. Suspected witches could be significant and powerful people in Zande culture, but they were not often formally accused. The Zande did not often ask their oracles whether important persons were causing their suffering. Rather, they were more likely to consider the weak—who were not in a position to retaliate—to be witches. Evans-Pritchard recounted the case of a man named Tupoi who was widely considered to be a witch and who used this reputation to intimidate others and extract certain benefits from them. People were often hesitant to offend or reject reputed witches out of fear that the witches might later attack them. Evans-Pritchard noted that the witchcraft beliefs provided a corrective to people's uncharitable tendencies, restraining meanness and hostility because the consequence might be resentment from a witch who could cause illness or death.

Witchcraft and Sorcery Among the Dobu

The Dobu distinguished sorcerers from witches on the basis of gender. All females were witches, and all males were sorcerers. Thus, all adult members of Dobu society had some type of supernatural power that they could utilize to affect others. This power affected many aspects of Dobu life and contributed to the widespread fear, mistrust, jealousy, and suspicion that people exhibited toward everyone who was not a member of their own matrilineal kin group, known as a *suso* (which means "mother's milk").

Reo Fortune (1963) was struck by the fear and lack of trust that the Dobu exhibited toward those who did not belong to their *suso*. Because they come from a different lineage, even a person's spouse was regarded with suspicion. Poisoning of food and drink was common, and sharing food, drink, or even cigarettes was a sign of great trust. In the Dobu worldview, the concept of "accidents" was unknown. All misfortunes, including illness or injury, were considered the result of sorcery or witchcraft. Only persons who died at an extremely advanced age were considered to have died "naturally"; all others were the victims of either sorcery or witchcraft.

In the Dobu worldview, males (sorcerers) possessed magical formulas (spells) that they could use to cause or cure illness, gain success in trade or gardening, and seduce women. These magical formulas had been given to the first Dobu by the *kasa sona*, the supernatural beings who were born at the same time as the sun and the moon, and who used these formulas to control the weather, affect health, and cause plants and animals to flourish. The *kasa sona* passed some formulas on to humans whom they liked—formulas that were important sources of wealth and success and were generally not shared with others. Men often bragged of the formulas they owned and of the illnesses and misfortunes they were able to cause. But they never shared them until it was time to teach them to the next generation. Even brothers would not share their formulas, and men were expected to pass them on to their sisters' sons and not their own children (who were members of a different *suso*).

The Dobu believed that a formula needed to be recited exactly as it had been received from the *kasa sona*, for the effectiveness of a particular formula depended on how precisely it was recited. But this was becoming increasingly difficult to achieve as the time between the *kasa sona* and the living Dobu increased. Success or failure in endeavors could be attributed to the relative accuracy of a man's knowledge of a formula, and even slight variations could reduce the formula's effectiveness. When a man wanted to use a magical formula, he would go to a place where he was certain that no one could overhear him. Once there, he would recite the formula, often after drinking seawater or chewing a large amount of ginger, both of which were thought to amplify the formula's effectiveness. If a sorcerer wished to cause harm to a person or seduce a woman, it was important for

him to have some object that had once been in contact with that person, such as some remnants of food, an article of clothing, or even a leaf that the person had stepped on. (Recall the discussion of the laws of similarity and contagion in Chapter 7.)

The Dobu men could practice sorcery only by day, and their sorcery activities always left some type of physical evidence. In contrast, the female witches worked at night, in their sleep. Whereas the men openly claimed to own certain types of magic, the women kept silent about their abilities. Because they performed magic while they were sleeping, they left no trace of their activities.

The Dobu beliefs in sorcery and witchcraft provided a means for explaining illnesses and other misfortunes. If a person was afflicted with a certain disease (such as malaria), the blame might be placed on a certain man who was believed (and had perhaps claimed) to own the formula for that disease. Others could demand that he remove the ailment. But if he would not or could not do so, then the victim's relatives might petition others who were also known to own the formula for the disease. If none could be found, then they would suspect that a woman—a witch—was causing the illness. But in contrast to accusations of sorcery, which placed the blame on a specific individual, witchcraft accusations were general and usually did not single one woman out for blame.

The Dobu system of sorcery and witchcraft provided a means to deal with social tensions, and it also discouraged people from causing envy or jealousy. Because one person's success in an endeavor (such as harvesting yams or seducing people) was regarded as another person's failure, most people were careful not to brag too much about their successes or to violate social norms—unless, that is, they felt their magic was so strong that they need not fear anyone else's.

Can a Hex Kill? The Biological Bases of "Voodoo Death"

Underlying the various etic explanations of sorcery and witchcraft—such as controlling social conflicts or providing explanations of certain events—is the assumption that humans cannot actually inflict or become the victims of a supernatural spell because such supernatural powers do not exist. For more than a century, however, evidence has been accumulating that both positive and negative magic can have powerful effects on people's well-being. Because these beliefs can affect our emotions, the symbolic manipulations of witchcraft can affect biological mechanisms and produce death.

Although many regard the idea that a hex can actually kill a person to be mere superstition, it is a fact that has long been recognized in anthropology and medicine. In the course of analyzing reports of hexing, the physician Walter Cannon (1942) developed a model of the psychophysiological mechanisms that can lead to death. His article, entitled "Voodoo Death," first appeared in *American Anthropologist* in 1942. The accuracy of Cannon's predictions was underscored six decades later, when the *American Journal of Public Health* reprinted the article, praising Cannon's astute perception of the mechanisms of voodoo death long before these were directly confirmed by laboratory studies.

Our current knowledge of the brain indicates that these effects are elicited by fear responses that shape the wiring of nerve cells for even more powerful future responses. Hormonal responses activated by the brain's fear centers can trigger detrimental chemical reactions in the brain producing cardiac arrhythmias and cardiovascular collapse. Our emotions link all these physiological responses, and, as we have seen repeatedly throughout this text, our emotions can be greatly affected by our cultural beliefs.

Cultures throughout the world believe that voodoo, hexes, and sorcery can result in the death of an intended victim. Cannon pointed out that the medical reports about these deaths, written by competent observers (including physicians), often noted that a person had died with no other explanation than their emotional responses to their cultural beliefs. Cannon explained the mechanisms of voodoo death by pointing out the effects that the extreme emotions of fear and terror can have on the autonomic nervous system. These emotional reactions lead to physiological changes that can disrupt the balance between the sympathetic and parasympathetic systems by causing hyperactivation of the sympathetic nervous system. The victim's belief in the efficacy of voodoo can result in extreme emotional excitation, triggering the fight or flight response and persistent sympathetic activity. The sustained production of adrenaline and other hormones can exhaust the body's resources (also see the discussion of the general adaptation syndrome in Chapter 6) and cause a drop in blood pressure similar to that produced by shock. Stimulation of the sympathetic nervous system constricts the blood vessels supplying the vital organs, thereby reducing circulation. These physical insults to the victim's body may be compounded if the victim's friends and relatives turn their backs on him or her. Since the people who are the victims of hexing have normally committed some type of social transgression, their relatives often accept and even support the hexing of the victim. As a result, the victim's relatives may reinforce his or her despair and withdrawal from society, and they may also withhold food, water, and care. These physical deprivations exacerbate the shock to the nervous system, further contributing to the victim's death unless action is taken to reverse these physiological responses.

Since Cannon first proposed this mechanism of voodoo death, other factors have been proposed that can contribute to the process. Among these is the "giving-up" response, a resignation to death that hastens the collapse to parasympathetic dominance. The family of the victim might begin mourning rituals while the person was still alive, reinforcing his or her giving-up response. Lester (1972) suggested that voodoo death was part of a "giving-up–given-up" complex in which both the individual and the social group come to accept the individual's inevitable demise.

Laboratory studies suggest that severe trauma can lead to a sense of hopelessness in animals, causing them to succumb rapidly to physical challenges (e.g., drowning) rather than continuing to struggle. This giving-up syndrome may also affect the ways that some humans respond to the deaths of significant others, explaining why a great increase in mortality occurs following the loss of a spouse. Humans experience this giving-up complex as feelings of hopelessness, worthlessness, and helplessness, and as a lack of meaningful interpersonal relationships and personal gratification. The condition can also lead to a diminished desire to resist disease and increase a person's susceptibility to disease. The giving-up model suggests that an additional mechanism distinct from Cannon's view may also be involved in voodoo death. In addition to experiencing the overstimulation of the sympathetic nervous system, people who die from voodoo experience the subsequent phase of the general adaptation syndrome: the excessive parasympathetic responses and a shutting down of the autonomic nervous system.

Garrity (1974) introduced yet another mechanism of voodoo death, involving acceptance. Here, individuals accept their impending death with peace and calmness, rather than with fear. Evidence of this model comes from studies that show mortality rates increase following certain important days (birthdays or holidays), suggesting that people have some degree of personal control over the timing of their deaths. Garrity proposed that the underlying mechanisms may reflect a biofeedback model in which a will to die can result in the modification and termination of vital functions.

The various aspects of voodoo death illustrate how social factors, such as the withdrawal of support and the acceptance of the victim's demise, also play a significant role. Symbolic processes and meaning are central to the three mechanisms for voodoo death that Garrity posits: the elicitation of physiological responses; the effects of depression, apathy, and withdrawal; and the acceptance response. Ethnographic accounts of the ability of healers to remove a hex and prevent death indicate that cultural mechanisms can also reverse the psychophysiological responses.

Symbolic Effects on the Nervous System: Stress and Nocebo Phenomena

The idea that religious beliefs can affect our well-being is not an illusion, but a psychophysiological fact. The ability of religious symbols to affect our physiological functioning is one of the most important adaptive functions of religion we discussed in Chapter 6 in relation to the stress responses. Stress is a consequence of how people perceive a situation and respond. Beliefs about evil supernatural beings and humans evoke profound fear, and consequently physiological responses to perceived threats to one's well-being. These responses can debilitate or kill through the stress that results from the perceived inadequacy of the individual's coping resources.

The Physiological Response to Stress: The General Adaptation Syndrome. Our body's general reaction to all stressors is known as the **general adaptation syndrome**. First discovered by the German physiologist Hans Selye (1936), this "fight or flight" response consists of three stages of physiological response to stress:

- stress or alarm reaction of the body,
- resistance to the threat with a new adaptation at an increased level of pituitary/adrenal activity, and
- exhaustion from resource depletion, leading to disease or death.

The physiological responses to stress begin with increased sympathetic activity. This general arousal of the sympathetic nervous system is basic to all emotions and induces a series of physiological responses that prepare an organism for action (fight or flight). However, prolonged activation exhausts the resources of the body and makes it more susceptible to disease. This excessive sympathetic activity contributes to pathological conditions by provoking increased cardiovascular function and disrupting the overall balance between the sympathetic and the parasympathetic systems. Prolonged sympathetic hyperactivity can damage organs and lead to cardiac failure and death. The general adaptation syndrome causes the pituitary-adrenal cortex to secrete hormones and stimulate the release of epinephrine and norepinephrine. These mobilize fatty acids for use as energy, accelerate cardiac activity, and raise blood pressure and corticosteroid levels. The release of adrenocorticotropic hormone (ACTH) and stimulation of cortisol has negative effects on the immune system, increasing susceptibility to infection and contributing to depression and anxiety. Sustained stress results in the exhaustion of neurotransmitter resources and wears down pituitary and adrenal defenses and other aspects of the endocrine system, leading to a collapse in the weakest aspect of the organism.

Situations that elicit this stress response leave a person's body activated and mobilized. If that person is unable to respond through physical exertion (hence the term *fight or flight*) to the stressful situation, he or she can develop ulcers, hypertension, cardiovascular problems, and migraine headaches. Simply fearing a situation can produce the same physiological responses as the actual situation. Symbolic threats, however, do not involve physical struggle, so the body does not consume the substances released into the bloodstream, which are instead deposited in arteries, causing arteriosclerosis.

Nocebo Effects. Another way in which our mental expectations can affect our health is demonstrated by the **nocebo effect**. The opposite of the placebo effect, the nocebo effect can induce sickness and death by negative expectations. The nocebo has been characterized as a side effect of human culture in which negative emotional expectations produce effects that are responsible for disease (Hahn 1997). There is evidence, for example, that belief in personal susceptibility to cardiac arrest is a risk factor for coronary death even in patients who do not have recognized cardiac symptoms. What are the implications of a fear of death due to sorcery or witchcraft, or as punishment from ancestor ghosts? Can we die from our religious beliefs? Voodoo death and the nocebo effect indicate that we can.

Nocebos are able to cause these effects because they increase the likelihood that a person will fall sick through negative expectations. Negative expectations can come from many sources: personal beliefs, medical diagnoses, sociogenic-induced mass hysteria, or other social influences (Hahn 1997). Cultural conceptions of the world and its condition, particularly ethnomedical categories describing sickness, may induce people to have those kinds of experiences. A disease may also worsen because we expect it to. For example, studies have shown that telling a patient that he or she has been diagnosed with cancer can cause the person to die sooner than if the person were not told about the disease. This may be a manifestation of a general effect of pessimistic attitudes as a risk factor for disease outcomes. Negative perceptions can undermine a person's morale and contribute to an attitude of learned helplessness in which a person believes that future events are out of his or her control, a perception that can undermine the individual's immune system. Spiegel (1997) suggests that studies of hypnotic phenomena indicate that imagination and its effects involve three interactive components: dissociation from ordinary awareness of the world; absorption in internal states and imagery; and suggestibility, a susceptibility to following direction of others. Our ability to construct alternative realities, focus on them, and suspend critical judgment to engage these constructions with our emotions provides mechanisms for placebo and nocebo effects.

Nocebo effects may be activated through a variety of mechanisms. The ways in which a culture classifies illnesses create expectations about what can occur, producing negative social messages that affect the patient's psychological status. These culturally based illness systems provide models that tell a person how to act when they are afflicted with a particular ailment. These cultural "scripts" can be particularly effective when there are other victims of the illness with whom the individual identifies.

But humans are not automatons, and bad news—and hexing—can be countered. The negative messages that elicit nocebo responses can be countered by the presence of supportive group dynamics and the positive message they communicate. Support groups contribute to the ability to resist negative comments, enhancing coping skills, and improving resistance to learned helplessness. The social effects of voodoo death may be reversed by close personal bonds with family or friends and by the assurances elicited by shamanic community rituals.

Supernatural Human Evils and Social Conditions

As the examples of the Zande and Dobu showed, not all societies view witches and sorcerers in the same way. In some cultures, concepts of supernatural evil combine characteristics of both witches and sorcerers, while other cultures emphasize one figure over the other. The human tendency to attribute human or supernatural figures with responsibility for the natural cycles and phenomena of nature and the inevitability of human sickness and death can take a variety of forms. The different concepts and attitudes about sorcery and witchcraft mirror the ways in which societies structure social relations and explain misfortunes.

The images of hell portrayed in the work of Hieronymus Bosch are both imaginative and terrifying. (Hieronymous Bosch, "The Last Judgement," 1504.)

Why do some cultures blame witches for misfortunes and seek them out to kill them, while others believe that disease and accidents are punishments for our disobedience to the rules of God?

The anthropological literature has emphasized the distinction between sorcerers and witches. Although both are malicious persons who are able to damage a person's health and well-being, they differ in important ways. In sorcery, health and well-being are intentionally harmed by the deliberate and aggressive use of magic. In witchcraft, the involuntary actions of special types of humans with innate powers cause harm.

Sorcery and witchcraft thus represent complementary explanations of illness due to human malevolent magic. Whereas sorcery refers to practices that are actually carried out, such practices are likely absent in the case of witchcraft. Although the particulars of sorcery vary from culture to culture, there are a few universal features, including the principles of sympathetic magic, imitation, and the ritual use of items that have been in close contact with the victim. The imitation often involves using objects to simulate the death of the intended victim, jabbing arrows, swords, pointed spines, or other sharp objects in the direction of the victim. In other cases, stones, worms, or other objects are projected into the victim and thought to lodge within their body. One widespread, and perhaps universal idea, is that the sorcerer or witch will send an animal familiar who will carry out their task by frightening or attacking the individual. In traditions where sorcery involves ritual, a frequent practice is **exuvial magic,** the ritual use of substances exuded from the body (such as nail clippings, feces, saliva, or other excretions). These evil rituals normally include verbal incantations or spells that express the desired consequences: "your blood boils, your brain throbs with pain, pus oozes from your wounds." The practitioner utters the verses and performs the ritual with an emotional fury thought to drive the power of the words to the victim.

Sorcery is believed to be an important cause of illness in most societies of the world (Murdock 1980), but others emphasize witchcraft. One type of witchcraft is the "evil eye" (Maloney 1976), the belief that one person can inadvertently cause harm by looking at another's property or person. Evil eye power is frequently thought to emanate from a person's eyes (or mouth) as a result of that person's feelings of envy. Like witchcraft in general, the idea is that a person is able to cause harm without engaging in a ritual. A person's desires and emotions alone are sufficient to cause the harm, and harm may result without the person even intending to cause it.

Cross-cultural studies (Murdock 1980, Winkelman 1992) show that witchcraft and sorcery beliefs tend to be found in different types of societies. Witchcraft is found in more complex societies characterized by political integration and the presence of social classes, as well as patrilineal descent and substantial bride price; they predominate in Africa and the Mediterranean regions. Evil eye beliefs are found in all major cultural regions of the world (Roberts 1976), but they are especially common in the Mediterranean region. They, too, are mostly associated with complex societies.

In contrast, sorcery beliefs are most likely to be found in small-scale preliterate societies without jurisdictional hierarchies, such as those found in aboriginal America and in other small-scale societies around the world. Sorcery serves as an important form of retaliation in societies that lack more formal control mechanisms, such as a government that can produce a system of social control and enforcement (Whiting 1950). In these societies, the threat of accusations of sorcery or witchcraft serve as a regulating mechanism, keeping people from engaging in serious social violations that might incite the anger and supernatural malevolence of others. The presence of frequent social contacts and relations, where there are no authorities to appeal to in case of transgressions, engenders the use of sorcery or the threat of its use as a mechanism for social control. Accusations of sorcery and witchcraft, therefore, can help ensure that people adhere to social norms, and they reinforce the social order because they leave

This hand hanging over the entry to a shop in the Cairo market of Khan el-Khalili helps to protect the shop from the envious gaze of others—the "evil eye."

open the possibility that people who transgress social codes will suffer retaliation.

Although we often think that the persons most likely to be accused of witchcraft occupy "weak" or "outsider" positions in their society, this is not always the case. In some cultures the people who are accused of witchcraft are upwardly mobile individuals who have been acquiring greater resources by participating in new economic activities. Most witchcraft accusations occur in societies in which the worldview is dominated by notions of a "limited good." That is, the available resources are thought to be limited, so that one person's success must always come at another person's cost. In these societies, witchcraft accusations serve as **leveling mechanisms** that keep people from accumulating significantly more resources than the other members of their society and induce those who are successful to share with their less fortunate kin in an effort to avoid any resentment that might lead to witchcraft accusations. Wherever we look at witchcraft, sorcery, and related beliefs, we find that the accusers are normally kin or other individuals who have social contact with the people being accused. These accusations often point to failures in kinship relations, a lack of propriety, and a failure to live up to social expectations (see Box 10.1: How to Make a Zombie).

Functional and Evolutionary Assessments of Beliefs in Supernatural Evil

Most explanations of witchcraft focus on the social and psychological functions fulfilled by suspicions and accusations and their consequences (Stevens 1996). A principal social function of witchcraft is its effect of compelling people to adhere to social norms lest they be

Box 10.1 HOW TO MAKE A ZOMBIE

One of the best-known beliefs about supernatural evil comes from Haiti: the "zombie." A **zombie** is a person whose body and mind are under the control of a sinister supernatural power. To make a zombie, a person known as a *bokor* magically poisons the victim, causing the person to apparently die. After the person's funeral and burial, the *bokor* digs up the person, revives him or her, and then keeps the person in a drugged state to use as a slave.

Although many outsiders believe that zombies are nothing more than a superstition, accounts of real-life zombies have been verified numerous times. Incidents have been reported in which a person long thought dead returns to society after years in captivity as a zombie slave. Wade Davis, an anthropologist who has conducted fieldwork among Haitian secret societies, has obtained other evidence of the reality of these practices (Davis 1988). He found that the deathlike stupor and the state of mental control that characterize a zombie slave are the products of poisoning with a number of toxic compounds.

Laboratory analyses of the ingredients in several samples of the zombie poison that Davis obtained found that the potions prepared by the *bokor* contain very powerful neurotoxins. One key ingredient, tetrodotoxin, comes from the puffer fish (*Fugu* spp.), a Japanese delicacy that is lethal if not prepared properly. The first signs of tetrodotoxin poisoning are a loss of motor control and a paralysis of the body. Blood pressure and body temperature both drop, and nervous system functions decline to the point where there is no longer a discernible pulse and the skin turns bluish from lack of oxygen. In spite of these effects, the victim may remain fully conscious of what is going on around him or her— while paralyzed. Overdoses of tetrodotoxin can cause respiratory failure. Some of the other compounds present in the potion came from a toad (*Bufo marinus*) that secretes neurotoxins as a defense mechanism. These substances have cardiotoxic effects and can induce confusion, psychotic states, and other effects. Clearly, zombie poison contains some very potent chemical compounds.

To test the effects of zombie poison, researchers made samples into a paste that was applied to shaved areas on the backs of laboratory rats. The rats quickly became comatose and unresponsive. Although they appeared to be dead, electronic monitoring devices indicated that the rats still had faint heartbeats and brain waves.

In the zombie tradition of Haiti, when a victim is exhumed, the *bokor* feeds him or her a new plant poison made from *Datura*, known in Haiti as the "zombie's cucumber." This plant contains potent substances (tropane alkaloids) that can cause confusion, hallucinations, and disorientation, making it easy to assert control over and enslave the victim. From time to time, the *bokor* gives the victim additional preparations of the plant to maintain the drugged condition.

Zombie victims are not chosen randomly. They are usually people who have violated a social norm or mistreated a family member. Like many other forms of sorcery, the creation of zombies serves as a form of social control. In this case, the beliefs have a clear and identifiable basis in the ways that the various compounds used by the *bokor* affect biological functioning.

accused of witchcraft, especially for failures regarding generosity and sharing. These social control functions lead people to avoid antisocial behaviors in order to avoid being suspected of witchcraft. Sorcery and witchcraft accusations reflect the dynamics of society in general, and accusations generally reflect the nature of social relationships that involve tension or competition. Such accusations generally increase in periods of stress, providing a profile of these accusations as a reflection of other societal dynamics involving strains. "Witch hunts" may provide cathartic effects for the perpetrators; however, their results can be devastating both for the victims and the society in general. Traditional witchcraft beliefs have given rise to regional witch hunts that have resulted in the deaths of tens of thousands.

The social characteristics and psychodynamic attributes of sorcery and witchcraft reveal that they not only reflect social tensions, frustrations, and anxieties, but that they serve important functions in social control (Marwick 1970; Middleton and Winter 1963; Whiting 1950), providing mechanisms for social enforcement of normative behavior through magical threats. They also have dysfunctional aspects because they disrupt social relations (Finkler 1985).

These findings demonstrate how such beliefs serve to ensure socially acceptable behavior, illustrating one important social function of religion. The use of witchcraft beliefs as a tool for enforcing social conformity illustrates that they are social adaptations whose value comes from their latent functions rather than from the manifest functions of eliminating evil from society. However, as Stevens notes, explanations of witchcraft in terms of their likely social and psychological functions reflect the dynamics that elicit the accusations, but do not reveal the origins of the beliefs. What is the source of their cross-cultural presence and similar—in some cases identical—features? Stevens suggests that while witches in each culture have unique traits, universal characteristics of witches found in cultures around the world include

- nighttime activities, particularly a community ceremony held in nature or in a cemetery;
- association with an animal familiar that carries out activities for the witch;
- the ability to transform into an animal;
- the ability to fly, including separation of the soul from the body;
- social subversion and contravention of human rules and norms, especially illicit sexual activities;

- the ability to cause disease and death; and
- cannibalism and vampirism, both literal as well as imagined consumption of the victim's spirit, soul, and organs, often focusing on the abduction of children.

It is useful to evaluate these beliefs in terms of our mental hardware. Some of the universal attributes of the witch may have adaptive consequences in terms of behavior, while others reflect human fears (Stevens 1996). The perspective of evolutionary psychology suggests that witchcraft beliefs involve exaptations of rational fears, a "standardized nightmare" reflecting deep human fears. Universal fears of the danger of the night reflect our poor adaptation for night-vision, while fear regarding the abduction of our children is an adaptive trait encouraging parents to supervise them closely, especially at night. Cannibalism is also a legitimate fear in some contexts, perhaps reflecting a past in which sacrificial cannibalism was practiced in many societies. Certain beliefs regarding the mechanisms that supernaturally evil humans use to cause disease include the use of exuvia cast off from the victim's body, including feces, old clothing, and hair. Such beliefs motivate a desire among people to hide these objects, normally burying them, which facilitates the control of diseases that are often attributed to witches. The social subversion features of witchcraft play a role in ensuring altruistic and prosocial behaviors, as well as providing a mechanism for eliminating members of the group who do not have such qualities. Control of sexual deviance is a significant feature of all cultures, reflecting the need to maintain stable sexual relations that minimize conflict and aggression over sex. The idea of transformation into animals and magical flight do not appear to have adaptive functions in witchcraft, but, as we have seen in the discussion of shamanism, they are part of the universal shamanic culture.

The Sorcerer/Witch as a Social Universal of Religion

The cross-cultural study of magico-religious practitioners carried out by Winkelman (1992) identified a group of religious practitioners distinct from shamans and priests, which he called the "sorcerer/witch," based on the most frequent labels applied to their translations into English. The sorcerer/witch is a social universal of religion not found in all societies, but only in those in which political power is integrated with several levels of hierarchy beyond the local community. The societies in which sorcerers/witches are found believe that these figures are involved only in malevolent activities, such as causing illness and death or destroying crops and livestock. Unlike shamans, who may heal as well as kill, the sorcerer/witch is devoid of any socially redeeming features. These sorcerers/witches are believed to slowly eat the internal organs of their victims from a distance. They can transform themselves into animals to fly through the spirit worlds to capture and consume the souls of their victims. They are generally thought to engage in the most immoral of activities—cannibalism, incest, eating corpses, and killing kin. A sorcerer/witch can be male or female, although the prevalence varies considerably from one culture to another. The accused—whether or not they are guilty—may be killed for their actual or suspected activities. While some individuals deliberately engage in ritual activities to cause harm, many are thought to act unconsciously, particularly as a consequence of envy, jealousy, anger, greed, or desire for revenge.

The Shamanic Roots of Sorcery and Witchcraft

Although they engage in some sorcery activities, this is not the principal focus of shamanism. Nonetheless, shamanism must be seen as the origins of humans' supernatural evil power since shamans engage in many activities associated with sorcery and witchcraft. Consequently, a study of shamans can help us to understand both the origin of many universals of witchcraft beliefs and the reasons for the demise and disappearance of shamanism in the modern world. While most of the activities of the shaman are very different from those of sorcerers and witches, several lines of evidence indicate that these evil supernatural practitioners have their origins in shamanism. Common features of shamans and sorcerer/witches include being active primarily at night; being able to fly; personally entering and interacting with the spirit world; being able to control spirits, having animal familiars; being able to transform themselves into animals; and being able to cause illness and death by stealing the victim's soul or by projecting objects or malignant spirits into the body of the victim. Significant differences include being found in different kinds of societies; shamans occur in foraging and simple agricultural societies, while sorcerer/witches are found in complex, politically integrated societies.

The Dark Side of Shamanism. The popular image of the shaman as a spiritual healer has led many people to overlook shamans' negative use of power. In cultures around the world, shamans were thought to have

a dual nature: they could specialize in a good path of healing or an evil path of causing harm. But even when shamans choose "good" healing paths, they acquire the basic power and skills used to cause harm to others. For example, when performing a healing ritual, a shaman may return the illness-causing spirits or objects (for example, magical darts) to the person who sent them to the victim. The process by which an illness-causing agent is returned to the person who sent it is the same as that used to originally send it, and can lead to the death of the person who originally sent the illness.

The Jívaro, a horticultural group of the Peruvian and Ecuadorian Amazon that we met in Chapter 7 (see Box 7.1: How Many Souls Do We Have?) provide a good illustration of the dual powers of shamans and the distinction between curing (good) shamans and bewitching (bad) shamans (Harner 1973a). Both types of shamans acquire their power by purchasing "magical darts" from other shamans, who then teach the purchaser how to use them. These magical darts—which work as spirit servants—grow from seeds of saliva that have been regurgitated by the teachers and swallowed by their pupils. Both individuals who are training to cure and those who are learning to bewitch swallow the magical darts given to them by their teachers. The initiates who become bewitching shamans are those who cannot resist the desire to use the darts to bewitch others when the darts later emerge from their mouths. In contrast, those who become healers are able to resist the impulse to use the dart to bewitch, and, instead, reswallow them. Bewitching shamans cause illness and death by projecting the darts into the body of their enemies, while curing shamans cure by using their own darts to form protective shields that capture and incorporate the darts of bewitching shamans. Curing shamans extract the darts of bewitching shamans by regurgitating their own darts that are identical to those that they see within the patient. The healing shamans hold these regurgitated darts in their mouth to capture and incorporate the darts that they suck out of the patient's body.

The evil capacities of the shaman are manifested when the curing shaman returns the extracted dart to the bewitching shaman, potentially killing the bewitching shaman or the client on whose behalf the darts were sent. Consequently, in most shamanic cultures, even a curing shaman may be suspected of also being a bewitching shaman capable of causing death. This integration of evil and healing capacities is also seen in the Zande healers, who were often suspected of being witches or sorcerers. Their ability to detect witches came from a special substance placed within their bodies by their teachers, and they returned sorcery attacks by using the same power that sorcerers used.

Although they might perform sorcery, the general features of shamans are quite different from those of witches. How can they be connected? Shamans and sorcerer/witches are the only types of religious practitioners who have a major involvement in malevolent activities as significant aspects of their professional role. Since shamans existed prior to witches, the figure of the sorcerer/witch must have had its origins in the malevolent functions of shamanism. Some cultures have mechanisms for transforming shamans into witches, as illustrated in cross-cultural research (Winkelman 1992) which indicates that the persecution of shamans as witches is part of the process of political integration that happened in the distant past (see Shamanic Features of European Witches). We will see this in more detail later when we consider the Inquisition and the Salem witch trials.

Linguistic Roots for the Shamanic Origins of Witchcraft

Weik- is an Indo-European root referring to magico-religious practices. The English words "witchcraft," "wizard," and "victim" are all derived from this root. While the word witch is generally used in connection with the negative aspects of the supernatural, its root *weik-* has a range of meanings that are unrelated to the negative stereotypes of witchcraft, but which point to shamanism. This can be seen in five general meanings

that *The American Heritage Dictionary* lists for the Indo-European root *weik-* (Morris 1981, p. 1548):

- "Words connected with magic and religious notions" such as wizard and bewitch, but also divination and sacrificial victims.
- "Clan (social unit above the household) . . . dwelling, house, . . . settler." This meaning bears no relationship to witches, but does reflect the social leadership roles of shamans.
- "To be like . . . likeness, image, icon." These meanings are connected with the shamans' use of enactment and imitation and the fundamental role of imagery in their visions.
- "To bend, wind . . . turn." These meanings are widely associated with the roots of the term shaman in the languages of Asia and are also associated with unseen powers.
- "To conquer." This meaning is unrelated to witchcraft, but does reflect both the shamans' battle with spirits and their hunter/warrior role.

Linguistic roots of the word witch have little association with the evil supernatural power of witches. But the concepts of magic, religion, divination, and imitative magic refer directly to shamanistic activities. The shaman is also a clan leader, and the diverse leadership roles of shamans persist in the roles of prophets in more complex societies.

An accurate appraisal of witchcraft reveals numerous shamanic connections in contemporary society and in antiquity, reflecting the shamanic roots of the Indo-European root *weik-*. These recognitions are core

SHAMANIC FEATURES OF EUROPEAN WITCHES

The shamanic roots of some of the phenomena associated with European witchcraft were pointed out by Michael Harner (1973b), who documented the use of hallucinogenic plants by many who were persecuted as witches by the Inquisition. He suggested that the beliefs about witches flying and transforming into animals were based on the experiential effects of these hallucinogens. Claims about witches flying on brooms may have reflected actual ritual practices. It is known that some people made "flying ointments" from plants that they then smeared onto their mucous membranes using small brushes. Among the plants were several members of the Solanaceae (nightshade) family that contained atropine, scopolamine, and other hallucinogenic substances. These plant compounds, which had been used since antiquity for religious and medicinal purposes, are oil soluble and can be absorbed directly through the skin. In high doses, they can produce sensations of flying and of transforming into an animal, properties that made them useful in many pre-Christian shamanistic and healing practices. Because of the Church's antipathy toward non-Christian practices in general and altered states of consciousness in particular, these practices were demonized, and the lurid descriptions of their use that were publicized fueled the emotions associated with the Great Witch Craze.

to the aspects that have been revived in the contemporary religion of Wicca. The characteristics that are associated with sorcerers and witches originated in shamanistic healers, but were transformed as local communities were forcibly subjugated and integrated into the political and religious structures that are typical of complex societies. As shamanism was repressed and eliminated from public life, some of the ideas surrounding it survived. Both the original characteristics of shamanistic practitioners (e.g., soul flight, capturing souls, animal associations, nighttime activities) and the products of persecution (distortion, negative attributions) were applied to sorcerers/witches. These connections are seen in the Inquisition.

Witchcraft and Heresy in Europe

During the fifteenth through eighteenth centuries, Europe was shifting from a rural and agrarian way of life to one that was more urban and commercial. The resulting changes—as well as other threats to the personal and social order, such as the many waves of the "black death" and other diseases that spread across Europe—were often interpreted in supernatural terms. Many mass social reactions occurred, including some in which people were accused of practicing and committing horrible crimes against their fellow citizens. These accusations focused on the alleged interaction of witches with the devil, particularly their clandestine meetings with this perverse beast in Black Sabbath and demonic rituals in which all kinds of atrocities were allegedly committed. The witches were said to fly on broomsticks, transform themselves into animals, and perform perverse and offensive acts, including the torture and cannibalism of infants; sexual acts with animals, the devil, and with one another; and all forms of **social inversion.**

In the eyes of the Church—and thus the law—worshipping the devil and practicing witchcraft were both heretical and criminal activities. The resources of the church and legal systems of the states were used to persecute alleged witches, who were often tortured until they "confessed," after which many were gruesomely executed for their offenses.

When we consider the history of the European witch hunts, several patterns emerge. Most of the people accused of witchcraft were marginalized women who had little social support and few family, kin, or friends. While many of these women had no husbands or children, they often controlled significant property that they had inherited. Accused witches were often tried in courts of law that allowed the prosecutors to seize the property of persons who were found guilty of witchcraft. Great personal rewards were therefore available to those who were able to successfully prosecute witchcraft charges against individuals who held significant land resources but were politically powerless.

Estimates of the number of witches who were actually killed in the "Great Witch Craze" of early modern Europe vary from conservative figures of as few as 50,000 people to upper-end estimates of half a million or more. Many of the accused had been practicing ancient healing, divination, and fertility rituals, or continuing other "pagan" beliefs rooted in the shamanistic traditions of Europe. The Church had a simple way to assert its claims of doctrinal superiority: it defined the ancient fertility cults, pre-Christian community religious practices, nature and agricultural rituals, and the spiritual and healing practices associated with women's traditions as the work of Satan. These practices and beliefs were also condemned because they stood in the way of the larger struggle for ideological and political supremacy in early modern Europe.

Many of the features of these witch hunts resembled the manners in which other minorities were persecuted in Europe. During the Roman Empire, the early Christians were often accused of ritual cannibalism because of their great emphasis on the sacrifice of Jesus on the cross. The Jews, too, were sometimes accused of conducting cannibalistic rituals. Other minorities within Europe were systematically persecuted by people in positions of political power when it served their purposes. As European leaders adopted Christianity, the rule of law was used to enforce Christianity and its rules on non-Christians, who were referred to as pagans (from the Latin term *paganus*, meaning "villager, rustic," referring to the people of the country who did not adopt Christianity as quickly as the people in urban areas). In this way, non-Christian beliefs were eradicated, ensuring both conformity of belief and the gratitude of the Church.

The early Church was forced to deal with a number of heresies (from the Greek term *hairesis*, meaning "choice"). One of the most significant was the Cathar heresy, which rose in southern France in the early tenth century. Also known as the Albigensian heresy (from the town of Albi, a center of the movement), the followers of this heretical movement believed that the God of the Old Testament was a lesser God (identified with Satan) and disputed the physical incarnation of the God of the New Testament—Jesus. The Cathars believed that the material world was a prison from which the spirit needed to liberate itself. They also believed that the Catholic Church had become beholden to the lesser God (Satan) and to the material world. These doctrines did not sit well with the Roman Catholic Church, but they did attract thousands of followers in southern France.

After several attempts to suppress this heresy, Pope Innocent declared a "crusade" against the Albigensians in 1207. It lasted until 1229. During the two decades of the Albigensian Crusade, tens of thousands of people were killed in military action and in the executions that often took place after the Crusaders had captured a city or town. Hundreds of "unrepentant heretics" were thrown into fires. Persons who repented were sometimes driven from their towns with only the clothes they were wearing, while others were forced to wear a "cross of infamy" that was made of yellow cloth and sewn onto the front and the back of a person's outer garments.

The Church's crusade succeeded in crushing the Albigensian movement, and became a model for eradicating dissent and opposition. As the Church became increasingly intertwined with the different states in Europe and rulers declared their faith in Christianity, religious beliefs and rules were increasingly adopted into political ideologies. The desire for doctrinal conformity provided a standard against which rival groups, deviants, the marginalized, and other minorities within the expanding state systems of Europe could be judged. Witchcraft accusations were a powerful tool for asserting political and religious control over the rural countryside and for eliminating local leaders who were resisting the expansion of both centralized political power and Christian beliefs.

The Inquisition Begins

In February 1231, in an effort to ward off future heretical movements and to consolidate the power of Rome, Pope Gregory IX issued *Excommunicamus*, a document that removed the power for persecuting heresy from the local bishops—who often did not even live in the areas under their charge—and assigned the responsibility to the Dominicans and Franciscans, two monastic orders whose members answered directly to Rome. This document described the procedures for determining heretics and the punishments that were to be used against them. Those found guilty were denied any formal right of appeal to the Pope (although there were informal ways to appeal), effectively making the tribunals of the Inquisition the sole executors of justice.

Each tribunal was headed by two judges known as Inquisitors. The Inquisition courts were originally circuit courts, and the Inquisitors would travel from place to place to hear and try charges of heresy and other crimes against the Church. Later, the Inquisitors were given the power to summon accused persons to a permanent location.

Anyone—even a convicted criminal or heretic—could accuse another person of heresy, witchcraft, or various other offenses. Charges could be brought against anyone on the basis of mere rumor. All that was necessary was that the accuser convince a judge that his or her accusations were valid. The accused persons were required to take an oath to tell the truth, and refusing to do so was taken as an indication of their guilt. They were not provided with any information about the persons who had accused them, many of whom were criminals, persons who had already been excommunicated from the church, and other heretics. The accused were not allowed legal counsel or even clerical assistance, as these persons could be accused of being accomplices. The only tactic that was open to an accused person was to reveal the names of his or her enemies to the Inquisitors. Accused individuals were often interrogated in secret to extract confession. Those who failed to confess were subjected to increasingly painful tortures until confessions were extracted or until the resistant witch died or was formally put to death.

The people who confessed, however, were not always executed as witches, but were often given the opportunity to do penance for their sins and to implicate others. The church might allow for a reconciliation and forgiveness if the person confessed and repented. But those who refused to confess, as well as many who did admit—usually under torture—to nocturnal conspiracies, cannibalism, and bestiality, were often executed by hanging or burning. Often, these took the forms of public burnings, at which the accused were asked a final time if they were repentant. Those who did repent were usually strangled before they were burned, but unrepentant individuals, as well as people convicted of particularly heinous acts, were not allowed this option and were burned alive.

In its efforts to eradicate any form of nonapproved thinking, the Inquisition even policed the scholarly arena. One of the most famous victims was a monk named Giordano Bruno, a mystic and mathematician who had been accused—among other things—of teaching Copernicus' ideas that the earth went around the sun, in violation of the Church's accepted dogma that the sun went around the earth. Another famous victim was Galileo Galilei, who discovered the rings of Saturn, the four largest moons of Jupiter, sunspots, and other features of the solar system. But Galileo also taught Copernicus' ideas, and in 1632 he was found guilty of

Box 10.2 ORDEALS IN WITCHCRAFT INQUIRIES

Ordeals are processes for determining guilt or innocence by subjecting a person to a painful and potentially lethal activity. If the person survived the activity or appeared to have no serious injuries, this was taken as a sign of divine intervention and an indication of innocence. One ordeal described in the Old Testament (Numbers 5:12–31) was used to determine whether a woman had committed adultery. A priest would force the woman to drink "bitter water," and if her belly swelled or her thigh "rot[ted]," this was taken as a sign of her guilt.

Ordeals were common in Medieval Europe. Sometimes persons accused of heresy or witchcraft were tightly bound and then thrown into a body of water. If they were not burdened by guilt, then they would sink. After an appropriate period of time, they would be brought back to the surface and revived. Another ordeal involved forcing the person to retrieve objects from boiling water; if a person was innocent, any wounds that he or she received would quickly heal.

The practice of ordeals in Christian Europe was curtailed by Pope Innocent III and the Fourth Lateran Council of 1215. The Council prohibited priests from participating in such activities, thereby removing much of their religious legitimacy. However, the rise of the Inquisition and the development of ever more imaginative methods of extracting confessions from accused heretics and witches led to the reintroduction of many of these practices, often with new explanations.

Today, the practice of placing one hand on the Bible while swearing an oath recalls the ordeals of the past. Invoking the supernatural implies that giving false testimony in a courtroom or failing to live up to the requirements of an oath of office will result in supernatural sanctions. Of course, criminal penalties for perjury and impeachment as a means for removing someone from office supplement these supernatural punishments with more down-to-earth punishments.

heresy as well. Yet because Galileo was well known and politically well connected, he was not sentenced to execution. Instead, he spent the next ten years—and eventually died—under house arrest for the crime of teaching that the earth goes around the sun (see Box 10.2: Ordeals in Witchcraft Inquiries).

The Spanish Inquisition

Probably the most infamous examples of the Roman Catholic Church's persecution of nonbelievers and heretics were carried out by the Spanish Inquisition, which was established in 1478 by Pope Sixtus IV to aid in the *reconquista,* or reconquest of Spain from the Muslims. The Muslim occupation of the Iberian Peninsula began in 711, when an initial force landed at Gibraltar. By 732, the Muslim armies had passed the Pyrenees and were moving northward. In one of the decisive battles of European history, Charles Martel and his army defeated the Muslim army at the Battle of Poitiers. Following this defeat, the Muslims withdrew south, and they ruled what is now Spain and Portugal for the next several centuries.

It took hundreds of years for Christian forces to reconquer the entire peninsula. On January 2, 1492, the forces of Ferdinand and Isabella, the Spanish king and queen, conquered the last Muslim stronghold of Grenada. Just three months later, on March 31,

Ferdinand and Isabella issued an expulsion decree ordering all Jews either to leave their lands by July 31 of that year or to convert to Christianity. Those who left were not allowed to take any gold or silver with them, but could negotiate bills of exchange that they could cash abroad. These conditions, and the speed with which the transactions had to be completed, forced many Jews to accept very small amounts for their goods and lands. It is estimated that between fifty and one hundred thousand left Spain.

A larger number remained, and, although they publically accepted Catholicism and were forced to be baptized, many continued to practice their religion secretly. Even after the other Jews had left, these *conversos* were the object of frequent suspicion, and many were accused of clandestinely conducting Jewish rituals in their homes. Rooting out these "Judaizers" kept the tribunals of the Inquisition busy for some two decades. Many *conversos* were forced to appear before the Inquisitors, and those found guilty of the more serious offenses were burned in public ceremonies known as *auto de fe* (from the medieval Spanish term for "act of faith"). These large-scale events were designed as much to ensure the conformity of the citizenry as to punish heretics.

After the Jews had been essentially exterminated in Spain, the Inquisition turned its eye to other groups. One of the first to be persecuted were the *moriscos*, Muslims

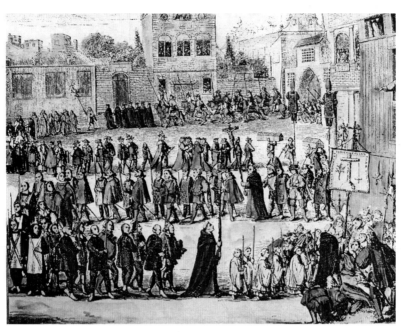

A procession of heretics and other religious criminals on their way to an *auto de fe*. Each prisoner's crime is evident from the garb that he must wear.

who had converted to Christianity. Another suspect group was the *alumbrados* ("the illuminated ones"), Christian mystics who believed that they could communicate directly with God. As the Protestant Reformation spread across northern Europe, Protestants who entered Spain also came into the cross-fire of the Inquisition. To ensure doctrinal conformity, the Inquisition carried out periodic mass book burnings, focusing especially on religious books and translations of the Bible into the vernacular (Pérez 2005).

To extract confessions, the Inquisition used three primary methods of torture. In the "waterboarding" technique, the accused was tied to a ladder that was slanted so that the person's head was lower than his or her feet. The person's mouth was forced open, and a cloth was placed over the mouth. Water was poured onto the cloth, forcing the accused to swallow it and experience a sense of drowning. Another method was to tie the person's wrists together, hang the person from a rope, and then attach weights to his or her feet. The third method of torture was the rack, a device that allowed the Inquisitors to tie the arms and the legs of the accused and then tighten the ties by twisting the ropes.

The Spanish Inquisition ultimately made its way to the Americas, where it was instrumental in the conquest of Native peoples and the destruction of their cultures. The *conquistadores* who traveled to the New World were accompanied by priests who extensively docu-

mented the local people they were encountering while simultaneously destroying as many of the native religious objects and practices as they could uncover. In California, the Franciscans established a mission system to indoctrinate Catholic and Spanish ideas in the local populations. The strategy of the California mission system was known as *reducción* ("reduction"). The priests forced their Indian converts to abandon their traditional ways of life and live in the missions, avoiding all contact with nonconverts. Men and women were required to live in dormitories at the missions, and married couples were separated from one another. The close living conditions—and the rape of Indian women by the soldiers and priests—helped to spread diseases brought by the Europeans. Although many modern histories of these missions claim that the converts welcomed the missionaries and were grateful to them for introducing improvements in agriculture and for bringing word about the "true" God, insurrections occurred at many of the missions. However, these revolts were quickly suppressed by the Spanish soldiers that were garrisoned near the missions.

The Salem Witchcraft Trials

In the New World, the efforts to root out witchcraft and other "diabolic" practices also focused on the imported slaves and colonists. One of the most famous examples

The Inquisition used a variety of methods of torture to extract confessions from its victims.

of a "witch craze" in the New World occurred in Salem, Massachusetts, in 1692. The Massachusetts colony had been settled largely by Protestants who had left England both for religious and for commercial reasons. Once they reached New England, they established the Massachusetts Bay Colony, which was guided by "Puritan" principles of universal education (so that each person would be able to read the Bible), simplicity in dress and worship, and the belief that all aspects of life should be guided by the words of the Bible. These principles were developed in England in reaction to what the Puritans perceived as the "worldly" focus of society and the excesses of the Church. Because they were so numerous, the Puritans who settled in Massachusetts were able to create a society based largely on their own religious tenets. Many of those who disagreed left the Massachusetts Bay Colony and moved to neighboring areas, eventually helping to establish other colonies, including New Hampshire, Rhode Island, and Pennsylvania.

In addition to their other beliefs, the Massachusetts settlers brought their English heritage of witchcraft beliefs to the New World. These included ideas about the types of people who were likely to be witches, the practices of witchcraft, the ways in which a person could become a witch, and the means by which a witch could be detected. The first witchcraft trials in the colony occurred in the 1640s, and other trials—and even some executions—took place over the next several decades.

The events for which Salem is so renowned began in late 1691. Several young women and girls had been using a makeshift crystal ball in an attempt to find out about their future husbands. But instead of seeing faces or other clues, they saw something resembling a coffin. Soon, several of the women, including Betty, the daughter of Reverend Parris, and her cousin, were beset by "fits" and other signs of possession. When the girls did not improve and the symptoms began to spread, the girls were pressured to reveal who had bewitched them.

Eventually, the girls named three women: Sarah Good, Sarah Osborne, and Tituba. Sarah Good was a poor woman who depended on others for her survival. She professed her innocence and blamed Sarah Osborne for the outbreak. Sarah Osborne, an argumentative woman who had stopped going to church, was the only one of the three women who was not poor. She argued that she was more likely to be bewitched than to be a witch. Tituba, a slave woman who had been brought from Barbados and had maintained some of the rituals of her Yoruba religion, worked in the home of Reverend Parris. She confessed to having conducted un-Christian activities, including helping the girls of her household to see their future husbands. In an apparent effort to please her master, she elaborated on (and contradicted) her initial answers, implicating both Sarahs and an increasingly large group of other people. Tituba was eventually freed for having confessed and begged forgiveness. But her accusations implicated dozens of people—including some of the most respectable and religious people of Salem—and led to many people being sent to jail in chains. Ultimately, almost two dozen people were executed for witchcraft, including Sarah Good. Sarah Osborne died in prison while awaiting trial.

A closer look at these events reveals that the accusers and the accused were members of two different families in the village: the Putnams and the Porters. Most of the accusations of witchcraft were made by girls of the Putnam family, which had seen its economic status decline in the years preceding the Salem outbreak. In contrast, the Porter family—the group principally accused of witchcraft—had prospered. The Porters were not the only locals to object to the witchcraft accusations. Other men opposed the trials instigated by Reverend Samuel Parris, the minister of the Salem church, but they were not accused—perhaps because they had relatively high status in the village and possessed wealth. Powerful men were accused of witchcraft in these trials, but they were not the local people; some had never even visited the village.

Although the Salem outbreak was not the first occurrence of witchcraft accusations in the colony, the extent of the accusations and the brutality of the trials in Salem were unprecedented in the history of English colonial America. A variety of factors contributed to these events, including the longstanding cultural beliefs in witches, the presence of people who could be accused as witches, the local schisms that had led to the economic distinctions between the accusers and the accused, laws that prohibited witchcraft, and powerful local political systems that could impose and carry out sentences of death. These factors had long been present in Salem and in many other colonial towns. But the stage for the Salem outbreak appears to have been set by several other chance events. A new minister (Parrish) had recently arrived in the settlement, and he had brought with him a slave (Tituba) acquainted with West Indian voodoo lore. In addition, many of the young people of the colony did not share their parents' religious zeal, and several of them developed an interest in fortune-telling and the occult.

The first person to face trial, Bridget Bishop, was an old and cantankerous woman who owned the local tavern, which she kept open even on the Sabbath. She was found guilty and hanged on June 10. Eventually, nineteen people were convicted and executed as witches. Four others died in prison. One man, the 80-year-old Giles Corey, openly scorned the proceedings and refused to stand trial. If he was convicted, he knew that his farm would be confiscated from his family. His refusal resulted in a different kind of punishment. On September 19, 1692, Corey was stripped naked and a large board was laid over his body. Large stones were then stacked on the board until Corey was crushed to death. Three days later, Corey's wife, Martha, was hanged together with seven other convicted witches.

The witchcraft accusations in Salem in 1692 were unusual in many respects. Although there had been some local trials and executions, there had been no major witchcraft trials in England for almost half a century. The tensions in the community were similar to those in other settlements. So why did they occur in the Salem area, and why in 1692? Could other factors have contributed to the outbreak of witchcraft?

The Ergot Hypothesis. The idea that the Salem witchcraft outbreak may have been due to an outbreak of ergotism was first proposed by Caporeal (1976). **Ergotism** is caused by consuming a naturally occurring fungus known as ergot (*Claviceps purpurea*). The fungus is known to infect a number of cereal grains and wild grasses, including rye. Ergot contains a number of different alkaloids, some of which induce uterine contractions. Since the Middle Ages, European midwives have exploited this effect by giving small amounts (1–2) of ergot-infected grains to induce labor. This treatment was not without its perils, for ergot also contains numerous compounds that can affect circulation and individuals with pronounced psychoactive effects. Ergotism is known to have produced at least a hundred outbreaks of mass illness in Europe, some of which left thousands dead. These outbreaks are now known to have been caused by the consumption of bread or other products made with grains infected with ergot, which was not clearly associated with the disease until the seventeenth century.

Ergotism occurs in two forms. Gangrenous ergotism first appears as vomiting and diarrhea, accompanied by itching, skin inflammations, and burning pains. After a few days, the fingers and toes begin to change to a blue-black color. If the disease continues to progress, this discoloration may move into the arms and legs. As the tissues die, the affected area may even fall off the body. Convulsive ergotism begins with many of the same symptoms but proceeds to severe disturbances of the nervous system. Involuntary muscle contractions, particularly in the arms and legs, may cause an affected person to twitch in pain. Other effects include loss of speech, dysfunction of the visual system, and a variety of central nervous system affects including dizziness, drowsiness, hallucinations and delusions, confusion, psychotic episodes, and periods of unconsciousness. The ergot alkaloids also have a variety of

The ergot fungus (*Claviceps purpurea*) infests cereal grains, including rye (shown here). It has been suggested that the events of the Salem witchcraft trials may have been triggered by the consumption of bread contaminated with the fungus. Ergot contains dozens of active substances. Some of these are toxic; others have hallucinogenic effects.

effects on the cardiovascular system, motor system, and gastrointestinal system, and can produce sensations of alternating hot and cold, numbness, deafness, blindness, sense of being pinched, or of being suffocated or choked, a tingling and itching of the skin, skin discoloration, and blistering. These kinds of symptoms were among the principal experiences reported by the people of Salem who made the witchcraft accusations.

Ergotism is also known to produce both temporary or long-lasting psychotic states, as well as other mental disorders, particularly among adolescents. The symptoms—including spasms and convulsions, hallucinations, panic, depression, and sensations of prickling or things crawling on the skin—exhibited by many of the Salem accusers are typical of the recognized toxic effects of the ergot alkaloids (Matossian 1989).

The ergot fungus is most likely to form in cold years, and on grain that is grown in or near wetlands. Both conditions appear to have been met in the growing season that preceded the Salem outbreak. Moreover, the families that exhibited the symptoms of

witchcraft were all living in areas suitable for rye production. Further evidence supporting the hypothesis that ergotism was responsible for the Salem outbreak include the fact that the preponderance of people who made the accusations were children and teenagers, the age group that generally suffers the more severe consequences of ergot poisoning.

In Salem, most of the people who were accused of witchcraft were political outsiders. While social analyses can help us to understand who was accused of witchcraft and why, they cannot account for the experiences of the accusers and their motivations. Could the physical symptoms the accusers reported—including convulsions, fits, and the sensations of being pinched and pricked, all of which are noted in the court records—have been the result of ergotism? Court records indicate that many of the other symptoms of ergotism were also present, such as blindness, deafness, burning sensations of the skin, swelling and pain in the extremities, episodes of speechlessness, gastrointestinal complaints, and hallucinations, including out-of-body experiences. There were also reports of deaths of people who had no connection with the witchcraft accusations—and of cattle—that are consistent with ergot poisoning. It was also said that the accused witches had consumed a red-colored bread (ergot is reddish in color).

All of this evidence supports the hypothesis that the Salem outbreak was triggered by the mass consumption of a toxic substance. The unusual symptoms and manifestations caused by ergotism were, in turn, interpreted within a cultural framework that accepted that witches exist and described how their effects would become manifest.

Summary: Supernatural Evil and Outside Groups: The Limits of Religious Adaptation?

The term *witch* has come to embody many different concepts of supernatural evil. Over time, witches have varied from being people who actually did engage in supernatural practices to others who were merely the unfortunate victims of scapegoating. Across a spectrum of times and places, similar characteristics of witches emerge, a reflection of both their shamanic origins and their persecution in processes of political subordination and incorporation. Today, witchcraft survives in many forms, but the most popular conceptions of it are the witch who harms through envy and jealousy; and the witch who conducts the revived shamanistic nature practices that reflect a postmodern reconstruction of the past (see Box 10.3: Wicca Today: A Reconstruction).

Box 10.3 WICCA TODAY: A RECONSTRUCTION

The contemporary "neo-pagan" practices referred to as **Wicca** encompass a wide variety of activities. Most aspects of contemporary European and American "witchcraft" are a reinvention, a reconstruction of ancient witchcraft practices combined with modern notions of magic and melded together by people in the twentieth century. One important source of inspiration for modern witchcraft is a nineteenth-century group, the Order of the Golden Dawn, which combined ancient knowledge about the power of the mind with modern philosophies about the capacity of the human will to bring about supernormal effects. The Golden Dawn derived many of its ideas from Freemason and Rosicrucian practices that integrated esoteric knowledge from cultures around the world and that were considered to be practices-of-nature religions.

The modern Wiccan traditions are largely the creation of a British civil servant named Gerald Gardner, who reconstructed these old nature religions in publications that would become twentieth-century handbooks for the practice of witchcraft. Gardner's ideas provided the basis for formation of covens and other secret rituals that produced a variety of effects and guided people's lives. Many different traditions were used for giving protection, healing, achieving personal goals, engaging in a developmental relationship with divine forces, and transforming personal consciousness.

By the 1950s, Gardner's books about ancient pagan rites and the worship of the earth and Goddesses had led to the formation of many groups of witches, or Wiccans. Their focus on ancient nature religions and Goddesses made them attractive to new converts and led to the formation of many covens, each under the leadership of a "high priestess." Following the guidance in Gardner's books while eclectically adopting information about practices around the world, these modern covens have incorporated a wide range of practices. They follow ritual cycles organized around the solar and lunar cycles as well as other patterns of nature. A full moon is a particularly important time for rituals designed to cure illness and help achieve worldly goals.

Gardner and his contemporaries drew on many sources of information about the European past and practices in cultures around the world. One central feature of these reconstructions was the notion of a sacred earth mother who had a special relation to nature and fertility. As concepts of shamanism became part of the intellectual and popular culture of Europe and the United States, these new witches often reconceptualized their ancient roots in terms of shamanic practices and their healing rituals.

One aspect of these Wiccan rituals that reveals their connections to shamanism is the use of altered states of consciousness and visualization as tools to achieve magical ends. Drawing on both ancient and modern concepts, today's Wiccans strive to manipulate and use the subtle energies of the Universe to affect their lives. Many use ritualized visualization exercises to help themselves achieve better lives. Their practices often resemble the meditative traditions much more than the ancient practices attributed to witches.

The Wiccans, the "witches" of today, bear little resemblance to the ancient shamanic practices from which they draw their inspiration, and even less to the horrid caricatures of social inversion that were persecuted by the Inquisition. Yet, the long-held animosity toward and ignorance concerning non-Christian practices continues to resurface from time to time. In the 1980s, charges were raised that satanic ritual child abuse was occurring across the United States. Although these charges proved to be unfounded, many aspects of the cases resemble earlier witchcraft crazes. People who considered themselves experts in ritual abuse were appointed to child welfare agencies and legal organizations to carry out investigations. In some areas, the statute of limitations was altered to allow the prosecution of crimes alleged to have occurred decades before. Children who were reluctant to admit that crimes had been committed against them were often given suggestions as to what had happened. Some of the children were repeatedly questioned and even intimidated to coerce testimony from them about crimes against them, crimes that they had repeatedly denied ever occurred. Clearly, the old ideas about "witches" continue to haunt people.

Given the universal belief in the capacity of humans for "supernatural evil," how can we interpret this capacity from the biocultural perspective? Is there an adaptation involved in the foundations of these beliefs, or are they just unfortunate by-products of other human capabilities? Are there any adaptive advantages of witchcraft accusations? Or is it just something at the basis of human psychology that makes these scapegoating procedures so compelling and satisfying? Wright points to a disturbing aspect of our mental hardware: "moral sentiments are used with rule flexibility, switched on and off in keeping with self interest" (1994, p. 13). Witchcraft accusations exemplify this moral double standard, for they are applied with discriminating self-interest in differentiating how to behave among the in-group from how to behave with "others"—pagans, heathens, and foreigners. Witchcraft accusations clearly involve an attribution of "out-group" status to specific members of the in-group.

To assess the possible role of evolutionary adaptations in witchcraft beliefs, it is important that we focus on the components of our mental hardware or the functions. We must also keep in mind that our mental hardware may have produced behaviors that were adaptive in the environment of our early ancestors, but that are no longer adaptive in the changed environment of our own time. The existence of a powerful mechanism to remove "in-group" members suggests that the underlying mental processes of witchcraft accusations are related to our innate tendencies to engage in a definition of "us" versus "them." Since many of the functional adaptations of religion are related to procedures for creating "in-group" membership and solidarity, witchcraft accusations can be seen as a mechanism for expelling group members who refuse or fail to conform to the groups' standards of behavior. Moreover, announcing the reasons why a person is considered a witch simultaneously underscores cultural ideas about the boundaries of acceptable behavior.

This suggests that some of our innate social tendencies may now engage these components of our mental hardware in ways that drive intergroup conflict. Like the Inquisition and the outbreak of witchcraft in Salem, our modern wars, nationalism, religious crusades, and intolerance may also reflect a hard-wired tendency for people to act differently toward outsiders than to members of their own group. Our feelings of collective indignation, grievance, and hostility toward outsiders likely originated in adaptations that occurred among bands of early humans. These ancient roots of our modern conflictive intergroup dynamics appear to derive from adaptations to the dynamics of "conflicts among coalitions of males for status" (Wright 1994, p. 285). As has been dramatically recorded in chimpanzee coalition politics, subordinated females are often the opportunistic victims of group struggles. This suggests that witchcraft *accusations* are primarily by-products of other social dynamics that involve competition. The use of supernatural mechanisms extends this, engaging the power of the "spiritual other" to further social competition.

The universality of religious beliefs and the many social and political similarities among religions in different cultures raise questions about the basis of religion in specific aspects of human nature and the mind. Do religious universals attest to their adaptive features? Do the billions of Christians, Muslims, and Hindus in the world provide an irrefutable body of evidence that these traditions contribute to human survival and reproduction? Isn't the numerical success alone of these religious traditions proof that they are adaptive? Or should we be cynical about religion, seeing it as a parasite or virus that invades and takes over our brains and bodies? Do religions prey on our innate tendencies derived for other purposes, just as drug addictions feed on our innate drives for natural chemicals that drive brain mechanisms underlying our basic sense of well-being? Is "God" no more than a symbol for dominance behavior that meets human needs for submissiveness?

By seeing religion as providing mechanisms that enhance the effectiveness of one group in competition with other groups, we can see how behaviors that were once adaptive no longer provide adaptive advantages in the current context of adaptation. Or can religion also help in encouraging interactions among societies, as it apparently did on the evolutionary origins of shamanic group rituals?

First, let us examine the advantages to the group that religion confers. Clearly, it provides "superior social being" symbols that help us create and function as a part of large social groups. This is an adaptation of significant importance in increasing the scale of human societies. Religion also has played an important role in expanding the human capacity for compassion beyond the innate kinship bonds of family and the immediate personal relations. Brotherly love becomes an adaptive religious ideology, a pattern of helping others whether or not they are related to us or are likely to help us in return. Philip Singer's book *The Expanding Circle* addresses how we move from our primitive bonds to identify with successively larger groups through the idea of behavior not motivated by self-interest. This has enabled societies to extend subordination of personal self-interest on behalf of collective self-interest to larger social groups, expanding to the level of the current nation–state and to global religions. Singer suggests that long ago, selection favored those individuals who could hide their self-interest by using language to create a system of morality that suggested personal motivations were driven by broader group interests rather than narrow personal self-interest. This evolutionary impulse was noted by Darwin: "As man advances in civilization, and small tribes are united into larger communities, the simplest reason would tell each individual that he ought to extend his social instincts and sympathies to all the members of

Osiris enthroned in the Underworld, judging the dead. On the right, the jackal-headed God Anubis leads the deceased before Osiris. He then weighs the heart of the deceased against a feather to determine his fate after death. (Hunefer Papyrus, ca. 1317–1285 B.C.E.)

the same nations, though personally unknown to him. This point being once reached, there is only an artificial barrier to prevent his sympathies extending to the men of all nations and races" (Darwin 1882, cited in Wright 1994, p. 340).

Did we evolve to sacrifice our lives for the nation–state, as so many young men and women do who volunteer for military service? Is self-sacrifice for the nation a non-functional by-product of our more mammalian tendencies to sacrifice our own lives in an altruistic way to defend our kin? Certainly, we did not evolve to protect some idea of a nation, but rather to protect smaller, kinship-related groups. Religion has extended these tendencies, exemplified in the practices of self-sacrifice.

Human Sacrifice

While none of the major religions of the world explicitly practices human sacrifice today, many of them have elements that suggest they once did. Contemporary religious practices that involve self-sacrifice, such as religiously motivated suicide bombers, as well as the self-sacrifice of military volunteers in wartime, might be seen as a continuation of this ancient practice. While we are inclined to view today's conflicts—such as the wars in Afghanistan and Iraq—in strictly political terms, some generals and politicians have used the term *crusade* to describe them, evoking images of earlier religiously inspired military activities.

Myths and metaphors of murder and sacrifice abound in ancient texts. In the *Rig Veda,* the myth of Purusa describes how the original primordial being was killed and dismembered, his body parts giving rise to the various groups that make up Hindu society. Ancient Egyptian texts recount the murder of Osiris, the God who—as the first pharaoh—introduced agriculture, law, and religion to humans and convinced them to cease the practice of cannibalism. In gratitude for these gifts, humans venerated Osiris, provoking envy and rage in his brother Seth, the God of Evil and Darkness. Seth killed his brother and hid the body, but Isis, Osiris's wife, found it and brought it back home. Enraged, Seth chopped the body into several pieces and scattered them. Isis patiently collected all the pieces except the penis—which she was unable to find—and reassembled them, creating the first mummy. Osiris was revived, but without his penis; consequently, he could no longer ensure the fertility of the earth. Osiris became the God of Death and the Underworld, and his son Horus became the pharaoh.

In the Old Testament, God ordered Abraham to sacrifice his son Isaac, and did not stop Abraham's preparations for the task until he was just about to cut his son's throat. Only after Abraham had demonstrated his complete obedience to God did God provide him with a ram to sacrifice in Isaac's place. This story is central to the Jewish, Christian, and Islamic religions and continues to echo in many of their practices. Jews have not performed animal sacrifices since the time of the Jewish Wars in the second century. Prayers are now offered in place of sacrifice, but many Orthodox Jews look forward to the rebuilding of the temple and the resumption of "burnt offerings" and other sacrifices.

An act of ritual sacrifice—and cannibalism—stands at the center of the Christian belief system (Levenson 1993). The Christian Savior, Jesus Christ, is explicitly said to have been sacrificed to atone for the sins of humanity. This deed is metaphorically and symbolically reenacted when the priest (and sometimes the congregation) consumes the body and blood of Jesus in the form of bread and wine. But the practice of human sacrifice is not just symbolic in nature: Jesus was actually killed by the standard Roman method of executing criminals at the time—crucifixion.

Some of the most dramatic human sacrifice rituals were the practices of the Aztecs. During ceremonies that might last for days, Aztec priests would bend human victims over altars and cut out their hearts. A priest would then lift the still-beating heart toward the heavens, offering it with prayers to the Gods. The body of the victim would then be removed, and another victim would step up to take his or her place. The flesh of the victims was consumed by many sectors of society, particularly the warriors and nobility. The skulls of the sacrificial offerings were stacked up in special racks known as *Tzompantli*.

The numbers of victims varied, but some rituals may have involved as many as 30,000–40,000 human sacrifices (although these numbers were likely exaggerated by the Spanish to make the Aztecs appear more brutal). Some of those who were sacrificed were volunteers who offered to take the glorious roles of messengers to the Gods, but most had been captured in neighboring kingdoms during "flower wars"—raiding expeditions designed to acquire victims for the sacrifices. These raids often took place months before the sacrificial ceremonies, and the Aztecs needed to house and feed their prisoners before they were sacrificed. Since the victims were carrying messages to the Gods, it was necessary that they be treated well and experience the grandeur and wealth of Aztec society. To aid in their transition from this world to that of the Gods, the victims were given specially prepared psychoactive beverages that were supposed to bring them into closer contact with the supernatural domain and also make them more docile.

These elaborate practices consumed time and enormous amounts of resources. The Aztecs believed that human sacrifice was required by their Gods, who demanded blood in exchange for life and fertility. But is this emic explanation sufficient? While many anthro-

pologists have accepted it, Michael Harner (1977a, 1977b) has suggested that the unparalleled scope of Aztec human sacrifice and cannibalism was the result of something much more down to earth: a chronic shortage of the protein needed to feed a growing population. That is, Aztec cannibalism was the result, not of the demands of bloodthirsty Gods, but of a combination of unfavorable agricultural conditions, seasonal crop failures, the lack of domesticated animals, the depletion of wild game in the region, food scarcity, famine, and limits on the amount of land that could be used for agriculture.

The fertile central valley of Mexico is surrounded by poor farming land. The Aztecs also were surrounded by other powerful groups, making it very difficult for them to expand their agricultural practices. While the staple Aztec combination of corn and beans does provide sufficient complementary amino acids to make up for a lack of meat, it lacks certain fatty acids that are essential for the human diet. Food crops are also scarce at some times of the year. Consequently, Harner hypothesized that protein insufficiency led the Aztecs to sacrifice and eat humans as a way to supplement their protein sources.

But there are problems with Harner's arguments. Ortiz de Montellano (1978, 1990) noted that a wide range of meat proteins was, in fact, available to the Aztecs. The Aztecs also received an enormous amount of food in tribute from their neighbors, and they stored great quantities of food to assure an adequate diet. Moreover, the total amount of human protein available from human sacrifice was insignificant, and the largest of the human sacrifices occurred during the harvest season and not during periods of protein scarcity. Ortiz de Montellano argued that the preponderance of human sacrifice during harvest periods indicated that it was "a gesture of thanks and reciprocity to the gods" (1978, p. 614) rather than a means for satisfying a need for protein.

This explanation echoes the Aztecs' own explanation for human sacrifice: that it was required by their Gods. While this religious explanation is obviously true at some level, it leaves many questions unanswered. Why were these beliefs and practices found among the Aztecs and some other societies, but absent in most societies? Are there predictable conditions that lead a society to institutionalize human sacrifice in its religion? Is human sacrifice normative under some specific ecological or social conditions? Or is it just an aberrant practice that is unrelated to the adaptations of societies?

As we saw in Chapter 9, Émile Durkheim argued a position that has become one of the dominant perspectives of the social sciences: that religious beliefs and practices derive from and reflect social conditions. This perspective is supported by other researchers who have proposed that the determinants of Aztec human sacrifice were to be found in the social conditions that structure religious beliefs, the economic networks and political conditions of state activities, warfare, and class stratification.

Price (1978) characterized cannibalism as a "stylistic" trait, a way of reinforcing the existing social stratification and political power. Isaac (1983) hypothesized that human sacrifice served an internal ideological function in Aztec society by uniting the class interests of nobles and upwardly aspiring lower class warriors, who received the right to participate in the elite privilege of consuming flesh. Hassig (1990) linked Aztec human sacrifice to their precarious social and political adaptation, arguing that the "flower wars" were actually a strategy of empire building that enabled the Aztecs to expand their influence. By allowing dependent areas to be self-administered and tribute paying, the Aztecs avoided the higher political and administrative costs of directly administering the conquered areas. Price (1978) and Isaac (1983) similarly suggested that the "flower wars" reflected the Aztec inability to conquer the Tlaxcala–Pueblan Valley. Price suggested that human sacrifice was an ideological mechanism to explain away the failure of military conquest under the guise of ritual pursuits. Montezuma's characterization of the wars as rituals for obtaining captives and providing military training for soldiers was a strategic ruse to direct the Spaniards' attention away from the political and military weaknesses of the Aztecs (Isaac 1983).

Aztec human sacrifice was clearly related to geopolitical dynamics, political and military instabilities, economic production, and distribution networks. But these studies did not use a cross-cultural sample of societies to systematically examine the hypothesized relationships, and consequently, no convincing data is available to demonstrate that any of these factors played a role in establishing a culture of human sacrifice. If these social conditions lead to ritualized human sacrifice, human sacrifice should be present in similar societies around the world.

Cross-Cultural Assessments of Human Sacrifice

Winkelman (1998, 1999) carried out cross-cultural analyses on societies in the Standard Cross-Cultural Sample (SCCS; Murdock and White 1969) to determine if ecological factors, religious conditions, and social complexity play a part in determining whether a society is likely to practice human sacrifice. He examined a wide range of measures, including social complexity variables, agricultural potential, meat protein in the diet, domestic animals, total foods, food storage adequacy, the threat of famine, population pressure, and environmental circumscription, assessed through warfare for land and resources.

The analyses showed that societies that practiced human sacrifice were typically at the mid-range of cultural complexity, neither the simplest hunter–gatherer or horticulture societies nor the most complex agricultural societies. Although they relied on domesticated animals for food, they were not pastoral societies, nor did they make great use of milk products. Most societies that sacrificed humans had good agricultural land and faced low threats of famine or food resource problems. However, population pressure or population stress, a measure of the density of the population, is significantly correlated with human sacrifice. These societies generally had very high population density, and both population pressure and an overall measure of war for land and resources were statistically significant predictors of human sacrifice. Societies with human sacrifice were relatively complex, but with low religious integration, suggesting that human sacrifice promotes religious integration, as postulated by Isaac (1983) and Price (1978) in their discussion of Aztec human sacrifice and cannibalism. If I eat my enemies, would you want to ally with me or be my enemy?

Human sacrifice was found in societies with an intermediate level of political complexity (politically semi-autonomous) but were affected by other societies, with political integration involving alliances and confederacies. In subsequent analyses Winkelman (1999) found both ecological and social conditions were associated with human sacrifice: ecological circumscription and weak political integration. These analyses suggest that ritualized human sacrifice was motivated by specific political dynamics compounded by ecological circumscription. Significant correlations of human sacrifice with population pressure and warfare for land and resources support the ecological hypothesis. The ecological predictors of human sacrifice related to population pressure suggest that it was not the sheer number of people, but the stresses that resulted from population density, that promoted human sacrifice. Specific political dynamics that prevent a society from effectively controlling independent neighboring groups may make human sacrifice a particularly adaptive strategy for dealing with fickle political neighbors. These processes are exemplified in the case of the Aztecs.

Aztec Human Sacrifice in Cross-Cultural Perspective

These general ecological and political motivations for human sacrifice are illustrated by the broader dynamics of Aztec sacrifices. The psychosocial effects of cannibalism are suggested by the Aztecs' dynamics of in-group and out-group relationships with respect to consumption for sacrifice, since the Aztecs generally did not consume members of their own group. Furthermore, only the elite class was allowed to consume human flesh, but warriors could earn their right and share these benefits with their lineage members. Human sacrifice can produce social integration by eliciting group commitment. The Aztecs did not normally consume members of their own group, so people who united with them in wars for sacrificial victims were able to establish in-group membership and hence achieve protection. Human sacrifice promoted the allegiance of the lower class, intimidating them, and helping assure their commitment. The Aztec lower class may have lacked allegiance because they were non-kin, but the likelihood that they would defect and ally with not-too-distant enemies of the nobility was undermined by the Aztecs' practice of sacrificing members of other polities.

The association of human sacrifice with population density and stress suggests that it functioned as a means of population control. Aztec human sacrifices reduced population pressure by causing fatalities among young males and relieving pressure on the land tenure system. As Ortiz de Montellano notes, Aztec cannibalism contributed little to the overall food supply; however, the practices could have provided mechanisms by which the perception (and perhaps long-term impact) of competing populations were reduced. The internal ideological and political functions of Aztec human sacrifice are supported by the cross-cultural findings. The highest level of political integration in societies with human sacrifice was provided by alliances and confederacies, lending support to the hypothesis that human sacrifice played a role in the management of inconclusive intergroup struggles. Relationships between the Aztecs and their neighbors were not stable; the local groups normally had semi-, de facto, or fully autonomous political status, so human sacrifice may have played a role in the persuasion and intimidation of the groups linked through alliances and confederacies. This is illustrated in the behavior of the Aztecs, who would invite the kings and lords of the other states to their ceremonies of massive human sacrifice as a form of intimidation (see Carrasco 1987). The sacrificial rituals were theatrically managed to maximize the terror and fear felt by these spectators, inducing them to cooperate with the Aztecs instead of risking being their enemies and sacrificial victims. A particularly dramatic example of this occurred when a neighboring ruler gave his daughter to the Aztecs as a wife. Instead of marrying her to one of their own, the Aztec priests ritually killed her, had her body flayed, and then donned her skin to dance before her horrified father.

In examining ritualized cannibalism in prehistoric America, Turner and Turner (1995, 1999) come to similar conclusions regarding the political functions of cannibalism among the prehistoric Anasazi (who lived in what is now the Southwest United States). The Turners assess five major hypotheses for cannibalism: sociobiological explanations, starvation, social control, ritual, and social pathology. Sociobiological explanations argue that among nonhuman animals, violence and aggression—including eating one's competitors—can, under certain conditions, be adaptive. Among humans, however, institutionalized cannibalism is relatively infrequent, so a sociobiological explanation does not explain why it occurs in some societies but not in others.

Turner and Turner (1999) suggest that social control, ritual, and social pathology constitute a set of interrelated hypotheses accounting for the practices of human cannibalism. They argue that the social control hypothesis fits well with evolutionary explanations, which suggest that the use of fear and terror to control the behavior of unrelated competitors is adaptive. Turner and Turner emphasize the role of cannibalism in "violent social control, possibly initiated by socially-pathological individuals." They suggest that these Southwest complexes began with prehistoric immigrations from the fall of the Toltec state at Teotihuacan (between 800 and 1000 C.E.) of "cultists, priests, warriors, pilgrims, traders, miners, farmers and others fleeing or displaced by the widespread unrest and civil war in Central Mexico" (Turner and Turner 1999, p. 463). The Turners propose that a group of the immigrants, probably the warrior–cultists of the Tezcatlipoca-Xipe-Toltec complex which practiced human sacrifice and cannibalism, used cannibalism to terrorize into submission the population, which lacked the central control necessary for effective resistance.

Asante and Modern Perspectives: Sacrament or Capital Punishment?

The work of Wilks (1975, 1988) on human sacrifice among the Asante of Africa similarly argues that human sacrifice provides a variety of internal control mechanisms. These include the intimidation of the population and opponents, as well as a mechanism for removing individuals or groups who are considered threats. These political dimensions of human sacrifice are illustrated in Wilks's assessments of Asante human sacrifice as state executions. He suggests that "human sacrifices" were really affairs of state in which criminals and prisoners of war were ceremonially executed in public events that also served to subjugate the populace. Williams (1988) also suggests that Asante human sacrifice provided a deterrent against challenges to the Asante state, a mechanism for eliminating opponents and legitimizing purges. In addition, the payments that captives or their families made to quash death sentences also were a source of revenue.

But Williams (1988) rejects Wilks's notion that all Asante human sacrifice was actually a form of capital punishment. His review of who was sacrificed and why illustrates that there were, indeed, judicial executions, but decapitations of slaves and servants at certain festivals for the ancestors indicate that these sacrifices were more than capital punishment. The belief that human sacrifice was necessary so that the king would be accompanied by servants into the next world was an important part of Asante religion. This was reflected by the fact that servants who volunteered or were chosen to accompany the deceased king received great privilege and honor. However, since the majority of those sacrificed were criminals and prisoners of war, Wilks suggests that the British characterized these practices as "human sacrifice" to justify their interference in the Asante nation. The fact remains that the Asante affairs of state incorporated religious practices of sacrifice.

The relationship of human sacrifice to capital punishment is explicitly addressed by Purdum and Parades (1989) in their article "Rituals of Death: Capital Punishment and Human Sacrifice." The authors point out a set of similar underlying rationales between Aztec sacrifice and modern bureaucratically regulated executions. Even members of modern societies offer unabashedly religious rationales for capital punishment, such as a God-given right to take human life in retribution for violations of God's laws. Arguments similar to ecological hypotheses of Aztec sacrifice are paralleled in justifications of the death penalty on the basis of the high costs of lifetime incarceration. But they also point to another function of modern execution that parallels some of the demographic hypotheses regarding Aztec sacrifice: "the universal ancient human impulse to do something in times of stress, even if it is only ritual" (Purdum and Parades 1989, p. 153).

Summary: Biological and Social–Ecological Determinants of Human Sacrifice

Harner's original hypothesis that Aztec human sacrifice and cannibalism were products of ecological factors receives partial, but significant, support from the present cross-cultural analysis. While discussions of Aztec human sacrifice and cannibalism have typically emphasized these practices as unique features of Aztec society, the cross-cultural analyses presented here suggest that the Aztecs typify patterns of human sacrifice found cross-culturally. But the Aztecs might have been particularly motivated to consume human flesh as a consequence of ecological pressure and population pressure. Compared with other societies that also practiced human sacrifice, the Aztecs were extreme in several ways: they were the only human sacrifice society that faced a high risk of famine, they were the highest on several measures of population pressure, they were in the highest category of population density (over 500 persons/square mile), and they had the highest levels of overall warfare for land and resources. The magnitude of Aztec sacrifice and cannibalism may reflect their extreme conditions on many ecological variables.

The findings of specific demographic and political conditions motivating human sacrifice do not make it any more personally palatable, but they do remind us of a long-standing axiom of anthropology and cultural relativism—that to understand cultural behavior, we must understand the cultural context in which that behavior takes place. These emic explanations can be expanded by cross-cultural research that identifies the associated structural conditions.

Such perspectives can help us refine Rene Girard's perspectives on sacrifice, namely, that they reflect a broader human impulse toward violence. Human sacrifice may take many less obvious forms in the practice of scapegoating, in which an individual is made the "other," an outsider to be killed for the sins of the group. Violence against the "other" has many functions, from releasing our innate aggressive tendencies to making the "other" responsible for our own sins, an appropriate victim to be offered to the Gods for atonement. Sacrifice is a way of channeling human aggression into safe victims, a ritualization that directs our violent tendencies in socially acceptable ways. Many of the global trends that are visible today have their roots in conflicts between groups that have been motivated by religions. In the final chapter of this book, we will consider how our ancient tendencies to favor our own group while displaying aggression to outsiders are currently manifested.

Conclusions: The Limits of Religious Adaptations?

All societies have concepts of "supernatural evil" involving both the capacities of humans and the spirit world. By defining the types of behaviors that are not approved within the group, these ideas may serve to establish and reinforce social norms. Concepts of supernatural evil can also provide the rationale for promoting the interests of one's own group over the interests of other groups. These dynamics point to the limits of religious adaptations that facilitate in-group processes, but produce conflicts with other groups.

As we have examined the numerous features and manifestations of religiosity, we have repeatedly encountered features that were adaptive or that supported adaptive behaviors. We can point to many features of beliefs in supernatural evil that provide some of the same social control and integration mechanisms that we discussed in Chapter 9 in reference to the ways in which ritual, moral systems, and High Gods assist in the maintenance of social order. Witchcraft can be a powerful force for reinforcing the value structure of society, punishing deviants, and providing visible reminders of the consequences of transgressions. Threats of supernatural punishment can motivate us to be prosocial, altruistic, and group-oriented.

On the other hand, witchcraft beliefs and practices bring to the forefront some of the same issues we addressed in the conflict perspectives in Chapter 9. Religious beliefs can be used to favor one subset of the group over another, such as when they are used to justify exploitation and subordination of the lower classes. What is adaptive for one group is clearly a disadvantage for another. These dynamics of group favoritism used to exploit others become very obvious in the context of witchcraft beliefs and human sacrifice. In these situations, what benefits the survival or members of one group is clearly at the expense of another group's very existence.

This discussion brings us to the fundamental limits of group adaptations enhanced by religiosity. While religion clearly has helped humans survive in many ways—in particular, by increasing the role of group selection—this effect is clearly at the expense of others' survival and reproduction opportunities. Religion today may still enable "us" to function more effectively as groups and to reproduce and survive as individuals, but we do so by denying those same advantages to the "other" whom we demonize. And, conversely, religious beliefs may threaten our very survival when the out-groups seek our extermination as their own supernatural evil. These shifts in the functional adaptiveness of the group dynamics provided by religion serve to remind us of a fundamental fact about adaptations. Adaptations are relative to an environment, and when environments change, so, too, do the behaviors that are adaptive.

Questions for Discussion

- What types of groups within your society are currently treated as if they were "evil"?
- What groups outside your society are treated this way?
- Have you ever been treated as an "outsider"? If so, what was it that made you different?

Glossary

ergotism an illness caused by ingestion of ergot, a type of fungus that grows on rye and other grains, that provokes a variety of neurological symptoms, and that may have been a factor in the events of the Salem witchcraft trials

exuvial magic a type of sorcery that involves the use of parts of the body or items excreted from the body

general adaptation syndrome the body's reaction to stressors, also known as the "fight or flight" response

leveling mechanisms cultural behaviors that help to ensure that every member of a society has a relatively equal share of resources

nocebo effect harmful consequences to the body resulting from negative expectations (the opposite of the placebo effect)

ordeals processes for determining guilt or innocence by subjecting a person to a painful and potentially lethal activity

social inversion the practice of performing illicit or unapproved rituals or other behaviors whose structure or content is the antithesis of accepted rituals or behaviors

Wicca a modern "neo-pagan" religion that draws from a reconstruction of ancient European beliefs and rituals

zombie a person in Haitian folklore whose body and mind are under the control of a sinister supernatural influence; real-life zombies are poisoned by a combination of toxins that stupefy them and render them easy to control

Conclusions: Religion in Evolutionary Perspective

CHAPTER OUTLINE

CHAPTER OBJECTIVES

- Use the perspectives of evolutionary science to assess various features of religion and to illustrate their evolutionary status.
- Establish a framework for assessing the evolution of human ritual capacities by illustrating the prior adaptations manifested in the ritualized behavior of animals.
- Examine adaptations of religiosity provided by altered states of consciousness, shamanism, and spiritual healing.
- Describe the ways in which the supernatural concept provided a range of social adaptations that enhance the functioning of large groups.
- Examine the limits of the adaptiveness of religion in the modern world context, and present perspectives for overcoming its maladaptive aspects.

THE LAST PERSON WHO HAD GONE INTO THE CAVE had not come back. Most of the people who went in did not come back. Some of the ancient myths did tell of ones that had returned, but none of these stories had a happy ending. All of them described the unpleasant deaths suffered by those who had dared to pass the boundary and enter into the forbidden world. They returned in pain, nauseated, weak, and unable to eat. Their skins peeled away from their flesh, and they bled profusely. Sometimes, their families and friends suffered the same fate. It was clear that the land was poisoned, they were certain of that. But no one knew why. Were the Gods angry? Had the earth itself turned its back on them?

* * *

In 1980, a group of thirteen scientists and scholars met to come up with some ideas to ensure the safekeeping of the thousands of tons of radioactive waste that have been produced since the dawn of the atomic age (Time 1984). They considered a variety of problems, including where to store the waste, what types of engineering problems would need to be solved, and how to most safely transport the waste to a dump site.

They also pondered the human problem. Radioactive waste can remain dangerous for tens of thousands of years. No society or language of the past has existed that long, so the group had few models to draw on as it considered how to keep people out of a place that would be deadly for at least 300 generations. But the group was not at a complete loss for ideas: One human institution—religion—did offer some solutions to the problem.

It was suggested that the entry to the waste sites should be marked by a triangular pattern of three artificial hills. In their midst would be a set of images as universally compelling as those found in the caves of Europe. One of the images would show three people standing by the three hills and drinking from a well. Next to it would be an image of them dying.

As a further assurance that the area would remain off limits, the group proposed establishing an "atomic priesthood." This priesthood would pass on a tradition that taught that waste dumps were taboo and that divine retribution awaited those who violated the taboos. As time passed, myths and other tales would emerge that described the fate of those who dared to pass the forbidden boundaries and enter into realms in which no human belonged. To date, little has come of the suggestion to create a new religion to ensure that the deadly waste buried thousands of feet below the ground will remain forever out of human reach. Yet the very idea is intriguing and reflects the fundamental insight that religion is here to stay.

Introduction: Does Religion Have a Future?

The scientific debate regarding whether religion is on its way to extinction seems to be over. Religion is not going away any time soon, even if some features of religion are not adaptive. While the rationality of science might seem to supersede the magical thought of our primitive ancestors, we have seen that religious thought and behavior have many rational adaptive elements and that they continue to guide people's perceptions, thoughts, beliefs, and behaviors in cultures across the globe. In this book we have used a biocultural approach to help us understand why people continue to be religious, why we are "wired for religiosity," and why religiosity will continue to be an important feature of our species world. We truly are the "spiritual ape."

Religious beliefs and practices, as we have seen throughout this text, help humans to feel at home in the Universe, as well as to survive and reproduce. Religions organize people into cooperative groups. They provide us with moral guidelines that help us get along with one another. They provide us with conceptual frameworks that help us understand the world around us, and they offer principles which we can use to navigate our ways through the challenges of daily life. All these functions of religion have remained vitally important for humans in societies throughout human existence.

In this final chapter, we will summarize and discuss how the features of religion emerged out of a variety of prior adaptations that in humans led to new adaptations and co-options of evolutionary by-products. By drawing together the many threads of evidence presented throughout this text, we will see how both biological and cultural evolution led to religious beliefs and behaviors that provided a variety of adaptive functions which contributed to human survival and reproduction. Our focus will not be on the religious institutions that we know of today, but rather on the various components of religiosity we have examined over the last chapters. As before, we will use the perspectives of evolutionary science to understand how and why these elements of religiosity emerged.

We also will attempt to identify the sources of the adaptations that produced the universal features of religions. Did natural selection favor these features because they enhanced survival and reproduction? Were they selected for because they enhanced our capacities for religious experience? Or do these universal features of religion reflect other psychological processes that evolved for nonreligious purposes and which were later co-opted by religion? If religion is based on prior adaptations, do they constitute nonfunctional by-products? Or does religious practice provide a context in which further adaptive advantages are obtained from prior adaptations?

Finally, we will ask whether religion is now more maladaptive than adaptive. Has religion become a parasite on the human biological and cultural landscape, something that has begun to undermine our ability to survive as a species? Or do features of religion still have adaptive roles in the current environment of global adaptations? While religious features may have had many adaptive functions in the past, such as integrating groups and distinguishing them from one another we have to ask whether these social effects of religious beliefs still offer adaptive advantages in the world today, or whether they have become maladaptive in the environment of the modern world, with its international interdependencies in politics, commerce, and the acquisition of resources. Our answers may be troubling, for even if some aspects of religiosity are now indeed maladaptive, we cannot easily abandon them. Because religious institutions engage and meet so many of our psychological needs, they can prey on human needs with practices that are clearly maladaptive for the individual and groups, perhaps even our species. But because we are "wired" for religiosity, it will continue to be a potent force in human life even if it is maladaptive in some situations.

The Conceptual Frameworks of Evolution

Many types of evidence are necessary to assess the biological bases of religion. In this section, we will expand our earlier considerations of the key concepts of evolutionary theory to illustrate the evidence that helps us understand whether universal features of religion involve adaptations. Even by-products can evolve into adaptations that produce cognitions and behaviors that enhance survival and reproduction. Evolutionary perspectives also illustrate that other biological features, such as co-opted exaptations and co-opted spandrels, also are functional and forms of adaptation (Buss et al. 1998).While many communal and ritual features of religion reflect hominin adaptations that were continued in humans, religion also involves new features and functions. Religious institutions combined the ritual adaptations of our primate heritage with new systems of thought and identity, including symbolism and culture that enabled human religion to emerge and vastly expand the functional integrative capacity of ritual.

The Emergent Nature of the Universe

As the Universe has evolved, phenomena emerged whose principles and properties were distinctly different from the principles and properties of the phenomena that produced them. **Emergence** refers to situations in which new levels of phenomena arise out of the interactions among lower level phenomena. The properties of these higher level phenomena cannot be accounted for solely in terms of the properties of lower levels. For example, living organisms depend on the physical and chemical processes that make life possible, but they also have characteristics that cannot be explained solely on the basis of processes at the atomic or chemical levels.

Similarly, the principles of physics can explain the impact of a chimpanzee's foot on the forest floor and the dynamic movements of the leg, but physics does not explain the path the chimpanzee takes or why it does so. Although living organisms are still constrained by the physical and chemical laws that affect the molecules of which they are composed, they have emergent features and operating principles that are qualitatively different than the features of molecules. Living organisms sleep, eat one another, and squabble over resources. Molecules do not do these things (but some cells do). While living organisms remain dependent on the biological level, they also have new properties that extend the capacities of their biological components.

Just as life is an emergent property of chemical processes, social behavior is an emergent property of life. Societies function according to principles and properties that are qualitatively different than those which gave rise to living organisms. Societies have their own operating principles, including dominance hierarchies and territorial defense. In at least one lineage of animals, social living eventually led to the emergence of a new phenomenon: culture. In cultural systems, traditions are passed down from one generation to the next not because they are encoded in molecules, but because they are learned by individuals during their lifetimes. Humans have many biologically driven behaviors. But more than any other species, humans have biological capacities that are molded and modified by **learning**, our ability to acquire knowledge during our own lifetimes. This learning capacity is based on innate capabilities, but it provides a new level of adaptation.

Consider our innate human capacity to acquire a language. Small children start to make sounds as soon as they can control the muscles of their vocal cords. But the random sounds they start with soon change to resemble the sounds they hear around them. This mimicking of the sounds around them is the first step in learning to speak the specific language they will acquire. A variety of similar innate capacities enable humans to learn culture—the most important of all human adaptations—and the first stage of learning our culture also involves mimicking others.

Our capacity for culture was expanded most significantly by the emergence of symbols. The human capacity for symbolism has provided a way for cultural knowledge to be encoded in material objects and transferred among generations. Symbols enable cultural traditions to be communicated across time and space and among individuals who have never met. Like the levels that emerged before it and that make it possible—including the chemical, the living, and the social—symbols are a qualitatively new phenomenon that has its own operating principles and contributes to human adaptation in unique ways.

While the capacities for cultural learning are not exclusive to humans, the gap in learning potentials among humans and even human-socialized chimpanzees is so great that it is clear that genetic differences are responsible for humans' cultural capacity. Today, every *Homo sapiens* lives in an environment created by culture. In a very real sense, culture stands between ourselves and the natural world. Culture provides us with many of the ideas we use to make sense of the world and even shapes the emotions that help us distinguish between the desirable and undesirable aspects of the world.

As we have seen throughout this book, religion plays an important role in shaping culture and communicating these ideas and emotions. Across human evolution, religion has provided systems that have enhanced the transmission of culture. Consequently, we may regard modern forms of religiosity to be cultural adaptations. However, many common features of religiosity reflect human psychological and social adaptations enabled by many features of our complex brains and minds. As we have seen, religions can help to define and provide structure and consistency to our social groups. By promoting allegiance to a particular group and providing mechanisms for ensuring the perpetuation of the group, religiosity became a key tool in cultural evolution. Because of the power of religious belief systems to mold large numbers of people into self-sacrificing actions on behalf of the group, religion is perhaps the most powerful ideological system for enhancing human potentials for survival and reproduction.

It may seem like quite a long way from the submission displays, the pant–hooting, and the occasional drumming of chimpanzees on tree trunks to the forms of prayer, chanting, and music in contemporary religions. And it is, for it took our ancestors some 5–7 million years to make that journey. Along the way, they acquired numerous new traits, some of which gave rise to our cognitive abilities to create models of the Universe. While the behavioral roots of our propensity for religiosity lie in the 98.46% of our genes that we share with chimpanzees, the flowering of religiosity and its expression in material and ideational culture is due to the changes that occurred in the remaining 1.54%.

Religiosity as an Emergent Phenomena. Sometime in our past, a combination of biological, psychological, and social traits gave rise to something new—the human capacity for religiosity. This capacity provided the basis for shamanism, a complex religious feature of all early human societies. This and other religious practices involve many traits that have established adaptive value. But this does not demonstrate that we evolved to be religious through natural selection. The process of emergence makes it difficult to identify if there are specific biological features related to religious features because the exact basis of any complex behavioral functions that are characteristic features of a species is somewhat elusive.

Assessing whether a specific behavior and its underlying trait is a biological adaptation that confers survival benefits is difficult to determine for many reasons.

Genes code for proteins, not behaviors. Furthermore, a particular human behavior is not the product of a specific gene but arises through the interactions of numerous behavioral capacities that are themselves shaped by many genetic influences. In contrast to a trait such as blood type, a behavioral trait typically is not the product of a specific single gene, but results from the complex interactions between numerous genetically based traits that enable the complex behaviors that organisms use as they interact with their environment.

For example, the ability to hit an animal with a stick is based not on a single gene, but on the complex outcome of the behavioral capacities of our bodies and the ways in which our brains are able to control them. These capacities include not only the range of motion of our fingers and thumbs, hands, arms, shoulders, and back muscles, and the support system provided by our skeleton and legs. They also involve our abilities to finely control and coordinate these movements, and they require us to use our highly evolved visual system and many other components of our brain. We can safely assume that none of these areas evolved specifically to hit animals.

Just because a behavior is universal or involves something adaptive does not establish that the behavior is a product of natural selection. Novel behavioral functions can derive from the interactions among many preexisting biological adaptations established by previous processes of natural selection and adaptation. Adaptations may be used for novel behaviors without having any functional relevance for survival. This can be seen in the ways we use our hands for playing tennis. Human adaptations can be co-opted by other motivational mechanisms and combined with other cognitive and physical capacities in order to produce behaviors that are universal, such as soccer, but that are not products of natural selection.

Consequently, it can be difficult to determine whether a new behavior constitutes a unique genetically-based adaptation. Are new behavioral functions the products of newly selected genes or gene interactions producing a trait, or do new behaviors derive from different recombinations of previous potentials that are now being adapted to different environmental circumstances? Since our potentials are self-organizing and take a particular configuration as a result of environmental influences, different environmental dynamics can produce different forms of organization from the same potentials through new recombinations of prior traits rather than new genes. How can we tell what produces the new trait and behavior, a new gene or a new effect generated by environmental influences acting on an existing combination of existing genes? Without evidence of specific gene–behavior linkages, these questions are difficult to answer.

It is apparent that many behavioral features of religion result from emergence, in which a new behavioral characteristic arises independently of changes in the genetic makeup, but is instead a product of recombinations of prior capabilities. For instance, while we did not evolve to build religious structures such as churches, it is now "natural" for religions to do so because of a variety of prior psychological and social adaptations. Many aspects of modern religions are cultural adaptations that meet human biological, social, and psychological needs by transmitting learned traditions rather than genetically determined capacities.

It is also clear that biological evolution has resulted in traits that have made religion possible. Specific features associated with religions, such as altered states of consciousness, spirit beliefs, and healing can be assessed with respect to their evolutionary origins as adaptations. But some of these assessments lead to the conclusion that specific features of universal religious practices evolved for reasons other than those related to religion. For instance, the hypnotic and placebo responses appear to have evolved not for religious purposes, but for other adaptive reasons. Nonetheless, there is support for the argument that some features of the human genome evolved because their religious uses facilitated human survival and reproduction and that adaptive aspects of religiosity drove specific aspects of human evolution.

Symbolism and Spirituality. In his book *The Symbolic Species*, Terrence Deacon (1997) explains how emergent processes and the creative dynamics of evolution provide an understanding of the spiritual in terms of humans' symbolic capacities. Social species understand reality through information derived from others, using a "theory of mind" to model and understand the perceptions of others. Symbols expand this ability to access other minds and their intents and form a substrate for maintaining awareness of others' perspectives, knowledge, and intents.

Deacon suggests that symbolic abilities give us a deep insatiable tendency to experience the spiritual in our quest for meaning, attempting to find the purpose and intentionality behind our experience of the Universe. The adaptive advantages of symbolic relationships involve broader evolved predispositions to seek out patterns and look for reasons beyond what we can perceive, searching for meaning beyond the obvious surface features in the minds of "behind the scenes actors." We view patterns in the natural world

as cryptic messages, symbols from an unseen communicator whom we attempt to understand. Human nature has an irrepressible need to find meaning in unseen intentional meaningful agents that we experience as the spiritual.

The spiritual shares fundamental features with the symbolic. The meanings to which spiritual concepts refer are not intrinsic to their representation, form, or sound, nor are they found in mechanisms of the brain; rather, they are found in an associational network of understandings entertained by the minds of a cultural and linguistic community. Symbolic reference is not in the physical reality, but in an imagined one. This experience of spiritual meaning has a foundation in our experience of shared meaning in symbol systems expressed in the imagined minds of others, disembodied abstractions like the spirit world. Deacon suggests that human intuitions of our selves or our minds that exist independently of our bodies are produced through symbols that give us a kind of a virtual identity separate from the corporeal basis of our existence.

Symbolic representation extended the ability of humans to have experiences in virtual reference, a capacity that allows us to use internalized abstract models to engage in the trial-and-error exploration of different possible circumstances. Symbols provide a processing medium beyond the capacities of genetic evolution in their engagement with different possibilities, a risk-free method for exploring different options and a capacity for forethought and extended planning. These symbolic capacities free a thinker from the constraints of the here and now, allowing imagined goals to take precedence over the immediate context in guiding adaptive behaviors. These experiences result not from biological capacities alone, but from the emergent properties derived from cultural systems of belief.

The concept of emergence does not refute the possibility of further religious-based evolution, including selective pressures favoring religiosity and the adaptation of both biological and cultural traits to new religious purposes. Religious practices changed humans' cultural niche, allowing a new level of gene–culture co-evolution. Religion did so by expanding our capacity to represent and relate to others, to "read their minds," and to make use of this information in coordinating larger, more effective social groups. Religion can be seen as an extension of our general social capability to manage relationships among people and to form social groups. This emphasizes the notion that there are many levels of influence affecting selection.

Multilevel Selection Processes in Evolution

Most discussions of natural selection focus on **individual selection**: how the particular traits of an organism favor its survival and affect the relative number of offspring it contributes to the next generation. This focus has led some investigators to reject the idea that religion is adaptive because it may lead people to do things that do not enhance fitness. For example, religious beliefs may lead people to sacrifice their lives for their Gods, religion, or group. How can something be adaptive if it leads you to kill yourself? The concept of **inclusive fitness** recognizes that these sacrifices may actually enhance the survival of one's own genes by enhancing the survival of descendants and other related members of one's group. Inclusive fitness is an assessment of fitness that considers not only your own survival and reproduction, but also the fitness of your relatives who share your genes. If your act of self-sacrifice increases the likelihood that your offspring and close relatives will survive and reproduce, then this act will enhance your fitness. Thus, a man who lays down his life in defense of his family or kin group may actually help these relatives to live longer and produce more offspring. Although he may not have produced any children, his close relatives will. And since these relatives will share many of the deceased's genes, his act of sacrifice can lead to his genes becoming more numerous in the next generation.

It was the recognition of these kinds of altruistic sacrifices that inspired the idea that evolution can also operate through group selection. This idea is controversial for many reasons, but the basic idea is sound. Natural selection operates on features and behavioral characteristics across the different levels of the biological hierarchy—not only at the level of the individual organisms and specific genes, but also in terms of various populations, including local groups, colonies, as well as entire species (Okasha 2003). Natural selection operates on differences in fitness among individuals (gene-level selection), differences in fitness among individuals within a group (individual level selection), and differences in fitness among groups (group level selection). Evolution occurs at all levels of selection. Acquired traits can produce behaviors that increase an individual's fitness within the group, or that enhance the group's internal coordination and effectiveness in competition with other groups.

The roles of religion in intergroup competition emphasize the ability of religious strategies to favor the members of one group to compete with members of outside groups. The closed breeding populations that are characteristic of many religious groups allow for certain traits concentrated within groups to increase in frequency, producing between-group genetic differences. However, while religion may be good at producing group differences and facilitating intergroup competition, universal features of religiosity cannot be the product of group differences. The basic traits for religiosity shared by humans across cultures provide a clear example of a human strategy designed to enhance between group competition by enhancing in group effectiveness.

Darwinian processes of evolution through natural selection also result from the cultural effects of religion on survival and reproduction. Individual and group fitness are affected by the crucial ways in which culture mediates our relationships with the environment—for example, acquiring food, escaping predation, forming alliances, obtaining a spouse, reducing conflict, achieving social status—that can confer advantages for reproduction and survival. Cultural traits can produce specific kinds of behaviors, such as conflict reduction processes or group protection strategies, that can enhance the survival and reproduction of the members and the group. This effect makes cultural traits—including religious beliefs—agents in the processes of biological evolution. Religion, like culture in general, is not a feature possessed by one individual alone, but is a trait that is shared by a group. Consequently, it can contribute to the survival of members of the group, even if it does not contribute to the reproduction of the individuals who express it (e.g., by motivating them to self-sacrifice for others).

Religious institutions are part of the cultural environment that has had the potential to exert selective pressures on the genome, favoring people who have traits that facilitate their ability to function in large groups. To some, this also constitutes one kind of group selection, one involving individual adaptations that enhance our capacity for effective social interaction. Enhanced skills for general in-group functioning are acquired potentials that religions exploit, and which religions select for because they enhance coordinated group functioning. Social evolution requires enhanced mechanisms for processing behavioral and social information about others in one's group and the personal ability to use that information in selecting among options in interacting with other group members. Religion and ritual provide a range of mechanisms for structuring interactions to optimize coordination of information and intentions.

Evaluating Adaptations, Exaptations, and Spandrels

An evolutionary functional analysis is necessary to determine (1) whether a universal trait is the product of natural selection, (2) whether selection for the trait was the consequence of its adaptive features or its association with other adaptive traits, and (3) whether other cognitive or motivational processes are responsible for co-opting that feature. Whether something is an adaptation, exaptation, spandrel, or functionless by-product depends on the origins of the feature and its relationship to the processes of natural selection in fixing the trait in the population. In the case of adaptations, these traits became universally established features of the species because they were adaptive. For instance, hypnotic susceptibility was apparently the result of natural selection for the adaptive features associated with dissociation, extreme focus of attention, and engagement with alternative realities. Hypnotic susceptibility is not religion, although it supports religious beliefs; and the social support effects of religious practices can enhance selection for people who are hypnotically disposed. These original adaptations, as well as their selected and non-selected associated features, are the basis for further adaptations called exaptations, as well as spandrels. These features may acquire the status of functional adaptations under specific environmental conditions.

Proximate and Ultimate Mechanisms. To establish that a feature is an evolutionary adaptation, we must show both biological and environmental mechanisms involved in the selection and establishment of a trait (Preston and deWaal 2002). These two levels of analysis—proximate and ultimate—that are involved in the assessment of the processes of evolutionary adaptation involve, respectively: the genetic variation in the species that allows for selection of new adaptive features for the species as a whole; and the influences in the environment that exert the selective influences that favor some features over others. The proximate mechanisms are concerned with the variation in physiological structures and cognitive processes that provide the underpinnings for specific adaptive behaviors and autonomic and somatic nervous system responses. The focus on the environment addresses questions of ultimate mechanisms that provide evolutionary explanations, illustrating the historical trajectory of the development of a trait in a functional account related to the organism's enhanced reproductive success in its environment. Ultimate mechanisms select for variation in the species on the basis of advantages that individuals receive through their ability to engage in behaviors that enhance fitness. Thus, while adaptations are, by definition, inherited features, the environment plays a critical role in their manifestation and development. The environment then can change the status of a feature over

In this image, a female chimpanzee carrying an infant attacks a stuffed leopard with a branch. This leopard is holding a baby chimpanzee doll in its front paws. This proclivity for even female chimps to attack predators who are threatening their group illustrates ways that aggression toward predators and other outside threats can enhance the fitness of members of the group.

time from adaptive to maladaptive (for example, skin coloring) or change something that is neutral in its original context into an important adaptation. The environment may affect whether or not a genetic trait is even expressed.

Biological mechanisms can be implied by behaviors that are a universal feature of a species. There must also be evidence that the behavior that the trait produces increases an individual's fitness—that is, his or her ability to survive and reproduce. We also need to step back from the present day and consider the benefits that the trait offered in the environment in which our ancestors lived: the small-scale foraging groups that characterized most of our prehistory. We can demonstrate the adaptiveness of a trait by producing independent and corroborating evidence from several different perspectives (cognitive sciences, ecology, ethology, biodynamics, etc.; see Wildman [2006]). We must integrate many forms of information in order to assess the evolutionary adaptations in human behavior, since the complexity of the human brain allows traits to produce a wide range of behaviors as a function of emergence, recombinations, and environmental circumstances.

To determine whether a new trait involves a co-opted exaptation or a co-opted spandrel with new adaptive features—and thus constitutes a new adaptation—we need to establish evidence that the later functions are distinct from the original functions. To establish new adaptive features, one first specifies causal processes recognized by evolutionary biology and then shows that an adaptive problem can be solved by the psychological mechanisms that have been proposed (Buss et al. 1998). Common features of adaptations and exaptations (including co-opted adaptations and co-opted spandrels) are selection for specialized functions for solving a specific adaptive problem with a special design that could not have arisen by chance because of its complex features.

To determine that a feature is a functionless by-product also requires an evolutionary analysis to establish, first, the evolved mechanisms underlying the particular religious capability or behavior; and second, the cognitive and motivational mechanisms that allow humans and religions to co-opt and exploit those capabilities. By-products do not solve adaptive problems, because they lack a functional design to achieve a feature that enhances survival and reproduction. If, on the other hand, a feature can enhance survival and be transmitted to the subsequent generation, then it is an adaptation. These are functional adaptations whether they are **co-opted exaptations** that use features selected initially for different functions or whether they are **co-opted spandrels**, features that emerged as side effects of adaptations produced through natural selection; or whether they are cultural institutions that exert influences on individual selection.

We thus have several distinct aspects of the possible roles of religiosity in evolutionary adaptations: (1) features of religiosity resulted from natural selection because they favored survival and reproduction (e.g., contagion avoidance); (2) features of religiosity resulted from natural selection favoring other adaptive strategies (i.e., social integration); (3) features of religiosity derived from by-products associated with adaptive features which later acquired functional adaptations on their own (co-opted exaptations; co-opted spandrels, such as the parental qualities of protection and love attributed to some spirits); and (4) religious practices functioned as group-level environmental influences in natural selection for individual social and cognitive features that were adaptive in enhancing group coordination and individual well-being.

Assessing the Evolutionary Status of Religious Features

The status of religion as a whole is assessed here from the perspective of evolutionary sequences of the emergence of religious features covered in the previous chapters. This analysis allows us to show how a variety of specific aspects of religion provided adaptive advantages. It also reveals that many of the features that are associated with religion evolved for reasons other than their religious functions, such as healing; religious beliefs may have, however, exapted and extended their functions.

Ritualized Animal Behaviors: The Preadaptations and Origins of Religiosity

The biocultural approach illustrates that our ancestors developed their capacity for religiosity in a context of community ritual; this reveals principles different from most contemporary conceptualizations and definitions of religion. The biocultural perspective and its explicit evolutionary focus point to the roots of religiosity in the homologous behaviors of the animal world. This evolutionary approach suggests that we understand religiosity as an expansion of the functions of ritualized behaviors. The many homologies between ritualized animal behaviors and our own rituals provide a framework for examining the precursors to and prior adaptations required for religious behaviors.

The traditional approach to studying religions that focuses on concepts such as "transcendence," "cosmology," "ultimate explanations," and "supernatural beings" exemplifies a cognitive emphasis that generally overlooks the importance of behavior. In traditional evolutionary terms, it is behavior—what we do—that enhances survival and reproduction. Beliefs don't affect survival unless they influence behavior or other responses of the organism, such as managing stress, that do affect survival and reproduction. A focus on animal behavior provides us with an understanding of the foundations of the religious impulse in the behavioral and cognitive systems that manage social life.

The ritual precursors of human religiosity manifested in animal behaviors and their common functions in organizing and coordinating social life illustrates (1) that religion as ritual involves capacities to enable larger groups to function more effectively; and (2) that ritual evolved for nonspiritual purposes. From this perspective, the fundamental aspects of human religious ritual are a continuation of the same ritualized functions in animals, whereas the unique evolution of human religiosity involves spirituality. Human ritual capacities also involve additional adaptive mechanisms through exaptations of prior features (such as mammalian opioid–mediated bonding) and the acquisition of new capacities for utilizing ritual and supernatural functions (i.e., integrating unrelated people and establishing moral systems).

Ritualized animal behavior itself is an exaptation, for it involves the use of behaviors that evolved for another purpose to do something new—communicate intention. The behavior itself is directly related to enacting the intention. For example, when one wolf snarls and shows its teeth to another, it is generally intending to use its teeth. But in this behavior—a dominance display—the use stops short of enactment. Through a display, the wolf signals its intent to engage in an act (e.g., using its teeth to express a willingness to dominate the other animal), but it does not need to carry out the action if the subordinate animal ritually signals submission. Thus, ritualized communication is an animal exaptation of initiatory behavioral movements that are used now to signal intentions in ritualized acts. Animal ritualized behaviors are co-opted exaptations of behaviors that acquired new adaptation functions in communication and social integration.

Animals also exhibit other precursors of religiosity. They are able to distinguish animate from inanimate objects (animacy detection). They establish and maintain dominance and submission relationships with other members of their species and—perhaps—with "unseen others" (hierarchical reasoning). They use group-bonding rituals to extend their natural preference to favor their own relatives to also favor "social others" (inclusiveness), and they may take risks or even give up their own lives in the defense of others (costly signaling and sacrifice). Some animals are even capable of at least the rudiments of "symbolism." When a mother bird tries to divert a predator from her nestlings by hopping away from the nest and dragging one of her wings, she is using a sign that falsely signals—symbolizes—that she is impaired, in order to lure the predator away from the nest. By doing so, she enhances her nestlings' chance of survival and thus her own reproductive success.

Some human religious traits also appear to be exaptations of the same hominin capacities that are manifested in chimpanzee ritualization. These involved excited group displays led by alpha males who used vocalization, drumming, and "dancing," which are manifested in the basic dynamics of shamanic ritual. Even before hominans evolved, our hominid ancestors incorporated a number of new elements into the kinds of ritualized behaviors found in chimpanzees. Community rituals involve a variety of adaptive features protecting and integrating the group. The preshamanic rituals exapted many preexisting aspects of the ritual capacity, particularly those focused on emotional group activities involving vocalizations. Newly evolved hominan capacities expanded on the original functions of coordinating and integrating members of society through the expressive capacities provided by imitation (mimesis), which expanded the ways in which individuals could communicate their experiences and intentions to one another.

These are adaptive functions involving group protection and integration, but these ritual activities are not sufficient to constitute human religion. Group ritual activities involving prolonged vocalizations and drumming also produced altered states of consciousness. Drumming is a behavior that was emergent from hominin capacities; but drumming for hours, rather than the few second bursts characteristic of chimpanzee drumming, is obviously the result of further adaptations. The phylogenetic depth of drumming and its multiple functional effects place it at the core of the precursors that were selected for shamanism and the production of altered states of consciousness (ASC).

Mystical Experiences and Altered States of Consciousness

The initial focus on religiosity in terms of experiences rather than beliefs might seem strange, but evolution is concerned with adaptive behaviors rather than thoughts. Behaviors, however, are produced by mental traits, and our beliefs are developed to account for our experiences. So, focusing on the origins of religious experiences and, in particular, on what we call spirituality, as embodied in mysticism, makes good sense. Chronologically, experiences emerge first and produce behavioral responses (rituals) that then require beliefs (myths) to account for them. As we illustrated in Chapter 3, many effects on our biology—trauma, starvation, long-distance running, and plant and fungal chemicals—all produce a range of mystical experiences. There are many aspects to these altered states of consciousness. The adaptive features of ASC must be understood first in terms of their effects on humans and their behavior, including cognitive and physiological responses. The experiences themselves may have initially been spandrels which later provided further adaptive consequences.

The concept of ASC as a special mode of consciousness—the integrative mode of consciousness—helps to explain their adaptiveness. Many different forms of ASC involve an enhanced capacity for transmitting information from the normally unconscious levels of the brain into conscious experience. Diverse forms of ASC allow this enhanced capability to access the output of the unconscious mind and our innate cognitive modules. These ASC typically involve an engagement with a special visual depiction of information, which is involved in dreaming, and typically engage a holistic presentational symbolic capacity. Thus, ASC exapt prior functional capacities of dreams to extend and focus their information integration capacities to additional domains of human concern, providing a co-opted exaptation.

A central feature of human cognitive evolution involving the development of specialized innate modules produced a fragmentation of consciousness, a functional dissociation of our automatized systems from our conscious stream of awareness. Ritually induced ASC provide mechanisms for reintegrating these processes and linking their outputs into the visual symbolic systems engaged by dreams, visions, and hallucinations. This adaptation allows for the transfer of information into consciousness. In this sense, religious consciousness, conceptualized in terms of visionary mystical and spiritual experiences, is an evolution of human consciousness to higher levels of integration of the modular and innate structures into consciousness. These capacities evolved as a consequence of the selective advantages for humans who were more labile to these influences, manifested in hypnotic susceptibility; or who could more effectively

metabolize exogenous sources of the substances that produced the same effects. These processes and capacities were selected because they reflected enhanced systemic integration of information, particularly by the serotonin system.

The human divergence from our hominin ancestors involved an enhanced integrative functioning of the nervous system. Humans acquired mechanisms for greater absorption of exogenous serotonergic-mimicking and -enhancing substances, as well as mechanisms for enhanced opioid reception. The failure of chimpanzees to self-administer psychedelic drugs, in contrast to their easy addiction to other drugs, illustrates something unique about human neuroreceptor systems. In humans, natural selection clearly favored some capacities for dissociation as a capacity for managing emotional life through symbols and expectations engaged in our unconscious imaginary worlds of the spirits and unconscious. These dissociative features were selected for their ability to provide emotional relief and psychological compartmentalization, providing healing. Religions provide ritual contexts in which these dissociative potentials could be safely and therapeutically channeled, constituting an environment that favored selection for hypnotic and dissociative capacities.

Managing Consciousness. Consciousness is a dynamic process, a product of the interplay among our brains, mind, and behavior. Religious consciousness draws on many important mammalian preadaptations and extends their potentials into the symbolic capacities that humans possess. In contrast to the role of baseline consciousness in ensuring that we remain engaged with the external Universe, processes associated with integrative consciousness are adaptations designed to help us process information within our inner worlds and to understand our emotions and relations with others in the outside world. Religious states of consciousness use these potentials to integrate our inner worlds with our conscious mind. This integrative mode of consciousness can provide people with religiously inspired insights that fundamentally change the way they view their societies. Numerous examples from religion, as well as a growing body of scientific evidence, demonstrate that individuals may spontaneously reconfigure the ways in which they look at themselves and the Universe. This effort can lead to more personally meaningful interactions with the Universe and with the other members of society. When one person's insights help others to make sense of their lives, these insights can even give rise to a new religion.

Thus, the religious management of ASC represents an important human adaptation that provides a constructive context for updating and rewriting the cultural software that helps us to relate to the Universe and to our group.

Spirits as Spandrels of ASC. Many of the phenomenological features produced by ASC contribute to a neurotheology, a set of beliefs about personal spiritual qualities and essences that caused them to develop a spirit belief system. ASC produce a spiritual experience of the self, exemplified in the near-death and out of body experiences. These experiences give the person a sense of personal qualities generally conceptualized as the soul. These aspects of ASC provide an experiential basis for the spirit world, a neurophenomenology which requires explanation. As humans endeavored to understand these ASC experiences and other features of their Universe, we inevitably projected our own human personal and social qualities onto the unknown others. These spirit experiences and beliefs consequently involve intuitions that reflect our human nature, imbuing spirits with the familiar and reassuring qualities of protecting parents. The personal and social features of spirits are a consequence of projecting prior adaptations for "knowing others;" and their presence in spirit concepts involves co-opted exaptations and spandrels that provided a basis for new functional adaptations. The capacity for representing and responding to personal and social features of people who met our dependency needs provided the basis for a co-opted spandrel in the construction of the concepts of spirits with personal and social qualities; these could be used for new functions as models for identification and social integration. Personal and social qualities also provided bases for extensions of other previous features of parental dynamics such as authority and submission to Gods. Beliefs in a powerful protective "other" elicit altruistic and protective behaviors, enhancing general well-being for groups and for the individual. These beliefs also provided mechanisms for activating healing mechanisms manifested in placebo effects. A variety of cultural adaptations enhancing reproduction and survival were facilitated by these beliefs in spirit beings.

Shamanism

Shamanism represents the continued enhancement of ritual group integration capacities that conferred selective advantages. These expanded across hominan evolution into more intense and elaborate community rituals that engaged adaptive mechanisms and exerted selective influence for those who could take advantage of the ritual effects (such as placebo responses and hypnotic susceptibility). Shamanism dramatically expanded the capacities for ritualized communication and social coordination displayed by other animals in new dimensions involving visual symbols and the representation of the self and others as spirits. Shamanism involves exaptations of ancient ritual capacities of drumming, dancing, and vocalizing, extending them from their original socially integrative functions to enhance the production of ASC experiences and engage the hypnotic capacity in alternate scenario exploration in the symbolic world of spiritual and cosmological beliefs and behaviors. Shamanism enhances the expression of our internal visionary capacities—our primordial symbolic substrate—through ritually-elicited experiences of the dream capacities.

Shamanic practices expanded the capacities and functions of ancient group vocalization practices in the human acquisition of a capacity for music, singing, melodies, rhythm, and the emotional effects they produce. Music has many preadaptations in emotional vocalizations, expanding them to include a greater range of tones and to generate longer productions. This enlargement enhances brain and body synchronization, as well as psychological healing and emotional management. Music improves the coordination of emotions in ways that enhance the power of a group, extending a sense of unity, connectedness, and common purpose. These musical abilities were part of a central suite of activities which enhanced human adaptation, well-being, and reproductive success, with benefits for group cohesion, social coordination, emotional communication, and healing. Music was selected because of these adaptive features, not because it was associated with belief in the supernatural. Both music and religiosity were, however, adaptive for the same ancient function of ritual, namely, group integration. If we consider this to be the fundamental purpose of religion, then musical abilities likely evolved because they supported the adaptive functions of ritual (group integration), and hence, religion.

Key symbolic features of shamanism illustrate how religious beliefs use the by-products of the integration of different modalities for thinking. Combining human personal and social qualities is a by-product or spandrel of these integrative brain processes, but it provides new forms of personal and social representation that have new adaptive functions in managing personal and social life. Evolved components of our mental hardware that we use to perceive and interpret existentially important phenomena in the Universe (such as animals, "others," and "spirits") provide much of the ideational content of shamanic beliefs. Shamanism manifested new forms of cognition and symbolic processes in animal spirit concepts that defined personal and social identities, such as totemism. These representations also provided mechanisms for healing through personal individuation (identity formation), social integration, emotional awareness, and symbolic transformations of self. The roles of shamans in the emergence of these capacities are exemplified in shamans' transformation of identity through animal familiars and guardian spirits and their social intelligence as charismatic group leaders and intergroup mediators.

The use of animal spirit concepts to represent personal and social identity has its origins in the visionary images of shamanic states of consciousness and their capacity to integrate the products of different components of our mental hardware. Such integrated products are exemplified in shamans' visionary experiences, which are complex models incorporating the integrative information capacities of dream cognition for rehearsal and planning. Shamanic ASC integrate the mental hardware that originally evolved to help us respond to the social and natural environments, using these new experiences to serve other functions of social representation and psychological manipulation. Shamanic practices engage and integrate into the individual's experience the innate processes and structures underlying attachment and bonding, kinship and unconscious psychological integration. Shamanic rituals activated various components of our mental hardware that offered our ancestors adaptive advantages, helping them in the management of emotions that affected group-inclusive social interactions.

The universality of shamanism in modern foraging societies indicates that shamanistic practices and beliefs emerged from some constants in the ancestral hominin populations that gave rise to hominans and modern *Homo sapiens*. It also suggests that the genetic bases of the behavioral dispositions and cognitive abilities that underlie shamanism were—and still are—common throughout our species. Shamanic ritual activities engaged uniquely human ways of understanding the Universe and facilitated both individual (psychological) and group (social) integration. By examining the new cultural elements associated with shamanism and understanding the preadaptations that made these possible, we can begin to sketch out the sequence in which different aspects of religiosity appeared. This sequence, in turn, can help to assess whether aspects of religiosity arose as adaptations, exaptations, or co-opting of biological functions acquired for other purposes.

The various features of shamanism examined in the previous chapters suggest the following sequences in the evolution of religiosity:

1. The communicative and social coordination functions of ritualized animal behaviors are expanded in shamanic rituals and beliefs with new adaptations that expanded their functional capacity to integrate unrelated humans into larger groups.

2. The ritualized capacities of hominins were expanded through community rituals that manipulated mammalian attachment processes, elicited the opioid-attachment mechanisms, and helped assure well-being by enhancing individuals' access to resources and support. Opioid receptivity was selected because it had advantages for immune functions, enhanced social bonding, and integration. Community rituals further expanded access to the advantages provided by enhanced opioid receptivity.

3. Humans developed the ability to enter into the integrative modes of consciousness, as manifested in shamanic soul flight, visionary experiences, and mystical experiences. This reflected an integration of information from multiple areas of the brain, producing new forms of representation. ASC enhanced the transfer of integrated visual information from the unconscious. They also involved a decentering of perspective—a detachment of the perceiving self from the body that provided new views of the self and new perspectives on the Universe.

4. These ASC also produced experiences interpreted as the soul and spirits; these and other anomalous experiences gave rise to an explanation— the supernatural assumption that spirits exist and that they can have an effect on our lives. Our innate tendencies to perceive animals, "self," "others," and "spirits" were applied to develop new understandings of the self and the group. These spirit concepts were co-opted spandrels that acquire new adaptive functions in helping people to psychologically and socially manage death anxiety and grieving through spiritual beliefs, enhancing survival and reproduction by curtailing potentially fatal stress responses.

5. Development of spiritual healing practices occurred through expanding concepts of altruism to benevolent spirit others, enabling them to evoke placebo effects through engagement of our hopes and positive expectations in ways that had

powerful effects in eliciting endogenous physiological healing mechanisms.

6. Shamanic experiences, particularly those induced by ritual ASC, enhanced the capacity for visual symbolism and metaphoric thought, manifested in shamanic universals such as soul flight, animal allies, spirit others, and personally transforming death-and-rebirth experiences. These shamanic universals may be seen as co-opted spandrels, originally by-products of the nervous system and integration of innate modules that provided new cognitive capacities embodied in visual symbolism.

7. Societies began to use sacred symbols such as Gods that provided benefits from their social integration effects that were derived from their emergent properties such as group identity and internalization of ideal models.

8. Supernatural agents began to serve as moral standards and observers, epitomized in moral High Gods who maintained social adherence to normative ideals and subordinated individual interest to the collectivity. Gods reflect co-opted spandrels that provided new functional adaptations in enabling the expansion of group membership dynamics and the establishment of moral systems that could be expanded beyond the immediate group of those engaged in face-to-face contact.

Thus, the biological bases of adaptation underlying the core aspects of shamanism involve the exapted and newly evolved mechanisms involved in community rituals, which have a variety of social integration effects; the co-opted spandrels of ritual, such as vocalization and drumming, that induce altered states of consciousness that produce an integration of consciousness; co-opted exaptations involved in spirit relations that involve forms of self and other representation; a variety of healing capacities involving a range of origins and functions; and the evolved capacities of metaphoric thought produced by integration of different innate representational systems.

Healing Functions. The many healing mechanisms involved in hypnotic engagement, placebo effects, musical expression, and a variety of other forms of emotional healing are not of religious origin, nor are they for religious purposes. Rather, they evolved for their functions in self-healing. Religious beliefs, however, do enhance these self-healing capacities. The properties of the supernatural appear to be particularly effective at eliciting the placebo and other coping responses. The parental qualities of spirits are spandrels of the dominance and attachment dynamics that are not selected for, but that have new adaptive functions for healing and social integration. Hence, the capacity for belief in a supernatural being involves many preadaptations (the concept of the other, mind-reading, dominance–submission relations). Spirits also have nonselected side features, such as parental and omnipotent qualities, which provide a basis for co-opted spandrels that have new functions in eliciting a variety of calming influences through the placebo effect, stress reduction, the effects of opioids, and enhanced coping. These features were favored, not for religious purposes, but for the health benefits they provide. Religious belief, however, facilitates these effects and could have been selected because of its ability to elicit these healing responses. In that case, selective pressures would have favored the capacity to integrate all the separate features (dominance–submission, animism, self-identification, other identification, nurturing qualities, parental qualities, etc.) that are present in supernatural beings. These integrative processes had many adaptive effects in enhancing healing, cognition, emotional management, and social life.

The healing capacities associated with religion have their foundations in the altruistic behaviors found in many animals. These healing capacities were dramatically expanded during the evolution of modern humans, providing one of the zones of development for the evolution of uniquely human capacities, including religious healing. The many ways in which religious beliefs and practices affect our psychology—and especially our emotions—reveal a number of particularly adaptive healing processes derived from religiosity. Religion makes use of our uniquely human capacities for emotional responses to the world and endows them with healing potential by conferring meaning on events, evoking emotions through group rituals, and extending our social network into the supernatural domain. These connections enable metaphors embodied in supernatural beliefs to evoke emotions and emotions to be managed by symbols. Our capacity to engage positive and hope-inspiring symbols can profoundly affect our emotions and virtually all aspects of our physiological functioning. Religion's management of emotions and social life also provides a variety of other adaptive effects.

Religion as an Emotional Adaptation

Religion is particularly effective at addressing many problems for which science is not well suited to produce solutions. Issues such as death, catastrophe, love, loneliness, and justice cannot be addressed by science in a way that fulfills the emotional needs those issues entail. Religion is a more effective tool for addressing these deep emotional needs of individuals and satisfying our collective societal needs for community, collective identification, and frameworks for normative and moral behavior. Atran (2006) points out that there is good evidence that religious beliefs can alleviate stress and anxiety and maintain social cohesion in the face of conflict. Individuals who participated in shared assumptions about benevolent supernatural entities that provide for them are able to resolve their existential anxieties and make costly commitments to a community that reciprocally supports them. Religion is an effective tool for countering extreme self-interest and, instead, encouraging people to support group interests that have the potential to benefit the individual.

The ways in which belief in the supernatural helps to manage human emotional and cognitive challenges demonstrate that it constitutes new adaptations. Such dramatic evidence of success counters the hypothesis that religions involve only evolutionary by-products that lack adaptive functions in enhancing reproduction and survival. The by-product arguments would require us to establish that the emotional functions of religious behavior borrowed prior adaptations, used them only for the originally selected functions, and did not meet other new needs or social functions in ways that enhanced survival and reproduction.

In our discussion of the emotional functions of religion, the significance and effects of a benevolent supernatural other are central. Our mammalian heritage of bonding with our protective and nurturing mothers is an adaptation that was exapted in the concept of a benevolent supernatural other that provided humans with protection and resources. Is the supernatural other just a projection of this mammalian dynamic of dependence on our mothers? Or do religion and the supernatural premise involve an extension of attachment dynamics in ways that constitute a new adaptation? Kirkpatrick (2005) emphasizes the importance of separating factors that enhance reproductive fitness from those which provide psychological benefits. Religions can provide psychological benefits such as comfort, security, and well-being, but can they enhance an individual's reproductive opportunities? The answer is an unequivocal "Yes!"

When we examine the dynamics of religious coping and its ability to deal with emotional crises and other aspects of stress in our lives, we find overwhelming evidence that religious beliefs are protective and help people to cope. People who can cope with adversity have enhanced opportunities for survival and reproduction. The many detrimental effects of uncontrolled stress—psychosomatic disease, infertility, the triggering of the general activation syndrome, nocebo death, ulcers, cardiovascular disease, and others—indicate that the coping mechanisms provided by religion can bring substantial benefits not only to our outlook on life, but also to our ability to survive and reproduce. The supernatural assumption is a key aspect of this healing response provided by religion. Yet, insofar as our beliefs in powerful but invisible beings enable us to deal effectively with existential anxieties (such as death) not addressed by our preexisting cognitive adaptations, the supernatural premise itself is an adaptation. This fact is illustrated by the special emotional adaptations that supernatural beliefs produce.

Religion clearly provides a means for coordinating the emotional dynamics of individuals into collective patterns that validate emotional attachments and commitments. Religions also have played substantial functional roles in the creation of positive emotional experiences and interpretations of events and in enhancing people's abilities to deal with adversity. Some of the ways that religions achieve this are clearly elaborations of other capacities, making them exaptations, but since they provide new functional adaptations, they qualify as co-opted exaptations.

Central to the healing processes of religion is the use of religious symbols to manage the physiological consequences of stress. By helping to manage our emotional reactions of anxiety, religious beliefs enhance many aspects of health, well-being, and, ultimately, survival. Social relations and symbols can evoke the relaxation response, which activates the parasympathetic nervous system and its physiological changes that mediate rest, recuperation, and maintenance of homeostatic (internal biological) balance. Religious beliefs can promote a sense of serenity and tranquility that has positive psychological effects on our emotions and may prevent stress. In its ability to relieve anxiety and stress, religion provides a sense of control, and may evoke automatic—and autonomic—responses, inspiring self-confidence and mobilizing personal defenses. Religious healing provides a unified psycho-socio-physiological response to the world in which the attribution of personal meaning to events and awareness of potential social support help to control and manage stress.

Ritual activities and religious symbols and social processes can have direct physiological effects on the autonomic nervous system. A ritual can reduce high levels of stress hormones by creating positive hope and expectations, countering anxiety, altering our emotional responses, and, consequently, changing our stress responses. This reduction of stress and its physiological concomitants enhances the immune system and the body's capacity for recovery. Religious coping is associated with enhanced outcomes in the face of negative events, indicating that belief in benevolent deities is particularly adaptive when the demands on a person exceed that person's abilities to cope. Spirit assumptions are adaptive because they provide positive hope and expectations regarding the adequacy of resources for managing stress. Thus, religion involves an adaptive set of beliefs that directly favor survival through functions that can be characterized broadly as healing.

The Supernatural as a Cognitive Adaptation

Certainly, the universality of religious beliefs regarding supernatural agents reflects their ability to play a central role in addressing some of the elements of the human condition, including our needs to understand the Universe, establish and maintain groups, heal, and cope with death. But how did religiosity come to fulfill these needs? Did natural selection favor those of our ancestors who had the cognitive abilities to conceive of active beings existing in a supernatural world? Or were these cognitive abilities exapted from other abilities that were more directly related to everyday life in the natural world? We think there is some truth in both explanations.

Many of the universal features of religious thought—including animism, contagion, and the principle of similarity—are reflections of broader adaptive principles that were favored by natural selection because of their obvious benefits for survival. Our ancestors' abilities to draw associations between different concepts offered them many advantages, such as an increased capacity to avoid contagious agents (what we call germs). We can clearly see the survival value of assuming that unseen agents are able to affect us. These unseen agents can be conceived of as impersonal forces (mana) or as personal forces (anima), both of which are universal features of religious belief systems. Both postulate the action of unseen agents with profound empirical—observable—consequences for human life.

Our capacity to conceive of supernatural agents is clearly based on our abilities to detect agency, develop and recognize personal and social identities, make inferences about the mental processes of others, and

internalize the social and personal expectations of others as models for the self. We share some of these abilities with other animals, while other abilities did not appear until the appearance of the hominan line leading to modern humans. Consequently, our cognitive abilities to conceive of supernatural beings involves preadaptations. But is there something more to the supernatural concept than just the sum of these prior features? Does the supernatural concept represent the acquisition of some new and different abilities?

Supernatural Agent Concepts. The focus of religion on supernatural agent concepts reflects the general role of agent concepts as central constructs in a universally human folk psychology or theory of mind. Our highly evolved tendency to attribute agency—an intentional actor—is a consequence of our adaptation to deal with intelligent predators. Our "agency detection mechanism," which evolved to respond to things "out there" that were vitally important for our ancestors to recognize, was then extended to explain other phenomena involving complex designs and agents of unknown origins.

Our tendency to attribute agency to unseen others can also be seen as an extension of our ability to understand others in terms of ourselves. Our need to detect important and active features of the natural world may account for our ability to perceive intentional agents, including their social qualities. These qualities may be seen as spandrels, side-effects of our general assumptions about other humans, and the consequently human qualities we project onto the Universe. However, spirit beings also exhibit a number of nonintuitive properties that apparently contradict both the ordinary principles of the Universe and the ways in which our brains understand the Universe. For example, spirits have supernatural abilities—an expanded set of behavioral capacities that outreach our own. What in the real world, physical or social, would constitute the basis for the exaptation providing the basis for supernatural beings' *super*-human capabilities? The lack of a ready answer to this question suggests that religion may provide a co-opted spandrel constituting a new adaptation provided by those aspects of the supernatural premise that relate to nonintuitive, contradictory, and superhuman capabilities. The counterintuitive properties of religious beliefs are adaptive in spite of their contradictions with factual knowledge because they suggest possibilities not found in our mental hardware, enabling them to facilitate the integration of heretofore unconsidered possibilities and the knowledge they provide. This feature makes them adaptations that exceed the capacities of our innate modules with new assumptions that go beyond ordinary human limits.

The supernatural concept represents an extreme manifestation of the symbolic process that makes it possible for us to represent and thereby conceive of "things" we can never actually see or touch as empirical objects. This realization points out another way in which religion's supernatural assumption is adaptive: The belief that "supernatural others" have access to our thoughts helps to inhibit deception and encourage group loyalty and sacrifice. Wildman (2006) points out that this belief provides a basis for a compelling interest in adhering to moral standards established by our society's conception of the supernatural. As the German philosopher Immanuel Kant contended, moral reasoning requires a religious framework in order for it to be rational, assuming an ultimate moral authority that establishes objective standards and allocates rewards and punishments. To the extent that the omniscient (all-knowing) properties of the supernatural engage possibilities beyond those of our innate mental hardware, religious thought provides an adaptation. The supernatural concept may offer an additional advantage by expanding our ability to internalize these "supernatural others" and their super-human capabilities, thereby providing a basis for addressing problems of similar value orientations. The super-human capabilities that enable omniscience can provide a policing function and ensure the adherence of individuals to normative expectations, even if normal social others—the other members of society—are not capable of detecting any deviant behavior.

Supernatural Concepts as Social Mechanisms. Supernatural concepts also exert significant influences in helping individuals function within a group. Spirit concepts may serve as role models in self-development and can aid individuals in internalizing social ideals by providing a mechanism through which an individual can identify with and internalize the social "other" represented in the spirit world. Thus, one important co-opted exaptation provided by the "supernatural social other" involves functions extending the functions of the social other in socialization. This contributes to group integration in the supernatural models provided for individual socialization. The supernatural social other provides something that is not provided by the ordinary social other: the "Perfect Other Model." The qualities of the spirit other provide a key mechanism in a complex system for managing and coordinating an individual's emotional and psychological dynamics with those of the other members of the group. The religious presumption that a superior deity—a superordinate social other—exists provides a model for the roles and expectations for individual behavior, making this conception an effective adaptation that fulfills a variety of human individual and social needs. The preadaptations for this evolved capacity may be found in a variety of previously evolved structures, including dominance–submission behaviors, dependency bonding on a nurturing other, and the attribution of agency and intentionality to unseen others.

The Explanatory Functions of Religiosity: Myth and the Structure of the Universe. A religion provides a cognitive framework that places human life into a meaningful context. Myths provide both a description of the Universe and statements about the "laws" that govern the Universe and human life. The compelling qualities of myths contribute to the persistence of worldviews, thereby contributing to the survival of those whose myths teach them stable and effective adaptations to their local environments. The models of the environment provided by mythologies create a cognitive space within which to make other empirical, material, and ultimately scientific adaptations.

Similarities in different cultures' myths reflect structures of the human mind manifested in universal archetypes manifesting intrinsic ways in which humans understand the Universe. Myths encompass a natural language of the self and the unconscious, a system for representing our most fundamental conceptualizations of our own nature and the universe. Consequently, since myths provide a language for representing many of the inaccessible aspects of human nature and tendencies, they create a system within which the individual can understand his or her unconscious and subconscious tendencies and those of others and adjust to them. Mythological traditions are universals of human culture because they reflect aspects of our innate capacities—our drive to explain the Universe that is manifested in our "storytelling" capacity. In this sense, our tendencies to provide mythological accounts reflect an ancient evolutionary accomplishment, the embodiment and expression of a framework for making sense of the Universe, including our own human nature.

These tendencies to provide an orderly system of explanation also fulfill a vital socialization function because they describe an order in the outside world that can be internalized in the individual psychology of the members of a culture. Consequently, myths shape the psychological reality of individuals by providing models for how to adapt to the Universe and what it means to belong to their particular groups. Myths also lay out expectations for behavior that are internalized during the process of socialization. By making use of our "storytelling" capacity, myths also provide a means of creating bonds between people, even those who do not know one another. Our storytelling need and capacity—the basis for the universal presence of mythologies—reflects one of the adaptive aspects of religion. Mythologies provide models that make life coherent and systematic, and they embody these in an authoritative system of explanation that makes them compelling. Although mythologies necessarily embody supernatural concepts, the mythic capacity did not evolve for religious reasons. Mythological capacities evolved from the pre-existing matrix of spiritual beliefs and needs for understanding the Universe. Because myths use those same prior capacities, we propose that myths be understood as co-opted spandrels which provide new functions in managing our understanding of ourselves, others, and the Universe.

Socialization. Religion is an important tool for teaching individuals about the proper ways to live in a society. Its ubiquity in socialization in premodern societies suggest that religion is one of the most effective tools of socialization and cultural transmission of traditions. Religion helps to define what it means to be a child or an adult, a man or a woman, alive or dead. In this way, religious beliefs help to "build" a person. Religious rituals help individuals to make the transition from one stage of life to the next, and channel and manage the emotions that are involved in changing status. Religions even shape our sexuality and create ritually sanctioned bonded pairs that control one of the most important aggressive and dangerous in-group features of primate life—sexual access. In most respects, religion is an optimal tool for fostering cultural conformity.

Religions worldwide consider adolescence to be the most significant part of the developmental cycle for the transmission of religious beliefs. Religions have provided adaptations for managing this natural "experience-expectant" period in order to provide socializations for integrating youth into society. Adolescent socialization rituals in cultures around the world focus on redefining and conforming initiates' social roles and identities to the ideals of society. Both sacred and secular socialization are combined in the psychological transformation of adolescents into adults. Deep in the hominin evolutionary past, religious adaptations helped to meet societal needs to integrate the male children reared in female-centered family groups into the male alliances and coalitions that dominated social life at the macrolevel of the group.

The neurological properties of the adolescent period produce intense emotional reactions and responses that need to be organized and controlled within cultural patterns. During adolescence, brain development is profoundly open to cultural influences. This cultural shaping can especially affect the prefrontal cortex and the frontal and temporal cortices, all of which play central roles in managing social behaviors and in integrating a variety of emotional and social cues in producing appropriate behavior. The prefrontal cortex also plays an important role in impulse control, as well as in planning and social judgment that is based on the integration of social information with the immediate context. Many of the crucial brain interconnections that are developed during adolescence engage the control of emotional inputs and apply them to manage personal and social life. The role of religion within this expectant period of development is to provide essential models and identifications for supra-individual identification and personality formation. The spirit assumption provides important agent qualities for enhancing the transmission and retention of cultural patterns.

Social Politics and Religion

Religious solutions to cooperative living have their roots in the roles that ritualized behaviors play in maintaining cooperation and reducing conflict in animal societies. These capacities of religion and ritual have been expanded as humans have acquired other needs and abilities as the members of larger and more complex social groups. Other features of religious behavior derived from supernatural beliefs made it possible for societies to survive and expand; beliefs in supernatural beings enabled social evolution.

While the dominant approaches in evolutionary biology have tended to emphasize individual selection in terms of the acquisition of innate characteristics and dispositions, individual selection takes place within a group context in which powerful collective forces affect an individual's success and reproduction. These collective forces favor individuals who are well suited to be integrated into a collective culture—who demonstrate a capacity for integrating themselves into collectively shared patterns and dispositions. Thus, we must address the mechanism by which participation in religious groups enhances individual survival and reproduction. How do religions collectively and individually provide adaptations that enhance survival and successful reproduction?

The concept of a supreme deity provides an important mechanism for forming connections between individual and collective psychology. A shared significant "other" provides a basis for expansive group identity, particularly by encouraging humans to extend acts of reciprocal altruism to others besides close kin. Religions justify positions of leadership, and they help to regulate and coordinate the interactions among individuals (reinforcing societies) as well as coordinating interactions between individuals and their environment (reinforcing ecological relationships). Religious rules associated with supernatural punishments and rewards promote appropriate behavior in both social and ecological contexts. The evolution of religious behavior must be understood in the context of a variety of factors that have contributed to the evolution of the human propensity to help other humans. But religions also function in defining and maintaining distinctions between the "in-group" and the "out-group."

Witchcraft, Voodoo Death, and Human Sacrifice: Adaptation or Maladaptation?

The positive power of religious beliefs to enhance our emotions and to heal is balanced by the negative power of religious entities to cause illness, punish, and even kill a person. Are these events evidence of adaptation, exaptation, or maladaptation of our religious potentials? The evil side of the supernatural is a human universal, and beliefs in witchcraft, sorcery, and other forms of supernatural malevolence and punishment have many effects on individuals and societies. The ability of religious symbols to manipulate our emotions through concepts and symbols that are "evil" and that represent behaviors or attitudes of which society does not approve are powerful tools for socialization and the enforcement of conformity. Yet we often find that witchcraft and sorcery beliefs do not level the playing field by providing a supernatural threat to deter people from attacking individuals thought to possess such powers. Instead, beliefs about supernatural evil—witches in particular—provide a basis for scapegoating, persecuting, and eliminating other groups or individuals in society. Rather than a mechanism for assuring fairness, supernatural beliefs can clearly be tools for exploitation.

Today, concepts of supernatural evil and the behaviors they justify demonstrate clearly the role of the environment in assessing the adaptive—or maladaptive—aspects of religion. Our tendency to attribute blame to outsiders and to view their activities as evil may have

been adaptive in the past—when groups were small and were able to avoid one another—but it now exacerbates conflicts between groups that are linked together within the global economy and that must live in close proximity to one another. While the concepts of evil that one group attributes to an outsider group (or groups) serve to define and mark groups as distinct from one another, these concepts become maladaptive in the face of our modern need to interact with people who belong to different groups and adhere to very different religions.

Religion's tendency to become maladaptive occurs clearly with respect to relations with the out-group. Historical examples of religion's abuse of the out-group include the capture and ritual sacrifice of individuals from other tribes and the persecution of subordinated classes and individuals within society through witchcraft accusations. The ancient practices of scapegoating are clearly extended to a whole new level today, the world system, where demonization of the religious other drives many of the current conflicts of the world.

Why Must We Learn to Disagree?

By almost any measure, the human species is phenomenally successful. Humans have spread into nearly every environmental niche found on earth, and we have envisioned migrations to new planets. This dream of spreading to other worlds may soon become a necessity. During the past two centuries, the number of humans has grown from around one billion to almost seven billion. Today, the population of the world is increasing by *over 200,000 people per day*. These increases are leading to ever greater demands for food, housing, energy, and employment. Unfortunately, while our numbers are growing at an ever faster rate, the resources on which we depend are not.

Our growing recognition that the earth's natural resources are limited has already led to wars for oil and other mineral wealth. In the past and, we can expect, in the future, wars will be fought over such basic needs as water and food. Our widespread alteration of the environment for short-term economic gain is creating long-term problems as global warming affects patterns of rainfall and alters hunting, fishing, and growing conditions around the world. Traces of plastics, pesticides, and other chemicals that did not exist a century ago are now found across the planet, and we are only beginning to understand how some of these substances are causing additional changes in the web of life upon which we depend. Historical and

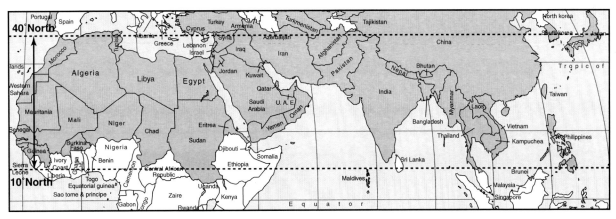

Figure 11.1 Over half the world's population lives in the "10/40 Window," and most are not Christians. Some Christian Evangelical groups have targeted this region as the focus of their missionary activities.

other factors have led to such an unequal distribution of wealth that the "golden billion" (the people of North America, the European Community, and Japan) have access to more resources than the remaining people of the Earth combined.

All of these changes are playing out in a world in which news about an event occurring on the other side of the globe is instantaneously available, leading to an unprecedented stream of information about natural disasters, political turmoil, and new epidemic diseases. The same satellites that beam this news into our homes also broadcast Western movies, music videos, situation comedies, and documentaries into the homes of people in very different societies, directly challenging their worldviews. Traditional cultures—and their religious beliefs and practices—are also being challenged as the global economy expands and as soldiers, missionaries, and other outsiders arrive to "liberate" traditional peoples from their "unproductive" ways of life and "superstitious" beliefs. Even the formerly safe geographical bastions of the world religions are experiencing new challenges as people of other faiths arrive and bear witness to their beliefs.

The first Muslims in the New World arrived on slave ships. For centuries, American Muslims were virtually invisible and Islam was little understood. This is no longer the case: Five percent of the population of the United States (over six million people) now call themselves Muslims, and Islam will soon be the second-largest religion in the country. Other religions are growing as well. The influx of Buddhists, Hindus, Sikhs, and people of other faiths, and the emergence of new religions and the reinterpretation of older beliefs, has made the United States into the most religiously diverse nation on Earth (Eck 2001). Yet many Americans continue to think of the United States as a "Christian" nation, and from time to time, there are attempts to amend the U.S. Constitution to legally enshrine this view.

Meanwhile, thousands of Christian missionaries have targeted the almost three billion non-Christians who live in the **10/40 Window** for concerted conversion efforts. The name of this region—which extends from Western Africa to Eastern Asia and which is home to Muslims, Buddhists, Hindus, and many other religious traditions—derives from the fact that it lies roughly between 10 degrees and 40 degrees north latitude (see Fig. 11.1). Christian evangelicals see this region, which they also call "The Resistant Belt," as a stronghold of Satan and an important battleground in their attempts to spread the Christian Gospel throughout the world. At the same time, there are Islamic fundamentalists who dream of restoring and even expanding the **caliphate.** This single worldwide Muslim state would consist of all of the lands that had ever been under Islamic jurisdiction, and its society would be based on the Shari'a, or Islamic law. Many of these lands fall within the 10/40 Window (see Fig. 11.2).

It is no coincidence that Christianity and Islam are the world's two largest religions. Of all the world's religions, these are the two that have been the most assertive in their claims of religious exclusivity and their zeal to convert others. Between them, they now account for over half the religious believers on Earth. Given the divergent views of their followers, we should not be surprised that some of the most heated religious conflicts of today occur in areas where the two meet. Of course, most Christians and Muslims favor more peaceful forms of religious engagement. But when a group of people feels that its own way of

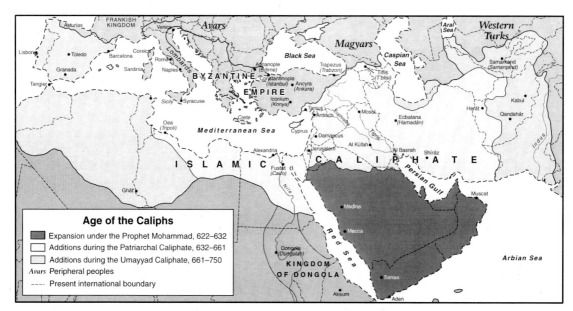

Age of the Caliphs

- Expansion under the Prophet Mohammad, 622–632
- Additions during the Patriarchal Caliphate, 632–661
- Additions during the Umayyad Caliphate, 661–750
- *Avars* Peripheral peoples
- - - - Present international boundary

Figure 11.2 Some Muslims dream of restoring the "Caliphate," the ancient empire ruled by the Islamic faith. Much of this area has also been targeted by Christian missionaries.

life in its traditional homeland is being threatened by outsiders with a different value system, we should not be surprised that some will react strongly.

However well-meaning the intentions of proselytizers may be, the destructive effects of their activities can last for centuries. And as we have already seen, a religion usually brings an entire cultural worldview with it, many of whose principles may be diametrically opposed to those of the existing local cultures. Here, religion can become a vehicle for forced culture change and imperialism. The Catholic Spanish came to the Americas with the explicit intention of destroying the native cultures and converting the survivors to Christianity. The native religions and cultures that survived did so by continuing their practices clandestinely or by moving into areas far removed from the centers of power. The Muslim invasion of India, which began in 1526, led to the conversion of millions of Hindus to Islam and the systematic destruction of thousands of Hindu temples and holy sites. The Muslim rulers (known as Moghuls) remained in India until 1857, when they were replaced by the British. During their rule, considerable efforts were made to Christianize India. In spite of repeated attempts, India did not gain independence from the British until 1947. As part of the agreement by which the British vacated India, elections were held in which Hindus and Muslims voted to determine whether their state would remain part of India (where Hindus dominated) or break off to form the state of Pakistan (where the state religion is Islam).

Following the elections, millions of Hindus and Muslims who were living in areas that were scheduled to become part of the rival religious state left their homes and journeyed to areas in which they could be part of the religious majority. Riots and fights broke out during this mass migration, leaving hundreds of thousands dead. Many of the current tensions between India and Pakistan—especially the conflict over the borders of Kashmir—date to this time. In addition, many of the current religious tensions within India are a direct result of the history of subjugation and religious oppression of Hindus during the Moghul period.

Today, some Christian and Muslim extremists view the geopolitical events of our time as the opening battles in a great war to establish the global supremacy of their own religion. A few have even attempted to speed up the process. Since Israel was founded in 1948, Israeli authorities have arrested a number of Jewish and Christian fundamentalists who were plotting to destroy the Al-Aqsa mosque, which sits on the site of the second Jewish temple. According to these people's interpretations of their religious scriptures, the Messiah will not come until the temple is rebuilt, and they believe that destroying the Islamic presence on the site will hasten that day.

What can the rest of us do to ease the tensions that will inevitably increase as the world's two largest and most emphatically proselytizing religions increasingly confront one another in their own traditional territories? Unfortunately, there are no easy answers. In a very real sense, history as we have come to understand it is drawing to a close. The nation–state system that has dominated world politics and trade for the last five hundred years has given way to a transnational economy in which multinational corporations readily shift resources and production from one area to another in their efforts to maximize their profits and increase their market share. In the process, local economies are transformed as jobs are created and then outsourced once more, often leading to the economic collapse of an entire region. Meanwhile, new factories are being opened in regions in which farming was the principal livelihood just one generation ago.

To meet the tensions and fears that all these changes are producing, people continue to turn to one of the most important of all human adaptations: religion. As we have seen, religions can help people channel their emotions in ways that mitigate fears and offer hope. Religious symbols are potent sources of group identity, and shared beliefs and practices help to keep a group together, enabling its members to understand and survive change. The shared worldviews that religions provide now make it possible for people to see themselves as members of groups that are so large that their "brothers" and "sisters" may live on the other side of the globe. These features of religion have helped to create the modern world of nation–states and global faiths. They have motivated people to perform great acts of charity and to stand up for others who have little power or wealth. But we have also seen the other side of religion: the demonization of nonbelievers and other outsiders that can occur, and the violence that religious beliefs can engender. In the past, the dark side of religion has led to witchcraft persecutions and holy wars. What will it engender in our modern world, with our many weapons of mass destruction? Have the *adaptive* functions that religions have long fulfilled now become *maladaptive* as different groups are forced to interact and live with one another?

The answer to this question depends on how the followers of a religion construe their faith. Most religious people share the same desires for themselves and their families as do people who are not religious. They desire to raise their families in peace, with access to adequate food, housing, and health care. They hope to see their children grow up and have children of their own, and they wish to see their traditions carried on by their children and grandchildren. For most people—whatever their religion or culture—religious beliefs and practices continue to offer a solution to the problems and challenges of life. But history has shown that people can justify violence in the name of any faith,

particularly when they believe that their religion is the only one that is "true."

The Five Warning Signs of a "Bad Religion"

As we have seen, religion is a double-edged sword, with power to do harm as well as good. The supernatural evil practiced by sorcerers and witches now has a new counterpart: the terrorism of religious extremists. What is it that causes people to misuse their religions for harmful purposes, to reinterpret the generally peaceful and constructive messages of their founders into something that condones or even demands violence?

Charles Kimball (2003), a Baptist minister who studies religions from a comparative perspective, has identified five warning signs that indicate when a particular religious tradition is in danger of being corrupted and turning violent. These five can appear in any religion, although Kimball himself noted that they are most likely to arise in monotheistic traditions with exclusivist claims to the truth.

The first warning sign occurs when the adherents of a religion begin to assert that they alone possess the absolute truth. As we have seen, the religious wars and witchcraft persecutions of Europe grew out of absolute truth claims and the desire to eradicate all competing religious views. These same absolute truth claims led to the forced conversions of "heathens" and "pagans" at the hands of missionaries. Today, rigid truth claims—often involving narrow interpretations of certain sacred texts—have led to suicide bombings by radical Muslims and to the killing of abortion providers by fundamentalist Christians.

A second warning sign is the requirement for blind obedience to a particular leader or religious viewpoint. Jim Jones, who began his career as a Christian minister in the 1950s by preaching a message of racial integration and social justice, faced numerous challenges from people who were not yet open to such ideas. His ministry attracted families from numerous ethnic backgrounds, and he was forced to relocate his church several times in an effort to find a more receptive location for his understanding of the Christian message. In their desire to create a "perfect" society, Jones and his followers eventually obtained a parcel of land in the jungle of Guyana, and in 1974 they established the community of Jonestown. But Jones himself had changed, as the years of hostility he had faced caused him to become increasingly self-centered and paranoid. By the time he and his followers arrived in Jonestown, Jones had abandoned his Christian roots and was proclaiming himself a new God. On November 18, 1977, Jones's demand for complete obedience to his word led his followers to murder a United States congressman who had flown to Jonestown at the request of the concerned relatives of some of Jones's followers. The congressman's arrival apparently confirmed Jones's fear that his opponents were intending to destroy the community. Convinced that the end was near, Jones then ordered his followers to commit suicide. While a few balked and managed to escape into the jungle surrounding the compound, most willingly drank the cyanide-laced punch that was passed around, and many even administered it to their own children. Those who refused were shot by the guards, who were supposed to protect the group from outsiders. In a single day, over 900 members of Jonestown died out of blind obedience to their leader.

A third warning sign occurs when the followers of a religion begin to actively work to establish an "ideal time" here on Earth. Although most religions believe in some form of ideal time, they usually associate it with their conceptions of afterlife or ultimate spiritual achievement (heaven, nirvana). When the adherents of a religion work to usher in what they consider to be a "perfect" society on Earth by applying their religious principles to everyone, that religious movement can become dangerous. The attempts of Jewish and Christian fundamentalists to destroy the Al-Aqsa mosque in Israel so that the Messiah can return is an example of religious believers attempting to create a "perfect" society.

Another warning sign that is closely related is the idea that "the ends justify the means." In any religious movement, a particular component of the religion (such as the sanctity of a holy site, or a particular interpretation of a scriptural passage) may become elevated into a principle that must be defended by any and all means. The acts that have been perpetrated to defend the faith have included the torture and murder of nonbelievers (the European witch crazes), as well as the numerous Christian Crusades into the Holy Land to "liberate" Christian religious sites from the Muslims. One of the main reasons given by Osama bin Laden to justify the terror attacks of September 11, 2001, was the Saudi government's decision to allow the United States to establish military bases in Saudi Arabia, thereby defiling the sacred lands in which Mohammed had received the Qur'an and had first shared his revelation from Allah.

Both the medieval crusades and the 2001 attacks were also expressions of the fifth warning sign: a call for a "holy war" against the enemies of the true faith. Certainly, the attacks on New York and Washington merited a strong response by the United States government. But a bad situation was made worse by the government's poor choices of words to justify its response, including language that was disturbingly similar to that of the people who had planned and carried out the attacks. Osama bin Laden and the al-qaida organization were not only branded as "terrorists" (a political term), but also as "evil" (a religious concept). Several U.S. government and military officials then characterized the "war on terror" as a "crusade" against Islamic extremism. This unwise choice of words compounds the problems of today by reopening centuries-old wounds in the Muslim world. Irrespective of the political reasoning that led to war, the use of religious rhetoric only confirmed the suspicions of many moderate Muslims that the terror attacks were being used to justify a renewed Christian war on Islam.

When it comes to religious conflict, language is all-important. Words carry a great deal of weight and can mobilize powerful emotions in support of one's cause. The Palestinian Intifada, or uprising, against Israel has been described as a "holy war" (by its supporters) and as "evil" (by its opponents). Once again, the rhetoric of religious justification glosses over the underlying causes of the conflicts: the appropriation of land, the competition for resources, the expression of ethnic and cultural rivalries, and the eruption of long-standing nationalist tensions. Here we can see how one of the most important adaptive features of religiosity—helping people to manage and channel their emotions—can lead people to overlook one of our other important human means of adaptation: our ability to objectively analyze a situation and to rationally consider the implications and likely success of alternative strategies. During the course of human evolution, this ability of our emotions to temporarily suppress our reason—to allow the "fight or flight" response of the older paleomammalian brain to preempt the model-making abilities of the newer neocortex—certainly aided in our ancestors' survival. When we are facing an immediate threat to personal safety, every second counts, and there is no time to ponder the reasons that have led to the appearance of the threat. But the dangers we face today are of a different kind, and many are of our own making. To meet these threats effectively, we need to see beyond the black-and-white world of friend or foe and to see the many shades of gray that lie between. In today's global world, we need to understand diverse viewpoints and accept the fact that other people do not share our beliefs and values. We need to learn to agree to disagree.

Moving Beyond Exclusivism

There are only a few ways that a person belonging to one religion can regard the beliefs of a person who belongs to another. One approach—exclusivism—asserts that one's own religion is true while all of the others are false. Another approach is to recognize that all religions are true in some sense. A third possibility is to regard one religion as more true than the others. Nonbelievers often point to a fourth possibility: All religions are false.

The biocultural approach of anthropology provides a perspective from which to see that all of these assertions have some validity. It also proposes a framework for expanding these perspectives. Cultural relativism allows us to understand that some religious claims are true for some specific groups while false for others. Ecological perspectives allow us to see that some religious practices are adaptive and that some provide better or worse adaptations, a perspective for grasping relatively greater truths. The anthropological approach, rather than considering all religious beliefs to be false, provides two principal perspectives on the "truth" of religious claims: (1) Religions are true in a symbolic and social sense because they create realities that people perceive and on which they act, and (2) some religious claims reflect something true about human nature. This neurognostic (neurological basis of *gnosis*, "knowing") perspective sees religious claims as a reflection of our evolved psychology, the mental hardware that we use to understand and live within the Universe.

Most people feel strongly about their own particular views regarding religion. And many of us wish that everyone else would see things the *right* way, the way we see them. But this will never come to pass. The biocultural insight that each and every one of us spends our entire life in a unique, ever-changing, and unavoidably personal world reminds us that no two people will ever see things in precisely the same way. Faced with this basic fact of existence, what can we do?

Events around the world make it abundantly clear what we *cannot* do. We can no longer afford to ignore other peoples' beliefs, or to discount them on the basis that they are misguided versions of our own "correct" and true beliefs. So how should we deal with the fact that other people hold beliefs very different from our own without calling our own beliefs into question? This question addresses one of the central issues of our time, and the lessons of the past are not all promising.

Consider the fact that the nearly two billion Christians in the world do not all interpret the Bible in the same manner. Today, twenty-seven books make up the official canon known as the New Testament. None of these were written during the time of Christ. During the early Christian period, there were many other gospels, epistles, and books of revelation in addition to the ones that are now found in the Bible. It was only in 367 C.E. that Athanasius, the bishop of Alexandria, wrote to his followers urging them to recognize the twenty-seven books that now make up the New Testament as canonical ("official") and to repudiate the other books—and the myths and ideas they contained. With this act, the core dogmas of the Christian faith as we know it today were codified. Alternative interpretations of the Christian message were declared heretical, and the scriptures on which they were based were burned. Yet, over the next sixteen centuries, these alternative interpretations have continued to resurface, leading to numerous disagreements about the relative importance of faith versus acts, the proper age to be baptized, the types of governance structures that should guide the community of the faithful, and other aspects of the Christian religion. Although the members of the Inquisition worked hard to eradicate these alternative interpretations, their efforts clearly failed. Today, the many repeated schisms within the Christian world have given rise to well over 30,000 recognized Christian denominations, each with its own idiosyncratic interpretation of the Christian message.

Such problems are not as acute for Muslims, whose Qur'an was codified during the lifetime of the Prophet Mohammed, the man who claimed to have received it directly from God. The fundamental agreement that all interpretations of the Qur'an must be based on the original Arabic texts has led to far greater doctrinal agreement than in Christianity. The most important schism in Islam—that between the Sunni and the Shia—occurred not because of differences between interpretations of scriptures, but because of disagreements concerning who should lead the *umma*—the community of the faithful—following the death of the Prophet. But there are alternative interpretations of Islam as well, and some of these—such as Wahhabism, the dominant form of Islam in Saudi Arabia—advocate the return to a strict and traditional way of life in which music and other forms of entertainment are prohibited, praying at tombs (even the tomb of Mohammed) is regarded as "polytheistic," and all forms of religious innovation are proscribed. It goes without saying that for a Wahhabi, there can be no new revelations from God.

It is a curious fact that although both Christianity and Islam are based on revelations, and each claims to

According to Mormon tradition, Moroni was a prophet-warrior who had lived in the Americas prior to the arrival of Europeans. Moroni was the last to write in the golden plates that contained what is now known as the *Book of Mormon*. Moroni revealed their hidden location to Joseph Smith in a series of visions.

offer corrections and refinements to the traditions from which it arose, once they were established, both effectively shut the door on future revelations and innovations of the faith. Individuals who have claimed to have received a subsequent revelation from the supernatural world often have been subjected to extreme hostility and persecution. Two famous examples are Joseph Smith, Jr., and Bahá'u'lláh, both of whom attempted to reform their respective traditions.

Joseph Smith and the Birth of Mormonism. Joseph Smith, Jr., (1805–1844), the founder of the Church of Jesus Christ of Latter Day Saints, came from a deeply religious family, several members of which had themselves received visions from God. While still in his teens, Smith had a vision in which he saw both Jesus and God the Father. Soon thereafter, an angel named Moroni showed Smith the location of several golden plates covered with unusual writing. Between 1827 and 1831, Smith transcribed the plates with the help of a friend and benefactor, and the resulting texts, known as the *Book of Mormon*, were seen as a third

testament that corrected and amended the corruptions that Smith believed had crept into the first two: the Old and the New Testaments.

Although Smith's teachings attracted some followers, most Christians were appalled by his claims to have received a new revelation. After violent encounters in New York and Pennsylvania, Smith moved his nascent church to Kirtland, Ohio, in 1831. In 1832, Smith and his family were attacked in the middle of the night. His adopted daughter died just five days later. In 1838, the Mormons were forced to leave Ohio and settled in Missouri. The governor of Missouri issued an "Extermination Order" that led to Smith being jailed for several months and his followers leaving for Illinois. He rejoined them in 1839, but was arrested again in 1844 for attempting to suppress a newspaper critical of him and his beliefs. While he was in jail, a mob of some 200 people stormed the building and shot Smith repeatedly, killing him on the spot. His followers left Illinois soon thereafter. By 1847, many were settling in Utah, which was a territory of Mexico at the time. Utah became a U.S. territory in 1848, but was not admitted to statehood until 1896, after a ban on the Mormon practice of polygamy had been written into the state constitution.

Today, there are some 13 million Mormons. Most follow the teachings set forth by Joseph Smith and are members of the church established by his follower, Brigham Young. But the followers of the *Book of Mormon* have already separated into several smaller groups, some because of disagreements as to who should lead the church and others because they refused to accept the ban on polygamy that was imposed by the U.S. government.

Bahá'u'lláh and the Rise of the Bahá'í Faith. The history of the Church of Jesus Christ of Latter Day Saints has some parallels with the Bahá'í Faith, which was founded by a man named Bahá'u'lláh in Persia in the nineteenth century. Born Mírzá Ḥusayn-`Alí, he was influenced by another Persian, Siyyid `Alí-Muhammad, who took the Shia title of the Báb (meaning "gate") to support his claim that divine revelation could still flow into the world. This heresy contradicted the Muslim view that the late-sixth-, early-to-mid-seventh-century Muhammad was the "seal" (last) of the Prophets, and the Báb was executed by firing squad in 1850.

A subsequent assassination attempt on the Shah of Persia by several followers of the Báb led to the imprisonment of most of the members of the Bábí community and the execution of several thousand people. Bahá'u'lláh was imprisoned, but he was eventually found to have played no role in the assassination attempt and was released. While he was in prison, he received a vision from a Maiden from God, who told him that he would impart a new series of messages from God. During the next several years, Bahá'u'lláh kept this vision secret while he wrote the *Kitáb-i-Íqán* ("the *Book of Certitude*"), the central scripture of the Bahá'í Faith. In this book, Bahá'u'lláh described divine revelation as a progressive event. He described how each of the Western monotheistic religions contained the seeds of its successor, which would offer a newer and more comprehensive revelation for humankind. Because he claimed to have received a new revelation from God, Bahá'u'lláh spent the remainder of his life either moving from one area to another or under arrest.

Like his predecessors Jesus and Mohammed, Bahá'u'lláh universalized and extended the teachings he had learned as a child to include people of numerous faiths. Although the total number of Bahá'í followers today is only about six million, the appeal of his message is worldwide. The followers of Bahá'u'lláh's message can now be found in over 200 countries, making the Bahá'í Faith one of the most widely spread religions in the world. Religious services include the reading of sacred scriptures from around the world, and the Bahá'í acknowledge that many paths lead to the one true God in which they believe.

Finding a Way to Disagree: Pluralism

The histories of the Church of Jesus Christ of Latter Day Saints and the Bahá'í Faith remind us that religions rise as a result of personal experience, and they spread because the messages of their founders attract followers. This dynamic of religious rebirth and renewal represents another important adaptive aspect of religiosity as a source of new cultural models to fit changing times. It also reminds us why religion is not going to "go away" anytime in the near future. For those who believe that all religions are false, this poses a problem. How can people continue to accept all these new and obviously *irrational* beliefs? For religious people, the problem is somewhat different. Why are so many people attracted to such obviously *wrong* beliefs?

These questions bring us back to the logical responses people may have when they encounter other belief systems. We have already noted religious exclusivism, the view that only one's own religious beliefs and practices are valid. In Chapter 1, we saw how this view led to the excesses of the many European religious wars and the persecution of people who did not have the "proper" beliefs. We have repeatedly seen how exclusivistic assumptions have also led to violence and warfare in other places and times.

The solution the Deists offered was a kind of inclusivism—the idea that all beliefs are partially true because they all contain the same core ideas. The Deists expanded the Christian concept of God and made it less personal. In their way of thinking, the beliefs of Europeans, Native Americans, Christians, Jews, Protestants, and Catholics all had elements of truth. The Mormons and Bahá'í follow an inclusivist view as well. Because they believe that each successive revelation in the Western monotheistic tradition represents a refinement and improvement over the previous revelations, they can interpret these other traditions as versions of their own.

But in some ways, inclusivism also represents a rather narrow view of religions, for it reinterprets other beliefs and practices using the terms of one's own tradition. Although it does often attempt to bridge the differences between faiths, inclusivism is still an ethnocentric position that fails to recognize that other traditions can be based on very different assumptions and worldviews and yet be as rich and as dynamic as one's own.

Rather than viewing other religions as being partially true because they contain some of the same ideas as our own, we may hold the view that all religions are equally true. This viewpoint, known as **pluralism,** is based on the notion that God, Allah, the Divine Source, or whatever other name may be given, is beyond human comprehension. If we can accept the idea that all religions represent attempts to understand that which is ultimately beyond understanding, then we can also see that no religion has a monopoly on the "truth."

It is natural to judge other cultural models from the perspective of our own. This impulse is an inevitable outcome of the ways that we use our own acquired and personally developed models to understand the Universe. One of the great achievements of anthropology has been to point out our tendency to be ethnocentric and to offer a corrective: cultural relativism. As we have already noted, cultural relativism does not say that "anything goes." Instead, it requires that we attempt to understand the concepts, values, behaviors, and material objects of people in another culture from the perspective of those people. In a very real sense, cultural relativism asks us to step out of our own limited cultural point of view and look at things from a more all-encompassing perspective. This allows us to gain a deeper appreciation of the ways that other people live, and to see our own way of life as one of the many possibilities that humans have developed for making and understanding the journey between birth and death. From this perspective, we may discover that our own culture does not always offer the "best" approach to a particular set of human needs, and the people of different cultures may even be able to share

This is the first photo of an "earthrise" over the moon ever taken by a human as it was occurring. It depicts the earth and moon as they were seen by the Apollo 8 astronauts, whose orbit made the moon appear to their right. (In the more famous color photo, taken just moments later, the image was rotated clockwise 90° so that the earth would appear "above" the moon). All of human history and prehistory has taken place on these two small objects.

their own best ideas and abandon those which are no longer appropriate to the modern world.

This same approach can be applied to religion. If we can just begin to step back a bit from the blind acceptance of our own beliefs and practices and look at other people's faith traditions from a more all-encompassing perspective, we might be able to see how each is the product of personal experiences, historical events, ecological influences, and cultural processes. If we can learn to view our own religion from both the insider's and the outsider's points of view, we may be able to see that we are all members of the same group—the group we call human—while simultaneously recognizing that we are also different and that these differences can be a source of strength rather than weakness.

Like any worldview, this more all-encompassing perspective can benefit from a symbol that can evoke the emotions and ideas associated with seeing all humans as members of the same group. For many people, such a symbol appeared on December 24, 1968, after the astronauts of Apollo 8 had rounded the far side of the moon and saw the earth rising above the lunar surface. This poignant image of our small and

fragile planet—the only home we humans have ever known, and the home we share with the members of all faiths—reminds us why we must find a way to live with our differences and learn to agree to disagree.

The pluralist perspective permits us to interact with people of different faiths and to ask one another what happens to us after this life without causing problems to one another in this life. It allows people to find words of wisdom in all traditions, and to see one another as members of the same human family. Making any family work requires patience, empathy, and a deep desire to understand others on their own terms. This is true for the families of our birth, the families we create through marriage, and the families that are created through shared histories and beliefs.

The positive qualities of religiosity have long helped people to cope with change, to heal physical and psychological ailments, and to channel our emotions in ways that create deep bonds with the other members of our group. If we can learn to combine these qualities with our amazing human ability to create new models of the Universe and abandon old ones that are no longer appropriate, then we may, indeed, find solutions to the many problems that face us today. We can begin by focusing on what is universal about the nature and roles of religiosity in human life, including its powerful role in creating groups.

Conclusions: A Universalist Perspective

If the human past tells us anything about our future, it is that religiosity is here to stay. It is natural for humans to think about the supernatural, to conceive of and then to develop relationships with unseen beings and powers. It is natural for some people to see and hear supernatural beings more than others. And for some people, it is completely natural to reject or doubt the supernatural. Whatever our individual beliefs may be, we need to recognize that these beliefs are "normal" products of both our biology and culture.

The persistent importance of religion in the affairs of the modern world reflects its engagement with deep-seated and ancient aspects of humans' personal, emotional, and social natures as mammals. Because we cannot escape that past, we must learn to deal with it in nondestructive ways. We are a religious species because humans are the most social of all primates. Religion has been a central tool in adapting to our social environment and expanding our social nature, enhancing our conspicuous ability to live in large, socially unified groups that distinguish themselves from outsiders. By providing a dominant and coherent system of social relations, religion produces mechanisms for uniting people. But because of its uniting force, it also produces strong group boundaries. Religion separates as well as joins.

Religion's tendency to divide people into separate groups evokes our in-group versus out-group dynamic, contributing to its ability to create enduring emotional commitments to a group and rejecting outsiders. The processes by which our individual needs are realized as part of a group need to be extended to form more positive relationships between groups. As we increase our understanding of why religion holds such power to shape us, we can begin to use the ancient evolved dynamics of ritual to unite different belief communities.

As science examines religious experiences and phenomena, it is important to remind ourselves that science cannot explain away the spiritual world. Understanding the brain mechanisms associated with spiritual experiences does not explain them "away" any more than understanding how a television works will explain or explain away the content of the programs you watch. The biological sciences may be able to explain the biological mechanisms associated with spiritual experiences, but biology is at present no more able to explain the contents of spirituality than it is able to explain the contents of culture.

Religion has in many cases provided a basis for supporting some of what is best about humans, our altruism and prosocial qualities that lead us to produce well-integrated communities and to help those less fortunate than ourselves. The universality of modern world religions as charitable organizations—often the most important source of charity in a society—points to the persistent positive value that religions have in the contemporary world. Unfortunately, our drive to define the group with whom we can identify and whom we will protect can also evoke its evil twin: the excluded and demonized other. But many universalist religious traditions provide examples that religion does not have to demonize the other. Rather, these traditions provide models for how religion can remain adaptive in a postmodern world when the power of secularism still falls far behind the power of religion as a catalyzing and motivating force for humans.

Whether you are devoutly religious or deeply skeptical, a "true believer" or an "infidel," an agnostic or an atheist, you are affected by the religious side of human nature. Whether you embrace the religious doctrines of your ancestors or reject all religion, religion affects your life today. Our country's "war on terrorism" is a thinly disguised war of religious extremism, and regardless of who is "right" and what is "true," we all stand to suffer from unconstrained global violence that has the potential to destroy humanity and our planet. One of the main challenges facing humans today and in the future will be to come to grips with religiosity, this double-edged sword of human nature that has the power both to divide and to unite.

Questions for Discussion

- Do you believe that there will ever be a single world religion? Why or why not?
- What possibilities do you see for ending religious conflict?
- Is religion necessary in your life? Is spirituality?

Glossary

caliphate the old Islamic Empire, which some Muslims wish to restore

co-opted exaptations traits that were originally selected for one purpose and were then applied to fulfill a different purpose

co-opted spandrels traits that originated as side-effects of natural selection but later came to fulfill a biological function

emergence the idea that interactions among the phenomena at one level of existence can give rise to qualitatively new phenomena at a higher level

inclusive fitness the idea that an individual's sacrifice may nevertheless enhance the survival of that individual's genes because the sacrifice increases the likelihood that the individual's descendants and other relatives will survive and reproduce

individual selection an evolutionary process that focuses on a specific organism and the ways in which its traits affect its own survival and reproductive success

learning the ability of an organism to acquire knowledge during its own lifetime

pluralism the idea that all religious traditions offer truths to their members and that no one religion possesses the entire truth

10/40 Window an area of Africa, Europe, and Asia that extends from roughly 10 degrees north latitude to 40 degrees north latitude and is the object of Christian Evangelical proselytizing.

Assessing Mystical Experiences:
Hood's Mysticism Scale

Score each of the following questions using the scale descriptors and values below.

+2 This description is definitely true of my own experience or experiences.

+1 This description is probably true of my own experience or experiences.

−1 This description is probably not true of my own experience or experiences.

−2 This description is definitely not true of my own experience or experiences.

 0 I cannot decide.

____1. I have had an experience which was both timeless and spaceless.

* ____2. I have never had an experience which was incapable of being expressed in words.

____3. I have had an experience in which something greater than myself seemed to absorb me.

____4. I have had an experience in which everything seemed to disappear from my mind until I was conscious only of a void.

____5. I have experienced profound joy.

* ____6. I have never had an experience in which I felt myself to be absorbed as one with all things.

* ____7. I have never experienced a perfectly peaceful state.

* ____8. I have never had an experience in which I felt as if all things were alive.

* ____9. I have never had an experience which seemed holy to me.

* ____10. I have never had an experience in which all things seemed to be aware.

____11. I have had an experience in which I had no sense of time or space.

____12. I have had an experience in which I realized the oneness of myself with all things.

____13. I have had an experience in which a new view of reality was revealed to me.

* ____14. I have never experienced anything to be divine.

* ____15. I have never had an experience in which time and space were nonexistent.

* ____16. I have never experienced anything that I could call ultimate reality.

____17. I have had an experience in which ultimate reality was revealed to me.

____18. I have had an experience in which I felt that all was perfection at that time.

____19. I have had an experience in which I felt everything in the world to be part of the same whole.

____20. I have had an experience which I knew to be sacred.

* ____21. I have never had an experience which I was unable to express adequately through language.

____22. I have had an experience which left me with a feeling of awe.

____23. I have had an experience that is impossible to communicate.

* ____24. I have never had an experience in which my own self seemed to merge into something greater.

* ____25. I have never had an experience which left me with a feeling of wonder.

* ____26. I have never had an experience in which deeper aspects of reality were revealed to me.

* ____27. I have never had an experience in which time, place, and distance were meaningless.

* ____28. I have never had an experience in which I became aware of the unity of all things.

____29. I have had an experience in which all things seemed to be conscious.

* ____30. I have never had an experience in which all things seemed to be unified into a single whole.

_____ 31. I have had an experience in which I felt nothing is ever really dead.

_____ 32. I have had an experience that cannot be expressed in words.

Transform scores: First you need to reverse the values of each of the items with an asterisk (*) (2, 6–10, 14–16, 21, 24–28, and 30); e.g., +2 → −2; +1 → −1; −1 → +1; and −2 → +2).

Then add 3 to the score for each item.

Overall Mysticism Scale: Add all of the items after transforming them as directed. The scale ranges from 32 (low) to 160 (highest), with 109 being the norm for males and 120 being the norm for females.

Mysticism Subscales (make sure you first transformed/reversed all of the * items as stated above):

Extrovertive Mysticism: Add 6, 8, 10, 12, 15, 19, 24, and 27–31.

Introvertive Mysticism: Add 1–4, 11, 21, 23, and 32.

Religious Interpretation (Noetic Experience): Add 5, 7, 9, 13–14, 16–18, 20, 22, 25, 26.

Unity Experience: Add 1 + 2 + 4 + 6 + 8 + 10 + 11 + 12 + 15 + 18 + 19 + 21 + 23 + 24 + 27 + 28 + 29 + 30 + 31 + 32.

Affective Religious Revelation: Add 3 + 5 + 7 + 9 + 13 + 14 + 16 + 17 + 20 + 22 + 25 + 26.

"Hood's Mysticism Scale" from "Dimensions of the Mysticism Scale: Confirming the Three-Factor Structure in the United States of Iran" by R. W. Hood, Jr., N. Ghorbani, P. J. Watson, A. F. Ghramaleki, M. N. Bing, et al., *Journal of the Scientific Study of Religion* 40(4): 691–705. Copyright © 2001. Reprinted by permission of Wiley-Blackwell.

References

Achterberg, J. 1985. *Imagery in healing: Shamanism in modern medicine.* Boston: Shambhala.

Alcorta, C. 2006. Religion and the life course: Is adolescence an "experience expectant" period for religious transmission? In *Where God and science meet: How brain and evolutionary studies alter our understanding of religion. Volume 2: The neurology of religious experience,* ed. P. McNamara, 55–80. Westport, CT: Praeger.

Alexander, C., J. Davies, C. Dixon, M. Dillbeck, R. Oetzel, S. Drucker, J. Muehlman, and D. Orme-Johnson. 1990. Growth of higher stages of consciousness: The Vedic psychology of human development. In *Higher stages of human development: Perspectives on adult growth,* ed. C. Alexander and E. Langer, 286–341. New York: Oxford University Press.

American Psychiatric Association. 1994. *Diagnostic and statistical manual of mental disorders.* 4th ed. (DSM-IV). Washington, D.C.: American Psychiatric Press.

American Psychiatric Association. 2000. *Diagnostic and statistical manual of mental disorders.* 4th ed., text rev. (DSM-IV-TR). Washington, D.C.: American Psychiatric Press.

Aniruddh, P. 2003. Language, music, syntax and the brain. *Nature Neuroscience* 6 (7): 674–681.

Applegate, R. B. 1975. The Datura cult among the Chumash. *Journal of California Anthropology* 2 (1): 6–17.

Arcadi, A. C. 1996. Phrase structure of wild chimpanzee pant hoots: Patterns of production and interpopulation variability. *American Journal of Primatology* 39 (3): 159–78.

Arcadi, A. C., D. Robert, and C. Boesch. 1998. Buttress drumming by wild chimpanzees: Temporal patterning, phrase integration into loud calls, and preliminary evidence for individual distinctiveness. *Primates* 39 (4): 505–18.

Atran, S. 2006. The cognitive and evolutionary roots of religion. In *Where God and science meet: How brain and evolutionary studies alter our understanding of religion. Volume 1: Evolution, genes, and the religious brain,* ed. P. McNamara, 181–208. Westport, CT: Praeger.

Averill, J. 1996. An analysis of psychophysiological symbolism and its influence on theories of emotion. In *The emotions: Social, cultural, and biological dimensions,* eds. R. Harre and W. Parrott, 204–28. Thousand Oaks, CA: Sage.

Bachner-Melman, R., C. Dina, A. Zohar, N. Constantini, E. Lerer, et. al. 2005. AVPR1a and SLC6A4 gene polymorphisms are associated with creative dance performance. *PLoS Genetics* 1 (3): e42.

Baker, J. R. 1994. The old woman and her gifts: Pharmacological bases of the Chumash use of *Datura. Curare* 17 (2): 253–76.

Barry III, H., & Schlegel, A. (Eds.). 1980. *Cross-cultural samples and codes.* Pittsburgh: University of Pittsburgh Press.

Beattie, J. 1964. The ghost cult in Bunyoro. *Ethnology* 3 (2): 127–51.

Beauregard, M., and V. Paquette. 2006. Neural correlates of a mystical experience in Carmelite nuns. *Neuroscience Letter* 405:186–90.

Benedetti, F., and M. Amanzio. 1997. The neurobiology of placebo analgesia: From endogenous opioids to cholecystokinin. *Progress in Neurobiology* 51:109–25.

Bering, J. M. 2006. The cognitive psychology of belief in the supernatural. In *Where God and science meet: How brain and evolutionary studies alter our understanding of religion. Volume 1: Evolution, genes, and the religious brain,* ed. P. McNamara, 123–34. Westport, CT: Praeger.

Berkman, L. 1984. Assessing the physical health effects of social networks and social support. *American Review of Public Health* 5: 413–32.

Berkman, L. 1985. The relationship of social networks and social support to morbidity and mortality. In *Social support and health,* eds. S. Cohen and S. Syme, 241–62. New York: Academic Press.

Berkman, L., and I. Kawachi. 2000. *Social epidemiology.* New York: Oxford University Press.

Berry, H., and A. Schlegel. 1980. *Cross-cultural samples and codes.* Pittsburgh: University of Pittsburgh Press.

Bird-David, N. 1999. "Animism" revisited: Personhood, environment, and relational epistemology. *Current Anthropology* 40:67–91.

Blanke, O., T. Landis, L. Spinelli, and M. Seeck. 2004. Out-of-body experience and autoscopy of neurological origin. *Brain* 127 (2): 243–58.

Blanke, O., and C. Mohr. 2005. Out-of-body experience, heautoscopy, and autoscopic hallucination of neurological origin. *Brain Research Reviews* 50 (1): 184–99.

Bourguignon, E. 1968. *Cross-cultural study of dissociational states.* Columbus: Ohio State University.

Bourguignon, E., and T. Evascu. 1977. Altered states of consciousness within a general evolutionary perspective: A holocultural analysis. *Behavior Science Research* 12 (3): 197–216.

Boyer, P. 2001. *Religion explained: The evolutionary origins of religious thought.* New York: Basic Books.

Bramble, D. M., and D. E. Lieberman. 2004. Endurance running and the evolution of *Homo. Nature* 432:345–52.

Brereton, D. 2000. Dreaming, adaptation, and consciousness: The social mapping hypothesis. *Ethos* 28 (3): 379–409.

Brody, H. 1987. *Stories of sickness.* New Haven, CT: Yale University Press.

Brown, S. 2000. The "musilanguage" model of music. In *The origins of music,* eds. N. Wallin, B. Merker, and S. Brown, 271–300. Cambridge, MA: MIT Press.

Bulbulia, J. 2006. Nature's medicine: Religiosity as an adaptation for health and cooperation. In *Where God and science meet: How brain and evolutionary studies alter our understanding of religion. Volume 1: Evolution, genes, and the religious brain,* ed. P. McNamara, 87–122. Westport, CT: Praeger.

Buss, D., M. G. Haselton, T. K. Shackelford, A. L. Bleske, and J. C. Wakefield. 1998. Adaptations, exaptations, and spandrels. *American Psychologist* 53 (5): 533–48.

Cannon, W. B. 1942. Voodoo death. *American Anthropologist* 44 (2): 169–181.

Caporeal, L. 1976. Ergotism: The Satan loosed in Salem? *Science* 192:21–26.

Carrasco, D. 1987. Myth, cosmic terror, and the Templo Mayor. In *The great temple of Tenochtitlan,* eds. J. Broda, D. Carrasco, and E. M. Moctezuma, 124–62. Berkeley: University of California Press.

Castillo, R. 1991. Divided consciousness and enlightenment in Hindu Yogis. *Anthropology of Consciousness* 2 (3–4): 1–6.

Castillo, R. 1995. Culture, trance and the mind-brain. *Anthropology of Consciousness* 6 (1): 17–34.

Castillo, R. 1997. *Culture and mental illness: A client-centered approach.* Pacific Grove, CA: Brooks/Cole.

Chagnon, N. 1997. *Yanomamö.* 5th ed. Fort Worth, TX: Harcourt Brace.

Chimpanzee Sequencing and Analysis Consortium. 2005. Initial sequence of the chimpanzee genome and comparison with the human genome. *Nature* 437: 69–87.

Clottes, J., and D. Lewis-Williams. 1998. *The shamans of prehistory: Trance and magic in the painted caves.* New York: Harry Abrams.

Colby, B. N. 2004. Calendrical divination by the Ixil Maya of Guatemala. In *Divination and healing: Potent vision,* eds. M. Winkelman and P. M. Peek, 81–102. Tucson: University of Arizona Press.

Crowe, B. 2004. *Music and soul making toward a new theory of music therapy.* Lanham, MD: Scarecrow Press.

Csordas, T. 1994. *The sacred self: A cultural phenomenology of charismatic healing.* Berkeley: University of California Press.

D'Aquili, E., and A. Newburg. 1999. *The mystical mind.* Minneapolis, MN: Augsburg Fortress.

Davidson, J. 1980. The psychobiology of sexual experience. In *The psychobiology of consciousness,* eds. J. Davidson and R. Davidson, 271–332. New York: Plenum Press.

Davis, W. 1971. *Societal complexity and the nature of primitive man's conception of the supernatural.* University Microfilms #72–10: 707.

Davis, W. 1988. *Passage of darkness: The ethnobiology of the Haitian zombie.* Chapel Hill: The University of North Carolina Press.

Deacon, T. 1997. *The symbolic species: The co-evolution of language and the brain*. New York: Norton.

De Ridder, D., K. Van Laere, P. Dupont, T. Menovsky, and P. Van de Heyning. 2007. Visualizing out-of-body experience in the brain. *New England Journal of Medicine* 357 (18): 1829–33.

De Waal, F. 1997. *Bonobo: The forgotten ape*. Berkeley: University of California Press.

Dietrich, A. 2003. Functional neuroanatomy of altered states of consciousness: The transient hypofrontality hypothesis. *Consciousness and Cognition* 12:231–56.

Dobkin de Rios, M. 1984. *Hallucinogens: Cross-cultural perspectives*. Albuquerque: University of New Mexico.

Dobkin de Rios, M., and B. Hayden. 1985. Odorous differentiation and variability in the sexual division of labor among hunter/gatherers. *Journal of Human Evolution* 14: 219–28.

Donald, M. 1991. *Origins of the modern mind*. Cambridge, MA: Harvard University Press.

Donald, M. 2001. *A mind so rare: An evolution of human consciousness*. New York: W.W. Norton and Company.

Dow, J. W. 1986. Universal aspects of symbolic healing: A theoretical synthesis. *American Anthropologist* 88: 56–69.

Dulaney, S., and A. Fiske. 1994. Cultural rituals and obsessive–compulsive disorder: Is there a common psychological mechanism? *Ethos* 22:243–83.

Dumezil, G. 1988. *The destiny of a king*. Trans. A. Hiltebeitel. Chicago: University of Chicago Press.

Dunbar, R. 1997. *Grooming, gossip, and the evolution of language*. Cambridge, MA: Harvard University Press.

Dunbar, R. 2004. Language, music, and laughter in evolutionary perspective. In *Evolution of communication systems*, eds. D. Kimbrough Oller and Ulrike Griebel, 257–73. Cambridge, MA: MIT Press.

Durkheim, É. 1964. *The elementary forms of the religious life*. Trans. J. Ward Swain. London: G. Allen & Unwin.

Eck, D. L. 1993. *Encountering God: A spiritual journey from Bozeman to Benares*. Boston: Beacon.

Eck, D. L. 2001. *A new religious America: How a "Christian country" has become the world's most religiously diverse nation*. New York: Harper Collins.

Ehrman, B. D. 2003. *Lost Christianities: The battles for scripture and faith we never knew*. Oxford: Oxford University Press.

Elfstrom, G. 2002. The origin of science. *Journal of the Alabama Academy of Science*. 73 (1): 30–37.

Eliade, M. 1964. *Shamanism: Archaic techniques of ecstasy*. New York: Pantheon Books.

Emmons, R. 2005. Sacred emotions. In *Soul, psyche, brain: New directions in the study of religion and brain–mind science*, ed. K. Bulkeley, 93–112. New York: Palgrave Macmillan.

Ernandes, M., and S. Giammanco. 1998. MacLean's triune brain and the origin of the "Immense Power Being" idea. *Mankind Quarterly* 39 (2): 173–201.

Evans-Pritchard, E. 1937. *Witchcraft, oracles and magic among the Azande*. Philadelphia: Clarendon.

Fábrega, H. 1997. *Evolution of sickness and healing*. Berkeley: University of California Press.

Fessler, D. 2002. Starvation, serotonin, and symbolism: A psychobiocultural perspective on stigmata. *Mind and Society* 3:81–96.

Finkler, K. 1985. *Spiritualist healers in Mexico*. South Hadley, MA: Bergin and Garvey.

Fischer, R. 1971. A cartography of the ecstatic and meditative states. *Science* 174: 897–904.

Fischer, R. 1992. A cartography of cognitive and non-cognitive states of consciousness. *Anthropology of Consciousness* 3 (3–4): 3–13.

Fiske, A., and N. Haslam. 1997. Is obsessive–compulsive disorder a pathology of the human disposition to perform socially meaningful rituals? Evidence of similar content. *The Journal of Nervous and Mental Disease* 185 (4): 211–22.

Flaten, A., T. Simonsen, and H. Olsen. 1999. Drug-related information generates placebo and nocebo responses that modify the drug response. *Psychosomatic Medicine* 61:250–55.

Fortune, R. 1963. *Sorcerers of Dobu: The social anthropology of the Dobu Islanders of the Western Pacific*. London: Routledge and Kegan Paul.

Frazer, J. 1890/1911/1929. *The golden bough: A study in magic and religion*. New York: St. Martins Press.

Frecska, E., and Z. Kulcsar. 1989. Social bonding in the modulation of the physiology of ritual trance. *Ethos* 17 (1): 70–87.

Freud, S. 1913. *Totem and taboo: Resemblances between the psychic lives of savages and neurotics.* New York: Dover Publications.

Freud, S. 1927. *The future of an illusion.* New York: W.W. Norton and Company.

Friedrich, P. 1991. Polytrophy. In *Beyond metaphor: The theory of tropes in anthropology,* ed. J. W. Fernandez, 17–55. Stanford, CA: Stanford University Press.

Fuller, R. C. 2000. *Stairways to heaven: Drugs in American religious history.* Boulder, CO: Westview Press.

Garrity, T. 1974. Psychic death: Behavioral types and psychological parallels. *Omega 5* (3): 207–15.

Gartz, J. 1992. Der alteste bekannte Pilzkult–ein mykologischer Vergleich. In *Jahrbuch des Europäschen Collegiums für Bewubtseinsstudien* (ECBS), 91–94. Berlin: VWB.

Gartz, J. 1996. *Magic mushrooms around the world: A scientific journey across cultures and time.* Los Angeles: LIS Publications.

Geertz, C. 1966. Religion as a cultural system. In *Anthropological approaches to the study of religion,* ed. M. Banton. A.S.A. Monograph No. 3. London: Tavistock Publications Limited.

Geissmann, T. 2000. Gibbon songs and human music from an evolutionary perspective. In *The origins of music,* eds. N. Wallin, B. Merker, and S. Brown, 103–23. Cambridge, MA: MIT Press.

Giddens, A. 1979. *Emile Durkheim.* New York: Viking Press.

Goddard, D., ed. 1970. *A Buddhist bible.* Boston: Beacon Press. Quoted in McFarlane, T. J., ed., 2001. *Einstein and Buddha: The parallel sayings.* Berkeley, CA: Seastone.

Goodall, J. 1986. *The chimpanzees of Gombe: Patterns of behavior.* Cambridge, MA: Belknap Press of Harvard University Press.

Graffin, N., W. Ray, and R. Lundy. 1995. EEG concomitants of hypnosis and susceptibility. *Journal of Abnormal Psychology* 50:846–58.

Green, E. C. 1999. *Indigenous theories of contagious disease.* Lanham, MD: Rowman & Littlefield.

Greyson, B. 2000. Near-death experiences. In *Varieties of anomalous experience: Examining the scientific evidence,* eds. E. Cardella, S. J. Lynn, and S. Krippner, 315–52. Washington, DC: American Psychological Association.

Griffiths, R. R., W. A. Richards, U. McCann, and R. Jesse. 2006. Psilocybin can occasion mystical-type experiences having substantial, sustained personal meaning and spiritual significance. *Psychopharmacology* 187 (3): 268–83.

Gould, S. J. 1997. The exaptive excellence of spandrels as a term and prototype. *Proceedings of the National Academy of Sciences of the United States of America* 94 (20): 10750–55.

Guthrie, S. E. 1993. *Faces in the clouds: A new theory of religion.* New York: Oxford University Press.

Guzman, G., J. Allen, and J. Gartz. 1998. A worldwide geographical distribution of the neurotropic fungi, an analysis and discussion. *Annali del Museo Civico di Rovereto* 14:189–280.

Hahn, R. 1997. The nocebo phenomenon: Concept, evidence, and implications for public health. *Preventative Medicine* 26:607–11.

Hamer, D. 2004. *The God gene: How faith is hardwired into our genes.* New York: Doubleday.

Hancock, G. 2006. *Supernatural: Meetings with the ancient teachers of mankind.* New York: Disinformation Company.

Harner, M. J. 1962. Jívaro souls. *American Anthropologist.* 64:258–72.

Harner, M., ed. 1973a. *Hallucinogens and shamanism.* New York: Oxford University Press.

Harner, M. 1973b. The role of hallucinogenic plants in European witchcraft. In *Hallucinogens and shamanism,* ed. M. Harner, 125–50. New York: Oxford University Press.

Harner, M. 1977a. The ecological basis for Aztec sacrifice. *American Ethnologist* 4:117–135.

Harner, M. 1977b. The enigma of Aztec sacrifice. *Natural History* 86 (4): 47–51.

Harris Interactive. 2005. Harris poll #90. http://www.harrisinteractive.com/harris_poll/index.asp?PID=618 (accessed March 20, 2008).

Harris, M. 1974. *Cows, pigs, wars, and witches: The riddles of culture.* New York: Vintage.

Hassig, R. 1990. Aztec warfare. *History Today* 40:17–24.

Hauser, M., and J. McDermott. 2003. The evolution of the music faculty: A comparative perspective. *Nature Neuroscience* 6:663–668.

Hayden, B. 2003. *Shamans, sorcerers, and saints: A prehistory of religion*. Washington, DC: Smithsonian Books.

Heaney, C., and B. Israel. 2002. *Social networks and social support. Health behavior and health education: Theory, research, and practice.* 3rd ed. San Francisco: Jossey-Bass.

Heelas, P. 1981. Introduction: Indigenous psychologies. In *Indigenous psychologies*, eds. P. Heelas and A. Lock, 3–18. London: Academic Press.

Helman, C. 1994. *Culture, health and illness*. Oxford: Butterworth Heinemann.

Hillgarth, J. N., ed. 1969. *Christianity and paganism, 350–750: The conversion of Western Europe.* Philadelphia: University of Pennsylvania.

Hinton, A. 1999. *Biocultural approaches to emotions.* New York: Cambridge University Press.

Hodgson, D., and P. Helvenston. 2006. The emergence of the representation of animals in Palaeoart: Insights from evolution and the cognitive, limbic and visual systems of the human brain. *Rock Art Research* 23 (1): 3–40.

Hofer, H., J. Carroll, J. Neitz, M. Neitz, and D. R. Williams. 2005. Organization of the human trichromatic cone mosaic. *Journal of Neuroscience* 25 (42): 9669–79.

Hood, R. W., Jr., N. Ghorbani, P. J. Watson, A. F. Ghramaleki, M. N. Bing, H. K. Davison, R. J. Morris, and W. P. Williamson. 2001. Dimensions of the mysticism scale: Confirming the three-factor structure in the United States and Iran. *Journal for the Scientific Study of Religion* 40 (4): 691–705.

Horton, R. 1967a. African traditional thought and Western science 1. *Africa* 37:50–71.

Horton, R. 1967b. African traditional thought and Western science 2. *Africa* 37:155–87.

Hubbard, T. 2002. Some correspondences and similarities of shamanism and cognitive science: Interconnectedness, extension of meaning and attribution of mental states. *Anthropology of Consciousness* 13 (2): 26–45.

Hughes, H. C. 1999. *Sensory exotica: A world beyond human experience.* Cambridge, MA: MIT Press.

Humphrey, N. 2002. *The mind made flesh essays from the frontiers of psychology and evolution.* Oxford: Oxford University Press.

Hunt, H. 1995. *On the nature of consciousness.* New Haven, CT, and London: Yale University Press.

Irons, W. 2001. Religion as a hard to fake sign of commitment. In *Evolution and the capacity for commitment*, ed. R. Neese, 292–309. New York: Russell Sage Foundation.

Irons, W. 2005. How has evolution shaped human behavior? Richard Alexander's contribution to an important question. *Evolution and Human Behavior* 26 (1): 1–9.

Isaac, B. 1983. The Aztec "Flowery War": A geopolitical explanation. *Journal of Anthropological Research* 39:415–32.

Janata, P., and S. Grafton. 2003. Swinging and the brain: Shared neural substrates for behaviors related to sequencing and music. *Nature Neuroscience* 6 (7): 682–91.

Johnson, D., and J. Bering. 2006. Hand of God, mind of man: Punishment and cognition in the evolution of cooperation. *Evolutionary Psychology* 4:219–233.

Jones, P. 2005. Ultrarunners and chance encounters with "Absolute Unitary Being." *Anthropology of Consciousness* 15 (2): 39–50.

Katz, R. 1982. *Boiling energy: Community healing among the Kalahari !Kung.* Cambridge, MA: Harvard University Press.

Kawachi, I., and L. Berkman, eds. 2003. *Neighborhoods and health.* New York: Oxford University Press.

Kimball, C. 2003. *When religion becomes evil.* New York: Harper Collins.

King, B. 2007. *Evolving God: A provocative view of the origins of religion.* New York: Doubleday.

Kirkpatrick, L. 1997. An attachment-theory approach to psychology of religion. In *The psychology of religion*, eds. B. Spilka and D. N. McIntosh. Boulder, CO: Westview Press.

Kirkpatrick, L. 2005. *Attachment, evolution, and the psychology of religion.* New York: Guilford Press.

Kirmayer, L. 1993. Healing and the invention of metaphor: The effectiveness of symbols revisited. *Culture, Medicine, and Psychiatry* 17:161–95.

Kirsch, I. 1997. Specifying nonspecifics: Psychological mechanisms of placebo effects. In *The placebo effect: An interdisciplinary exploration*, ed. A. Harrington, 166–86. Cambridge, MA: Harvard University Press.

Kjaer, T. W., C. Bertelsen, P. Piccini, D. Brooks, J. Alving, and H. C. Lou. 2002. Increased dopamine tone during meditation-induced change of consciousness. *Cognitive Brain Research* 13 (2): 255–59.

Kleinman, A. 1973. Medicine's symbolic reality. On a central problem in the philosophy of medicine. *Inquiry* 16: 206–13.

Koenig, H., J. Hays, D. Larson, L. George, H. Cohen, M. McCullough, K. Meador, and D. Blazer. 1999. Does religious attendance prolong survival? A six-year follow-up study of 3,968 older adults. *Journal of Gerontology, Series A* (54):370–77.

Koenig, H., M. McCullough, and D. Larson. 2001. *Handbook of religion and health.* Oxford: Oxford University Press.

Koenig, L. B., and T. J. Bouchard, Jr. 2006. Genetic influences on the traditional moral values triad—authoritarianism, conservatism, and religiousness—as assessed by quantitative behavior genetic methods. In *Where God and science meet: How brain and evolutionary studies alter our understanding of religion.* Vol. 1, Evolution, genes, and the religious brain, ed. P. McKenna, 31–60. Westport, CT: Praeger.

Köhler, W. 1925. *The mentality of apes.* 2nd ed. Trans. Ella Winter. New York: Harcourt, Brace.

Krebs, D. L. 2005. The evolution of morality. In *The handbook of evolutionary psychology,* ed. D. Buss, 747–71. Hoboken, NJ: John Wiley & Sons.

Krebs, D. L. 2008. Morality: An evolutionary account. *Perspectives on Psychological Science* 3:149–72.

Krebs-Thomson, K., E. Ruiz, V. Masten, M. Buell, and M. Geyer. 2006. The roles of 5-HT$_2$ receptors in the effects of 5-MeO-DMT on locomotor activity and prepulse inhibition in rats. *Psychopharmacology* 189:319–29.

Krippner, S. 1987. Cross-cultural approaches to multiple personality disorder: Practices in Brazilian spiritism. *Ethos* 15 (3): 273–95.

Kroll, J., and B. Backrach. 2005. *The mystic mind: The psychology of medieval mystics and ascetics.* New York: Routledge.

LaBarre, W. 1972. Hallucinogens and the shamanic origins of religion. In *Flesh of the gods,* ed. P. Furst, 261–78. New York: Praeger.

LaBerge, S., and J. Gackenbach. 2000. Lucid dreaming. In *Varieties of anomalous experience: Examining the scientific evidence,* eds. E. Cardeña, S. Lynn, and S. Krippner, 151–82. Washington, DC: American Psychological Association.

Lang, A. 1897. *The book of dreams and ghosts.* London: Longmans, Green.

Lang, A. 1901. *Magic and religion.* London: Longmans, Green.

Lang, A. 1905. *The secret of the totem.* London: Longmans, Green.

Lansing, S. J. 1991. *Priests and programmers: Technologies of power in the engineered landscape.* Princeton, NJ: Princeton University Press.

Laughlin, C. 1992. *Scientific explanation and the lifeworld. A biogenetic structural theory of meaning and causation.* Sausalito, CA: Institute of Noetic Sciences.

Laughlin, C. 1997. Body, brain, and behavior: The neuroanthropology of the body image. *Anthropology of Consciousness* 8 (2–3): 49–68.

Laughlin, C., J. McManus, and E. d'Aquili. 1992. *Brain, symbol and experience: Toward a neurophenomenology of consciousness.* New York: Columbia University Press.

Lawick-Goodall, J. Van. 1968. The behaviour of a free-living chimpanzees in the Gombe Stream Reserve. *Animal Behavior Monographs* 1 (3): 161–311.

LeDoux, J. 1995. Emotion: Clues from the brain. *Annual Review of Psychology* 46:209–35.

Lee, B., and A. Newberg. 2005. Religion and health: A review and critical analysis. *Zygon* 40 (2): 443–68.

Lester, D. 1972. Voodoo death: Some thoughts on an old phenomena. *American Anthropologist* 76: 818–23.

Levenson, J. 1993. *The death and resurrection of the beloved son: The transformation of child sacrifice in Judaism and Christianity.* New Haven, CT: Yale University Press.

Lévi-Strauss, C. 1962. *Totemism.* Boston: Beacon.

Lévi-Strauss, C. 1966. *The raw and the cooked (Le cru et le cuit).* New York: Harper & Row.

Levin, J. 1994. Religion and health: Is there an association, is it valid, and is it causal? *Social Science and Medicine* 38 (11):1475–1482.

Levin, J. 2001. *God, faith, and health: Exploring the spirituality-healing connection.* Hoboken, N.J.: Wiley.

Lévy-Brühl, L. 1926. *How natives think.* London: George Allen and Unwin, Ltd.

Lévy-Brühl, L. 1978. *Primitive mentality.* 3rd ed. Trans. L. A. Clare. New York: AMS Press.

Lewis-Williams, D. J., and J. Clottes. 1998. The mind in the cave—the cave in the mind: Altered consciousness in the Upper Paleolithic. *Anthropology of Consciousness* 9 (1): 13–21.

Lock, A. 1981. Universals in human conception. In *Indigenous psychologies*, eds. P. Heelas and A. Lock, 19–36. London: Academic Press.

Long, J. K. 1977. *Extrasensory ecology*. Metuchen, NJ: Scarecrow Press.

Ludwig, A. 1966. Altered states of consciousness. *Archives of General Psychiatry* 15:225–34.

Luhrmann, T. 1989. *Persuasions of the witch's craft: Ritual magic and witchcraft in present day England*. Oxford: Blackwell.

Lynn, C. 2005. Adaptive and maladaptive dissociation: An epidemiological and anthropological comparison and proposition for an expanded dissociation model. *Anthropology of Consciousness* 16 (2): 16–50.

MacLean, P. 1990. *The triune brain in evolution*. New York: Plenum.

MacLennan, B. 2002. Evolutionary neurotheology and the varieties of religious experience. In *Neurotheology: Brain, science, spirituality, religious experience*, ed. Rhwan Joseph, 305–14. San Jose, CA: University Press.

Malinowski, B. 1926. *Myth in primitive psychology*. New York: W.W. Norton and Company.

Malinowski, B. 1954. *Magic, science, and religion*. New York: Anchor.

Maloney, C., ed. 1976. *The evil eye*. Columbia: University Press.

Mandell, A. 1980. Toward a psychobiology of transcendence: God in the brain. In *The psychobiology of consciousness*, eds. D. Davidson and R. Davidson, 379–464. New York: Plenum.

Marshack, A. 1997. The Berekhat Ram figurine: A late Acheulian carving from the Middle East. *Antiquity* 71:327–ff.

Marwick, M., ed. 1970. *Witchcraft and sorcery*. Baltimore: Penguin.

Massimini, M., F. Ferrarelli, R. Huber, S. K. Esser, H. Singh, and G. Tononi. 2005. Breakdown of cortical effective connectivity during sleep. *Science* 309 (5744): 2228–32.

Matossian, M. K. 1989. *Poisons of the past: Molds, epidemics, and history*. New Haven, CT: Yale University Press.

Mauss, M. 1950. *A general theory of magic*. New York: Routledge.

Mauss, M. 1972. *A general theory of magic*. 2nd ed. New York: W.W. Norton and Company.

McClenon, J. 1997. Shamanic healing, human evolution, and the origin of religion. *Journal for the Scientific Study of Religion* 36 (3): 345–54.

McClenon, J. 2002. *Wondrous healing: Shamanism, human evolution and the origin of religion*. DeKalb, IL: Northern Illinois University Press.

McClenon, J. 2006. The ritual healing theory: Therapeutic suggestion and the origin of religion. In *Where God and science meet: How brain and evolutionary studies alter our understanding of religion. Volume 1: Evolution, genes, and the religious brain*, ed. Patrick McNamara, 135–58. Westport: Praeger.

McGrew, W. C. 1992. *Chimpanzee material culture: Implications for human evolution*. Cambridge: Cambridge University Press.

McNamara, T. E. 2004. *Evolution, culture, and consciousness: The discovery of the pre-conscious mind*. Dallas, TX: University Press of America.

Meyer, J. S., and L. S. Quenzer. 2005. *Psychopharmacology: Drugs, the brain and behavior*. Sunderland, MA: Sinauer Associates.

Middleton, J., and E. Winter, eds. 1963. *Witchcraft and sorcery in East Africa*. London: Routledge and Kegan Paul.

Mithen, S. 1996. *The prehistory of the mind: A search for the origins of art, religion and science*. London: Thames and Hudson.

Moerman, D. 2000. Cultural variations in the placebo effect: Ulcers, anxiety, and blood pressure. *Medical Anthropology Quarterly* 14 (1): 51–72.

Molino, J. 2000. Toward an evolutionary theory of music. In *The origins of music*, eds. N. Wallin, B. Merker, and S. Brown, 165–76. Cambridge, MA: MIT Press.

Montgomery, G., and I. Kirsch. 1997. Classical conditioning and the placebo effect. *Pain* 72:107–13.

Moody, R. 1975. *Life after life*. Atlanta: Mockingbird Books.

Mori, Fabrizio. 1974. The earliest Saharan rock-engravings. *Antiquity* 48 (197): 87–92.

Morris, W. 1981. *American heritage dictionary of the English language*. Boston: Houghton Mifflin Company.

Murdock, G. P. 1980. *Theories of illness: A world survey*. Pittsburgh: University of Pittsburgh Press.

Murdock, G. P. 1981. *Atlas of world cultures*. Pittsburgh: University of Pittsburgh Press.

Murdock, G. P., and D. R. White. 1969. The standard cross-cultural sample. *Ethnology* 8:329–69.

Nanda, S. 1998. *Neither man nor woman: The hijras of India*. Florence, KY: Wadsworth.

Nemeroff, C., and P. Rozin. 2000. The makings of the magical mind. In *Imagining the impossible: Magical, scientific, and religious thinking in children*, eds. K. S. Rosengren, C. N. Johnson, and P. L. Harris, 1–34. New York: Cambridge University Press.

Neppe, V. 1981. Review article: The non-epileptic symptoms of temporal lobe dysfunction. *South Africa Medical Journal* 60:989–91.

Neppe, V. 1983. Temporal lobe symptomatology in subjective paranormal experiences. *Journal of the American Society for Psychical Research* 77:1.

Newberg, A., A. Alavi, M. Baime, M. Pourdehnad, J. Santanna, and E. d'Aquili. 2001. The measurement of regional cerebral blood flow during the complex task of meditation: A preliminary SPECT study. *Psychiatry Research: Neuroimaging Section* 106: 113–22.

Nicholas, H. 2002. *The mind made flesh: Essays from the frontiers of psychology and evolution*. Oxford: Oxford University Press.

Noakes, T. 1991. *Lore of running: Discover the science and spirit of running*. Champaign, IL: Leisure Press.

Noll, R. 1983. Shamanism and schizophrenia: A state-specific approach to the schizophrenia metaphor of shamanic states. *American Ethnologist* 10 (3): 443–59.

O'Flaherty, W. D. 1975. *Hindu myths: A sourcebook*. Penguin: New York.

Oldham, M., S. Horvath, and D. Geschwind. 2006. Conservation and evolution of gene coexpression networks in human and chimpanzee brains. *Proceedings of the National Academy of Sciences of the United States of America* 103 (47): 17973–78.

Okasha, S. 2003. Recent work on the levels of selection problem. *Human Nature Review* 3:349–56.

Ortiz de Montellano, B. 1978. Aztec Cannibalism: An ecological necessity? *Science* 200:611–617.

Ortiz de Montellano, B. 1990. *Aztec medicine, health, and nutrition*. New Brunswick, NJ: Rutgers University Press.

Otto, R. 1958. *The idea of holy*. 2nd ed. London: Oxford University Press.

Oubré, A. 1997. *Instinct and revelation: Reflections on the origins of numinous perception*. Amsterdam: Gordon and Breach.

Pahnke, Walter N. 1966. Drugs and mysticism. *International Journal of Parapsychology*, 8 (2): 295–313.

Pandharipande, R. 1996. *The eternal self and the cycle of Samsara: Introduction to Asian mythology and religion*. New York: Simon & Schuster.

Pandian, J. 1997. The sacred integration of the cultural self: An anthropological approach to the study of religion. In *The anthropology of religion*, ed. S. Glazier, 505–514. Westport, CT: Greenwood Press.

Park, G. 1963. Divination and its social contexts. *Journal of the Royal Anthropological Institute* 93 (2): 195–209.

Peek, P. 1991. The study of divination, present and past. In *African divination systems: Ways of knowing*, ed. P. Peek, 1–22. Bloomington: Indiana University Press.

Peregrine, P. 1996. The birth of the gods revisited: A partial replication of Guy Swanson's (1960) cross-cultural study of religion. *Cross-Cultural Research* 30:84–122.

Peretz, I., and M. Coltheart. 2003. Modularity of music processing. *Nature Neuroscience* 6 (7): 688–691.

Pérez, J. 2005. *The Spanish Inquisition: A history*. Trans. J. Lloyd. New Haven: Yale University.

Persinger, M. 2003. *Neurotheology: Brain, science, spirituality, religious experience*. Lanham, MD: University Press.

Pinker, S. 2006. The evolutionary psychology of religion. In *Where God and science meet: How brain and evolutionary studies alter our understanding of religion. Volume 1: Evolution, genes, and the religious brain*, ed. P. McNamara, 1–10. Westport: Praeger.

Popper, K. 1959. *The logic of scientific discovery*. London: Hutchinson.

Popper, K., and J. C. Eccles. 1981. *The self and its brain: An argument for interactionism*. Heidelberg: Springer.

Pregenzer, J. F., G. L. Alberts, J. H., Bock, J. L. Slightom, and W. B. Im. 1997. Characterization of ligand binding properties of the 5-HT1D receptors cloned from chimpanzee, gorilla and rhesus monkey in comparison with those from the human and guinea pig receptors. *Neuroscience Letters* 3 (17): 117-120.

Preston, S., and F. de Waal. 2002. Empathy: Its ultimate and proximate bases. *Behavioral and Brain Sciences* 25:62–72.

Price, B. 1978. Demystification, enriddlement, and Aztec cannibalism: A materialist rejoinder to Harner. *American Ethnologist* 5 (1): 98–115.

Purdum, E., and J. Parades. 1989. Rituals of death: Capital punishment and human sacrifice. In *Facing the death penalty*, ed. M. Radelet, 139–55. Philadelphia: Temple University Press.

Radcliffe-Brown, A. R. 1965. *Structure and function in primitive society: Essays and addresses*. New York: The Free Press.

Raghanti, M. A., C. D. Stimpson, J. L. Marcinkiewicz, J. M. Erwin, P. R. Hof, and C. C. Sherwood. March 2008. Differences in cortical serotonergic innervation among humans, chimpanzees, and macaque monkeys: A comparative study. *Cerebral Cortex* 18: 584–597.

Randall, J. 2001. Evolution and function of drumming as communication in mammals. *American Zoologist* 41 (5): 1143–56.

Rapoport, J., and A. Fiske 1998. The new biology of obsessive–compulsive disorder: Implications for evolutionary psychology. *Perspectives in Biology and Medicine* 41 (2): 159–75.

Rappaport, R. A. 1999. *Ritual and religion in the making of humanity*. Cambridge, U.K., and New York: Cambridge University Press.

Rätsch, C. 2005. *The encyclopedia of psychoactive plants: Ethnopharmacology and its applications*. Trans. J. Baker. Rochester: Park Street Press.

Reynolds, V. 2005. *The chimpanzees of the Budongo Forest*. New York: Oxford University Press.

Ring, K. 1981. *Life at death: A scientific investigation of the near-death experience*. New York: Coward, McCann and Geoghegan.

Ring, K. 1986. *Heading toward omega*. New York: Morrow.

Roberts, J. 1976. Belief in the evil eye in world perspective. In *The evil eye*, ed. C. Maloney, 223–78. New York: Columbia University Press.

Rockman, M., M. Hahn, N. Soranzo, F. Zimprich, D. Goldstein, and G. A. Wray. 2005. Ancient and recent positive selection transformed opioid *cis*-regulation in humans. *PloS Biology* 3 (12): e387.

Roes, F. L., and M. Raymond. 2003. Belief in moralizing gods. *Evolution and Human Behavior* 24:126–35.

Rossano, M. 2006. The religious mind and the evolution of religion. *Review of General Psychology* 10 (4): 346–64.

Rudgley, R. 1993. *The alchemy of culture: Intoxicants in society*. London: British Museum Press.

Samorini, G. 1992. The oldest representations of hallucinogenic mushrooms in the world (Sahara Desert, 9000–7000 B.P.). *Integration* 2/3:69–78.

Schlegel, A., and H. Barry III. 1991. *Adolescence: An anthropological inquiry*. New York: Free Press.

Schultes, R., and A. Hofmann. 1979. *Plants of the gods: Origins of hallucinogenic use*. New York: McGraw-Hill. (Reprinted 1992 by Healing Arts Press, Rochester, Vermont.)

Selye, H. 1936. A syndrome produced by diverse nocuous agents. *Nature* 138: 32.

Selye, H. 1976. *Stress in health and disease*, 2nd ed. Boston: Butterworth-Heinemann.

Shanon, B. 2002. Ayahuasca visualizations: A structural typology. *Journal of Consciousness Studies* 9 (2): 3–30.

Sherrington, C. S. 1947. *The integrative action of the nervous system*, 2nd ed. Cambridge: Cambridge University Press.

Shi, P., M. A. Bakewell, and J. Zhang. 2006. Did brain-specific genes evolve faster in humans than in chimpanzees? *Trends in Genetics* 22: 608–613.

Shweder, R. A. December 1977. Likeness and likelihood in everyday thought: Magical thinking in judgments about personality. *Current Anthropology* 18 (4): 637–658.

Singer, P. 1981. *The expanding circle: Ethics and sociobiology*. New York: Farrar, Straus & Giroux.

Sloan, R., E. Bagiella, and T. Powell. 1999. Religion, spirituality and medicine. *Lancet* 353:664–67.

Smith, H. 2000. *Cleansing the doors of perception: The religious significance of entheogenic plants and chemicals*. Los Angeles: Tarcher.

Solecki, R. S. 1975. Shanidar IV, a Neanderthal flower burial in N. Iraq. *Science* 190 (28): 880–881.

Sosis, R. 2004. The adaptive value of religious ritual. *American Scientist* 92 (2): 166–72.

Sosis, R. 2006. Religious behaviors, badges, and bans: Signaling theory and the evolution of religion. In *Where God and science meet: How brain and evolutionary studies alter our understanding of religion. Volume 1: Evolution, genes, and the religious brain,* ed. Patrick McNamara, 61–86. Westport, CT: Praeger.

Spiegel, H. 1997. Nocebo: The power of suggestibility. *Preventative Medicine* 26:616–21.

Spilka, B., and D. McIntosh, eds. 1997. *The psychology of religion: Theoretical approaches.* Boulder, CO: Westview Press.

Stace, W. T. 1960. *The teachings of the mystics.* New York: The New American Library.

Stace, W. T. 1961. *Mysticism and philosophy.* London: Macmillan.

Stark, R. 1997. A taxonomy of religious experience. In *The psychology of religion: Theoretical approaches,* eds. B. Spilka and D. McIntosh, 209–21. Boulder, CO: Westview Press.

Stark, R. 2001. Gods, rituals, and the moral order. *Journal for the Scientific Study of Religion* 40 (4): 619–36.

Steadman, L., C. Palmer, and C. Tilley. 1996. The universality of ancestor worship. *Ethnology* 35: 63–76.

Stevens, A. 2002. *Archetype revisited: An updated natural history of the self.* Toronto: Inner City Books.

Stevens, P., Jr. 1996. Sorcery and witchcraft. In *Encyclopedia of cultural anthropology,* eds. D. Levinson and M. Ember, 1225–31. New York: Henry Holt.

Strawbridge, W. J., R. D. Cohen, S. J. Shema, and G.A. Kaplan. 1997. Frequent attendance at religious services and mortality over 28 years. *American Journal of Public Health* 87 (6): 957–961.

Sullivan, R., and E. Hagen. 2002. Psychotropic substance-seeking: Evolutionary pathology or adaptation? *Addiction* 97:389–400.

Sullivan, R., E. Hagen, and P. Hammerstein. 2008. Revealing the paradox of drug reward in human evolution. *Proceedings of the Royal Society B.* Under review.

Swanson, G. 1960. *The birth of the gods.* Ann Arbor: University of Michigan Press.

Thagard, P. 2005. The emotional coherence of religion. *Journal of Cognition and Culture* 5 (1–2): 58–74.

Time. 1984. Warning Signals. November 26.

Turner, C., and J. Turner. 1995. Cannibalism in the prehistoric American Southwest: Occurrence, taphonomy, explanation and suggestions for standardized world definitions. *Anthropological Science* 103 (1): 1–22.

Turner, C., and J. Turner. 1999. *Man corn: Cannibalism and violence in the pre-historic American Southwest.* Salt Lake City: University of Utah Press.

Tylor, E. B. 1871. *Primitive culture: Researches into the development of mythology, philosophy, religion, language, art and custom.* New York: Henry Holt.

Tyrrell, G. N. M. 1953. *Apparitions.* London: Gerald Duckworth & Co.

Uhl, G. R., and P. S. Johnson. 1994. Neurotransmitter transporters: Three important gene families for neuronal function. *Journal of Experimental Biology* 196:229–36.

Valle, J., and R. Prince. 1989. Religious experiences as self-healing mechanisms. In *Altered states of consciousness and mental health: A cross-cultural perspective,* ed. C. A. Ward, 149–66. Newbury Park, CA: Sage.

Van Gennep, A. 1960. *The rites of passage,* 2nd ed. Chicago: University of Chicago Press.

Van Lawick-Goodall, J. V. 1968. Behaviour of free-living chimpanzees in the Gombe Stream Reserve. *Animal Behavior Monographs* 1 (3): 161–311.

Walker, D., ed. 1970. *Systems of North American witchcraft and sorcery.* Moscow: University of Idaho.

Wallace, A. F. C. 1956. Mazeway resynthesis: A biocultural theory of religious inspiration. *Transactions of the New York Academy of Sciences* II; 18: 626–638.

Wallace, A. F. C. 1966. *Religion: An anthropological view.* New York: Random House.

Wallin, N., B. Merker, and S. Brown (Eds.). 2000. *The origins of music.* Cambridge: MIT Press.

Walsh, R. 1983. Meditation practice and research. *Journal of Humanistic Psychology* 23 (1): 18–50.

Walsh, R. 1990. *The spirit of shamanism.* Los Angeles: Tarcher.

Walton, K., and D. Levitsky. 1994. A neuroendocrine mechanism for the reduction of drug use and addictions by transcendental meditation. In *Self-recovery: Treating addictions using transcendental meditation and Maharishi Ayur-veda*, eds. D. O'Connell and C. Alexander, 89–117. New York: Hayworth Press.

Wang, Y.-Q., Y.-P. Qian, S. Yang, H. Shi, C.-H. Liao, H.-K. Zheng, J. Wang, et al. 2005. Accelerated evolution of the pituitary adenylate cyclase-activating polypeptide precursor gene during human origin. *Genetics* 170: 801–6.

Waxman, S., and N. Geschwind. 1974. Hypergraphia in temporal lobe epileptics. *Neurology* 24: 629–36.

Weber, M. 1958. *The Protestant ethic and the spirit of capitalism.* Trans. T. Parsons, New York: Scribner.

Weber, M. 1993. *The sociology of religion*, 3rd ed. Trans. E. Fischoff. Boston: Beacon Press.

West, M. 1987. Traditional and psychological perspectives of meditation. In *The psychology of meditation*, ed. M. West, 59–80. Oxford: Clarendon Press.

Whiting, B. 1950. *Paiute sorcery.* New York: Viking Fund.

Whitley, D. 1998. Cognitive neuroscience, shamanism, and the rock art of native California. *Anthropology of Consciousness* 9 (1): 22–37.

Wigner, E. P. 1967. *Symmetries and reflections.* Bloomington: Indiana University Press. Quoted in McFarlane, T. J., ed. 2001. *Einstein and Buddha: The parallel sayings.* Berkeley, CA: Seastone.

Wildman, W. 2006. The significance of the evolution of religious beliefs and behavior for religious studies and theology. In *Where God and science meet: How brain and evolutionary studies alter our understanding of religion. Volume 1: Evolution, genes, and the religious brain*, ed. P. McNamara, 227–72. Westport, CT: Praeger.

Wilks, I. 1975. *Asante in the nineteenth century.* Cambridge: Cambridge University Press.

Wilks, I. 1988. Asante: Human sacrifice or capital punishment? A rejoinder. *The International Journal of African Historical Studies* 21 (3): 443–52.

Williams, C. 1988. Asante: Human sacrifice or capital punishment. *The International Journal of African Historical Studies* 21 (3):433–441.

Williams, G. C. 1966. *Adaptation and natural selection.* Princeton, NJ: Princeton University Press.

Williams, G. C. 1992. *Natural selection.* New York: Oxford University Press.

Williams, L. 1980. *The dancing chimpanzee.* London and New York: Allison and Busby.

Wilson, D. S. 2002. *Darwin's cathedral: Evolution, religion, and the nature of society.* Chicago: University of Chicago Press.

Wilson, E. O. 1975. *Sociobiology: The new synthesis, twenty-fifth anniversary edition.* Cambridge, MA: Belknap Press.

Winkelman, M. 1982. Magic: A theoretical reassessment. *Current Anthropology* 23: 37–44, 59–66.

Winkelman, M. 1986. Magico-religious practitioner types and socioeconomic conditions. *Behavior Science Research* 20: 17–46.

Winkelman, M. 1990. Shamans and other 'magico-religious' healers: A cross-cultural study of their origins, nature and social transformations. *Ethos* 18 (3): 308–52.

Winkelman, M. 1992. Shamans, priests and witches: A cross-cultural study of magico-religious practitioners. *Anthropological Research Papers* No. 44. Tempe: Arizona State University.

Winkelman, M. 1994. Multidisciplinary perspectives on consciousness. *Anthropology of Consciousness* 5 (2): 16–25.

Winkelman, M. 1995. Cultural shock and adaptation. *Journal of Counseling and Development* 73:121–26.

Winkelman, M. 1996. Psychointegrator plants: Their roles in human culture and health. In *Sacred plants, consciousness and healing. Yearbook of cross-cultural medicine and psychotherapy*, Vol. 5, eds. M. Winkelman and W. Andritzky, 9–53. Berlin: Verlag.

Winkelman, M. 1997. Altered states of consciousness and religious behavior. In *Anthropology of religion: A handbook of method and theory*, ed. S. Glazier, 393–428. Westport, CT: Greenwood.

Winkelman, M. 1998. Aztec human sacrifice: Cross-cultural assessments of the ecological hypothesis. *Ethnology* 37 (3): 285–98.

Winkelman, M. 1999. *Ethnic sensitivity in social work.* Dubuque: Eddie Bowers.

Winkelman, M. 2000. *Shamanism: The neural ecology of consciousness and healing.* Westport, CT: Bergin and Garvey.

Winkelman, M. 2002a. Psychointegrators: Multidisciplinary perspectives on the therapeutic effects of hallucinogens. *Complementary Health Practice Review* 6 (3): 219–37.

Winkelman, M. 2002b. Shamanism and cognitive evolution. *Cambridge Archaeological Journal* 12 (1): 71–101.

Winkelman, M. 2007a. Therapeutic bases of psychedelic medicines: Psychointegrative effects. In *Psychedelic medicine*, Vol. 1, eds. M. Winkelman and T. Roberts, 1–19. Westport, CT: Praeger/Greenwood Publishers.

Winkelman, M. 2007b. Shamanic guidelines for psychedelic medicines. In *Psychedelic medicine*, Vol. 2, eds. M. Winkelman and T. Roberts, 143–68. Westport, CT: Praeger/Greenwood Publishers.

Winkelman, M. 2008. Cross-cultural and biogenetic perspectives on the origins of shamanism. In *Belief in the past: Theoretical approaches to the archaeology of religion*, eds. D. S. Whitley and K. Hays-Gilpin. Walnut Creek, CA: Left Coast Press.

Winkelman, M., and P. Peek, eds. 2004. *Divination and healing: Potent vision*. Tucson: University of Arizona Press.

Winkelman, M., and D. White. 1987. A cross-cultural study of magico-religious practitioners and trance states: Data base. In *Human relations area files research series in quantitative cross-cultural data*, Vol. 3, eds. D. Levinson and R. Wagner. New Haven, CT: HRAF Press.

Winkelman, M., and C. Winkelman. 1991. Shamanistic healers and their therapies. In *Yearbook of cross-cultural medicine and psychotherapy*, Vol. 1 (1990), ed. W. Andritzky, 163–182, Berlin: VWB.

Winson, J. 1985. *Brain and psyche: The biology of the unconscious*. Garden City, NY: Anchor Press/Doubleday.

Winson, J. 1990. The meaning of dreams. *Scientific American*. November, 86–96.

Wooding, S., and L.B. Jorde. 2006. Duplication and divergence in humans and chimpanzees. *BioEssays* 28:335–338.

Wright, R. 1994. *The moral animal: Why we are the way we are: The new science of evolutionary psychology*. New York: Vintage Books.

Wyttenbach, R. A., L. M. Michael, and R. H. Ronald. 1996. Categorical perception of sound frequency by crickets. *Science* 273 (5281): 1542–43.

Photo Credits

Cover

Stefano Scata. Getty Images Inc.—Stone Allstock.

Chapter 1

Page 9 Hulton Archive/Stringer. Getty Images; **10** The Trustees of the British Museum; **13** The LIFE Picture Collection/Getty Images; **19** Dr. Giacomo Giacobini.

Chapter 2

Page 43 GSFC/METI/ERSDAC/JAROS, and U.S./Japan ASTER Science Team.. NASA; **47** Getty Images/De Agostini Editore Picture Library; **54** (top) SPL. Photo Researchers, Inc.; (bottom left) Dr. Andrew Newberg ; (bottom right) Todd Handy. Cathy Margetts.

Chapter 3

Page 79 Snark/Freies Deutches Hochsift-Frankfurter Goethe-Museum. Art Resource, N.Y.

Chapter 4

Page 91 Jane Goodall Institute; **94** Kim Taylor. Minden Pictures; **100** Leszczynski, Zig. Animals/Earth Scenes; **102** EyeWire Collection. Getty Images—Photodisc; **104** Jane Goodall Institute; **107** Frans B. M. de Waal, Ph.D.

Chapter 5

Page 118 Richard Katz; **126** Jean-Dominique Lajoux. Photo Researchers, Inc.; **134** Israel Museum Jerusalem; **137** The Print Collector. Alamy Images; **145** bpk, Berlin/Bildarchi v Preussischer Kulturbesitz/Lutz Braun/ Art Resource, NY.

Chapter 6

Page 153 Pascal van Heesch / Alamy; **157** Jane Goodall Institute; **167** Tomas del Amo/Pacific Stock; **168** John R. Baker.

Chapter 7

Page 182 Jacopo Robusti. The Columbia Museum of Art; **183** Private Collection/Bridgeman Images; **191** John Woodcock © Dorling Kindersley.

Chapter 8

Page 210 Dr. David Whitley; **217** Picture Desk, Inc./Kobal Collection; **230** (top left) Peter Blackwell. Nature Picture Library; (top right) Bruce Davidson. Nature Picture Library; (bottom) Bruce Davidson. Nature Picture Library.

Chapter 9

Page 242 Brooks Kraft. Corbis/Sygma; **253** © Mira / Alamy; **255** © Robert Sablan/Pacific Stock; **258** Scala. Art Resource, N.Y.

Chapter 10

Page 276 Akademie der Bildenden Kunste, Vienna, Austria/Bridgeman Images; **277** John R. Baker; **285** Ancient Art & Architecture. Danita Delimont Photography; **286** Kunsthistorisches Museum, Vienna, Austria/Bridgeman Images; **288** Ken Liska; **291** The Trustees of the British Museum.

Chapter 11

Page 303 Dr. Adriaan Kortlandt; **320** Library of Congress; **322** NASA.

Author Index